Who's Who
IN THE ROMAN WORLD

Who's Who in the Roman World is a wide-ranging biographical survey of one of the greatest civilizations in history. Covering a period from the fifth century BC to AD 364, this is an authoritative and hugely enjoyable guide to an era which continues to fascinate today. The figures represented come from all walks of Roman life and include some of history's most famous – not to mention infamous – figures as well as hitherto little-known, but no less fascinating, characters.

- The notorious emperors – Caligula, Nero, Elagabalus, Commodus
- The great poets, philosophers and historians – Virgil, Tacitus, Seneca, Ovid
- The brilliant politicians and soldiers – Hannibal, Scipio, Caesar, Mark Antony, Constantine
- Noteworthy personalities – Acte, mistress of Nero; Catiline, the revolutionary; Spartacus, champion of the slaves; Gaius Verres, the corrupt governor of Sicily

The inclusion of cross-referencing, a glossary of terms, select bibliographies, a chronology and list of emperors, maps, and an author's preface complete what is at once a superb reference resource and an enormously entertaining read.

John Hazel, M.A. (Oxon.), taught Classics at the French Lycée in London and later at the City of London School. He is the author of *Who's Who in Classical Mythology* (in collaboration with Michael Grant) and *Who's Who in the Greek World*, both published by Routledge.

WHO'S WHO SERIES

Who's Who in Ancient Egypt
Michael Rice

Who's Who in the Ancient Near East
Gwendolyn Leick

Who's Who in Christianity
Lavinia Cohn-Sherbok

*Who's Who in Classical Mythology**
Michael Grant and John Hazel

Who's Who in Contemporary Gay and Lesbian History
Edited by Robert Aldrich and Garry Wotherspoon

Who's Who in Contemporary Women's Writing
Edited by Jane Eldridge Miller

Who's Who in Contemporary World Theatre
Edited by Daniel Meyer-Dinkegräfe

Who's Who in Dickens
Donald Hawes

Who's Who in Europe 1450-1750
Henry Kamen

Who's Who in Gay and Lesbian History
Edited by Robert Aldrich and Garry Wotherspoon

Who's Who in the Greek World
John Hazel

*Who's Who in Jewish History**
Joan Comay, new edition revised by Lavinia Cohn-Sherbok

Who's Who in Military History
John Keegan and Andrew Wheatcroft

Who's Who in Nazi Germany
Robert S. Wistrich

*Who's Who in the New Testament**
Ronald Brownrigg

*Who's Who in Non-Classical Mythology**
Egerton Sykes, new edition revised by Alan Kendall

*Who's Who in the Old Testament**
Joan Comay

Who's Who in Russia since 1900
Martin McCauley

*Who's Who in Shakespeare**
Peter Quennell and Hamish Johnson

Who's Who in Twentieth Century World Poetry
Edited by Mark Willhardt and Alan Michael Parker

Who's Who in World Politics
Alan Palmer

*Who's Who in World War Two**
Edited by John Keegan

*Available in the USA from Oxford University Press

Who's Who IN THE ROMAN WORLD

John Hazel

London and New York

First published 2001
by Routledge
11 New Fetter Lane, London EC4P 4EE

Simultaneously published in the USA and Canada
by Routledge
29 West 35th Street, New York, NY 10001

Routledge is an imprint of the Taylor & Francis Group

Typeset in Sabon by Taylor & Francis Books Ltd
Printed and bound in Great Britain by TJ International Ltd, Padstow, Cornwall

British Library Cataloguing in Publication Data
A catalogue record for this book is available from the British Library

Library of Congress Cataloging in Publication Data
A catalog record has been requested for this title.

ISBN 0-415-22410-1

TO MY SONS AND GRANDCHILDREN

Contents

Preface

Roman history is a huge subject and its timespan is enormous. In compiling this work of reference, I have tried as far as possible to avoid overlap with its two sister volumes, *Who's Who in Classical Mythology*, which I wrote many years ago in collaboration with Michael Grant, and *Who's Who in the Greek World*, freshly published as I write. The latter has provided the harder task, as there are inevitably personages of historical, philosophical or scientific interest who can reasonably claim a place, so to speak, in both the Greek and the Roman 'worlds', such as the later kings of Macedonia, the later Seleucids and Ptolemies, and Pyrrhus; philosophers like Plotinus and Porphyry; scientists like Galen; and historians such as Plutarch and Polybius.

Inevitably our information is much greater and our sources better for some periods than for others, and much depends on the survival of documents, especially historical accounts, from the ancient world. In this respect we are particularly fortunate in the coverage of the last century BC and the first AD. Our knowledge of the period of the Punic Wars is also good. From what we can discern, we have been lucky in that those are surely the most interesting periods from a historic and cultural point of view. It is almost impossible to distinguish history from myth in the days of the monarchy; the 'enlightened' Age of the Antonines does not offer much to excite; and the succession of short-lived emperors of the third century is tedious. The period of time from Diocletian to Julian, however, provides much variety, being a time of important development and retrenchment. I decided to limit the scope of the book by ending with the deaths of the last non-Christian emperor, Julian, and his short-lived successor, which mark the passing of the world that the great Romans of earlier days might have recognised as having an affinity with their own.

Cross-referencing has been made easy by the printing of q.v. items in small capitals, with a figure in brackets where necessary to indicate which subentry is in question. The spelling of Greek names adopted is conventional, the Latinised forms (with c rather than k) being given. As Romans always had more than one name, I have chosen to enter best known, usually the cognomen or last of the three names. Sometimes an English form exists, such as Livy, Ovid or Virgil, and these are adopted, though in cases where several entries are made under the same name, the Latin form may be the one found, such as Antonius (for Antony) and Pompeius (for Pompey). Strict chronological order is followed where there is more than one personage with exactly the same name, but is broken in the case of a few emperors with long and detailed entries, who are placed first: this applies to Claudius and Nero. A few well known nicknames are used, such as Caligula and Caracalla. Brief bibliographies are appended to articles on major personages where suitable works exist.

I should like to thank Roger Thorp of Routledge for his patience and unfailing encouragement during the writing of this book and its Greek predecessor. I should also like to thank Richard Stoneman for his valued support. I am grateful to my friend and former colleague Geoffrey Rider for help with a couple of articles. I should also like to acknowledge use made of, for establishing the factual basis of certain entries, the *Oxford Classical Dictionary*, 3rd edn, and *A Dictionary of Ancient History*, edited by Graham Speake. The errors and deficiencies in the book are entirely my own.

John Hazel
London, 2000

Acknowledgements

We acknowledge with thanks the kind permission granted us to use maps from the *Atlas of Classical History* edited by Richard J. A. Talbert, first published in 1985 by Croom Helm Ltd, and for the chronological tables and lists of rulers based on tables and lists in *Chronology of the Ancient World* by Elias J. Bickerman, revised edition published 1980 by Thames & Hudson.

Note on Roman names

Most Roman citizens had three names, first a *praenomen*, usually chosen from a rather limited set of traditional forenames, which were very often abbreviated in written documents (see below); then the *nomen*, a gentile or clan name, almost always characterised by the termination -ius; and lastly, to distinguish divisions of large clans or families (*gentes*), a *cognomen*, often originally a nickname, as many such names show derivation from some physical peculiarity e.g. *Crassus* 'thick', 'fat'; *Lepidus* 'neat', 'elegant'; *Rufus* 'red-haired'. A few men of ignoble family, such as Antonius, Marius and Livy, had no *cognomen*. Some men also bore an extra name, an *agnomen*, to distinguish sub-branches of large families, such as Scipio Nasica. In the later imperial period, we find men with five or more names. An extra name was also added to show adoption, derived from the adoptee's original *nomen*, such as Aemilianus, Julianus, Octavianus. Freed slaves or foreigners took the first two names of the man who freed or emancipated them and added their original servile or foreign name as a *cognomen*. Women were officially endowed with the feminine form of their father's *nomen*, e.g. Julia, Livia; but as this practice must have led to much confusion other names were often added or substituted, such as a feminine form of his *cognomen* such as Metella, Fausta, or a diminutive such as Livilla or Domitilla. In imperial times, the mother's name was often added.

The most common forenames were abbreviated as follows: A. Aulus, C. Gaius, Cn. Gnaeus, D. Decimus, L. Lucius, M. Marcus, M' Manius, P. Publius, Q. Quintus, Ser. Servius, Sex. Sextus, Sp. Spurius, T. Titus, Ti. Tiberius. Otherwise they were written in full.

A

Accius, Lucius (*c*.170–*c*.90 BC), a tragic poet, born at Pisaurum in Umbria, was befriended by PACUVIUS: both writers produced plays for the same festival in 140 though their ages differed by some forty years. CICERO (1) knew him and greatly admired his work. His patron was BRUTUS (1) Callaicus, for whom Accius wrote a verse dedication for the temple built to commemorate his victories in Spain. He translated Greek tragedies into Latin, and fragments of some forty-six named plays are extant. He also wrote other verse including *Annals* about annual Roman festivals. His *Didascalica* in nine books was a verse history of Greek and Latin literature. He also wrote erotic poetry. He was interested in the reform of Latin spelling, for which he was attacked by LUCILIUS (1). He had an important influence on the development of Latin literature and seems to have been a strong stylist and a powerful critic.

Acilius, Gaius (C2 BC), was a profoundly philhellene senator and historian who interpreted in the Senate for the three Greek philosophers, Carneades, Diogenes the Stoic and Critolaus, who came to plead for Athens in 155 BC. His *History of Rome* in Greek extended from the earliest times to his own day. LIVY suggests that it appeared around 142 BC; he used it as a source. CLAUDIUS (11) Quadrigarius was probably the person who translated it into Latin.

Acte, Claudia, a mistress of NERO (1), was used by his tutor SENECA (2) in AD 59 to try to prevent his incestuous behaviour with his mother AGRIPPINA (3), when, according to TACITUS (1), she was thought to be attempting to win power for herself by enticing him into sexual misconduct with her. Acte had been his mistress from 95, encouraged by Seneca; POPPAEA later supplanted her. She claimed descent from the royal family of Pergamon; she owned land in Italy and Sardinia. It was she who, after his suicide in 68, gave Nero's ashes burial in his ancestral tomb.

Adherbal *see* JUGURTHA.

Aelianus, Claudius (C2–3 AD), was a teacher of rhetoric from Praeneste. He worked at Rome and was a protégé of the empress JULIA (10) Domna. He wrote a number of moralising works in Greek of which a few fragments exist: *The Nature of Animals* is a collection of animal stories; his fourteen books of *True Stories* contain anecdotes about men and their customs. He is also the reputed author of twenty *Peasant Letters*. He was a very popular writer in later antiquity, being influenced by Stoic ideas and strongly opposed to Epicurean doctrines; he had an influence on Christian writers.

Aelius 1. Stilo, Lucius (*c.*150–*c.*75 BC), was the first Roman scholar of importance. An equestrian, he came from Lanuvium and became a Stoic. He wrote much, though his works have all perished. He was interested in literature, language including etymology, and historical matters. He wrote about ancient Latin texts, the *Carmen Saliare*, the Twelve Tables of early Roman law, the language of religious ceremonies, and a list of the works of PLAUTUS. He also wrote speeches for politicians, though he was not an orator. He taught and influenced VARRO (3), CICERO (1) and VERRIUS FLACCUS.

2. Paetus, Sextus, was consul in 198 BC. Nicknamed *Catus* 'clever', he wrote on law and published the *Tripertita*, a highly authoritative document including the famous Twelve Tables of Roman Law, a commentary, and the rules of procedure. His work, influential on later legal writers, does not survive.

3. Caesar, Lucius (*c.*AD 104–138), was a stepson of C. Avidius NIGRINUS who was executed at the start of HADRIAN's reign. He was originally named Lucius Ceionius Commodus. He was praetor in 130 and consul in 136; later in the same year he was adopted by the emperor Hadrian under the name L. Aelius Caesar as his son and successor. He governed Pannonia in 136 to 137, but died on 1 January 138, his place being taken by ANTONINUS Pius, who then adopted Lucius' son, LUCIUS VERUS.

Aemilia 1. Lepida was the daughter of LEPIDUS (6) and wife of DRUSUS (5) Julius Caesar. She helped SEJANUS to entrap and imprison her husband in AD 30. She was accused of adultery with a slave in 36, as a result of which she killed herself.

2. *See* JULIA (6).

Aemilianus *see* SCIPIO (11).

Aemilianus, Marcus Aemilius (emperor in AD 253), a Moor, was governor of Pannonia and Moesia under the emperor GALLUS (8). He drove the Goth Kniva out of Moesia and attempted to strike a bargain with the Senate to share power with it, but his own troops, who had proclaimed him emperor, murdered him three months after his accession. See M. Grant (1985) *The Roman Emperors*, London: Weidenfeld & Nicolson.

Aemilius *see* ASPER, LEPIDUS, MACER (1), PAULLUS, SCAURUS.

Aesopus, Clodius (C1 BC), was a tragic actor mentioned in the works of CICERO (1) and HORACE. Cicero tells us that Aesopus gave him elocution lessons and supported his return from exile in 57 BC. He made a late comeback to the stage at the dedication of POMPEIUS (2)'s theatre in 55, but his voice failed him and he had to leave the stage. Horace and QUINTILIAN both refer to him as *gravis*, 'serious', 'weighty'.

Afer, Gnaeus Domitius (died AD 59), was an orator and advocate from Nîmes, greatly admired by the critic QUINTILIAN, who had been his pupil. Quintilian quotes some of his *bons mots*, and says he wrote two books with the title *On Witnesses*. In AD 26 he successfully prosecuted Claudia Pulchra, the cousin of Tiberius' enemy AGRIPPINA (2), which lent him a distinguished but sinister reputation. In 39 he was prosecuted by CALIGULA, saved himself by flattery, and was made consul; he became superintendent of the water supply under NERO (1), and died as a result of his intemperate habits.

Afranius 1, Lucius (*c.*100 BC), was a comic poet who was popular down to imperial times for his comedies based on Roman and Italian middle-class life *(comoediae togatae)*. His best known plays were *The Divorce*, *The Letter*, *The Sis-*

ters-in-Law, *The Son-in-Law*, and *Vopiscus*. He admired TERENCE and borrowed from him, and was compared by HORACE with Menander. About 400 lines of his work survive.

2. (died 46 BC) was a supporter of POMPEIUS (2) in the Civil War. He served under Pompeius in Spain (76–72) and against MITHRIDATES (3) VI, was consul in 60 BC, and governed Hither (eastern) Spain as Pompeius's legate in 53. In 49 he and Marcus PETREIUS were defeated by CAESAR (1) at Ilerda and their lives were spared on condition that they took no further part in the war. But Afranius joined Pompeius at Dyrrhachium and Pharsalus. He escaped the latter, but was caught by SITTIUS and executed after the battle of Thapsus.

Africanus *see* SCIPIO, JULIUS, CAECILIUS (6).

Agathinus, Claudius (C1 AD), was a writer on medicine and an eclectic philosopher from Sparta. He was a pupil of the Stoic Pneumatist ATHENAEUS of Attalia and of the Stoic philosopher L. Annaeus CORNUTUS (1). He followed the medical teachings of the Pneumatic school and wrote on the pulse and other matters: our knowledge of him derives from references in GALEN and other authorities.

Agricola, Gnaeus Julius (AD 40–93), was a governor of Britain. He was born at Forum Julii (Fréjus) in Provence, son of Julius GRAECINUS and Julia Procilla, married Domitia Decidiana, and had a daughter who married the historian TACITUS (1). After education at Massilia (Marseilles), he entered the army in 61 as a military tribune under SUETONIUS (1) Paulinus. He became successively quaestor of Asia, tribune of the *plebs*, praetor in 68, commander of the Twentieth Legion in Britain between 71 and 73, governor of Aquitania from 74 to 77, consul in 77, and governor of Britain from 78 to 85. While in Britain he completed the subjugation of the island to Roman rule, though it proved impossible for the Romans to control the Highlands of Scotland. After his recall by the emperor DOMITIAN, he lived in retirement until his death. His efforts secured the pacification and civilisation of southern Britain, and he encouraged education and the founding of self-ruling cities. The Romans were greatly impressed by his circumnavigation of Britain and his sighting of Ireland. Our source for his career is his biography by Tacitus, who deplored his treatment at the hands of Domitian, though the emperor may have opposed Agricola's policy of expansion. See W.S. Hanson (1987) *Agricola and the Conquest of the North*, London: Batsford.

Agrippa 1, Marcus Vipsanius (*c*.63–12 BC), was a statesman and general of obscure family, a lifelong supporter of the emperor AUGUSTUS. At the time of CAESAR (1)'s assassination in 44 BC he and Caesar's great-nephew Octavian (see AUGUSTUS) were studying at Apollonia in Illyricum; he persuaded Octavian to return to Rome and helped him enlist a private army; he also prosecuted CASSIUS (2), one of Caesar's assassins. In 40 he became city praetor and played a leading part in the war against Lucius ANTONIUS (4). This was followed by the governorship of Gaul, in which he gained valuable military experience in Aquitania and on the Rhine. In 37 he was consul, and built a fleet for the war against Sextus POMPEIUS (3), converting Lake Avernus near Cumae into an artificial harbour. The following year he won important naval victories at Mylae and Naulochus, which destroyed Sextus Pompeius' power. In 35 and 34 he fought in Illyricum. In 33 he turned his attention to the city of Rome, and acting as aedile he beautified the city, winning valuable support for Octavian. In 31 he presented Octavian with the naval victory of Actium over ANTONIUS (7) and CLEOPATRA (4), which gave him undisputed mastery of the Roman world. Though Octavian was present at the battle, he was ill, and the main credit for success must be given to Agrippa. While Octavian was absent securing Egypt, Agrippa and MAECENAS took charge in Italy. In 29 he helped Octavian in his census and reconstruction of the Senate. In 28 and 27 Agrippa held the consulship for the second and third times and built the Pantheon. Augustus, as Octavian was now styled, gave him his signet ring in 23 when he was seriously ill, indicating his choice for the succession, but he lived. However, as MARCELLUS (7), Augustus' young nephew, was promoted in such a way as to be his obvious successor, Agrippa was sent on a mission to the east with special powers, and resided at Mytilene in Lesbos. Marcellus died the same year.

He returned in 21 and over the next years was ever more closely associated in Augustus' power, marrying Augustus' daughter JULIA (5). His first wife had been Caecilia, daughter of Cicero's friend ATTICUS, by whom he had a daughter, Vipsania AGRIPPINA (1), who married TIBERIUS. Agrippa's second marriage took place in 28 with Marcella, niece of Octavian, who bore him children. His divorce from her and marriage with JULIA (5) in 21 was forced on him by Augustus for dynastic reasons, to mark him out for succession. He had five children by Julia, two of whom, Gaius CAESAR (3) and Lucius CAESAR (8), were adopted by Augustus in 17 BC so as to be his heirs. His daughter AGRIPPINA (2) married GERMANICUS and bore the future emperor Gaius (CALIGULA). In 20 and 19 he was in Gaul and Spain asserting Roman power, and in 18 he received the power of a tribune, the mainstay of imperial power. He was sent east again in 17 and made several useful settlements; he became a friend of King HEROD (1) of Judaea, which led to his patronage of Herod's family (see 3 and 4 below). In 13 his tribunician power and his military command were renewed and he was sent in 12 to Pannonia, but died on his return and was buried in Augustus' mausoleum.

This talented man was used by Augustus in all sorts of crises, and provided a sure support when the emperor fell ill, as often happened at critical moments. He was undoubtedly seen by Augustus as a possible successor. He inherited great wealth from Atticus, his father-in-law, and spent it freely for the state, building, besides the Pantheon, the first public baths, a new bridge, and many constructions for the water supply of Rome. In his will he left large legacies to Augustus and to the Roman People. He supervised a survey of the Empire begun by Julius Caesar, and as a result of this work published a geography on the basis of which a map of the Empire was made, engraved on marble, and placed in Agrippa's Portico in the city. See E.T. Salmon (1968) *A History of the Roman World*, London: Methuen; R. Syme (1939) *The Roman Revolution*, Oxford: Clarendon; F.A. Wright (1937) *Marcus Agrippa, Organiser of Victory*, London: Routledge.

2. Postumus (12 BC–AD 14) was the youngest child of AGRIPPA (1) by his third wife JULIA (5), born after his death (*postumus* means 'last') and in AD 4 adopted, along with the much older TIBERIUS, by AUGUSTUS. But the character of the youth, who was very independent and outspoken, upset the emperor who banished him to Sorrento and finally in AD 7 made the Senate exile him to the island of Planasia. A conspiracy to bring him to power was put down. On the death of Augustus he was put to death.

3. I, Marcus Julius (*c.*10 BC–AD 44), was a king of Judaea and the tetrarchy of Palestine; he was also known as Herod Agrippa. His father, Aristobulus, a son of HEROD (1) the Great of Judaea, was executed by Herod in 7 BC. His mother Berenice then sent him to Rome where he lived at the imperial court in the house of ANTONIA (2) the Younger and took the name Agrippa from the fact that AGRIPPA (1) had been his grandfather's patron. He remained in Rome until the death of his friend, DRUSUS (4), son of Tiberius, in AD 23. He returned to Palestine, heavily in debt, and stayed there until 36 when he returned to Rome on borrowed money and became a close friend of Gaius Caesar (the future emperor CALIGULA). Tiberius imprisoned him in 36 for treasonable words heard and reported by a freedman, but Caligula released him on his accession in 37 and made him ruler of the tetrarchy of his uncle PHILIP (2), which was then vacant. Two years later he was appointed ruler of the tetrarchy of his uncle Antipas (see HEROD 2) as well, when the latter offended Caligula by claiming royal power and was exiled at Agrippa's instigation. He was bold enough to stand up to Caligula's threat to desecrate the temple at Jerusalem, and in 41 CLAUDIUS (1) made him king of Judaea and Samaria. He was popular with the Jews, but when he died in 44 his whole kingdom was annexed by the emperor. The writer of *Acts of the Apostles*, a hostile source, gives in ch. 12 an account of his death, which occurred in the amphitheatre at Caesarea, and also regards him as having executed James, a disciple of JESUS, and caused the imprisonment of another, Peter. His daughter Drusilla married the procurator FELIX.

4. II, Marcus Julius (*c.*AD 27–*c.*90), was the son of AGRIPPA (3) I and also known as Herod Agrippa. After his father's death in 44 he lived at CLAUDIUS (1)'s court until 50, when he was granted the kingdom of Chalcis in Ituraea (the Bekaa Valley in Lebanon) since his uncle Herod (a brother of his father) was now dead. In 53 he was, however, obliged to exchange Chalcis for the former tetrarchy of PHILIP (2), to which Claudius added Abilene and Arcene. NERO (1) gave him further powers in Galilee and Peraea. However, there were few Jews in his kingdom, though he inherited the right to appoint the high priests and control the Temple Treasury. The *Acts of the Apostles* gives a favourable account of his interview with PAUL at Caesarea. He was a strong supporter of Rome in the Jewish rebellion of 66, which he tried to prevent, and was present at the siege of Jerusalem. He was rewarded for his support by a grant of further territories. He received the status of a praetor in Rome and assisted JOSEPHUS with his history of the war, but died before its publication in 93.

Agrippina 1. (died AD 20) Vipsania Agrippina, daughter of Marcus Vipsanius AGRIPPA (1) by his first wife Caecilia (daughter of ATTICUS), was married to TIBERIUS, to whom she bore one son, DRUSUS (4). In 11 BC Tiberius was forced by AUGUSTUS to divorce her, much against his will, so that he could marry JULIA (5). Agrippina then married C. Asinius GALLUS (2), to whom she bore five sons.

2. (*c.*14 BC–AD 33) Vipsania Agrippina, daughter of M. Vipsanius AGRIPPA (1) by JULIA (5), was usually called 'the Elder' to distinguish her from AGRIPPINA (3). She married TIBERIUS' nephew GERMANICUS, probably in AD 5, to whom she bore nine children, among them the emperor Gaius (CALIGULA) and AGRIPPINA (3) 'the Younger', mother of NERO (1). She was highly regarded for her heroism and virtue, and accompanied her husband on all his campaigns. On his death in AD 19 she returned to Rome where she lived for ten years as a focus of opposition to SEJANUS. Tiberius refused her request in 26 to be allowed to marry again. In 30 she was banished to the island of Pandateria on the emperor's orders: she had never ceased to believe him to have been behind her husband's death. She starved herself to death in 33.

3. (AD 15–59) Julia Agrippina, daughter of AGRIPPINA (2), usually called 'the Younger', was born in Germany at Oppidum Ubiorum, later renamed Colonia

Agrippinensis after her, now Cologne. In 28 she married Gnaeus Domitius AHENOBARBUS (5), by whom she had a son, the future emperor NERO (1). She was banished by her brother, the emperor Gaius (CALIGULA), for involvement in the conspiracy of LENTULUS (6) Gaetulicus against him, but was recalled by CLAUDIUS (1) shortly after his accession and, after the fall of his third wife MESSALLINA in 48, he married her. In 50 she prevailed upon the emperor to adopt her son, so that he became Nero Claudius Caesar, and, being older than his own son BRITANNICUS, a likely successor. Agrippina was ambitious to gain power for herself through her son and, with the help of Claudius' freedman PALLAS, and of BURRUS and Nero's tutor, SENECA (2), she obtained the title of *Augusta*. In 54 Claudius died, almost certainly poisoned by her (see LOCUSTA). She exercised a powerful influence over Nero, and for a few years was almost his equal in power; but, after Pallas fell in 55, Seneca and Burrus turned against her and she lived in obscurity until Nero had her murdered in her own villa by Anicetus, a ship's captain. Tacitus reports a story that she tried to regain Nero's favour through incest. See A.A. Barrett (1996) *Agrippina, Mother of Nero*, London: Batsford.
See also ACTE.

Ahala, Gaius Servilius (C5 BC), a legendary Roman patriot, was said to have been the Master of the Horse when CINCINNATUS was dictator for the second (fictitious) time. The story that he saved his country by killing Spurius MAELIUS with a dagger in 439 BC may have been a myth to explain the origin of the family name (Ahala, 'armpit') because he hid the dagger there.

Ahenobarbus 1, Gnaeus Domitius (died 104 BC), consul in 122 BC, governor of Gaul the following year, defeated the Allobroges and Arverni and held a triumph in 120 in which he led the Arvernian chief Bituitus whom he had treacherously captured. He built the Via Domitia in Gaul and placed a garrison at Narbonne, which he founded as a Roman colony in company with L. Licinius CRASSUS (2). He was censor in 115.

2, Gnaeus Domitius, son of AHENOBARBUS (1), after his tribuneship in 104 BC, in a pique at not being co-opted to his father's priesthood, promoted a law transferring the election of priests from the colleges of priests to the people. He was consul in 96 and soon after was elected Pontifex Maximus, chief priest of the Roman state.

3, Gnaeus Domitius, son of AHENOBARBUS (2), married a daughter of CINNA (2) and was active against POMPEIUS (2)'s troops in Africa in 81 BC. See HIEMPSAL (2).

4, Gnaeus Domitius (died 31 BC), a son of AHENOBARBUS (6), was with him at Corfinium and likewise released by CAESAR (1). He was present at the battle of Pharsalus, and returned to Italy in 46 BC to be pardoned again by Caesar. In 44 he accompanied BRUTUS (5) to Philippi, and in 43 was condemned for being one of Caesar's assassins. In 43 and 42 he supported the republicans with a fleet in the Adriatic, but after the battle of Philippi he was reconciled to ANTONIUS (7), reinstated in his citizenship, and governed Bithynia from 40 BC. In 36 he joined Antonius on his Parthian campaign, was consul in 32 and fled to Antonius; but through hostility to CLEOPATRA (4) he deserted to Octavian (see AUGUSTUS) just before Actium and died of a fever shortly after.

5, Gnaeus Domitius (died *c.*AD 40), the son of AHENOBARBUS (6), was described by SUETONIUS (2) as 'entirely detestable'. In AD 28 he was betrothed to GERMANICUS' daughter AGRIPPINA (3) the Younger, and in 37 became father of the emperor NERO (1) by her. He was consul in 32.

6, Lucius Domitius (died 48 BC), was a republican politician, hostile to the 'triumvirs' and especially CAESAR (1). Expectant of the consulship of 55, he threatened Caesar's position in 56 during the latter's governorship and conquest of Gaul, so bringing about the conference of Luca that year at which Caesar's power was confirmed for the next five years. Consul in 54 BC, he married Porcia, sister of Marcus CATO (5). He presided at the trial of MILO in 52. The Senate appointed him to govern Gaul in 49 in succession to Caesar, but Caesar trapped him in Corfinium in central Italy and his own troops compelled him to surrender. Caesar released him and he joined the Pompeians, defending Massilia for a time and commanding the left of POMPEIUS (2)'s army at Pharsalus, where he perished.

7, Lucius Domitius (died AD 25), a son of AHENOBARBUS (4), was an arrogant man addicted to chariot-racing; in his aedileship in 22 BC he offended the censor, PLANCUS (1). He married ANTONIA (1), daughter of ANTONIUS (7) and of AUGUSTUS' sister OCTAVIA (1). He was consul in 16 and in 12 governor of Africa. As legate of Illyricum between 7 and 2 BC he marched to the Elbe, and was subsequently legate of Germany where he built a causeway between the Rhine and the Ems.

Albinovanus Pedo (C1 AD), was a poet and friend of OVID, who addressed to him one of his *Letters from the Black Sea* (4. 10). He is credited with an epic poem about Theseus and with epigrams which MARTIAL took for his models. During the reign of TIBERIUS he wrote a poem in honour of GERMANICUS' campaign in Germany, of which a fragment is preserved in the younger SENECA (2)'s *Suasoriae*, 1, 15. Seneca refers to him as a witty storyteller and recounts, in letter 122, a story about Pedo's neighbour Sextus Papinius, who turned night into day.

Albinus 1, Decimus Clodius Septimius (died AD 197), served under MARCUS AURELIUS with distinction in Dacia and Germany and was governing Britain at the time of COMMODUS' death in AD 193. Septimius SEVERUS (1) made him Caesar and promised him the succession, but changed his mind in 196 after the death of PESCENNIUS Niger. Albinus was hailed as emperor by his troops, and war broke out between the two. Albinus crossed to Gaul and prepared to march on Rome, but he was defeated and killed by Severus near Lyons.

2, Aulus Postumius (C2 BC), was a senator and historian who served under L. Aemilius PAULLUS (2) against PERSEUS. A praetor in 155, he used a procedural device to prevent the release of Achaean hostages, one of whom was POLYBIUS. He served in 154 on an embassy to the east, which reconciled ATTALUS (2) II and PRUSIAS II. He was consul in 151 when the tribunes imprisoned him and his colleague, Lucullus, for levying men too harshly. In 146 he was on a commission to settle the province of Achaia. He wrote a history of Rome in Greek, very little of which survives, which was admired by POLYBIUS though his own compatriots, including CATO (4) the Censor, were critical of its effusive philhellenism and verbosity. CICERO (1) praised him, calling him 'eloquent'. He also wrote a poem, *The Arrival of Aeneas.*

3, Spurius Postumius, as consul in 186 BC with PHILIPPUS (4), dealt with the threat he believed to be posed by the *Bacchanalia* or orgies of Dionysus, which had spread to Latium from southern Italy. At his instigation the Senate passed a decree, which is still extant, to suppress the cult. See Livy, *History of Rome*, 39, 8–18.

4, Spurius Postumius (C2 BC), as consul in 110 BC revived the war with JUGURTHA, king of Numidia, which BESTIA had given up. After a brief incursion he returned to Rome to organise elections, leaving his brother Aulus in command. The latter's winter campaign was ill conceived and ineffective and his camp was captured by the enemy. Jugurtha made his army go under the yoke. Spurius returned to Numidia as proconsul but was unsuccessful in recovering the situation, and was exiled by MAMILIUS (1)'s tribunal for corrupt dealings with Jugurtha.

5. (C2 AD) was a philosopher who taught at Smyrna (where GALEN was his pupil) and wrote a collection of his master GAIUS' lectures. His only surviving work is an introduction to Plato's dialogues, formerly attributed to Alcinous.

Albucius, Titus (C2 BC), was a senator, an Epicurean and philhellene, whom LUCILIUS (1) satirised for the ineptness of his prosecution of SCAEVOLA (3) for extortion in Asia. He held offices of state and governed Sardinia *c.*106 BC when he himself committed extortion: he was exiled and spent his time in Athens studying philosophy. CICERO (1) condemned his excessive fondness for Greek culture.

Alexander 1. Jannaeus (reigned 103–76 BC) was a king and high priest of the Jews, of the Hasmonean family, and the younger son of John HYRCANUS (1). He succeeded his brother ARISTOBULUS (1) and advanced the monarchical aspect of his rule, as shown by his coinage on which he placed Greek and Aramaic as well as Hebrew inscriptions. He expanded the Jewish state by conquering Galilee, Peraea, part of Ituraea, and a number of Greek cities across the Jordan and on the coast of Palestine. He had to face popular revolts and the anger of the Pharisees. On his death he was succeeded by his wife ALEXANDRA Salome, who reigned successfully until her death in 67. She recovered the favour of the Pharisees. Their sons were HYRCANUS (2) II and ARISTOBULUS (2).

2. (died 7 BC) was a son of HEROD (1) the Great and Miriamne, whom his father caused to be strangled with his brother Aristobulus in fear of their popularity.

3, Tiberius Julius (C1 AD), was an Alexandrian Jew, the son of Alexander the Alabarch and nephew of PHILO (2), and a Roman administrator of equestrian rank. He was procurator of Judaea between AD 46 and 48 and served under CORBULO in Armenia in 63. He became Prefect of Egypt *c.*65. He was close to VESPASIAN, and made his troops swear an oath of allegiance to him on the day of his accession, 1 July 69. He accompanied TITUS in his siege of Jerusalem as Commander of the Praetorian Guard and, though he was not a practising Jew, he vainly tried to save the Temple. He was briefly married to BERENICE (2).

4. of Abonuteichos (C2 AD) was a Paphlagonian mystic attached to the worship of Asclepius. He was attacked by Lucian in his work *Alexander or the False Prophet.* He taught that Asclepius, the god of healing, had been reborn in the shape of a serpent called Glycon, and he built a temple in which he delivered oracles with a large tame serpent wearing a human head-mask. He excluded Epicureans and Christians from his rites, and made a large fortune by his prophecies, even establishing an office in Rome. Lucian attempted to investigate his frauds, but was nearly assassinated for his pains. Alexander gained a large following including an influential Roman named Rutilianus. After he died, aged seventy, the cult survived him.

5. Aegaeus (C1 AD) was a Greek Peripatetic Philosopher who taught in Rome and a tutor to the future emperor NERO (1).

6. of Aphrodisias (C3 AD) was a Greek Peripatetic philosopher who came to Athens *c.*AD 198 and became the foremost commentator on the works of Aristotle and the head of the Lyceum. He dedicated his treatise *On Destiny* to the emperors Septimius SEVERUS (1) and CARACALLA. Much of his work, including commentaries on Aristotle's *Metaphysics*, I–V, *Topica, Analytica Priora*, I, *Meteorologica* and *On Sense*, survives. There is a translation of *On Destiny* by A. Fitzgerald, 1931.

7. Polyhistor (C1 BC) was a Greek writer, born at Mitetus, captured by Romans and emancipated *c.*80 by SULLA (2). He adopted the name L. Cornelius Alexander. He was tutor to a Cornelius Lentulus and to C. Julius HYGINUS (1). He wrote profusely on many subjects including travel, literary criticism and tales of wonder. He died accidentally in a fire at Laurentum.
See also BALAS.

Alexandra Salome *see* ALEXANDER (1) Jannaeus.

Alexianus *see* AVITUS.

Alfenus Varus, Publius (C1 BC), was a jurist, possibly originating from Cremona in Cisalpine Gaul, who may in his youth have been the Alfenus Varus mentioned by CATULLUS (1) (poems 10 and 30). If this identification is correct, he served on MEMMIUS (2)'s staff in Bithynia in 57 BC and would have been born some twenty years earlier. HORACE (*Sat.*, 1, 3) mentions an Alfenus who was a cobbler, and PORPHYRIO identifies him with the jurist. He was appointed commissioner with Asinius POLLIO (1) and Cornelius GALLUS (4) in 41 to confiscate land for the veterans of the Civil War in the land north of the Po. He may have been responsible for the confiscation of VIRGIL's family's farm, and is probably the Varus mentioned in the *Eclogues*. He was suffect consul in 39 BC, and was unique (together with his son) in gaining a consulship as a 'new man' under AUGUSTUS. He wrote a *Digest* of legal responses in forty books, some of which found its way into Justinian's *Digests* of Roman law.

Alimentus, Lucius Cincius (C3 BC), was a senator and historian, praetor in Sicily in 210 BC and captured there by HANNIBAL. He wrote a history of Rome in Greek and established a senatorial tradition of historiography, especially of the Second Punic War.

Allectus (died AD 296) was a pretender to the rulership of Britain. In AD 293 he assassinated CARAUSIUS, whose financial officer he had been, and himself ruled Britain for the next three years. Asclepiodotus, praetorian prefect of the emperor CONSTANTIUS (1) I, invaded Britain and killed him.

Ambiorix (C1 BC) was a chief of the Gallic Eburones of northern Gaul. Though CAESAR (1) had freed his nation from dependence on their neighbours the Atuatuci, Ambiorix and his colleague Catuvolcus rebelled against the Romans in 54 BC and destroyed the camp and forces of Sabinus and Cotta at Atuatuca. He incited the Nervii to besiege the winter camp of Quintus CICERO (2), which was only relieved by the timely arrival of Caesar himself. Ambiorix continued to resist and was never captured.

Ambivius Turpio, Lucius (C2 BC), was the producer of the comedies of TERENCE and of Statius CAECILIUS (7). He appears to have been an actor-manager somewhat in the Shakespearian mould.

Ambustus *see* FABIUS (1), FABIUS (2).

Ammianus Marcellinus (born *c.*AD 330) was a Greek historian of Rome who wrote in Latin; the last great historian of Ancient Rome. Born at Antioch of a middle class family, he may have studied under LIBANIUS. He joined the army and served on the eastern frontier and later in Gaul under the emperor JULIAN; he participated in Julian's final campaign in Persia in 363 and travelled in Greece and Egypt.

He settled in Rome in 378 and devoted himself to writing a Roman history in Latin for Roman readers. The history is a continuation of TACITUS (1)'s historical works, though his record of the period from AD 96 to 353 is lost. The rest, from 353 to 378, is detailed, interesting and accurate, and an invaluable source for social as well as political history. Ammianus, who followed the traditional religion and admired Julian, was also able to write dispassionately of other faiths. See W. Hamilton and A. Wallace-Hadrill (1986) *Ammianus Marcellinus: the Later Roman Empire*, Harmondsworth: Penguin; J. Matthews (1989) *The Roman Empire of Ammianus*, London, Duckworth.

Ammonius Saccas (*c.*AD 160–242) was an Alexandrian philosopher. PORPHYRY states that he was born a Christian but renounced that faith when he started to think for himself. He left no writings. His pupils are said to have included 'Longinus', ORIGEN (1) the Christian, ORIGEN (2) the Platonist, and PLOTINUS.

Amyntas (died 25 BC) was a client king of a large part of Asia Minor subject to Rome. As secretary of DEIOTARUS, king of Galatia, he took part in the campaign of Philippi in 42 BC but deserted to ANTONIUS (7) after the battle and the death of Deiotarus. In 40 he received the kingdom from Antonius, including also Lycaonia and parts of Phrygia, Pamphylia and Pisidia. In 35 Sextus POMPEIUS (4) surrendered to him. In 31 he was with Antonius at Actium where he again deserted and joined Octavian (see AUGUSTUS), to be rewarded with additional territories, Isauria and Cilicia. He died while fighting against mountain tribesmen on his southern border. Augustus turned his kingdom into the province of Galatia.

Androcles (C1 AD), more correctly Androclus, was a slave, probably of Greek origin. He lived during the reign of TIBERIUS, and his story is told by Aulus GELLIUS (1). He had fled from a cruel master in Africa and taken refuge in a cave, where a lion came and showed him its swollen paw, from which he extracted a large thorn. Subsequently recaptured, as a runaway slave he was thrown to the beasts in the arena, of which the lion happened to be one: it fawned upon him, and the emperor set him free.

Andronicus, Lucius Livius (C3 BC), was a writer and adaptor of plays and epic poetry. He was a Greek, born in Tarentum and taken prisoner when it fell to the Romans in 272 BC. After a period of slavery he was set free and took the name of his master (L. Livius SALINATOR), whose children he taught Greek and Latin grammar. He composed tragedies and comedies in Latin along Greek lines: according to VARRO (3) his first production was in 240 BC. He was an exact contemporary of NAEVIUS. The success of his plays persuaded the Roman authorities to allow a festival of drama to be held in the temple of Minerva on the Aventine. In 207 he was commissioned to write a hymn on a consultation of the Sibylline Books. He also wrote in verse an *Odyssey* which is part translation of Homer and part adaptation. Only scanty fragments survive of his plays, of which we know the titles of three comedies and ten tragedies, though rather more of the *Odyssey* is extant. He seems to have toned down those elements in the Greek which would have offended Roman sensibilities, and freely invented new Latin words.

Antigonus, Mattathias (C1 BC), was a son of ARISTOBULUS (2). Briefly king of Judaea, he was appointed by the Parthians in 40 BC and deposed and beheaded in 37 by ANTONIUS (7), who replaced him with HEROD (1) the Great.

Antinous (*c.*AD 111–130) was a favourite of the emperor HADRIAN. He was born at Claudiopolis in Bithynia (Asia Minor). He may have been a slave; his beauty won him the admiration and affection of the emperor who took him on all his travels. Antinous was drowned at Besa on the Nile and Hadrian was stricken with grief. He caused many cities to build temples in honour of the youth, and declared him a god. He founded a city in Egypt in his honour, Antinoöpolis. Antinous was widely honoured throughout the Empire with worship and statues.

Antiochus 1. III 'the Great' (*c.*242–187 BC) was a king of Syria and lands to the east. He was the second son of Seleucus II, and succeeded his brother Seleucus III in 223. The kingdom was then falling apart owing to secessions by a number of eastern nations, and Antiochus did much to restore it and give it manageable frontiers. He married Laodice, daughter of Mithridates II of Pontus, thus allying himself with a powerful neighbour. He fought a war against Egypt to recover the occupied parts of Syria and Palestine, but was defeated at Raphia near Gaza in 217. He besieged the rebel Achaeus in Sardis from 215 to 213, and by defeating and killing him won back lost territory in Asia Minor. In 212 he embarked on an eastern campaign that lasted seven years and earned his epithet 'The Great'. In 203–2 he made a secret treaty with PHILIP (1) V of Macedonia to share the overseas possessions of Egypt, and in 202–198 he conquered the parts of Syria and Palestine in Egyptian hands.

The hostility of the Roman Senate was aroused by the collaboration between Syria and Macedonia, especially when in 196 Antiochus invaded Europe to recover the Gallipoli peninsula in Thrace, where he rebuilt the city of Lysimacheia, and met an embassy from Rome, which had been sent to negotiate for peace. After fruitless negotiations lasting three years, Antiochus invaded Greece, and was defeated in 191 by the Romans at Thermopylae and compelled to abandon Europe. HANNIBAL, an exile from Carthage, had taken refuge at the court of Syria *c.*195 and had tried to persuade Antiochus to invade Italy.

Hostilities were renewed and in 190 Antiochus was defeated by Lucius SCIPIO (4) and Publius SCIPIO (7) Africanus at Magnesia near Mt Sipylus in Asia Minor. A treaty was made in 188 at Apamea, by which Antiochus gave up all his territory west of the Taurus range and paid 15,000 talents. He also lost Armenia, which rebelled and became a separate kingdom under Artaxias. He had previously lost eastern lands to Demetrius of Bactria. Thus Syria ceased to be a Mediterranean power. He was killed in Elymais (on the border of Persia) while trying to take treasure from a temple to meet the demands of the Romans. He was succeeded by his second son, SELEUCUS (1) IV. See P. Green (1990) *Alexander to Actium*, Berkeley: University of California Press; E.S. Gruen (1984) *The Hellenistic World and the Coming of Rome*, Berkeley: University of California Press.

2. IV Epiphanes ('the Glorious') (*c.*215–162 BC), the third son of ANTIOCHUS (1) III, was a king of Syria. He succeeded his elder brother SELEUCUS (1) IV in 175. He fought a successful war against Egypt (170–168) and was preparing to lay siege to Alexandria when Rome intervened and compelled him to retire. He concentrated his attention on Palestine, an important frontier province, which he attempted to hellenise. He installed a garrison in Jerusalem and dedicated the Temple to Olympian Zeus, but in doing so aroused the opposition of the Jews, which led to a rising under Mattathias and his sons the Maccabees. This came to a head after Antiochus' death. In 165 he defeated and captured Artaxias, king of Armenia. He died in 164 after trying, like his father, to plunder a temple in Elymais.

3. V Eupator ('of a good father') (173–162 BC), the son of ANTIOCHUS (2) IV, was nine years old at the time of his accession to the throne in 164. He reigned for two years through his regent Lysias, and in 162 was dethroned and killed in Antioch by DEMETRIUS (1) I when he came from Rome to claim the kingdom. During his reign Jerusalem was restored to its former Jewish position.

4. VI Epiphanes ('the Glorious') (*c.*148–138 BC) was a king of Syria, son of Alexander BALAS and Cleopatra Thea, daughter of PTOLEMY (2) VI. In fact he did not really reign at all, being nominated in 144 BC by the general DIODOTUS Tryphon as heir to the throne in oppositions to DEMETRIUS (2) II. In 142 Diodotus deposed and succeeded him, and in 138 killed him.

5. VII of Side (*c.*159–129 BC) was a king of Syria, the second son of DEMETRIUS (1) I and brother of DEMETRIUS (2) II, whom he succeeded after the usurpation of DIODOTUS Tryphon (see ANTIOCHUS 4). Born in and brought up at Side in Pamphylia, he attacked and defeated Diodotus in Antioch (138 BC), briefly reconquered Judaea, which had been an independent Jewish state, in 134, and in 130 took Babylon from the Parthians. In 129, however, he was killed in battle by the Parthians.

6. VIII Grypus (reigned 125–96 BC) A king of Syria, the younger son of DEMETRIUS (2) II, he succeeded his brother SELEUCUS V; however, his half-brother ANTIOCHUS (7) disputed the throne with him and they fought a war until 122 when they agreed to divide the kingdom. Grypus took all Syria except Phoenicia and Coele Syria. In 96 he was assassinated and succeeded by his son SELEUCUS (3) VI.

7. IX of Cyzicus (died 95 BC), in the division of the Seleucid kingdom in 122, took Phoenicia and Coele Syria; in 96 on his brother's death he tried to seize his brother's share, but had to face Grypus' son SELEUCUS (3) VI, fighting whom he was killed.

8. X 'the Pious', son of ANTIOCHUS (7) IX, in 95 BC routed SELEUCUS (3) VI who had killed his father; he then overwhelmed the brother of Seleucus, ANTIOCHUS (9) XI.

9. XI was drowned in the river Orontes in 95 while fleeing from ANTIOCHUS (8) X.

10. XII, the younger brother of ANTIOCHUS (9) XI, who called himself Dionysus but is known to history as Antiochus XII, claimed the throne after his death. He was killed in battle against the Arabian king ARETAS (1) III.

11. XIII 'the Asiatic' (reigned 69–65 BC), the last Seleucid king of Syria, was a Roman puppet until POMPEIUS (2) deposed him and made Syria into a Roman province.

12. I (C1 BC) was a king of Commagene, a small kingdom of northern Syria, now in Turkey. Antiochus I was the son of MITHRIDATES (3) VI of Pontus and of Laodice, daughter of ANTIOCHUS (6) VIII Grypus. POMPEIUS (2) awarded him the kingdom of Commagene in 64 BC and he supported Pompeius in the Civil War in 49. Later he changed his allegiance to the Parthians and in 38 was besieged in Samosata by VENTIDIUS and then by ANTONIUS (7), who probably removed him in favour of his brother Mithridates. He built himself a spectacular memorial, still visible, on the summit of Nemrut Dagh in eastern Turkey.

13. II (died 29 BC), a son of the above, was king of Commagene. He succeeded his father but was summoned to Rome by Augustus and put to death for having murdered an ambassador.

14. III (died AD17) succeeded Mithridates II of Commagene: his kingdom was then annexed by Rome.

15. IV (C1 AD) A king of Commagene, son of ANTIOCHUS (14) III, he spent his youth an exile in Rome, where the future emperor CALIGULA befriended him. In AD 38 Caligula restored him to his kingdom, but soon deposed him. Claudius restored him again in 41 and he proved a useful ally to Rome against the Parthians and Jews. In 60 he received part of Armenia for help rendered to CORBULO. In 72 VESPASIAN deposed him on suspicion of intriguing with the Parthians. He spent the rest of his life in exile, partly in Rome. Commagene was annexed to the province of Syria. It seems likely that the religion of Mithras (Mithraism) originated in his kingdom at about this time. See PHILOPAPPUS.

16. of Ascalon (died *c.*68 BC) was a Greek philosopher, a pupil of PHILO (2) of Larissa whom he accompanied to Rome in 88 BC, where he got to know Lucius LUCULLUS (2). He became head of the Academy in 79–78, when CICERO (1) attended his lectures. VARRO (3) had been his pupil in Athens or during his stay in Rome. His philosophy was eclectic and composed of Academic, Peripatetic and Stoic elements, and influenced Cicero's thought greatly.

Antipater 1. (*c.*100–43 BC) was an Idumaean ruler who supported Rome and influenced the history of Palestine. He was the son of an Idumaean nobleman whom ALEXANDER (1) Jannaeus had appointed governor of Idumaea. He married a Nabataean woman and became powerful with the aid of the Pharisees and king ARETAS (1) III of Nabataea. He supported the claim of HYRCANUS (2) II to the Jewish high priesthood and ethnarchate and received help from POMPEIUS (2). In 57 he was established in power as ethnarch of Judaea by GABINIUS (2), the governor of Syria, whom he helped in 55 to restore PTOLEMY (8) the Piper to the throne of Egypt. However, after the battle of Pharsalus, Antipater raised and led troops to support Julius CAESAR (1) at Alexandria in 48 BC. As a reward, Caesar obtained Roman citizenship for him and made him governor of Judaea. He was murdered while collecting funds for CASSIUS (2) and succeeded by his son, HEROD (1) the Great.

2, Aelius (C2 AD) was a Roman historian and civil servant. He was born in Phrygia and was a pupil of Claudius Hadrianus of Tyre. Septimius SEVERUS (1) promoted him to be his secretary and made him governor of Bithynia. He was the teacher and friend of the emperors CARACALLA and GETA (3). He wrote the history of Severus' reign, and died in about AD 212.

3, Lucius Caelius (C2 BC), was a Roman historian and author of a work, *Annals*, which contained a valuable account of the Second Punic War based on the works of Silenus and Sosylus.

4. of Thessalonica (C1 BC) was a Greek epigrammatist, author of many poems in the *Greek Anthology*. He was the client of L. Calpurnius PISO (6).

5. of Tyre (died *c.*45 BC) was a Greek teacher of philosophy who introduced CATO (5) of Utica to Stoicism.

Antonia 1. (born 39 BC) was the elder daughter of ANTONIUS (7) by Octavia, sister of Octavian (see AUGUSTUS). Her forthcoming birth probably inspired VIRGIL to compose his *Fourth Eclogue* in expectation of a son and heir for Antonius, the seal of the success of his political alliance with Octavian. She married Lucius Domitius AHENOBARBUS (5) and was the grandmother of NERO (1).

2. (36 BC–AD 37) was the younger sister of ANTONIA (1), married to DRUSUS (3), brother of the emperor TIBERIUS. She was the mother of GERMANICUS, LIVIA (3) (Livilla) and the emperor CLAUDIUS (1). When her husband died in 9 BC she refused to remarry. In AD 31 she gave Tiberius the information which brought about the fall of SEJANUS. She gave a home to the Jewish king AGRIPPA (3) I in his boyhood. Her grandson CALIGULA conferred upon her the title *Augusta*, but later turned against her.

Antoninus Pius (AD 86–161) was a Roman emperor, born at Lanuvium near Rome, the son of a consular, Aurelius Fulvus, who originated from Nîmes. His full name was Titus Aurelius Fulvus Boionus Antoninus. His mother was Arria Fadilla. He became consul of the year in AD 120, by which time he had married FAUSTINA (1). Under HADRIAN he held administrative posts in Umbria and Etruria where he owned land. He governed Asia as proconsul between 133 and 136, and was adopted by Hadrian in 138, on the death of Lucius AELIUS (3), as his son and heir, such was the emperor's esteem for his integrity. As part of the arrangement, he adopted M. Annius Verus, Faustina's nephew, afterwards the emperor MARCUS AURELIUS, and L. Aelius VERUS, as his sons.

Hadrian, having thus secured the succession with great foresight, died within a few months (during which Antoninus was virtual ruler) and Antoninus asked the Senate to confer divine honours on him, for which he was rewarded with the title *Pius*, 'dutiful'; Faustina was styled *Augusta*. He took three further consulships. His policy as emperor was mild and beneficent; he remitted considerable portions of the accession gifts that were normally paid to emperors. He stayed in Italy during his reign, gave the Senate control of Italy (ending Hadrian's arrangement of the country into four provinces), showed it respect but did not otherwise extend its powers. He supported good administration, leaving officials in their posts for longer periods, and centralising control. He also organised charities (see FAUSTINA 1), inaugurated a public building programme, and supported many communities with financial grants.

The situation on the Empire's borders was less peaceful during the reign: Germany was restless and he settled British colonists around the river Neckar. Dacia was troubled and had to be divided in three for closer supervision. North Africa, Egypt and Judaea revolted. Further afield, new client kings were appointed in Armenia and elsewhere. The Antonine Wall was built in north Britain. Antoninus died at Lorium in March 161, to universal mourning; he was deified by popular acclaim and succeeded by his adopted son Marcus Aurelius. See M. Grant (1994) *The Antonines*, London: Routledge.

Antonius 1, Gaius (C1 BC), known as Hybrida, 'mongrel', was the younger son of Marcus ANTONIUS (5). He served under SULLA (2) and was tribune in 72 BC. He was expelled from the Senate by the censors in 70, but was helped by CICERO (1) to the praetorship in 66. He was a friend of CATILINE and made a deal with him for the consulship of 63, but was elected with Cicero as his colleague. He deserted Catiline's cause when Cicero offered to resign to him the province of Macedonia for the following year. He was appointed, though reluctant, to lead an army against Catiline in Etruria: he left the conduct of the battle to his legate Marcus PETREIUS. He plundered his province and was prosecuted by Caelius RUFUS (1) on his return; defended by Cicero he was nevertheless condemned and retired to the island of Cephallenia. CAESAR (1) recalled him from exile; he was censor in 42 BC.

2, Gaius (died 42 BC), was the second son of ANTONIUS (6), and brother of the triumvir. He served CAESAR (1) in the Civil War, and in 49 BC was blockaded in the island of Curieta in the Adriatic and forced by POMPEIUS (2)'s fleet to surrender. He was praetor in 44 and then appointed to govern Macedonia, but was besieged in Apollonia by M. Junius BRUTUS (5) and captured in March 43. The next year, after he sought to incite Brutus' troops to mutiny, he was put to death.

3, Iullus (43–2 BC), second son of the triumvir ANTONIUS (7) and FULVIA, he was brought up at Rome by his stepmother OCTAVIA (2) in the household of the emperor AUGUSTUS. He married Octavia's daughter Marcella, who had previously been married to AGRIPPA (1); he was praetor in 13 BC, consul in 10, and proconsul of Asia *c.*7 BC. In 2 BC he committed suicide or was executed after being found guilty of adultery with the emperor's daughter JULIA (5), though the real reason may have been political. He wrote an epic poem and was the addressee of an ode of HORACE (4, 2).

4, Lucius (died 39 BC), third son of ANTONIUS (6), was a brother of the triumvir. He was consul in 41 BC and opposed Octavian (see AUGUSTUS) at the instigation of his sister-in-law FULVIA, so as to champion the interests of the Italians whom Octavian had dispossessed to give land to his veterans; he took the last name *Pietas* ('Loyalty') to impress his brother's followers. He marched briefly into Rome and then occupied Perusia but surrendered it the next year (40) and was spared by Octavian. He was sent to a command in Spain, where he died.

5, Marcus (143–87 BC), as praetor in 102 fought against the Cilician pirates, over whom he held a triumph in 100. He was consul in 99 and censor in 97. He was a friend and supporter of MARIUS (1), opposed the party of SATURNINUS (2), and as censor allowed Italians to become Roman citizens. He defended NORBANUS and AQUILLIUS (2). He later fell out with Marius and was prosecuted under the Varian Law for having incited Italians to rebel. On Marius' return to Rome in 87 he was killed. CICERO (1) introduced him as a participant in his treatise *On the Orator.*

6, Marcus (C1 BC), eldest son of ANTONIUS (5), was nicknamed Creticus, 'the Cretan', from his disastrous dealings with the islanders. When praetor in 74 BC he was given a special command to tackle the Mediterranean pirates. He campaigned with moderate success in the western Mediterranean but when in 72 he went east he was soundly defeated by the Cretan pirates with whom he then made a treaty.

7, Marcus (83–30 BC), was the Mark Antony of history and literature, eldest son of ANTONIUS (6) by JULIA (2), sister of Lucius Julius CAESAR (6), the consul of 64 BC. After his father's early death he was brought up in the house of his stepfather P. Cornelius LENTULUS (9) Sura. After a youth spent in dissipation, he served with distinction as a cavalry commander under Aulus GABINIUS (2) in Palestine and Egypt, and in 54 he joined the staff of Julius CAESAR (1) in Gaul and was elected quaestor in 51 through Caesar's influence. Apart from a short break in Rome, Antonius remained with Caesar until 50; in 49 he was tribune and defended Caesar's interests in Rome as long as he could. He vetoed a decree which would have deprived Caesar of his command, but when the 'Ultimate Decree' was passed by the Senate, he fled to join Caesar in his camp in Cisalpine Gaul. He used his power as a tribune to frustrate some of POMPEIUS (2)'s measures concerning bribery and was left by Caesar in command of Italy while the latter campaigned in Spain. In 48 he was with Caesar's forces in Greece and commanded the left wing of the army at the battle of Pharsalus, where Pompeius was routed. He was then sent back to Italy as Caesar's 'Master of the Horse' (the title of the dictator's deputy). He was active in suppressing riots started by Caelius RUFUS (1) and MILO to achieve cancellation of debts. He held no further position until his consulship with Caesar in 44, when he offered Caesar a crown at the festival of Lupercalia in February. After Caesar's assassination on 15 March, he was circumspect and cautious. He obtained Caesar's papers from his widow CALPURNIA

(1), and his speech at the funeral five days later, when he revealed Caesar's will to the populace, was moderate in tone but led to the cremation of the body in the forum and the flight of the conspirators.

Caesar had in his will adopted his young great-nephew C. Octavius (Octavian: see AUGUSTUS), who became a rival to Antonius for the leadership of Caesar's party. Antonius secured the support of an irregular army, and of the people, who voted a law giving him the governorship of Gaul for five years. Towards the end of the year he left for his province, but Decimus Junius BRUTUS (2), one of Caesar's murderers, to whom Caesar had promised the province, was already in Cisalpine Gaul and held the city of Mutina. Antonius besieged him there until he was attacked by a coalition led by Octavian and the consuls HIRTIUS and PANSA, whom the Senate had sent out to deal with Antonius, now through Cicero's eloquence declared a public enemy. Antonius was defeated in April 43 and retired across the Alps, but both consuls had been killed in the battle and the Senate turned against Octavian, who aligned himself with Antonius. After a conference in Gaul, the Caesarians had a law passed (*Lex Titia*) of November 43, by which Antonius, Octavian and LEPIDUS (4) were created triumvirs, that is, a specially constituted group with dictatorial powers to ensure the stability of the state for five years. They held a proscription of their enemies, including CICERO (1), who had mortally offended Antonius by executing his stepfather LENTULUS (9) in 63 and by his *Philippic* orations of 44. In 42 Antonius and Octavian crushed the forces of the republicans at the battle of Philippi in Macedonia, in which BRUTUS (5) and CASSIUS (2) fell.

By agreement with his colleagues Antonius went to organise the eastern half of the Empire. At Tarsus in Cilicia in 41 he met the queen of Egypt, CLEOPATRA (4), whom he followed to Egypt, where he spent the winter with her. He then had to return to Italy: his wife FULVIA and his brother Lucius had been defeated at Perusia (Perugia) in a war with Octavian, and Fulvia died after escaping to Greece. A new agreement was made between the triumvirs at Brundisium in southern Italy, by which Antonius surrendered Gaul to Octavian, which he had already occupied, and married Octavian's sister, OCTAVIA (1). Antonius remained in Italy until 39, when the triumvirs made a treaty at Misenum with Sextus POMPEIUS (4). He then returned with Octavia to the East, spending most of his time in Athens. His general VENTIDIUS twice, in 39 and 38, defeated the Parthians, who had taken advantage of Roman weakness by invading Syria. In 37 BC he made his last visit to Italy, meeting his colleagues at Tarentum; the triumvirate was renewed for a further five years. At Corcyra, however, angry and frustrated with Octavian, Antonius sent his wife back to Italy. He went to Antioch and renewed his relationship with Cleopatra, and established HEROD (1) as king in Judaea. His power base was thus strengthened, though he expected to receive reinforcements of troops from Italy. In 36 he invaded Parthia but suffered a disastrous defeat. The elimination of Lepidus and Sextus Pompeius from the scene highlighted the growing rivalry of Antonius and Octavian. In 35 Octavia went east, bringing a fraction of the troops that Antonius was expecting, and he refused to meet her. In 34 he seized Armenia and took its king ARTAVASDES (1) back to Alexandria as a captive; he celebrated a triumph and a ceremony in which he proclaimed the extension of Egypt's frontiers into Roman territory. He had now broken openly with Octavian, who used the full force of his propaganda machine against Antonius. Many former republicans now sided with Octavian, and in 33 there were angry exchanges. In 32 Antonius formally divorced Octavia and Octavian seized Antonius' will from the Vestal Virgins, which he published. It favoured his children by

Cleopatra and requested burial in Alexandria. Octavian now felt justified in declaring war on Egypt. Antonius' remaining powers were removed. The Egyptian fleet sailed west and met Octavian's fleet off the promontory of Actium; many of Antonius' Roman supporters had deserted him in fear of Cleopatra's power. After many months of delay he was decisively beaten in a naval battle in September 31 and fled with Cleopatra to Egypt, which he tried to defend. Octavian invaded the country and besieged Alexandria in 30 BC. Deserted by nearly all his friends, he killed himself in early August before Octavian entered the city.

He was a fine general but was somewhat hot-headed and no match in diplomacy for the hard coolness of Octavian. He had five legitimate children, and was the ancestor of three emperors by his daughters. See ANTONIA (1), ANTONIA (2). See J. M. Carter (1970) *The Battle of Actium*, London: Hamish Hamilton; E.G. Huzar (1978) *Mark Antony*, Minneapolis: Minnesota University Press; R. Syme (1939) *The Roman Revolution*, Oxford: Clarendon Press.

8, Marcus (died 30 BC), was the elder son of ANTONIUS (7) by FULVIA. He was betrothed to Octavian's (see AUGUSTUS) daughter JULIA (6) at the conference of Tarentum in 37 BC when he was about seven years old. Octavian slew him in 30 after his father's suicide.

Antony (AD 251–356) (Antonios) was a Christian ascetic and founder of monasticism. He was born in Upper Egypt and aged twenty became a hermit in the desert. In 305 he accepted the pleas of like-minded people and founded a community of hermits near Memphis. In 355, aged 104, he went to Alexandria to oppose Arianism, dying the following year in his cell. His *Life* was written by ATHANASIUS.

Antony (Mark) *see* ANTONIUS (7).

Apellicon (C1 BC) was a Peripatetic philosopher, a native of Teos, who had a valuable library, including many original works of Aristotle and Theophrastus, which he had bought from the heirs of Neleus of Scepsis. He edited them badly. In 84 BC SULLA (2) seized this library and took it to Rome. See TYRANNIO (1).

Aper, Arrius (died AD 284), was a Roman prefect of the Praetorian Guard under the emperor CARUS, father-in-law of the latter's son NUMERIAN, whom he murdered in Asia Minor in 284. He was put to death by DIOCLETIAN.

Apicius (C1 AD) is the name of two gourmets: one, M. Gavius Apicius, lived in the reigns of AUGUSTUS and TIBERIUS and left some writings about culinary science. The celebrated cookery book *De Re Coquinaria*, ascribed to Caelius Apicius, is of much later date.

Apion (C1 AD) was a Greek scholar and commentator on Homer, born in Alexandria and successor of Theon as head of the Alexandrian school. He went to Rome during the principate of CALIGULA to complain about the Jews in Alexandria, and was opposed by PHILO (2). He also wrote several books in the same vein, to which JOSEPHUS wrote a rejoinder (*Against Apion*). He later settled in Rome and taught rhetoric. He died in the reign of CLAUDIUS (1).

Apollodorus 1. (*c.*104–22 BC) was a Greek teacher of rhetoric from Pergamon: CAESAR (1) selected him as Octavian's (see AUGUSTUS) teacher in 45 BC. His *Art of Rhetoric*, which was translated into Latin by VALGIUS Rufus, laid down a rigid form for court speeches: introduction, narrative, evidence and conclusion, in precise order.

2. (C1 AD) was a Greek architect and town planner, born in Damascus, who worked in Rome. He planned TRAJAN's

Forum and built the Basilica and Column of Trajan, and HADRIAN's temple to Venus and Rome. He built a triumphal arch in honour of Trajan at Ancona (in 115). He was banished by Hadrian in AD 129 and later executed, because he dared to criticise Hadrian's architectural plans. He wrote an extant work *On Engines of War.*

Apollonius **1.** Malakos (C2 BC) was a teacher of rhetoric from Alabanda who founded a school at Rhodes, visited by SCAEVOLA (3) in 121 BC and Marcus ANTONIUS (5) in 98.

2. Molon (C1 BC) was a teacher of rhetoric from Alabanda who taught at Rhodes and visited Rome twice, in 87 and 81 BC, as ambassador of the Rhodians, when he also gave lectures which were attended by CICERO (1) and others. In 78 Cicero and CAESAR (1) attended his lectures in Rhodes.

3. (C1 BC) was an Athenian sculptor, son of Nestor. He signed the Belvedere Torso in the Vatican and a cult statue of Capitoline Jupiter, dedicated in 69 BC.

4. of Tyana (C1 AD) was a Neopythagorean philosopher from Cappadocia, an ascetic who went from place to place teaching. He claimed miraculous powers and pretended to be able to fly from place to place and to have foreknowledge of events such as the death of DOMITIAN. For this he was tried but acquitted. He settled in Ephesus, where he opened a school, and according to Flavius PHILOSTRATUS died in AD 97. A few fragments of his writings survive. Hierocles of Nicomedia compared his life with that of JESUS of Nazareth, to the detriment of the latter: EUSEBIUS wrote a surviving reply.

Appian (C2 AD) was a historian, born in Alexandria probably during DOMITIAN's reign, who held office in his native city before acquiring Roman citizenship and moving to Rome, where he practised as an advocate. During the reign of ANTONINUS Pius he wrote his *History of Rome* in Greek in twenty-four books, parts of which survive. He did not entirely understand the institutions of Republican Rome.

Apuleius, Lucius (born *c.*AD 123), was a writer, Platonic philosopher, and rhetorician, of a rich family at Madaurus in Numidia. He was educated at Carthage and Athens, and later at Rome. He travelled widely, especially in the East, having a strong interest in religion and magic. He practised for a time as an advocate at Rome but returned to Numidia; around AD 155 he set out for Egypt but fell ill on the way at Oea near Tripoli. While he was there he met a rich widow, Pudentilla, the mother of his friend Sicinius Pontianus, whom his friend persuaded him to marry; he was accused by the woman's older kinsmen of having enticed her by magic. His defence speech survives, *Apologia* or *On Magic*, which led to his acquittal in a trial which took place at Sabratha before the proconsul Claudius Maximus. He took his wife to Carthage where he prospered, writing poetry and philosophy and his novel *Metamorphoses*, and engaging in speech making; he also served as chief priest of the province. The picaresque *Metamorphoses* (often referred to as *The Golden Ass*) is important in being the only truly Latin novel to survive in its entirety. It has fine qualities of suspense and humour as well as a manifestation of powerful religious belief in its dénouement. Apuleius left other works also: his *Florida* or *Flowery Passages*, consisting of purple passages from his speeches containing interesting material including a moving description of the death of the Greek poet Philemon; a speech on the *God of Socrates*; and a translation of part of Menander's *Patient Man.* There were also other lost works whose titles are known. His Latin was influenced by the ideas of FRONTO. For a translation see Robert

Graves (1950) *The Golden Ass*, Harmondsworth: Penguin.

Aquila, Pontius (C1 BC), was one of the assassins of CAESAR (1). He was tribune in 45 BC when he insulted Caesar by refusing to stand up for his triumph after Munda, and served in the war of Mutina in 43 under Decimus BRUTUS (2). He drove T. Munatius PLANCUS (2) out of Pollentia but was killed in the battle of Mutina.

Aquillius 1, Manius (C2 BC), was consul in 129 BC. As governor of Asia he completed the work of PERPERNA (1) in the war against the allies of ARISTONICUS. He organised the province and gave it a road system. He held a triumph in 126 and was accused of extortion but acquitted.

2, Manius (died 88 BC), the son of AQUILLIUS (1), consul with MARIUS (1) in 101 BC, defeated the rebellion of slaves in Sicily. He was accused of extortion but corruptly acquitted with the help of Marius and Marcus ANTONIUS (5). He led a commission in Asia in 89 and precipitated the First Mithridatic War by restoring to their thrones ARIOBARZANES (1) I of Cappadocia and NICOMEDES IV of Bithynia and by provoking the king in various ways. After being overwhelmed by the onslaught of MITHRIDATES (3) VI in 88 he was captured and killed.

3. Gallus, Gaius (C1 BC), was a lawyer, a pupil of Q. Mucius SCAEVOLA (4), praetor in 66. Having withdrawn from active politics, he made new rules governing lawsuits in which a claim of bad faith could be invoked; he also reformed the law regarding the settlement of debts. See LABEO.

Archelaus 1. (C1 BC) was a Greek general from Cappadocia who served MITHRIDATES (3) VI, king of Pontus. He conquered Bithynia and central Greece in the First Mithridatic War from 88 to 85 BC and was decisively defeated twice by SULLA (2), at Chaeronea and at Orchomenus in Boeotia. Mithridates commissioned him to negotiate peace with Rome, which he continued to do until 83. He deserted to Rome on the renewal of war and helped LUCULLUS (2) in the Third Mithridatic War.

2. (C1 BC) was a ruler of Egypt, son of ARCHELAUS (1). He was favoured by POMPEIUS (2), who gave him the priesthood and rulership of Comana in Cappadocia, and married BERENICE (1), daughter of PTOLEMY (8) XII the Piper, with the result that in 58 BC when Ptolemy was deposed he became ruler of Egypt. In 55 he was deposed by Aulus GABINIUS (2), who restored Ptolemy for a huge bribe.

3. (C1 BC–C1 AD) was a king of Cappadocia, the grandson of ARCHELAUS (2). Around 36 BC the triumvir ANTONIUS (7) gave him the kingdom in his settlement of the East, which some attributed to the influence of his mother GLAPHYRA (1), whose sexual favours Antonius had enjoyed in 41. He offended TIBERIUS while he was living on Rhodes, who had assisted him with a speech in the Senate, and was consequently deposed by him in AD 17, after a reign of 54 years, his kingdom becoming a Roman province. The old man died while in Rome for his trial by the Senate. He was the author of a treatise describing the lands conquered by Alexander the Great. His daughter was GLAPHYRA (2).

4. (C1 BC–C1 AD) was a ruler (ethnarch) of Judaea, a son of HEROD (1) the Great, on whose death in 4 BC AUGUSTUS shared their father's kingdom among his surviving sons. With the support of NICOLAUS, Archelaus received Judaea, Samaria and Idumaea. However, his rule was so harsh that in AD 6 Augustus deposed him at his subjects' request and banished him to Vienna in Gaul: his kingdom became a Roman province. He married GLAPHYRA

(2), daughter of ARCHELAUS (3), and was her third husband.

Archias, Aulus Licinius (*c.*120–*c.*45 BC), was a Greek poet from Antioch in Syria. He came to Rome in 102 and was received in the house of LUCULLUS (2). He wrote poems in honour of MARIUS (1)'s victory over the Cimbri and Lucullus' victories in the Mithridatic War: the latter obtained for him citizenship of Heraclea in Lucania in 93. By the law of Plautius and Papirius of 89 BC he automatically became a Roman citizen, as Heraclea had an alliance with Rome. In 62 Gratius accused him of illegality in acquiring the citizenship, and in his trial he was defended by CICERO (1), whose speech (*Pro Archia*) is extant. It secured his client's acquittal and contains a magnificent panegyric of literature. Archias later fell out with Cicero and lived until at least 45, and may be the author of some of the poems in the *Greek Anthology* under his name.

Arellius Fuscus (C1 BC) was a teacher of rhetoric who taught OVID.

Aretas The Greek form of the name (Haritha) of several kings of the Arab kingdom of Nabataea, with its capital at Petra.

1. III (reigned *c.*87–62 BC) defeated ALEXANDER (1) Jannaeus and seized Damascus, which he surrendered to TIGRANES (1) II of Armenia. In 63 he besieged Jerusalem in support of John HYRCANUS (2) II against ARISTOBULUS (2). He was compelled to desist by POMPEIUS (2)'s lieutenant, SCAURUS (3), who pursued him to Petra, his capital, where he was bought off, and recognised Aretas' rights as king.

2. IV (reigned 9 BC–AD 39) had an eventful career, being recognised as king by AUGUSTUS only after the intriguer Syllaeus, who tried to replace him with a pretender, had fallen from favour and been executed. After the death of HEROD (1) the Great in 4 BC, Aretas assisted VARUS in pacifying Judaea. His daughter married HEROD (2) Antipas who *c.*AD 33 divorced her to marry his niece Herodias: in 37 Aretas invaded and seized Herod's kingdom of Peraea and defeated him. The timely death of TIBERIUS saved him from punishment for this disturbance of the peace. CALIGULA granted Aretas control of Damascus, and his governor ruled it at the time of PAUL's visit (see *II Corinthians*, 11, 32) in 37.

Ariarathes The name of several rulers of Cappadocia.

1. IV Eusebes ('the Pious') (reigned *c.*220–*c.*163 BC) married Antiochis, daughter of ANTIOCHUS (1) III, king of Syria; after the latter lost the battle of Magnesia against the Romans in 190, Ariarathes deserted him for an alliance with Pergamon and Rome: he married his daughter Stratonice to EUMENES II of Pergamon. He assisted Rome against the Gauls and Pharnaces I king of Pontus.

2. V Philopator ('loving his father') (reigned *c.*163–130 BC) was the son of ARIARATHES (1) IV. He rejected, on Roman advice, a marriage alliance with Syria, for which DEMETRIUS (1) I expelled him from his kingdom and replaced him with a usurper. He appealed to Rome, which divided the kingdom between the two; Ariarathes then (*c.*157) recovered the lost portion with the help of ATTALUS (2) II of Pergamon. He sacked Priene to recover the treasure he considered had been stolen from him. He fell in battle while assisting the Romans against ARISTONICUS of Pergamon.

3. VI (reigned 130–116 BC) was the son of ARIARATHES (2) V. During his minority his mother Nysa ruled harshly and the king of Pontus, MITHRIDATES (2) V, intervened and married him to his own daughter, Laodice. He was killed by GOR-

DIUS, a Cappadocian nobleman, who was in Mithridates' pay.

4. **VII** (died 101 BC) During his infancy his mother Laodice acted as regent; Cappadocia was invaded by the Bithynian king NICOMEDES III, whereupon Laodice's brother, MITHRIDATES (3) VI of Pontus, also invaded the country. Laodice married Nicomedes, and Mithridates, claiming to be the protector of Ariarathes, placed him on the throne. However, Ariarathes objected to the presence of his father's assassin GORDIUS, who was in league with Mithridates: the upshot was the murder of the king by Mithridates, his uncle, who replaced him with his own son, ARIARATHES (6) IX.

5. **VIII** was the younger brother of ARIARATHES (4) VII. The Cappadocian nobles rebelled against MITHRIDATES (3) VI and his son and drove them out, and chose this Ariarathes as their king. However, Mithridates soon returned and expelled him. He died shortly afterwards, the last of his line.

6. **IX** (died 86 BC) was a son of MITHRIDATES (3) VI of Pontus who was made king of Cappadocia by his father at the age of eight in 101 BC, with GORDIUS as regent. He was soon deposed by the Roman Senate, which allowed the Cappadocians to choose their own king. They chose ARIOBARZANES (1) I, whom Sulla installed in 95. Ariarathes was later restored after TIGRANES (1) I of Armenia had removed his rival, but once more deposed by the Romans in 89. He died fighting for his father in Thessaly (see ARIARATHES VII).

7. **X** (reigned 42–36 BC) succeeded his brother, ARIOBARZANES (3) III. In 36 ANTONIUS (7) deposed him, put him to death, and relaced him with ARCHELAUS (3).

Ariobarzanes The name of three kings of Cappadocia.

1. **I** (reigned 95–63 BC) was installed on the throne by SULLA (2), then governor (proconsul) of Cilicia, who gave him the title 'Friend of Rome', and he was deposed from *c.*94 to 89 when AQUILLIUS (2) restored him; he was driven out in 88 and restored by Sulla in 84. MITHRIDATES (3) VI's ally TIGRANES (1) I of Armenia drove him out twice, in 78 and 67, after which POMPEIUS (2) finally restored him, increased his kingdom and lent him large sums. In 63 in Pompeius' presence he abdicated in favour of his son, ARIOBARZANES (2) II.

2. **II** (reigned 63–52 BC), a son of ARIOBARZANES (1) I, married a daughter of MITHRIDATES (3) VI, the enemy of Rome. To maintain his throne, however, he required Roman help, which he received from GABINIUS (2) in 57. He was assassinated in 52 BC.

3. **III** (reigned 52–42 BC) was a son of ARIOBARZANES (2) II, recognised in 52 BC as king by the Senate; in 51 BC CICERO (1), when he was governor of neighbouring Cilicia, found Ariobarzanes in a sorry state, friendless and indebted to POMPEIUS (2). He supported Pompeius in the Civil War, but CAESAR (1) pardoned him and added part of Armenia to his kingdom. In 42 CASSIUS (2) accused him of conspiracy and had him killed.

Ariovistus (C1 BC) was a king of the German Suebi. In 71 BC he invaded Gaul on the invitation of the Sequani and attacked and defeated the Aedui. He proceeded to occupy large territories in Gaul. When *c.*61 the Gauls combined to expel him, he defeated them with reinforcements from Germany. The Roman Senate recognised his conquests and gave him the title of 'Friend'. CAESAR (1), however, on becoming governor in 58, was concerned by his power and was petitioned by the Gauls to expel him. He found a pretext for a quarrel and defeated him in a tough campaign in the lands near the Rhine.

Soon after, Ariovistus died a violent death, probably at Roman hands.

Aristides, Aelius (C2 AD), was a Greek writer and public speaker from Mysia who studied Greek literature under Alexander of Cotiaeon, the teacher of MARCUS AURELIUS. He also studied at Athens, perhaps under HERODES ATTICUS (2). On his visit to Rome aged twenty-six he fell ill and went for a cure to the shrine of Asclepius at Pergamon; he lived the rest of his life at Smyrna, within easy reach of the shrine. His writings survive: the most interesting are his account, in *Sacred Teachings*, of his experiences in the healing shrine of Pergamon and his own religious perspective. His other works are speeches, encomiums of gods, and essays. *The Art of Rhetoric* is wrongly attributed to Aristides. In AD 178 he addressed a memorial to the emperor Marcus Aurelius after the earthquake at Smyrna and persuaded him to rebuild the city.

Aristion (C1 BC) was a tyrant of Athens who, as ambassador of the democratic party in 88 BC invited MITHRIDATES (3) VI of Pontus to invade Greece in a campaign of liberation from the Romans. He succeeded the anti-Roman Athenion as tyrant in 87. After Mithridates sent a force under ARCHELAUS (1), SULLA (2) retaliated and besieged Athens. When the Acropolis fell in 86, Aristion was executed.

Aristo, Titius (C1–2 AD), a leading lawyer, was trained by CASSIUS (3) Longinus and was equally proficient in private and public law. He corresponded with the Younger PLINY (2), who admired him, and may have acted as an advisor to TRAJAN. He wrote and collected legal decisions, but though his work was collected by POMPONIUS (2) under the title *Digests*, we only know it through quotations.

Aristobulus 1. (reigned 104–103 BC) was a king and high priest of the Jews, the son of John HYRCANUS (1). He was the first of his family (the Hasmoneans) to assume the royal title. He was succeeded by his brother, ALEXANDER (1) Jannaeus.

2. (C1 BC) was a Hasmonean king and high priest of the Jews, son of ALEXANDER (1) Jannaeus and ALEXANDRA Salome. In 67 he drove out his elder brother HYRCANUS (2), who fled to Nabataea and received help from ARETAS (1) III. The latter was besieging Aristobulus in Jerusalem when, in 63, POMPEIUS (2) intervened and stormed the city, deposing Aristobulus, whom he took with him to Rome as a prisoner. Aristobulus later escaped and led Jewish resistance to Rome, but was recaptured by GABINIUS (2) in 57 and sent back in chains to Rome. After the outbreak of the civil war between Pompeius and CAESAR (1) in 49 BC, Caesar sent Aristobulus to Syria with the support of two legions, but he was murdered by the Pomp- eians. The Parthians installed his son Mattathias ANTIGONUS as king briefly in 40. See Josephus, *The Jewish Wars*.

Aristonicus (died 128 BC) was a pretender to the throne of Pergamon. He was probably an illegitimate son of King EUMENES II of Pergamon who, after the death of ATTALUS (3) III in 133 BC and the bequest of the kingdom to Rome, led a rising against the Romans in favour of his own claim to the throne. He wished to establish a 'City of the Sun' in Asia Minor, and may also have supported a socialistic reorganisation of the state in favour of the poor and servile classes. He fought and won a battle against P. Licinius CRASSUS (5) in 131, but was defeated in 130 by the consul PERPERNA (1) and executed at Rome.

Arius (*c.*AD 260–336) was a Christian theologian from Libya. He was a pupil of Lucian, presbyter of Antioch. After becoming a presbyter at Alexandria he began to propagate the theological view that the Son is less than the Father. After much heated controversy he was condemned as heretical by the Council of Nicaea in 325, where he refused to sign the statement of belief imposed by those who asserted the divinity of JESUS, the Alexandrians led by ATHANASIUS and backed by the emperor CONSTANTINE (1). He was banished and suffered persecution and his writings were burnt, but before he died he was restored to favour with the emperor by the intervention of EUSEBIUS. Three of his letters survive.

Arius Didymus (C1 BC) was a Stoic or Eclectic philosopher from Alexandria, AUGUSTUS' teacher of philosophy. He addressed a message of consolation to LIVIA (2) on the death of her son DRUSUS (3).

Arminius (*c.*18 BC–AD 21) was a chieftain of the Cherusci in northwestern Germany and an opponent of Rome. He led his people in the service of Rome, learnt Latin, and was granted Roman citizenship and equestrian status. However, he changed his view of Roman domination and came to prefer liberty. In AD 9 he led a rising against the Roman occupation force. He lured the Roman legate of Germany, Quinctilius VARUS, at the head of three legions, into an undefensible position near Detmold, in the *Teutoburgiensis Saltus*. There he massacred the legions and took their standards. In AD 15 he fought against his father-in-law Segestes, a pro-Roman who was supported by GERMANICUS; his wife Thusnelda was captured by the Romans. In 16 he was defeated by Germanicus and wounded, but continued his resistance, and was saved by TIBERIUS' recall of Germanicus in 17. In 19 he attacked MAROBODUUS, the king of the Marcomanni, who supported Rome. He then tried to make himself king, but was faced by an armed rebellion. A chieftain of the neighbouring Chatti offered to poison Arminius for Tiberius, but the emperor refused. He was finally killed by his own kinsmen.

Arnobius (C3 AD) was a Christian apologist. Originally a teacher of rhetoric in Numidia, North Africa, he suddenly converted to Christianity *c.*295. At his bishop's behest, he wrote seven books *Against the Pagans*, in which he makes almost no use of the Christian or Hebrew Scriptures but bases his attack on paganism upon a Platonic view of God and a Stoic view of the Soul. He seems to regard JESUS as an inferior deity. His Latin style is elegant and his work survives. He taught LACTANTIUS.

Arria 1. (died AD 42) and her husband, Caecina Paetus, both followed the Stoic philosophy. When Paetus was ordered by the emperor CLAUDIUS (1) to kill himself for his part in the conspiracy that led to the revolt of SCRIBONIANUS, she helped to stiffen her husband's resolve by first stabbing herself and then handing her husband the dagger with the words *Paete, non dolet*: 'It doesn't hurt, Paetus!'. See Pliny, *Letters*, 3. 16.

2. (C1 AD) was the daughter of ARRIA (1) and wife of P. Clodius THRASEA Paetus. She was the mother of FANNIA, who married HELVIDIUS (1) Priscus. Like her parents, she and her husband were leaders of the Stoic opposition to the imperial system. When in AD 66 her husband was condemned by NERO (1) to death for his outspoken views and writings, she wished to join him in death, but was prevented. DOMITIAN banished her but NERVA (4) recalled her and she was a friend of PLINY (2) the Younger. See Tacitus, *Annals*, 16, 21–35.

Arrian (*c.*AD 86–160) was the historian of Alexander the Great. Flavius Arrianus, born at Nicomedia in Bithynia, was a friend and pupil of Epictetus, whose *Discourses* he preserved and published at Athens. In 124 he received the Roman citizenship from HADRIAN, and in 133 was appointed prefect of Cappadocia; the following year he repulsed an invasion of the province by the Alans. He became consul in 146 under ANTONINUS Pius and died in the reign of MARCUS AURELIUS.

Arruntius 1, Lucius (C1 BC), was a Roman naval commander and historian who was proscribed by the triumvirs in 43 BC but escaped to join Sextus POMPEIUS (4). In 39 after the treaty of Misenum he was reconciled to Octavian (see AUGUSTUS) and in 31 led a section of his fleet at Actium. He was consul in 22 BC and wrote a lost history of the Punic Wars.

2, Lucius (died AD 36), was a senator and provincial governor, son of ARRUNTIUS (1). He inherited great wealth and was a successful and energetic man with a reputation for honesty. He was consul in AD 6 and, according to TACITUS (1), was seen as a possible and worthy successor to AUGUSTUS' principate. Consequently TIBERIUS saw him as a rival, but treated him with respect, appointing him governor of Eastern Spain, but making it difficult for him to go to his province, which he nevertheless ruled through legates for about ten years. In 31 Tiberius overruled an attempt by SEJANUS' friends to bring him to trial; but he committed suicide after being accused of treason and adultery. He adopted as his son SCRIBONIANUS, who led a rebellion against CLAUDIUS (1).

Artabanus 1. II (reigned AD 12–40) was a king of Parthia. In AD 12 he gained the throne by force from his predecessor, Vonones I. Artabanus, who was a member of the Arsacid house on his mother's side, was chosen by the nobles in preference to Vonones, who fled to Armenia. GERMANICUS supported Artabanus' claim and made a treaty with him, and, in AD 18, installed a Roman puppet on the throne of Armenia; but in 34 Artabanus challenged Rome and invaded Armenia, putting his own son Arsaces on the Armenian throne. TIBERIUS responded to this threat by encouraging rivals to seize the thrones of Armenia and Parthia. In 36 Artabanus, menaced by an Iberian invasion of Armenia, fled to Hyrcania. TIRIDATES (2), a Parthian usurper supported by Tiberius, advanced through Mesopotamia and was crowned at Ctesiphon, the capital, but Artabanus soon drove him out again. Being thus restored to his kingdom, he held a meeting on the Euphrates with VITELLIUS (2), the governor of Syria, at which he accepted Roman dominion over Armenia in return for Roman recognition of his claim to Parthia. Once again, under pressure from Parthian nobles, he had to flee, but was finally restored by Izates, king of Adiabene in Mesopotamia.

2. V (reigned AD 209–226) was the last Parthian king, the younger son of Vologeses IV. He rebelled against his brother Vologeses V, and the ensuing civil strife gave the Roman emperor CARACALLA a chance to attempt the conquest of the East. The latter invaded Parthia in 216 and 217 but was murdered by his officers; his successor MACRINUS was defeated but patched up a peace with Artabanus, leaving him in possession of Parthia and Armenia. In 226 Ardashir, an officer in the Parthian army who claimed descent from the Persian Achaemenid dynasty, and who had a sense of grievance against Artabanus, led a revolt which was widely supported, partly because of the leader's championship of the ancient Persian religion. He defeated and killed Artabanus and took the title King of Kings. See ARTAXERXES.

Artavasdes 1. II (reigned 55–34 BC) was a king of Armenia, the son of TIGRANES (1) II. He was an ally of Rome when CRASSUS (3) invaded Mesopotamia in 53. He turned against Rome, however, when ORODES II, king of Parthia, invaded Armenian territory: he made his peace with him and gave his sister to be married to Pacorus, the son of Orodes. Euripides' *Bacchae* was performed at the wedding feast: there is a story that the head of the dead Crassus was used to represent the head of Pentheus in the performance. After many years of neutrality, he assisted ANTONIUS (7) in 36 in his campaign against Parthia, but betrayed Antonius' trust by changing sides in mid-campaign. In 34 Antonius invaded Armenia, defeated and captured him, and took him to Alexandria for display in his triumphal procession. CLEOPATRA (4) VII had him killed in 31 BC.

2. (died 20 BC) was a king of Media Atropatene (Azerbaijan) whose kingdom ANTONIUS (7) attacked in 36 BC. He went over to the Roman side in hostility to ARTAVASDES (1), and received part of Armenia as his reward after Antonius conquered it in 34. His daughter Iotape was betrothed to Antonius' son Alexander Helios. In 30 BC, however, his kingdom and Armenia were overrun by the Parthians under PHRAATES (1) IV, and Artavasdes took refuge with Octavian (see AUGUSTUS). The latter appointed him king of Lesser Armenia, but he remained in Rome where he died.

Artaxerxes I (reigned AD 226–241) (Persian *Ardashir*) was the first Sassanid king of Persia; also the name of several of his successors. He was the son of Papak and claimed descent from the Achaemenid dynasty. He served with distinction in the army of ARTABANUS (2) V of Parthia and was dissatisfied with his reward and rebelled, leading an army of disaffected people whom he aroused by offering to restore the ancient Zoroastrian religion. He seized Persepolis, conquered other areas of the kingdom, and finally in AD 226 defeated Artabanus and took his capital of Ctesiphon. He then embarked on a war with Rome, claiming the return of all the territories which the Persians had held in the fifth century BC. SEVERUS (2) Alexander, the Roman emperor, fought an indecisive war against him from 230 to 232, though he recovered Mesopotamia. After the deposition and murder of Severus in 235, Artaxerxes invaded Mesopotamia again, and took Carrhae and Nisibis. He made his son SAPOR (1) I coregent in the last year of his life.

Artaxias or **Artaxes** Greek forms of the name of kings of Armenia.

1. A son of king ARTAVASDES (1) II of Armenia. He seized his father's throne in 33 BC, and avenged his father's fall by massacring all the Romans in his country. Ten years later he was murdered by a party of malcontents, and AUGUSTUS, at the request of the Armenians, replaced him with his brother TIGRANES (2) III.

2. (reigned AD 18–35) A son of POLEMO (1), king of Pontus, he was placed on the throne of Armenia by GERMANICUS.

Arulenus Rusticus, Quintus Junius (died *c.*AD 93), was a Roman senator and Stoic philosopher from Patavium (Padua), suffect consul in AD 92. He was a friend of the Stoics who opposed the emperors in the first century AD, and died for it. In 66 when Arulenus was a tribune, THRASEA Paetus persuaded him not to veto the decree of the Senate which condemned Thrasea to death. As praetor in 69 he was wounded while on a delegation for VITELLIUS (1) to VESPASIAN's army, and was put to death by DOMITIAN for his works in praise of the Stoics THRASEA Paetus and HELVIDIUS (1) Priscus. REGULUS (2) published his speech prosecuting him.

Asclepiades (died *c.*56 BC) was a Greek physician from Prusa in Bithynia who practised medicine at Rome. He represents a revolutionary approach in that he based his practice on the atomic theory of Epicurus as opposed to the tradition descending from Hippocrates, and used diet and the observation of appearances in his approach to healing. He was popular and successful and left writings of which we have considerable fragments. He died in his eighties.

Asclepiodotus *see* ALLECTUS.

Asconius Pedianus, Quintus (AD 3–88), was a Roman writer on history and literature and commentator on CICERO (1). He was born at Patavium (Padua), and probably knew C. Asinius GALLUS (2) and Junius BLAESUS; he went blind in 76. He wrote a (now lost) life of SALLUST, a *Symposium* on the virtues of physical exercise for a long life, and a defence of VIRGIL. We still have part of his historical commentary on some of Cicero's speeches, written between 54 and 57 for his two sons. A much later grammatical commentary on Cicero's Verrine orations was included in the manuscript of this commentary.

Asellio, Sempronius (C2 BC), was a historian who had been a military tribune at Numantia in 134 BC. He wrote a lost history of his own time in the manner of POLYBIUS. GELLIUS (1) quotes him (5, 18. 8). CICERO (1) had a low opinion of his style. His work seems to have been continued by SISENNA.

Asper, Aemilius (C2 AD), was a Latin grammarian and literary critic who wrote lost commentaries on the works of TERENCE, SALLUST and VIRGIL. He was used as a source for grammar by Donatus: fragments of his work suggest that it was of high quality.

Athanasius (*c*.295–373 AD) was a Christian theologian and leader who, in 325, though only a deacon, was prominent at the Council of Nicaea, where he argued forcefully for belief in the divinity of JESUS and his equality with God. In 328 he was elected bishop of Alexandria, where he vigorously opposed the standpoint of ARIUS. During this period he was deposed and exiled five times: two of his periods of exile he spent in the West, to which he introduced monasticism: he was influenced by ANTONY, the founder of monasticism, whose biography he wrote. Later in his life he tried to bring the opponents of Arianism together, and he elaborated the theology of the Holy Spirit. Many of his writings survive, including letters and polemical works.

Athenaeus (C1 AD) was a Greek physician and Stoic, founder of the Pneumatists. He originated from Attalia in Pamphylia and practised medicine at Rome under the emperor CLAUDIUS (1). Accepting the existence of four elements in the body, he added *pneuma*, breath, as the fifth: according to him health and illness depended on the mixture of the elements in the body. He insisted on the importance of diet and formulated elaborate rules of diet for people of different ages. He followed Aristotle's physiological doctrines. GALEN had a high opinion of his theories.

Athenodorus 1. (C1 BC) was a Greek Stoic philosopher and man of letters. Known as Cordylion, he came from Tarsus, and was head of the library of Pergamon. Marcus CATO (5) of Utica, however, took him to Rome on his return from the East and gave him hospitality until he died, an old man, *c*.47 BC.

2. (*c*.74 BC–AD 7) was a Greek Stoic philosopher like ATHENODORUS (1) and a man of letters; also associated with Tarsus. He was born at Canana near Tarsus, the son of Sandon. He studied under POSIDONIUS at Rhodes and himself taught at Apollonia in Illyricum where Octavius, the future AUGUSTUS, was his pupil at the time of CAESAR (1)'s assassination in 44 BC, and with whom he probably travelled back to Italy. He seems to have exercised a strong influence over Augustus; later in life he was sent by his patron to Tarsus to remove Boethus, the ruler whom ANTONIUS (7) had appointed, and take his place. Here he drew up a new constitution for the city. He was a friend of CICERO (1) and STRABO, and corresponded with the former, when he was writing *On Duties*, about the opinions of Posidonius.

Atia (died 43 BC) was the mother of the emperor AUGUSTUS. She was the daughter of M. Atius Balbus and of CAESAR (1)'s sister JULIA (2), and married OCTAVIUS (1), to whom she bore the future emperor. After her husband died in 58 BC she married L. Marcius PHILIPPUS (3). The couple opposed Octavian's acceptance of Caesar's bequest. On her death she received a state funeral, her son being consul.

Atilius, Marcus (C2 BC), was a Roman writer of comedy. He may be the same person as the Atilius whom CICERO (1) mentions in *On Ends* (*De Finibus*), 1. 5: he quotes Licinius as describing Atilius as a 'writer of steel' for his translation of the *Electra* of Sophocles.

Attalus The name of three kings of Pergamon.

1. I (269–197 BC) The founder of the kingdom, the son of Attalus who was a cousin of Eumenes I. In 241 he succeeded his cousin as ruler and stopped the policy of conciliating his Galatian neighbours by payment of tribute. Consequently he was faced with war against them: he defeated them thoroughly *c.*231, for which he earned the title *Soter* ('Saviour') and a monument which was surmounted with the well known statue of the 'Dying Gaul'. He also attacked Antiochus 'the Hawk' who had seceded from the kingdom of his brother Seleucus II and by 228 drove him out of Asia Minor except Cilicia. However, he lost most of what he had acquired to the prowess of Achaeus, a Seleucid general of ANTIOCHUS (1) III. He cooperated with Rome in her wars against the Macedonians, himself supporting the Aetolians who were trying to break away from PHILIP (1) V. In the Second Macedonian War (201–197 BC) he and the Rhodians joined forces with the Romans, who finally put an end to Philip's expansionist ambitions. Attalus died just before the final victory of Cynoscephalae.

Besides being an able general and diplomat, Attalus made his small kingdom an important power in Asia Minor and beyond. He was a great patron of the arts and philosophy. He was succeeded by his son, EUMENES II.

2. II (220–138 BC) was the second son of ATTALUS (1), and succeeded his brother EUMENES II in 159 as king of Pergamon. He was an able general and diplomat who outshone his brother, to whom, however, he remained loyal. When he became king he maintained the policy of supporting Rome, and caused trouble to Syria by his support of Alexander BALAS as pretender to its throne in 150. He won the support of Rome for his two wars against Bithynia. At Athens he beautified the marketplace by building the *Stoa* or colonnade which bears his name. He was nicknamed *Philadelphus* for his loyalty to Eumenes.

3. III (*c.*170–133 BC) was the son of EUMENES II and nephew of ATTALUS (2), he succeeded his uncle as king in 138 BC. He only reigned for five years; by his will he bequeathed the kingdom to the Roman Senate, having no child of his own. His death led to the insurrection of ARISTONICUS.

Attianus, Publius Acilius (C2 AD), the tutor and guardian of the emperor HADRIAN, was born at Italica in Spain of equestrian rank. He was prefect of the Praetorian Guard on the death of TRAJAN in AD 117, and probably assisted PLOTINA, Trajan's wife, to secure the succession for Hadrian. In 118 he was responsible for the execution of four senators of consular rank who were alleged to have conspired against Hadrian. In 119 Hadrian rewarded him with consular rank and a seat in the Senate, thereby depriving him of his power.

Atticus, Titus Pomponius (110–32 BC), was a Roman financier and man of letters. He was born in the equestrian class to a rich father, and was adopted by his childless maternal uncle, CAECILIUS (4), who left him ten million sesterces. He took his uncle's name on adoption, being known as Caecilius Pomponianus; *Atticus* was a nickname that his friends gave him for his love of Greek culture. He was a boyhood friend of CICERO (1), whose brother Quintus CICERO (2) married the sister of Atticus, Pomponia. In 85 BC, to avoid the coming civil strife in Italy, Atticus liquidised his assets and went to live in Athens. About twenty years later he returned to Rome, but being now a convinced Epicurean he refused to take any part in politics but devoted himself to money-making and the arts. In 56 he married Pilia, by whom he had one child, a daughter. Besides Cicero, he was on close terms with a string of statesmen from MARIUS (1) to Octavian (see AUGUSTUS), many of whom he helped financially, though keeping clear of all political involvement. He gave support to the family of ANTONIUS (7) during the campaign of Mutina and so escaped proscription in 42. Cicero's correspondence with him is famous, and through it we gain a considerable picture of the man. Cicero relied on his judgment and seems to have needed to be in constant communication with him. Atticus is thought to have himself edited the letters and published them. He married his daughter Caecilia to Marcus AGRIPPA (1), who inherited Atticus' fortune and used it to carry out an ambitious building programme. Atticus committed suicide by starving himself because he had fallen incurably ill. Cornelius NEPOS wrote his life. See D.R. Shackleton Bailey (1970) *Cicero's Letters to Atticus*, Cambridge: Cambridge University Press.

Aufidius Bassus *see* BASSUS (2).

Augustus (63 BC–AD 14) was the first Roman emperor (*Imperator*, *Princeps*), a title and concept which he himself created. Originally named Gaius Octavius, he was born at Rome on 23 September 63 BC, the son of a 'new man', Gaius OCTAVIUS (1), and of ATIA, the daughter of Julius CAESAR (1)'s sister JULIA (3), and hence was the great-nephew of Caesar. His father died in 59 and he was brought up by his mother in the household of his stepfather L. Marcius PHILIPPUS (3), though he had much contact with his great-uncle. He was given a good education and had a taste for literature and philosophy. When he was twelve his grandmother Julia died, and it fell upon him to deliver the speech at her funeral. Three years later he was appointed *pontifex*, and in 46 BC he took part in Caesar's triumphal procession. He visited Caesar in Spain in 45 and was at Apollonia in Illyricum studying under ATHENODORUS (2) when the news arrived of Caesar's assassination. He had been adopted by Caesar as his son by his will (an act of dubious legality), as the dictator had no legitimate child, and he hurried back to Rome with his friends AGRIPPA (1) and SALVIDIENUS Rufus to claim his inheritance.

Now officially styled C. Julius Caesar, to which the distinguishing extra name Octavianus could be added, he was nevertheless an unknown youth and one whom the great men of state, particularly the orator CICERO (1), thought they could manipulate. He allied himself at first with the senatorial party against ANTONIUS (7), who in 43 left Rome to govern part of Gaul. The Senate granted Octavian the rank of a senator and propraetor, and he led an army of Caesar's veterans, whose loyalty he nurtured, to defeat Antonius at Mutina in 43. The death of both consuls in this action enhanced Octavian's power and put him at the head of a large army, who marched to Rome and compelled the reluctant Senate to accept his status as Caesar's son and heir and nominate him consul for the rest of 43. He now made an accommodation with Antonius and Antonius' new ally M. Aemilius LEPIDUS (4), an ex-consul who was governing part of Spain and southern Gaul, both of whom he met at Bononia (Bologna) in Cisalpine Gaul. As a result of their compact, a law was passed in November 42, the *lex Titia*, granting the three Caesarian leaders, Octavian, Antonius and Lepidus, overriding dictatorial powers for five years: this was the second and official 'triumvirate'. They divided the western part of the Empire among themselves, leaving the East to the republicans under BRUTUS (5) and CASSIUS (2). Octavian was appointed to rule Africa, Sicily and Sardinia as his provinces. On 1 January 42 Julius Caesar was declared a god and Octavian was henceforth able to assume the title *Divi Filius*, 'Son of a god'. The triumvirs also held a proscription of their enemies, following the example of SULLA (2), drawing up lists of those who could be killed with impunity: Octavian was as ruthless as his colleagues and did nothing to prevent the death of Cicero. Many escaped by flight, and those who were not caught were later restored to their previous status. In 42 the triumvirs took on the republican army in Macedonia and defeated it at Philippi, though Octavian was afflicted by ill health, which often struck him at moments of military crisis. There remained Sextus POMPEIUS (4), who still defied the triumvirs with a strong navy, and Lucius ANTONIUS (4), Antonius' brother, who was consul in 41 and then proceeded with the support of FULVIA, Antonius' wife, to champion Italian landowners against Octavian's settlements of the veteran soldiers of Julius Caesar. A new distribution of provinces had given Octavian Spain as well as Africa and Sardinia, and he had been charged by his colleagues with the settlement of the veterans. During this time Octavian spent most of his time in Italy and relied on the support of Agrippa, MAECENAS and Salvidienus Rufus. He had been betrothed to Servilia, but now married Claudia, daughter of Publius CLODIUS and Fulvia: the marriage was probably not consummated. In 40 Octavian defeated L. Antonius at Perusia. He pardoned Antonius but Fulvia fled to her husband in Greece. In 40 he became SCRIBONIA's third husband: she bore him his only child, JULIA (5). He may have done this to win over Sextus Pompeius, as Scribonia was a kinswoman of his by marriage.

In 40 the triumvirs met at Brundisium: relations had been strained by the rebellion of L. Antonius and Fulvia, who was now dead, allowing Octavian to offer Antonius his sister OCTAVIA (1), the widow of C. Claudius MARCELLUS (4) and the mother of three children; Antonius married her at once. The Empire was redistributed and Octavian became ruler of the west while Italy remained open to all three triumvirs. At the pact of Misenum, Sextus Pompeius was granted a share in power, being given Sicily, Sardinia, Corsica and Achaea in return for lifting his blockade of Italy. In 39, however, Octavian divorced his wife, who was much older than himself and nagged him, and insisted on marrying in January 38 a woman already pregnant by her current husband, namely LIVIA (2) Drusilla, the wife of Tiberius Claudius NERO (4) and mother of the future emperor TIBERIUS. She proved to be his lifelong support, though she bore him no children. In the next two years Octavian was preoccupied with Sextus Pompeius, a painful thorn in his flesh, whom he accused of breaking the pact; but he suffered naval defeats at Cumae and Messina. He met Antonius again in 37 at Tarentum where they renewed their triumviral powers for five more years. In 36 Octavian was again defeated by Pompeius at Tauromenium (Taormina) though Agrippa had more success. Lepidus brought a vast army from Africa and defeated Pompeius' army soundly; Pompeius was finally defeated at sea by Agrippa at Naulochus and later killed in Asia. At the same time Octavian dealt with Lepidus, who ventured to claim Sicily for himself, forcing him to retire from the triumvirate and live under house arrest. Antonius was now his only rival.

Octavian's task at this time was to win the support of Rome and Italy in his struggle to become sole ruler. In this task he was aided by Agrippa, Livia, and able men like Maecenas and Valerius MESSALLA (4). By a process of propaganda and consolidation Octavian established himself in Italian minds as the supreme patron and sole guarantor of peace. By his campaigns east of the Adriatic he gained glory and strengthened the frontier system of Italy. In 33 the triumvirate ended and Octavian was in constitutional difficulties. He faced down the consuls of 32, who were Antonius' men and fled to him. Octavian extorted Antonius' will from the Vestal Virgins, to whom it had been entrusted, and read it to the Senate: it was scandalous in the gifts and privileges it granted to the family of CLEOPATRA (4). In October Roman citizens throughout Italy – the western provinces were added later – were made to swear an oath of allegiance to Octavian and thus became attached to him as clients. Meanwhile Antonius had rejected and divorced Octavia, by whom he had had two daughters (ANTONIA 1 and ANTONIA 2) and now openly called Cleopatra his wife. In 31 Octavian deprived Antonius of his powers and the consulship and took the office himself for the third time, and held it every year until 23. The Senate declared war on Cleopatra.

In September 31, after some months of skirmishing on land and sea in the region of Epirus, Octavian's fleet under the command of Agrippa overcame Antonius' in what may have been a negligible skirmish off the promontory of Actium in Greece. Antonius was deserted by most of his soldiers and sailors, and fled with Cleopatra to Egypt. Octavian now had to deal with the settlement of a huge army he no longer needed. In 30 he entered Egypt, defeated Antonius in battle, and took Egypt into the Empire on special terms. Otherwise he left Antonius' dispositions in the East very much as he found them. In 29 he returned to Italy to hold his triumph and closed the gates of the temple of Janus, symbolising the return of peace. The 20s were a time of intensive constitutional reform. In 28 he and Agrippa were censors and remodelled the Senate, reducing its numbers by 200. In 27 he formally 'restored the Republic', but in fact retained enough powers to maintain absolute control. He also took the honorific title *Augustus*, by which he is usually known and which emphasises a religious piety for which he wished to be known: the word meant 'divinely ordained' and is probably connected with *augur*. Augustus now commanded the entire Roman army, which he kept sweet with enormous gratuities, and was by far the most prestigious and influential man in the state. As victor at least in name of so many battles, he took and kept the old title *Imperator* ('Commander'), which he and his successors monopolised and which came to denote the general powers of the emperor. In 28 he had been elected *Princeps Senatus* ('Leader of the Senate'), and the title *Princeps* (sc. *Civitatis* 'of the citizen body') also gave a more civilian and presidential reference. In theory, the powers he held were to end after ten years.

At this period Augustus was striving to enhance his authority among a mostly willing populace. Worship of the emperor was encouraged, especially in the eastern provinces where worship of the monarch was already well established. The oath of allegiance was also extended widely in the East and elsewhere, and the military oath was now made to the person of the emperor. In the 20s much was done to consolidate the frontiers of the Empire, in Egypt, Gaul, and the Alps. Augustus fell seriously ill a couple of times, and his sister's son MARCELLUS (7), on whom he was building his hopes for the succession and had married to his own daughter Julia, died in 23. In this year Augustus decided that a new constitutional settlement was needed: he gave up the consulship, which he had now held twelve times, but took the power of a tribune ('tribunician power') for life, which gave him a constitutional right to propose and veto laws. He was also awarded seniority of command over every governor appointed by the Senate – and he kept the major provinces that were under military garrisons under his own governance. He rejected the title of dictator and seemed to have restored republican procedures while really usurping political and military power definitively to his office. In fact, his reign saw the transference of political and administrative powers of initiative from the Senate and magistrates to the court, which the emperor now gathered round him, a new concept in Roman government.

Now that Marcellus was dead, Augustus promoted the faithful Agrippa to provide for the succession. He caused him in 21 to divorce his wife Marcella, Augustus' own niece, in favour of his daughter Julia, who bore him five children. Augustus embarked on travels in Greece and Asia in the years between 22 and 19, and won diplomatic success in dealing with the Parthians who recognised Roman claims to control Armenia. In 18 and 17 he embarked on a programme of moral legislation, passing the laws that bore his name to make adultery a crime and marriage a virtual obligation. Another law was intended to reduce extravagant spending by private citizens. In 18 Agrippa was made his co-regent and in 17 Augustus adopted the latter's sons Gaius CAESAR (3) and Lucius CAESAR (8). In 17 he held 'secular' games, a great display that celebrated the end of every hundred years of the City. He spent the years 16 to 13 in Gaul, settling the affairs of the huge territory that his great-uncle Julius Caesar had conquered. In 12 a new campaign began to advance the frontier to the Danube, a process which Octavian and later Agrippa had begun. Tiberius was kept busy for three years completing the conquest of Pannonia and the Danube lands. Meanwhile at Rome Augustus reorganised the social classes, the senatorial and equestrian orders. He also appointed a council of senators and others to advise him (much later, in AD 13, their decisions were given the force of senatorial decrees). In 12 BC the death of Lepidus, the *Pontifex Maximus* or chief priest of the state, allowed him to take that title, which emperors thereafter nearly always held. Agrippa also died in 12, and Livia's sons, Tiberius and DRUSUS (3), now took on greater prominence. Tiberius, already a successful general, was compelled to divorce Agrippa's daughter Vipsania, whom he loved, to marry Agrippa's widow Julia, whom he came to detest. But he brilliantly executed the emperor's military plans or retrieved desperate situations in the East, the Danube, and Germany. In 6 BC Tiberius was granted the power of a tribune for five years, but soon afterwards went into retirement in Rhodes through jealousy of Augustus' promotion of Gaius and Lucius. In 2 BC on the proposal of Valerius Messalla Augustus was voted the title *Pater Patriae* ('Father of the Fatherland') by the Senate. Whatever military successes were won during Tiberius' absence, later historians seem deliberately to have ignored.

The remaining acts of the reign were mostly concerned with social legislation. He divided the city of Rome into fourteen regions, limited the rights of ex-slaves to the citizenship, and in 2 BC banished Julia to the island of Pandataria for immorality. His two grandsons, whom he had adopted, died, Lucius in AD 2, Gaius in 4. Tiberius came back to Rome in AD 2, and in 4 Augustus finally recognised him as his heir and adopted him, together with Agrippa's last child, AGRIPPA (2) Postumus, whom he soon banished. Augustus *c.*AD 5 reformed voting procedures, effectively abolishing the ancient electoral system of popular voting and replacing it with 'designation' by a group of members of the higher orders. In AD 6 a new arrangement came into force for paying off discharged soldiers from a military treasury instead of sending them to found colonies. He also set up a city police force and a force of night watchmen. A terrible disaster occurred in AD 9 in Germany when three legions under Quinctilius VARUS were ambushed and destroyed. Tiberius was given the task of restoring the situation.

Augustus died peacefully at Nola on 19 August AD 14, his reign of 45 years from 31 BC having been so long that he had outlived all opposition and had firmly established his new form of 'republican' monarchy. His ashes were buried in the mausoleum he had built on the Campus Martius and the Senate voted him divine, with a state cult, within a month of his death. He had been ruthless and hypocritical, but also tenacious and loyal, especially to his family and faithful supporters, and had given the Empire the inestimable gift of internal peace. Provincial government had been made honest and efficient, the Empire's borders fixed on defensible lines, and the succession assured. He was conservative in his preservation of the rigid class structure of earlier times and in his puritanical moral legislation. He most feared the old Roman aristocracy, which he deprived of its power and ability to compete with him, instead establishing his court of selected loyalists and his kinsmen. Yet he encouraged literature, especially poetry, if it favoured his regime. The works of VIRGIL, HORACE and LIVY are monuments to what was best in Augustus' Rome; but we cannot forget OVID languishing for years at Tomis. He left to posterity an account of his Empire, the *Achievements of Augustus* (*Res Gestae Divi Augusti*), probably brought up to date in AD 13 by Tiberius. See Suetonius' *Life of Augustus*; R. Syme (1939) *The Roman Revolution*, Oxford: Clarendon Press; M. Grant (1985) *The Roman Emperors*, London: Weidenfeld & Nicolson; A.H.M. Jones (1970) *Augustus*, London: Chatto & Windus; F.G.B. Millar (1977) *The Emperor in the Roman World*, London: Duckworth; H.H. Scullard (1982) *From The Gracchi to Nero*, London; Methuen; P. Southern (1998) *Augustus*, London: Routledge.

Aurelian (*c.*AD 215–275), the emperor Lucius Domitius Aurelianus, was born at Sirmium in Lower Pannonia of humble family and was involved in the plot that in 268 overthrew GALLIENUS and replaced him with CLAUDIUS (2) II 'Gothicus'. Claudius appointed him commander of the cavalry and he fought with great success in the war with the Goths of 269–70. Claudius fell ill and died in May 270, and though the army in Italy tried to replace him with his brother QUINTILLUS, the Balkan army insisted on the appointment of Aurelian to the purple. He finished the work begun by Gallienus and, by defeating the Goths and Vandals, restored the Danube frontier to its earlier strength; he also withdrew the Roman garrisons and doubtless much of the Romanised population from Dacia to the right bank of the river, leaving Dacia to the barbarians. In 271 the Alemanni, who had previously invaded Gaul, invaded Italy and got past Rimini. Though at first worsted, Aurelian drove them back and destroyed them in detail. He then went to Rome and organised the defence of the City by ordering the construction of a new city wall.

Meanwhile ZENOBIA, queen-regent of Palmyra in eastern Syria, had seized Egypt and nearly all Asia Minor. The emperor marched east, on his way clearing more Gothic invaders from the Balkans, and advanced through Asia Minor to meet Zenobia's forces near Antioch. He defeated the army of Palmyra both here and at Emesa, and after conveying his army through the desert to Palmyra he captured Zenobia as she made her way to Persia to seek reinforcements. In any case the Sassanids were preoccupied with the consequences of the death of SAPOR (1).

Aurelian brought the queen back to Rome for his triumph; on the way he again drove invading Carpi across the Danube, but was recalled to Palmyra by a rebellion: the kinsmen of Zenobia had massacred the Roman garrison and proclaimed a new king, Antiochus. In 273 he struck at Palmyra while off its guard and wiped it out. He also defeated an attempt by an Alexandrian merchant, Firmus, to save Zenobia.

He next turned to the west, where in Gaul Gaius TETRICUS had established himself at the head of a Gallic empire, including Spain and Britain, which had subsisted since the rebellion of POSTUMUS. He met Tetricus' army in 274 at Châlons-sur-Marne, where Tetricus hastened to surrender. The Roman Empire was reunited and both Zenobia and Tetricus walked in Aurelian's triumph. Both were treated with magnanimity; Aurelian was endowed with the title *Restitutor Orbis* ('Restorer of the World'). He set out in 275 to face the Persian threat but was murdered by a small group of officers led by his secretary, Eros. Few reigns as short have witnessed such brilliant success. He won by determination and strict discipline of himself and others who were in authority. He instituted the worship of the Unconquered Sun as a state cult and was hostile to Christianity. He attempted to reform the debased coinage. At his death, the army handed the choice of his successor to the Senate, who chose TACITUS (2). See M. Grant (1985) *The Roman Emperors*, London: Weidenfeld & Nicolson.

Aurelius Antoninus *see* CARACALLA.

Aurelius, Marcus *see* MARCUS AURELIUS.

Aurelius Victor, Sextus (C4 AD), was a Roman historian, born in Africa, governor of Pannonia Secunda in AD 361. About this time he published an extant volume of biographies of emperors called *The Caesars* along the lines of SUETONIUS (2)'s. He was city prefect in AD 389.

Aureolus, Manius Acilius (C3 AD), was a general of Dacian origin. In the reign of VALERIAN he was made commander of a new corps of cavalry in Northern Italy and assisted GALLIENUS in 258 to defeat Ingenuus in Pannonia. In 261 he defeated and killed MACRIANUS, who was a pretender to the purple, in Thrace. In 263 he opposed POSTUMUS, the usurping emperor of Gaul. But in 268 he tired of loyalty to his emperor and, with the support of Postumus, rebelled and seized Milan, where Gallienus besieged him. Gallienus, however, was murdered by members of his staff, and Aureolus surrendered to CLAUDIUS (2) II; he was shortly afterwards murdered by his troops.

Avidius Cassius, Gaius (died AD 175), was a general and provincial governor in the east. A native of Syria, the son of C. Avidius Heliodorus of Cyrrhus, he was suffect consul under MARCUS AURELIUS and commanded the army under VERUS in the Parthian War of AD 162–65, in which his efforts led to the conquest of Mesopotamia. He was subsequently appointed governor of all the eastern provinces. In 175, on hearing false news that Marcus Aurelius was dead, he had himself proclaimed emperor and ruled the East for three months. He was then murdered by a centurion.

Avienus (mid-C4 AD), otherwise Avienius, a poet and geographer, wrote in Latin hexameters poetry on various geographical, topological or mythological themes. He is far from reliable. His main extant works are *Description of the Earth* (*Descriptio Orbis Terrae*), based on Dionysius Periegetes, and *The Coast* (*Ora Maritima*), possibly part of a larger work in iambic metre, on the coastline of the northern Mediterranean west from Massilia.

He also translated Aratus' *Phaenomena* and *Prognostica*. Besides being a writer, he held political positions, belonging to a noble family from Volsinii. His full name was Postumius Rufius Festus. How he gained his extra name, Avien(i)us, is unclear.

Avitus Alexianus, Gaius Julius (late C2 AD), was a Syrian of equestrian rank from Emesa. He was raised to the Senate by Septimius SEVERUS (1) and governed Raetia: he held the consulship, acted as *comes* (companion) to Severus in Britain and was later governor (legate) of Dalmatia and proconsul of Asia until his death in 217. He married JULIA (11) Maesa, sister of Severus' wife JULIA (10) Domna, by whom he had two distinguished daughters, JULIA (12) Soaemias and JULIA (13) Mamaea, both mothers of emperors: he was thus the grandfather of ELAGABALUS and SEVERUS (2) Alexander.

B

Baebius Tamphilus, Marcus (C2 BC), was praetor in 192 BC and consul in 181. He assisted GLABRIO (1)'s invasion of Greece against ANTIOCHUS (1) III in 191, and in 181 transported 40,000 Ligurians to a new home near Beneventum. LIVY reports that he fixed the number of praetorships and passed a law against bribery at elections.

Balas, Alexander (reigned 153–145 BC), was an incompetent ruler of Syria who gained the throne by pretending to be the son of ANTIOCHUS (2) IV. He killed DEMETRIUS (1) I in battle with the help of the Jewish Maccabees. He had the support of Rome, Egypt and Pergamon, but was defeated and dethroned by DEMETRIUS (2) II with Egyptian help. He married Cleopatra Thea, eldest daughter of PTOLEMY (2) VI, but lost her to Demetrius.

Balbillus, Tiberius Claudius (C1 AD), was a Greek astrologer. While in Rome he met CLAUDIUS (1), and, when Claudius became emperor, returned from Alexandria where he had been head of the Museum to support him as a 'friend'. He accompanied the emperor to Britain in 43 in a military capacity: military tribune and commander of the engineers; he was later procurator of the province of Asia, and, under NERO (1), Prefect of Egypt from 55 to 59. He also found favour with VESPASIAN. He wrote a book about astrology, *Astrologumena*, of which fragments exist.

Balbinus, Decius Caelius and Marcus Clodius **Pupienus** Maximus were joint emperors, elected by the Senate in AD 238. After long senatorial careers the two were members of a council of twenty ex-consuls appointed to defend Italy against MAXIMINUS (1) the Thracian. They were elected emperors after the death of GORDIAN II in Africa, and divided the responsibilities of the post between them. Pupienus became military commander and on the murder of Maximinus went to Aquileia to send his troops back to their duties on the frontier. The two emperors, with their Caesar, GORDIAN III, then celebrated a triumph, but within three months of their accession were killed by the Praetorian Guard. See M. Grant (1985) *The Roman Emperors*, London: Weidenfeld & Nicolson.

Balbus 1, Lucius Cornelius (C1 BC), a statesman and literary figure, was born a citizen of Gades (Cádiz) in Spain. He was granted Roman citizenship in 72 BC by POMPEIUS (2) in recompense for services against SERTORIUS. He took his name from that of L. Cornelius LENTULUS (8) Crus. He returned to Rome with Caesar and around 59 BC was adopted by THEOPHANES of Mytilene, whose great wealth he inherited. Though widely unpopular as a rich foreign upstart, he lived for a time on close terms with both Pompeius and CAESAR (1), to the latter of whom he gradually attached himself. He became a close friend of CICERO (1), and corresponded with him. When he was accused in 56 of having gained the citizenship illegally, Cicero successfully defended him, aided by Pompeius and CRASSUS (3), with his extant speech *In Defence of Balbus* (*Pro Balbo*). During the Civil War he maintained a neutral stance, which he also urged on Cicero and Lentulus; but he remained in Rome, and after the battle of Pharsalus managed Caesar's personal affairs at Rome along with OPPIUS (2). After Caesar's assassination in 44, he supported Octavian, who raised him to the consulship in 40 BC, the first foreign-born holder of the office. He edited HIRTIUS' commentaries on the Gallic War. He lived until at least 32 BC: in his will he bequeathed 25 denarii to every Roman citizen.

2, Lucius Cornelius (C1 BC), the nephew of BALBUS (1), was also a political and literary figure. He became a Roman citizen at the same time as his uncle, and went to Rome with him where he became an agent of CAESAR (1). He served on POLLIO (1)'s staff in 43 when he was governing Further Spain and, according to a letter Pollio wrote to CICERO (1), embezzled the soldiers' pay after behaving in a high-handed fashion to the people of Cádiz, whose fellow-townsman he was. Later, AUGUSTUS gave him consular rank and made him proconsul of Africa around 20 BC: he won a triumph for his victory over the Garamantes which he held in 19 and which was commemorated in a theatre he built in Rome and dedicated in 13. He carried out large building works in his native Cádiz, including new docks. He wrote a historical play on a mission he performed for Caesar in 49 and other works, all lost.

Bar Kochba or **Cosiba** (died AD 135) in AD 131 led the second Jewish revolt against Rome. His real Hebrew name was Shimon bar Cosiba and the form 'Bar Kochba', 'son of a star', was used by Christian writers. HADRIAN had provoked the revolt by his ban on circumcision and his foundation of a Roman colony (Aelia Capitolina) at Jerusalem. The Roman commander, Sextus Julius Severus, exterminated opposition piecemeal throughout Judaea. Jews were forbidden access to Jerusalem, which was repopulated with Gentiles. Bar Kochba relied largely on guerilla tactics and had a base at En Gedi. Certain of his letters about the revolt survive. Some of his followers took refuge in caves near the Dead Sea, others made a final stand in 135 at Bethar, where he was killed.

Basil (C4 AD) was a Greek defender of Christianity and the founder of monasticism. He was born at Caesarea in Cappadocia in AD 330 of wealthy Christian parents, and received a good education in rhetoric at Constantinople and Athens: his teachers were HIMERIUS, Prohaeresius, and probably LIBANIUS. While he studied he came into contact with GREGORY (2) of Nazianzus. He was baptised in 356 and devoted himself to founding monasteries and establishing their rules; he resisted solitary asceticism. He became bishop of Caesarea in Cappadocia in 370 and died in 379. He wrote much and was deeply imbued with classical learning. His theological views owe something to the philosophy of PLOTINUS. His younger brother was GREGORY (3) of Nyssa.

Bassus 1, Quintus Caecilius (C1 BC), was a supporter of POMPEIUS (2) in the Civil War, of equestrian rank, who fought at the battle of Pharsalus. From there he fled to Syria where in a mutiny he encompassed the murder of Sextus CAESAR (9); he gained the allegiance of two legions and seized the town of Apamea, in which he was besieged by CAESAR (1)'s men from 46 to 44. After Caesar's murder, however, when CASSIUS (2) sought support in Syria, both armies went over to join him. Cassius released Bassus unharmed.

2, Aufidius (C1 AD), was a Roman historian and Epicurean who suffered from ill health. He wrote the history of TIBERIUS' German Wars and a general history of his times, covering the years from 44 BC to AD 50. PLINY (1) the Elder wrote a continuation of the latter. His works, of which QUINTILIAN thought highly, have not survived. TACITUS (1) may have used them as a source for his *Annals*.

3, Caesius (died AD 79), was a poet of the first century AD. In collaboration with CORNUTUS (1) he edited the satires of PERSIUS, who addressed his sixth satire to him. QUINTILIAN praised him for his poetry, which he considered to rank next to that of HORACE. He was killed in the eruption of Vesuvius.
See also QUADRATUS (1).

Bato 1. was a Dalmatian leader who rebelled against Rome in AD 6: he attacked the coastal towns on the northern Adriatic and penetrated the valley of the Save. He allied himself with the Pannonians under BATO (2), but after their surrender in AD 8 and a fruitless attempt to resist the forces of TIBERIUS, he surrendered in AD 9 and was imprisoned at Ravenna.

2. A Pannonian leader who rebelled at the same time as BATO (1), and, after trying to capture Sirmium, surrendered at the river Bathinus. He was, however, captured and killed by BATO (1). See H.H. Scullard (1982) *From the Gracchi to Nero*, London: Methuen, 264f.

Berenice 1. (died 55 BC) was a daughter of PTOLEMY (8) XII The Piper, the eldest sister of the famous CLEOPATRA (4). She was made queen in 58 BC when the people of Alexandria drove her father out. She married ARCHELAUS (2), but was put to death with her husband when GABINIUS (2) restored Ptolemy.

2. (born AD 28) was the daughter of AGRIPPA (3) I, and in 41 married Marcus Julius Alexander. In 46 she married her uncle, Herod, king of Chalcis, but on his death in 48 she lived with her brother, AGRIPPA (4) II, not without suspicion of incest. To counter this, she married Polemo, king of Olba in Cilicia in 53. In 66 she tried to prevent the Jewish revolt against NERO (1). TITUS, son of VESPASIAN, the future emperor, fell in love with her during his command in Judaea (67 to 70); he lived with her openly after she visited Rome with Agrippa in 75. We do not know how long the liaison lasted: on her second visit in 79 he ignored her, and out of respect for Roman public opinion did not marry her. She was defended in a court case by QUINTILIAN.

Bestia, Lucius Calpurnius (C2 BC), served as a Gracchan land commissioner, distributing land in Africa, and was tribune of the *plebs* in 120 BC when he obtained the recall of Publius Popillius LAENAS (3) from exile. Consul in 111 BC, he was despatched to Numidia with SCAURUS (1) to make war on JUGURTHA, but instead concluded a peace which was unacceptable to Rome. On his return to Rome he was condemned by a commission set up by the law of MAMILIUS (1), of which Scaurus was the president, and went into exile. He returned only to flee again, fearing prosecution under VARIUS' law.

Bibaculus, Marcus Furius (C1 BC), a poet, was born *c.*83 BC at Cremona, and is said by SUETONIUS (2) to have been a pupil of Valerius CATO (6). TACITUS (1) and QUINTILIAN assert that, like CATULLUS (1), he lampooned the Caesars but was ignored by them. If he was one of the 'new poets' associated with Catullus he was probably not the Furius attacked by Catullus in several of his hendecasyllabic epigrams. If, on the other hand, as is stated by scholia on HORACE (*Satires*, II, 5, 40) he was the author of an annalistic poem *The Gallic War*, he is unlikely to have been a friend of Catullus.

Bibulus 1, Marcus Calpurnius (died 48 BC), was CAESAR (1)'s colleague in the aedileship (65 BC), the praetorship (62) and the consulship (59). He was a traditional republican who opposed Caesar's agrarian law and, when prevented by force from vetoing it, retired from political life to 'watch the heavens' for omens, so as to block all further legislation: people therefore spoke of the consulship of 'Julius and Caesar'. However, he proposed POMPEIUS (2)'s consulship in 52 and, after governing Syria in 51, commanded Pompeius' Adriatic fleet in the Civil War when he strenuously tried to stop Caesar's forces reaching Epirus. He died while carrying out this duty. His wife was PORCIA, the daughter of CATO (5) of Utica.

2, Lucius Calpurnius (died *c.*32 BC), was the son of the above and PORCIA. He joined the forces of BRUTUS (5) at Philippi for which he was proscribed, but he evaded death and became a follower of ANTONIUS (7), who appointed him commander of his fleet and governor of Syria *c.*34 BC. He also acted as mediator between Antonius and Octavian (see AUGUSTUS). He died in Syria. Plutarch used his memoir of Brutus as a source.

Blaesus, Quintus Junius (died AD 31), was a general of local Italian extraction who held a suffect consulship in AD 10. As governor of Pannonia in 14 he was confronted by an army mutiny which DRUSUS (3), son of TIBERIUS, put down. In 21 as proconsul of Africa he defeated the Numidian rebel TACFARINAS, as a result of which his troops hailed him as *Imperator* (the last time this honour was gained by a private citizen). The fall of SEJANUS, his nephew, brought about Blaesus' death.

Blossius, Gaius (C2 BC), was a philosopher whose family came from Capua and had supported HANNIBAL; he studied Stoic philosophy and was associated with Tiberius GRACCHUS (3). When the latter was killed, he joined ARISTONICUS in Pergamon and killed himself after his defeat.

Bocchus 1. I (late C2 BC) was a king of Mauretania; he married his daughter to JUGURTHA, with whom he allied himself in 108 BC against Rome, though he had earlier offered an alliance to the Romans and been rejected. The two nearly defeated MARIUS (1), but in 105 Bocchus negotiated with SULLA (2) and abandoned Jugurtha in exchange for the title 'Friend of the Roman People' and the territory of western Numidia.

2. II (died 33 BC) was the son or grandson of BOCCHUS (1) I, and reigned jointly with his brother BOGUD: Bocchus ruled eastern Mauretania. In the Civil War they supported CAESAR (1) and Bocchus joined Publius SITTIUS in an attack on JUBA (1) I of Numidia. After Caesar's assassination they parted company: Bocchus favoured Octavian (see AUGUSTUS), Bogud ANTONIUS (7). Bocchus ousted his brother and was confirmed as sole client king by Octavian.

Bogud (died 31 BC) was the son or grandson of BOCCHUS (1) I, and shared the kingdom of Mauretania with his brother BOCCHUS (2) II: he ruled the west. He joined CAESAR (1)'s party in 49 BC and assisted him in Spain in 48 and in 45 at Munda. While he was intervening *c.*41 on ANTONIUS (7)'s behalf in Spain against Octavian's (see AUGUSTUS) supporters, there was a rebellion in his kingdom, which his brother took over. Bogud died in the campaign of Actium fighting for Antonius at Methone.

Bolanus, Vettius (C1 AD), served in AD 62 under CORBULO in Armenia, was a suffect consul *c*.66, and was sent to govern Britain by VITELLIUS (1) in 69. He was active in the north and was recalled in 71. He later became proconsul of Asia and was made a patrician by VESPASIAN.

Bomilcar (C2 BC) was a confidential agent of JUGURTHA who, while Jugurtha was in Rome in 111 BC, murdered the Numidian pretender Massiva, his cousin, who was also in Rome. He took part in the battle on the river Muthul in 108, but then tried to assassinate Jugurtha, for which he paid with his life.

Bonosus (died AD 280) was an admiral and rebel of the third century AD, of Gallo-British descent. He lost the fleet he was commanding in the Rhine to the Germans and, in fear of punishment, rebelled. The emperor PROBUS (1) overcame him in AD 280 after a struggle.

Boudicca (died AD 61) (also Boudica and less correctly Boadicea) was the wife of Prasutagus, the established king of the Iceni nation, which then inhabited Norfolk. He ruled autonomously under Roman protection. On his death in AD 60 he left his kingdom equally to the emperor NERO (1) and his daughters, but Roman officials abused his family and raped his daughters. Boudicca raised both the Iceni and the neighbouring Trinovantes, who lived in Essex and Suffolk, against the Romans who were detested for their harsh taxation and cruelty. The rebels sacked and burnt Colchester, St Albans and London, the three most important towns of southern Britain, and routed a section of the Ninth Legion from Lincoln while the governor, SUETONIUS (1) Paulinus, was occupied with the Druid rebellion in Anglesey. On his return they attacked his force but were quickly defeated: Boudicca took poison and the kingdom was assimilated into the province. See Tacitus, *Annals*, XIV, 31–37. See also G. Webster (1978) *Boudicca*, London: Batsford.

Brennus was traditionally held to be the name of the Gallic king who captured Rome *c*.387 BC, after defeating the Roman army on the river Allia. Then, after besieging the Capitol for six months, he agreed to leave Rome on condition that he received a thousand pounds of gold; while the gold was being weighed he tried to swindle the Romans by throwing his sword into the scales with the cry *vae victis!* ('Woe to the defeated!'). According to the legend, CAMILLUS (1) just then arrived and routed the Gauls.

Britannicus, Tiberius Claudius (AD *c*.42–*c*.56), the son of the emperor CLAUDIUS (1) by his third wife MESSALLINA, was born in AD 41 or 42. He was at first named 'Germanicus' and gained his better known name after Claudius conquered Britain in 43. In 48 his mother was killed as a result of her immorality and Claudius married his niece AGRIPPINA (3), whose son, Lucius Domitius, he adopted. Agrippina worked to remove Britannicus' supporters from the court, and when Claudius died in 54 her son, four years older than Britannicus, became the emperor NERO (1). Britannicus died a year or two later, poisoned on Nero's orders when his mother showed too much sympathy for her stepson.

Brutus 1, Decimus Junius, known as Callaicus (C2 BC), was an orator and general who, as consul in 138 BC and proconsul the following year, fought a campaign in the Iberian peninsula. He defeated the Lusitani of Portugal and the Callaici of Galicia, from whom he took his honorific name, and after his triumph built a temple to Mars. He went to Illyricum under Gaius SEMPRONIUS Tuditanus; he opposed Gaius GRACCHUS (1) and was the patron of ACCIUS.

2, Decimus Junius, known as Albinus (died 43 BC), a conspirator against CAESAR (1), was the son of Decimus Brutus (consul in 77 BC) and Sempronia. He was adopted by Postumius Albinus. He served on Caesar's staff in Gaul and in 56 won a decisive victory over the Veneti. He continued to support Caesar, commanding his fleet at the siege of Massilia in 49 and in 46 governing Transalpine Gaul and putting down a rebellion by the Belgic Bellovaci. Praetor in 45, in 44 he turned against Caesar and joined the plot to kill him; he then, in April, went to take up the command of the army in Cisalpine Gaul that Caesar had given him. In December 44 he refused to hand his province over to ANTONIUS (7), who had obtained it by a vote of the people and who now besieged him in Mutina. The siege was relieved in April 43 by the victory of the consuls, HIRTIUS and PANSA, and Octavian (see AUGUSTUS) over Antonius. The Senate appointed Brutus commander of the army, but the veteran troops preferred Octavian's banner. Brutus followed Antonius across the Alps and joined PLANCUS (1) for a while and then started to march to Macedonia to support Marcus BRUTUS (5). Deserted by his men, however, he was captured by a chieftain in the Carnic Alps and killed on Antonius' orders.

3, Lucius Junius, known as Damasippus (died 82 BC), a supporter of MARIUS (1), after being defeated by the youthful POMPEIUS (2) in 83, was city praetor in 82, when he killed Q. Mucius SCAEVOLA (4) and others before they could join SULLA (2). He made an unsuccessful attempt to relieve the younger MARIUS (2) at Praeneste, but was captured by Sulla in the battle at the Colline gate of Rome and put to death.

4, Marcus Junius (*c.*85–42 BC), the 'noblest Roman', helped to assassinate his friend and patron CAESAR (1). He was adopted by his maternal uncle Q. Servilius Caepio. He was greatly influenced by another uncle, CATO (5), whose daughter, PORCIA, he married in 45 BC. He served in Cyprus under Cato in 58, and was quaestor in Cilicia in 53 under Appius CLAUDIUS (8), whose daughter he married *c.*51 and later divorced. Though his mother, SERVILIA, was Caesar's mistress, he opposed Caesar in the Civil War and was pardoned by him after the battle of Pharsalus; he was then favoured by the dictator by his appointment as governor of Cisalpine Gaul in 46 BC and as praetor in 44. He was nevertheless the figurehead in the conspiracy to kill Caesar and the latter's dying words were addressed to him, in Greek, 'You too, child', seeming to some to imply that Caesar was his natural father. He insisted that nobody besides Caesar should be killed, and so spared ANTONIUS (7). Soon, however, Rome became too dangerous for him and he took on the commission of importing grain from Asia and then the governorship of Crete. He quarrelled with Antonius in August 44 and went to Greece. There he raised an army with money given him by the quaestors of neighbouring provinces and with the support of the governor of Macedonia, Q. Hortensius. In February 43 the Senate voted him command of all the armies in Macedonia, Greece and Illyricum, and he fought minor wars in Thrace and Lycia to raise funds. He and CASSIUS (2), governor of Syria, after plundering Asia Minor for cash, moved their forces in autumn 42 to Philippi in Macedonia to meet those of Antonius and Octavian (see AUGUSTUS). Two battles were fought, three weeks apart. In the first, Brutus beat Octavian but Cassius lost to Antonius and killed himself. In the second Brutus was routed and did likewise.

His friendship with CICERO (1) led to a correspondence, part of which has survived. Cicero dedicated several works to him and named a work on oratory after him. He himself wrote many works, including philosophical and historical material, that have not survived. Certain Greek letters written under his name are spurious. See Cicero, *Letters to Atticus* and *Letters to his Friends*; Plutarch, *Life of Brutus*.

Burebistas (C1 BC) was a king of the Dacians who extended his kingdom to include most of the Danube lands. He was a moral reformer, and with the help of Decaeneos, a priest, he stopped wine production. He fought the Celtic peoples to the northwest, notably the Boii, and threatened Thrace. POMPEIUS (2) tried to win his support in the Civil War and CAESAR (1) was planning a campaign against him in 44 BC, but both were assassinated. Burebistas' empire split into several smaller kingdoms.

Burrus, Sextus Afranius (died AD 62), was a commander of the Praetorian Guard and an adviser of NERO (1). He was born at Vasio in Provence and served in an equestrian capacity under the emperors from TIBERIUS to Nero, gaining the post of sole commander of the guard in AD 51 through the influence of AGRIPPINA (3). Together with SENECA (2), he guided Nero in the early days of his reign, and had some responsibility for Agrippina's murder in 59. After opposing Nero's plans in 62 to divorce OCTAVIA (3), he died, perhaps by poison, though TACITUS (1) questions this. See Tacitus, *Annals*, 14; Suetonius, *Life of Nero*.

C

Caecilia *see* ATTICUS, METELLA.

Caecilius 1. (C1 BC) was a poet from Como, known to us only from CATULLUS (1), who tells us in poem 35 that he wrote a poem on Cybele.

2. (C1 BC) was a Sicilian writer on rhetoric from Caleacte, whose book *On the Sublime* inspired the critic 'Longinus' to write his own treatise of the same name, in reaction against the standpoint of Caecilius, but using many examples from Caecilius' work.

3. Iucundus, Lucius (C1 AD), was a Pompeian auctioneer whose business dealings are recorded on an extensive collection of wax tablets showing receipts for sale proceeds.

4, Quintus (C1 BC), was a wealthy equestrian who adopted his nephew T. Pomponius and left him a fortune of ten million sesterces. See ATTICUS.

5. Epirota, Quintus (C1 BC), was a freedman of ATTICUS (he taught his daughter Caecilia) and a friend of Cornelius GALLUS (4), after whose death in 26 BC he opened a school and lectured on contemporary poetry.

6. Africanus, Sextus (C2 AD), was a lawyer from Tunisia, a pupil of JULIANUS. He wrote a rough-and-ready account of Julianus' responses to various legal questions in nine books entitled *Problems*, adding his own comments. His work was used as a source by the compilers of Justinian's code.

7, Statius (early C2 BC), was a writer of comedies. He was born in Milan of Insubrian stock and was brought to Rome as a slave after being captured in war *c.*223 BC. He was set free at some time before 180 and died in 168. He was a successful playwright and was supported by AMBIVIUS Turpio, who produced his plays and gave him encouragement to persevere when, early in his career, he seemed to be failing. He wrote at least forty plays and based several on Menander. About 300 lines of his *Necklace* survive in the works of GELLIUS (1) and can be compared with their Greek original. He encouraged ENNIUS and was highly esteemed by his successors. An anecdote relates his meeting with TERENCE which resulted in his inviting Terence to dinner.
See also METELLUS.

Caecina 1, Aulus (C1 BC), was a friend of CICERO (1) from Volaterrae in Etruria and an expert in Etruscan divination. Cicero defended his father in a lawsuit in 69 BC; the son joined the Pompeian party and published a libellous pamphlet against CAESAR (1) for which he was exiled in 48 after the battle of Pharsalus.

He recanted in 46 and through Cicero's intercession was pardoned. Cicero used his expertise in writing his *Divination*; SENECA (2) and PLINY (2) also used him as a source.

2. Severus, Aulus (early C1 AD), was an Etruscan from Volaterrae. He was suffect consul in 1 BC and governed Moesia in AD 6 when he rescued Sirmium from the rebellion in Pannonia and then had to return to his province to drive out Dacian invaders. In AD 7 together with M. Plautius Silvanus he won a resounding victory over the Pannonians near Sirmium. He was appointed by TIBERIUS in 14 to govern Lower Germany, where he put down a mutiny of the troops and in 15 narrowly escaped disaster when returning from the Ems to the Rhine by the 'long bridges'.

3. Alienus, Aulus (died AD 79), was a general from Vicentia active in the year of four emperors (AD 68–69). As quaestor in Baetica, southern Spain, he gave his support to GALBA (1), who appointed him to command a legion in Upper Germany. After Galba's fall, he gave his allegiance to VITELLIUS (1), leading troops over the Alps to fight OTHO's army in the neighbourhood of Cremona. Vitellius rewarded him for his support and put him in command of the army he sent to northern Italy to meet the Flavian threat. When he tried to make terms with the enemy his troops deposed him. After the battle of Cremona, he made himself acceptable to VESPASIAN. He was executed by TITUS for conspiring with EPRIUS Marcellus against the emperor.

Caepio 1, Fannius, was a plotter with Murena against AUGUSTUS, probably in 23 BC, who was prosecuted by TIBERIUS, tried to escape, was caught and executed.

2, Quintus Servilius, was a consul who in 140 BC persuaded the Senate to disavow its treaty with the Lusitani and renew the war; he was outmanoeuvred by VIRIATHUS but bribed his men to desert and murder their leader. The Lusitani were thus forced to submit to Rome.

3, Quintus Servilius (late C2 BC), a general and politician, was praetor in 109 BC, and as governor in Spain won a victory over rebels in 107. As consul in 106 he passed anti-Marian legislation to put a majority of senators on criminal juries. He was then dispatched to Gaul, where he defeated the Tectosages and took their chief town of Tolosa (Toulouse), capturing their sacred treasure (which may have been stolen by their ancestors from Delphi), part of which he pocketed. In 105 he was governor of Narbonese Gaul; he refused to cooperate with his successor the consul Gnaeus Manlius Maximus and caused the disastrous defeat of Arausio (Orange) at the hands of the Cimbri. He was deprived of his power and eventually prosecuted successfully by NORBANUS for his misconduct of the war, and went into exile at Smyrna.

4, Quintus Servilius (died 90 BC), a son of CAEPIO (3), was quaestor in 100 BC when he failed to thwart SATURNINUS (2). He was prosecuted for treason by NORBANUS in 95 and successfully defended by L. Licinius CRASSUS (1). Originally an associate of DRUSUS (2), whose sister he married, he quarrelled with him for private reasons and in 92 attacked SCAURUS (2) in the courts. In 91 he was one of Drusus' chief opponents and was killed by POPPAEDIUS during the Social War.

Caesar 1, Gaius Julius (100–44 BC), was the conqueror of Gaul, victor of the second Civil War, and dictator of Rome. He was of an ancient patrician family that had passed through a period of obscurity. His father of the same name died in 85 without becoming consul, and his mother was Aurelia of the Cotta family. His family had attached itself to the radical Marian party by the marriage of Caesar's aunt JULIA (1) to MARIUS (1). He had been betrothed to Cossutia but in 84 he married

Cornelia, the daughter of CINNA (2), who appointed him *Flamen Dialis* (priest of Jupiter). SULLA (2), who annulled all Cinna's decisions, proscribed him for this alliance, and Caesar hid in Sabine country until his friends obtained a pardon for him. He served in 81 in Asia on the staff of M. Minucius Thermus and won a decoration (a civic crown) at the capture of Mytilene for saving a man's life. On Sulla's death in 78 he returned to Rome and unsuccessfully prosecuted DOLABELLA (2) for extortion and then retired to Rhodes to study rhetoric under APOLLONIUS (2) Molon. On his way he was captured by pirates and ransomed for fifty talents; he subsequently raised a fleet, captured them, and later crucified them at Pergamon.

In 74 he was back in Rome and in 73 was co-opted to the priestly office of *Pontifex*. In 70 he was elected military tribune and supported POMPEIUS (2) in restoring the rights of tribunes and an amnesty for LEPIDUS (2)'s followers. He was elected quaestor for 69; his wife Cornelia died in 69 after bearing him a daughter and he married POMPEIA (1), a granddaughter of Sulla. However, he remained a committed Marian, and when his aunt Julia, the wife of Marius, died in the same year, he boldly paraded Marius' bust at the funeral. He was elected aedile for 65 when he restored the trophies of Marius to the Capitol. He spent lavishly on bribery of the electors, games, and new buildings, and ran up huge debts, some of which were paid by M. Licinius CRASSUS (3), whom he supported for a time. In 64 he was appointed to run the murder court and encouraged the prosecution of those who had killed people proscribed by Sulla; in this he was opposed by LUCCEIUS. In 63, after serving as commissioner to pass sentence on Gaius RABIRIUS (1) for treason, he was elected by lavish bribery but against powerful opposition to the prestigious post of *Pontifex Maximus*. He spoke very eloquently in the Senate against the execution of the fellow-conspirators of CATILINE, and would have won the day but for CATO (5). He was praetor in 62, but his office was suspended when he supported METELLUS (9) Nepos' proposal that Pompeius be given a command against Catiline; he was, however, soon restored. The following year he governed Further (western) Spain, though his creditors kept him in Rome until June 61. In May he had refused to give evidence against CLODIUS in the Bona Dea trial even though he divorced Pompeia who, he said, must be 'above suspicion'. His governorship helped to pay off his debts: he fought a campaign against the Lusitani for which he claimed a triumph, but fell foul of electoral law, for the rules of the triumph would have prevented him from standing for office. In fact he made a compact with two other magnates, Pompeius and Crassus, and with their support and much violence and bribery was elected consul for 59. This group has become known as the 'First Triumvirate', though there was nothing official about their partnership. Pompeius had become estranged from the aristocracy because the Senate would not ratify his settlement of the Asiatic provinces or his assignment of lands to his veteran soldiers. Crassus, immensely rich and ambitious, was reconciled with Pompeius by Caesar's diplomacy. In 59 Caesar married his third wife, CALPURNIA (1).

In his consulship Caesar had things his own way because his colleague, BIBULUS (1), was not strong enough to make his veto of Caesar's legislation stick, and because he had the firm support of his partners. He passed laws to give Pompeius the measures he desired. He turned Como into a colony, passed a law to counter extortion, and engineered a change in the province assigned to him for the following year. The tribune VATINIUS carried a proposal that he should govern Cisalpine Gaul and Illyricum with three legions for five years; the Senate added Transalpine Gaul and another legion. Pompeius was to stay in Rome and look after his interests there: Caesar gave him his daughter JULIA (4) in marriage. In early 58 Caesar left for his province.

We do not know how clearly formulated Caesar's plans were regarding the conquest of Gaul. At all events, he had secured a province offering the prospect of expansion and a strong army with which to defend himself in case of a power struggle at Rome. He had many enemies, real and potential. During 58 he responded to appeals from Gallic peoples, especially the Aedui, against their enemies the Sequani and invaders from the east, the Helvetii from Switzerland and the Germans of ARIOVISTUS, the Suebi and their allies. He defeated both sets of invaders and wintered in the north-eastern part of Gaul; the next year he subdued the Belgic peoples of that area and in 56 he moved to the Atlantic coast and conquered Armorica (Brittany) and the Veneti of the Vendée. In this way he encircled the nations of central Gaul and felt free to extend his area of activity. In 55 there was an invasion of Gaul by Germans who, under pressure from the Suebi, crossed the Rhine near its mouth: having thrown back these invaders, Caesar bridged the Rhine and made a demonstration of force in Germany. Then, late in the season, he prepared his first passage to Britain to reconnoitre the little-known island, sending COMMIUS ahead to win British support. He landed successfully in spite of opposition, but after his beached fleet was badly damaged by storms, he withdrew under pressure from the inhabitants.

Danger arose for Caesar in the intention of his enemy L. Domitius AHENOBARBUS (6), confident of the next year's consulship, to recall and prosecute him, a plan that had support from Cicero. To meet this crisis, Crassus sent Caesar information of the situation and together they summoned Pompeius to a meeting. In April 56 the three 'triumvirs' had met at Luca (Lucca) in northern Italy, and agreed that Caesar's command should be extended for five more years until the end of 49. Caesar used the loot of Gaul to enlist support at Rome and elsewhere in the Empire. His links with Pompeius dissolved as Julia died in childbirth in 54 and Crassus was killed in Parthia in 53. Meanwhile Caesar led a second expedition to Britain in 54 in which he penetrated beyond the Thames and overawed the native peoples. At the end of summer he withdrew, never to return. The Gauls rose against him at a number of places in northern Gaul during the winter, defeating his legates Sabinus and Cotta, and in 53 he pacified the Senones, Carnutes and Nervii, and again bridged the Rhine. He devastated the land of the Eburones. During his travels he wrote a treatise on rhetoric, *On Regularity* (*De Analogia*). A larger rebellion took place in 52 led by VERCINGETORIX the Arvernian. After much skirmishing and shifting of ground, Caesar managed to pin Vercingetorix down in the stronghold of Alesia, which he starved into submission. In 51 some minor revolts occurred, but the defeat and capture of Vercingetorix had broken the back of Gallic resistance. In 51 he reduced the Bellovaci and successfully besieged Uxellodunum.

Pompeius' firm action in 52 and his legislation giving tribunes back certain powers of veto, which could be used to protect Caesar, met with Caesar's approval. But in 51 Pompeius shifted his support to the aristocratic party which opposed Caesar's ambitions, and which now sought to bring him back to Rome without office and prosecute him for abuses of his command in Gaul. Caesar offered to lay down his command if Pompeius would do the same, but the Senate would accept no compromise, and voted on 1 January 49 that Caesar would be regarded as a public enemy unless he resigned his command. The veto interposed by the tribunes ANTONIUS (7) and CASSIUS (5) Longinus was disregarded and they fled to Caesar's camp. This abuse of the constitution afforded Caesar a pretext to act and ten days later he led his one available legion across the river Rubicon, then the boundary between Gaul and Italy. There was little opposition to Caesar's advance: Pompeius, entrusted by the Senate with the defence of Italy, had greatly overestimated his own popularity, and had two legions which were more loyal to Caesar than to himself. L. Ahenobarbus, the new governor of Gaul, was trapped by Caesar in Corfinium and forced by his troops to surrender. Pompeius and most of the Senate fled to Brundisium where they embarked for Greece with a large army on March 17, but Caesar had no ships in which to pursue them. Shortly afterwards, leaving Antonius in charge of Italy, he marched to Spain and there forced Pompeius's legates, AFRANIUS (2) and PETREIUS, to surrender near Ilerda in August. The writer VARRO (3), who was also a legate of Pompeius and held western Spain, went over to Caesar, and Massilia, held by Ahenobarbus, which Trebonius and Decimus BRUTUS (2) had been besieging for Caesar, capitulated. Caesar returned to Rome where he had been elected dictator on the proposal of the praetor LEPIDUS (4). He held elections for the consulship, passed some reforming legislation, and resigned the dictatorship eleven days later. He and SERVILIUS (2) Isauricus became the consuls for 48.

Caesar's next task was the defeat of the senatorial opposition led by Pompeius. To do this he had to take his army across to Epirus, where Pompeius awaited him with a formidable army. He crossed in January 48 with seven legions and besieged Pompeius in fortifications near Dyrrachium. Antony joined him with four further legions, but an attack by Pompeius' troops was repelled with heavy loss, and shortage of supplies forced Caesar to withdraw eastwards to Thessaly where grain could be obtained. Pompeius pursued him to Pharsalus, and on 9 August 48 engaged confidently as he had a larger force and better cavalry: but Caesar's tactics were superior and Pompeius fled. Caesar followed him to Egypt where he found that Pompeius had been murdered by the king. Caesar had a small force with him and quickly became involved in a war between PTOLEMY (9) XIII and his wife-sister CLEOPATRA (4) VII. The former had rejected Caesar's demand for the money owed by his father PTOLEMY (8) XII the Piper to the triumvirs, and blockaded Caesar in the palace, into which Cleopatra had herself smuggled. She became his mistress and bore him a son, CAESARION. Caesar was in a tricky predicament but reinforcements eventually reached him from MITHRIDATES (4) and ANTIPATER (1), and in spring 47 he defeated Ptolemy's army and made Cleopatra virtual ruler of Egypt. After a two-month tour with her up the Nile, on his return to Rome through Syria and Asia Minor he had to deal with PHARNACES II, son of MITHRIDATES (3) VI, who had been made king of Bosporos (Crimea) by Pompeius and had recently overrun Cappadocia and Lesser Armenia, defeated Caesar's legate Cn. Domitius CALVINUS (2) at Nicopolis, and seized his father's former kingdom of Pontus. Caesar defeated him at Zela after a campaign of five days: in his subsequent triumph he displayed the boastful declaration, 'I came, I saw, I conquered' (*veni, vidi, vici*).

In Italy there had been much confusion in his absence. In 48 his consular colleague Servilius had deposed a praetor, Caelius RUFUS (1), who objected to Caesar's debt reform, and fortified by senatorial support had killed him and MILO. In late 48 Servilius had Caesar appointed dictator again, for a year, with Antonius as his deputy. Many of Caesar's veterans were disgruntled at the delay in their discharge, and marched on Rome. Caesar addressed them and shamed them into submission. In autumn 47 Caesar had to go and quell the Pompeian forces which had gathered in Africa. He defeated them at the battle of Thapsus in April 46 after a four-month campaign. In summer 46 Caesar held a fourfold triumph at which he gave generously to both citizens and veterans, and was elected dictator for ten years. In 46 he was consul for the third time. He also installed Cleopatra and her son in a villa on the Janiculum Hill. But there was yet more opposition in Spain, where the two sons of Pompeius, Gnaeus POMPEIUS (3) and Sextus POMPEIUS (4), had gathered an army of thirteen legions. Leaving Lepidus in charge in Italy, Caesar in the winter of 46–5 took an army to Spain and routed the Pompeians in a bitter battle at Munda, from which Sextus Pompeius escaped. Caesar had meantime been elected sole consul.

In the last months of his life, honours were heaped on Caesar: the title *Liberator*, the sacrosanctity of a tribune, and emblems suggesting royalty and even divinity. In February 44, when he was consul for the fifth time, he was elected dictator for life. He refused the title of king, which had been long hateful to Romans, but controlled the offices of state in a way that was intolerable to the nobles who considered themselves his equals. On 15 March, the Ides, he was assassinated at a meeting of the Senate in the Theatre of Pompeius. He had been intending to go later in the year to the Balkans and the eastern frontier. The process of deifying him began.

He had been generous to a fault with his veterans, the common people of Rome, and his enemies, of whom several were spared more than once to renew the fight against him. He carried much useful reforming legislation, even though he spent so little time in Rome. In 46, with the help of Sosigenes, an Alexandrian astronomer, he reformed the calendar, and on 1 January 45 BC inaugurated the chronological system (the Julian Calendar) that has remained almost intact to the present day. He reformed provincial administration by his law of 59, which forced governors to publish accounts before leaving office. He greatly extended the citizenship and planted many new colonies. In 48 he abolished the tax farming of Asia and Sicily and substituted a land tax. However, he halved the number of citizens receiving free grain because he intended to send many of them abroad to found new colonies. He established basic rules for the government of municipalities.

He married three times and had numerous mistresses, including Cleopatra and Servilia. He was epileptic and probably bisexual. The medical term 'Caesarian' derives from the manner of his birth. He wrote and published seven books of commentaries (namely 'notes' to aid the future composition of history) on the *Gallic War* and three on the *Civil War*. His admirer HIRTIUS extended the former and probably added the *War at Alexandria*. The *African War* and the *Spanish War* were compiled by officers for Hirtius to publish. The style of his two commentaries is a masterpiece of lucidity and relevance, and the element of propaganda is not immediately obvious. He was also a fine orator, second in his time only to CICERO (1), and wrote a hostile reply to Cicero's pamphlet praising Cato, the *Anticato*, now lost. His lost *On Regularity* (53 BC), dedicated to Cicero, argued for a plain, straightforward style in speech and writing. He was a great radical and an untiring campaigner with a strong sense of his own vocation to rule, and in the end a lack of the sort of political caution shown by his successor, AUGUSTUS, deprived him of the chance to give the Roman state the stability it needed. See Cicero's *Letters*, *passim*; Suetonius, *Life of Julius Caesar*; lives by Appian and Plutarch; F.E. Adcock (1956) *Caesar as a Man of Letters*, Cambridge: Cambridge University Press; J.P.V.D. Balsdon (1967) *Julius Caesar*, London: English Universities Press; R. Syme (1939) *The Roman Revolution*, Oxford: Clarendon Press.

2. Strabo Vopiscus, Gaius Julius (died 87 BC), was an orator and wit, the younger brother of CAESAR (5) and stepbrother of

CATULUS (2). In his *Orator*, CICERO (1) makes him the principal speaker on humour. He was curule aedile in 90 BC, and without being praetor stood for the consulship for 88. This roused the anger of MARIUS (1), whom he had previously supported, and of SULPICIUS (1) Rufus. When Marius returned he had Caesar killed.

3, Gaius Julius (20 BC–AD 4), the eldest son of AGRIPPA (1) and JULIA (5), was adopted by AUGUSTUS as his son in 17 BC. He and his brother Lucius CAESAR (8) were the two bulwarks of Augustus' plans for the succession, Julia being his only legitimate child. In 5 BC he assumed the man's toga (came of age) and was given the title of Leader of Youth and a seat in the Senate. He married Livia (Livilla), daughter of DRUSUS (3), in 1 BC and in the same year was sent to the east under the eye of Marcus LOLLIUS with the powers of a proconsul. He was consul in AD 1, and in 2 conferred with the king of Parthia (PHRAATES 2) and appointed a king of Armenia. But he was wounded in the siege of Artagira and never recovered, dying eighteen months later in Lycia. As his brother Lucius was already dead, Augustus' plans for an heir of his own blood were shattered.

4. See CALIGULA.

5, Lucius Julius (died 87 BC), was the elder brother of CAESAR (2) and step-brother of CATULUS (2). After his praetorship he governed Macedonia *c.*94 BC and was consul in 90. He was involved as a general in the Social War with varying fortune, and afterwards proposed a law to grant citizenship to those of the Italian allies who had been faithful to Rome. He held the censorship in 89 but was killed by MARIUS (1), whom he had previously supported, along with his brother Gaius. His daughter JULIA (2), married to Marcus ANTONIUS (6), was the mother of ANTONIUS (7).

6, Lucius Julius (C1 BC), was a son of CAESAR (5) and uncle of ANTONIUS (7). He served in Asia as quaestor in 77 BC and was consul in 64. He was CAESAR (1)'s legate in Gaul during 52 to 49, and supported him in the Civil War. In 47 Caesar appointed him Prefect of the City to deputise for him during his consulship in his absence, but he was unable to cope with the Caesarian tribune DOLABELLA (4) who proposed a cancellation of debt. After Caesar's death he opposed his nephew Octavian (AUGUSTUS) and was proscribed, but was pardoned by his sister Julia's influence.

7, Lucius Julius (died *c.*46 BC), was a grandson of CAESAR (5). He supported POMPEIUS (2) in the Civil War. He was sent by Pompeius to negotiate with CAESAR (1) in 49 BC. Later that year, when in command of Pompeius' fleet, he failed to prevent CURIO (2)'s crossing from Sicily to Africa. He took part in the battle of Thapsus in 46, and was pardoned by Caesar, but died shortly afterwards, probably at the hands of Caesar's troops.

8, Lucius Julius (17 BC–AD 2), was the younger brother of CAESAR (3) above and second son of AGRIPPA (1) and JULIA (5), adopted at birth by AUGUSTUS as his son. He came of age at fifteen in 2 BC and Augustus granted him honours indicating possible succession, including designation as consul for AD 4. In AD 2 he was sent to his first command in Spain but died on the way at Massilia.

9. Nero, Tiberius Julius, generally known as Gemellus, 'twin' (AD 19–38), was a grandson of the emperor TIBERIUS; he was the surviving twin born to LIVIA (3) (Livilla) and her second husband DRUSUS (4). At Tiberius' death in 37 he was named in the will as co-heir with his older kinsman CALIGULA, his maternal uncle: the will, however was declared void by the Senate. Caligula adopted Gemellus and made him Leader of Youth (cf. CAE-

SAR 3). Caligula had him executed within a year of his accession.

Caesarion (47–30 BC) was the son of CAESAR (1) and CLEOPATRA (4) VII. This nickname means 'Caesar's son': his official name and style was Ptolemy XV Caesar Theos Philopator kai Philometor ('father-loving and mother-loving god'). He was his mother's first child. In 44 Cleopatra made him joint ruler with herself, and in 34 he was given the title 'King of Kings' at the donations made by ANTONIUS (7). Octavian (see AUGUSTUS) regarded Egypt as the principal threat to Rome, and as Antonius declared that Caesar had acknowledged Caesarion as his son, he had OPPIUS (2) write a pamphlet to disprove the claim. Cleopatra sent him to a place of safety after Actium, but he was tricked into returning to Alexandria and was killed on Octavian's order.

Calatinus, Aulus Atilius (C3 BC), as praetor won a victory over the Carthaginians in Sicily in 257 for which he was awarded a triumph. He had been consul for the first time in the previous year: he took Panormus (Palermo) during his second consulship in 254. In 249 he was appointed dictator and was the first such to lead an army outside Italy, again in Sicily. He dedicated a temple to Hope in the vegetable market at Rome.

Calenus, Quintus Fufius (died 40 BC), was a tribune in 61 BC when he aided CLODIUS in the scandal of the *Bona Dea* festival. A supporter of CAESAR (1) in the Civil War, he served on Caesar's staff in Gaul and in the Civil War and was consul in 47 with VATINIUS. After the assassination of Caesar he followed ANTONIUS (7), on whose behalf he governed Gaul until his death. His son then joined Octavian (AUGUSTUS) with the eleven legions stationed in Gaul.

Calidius, Marcus, a friend of CICERO (1), as praetor in 57 BC supported Cicero's restoration from exile. Cicero in his *Brutus* praised Calidius' powers as a speaker.

Caligula (AD 12–41), the third emperor, who reigned from AD 37–41, was the youngest son of GERMANICUS and AGRIPPINA (2) the Elder. The nickname *Caligula*, 'little-boot', which he hated, was given him by the soldiers in his father's camp on the Rhine on account of the small military boots he wore: his real name was Gaius Julius Caesar Germanicus and he is known as the emperor Gaius. He was born on 31 August at Antium and was taken by his parents on tours of duty to the Rhine frontier and later, in AD 18, in the east. When his father died in 19 his mother looked after him until her arrest in 29. He then lived first with LIVIA (2) and later ANTONIA (2) the Younger before going in 32 to stay with TIBERIUS in his retirement on Capri. After the death of his brother DRUSUS (5) in 33, probably at the hands of SEJANUS, he was, along with Tiberius' grandson Gemellus (CAESAR 9), seven years his junior, next in succession. Tiberius died in March 37, and with the support of MACRO, prefect of the Praetorian Guard, Gaius was proclaimed the new emperor. He adopted his cousin Gemellus, though the Senate declared the late emperor's will invalid and Gemellus was disinherited. Gaius affected dislike of Tiberius and won popular support by extolling the memory of his father and mother. He made CLAUDIUS (1) his colleague in the consulship. He put on a series of entertainments to win popular support. He had a serious illness in October 37 which many thought left him mentally deranged. He developed megalomania and decreed that he be worshipped as Jupiter Latiaris, and appointed priests to administer his cult. In May 38 he executed Macro and Tiberius Gemellus. When his favourite sister, JULIA (7) Drusilla, whom he had nominated as his heir, died in 38, he ordered public mourning throughout the Empire, and proclaimed her deified, an unprecedented honour for a woman. He forced MEMMIUS (3) Regulus to give up his rich wife LOLLIA Paulina so that he might marry her himself, but divorced her in 39 when he married Milonia Caesonia, who had already borne him a daughter. In autumn 39 he went to Gaul and the Rhine, discovering a plot against his life at Mainz, and executed its leaders, Cornelius LENTULUS (6) Gaetulicus and M. Aemilius Lepidus. The emperor's sisters AGRIPPINA (3) and JULIA (8) Livilla were suspected of being implicated in the plot and exiled. He planned an invasion of Britain, but abandoned it, merely making his troops pick up seashells which he called 'spoils of the ocean'. He returned to Rome in August 40 to an ovation, though he had won no victory. On 24 January the next year he was assassinated in the palace together with his wife and daughter by a group of soldiers led by the praetorian tribune Cassius CHAEREA.

His reign was marked by a move to greater autocracy and a failure to control spending, leading to increased taxes. He behaved with unpredictable swings of mood towards his close family, especially his sister Drusilla, whom he associated in his personal cult. He married four times. He offended the Jews by demanding that his image be set up for worship in the temple at Jerusalem, which caused unrest both in Judaea and Alexandria. He was dissuaded from this act by Marcus AGRIPPA (3) I. He was succeeded by his uncle Claudius. See J.P.V.D. Balsdon (1934) *The Emperor Gaius*, Oxford: Clarendon Press; A.A. Barrett (1989) *Caligula, the Corruption of Power*, London: Batsford; M. Grant (1985) *The Roman Emperors*, London: Weidenfeld & Nicolson.

Callicrates (died *c.*148 BC) was an Achaean statesman from Leontium in the northern Peloponnese. After the death of PHILOPOEMEN (182) he declared his absolute support for Rome, and a couple of years later, as general of the Achaean Confederacy, he recalled Spartan exiles and gave Sparta back her local autonomy. The Romans supported his rule after the close of the Third Macedonian War, despite his unpopularity with the Achaeans, until his death. POLYBIUS, whose father LYCORTAS Callicrates had opposed, was extremely hostile to him in his *History.*

Callistus, Gaius Julius (C1 AD), was a freedman of CALIGULA who took part in the plot of Cassius CHAEREA to assassinate him. Under his successor Claudius he prospered as the secretary *a libellis* who dealt with petitions to the emperor. He tried to promote LOLLIA Paulina to be CLAUDIUS (1)'s fourth wife after the fall of MESSALLINA; he disappears from the scene after AGRIPPINA (3) took that role. The physician Scribonius Largus dedicated his work on prescriptions to him.

Calpurnia 1. was CAESAR (1)'s third wife, the daughter of Lucius Calpurnius PISO (6) Caesonianus. He married her in 59 BC to strengthen his friendship with her father, but was prepared to divorce her in 53 to marry POMPEIUS (2)'s daughter; however, he kept her and she tried to prevent his going to the meeting of the Senate at the Theatre of Pompeius on the Ides of March 44. After his murder she gave his papers, including his will, and his private fortune of 4,000 talents, to ANTONIUS (7).

2. was the third wife of the Younger PLINY (2), whose affection for him he describes graphically in his letters. She was the daughter of a Roman knight from Como, L. Calpurnius Fabatus, and accompanied him on his tour of duty in Bithynia. They had no children.

Calpurnius Siculus, Titus (C1 AD), was a poet who wrote extant pastoral poems in Latin in the manner of Theocritus. A contemporary of NERO (1), he refers to the comet of AD 54, the amphitheatre opened in 57, and to Nero's speech on behalf of Ilium. There are seven eclogues in the collection, of which the first, the middle and the last, containing long monologues, deal with concerns of the court, whereas the rest, in dialogue form, relate to the countryside. He acknowledges his debt to VIRGIL, whom he calls Tityrus, in 4. The cognomen *Siculus* may represent a homage to Theocritus or indicate his actual origin in Sicily.

Calvinus 1, Gaius Sextius, was the founder of Aquae Sextii (Aix-en-Provence), consul in 124 BC and in the next year proconsul of Gaul. He defeated the Ligurians, and the Vocontii and Salluvii of southeastern Transalpine Gaul. He held a triumph in 122.

2, Gnaeus Domitius (mid-C1 BC), having served in Asia in 62 BC, was tribune of the *plebs* in 59, when he supported BIBULUS (1) against CAESAR (1); he was praetor in 56 and consul in 53, being elected only in mid-year after the revelation of a fraudulent plot with the consuls of the previous year to fix up certain posts without senatorial authority. In the Civil War he was on the side of Caesar, who sent him in 48 to intercept Scipio's approach from the east; he opposed him in Thessaly. He commanded the centre at the battle of Pharsalus, and was then dispatched with three legions to seize the province of Asia. In late 48 he was defeated by PHARNACES II at Nicopolis: Caesar then sent him to Africa. In 44 Caesar designated him to be his Master of the Horse in his dictatorship. He was the only noble to support Octavian (see AUGUSTUS) until the establishment of the triumvirate, and was in charge of transporting two legions to Macedonia for the Philippi campaign but was prevented by AHENOBARBUS (4) and MURCUS and lost his fleet. He held a second consulship in 40 BC, and was Octavian's legate governing Spain from 39 to 36, gaining a triumph on his return: he rebuilt the Regia, the house of the Chief Priest (*Pontifex Maximus*) in the Roman forum.

Calvisius *see* SABINUS (1).

Calvus, Gaius Licinius (82–*c*.47 BC), was a poet of the neoteric school and an orator, the son of the historian Gaius Licinius Macer whom CICERO (1) prosecuted for extortion and who committed suicide in 66 BC. As an orator he was much admired by CATULLUS (1), Cicero (though he felt that Calvus' austere Attic style spoilt his effectiveness) and by the critic QUINTILIAN. In 54 BC he unsuccessfully prosecuted VATINIUS for bribery: Cicero spoke for the defence. TACITUS (1) also speaks highly of his oratorical powers in the *Dialogue on Orators*, and mentions three speeches against Vatinius. Catullus and SENECA (2) represent Calvus as being of short stature, and portray him as a speaker whose force and rapidity told against his opponents. Vatinius protested at his trial that it was unjust that he should be condemned simply because Calvus was so eloquent. Catullus was an intimate friend of his, with whom he composed witty poems in light-hearted rivalry. Calvus was married to Quintilia: after her early death he wrote an elegy in which he reproached himself for his infidelities: in reply to this Catullus wrote a consolation. Of Calvus' works almost nothing has survived. In antiquity twenty-one speeches were known, as well as poetry: an epyllion entitled *Io*, epithalamia, elegies and epigrams: like Catullus, he attacked CAESAR (1) and POMPEIUS (2). His name was often linked with that of Catullus by later critics and writers. See T.P. Wiseman (1985) *Catullus and his World*, Cambridge: Cambridge University Press.

Camillus 1, Marcus Furius (C4 BC) It is hard to distinguish the historical from the mythical in the picture we have of the statesman Camillus. He conquered the Etruscan city of Veii in 396 BC and took Falerii soon afterwards. He is said to have been exiled from Rome for unfair distribution of the booty and to have taken refuge in Ardea, from which, after being elected dictator, he attacked the Gauls who had descended on Rome in 390 and recovered the gold with which they had been bought off. Whether that is true or not, he played a great part in reconciling the patricians and plebeians, and in reforming the Roman army. He led Roman forces against the Aequi and the Volscians in the 380s and defeated both. In 367 he vowed to build a temple to the goddess Concord when conflict between the classes seemed to be threatened by the measures taken by the tribunes Licinius and Sextius; he built it at the foot of the Capitol. Tradition states that he died of plague in 365 at the age of eighty-two. LIVY called him the father of his country and the second founder of the city.

2, Lucius Furius (C4 BC), was a general, the son of CAMILLUS (1). As consul in 349 he won a victory over the Gauls, and dedicated a temple to Juno Moneta.

3, Lucius Furius (C4 BC), was a general, the grandson of CAMILLUS (1). In 338 he overthrew the Latin League for which, LIVY states, a statue was erected for him in the forum.

Candace was the title of a queen of Nubia, Ameniremas, who defended her territory in 22 BC when it was invaded by the prefect of Egypt, C. Petronius. AUGUSTUS subsequently withdrew to the first cataract.

Canuleius, Gaius (C5 BC), as tribune of the *plebs* in 445 BC, passed a law allowing marriages between patricians and plebeians, in which the sons of plebeian mothers were to have patrician status.

Canus, Julius (C1 AD), was a Stoic philosopher praised by the younger SENECA (2) for his courage in engaging in argument with the emperor CALIGULA before his execution. See Seneca, *Tranq.*, 14, 4ff.

Capito 1, Gaius Ateius, as tribune of the *plebs* in 55 BC opposed CRASSUS (3)'s Parthian expedition by declaring adverse omens, for which in 50 he was condemned by the censors as having invented them. CAESAR (1) gave him the task of distributing lands to his veterans in 44 BC.

2, Gaius Ateius (died AD 22), the grandson of a centurion in SULLA (1)'s army, was a jurist of the Augustan period. He was consul in AD 5, and from 13 to his death was in charge of the Roman water supply. He was conservative in his legal thinking and had little influence on posterity, being eclipsed by his contemporary M. Antistius LABEO. He was regarded by the historian Sextus POMPONIUS (2) as the inspiration behind the Sabinian law school (see SABINUS 4). His writings have not survived.

Caracalla (AD 188–217), the elder son of Septimius SEVERUS (1), reigned as emperor from 211 until his death. He was born at Lugdunum (Lyons), and was later given the official name Marcus Aurelius Antoninus after his adoptive grandfather, the emperor of that name. His nickname Caracalla derives from the hooded Gallic military greatcoat (*caracallus*) which he often wore after he became emperor in defiance of the law that military garb could not be worn in the city. He was created *Caesar* by his father in 196 and *Augustus* in 198. In 202 he married Fulvia Plautilla, the daughter of the praetorian prefect, PLAUTIANUS, but he caused the death of her father in 205, and killed her in 212 after a long exile. He accompanied his father to Britain in 208: even before Septimius died at York in February 211, Caracalla was at odds with his brother GETA (3), and when on Septimius' death the two became joint rulers through his will, their mother, JULIA (10) Domna, prevented a partition of the Empire. But Caracalla murdered his brother in 212 and carried out a reign of terror against his brother's supporters. The same year he issued an imperial edict (the *Constitutio Antoniniana*) extending the franchise to all free men in the Empire, probably with little practical effect. He completed the building of the baths at Rome named after him, which his father had begun. In 213 he went to Germany, where he defeated the Alemanni and strengthened the wall along the frontier. In 214 he was on the Danube frontier on his way to the east and fought the Carpi. He also levied an army based on that of Alexander the Great, whom he admired and wished to emulate. The next year he attacked Armenia unsuccessfully, and in 216 he moved against Media, spending the following winter at Edessa, which he had added to the province of Osroene. In April 217 he was about to set out again for the east when he was assassinated near Carrhae by the praetorian prefect, MACRINUS, who succeeded and deified him. See M. Grant (1985) *The Roman Emperors*, London: Weidenfeld & Nicolson.

Caratacus (C1 AD) was a British king, a son of CUNOBELINUS, king of the Catuvellauni and the Trinovantes. With his brother Togodumnus he resisted the Roman occupation in AD 43 and fought against VESPASIAN on the Medway, where he was defeated and forced to retire over the Severn and seek the help of the Silures. He was later defeated in North Wales at Caersws by the Roman governor OSTORIUS SCAPULA and fled to the north, taking refuge with CARTIMANDUA, queen of the Brigantes. She surrendered him in 51 to the Romans and he was taken to CLAUDIUS (1) in Rome, who treated him well.

Carausius, Marcus Aurelius (died AD 293), was a Gaul of Menapian origin who was appointed commander of the Channel *c.*AD 287 by the emperor MAXIMIAN. After being accused of complicity with the Germanic enemies of Rome whom he was appointed to oppose, he was condemned to death by the emperor and fled to Britain, where he established himself as an independent ruler and claimed to be emperor. Maximian sent a fleet to overthrow him, but it was wrecked in a storm and failed in its mission. Maximian was then (*c.*290) compelled to recognise Carausius as a colleague, and his rule extended to north-eastern Gaul. He seems to have had the support of the Franks and continued in power until CONSTANTIUS (1) I Chlorus attacked him and he was murdered by his subordinate ALLECTUS. See P.J. Casey (1994) *Carausius and Allectus*, London: Batsford.

Carbo 1, Gaius Papirius (died 119 BC), a supporter of the Gracchi, served on the commission (to which he was appointed in 130 BC) to give effect to the agrarian law of Tiberius GRACCHUS (4). He had been tribune of the *plebs* the year before, when he had enacted a law to extend secret voting to the lawmaking Assembly of the People. He failed in an attempt to legalise re-election to the tribunate, and changed sides to the aristocratic party, becoming consul in 120. He successfully defended OPIMIUS, the murderer of Gaius GRACCHUS (1) that year, but was prosecuted by the youthful L. Licinius CRASSUS (2) the next year for putting citizens to death without trial, and committed suicide. He was alleged to have been among the assassins of SCIPIO (11) Aemilianus.

2, Gaius Papirius (died 81 BC), a nephew of CARBO (1), was a tribune of the *plebs* in 89 BC when he and his colleague M. PLAUTIUS (3) Silvanus passed the law *Plautia Papiria* which offered Roman citizenship to every Italian ally of Rome domiciled in Italy provided he made a personal application to the praetor in Rome within sixty days. Carbo died in the siege of Volaterrae.

3. Arvina, Gaius Papirius, a son of CARBO (1), was tribune of the *plebs* in 90 BC and a supporter of CINNA (2) during the Civil War. He was executed in 82 by

BRUTUS (3) Damasippus on the orders of MARIUS (3) Graditanus on suspicion of wishing to change sides.

4, Gnaeus Papirius, as consul in 113 BC was sent with an army to ward off the advance of the Cimbri and Teutones on the eastern frontier of Cisalpine Gaul, and attacked them after they had agreed to withdraw, but they repulsed him.

5, Gnaeus Papirius (C1 BC), brother of CARBO (2), was tribune of the *plebs* in 92 BC. He fought in the Social War and later became the henchman of CINNA (2) who in 85 chose him as his colleague for the consulship and retained this arrangement for the following year. Cinna was killed by his troops in 84, and Carbo as sole consul had to face a vengeful SULLA (2). He raised 100,000 Italian troops, but they were unenthusiastic and untrained: Sulla was reinforced by ardent supporters. Carbo failed to prevent Sulla's advance to Campania. He became consul for the third time in 82 with MARIUS (1)'s son as his colleague. He deserted Rome in spring 82 after massacring aristocratic senators including C. Mucius Scaevola. He retired northwards and was defeated by METELLUS (6) Pius near Faventia. He then fled to Africa. He was proscribed: POMPEIUS (2) caught him off Sicily and executed him at Lilybaeum, though he was still consul and had assisted Pompeius in a trial.

Carinus, Marcus Aurelius (reigned AD 283–285), was an emperor, the elder son of CARUS, who left him with the title *Caesar* in charge of the western provinces of the Empire while he marched on Persia. Carinus won some successes on the German frontier and then retired to Rome, where after the death of his father he became emperor together with his brother NUMERIAN. In the north of Italy at Verona, Carinus defeated the pretender Julian. The following year Numerian was murdered in Bithynia and DIOCLETIAN was elected by the army to succeed him. Carinus met him in Moesia at the river Margus and was defeated in a hard-fought battle: one of his officers assassinated him.

Carrinas, Gaius (C1 BC), was a pro-Marian politician. In the campaign of 83 BC he led an army against SULLA (2) and suffered several defeats in central Italy. After the flight of CARBO (3) in 82 he failed to reach MARIUS (2) the Younger at Praeneste, but joined Pontius in a dash for Rome, and was among those caught by Sulla's army at the Colline Gate and later executed.

Cartimandua (C1 AD) was a queen of the Brigantes, the British nation that occupied most of Yorkshire, Lancashire and Cumbria. Her husband was Venutius, who in AD 51 rebelled against her when she surrendered CARATACUS to CLAUDIUS (1) in compliance with the treaty of friendship between them establishing her as a 'client' ruler under the Romans. During the years 52–57 she relied on the support of the Roman governor, Aulus Didius GALLUS (5), to maintain her position against her husband. She subsequently divorced him and married Vellocatus. In 68, when the Romans were preoccupied at home, Venutius rose against her and expelled her. VESPASIAN accordingly seized Brigantia and incorporated it in the Roman province. See B.R. Hartley (1988) *The Brigantes*, Gloucester: Alan Sutton.

Carus, Marcus Aurelius (reigned AD 282–283), an Illyrian, born at Narona, was an emperor. He was a senator and the praetorian prefect of the emperor PROBUS (1). After the murder of Probus by his troops, Carus was proclaimed emperor by his army. He left his son CARINUS to deputise for him in Rome and the western provinces, and himself moved against the Persian empire with his younger son, NUMERIAN. On the way he fought successful campaigns against the Quadi and Sarmatians on the upper Danube. In

Persia he captured the capital, Ctesiphon, took Mesopotamia, and crossed the river Tigris, but was assassinated by his troops, probably instigated by his praetorian prefect, Arrius APER. He was succeeded by his sons Carinus and Numerian, the latter of whom Aper also murdered in 284. See M. Grant (1985) *The Roman Emperors*, London: Weidenfeld & Nicolson.

Carvilius *see* MAXIMUS (1).

Casca (C1 BC) **1.** Two brothers named Casca were implicated in the plot to kill Julius CAESAR (1) in 44 BC. Publius Servilius Casca Longus struck the first blow in the assassination. He was a tribune in 43 but fled to join the army of BRUTUS (5) and committed suicide with his brother after the battle of Philippi.

2, Gaius, a tribune of 44 BC, unrelated to CASCA (1), published a denial of complicity in the plot to kill Caesar.

Cassius 1. Dio (*c.*AD 164–*c.*230) was a historian of Rome who wrote in Greek. His full name was Lucius Cassius Dio. Born in Bithynia, he was the son of Cassius Apronianus, a Roman senator and governor, first of Dalmatia and then of Cilicia under MARCUS AURELIUS; his maternal grandfather was DIO CHRYSOSTOM, whose name he took. He went to Rome in 180 and held many offices, becoming a senator under COMMODUS, praetor in 194, suffect consul *c.*205 and consul with SEVERUS (2) Alexander in 229, though he had to live outside Rome while holding this office for fear of the wrath of the Praetorians. He composed his greatest work, a *History of Rome*, in eighty books over a period of twenty-two years. Some parts have survived intact, others were summarised in epitomes. The surviving books are 36–54 (68–10 BC) in full, 55–60 (9 BC–AD 46) in an abridged version, and 17 and 79–80 in part. The contents of much of the rest are known from the eleventh century epitome by Xiphilinus and the twelfth-century *Epitome of Historical Works* by Zonaras. Dio was unfamiliar with republican institutions, relying on LIVY and his sources; he is more reliable on the principate. His narrative shows strong interest in political developments and has a rhetorical style in the Atticist tradition. He also wrote a biography of the writer ARRIAN and a book about the dreams of Septimius SEVERUS (1).

2. Longinus, Gaius (died 42 BC), was a Roman politician and general, and an assassin of CAESAR (1). He began his career as quaestor of Marcus CRASSUS (3) and escaped from the battle of Carrhae (Harran) in 53 BC, leading the withdrawal of the fragmented army. He organised the defence of Syria, crushed a rebellion in Judaea in 52, and drove back a Parthian invasion in 51. In 49 he was tribune of the *plebs*, supporting POMPEIUS (2), who appointed him commander of his fleet. On hearing the news of Pharsalus in 48 he made his peace with Caesar and was appointed *legatus*. He was praetor in 44 when he organised the conspiracy to murder Caesar: he wished to extend the plot so as to kill ANTONIUS (7) as well, but BRUTUS (5) vetoed the plan. Popular anger against the conspirators made him leave Rome, and in June he was commissioned by the Senate to supervise the import of grain from Sicily. His next appointment was to govern Cyrene, but Cassius quarrelled with Antonius and sailed to Asia and then to Syria, which Caesar had promised to appoint him to govern. But the Assembly of the People had granted the province to the Caesarian DOLABELLA (4) for five years: Cassius won the support of the armies of Bithynia and Syria which were besieging Caecilius BASSUS (1) in Apamea and also Bassus' own troops. He intercepted troops coming from Egypt and forced them to join him, and, after taking Laodicea where Dolabella had taken refuge, he acquired his army. After the battle of Mutina the

Senate appointed Brutus and Cassius to command the eastern provinces, but the law of PEDIUS (2) outlawed them for the murder of Caesar. Cassius sent Quintus LABIENUS (1) to Parthia to raise troops to help defeat the triumvirs. Cassius levied troops and money as he went through Syria and Asia to Macedonia to join Brutus and stormed Rhodes on the way. When the Caesarians reached Philippi in 42 they found Brutus and Cassius well fortified, but turned their position. At the first battle Cassius had himself killed somewhat prematurely after losing his camp: he did not know that Brutus had beaten Octavian (see AUGUSTUS). His wife Junia, the half-sister of Brutus and daughter of Caesar's mistress SERVILIA, survived until 22 BC.

3. Longinus, Gaius (C1 AD), was a legal expert and teacher of law. He was suffect consul in 30, proconsul of Asia in 40 and 41, and legate of Syria from 45 to 49. NERO (1) exiled him in 65 for treason as he owned an ancestral bust of the 'tyrannicide' CASSIUS (2), but he was recalled by VESPASIAN. His *Books of Civil Law* are lost, but are known to us through JAVOLENUS' comments recorded by Justinian's compilers. He was taught by SABINUS (4) and succeeded him as head of the school, which was consequently called the Cassian School. See PROCULUS.

4. Longinus Ravilla, Lucius (C2 BC) was a judge and reformer. As tribune of the *plebs* in 137 he passed a law introducing secret ballots in all legal cases before the popular courts except those for treason. He was consul in 127 and censor in 125, and extended the Tepula Aqueduct to Rome. As a judge he was known as the 'defendants' shipwreck', and formulated the famous maxim *cui bono?*, 'who profits?'. He condemned the three Vestal Virgins accused of unchastity in 113 BC, even though two had been acquitted by the *Pontifex Maximus* (Chief Priest).

5. Longinus, Lucius (died AD 40), after a consulship in 30 was appointed governor of Syria by CALIGULA. He was married to Drusilla, the daughter of GERMANICUS and sister of Caligula, with whom the latter committed incest. Caligula ordered his murder for fear of an oracle naming his future assassin as 'Cassius' (see CHAEREA).

6. Longinus, Quintus (died 47 BC), was notorious as a rapacious quaestor and governor of Spain. He served there under POMPEIUS (2) *c.*52 BC and in 49 as one of the two tribunes of the *plebs* who supported CAESAR (1) and tried to prevent the Senate from declaring him a public enemy. After their failure, he and his colleague ANTONIUS (7) fled to Caesar's camp. In April after the flight of Caesar's enemies Cassius summoned the Senate. He was made governor of Further Spain for 48 and had to cope with a rebellion that he put down with the help of BOGUD and LEPIDUS (4). At the end of his year of office he sailed away with his looted treasure but sank with it.

7. Longinus (*c.*AD 213–273), was an Athenian philosopher and rhetorician who in the early 270s moved to Palmyra, where he became the adviser of the queen, ZENOBIA, and her general ODAENATHUS. AURELIAN executed him when he sacked the city. A few fragments of his writings survive, mostly on rhetoric, though he also wrote a commentary on Plato's *Timaeus*. PLOTINUS denied him the name philosopher, but Eunapius described him as a 'living library'. He taught PORPHYRY.

8. Severus (died *c.*AD 35) was an orator and writer of the Augustan period. He was an outspoken critic of the regime, and prosecuted some of the emperor's friends. He wrote pamphlets, often libellous, which attacked various important people, and was widely hated. AUGUSTUS had him prosecuted by Paullus FABIUS (8) Maximus on a charge of treason and he was banished *c.*AD 12 to Crete, and removed in 24 to Seriphos, where he died.

9. Vecellinus, Spurius, was an early Roman statesman who held three consulships, in 502, 493 and 486 BC, and made a peace treaty with the Latins in 493 to the effect that both sides would defend each other on equal terms. The treaty held for more than a century until 380. According to tradition, he was put to death in 486 for attempting to make himself king, after he had proposed a law to distribute public land to the plebeians. The evidence for his consulships and the treaty is sound, though his name (Cassius) is plebeian.
See also AVIDIUS, CHAEREA.

Cassivellaunus (C1 BC) was the king of the Catuvellauni, the nation that inhabited land immediately north of the Thames when CAESAR (1) invaded Britain in 54 BC. He was chosen by the Britons of the south-east to lead them against the invaders: he was defeated in battle in Kent and subsequently avoided pitched battles, preferring to attack Caesar's foragers and fleet. But when his capital at Wheathampstead was overrun, he made terms with Caesar's agent COMMIUS, promising tribute and hostages and to leave the Trinovantes of Essex in peace. One of his eventual successors was TASCIOVANUS, who may have been his grandson.

Catiline (*c.*109–62 BC) Lucius Sergius Catilina was born into an impoverished patrician family at Rome. He fought in the Social War under POMPEIUS (5) Strabo and served under SULLA (2) in his assault on Rome and in the proscriptions in which he slew his brother-in-law Marcus MARIUS (3) at the request of Quintus CATULUS (3). He was quaestor in 77, praetor in 68 and governor of Africa in 67 and 66, when he wished to stand for the consulship. But he was accused of extortion in his province, and was disqualified until his trial was over. He was prosecuted by Publius CLODIUS, who colluded in his acquittal. He was said to have conspired in 66 to murder the new consuls on the day of their installation, but the date was postponed. Though guilty of the plot, which he did little to conceal, he was saved from prosecution by the machinations of M. Licinius CRASSUS (3). He was ambitious and embittered by frustration, and decided to win the support of disaffected young men and the dissatisfied veterans of Sulla to win power for himself. He would then obtain a cancellation of debts and a proscription of the rich. He made a pact with ANTONIUS (1) that they should both stand for the consulship for 63 and once elected, act in concert to bring about Catiline's programme. He was supported in his electoral campaign by CAESAR (1) and Crassus. In the meantime in 64 he was prosecuted unsuccessfully by LUCCEIUS for murder.

When, however, the voters chose CICERO (1) in place of Catiline, he stood again for 62, but was again defeated. In despair of gaining his ends, he formed a widespread conspiracy and won support from many disgruntled aristocrats, veterans and even slaves, collecting money and weapons. Catiline had a large following and was popular: he was a patrician, a Sullan, and a demagogue. Cicero could not easily move against him as he lacked evidence. Catiline then plotted to kill Cicero at his house on the morning of 7 November 63, but Cicero's spies kept him informed and he foiled the plot. The next day he delivered his first speech against Catiline in the Senate and frightened him into fleeing to his army in Etruria where the standard had already been raised by C. Manlius, a Sullan veteran. On the 9th Cicero spoke to the people in the Assembly and proposed that Catiline and Manlius be declared public enemies. Shortly afterwards, some Allobrogian ambassadors, who had been approached by the conspirators for help, gave Cicero written evidence of the plot, and he arrested the ringleaders still in the city. After a resolution of the Senate moved by CATO (5), which gave him authorisation, Cicero had these men, LENTULUS (9), CETHEGUS (1) and other senators, strangled in the prison. Meanwhile his colleague, Antonius, marched against Catiline and in early January defeated him with the help of METELLUS (8) Celer. PETREIUS led Antonius' army and killed Catiline as he fought bravely near Pistoria. See Sallust, *The War with Catiline*.

Cato 1, Gaius Porcius (C2 BC), was a grandson of CATO (4) and a supporter of the Gracchi. He was consul in 114 BC, when he lost a battle against the Scordisci in Macedonia, and was convicted of extortion on his return to Rome. Later, after being found guilty by MAMILIUS (1)'s commission of corrupt dealings with JUGURTHA, he was exiled and went to live at Tarraco in Spain.

2, Gaius Porcius, was an opponent of POMPEIUS (2) who as tribune of the *plebs* in 56 attacked him over his policy to restore PTOLEMY (8) XII the Piper in Egypt. He also proposed legislation to remove LENTULUS (10) Spinther from his command. He had the elections of that year postponed until after the triumviral conference of Lucca so as to favour CRASSUS (3).

3, Lucius Porcius (C1 BC), was a grandson of CATO (4) who supported Pompeius Rufus' attempt to recall METELLUS (5) *c.*99 BC after the death of SATURNINUS (2). He may have been the tribune who the previous year had opposed Saturninus. Cato was killed in the Social War during his consulship in 89 when fighting the Marsi in southern Italy.

4, Marcus Porcius 'the Censor' (234–149 BC), was a statesman, moralist and writer, born at Tusculum of peasant stock, who served in the Second Punic War as a military tribune and was at the victory over HASDRUBAL (2) on the river Metaurus in 207. He was quaestor in 204, and served in Sicily. On his return he passed through Sardinia, where he met ENNIUS and brought him back to Rome. He was plebeian aedile in 199 BC and governed Sardinia in 198, when he drove out the moneylenders. In 195 he was consul with Lucius Valerius FLACCUS (6), a neighbour of patrician rank who acted as a patron to the young 'new man'. In his consulship he was sent to Spain where Roman forces were under pressure from the natives. He subdued the north, winning a victory at Emporiae (Ampurias), and opened up communications between the two provinces. With a distinguished contribution to the Roman victory over ANTIOCHUS (1) III at Thermopylae in 191, his military career ended. He wrote an account of his campaign which LIVY drew upon.

During the rest of his life Cato took an unusually active part in civil affairs, opposing the growth of Greek influence at Rome as shown in the Scipionic circle, and emphasising the old Roman virtues of simple country living. He failed to be elected censor in 189, when he supported charges of bribery against GLABRIO (3), the victor of Thermopylae. His successful attacks on Lucius SCIPIO (2) and SCIPIO (7) Africanus helped secure him the censorship in 184; his colleague was again Valerius Flaccus. He applied himself vigorously to the task he had set himself, regardless of hostility and opposition, but all his efforts were fruitless and he failed to bring back the past. However, he revised the lists of senators and knights, and regulated the publican tax-gatherers; he put a tax on luxuries, but spent a vast sum on the sewerage system of Rome, and built the Basilica Porcia in 184, a lawcourt on the Hellenistic model. He supported the passage of Orchius' law to curb extravagance in 182, and opposed later attempts to repeal it; he also supported Baebius' law in 181 to reorganise the election of praetors. He was energetic in trying to maintain high standards against corrupt provincial governors, and prosecuted Publius Furius PHILUS in 171 for extortion in Spain. He supported

Voconius' law in 169, which limited the inheritance rights of women, opposed war against Rhodes in 167, and wished Macedonia to keep its independence. When the Athenians sent an embassy led by the philosopher Carneades in 155, Cato opposed reception of the embassy and proposed the ejection of Carneades from Rome. The following year he gave support to PTOLEMY (2) VI in his struggle against his brother. He led an embassy to Carthage in 153, which opened his eyes to the recovery of Rome's old enemy, and caused his implacable opposition to her continued existence. Any speech he made in the Senate on whatever subject, he always ended with the declaration that Carthage must be destroyed. On the pretext of helping MASINISSA, king of the Numidian Massyli, who had profited greatly from the Roman victory in the second Punic War, he urged his fellow-countrymen to attack, and in 150 the Senate had its excuse: Carthage was goaded into an attack on Masinissa. War was declared the next year, when Cato died at eighty-five, leaving two sons, Cato Licinianus by his first wife, Licinia, and Cato Salonianus by Salonia.

Cato was very influential as a writer and has been described as the founder of Latin prose writing. He wrote a historical work of great importance, the unfinished *Origins*, in seven books, on which he worked between about 168 and his death. It owed much to Hellenistic predecessors, but broke new ground and included the fruits of some real historical research; it covered Roman and Italian history from Aeneas and the times of the kings down to his own day. Of this work only fragments survive. He was passionately devoted to the countyside and wrote *c.*160 a treatise *On Agriculture*, which survives entire (it is also known as *On Country Life*): he drew on his own experience and described the cultivation of the major crops of Italy. He was aware of the virtues of capitalism and said that farmers should always aim to have a surplus to sell. He published many speeches (we have fragments of eighty) in which he displayed his mastery of Attic oratorical techniques. He knew Greek well and had mastered Greek literature: his objection was to Romans who were excessively philhellene. He also published a work on medicine. See A.E. Astin (1978) *Cato the Censor*, Oxford: Clarendon Press; E.D. Rawson (1985) *Intellectual Life in the Late Roman Republic*, London: Duckworth.

5, Marcus Porcius 'of Utica' (95–46 BC), was the great-grandson of CATO (4) by his second son, and known as Cato the Younger to distinguish him from the former; a statesman and philosopher of the first century BC. On the early death of both his parents he was brought up in the household of his maternal uncle, M. Livius DRUSUS (1), with his mother LIVIA (1)'s children by her marriage with Q. Servilius Caepio. As a young man he studied rhetoric and Stoic philosophy, both of which were powerful influences on his career. He was quaestor in 64 BC and in 63, after supporting the prosecution of MURENA, he spoke in the Senate to secure the execution of the Catilinarian conspirators which CICERO (1) demanded and CAESAR (1) opposed. Early in 62, when Cato was tribune of the *plebs*, he applied his veto to his colleague METELLUS (9) Nepos' proposal that POMPEIUS (2) should be recalled to head the fight against CATILINE: the issue soon faded as Catiline's army was quickly defeated. During his tribuneship Cato increased the corn-dole to the common people: in other respects he was obstructive of compromise with Pompeius and in 60 proved an outspoken opponent of a deal with the publican tax-gatherers. In 59 BC he opposed the formation of the 'triumvirate', which he had largely provoked, and suffered imprisonment for his pains. When Caesar was elected consul for 59, Cato approved of the bribery used to persuade the electorate to accept BIBULUS

(1) as his colleague. He persuaded the Senate to reject Caesar's agrarian bill to settle Pompeius' veterans, which Caesar then took to the Assembly of the People. In 58 Cato was removed from politics through the machinations of Publius CLODIUS, the populist demagogue, and sent to annex Cyprus from Ptolemy, its king, because the latter had aided the pirates. He sold the king's property, which fetched 7,000 talents. Although Cato lost his accounts during his voyage home, he was not suspected of corruption. He persuaded his brother-in-law L. Domitius AHENOBARBUS (6) to stand for the consulship of 55 in order to secure the recall of Caesar from his Gallic command, but the plan failed and the triumvirs made the compact of Lucca. Pompeius, through his powers as augur, prevented Cato standing for the praetorship of 55, in retaliation for his opposition to the bill to enact the decisions made at Lucca. He was, however, elected praetor for 54. In 53 he supported a bill proposed by Bibulus to make Pompeius sole consul for 52. He happily joined the common assault on Caesar's political position during 51, as he hated Caesar and saw him as representing everything he detested: opportunism, self-aggrandisement, betrayal of his class and contempt for the Republic. He failed in his attempt to be elected consul for 51, and when the Civil War broke out he reluctantly served the Senate's cause in Sicily, but abandoned his efforts there to Caesar's agent Curio in order to avoid bloodshed. He blamed Pompeius for having rushed into an unnecessary war. He next went to Asia, and at the time of the battle of Pharsalus (August 48) was in command of Dyrrhachium. He then joined the general movement of republicans to Africa, where he joined METELLUS (11) Scipio. He was appointed to govern Utica near Carthage, from which he was posthumously given his nickname *Uticensis*, and his moderate rule was appreciated by its citizens. In 46 however, following Caesar's victory at Thapsus, he realised that the republican cause was lost and committed suicide, even though he could surely have gained pardon from Caesar.

Cato was a genuine lover of the old Roman character and modelled himself consciously on his great-grandfather. But he was arrogant and unyielding, and must have been hard to live with. His first wife, Antistia, was unfaithful and he divorced her; he lent his second wife, Marcia, to HORTENSIUS (2). He left a son, and a daughter (PORCIA). Cicero wrote a pamphlet in praise of what he stood for, entitled *Cato*. Caesar responded with *Anticato*, but pitched his case too strongly. Cato was remembered as a patriot and a republican. See PLUTARCH, *The Younger Cato*.

Catullus 1, Gaius Valerius (*c.*84–*c.*54 BC), was a poet from Verona in Cisalpine Gaul. His family was equestrian, rich and notable in the area – his father entertained CAESAR (1) to dinner while he was governor – and Catullus and his elder brother were both intended for the senatorial career. But Catullus turned to the writing of poetry, in a wide variety of styles and metres, and introduced a new perspective into Latin literature which derived partly from the Alexandrian poets, especially Callimachus, to whose work he was introduced by PARTHENIUS, and partly from Greek lyric poets such as Sappho. His surviving work, preserved in a single manuscript found in Verona, consists of 114 poems which fall into three distinct groups, which he almost certainly published in three original volumes. The first is composed in a variety of metres, including hendecasyllables, scazons, pure iambics and Sapphics: this group of poems conveys a wide range of sometimes intense emotion. The second is a series of longer poems, some in the elegiac metre, but the longest, an epyllion (no. 64), in hexameters. The last is a book of epigrams, namely shorter elegiac poems. It has been argued cogently that the order in which we have them is the order in which Catullus published them. A dominant theme, running through all three books, is a desperate love affair with a married woman he calls Lesbia, whose real name was CLODIA (as reported by APULEIUS), and who was almost certainly one of the sisters of Publius CLODIUS. Around this affair he wrote a series of twenty-five poems scattered through the collection, expressing the whole gamut of feelings from ecstasy to desolation. There is also much wit and humour in his poetry, as well as tenderness towards friends, including a farewell elegy to his dead brother (no. 101), composed when he was on a visit to the Troad, as a dramatic monologue addressed to his brother's tomb there. Many historical and literary men feature in the poems: Caesar is lampooned, but is reported by SUETONIUS (2) to have forgiven Catullus and invited him to dinner; CICERO (1) also gives rise to a joke; Catullus is abusive of Caesar's chief engineer, MAMURRA, whom he calls *Mentula*, 'Prick'. He was a close friend of Licinius CALVUS and of other poets such as CINNA (1).

He settled in Rome *c.*62 BC and spent the rest of his life there, though he did not lose touch with his homeland, and in his poems often refers to Verona and its surroundings, including Lake Garda. He must have mixed in fashionable society as well as literary circles in Rome and developed close friendships and bitter enmities there: he mentions many of those he knew. In the year 57 BC he was in Bithynia in the retinue of the pro-praetor (governor), Gaius MEMMIUS (2), probably in a private capacity as a friend rather than as an official. He commemorates (no. 4) his return home in a yacht which he had built at Amastris and which he finally docked at Sirmio on Garda where his family had a villa. Nothing is known of his death: he certainly lived until 54 BC, the last date for any recognisable event in his extant poetry, but he may well have lived on after that and may even be identified with the writer of mimes, CATULLUS (2).

Catullus was a poet of great range of style and emotion, deeply aware of the tradition he was heir to. He translated Callimachus (no. 66) and earned the epithet *doctus*, 'learned', which later generations applied to him. Yet he also adapted Sappho (no. 51) and wrote a poem of great emotional power and originality in the *Atthis* (no. 63); he was never overawed by the past nor was he a slave to learning. He had a profound influence on his successors: VIRGIL's poetry contains many echoes of Catullus, HORACE's *Odes* owe him an unacknowledged debt, and OVID, PROPERTIUS and MARTIAL were each influenced by his work; Martial acknowledged his mastery. See E.A. Havelock (1939) *The Lyric Genius of Catullus*, Oxford: Blackwell; T.P. Wiseman (1985) *Catullus and his World*, Cambridge: Cambridge University Press; J.K. Newman (1990) *Roman Catullus*, Hildesheim: Weidmann; R.O.A.M. Lyne (1980) *The Latin Love Poets*, Oxford: Clarendon Press.

2. A writer of mimes, possibly to be identified with CATULLUS (1), though he could have lived up to a century later. His lost works included a mime, *The Apparition*, which JUVENAL described as 'noisy', and another, *Laureolus*, concerned with a highwayman whose crucifixion was shown on stage.

Catulus 1, Gaius Lutatius (C3 BC), was commander of the Roman fleet during his consulship in 242, when he occupied Lilybaeum and Drepanum with 200 ships. At the Aegates Islands off west Sicily, though wounded, he attacked and defeated the Carthaginian fleet in March 241 and so brought the First Punic War to a successful conclusion.

2, Quintus Lutatius (died 87 BC), was the half-brother of CAESAR (2) and CAESAR (5). He failed three times to be elected consul and only succeeded in 102 BC with the help of MARIUS (1), who was his colleague. He led an army against the Cimbri but was defeated on the Upper Adige and retreated, abandoning the Po valley. As proconsul the following year, he was joined by Marius and won the victory of Vercellae over the Cimbri; SULLA (2) was his legate. Catulus and Marius held a joint triumph, but Catulus became disillusioned with Marius, who received most credit for the victory, and switched his support to Sulla. He may have fought in the Social War under Lucius Caesar; Marcus MARIUS (3), after returning in 87, prosecuted him and he killed himself. Two of his epigrams survive. He was also an orator and delivered the funeral oration on his mother Popillia. He knew the Scipionic circle in his youth and was introduced as a character in CICERO (1)'s *On the Orator.*

3, Quintus Lutatius (died 61 BC), was the son of CATULUS (2) by Domitia. He supported SULLA (2) after his return from the east in 82 BC, and avenged his father's suicide by encompassing the death of Marcus MARIUS (3) which was accomplished by CATILINE. He was elected consul for 78 with Sulla's support, though he disapproved of the behaviour of Sulla's followers; he opposed the attempt of his colleague, Aemilius LEPIDUS (3), to overthrow Sulla's constitution, and defeated him with the aid of POMPEIUS (2). He passed a law against public violence. When Lepidus as proconsul of Gaul rebelled in 77 and led his army against Rome, Catulus outmanoeuvred and beat him. He rebuilt the temple of Jupiter on the Capitol and reopened it in 69. In 70 he accepted the modification of Sulla's constitution, whose defects he had come to recognise. He had broken with Pompeius in 77 and opposed the Gabinian and Manilian laws, which gave Pompeius commands against the pirates and MITHRIDATES (3) VI respectively. He was censor in 65 with Marcus CRASSUS (3) as his colleague, but opposed the latter's proposal to give citizenship to the Gauls living north of the Po. In 63 CAESAR (1) defeated him in the election to become *Pontifex Maximus*, and he died after being humiliated in the Senate. He failed to live up to his father's example as a public speaker and poet.

Celsus 1, Aulus Cornelius (*c.*25 BC–*c.*AD 50) A first-century AD encyclopaedist whose writings on medicine are extant. Though a layman in medical science, he showed great skill in the selection and presentation of his material. His eighth and final book, on surgery, shows that many delicate and serious operations were performed in his time. Only fragments of his other work survive. The style of his Latin is admired for its clarity and purity.

2, Publius (early C2 AD), was a jurist, provincial governor, and counsellor of HADRIAN. His full name was P. Juventius Celsus Titus Aufidius Hoenius Severianus (the name suggests adoption). He was praetor in AD 106 or 107, legate of Thrace, consul twice, in 129 for the second time, and proconsul of Asia. He succeeded his father (also Juventius Celsus) as head of the Proculian school of law, in partnership with NERATIUS Priscus, and wrote thirty-nine books of *Digests* partly based on earlier work of his own. JULIANUS followed his order in arranging his own *Digests*; Justinian's *Digests* cite 144 extracts from Celsus; ULPIANUS often quotes him. He had an original mind and deep knowledge of his sources.

3. (C2 AD) An anti-Christian writer of the Platonist school. He wrote in AD 176 an indictment of Christianity, no longer extant, entitled *The True Word*, which ORIGEN (1) quotes extensively in his book *Against Celsus*, dealing point by point with Celsus' arguments.

Censorinus (C3 AD) was a grammarian and chronologist whose surviving work, *On the Birthday*, dedicated to Q. Caerellius on his birthday in AD 238, discussed human life and its origins, the influence of the stars and various methods employed in the division and calculation of time. The major influences on this work were VARRO (3) and SUETONIUS (2). The manuscript of *On the Birthday* also contains an anonymous collection of articles on various subjects known as the *Fragmentum Censorini*.

Cerialis (C1 AD) was a governor of Britain whose full name was Quintus Petillius Cerialis Caesius Rufus. He may have been a Sabine and was a kinsman of the emperor VESPASIAN. He was commander of the Ninth Legion in Britain in AD 61 when it was almost annihilated by forces allied to BOUDICCA. In 69 he assisted Vespasian's forces in the capture of Rome. He was made suffect consul for AD 70, and in summer of that year was sent to put down the rebellion of CIVILIS and CLASSICUS in the German provinces. He won battles near Trier and Vetera and accomplished the destruction of the 'Gallic Empire' and the repulse of the German invaders under Civilis including the submission of the Batavi. Cerialis was appointed governor of Britain in 71 and subjugated the Brigantes of northern England before his recall in 74, when he was again suffect consul. A Petillius, possibly the same man, was consul in 83.

Cestius Gallus, Gaius (died AD 67), was suffect consul in AD 42 and legate of Syria from 63 to 67. In 66 he tried to put down an insurrection at Jerusalem and besieged the city, but lost his nerve and retreated, only to be routed by the Jewish partisans at Beth-horon.

Cestius Pius, Lucius was a rhetorician of the Augustan period from Smyrna who hated CICERO (1) and wrote ripostes to his speeches.

Cethegus 1, Gaius Cornelius (C1 BC), was one of the Catilinarian conspirators. He remained at Rome when CATILINE left the city on 8 November 63. He was executed on CICERO (1)'s orders with the other conspirators on 5 December.

2, Marcus Cornelius (died 196 BC), was a general and orator of the third century BC. He was consul in 204. In 203 he and the praetor P. Quinctilius Varus defeated Hannibal's brother MAGO in Cisalpine Gaul, and drove him back over the Alps. In 197 he defeated the Insubres.

3, Publius Cornelius (early C1 BC), was a supporter of MARIUS (1) who defected to SULLA (2) and was energetic in pursuing those whom Sulla proscribed. He became very powerful through intrigue and knowledge of procedure, though he failed to gain high office. It was by cultivating Cethegus and his mistress that ANTONIUS (6) Creticus and the Luculli (see LUCULLUS 2, LUCULLUS 3) obtained commands.

Chaerea, Gaius Cassius (died AD 41), as a tribune in the Praetorian Guard, being motivated by the emperor's mockery of him for his effeminacy, formed a conspiracy against CALIGULA which had support among his colleagues. He struck him down as he took a walk after attending the theatre on the morning of the 24 January 41. He was executed by Caligula's successor, CLAUDIUS (1).

Chrysogonus, Lucius Cornelius was a freedman of SULLA (2). He was implicated in a plot in 81 BC to obtain fraudulently for two of his kinsmen the property of Sextius ROSCIUS (1) of Ameria, by having his name put on the proscription list. He accused Roscius' son of having killed his father. CICERO (1) denounced the plot in his speech *For Roscius of Ameria*.

Cicero 1, Marcus Tullius (106–43 BC), Rome's greatest orator and writer, was born at Arpinum in central Italy on 3 January 106. His father, a rich equestrian, had the foresight to give him and his younger brother, CICERO (3), a good education in Rome where they were joined by their cousins Q. and L. Cicero. The four boys studied rhetoric and philosophy together, and here Cicero became friendly with Titus Pomponius, later to be called ATTICUS. He assumed the adult toga in 91 BC and served as a military tribune the following year under POMPEIUS (2)'s father, POMPEIUS (5) Strabo. In the next years he studied law, attending the consultations of both the elder and the younger Q. Mucius SCAEVOLA, and in 81 he defended P. Quinctius with a speech which is extant. He also studied philosophy under PHILO (2). The following year he successfully defended Sextius ROSCIUS (1) on a charge of parricide and made his name both by his eloquence and by his courage in attacking a protégé of SULLA (1) whom the dictator was forced to repudiate (see CHRYSOGONUS). Through fear of Sulla, Cicero then thought it wise to leave Italy for a while, and from 79 to 77 he was in Greece furthering his education. He spent six months in Athens where he renewed acquaintance with Atticus, and together with his brother and cousins they followed a course of philosophical studies. He also went to Rhodes where he attended lectures given by APOLLONIUS (2) Molon and POSIDONIUS, and to Smyrna where he met P. Rutilius RUFUS (4). His tour abroad improved his health.

In 77 he returned to Rome where he married and embarked on the senatorial career. He stood for the quaestorship and was elected to serve in Sicily for the year 75. He spent the next four years in pleading cases at the Bar: in 70 he was at the head of the team that prosecuted VERRES, who had governed Sicily from 73 to 71. It was due to Cicero's brilliant strategy as well as his oratorical power that Verres threw up his defence and fled. This amounted to a victory over the then leading advocate of the day, HORTENSIUS (2) Hortalus. Cicero was curule aedile in 69 and praetor in 66, a significant success for a 'new man', as he was climbing the ladder of office at the fastest possible speed. As praetor he made his first important political speech, *For Manilius' Law* (or *On Pompeius' Command*), in favour of POMPEIUS (2)'s being awarded command of the army against MITHRIDATES (3) VI. Cicero during this part of his career was associated with the popular party in politics, and sided strongly with Pompeius. With considerable support from Atticus he was elected consul for 63 along with ANTONIUS (1) to the detriment of CATILINE, who was defeated at the polls as the *Optimates*, the party of tradition and of the aristocrats, deserted him for Cicero. Henceforth Cicero transferred his allegiance to this party. Towards the end of his year of office Cicero had the task of dealing with Catiline's conspiracy, and did well to collect enough evidence against him to persuade the Senate of the seriousness of the situation. Catiline tried to have him murdered in his house on the morning of 7 November, but Cicero's foresight foiled the attempt. His colleague, Antonius, was suspected of secretly supporting Catiline, but Cicero, with the help of CATO (5), convinced the senators and the 'Ultimate Decree', authorising all means to put an end to the crisis, was passed. Catiline fled to the army he had organised in Etruria, where he was shortly afterwards defeated and killed. In Rome, Cicero arrested those who he had proof were fellow-conspirators with Catiline, five in all, including the praetor P. Cornelius LENTULUS (9), and had them strangled in the prison on 5 December. The act was strictly illegal, though it had been supported by the Senate and by all classes. Cicero was hailed as *Pater Patriae* (*Father of the Fatherland*) but was vulnerable to attacks by his enemies. He worsened his position, however, by publicising his deed and glorying in it over the next few years. In 60 he published the speeches he had made during the crisis; he wrote letters, including one to Pompeius who was still in the east, and harped on his one great success in further speeches. He also wrote a notorious poem, *On His Consulship*, in which he bragged of his achievement. In May 61, however, Cicero won the undying hatred of Publius CLODIUS Pulcher by accusing him of incest at his trial for sacrilege in the *Bona Dea* case. With the help of Caesar, Clodius became a plebeian and was thus made eligible for the tribuneship: as tribune in 58 he re-enacted a law which imposed exile on anyone who had executed a citizen without trial. Cicero well understood that the enactment was aimed at him and anticipated trouble by fleeing to Macedonia in March 58. Pompeius failed Cicero on this occasion. Clodius then passed another bill of dubious legality, which declared Cicero guilty and an exile. During his exile Cicero was helped financially by Atticus, who inherited CAECILIUS (4)'s wealth in September; in early 57 he appears to have spent some time with Atticus in Epirus, prior to his return to Italy in August. He now had an ally as violent as Clodius himself, T. Annius MILO, formerly a supporter of Pompeius, who as tribune had a law passed to recall him. Pompeius now looked kindly on the proposal.

Cicero entered Rome on 4 September 57 to public acclaim. He was faced with the task of winning compensation for the damage done to his property in his absence: his town house on the Palatine Hill had been destroyed and a 'temple of liberty' built by Clodius in its ruins; his country house at Tusculum had also suffered badly. Cicero's aim after his return from exile was to try to separate Pompeius from his alliance with Caesar and Crassus known as the First Triumvirate. Caesar, now campaigning in Gaul, used Clodius to oppose Cicero's tactics. For a time the triumvirate seemed doomed, but in April 56 the compact was renewed for five more years at Lucca, and Cicero was told to acquiesce. He recanted publicly in a speech, *On the Consular Provinces*, in which he praised Caesar warmly as if the two had been close political associates. He then withdrew from politics, expressing only in private, in letters to Atticus and other close friends, the hurt he felt at his subservience to the new order. He was compelled to accept unwelcome cases to plead at the behest of Pompeius and Caesar, such as his defence of VATINIUS and of GABINIUS (2), but in 53 Caesar and Pompeius drifted rapidly apart, and at the beginning of 52 Milo killed Clodius in an affray near Bovillae. Cicero was to have defended Milo on the charge of murder; Pompeius, however, now made sole consul to reestablish order, packed the courtroom with soldiers and cowed Cicero into silence. Milo went into exile at Marseilles, and after receiving a copy of the speech that Cicero had intended to make, expressed his gratification that Cicero's silence had allowed him to enjoy the fine mullets of that city.

Cicero was absent from Rome during the stormy period that led up to Caesar's invasion of Italy and the Civil War. As a result of Pompeius' Law on the Provinces of 52, he was appointed governor of Cilicia in Asia Minor from summer 51 to summer 50. The appointment was most unwelcome to Cicero, who had had enough of foreign travel during his exile, but he had no option but to go, and he performed his duties fairly and with some success, as his soldiers put down some brigands in a battle on Mount Amanus and so won him a public thanksgiving at Rome. He returned slowly, pausing at Athens on the way, and came to the neighbourhood of Rome on 4 January 49, hoping for a triumph, but Caesar's invasion was imminent, and the consuls sent Cicero to govern Capua and guard the coast of Campania. On the 28 March at Formiae he met Caesar, who invited him to rejoin the Senate, but the terms were unacceptable to him. He felt that Pompeius, for all his failings, was a friend, whereas Caesar was an aristocrat for whom he could feel no real affinity. After much heartsearching and consultation of Atticus, Cicero left Italy for Greece in June 49. On arriving at Pompeius' camp, however, he found little to admire and much to condemn; he took no part in the battle of Pharsalus but returned to Italy in October 48 with a pardon from Caesar. He had to wait in misery at Brundisium, however, until the two men met there in September 47, when Caesar treated Cicero respectfully and allowed him to return to Rome. He played no part in public life, but wrote, concentrating on philosophical and rhetorical works. He divorced Terentia, his wife of thirty years, in the winter of 47–46. She had supported him in crises, nerving him to take decisive action, but he had grown tired of her and accused her of systematically defrauding him. He now married a rich young woman, his ward Publilia, who divorced him almost immediately. He made one speech in the Senate in 46, in praise of Caesar's pardoning of Marcus MARCELLUS (6). In February 45 his daughter Tullia, the wife of DOLABELLA (4), died, which afflicted him deeply. He published a pamphlet in praise of Caesar's enemy Cato, to which Caesar responded with a rebuttal. He defended his friend king DEIOTARUS of Galatia against his grandson's accusation that he had tried to murder Caesar.

Cicero was not given prior knowledge of the plot to kill Caesar in March 44, but rejoiced when he heard of its success. He expected that with the dictator dead, political life as he had known it would return to Rome. He put himself at the head of a republican movement, being a senior ex-consul, and soon began to speak vehemently against Marcus ANTONIUS (7). By his *Philippics*, a series of speeches named after Demosthenes' attacks on Philip II, made between September 44 and April 43, he secured the Senate's decree which declared Antonius a public enemy. During the summer of 44 he tried to manipulate Caesar's heir Octavian (see AUGUSTUS) to his own ends, ignoring the fact that Octavian was implacably hostile to Caesar's assassins. In 43, after Antonius had been defeated near Mutina, Octavian marched on Rome and took power: the triumvirate of Antonius, Octavian and Lepidus was established in November 43 and Cicero was, at Antonius' insistence, among those proscribed. Octavian did nothing to save him, and he was caught by Antonius' men near his villa at Formiae while making a feeble effort to escape. He died bravely on 7 December, and by Antonius' orders his head and hands were exhibited on the speakers' platform in the Roman forum. He left a son, Marcus (CICERO 2).

Cicero could never rank amongst the most powerful or influential Romans of his age because, as a 'new man' without a military reputation, he lacked the army of clients that men like Pompeius and Caesar could command. Moreover, he fell between the two stools of the 'popular' party, which tried to work for reform through the Assembly of the People, and the *Optimates* or traditional aristocrats, who rightly felt he was not one of their number. He relied heavily for advice and support on Atticus and Cato, the two men he most admired and respected. Another close associate was his slave and later freedman TIRO, whom he treated well and freed in 53 and to whom he wrote twenty-one surviving letters. Milo's support, though useful, was a short-lived affair. As a character he was vain, self-advertising, and diffident, but nevertheless quite genuine in his devotion to republican institutions: as Augustus later observed, he was a good man who loved his country.

Cicero is most memorable for the huge literary legacy that he left to the world. His works, most of which survive, fall into the following categories by genre: speeches, letters, treatises on rhetoric, and philosophical works. He composed fifty-eight *speeches* that have come down to us more or less intact; a further forty-eight are known, though lost. Most were forensic speeches in defence of a client, such as his pleadings for MURENA, Milo,

Caelius RUFUS (1), SESTIUS, PLANCIUS and others. A few were speeches of prosecution, the most famous being those he made against VERRES. He also made significant political speeches, including his telling invectives against Catiline (*The Catilinarians*) and his self-destructive *Philippics* against Antonius.

His *letters*, of which we have more than 800, were written in all sorts of situations and range from the careful and politic to the hasty note dashed off to a friend. They are the more fascinating for being genuine revelations of the mind of a man central to the events of a revolutionary period of history. Most of them were private and frank and not meant for publication. They cover a period of twenty-six years and were published after his death in four groups: the sixteen books of *Letters to Atticus* were probably published in NERO (1)'s reign; they were seen by Cornelius NEPOS, who wrote Atticus' *Life*. Sixteen books of *Letters to Friends* (*Ad Fam.*) were published by Tiro in the Augustan period. There are twenty-seven *Letters to his Brother Quintus* and a collection of twenty-five letters of his correspondence with BRUTUS (5) in 43 BC.

Cicero's seven *rhetorical works* include a juvenile work, *Invention*, and a group written in the time after the establishment of the First Triumvirate: *On the Orator*, *Brutus*, *The Orator*, *The Best Kind of Orators*, *The Divisions of Oratory*, and *Topics*. In these works Cicero has much to say about the education and art of the orator, and offers much criticism of past and contemporary exponents of the art.

His *philosophical works* fall into two parts, political philosophy written in the mid-50s, including *The Republic* and *The Laws*, both written in dialogue form and very largely preserved, the former containing *Scipio's Dream* and the latter being an exposition of Stoic doctrine. A series of works produced in the short period between February 45 and November 44 display a more theological and ethical approach. Herein we may observe his great ability as a stylist, especially in the *Tusculan Disputations*, but, as he himself admitted in the introduction to his *Duties* (*De Officiis*), he was insufficiently trained as a philosopher. One of his principal motivations at the time of his philosophical activity was his grief over the death of his daughter (concerning whom he also wrote a lost *Consolation*, addressed to himself). *Duties*, a Stoic-influenced treatise on morals, based on a work by PANAETIUS, was written for his son Marcus who was studying at Athens. A work entitled *On Glory*, a eulogy of Cato, is lost. He also wrote on *Old Age* and *Laelius on Friendship*, which are preserved. His book *On Ends* (*De Finibus*) is an enquiry into the Highest Good. His theological speculations are contained in *The Nature of the Gods*, which favours Stoicism, and *Divination*, where he abandons Stoicism for a more basic paganism. In the fragmentary *On Fate* he admits, contrary to Stoic belief, the possibility of free will. His study of Academic philosophy under Philo led him to entertain a certain scepticism, and encouraged his eclecticism: under this influence he wrote the *Former and Latter Academics*, originally two books entitled *Catulus* and *Lucullus*. His translation of part of Aratus' *Phaenomena*, which LUCRETIUS read, has also survived.

See T.A. Dorey (ed.) (1980) *Cicero*, London: Routledge; A.E. Douglas (1968) *Cicero*, Greece and Rome New Survey 2; M. Fuhrmann (1992) *Cicero and the Roman Republic*, Oxford: Blackwell; C. Habicht (1990) *Cicero the Politician*, Baltimore and London: Johns Hopkins University Press; E.D. Rawson (1975) *Cicero, a Portrait*, London: Allen Lane; D. Stockton (1971) *Cicero, a Political Biography*, Oxford: Clarendon Press; D.R. Shackleton Bailey (1970) *Cicero's Letters to Atticus*, Cambridge: Cambridge University Press; (1977) *Ad Familiares*, Cambridge: Cambridge University Press; (1980) *Ad Fratrem Quintum* and *Ad Brutum*, Cambridge: Cambridge University

Press; texts and translations in the *Loeb Classical Texts* Series.

2, Marcus Tullius (born 65 BC), was the only son of CICERO (1) and TERENTIA. His father took him to Cilicia in 51; he served under POMPEIUS (2) in Greece in 49 as a successful cavalry commander. CAESAR (1) pardoned him after the battle of Pharsalus in 48, and he wanted to serve in Caesar's army, but his father sent him instead to Athens to study under CRATIPPUS. He was disappointing to his father and seems to have had a disposition to idleness and excessive drinking. After Caesar's murder he served under BRUTUS (5) in Macedonia as a military tribune; the defeat of the republicans at Philippi drove him to seek service with Sextus POMPEIUS (4) in Sicily, but in 39 he availed himself of the amnesty to return to Rome. Octavian (see AUGUSTUS), perhaps feeling guilty over the fate of his famous father, promoted him and he was elected *pontifex* and in 30 was Octavian's colleague as suffect consul for a month or two. During this time the official announcement of ANTONIUS (7)'s death was brought to him, and he had the task of destroying his statues. A little later he was governor of Syria and may have governed Asia, but nothing more is known of him.

3, Quintus Tullius (102–43 BC), was the younger brother of CICERO (1), with whom he was educated and whom he accompanied to Athens in 79. In 69 he married ATTICUS' sister Pomponia, with whom he had a tense relationship. He embarked on the senatorial career, becoming aedile in 65 and praetor in 62, his brother being in office on each occasion when the elections were held. He governed the province of Asia from 61 to 59 and later served POMPEIUS (2) in Sardinia in the winter of 57–56 and CAESAR (1) in Gaul from 54 to 51. In 51 he accompanied his brother to Cilicia where he was governor, taking his son Quintus. He acted as legate, commanding the troops and providing the military experience that his brother lacked. He joined Pompeius in 49 in the Civil War and was pardoned by Caesar after Pharsalus; he went with Caesar to Asia and with his son (see CICERO 4 below) tried to poison Caesar's mind against Marcus. In 43 he was betrayed by his slaves and killed in the proscriptions, just before Marcus. He was something of a writer: there remain his letters to his brother and to TIRO, and the interesting *Electioneering Guide* (*Commentariolum Petitionis*) was probably his work: it concerns Marcus Cicero's campaign to be elected consul for 63.

4, Quintus Tullius (*c*.67–43 BC) The son of CICERO (3), the victim of his parents' unhappy marriage. He was taken with his cousin to Cilicia when his uncle Marcus CICERO (1) was governor there in 51. Like his father, he supported POMPEIUS (2) at Pharsalus and was pardoned by CAESAR (1), and he went with his father to Asia (see **3** above). He was a *lupercus* at Rome in February 44 with ANTONIUS (7), when the latter offered Caesar a crown; he shared his father's fate.

Cilo, Lucius Fabius (C2–3 AD), was a Roman of Spanish extraction who served the emperors Septimius SEVERUS (1) and CARACALLA. He was governor of southern Gaul and parts of Asia Minor and suffect consul in AD 193, in which year he was with Septimius in his campaign against the rival emperor PESCENNIUS NIGER in the east. After the defeat of the latter, Cilo governed Moesia and Upper Pannonia until 202, being appointed the next year prefect of the city of Rome. He was consul in 204 and in 205 saved the life of the future emperor MACRINUS. In 212, when GETA (3) was murdered, Caracalla wished to kill Cilo but he was saved by his popularity.

Cincinnatus, Lucius Quinctius (C5 BC), was a Roman hero: historical fact about him is contaminated with legend. The tradition was that in 458 BC he relieved a force of Romans under MINUCIUS (1) who were under siege on Mount Algidus in the territory of the Aequi. As ex-consul he was ploughing his fields when a deputation arrived from the Senate to summon him to take up the duties of dictator. He accomplished his task in sixteen days, defeating the Aequi and liberating the Roman army; he then resigned and returned to his plough. A second dictatorship *c.*440, during which AHALA slew MAELIUS for aiming at tyranny, is fictitious.

Cincius Alimentus, Lucius (C3 BC), was a Roman historian. He governed Sicily in 210 BC and was afterwards captured by Hannibal. He wrote his *History of Rome* in Greek, from the foundation of the city to his own times. His book, which is not extant, together with that of FABIUS (11) Pictor, established the senatorial tradition of history writing.

Cineas (C3 BC) was a Thessalian diplomat who served PYRRHUS, king of Epirus. After the battles of Heraclea and Asculum in southern Italy in 280 and 279 BC, he was sent by Pyrrhus to Rome to negotiate peace. He offered terms, which were rejected by the Senate at the instigation of Appius CLAUDIUS (4). He is said to have remarked that the Senate was an assembly of kings and that fighting Rome was like fighting a hydra.

Cinna 1, Gnaeus Cornelius, known as Magnus (C1 BC), was the son of CINNA (3) and a grandson of POMPEIUS (2), whose daughter had married his father. He was a supporter of Sextus POMPEIUS (4) and of ANTONIUS (7), was pardoned by Octavian (see AUGUSTUS) and became consul in AD 5. There was a story that he plotted against Augustus during his absence in Gaul (perhaps *c.*16 BC) and was pardoned through the intercession of LIVIA (2).

2, Lucius Cornelius (early C1 BC), was a politician of undistinguished patrician birth who fought in the Social War and was elected consul for 87 BC despite the opposition of SULLA (2), who had recently seized Rome with his army. Cinna's colleague, Gnaeus OCTAVIUS (3), was a supporter of Sulla's pro-senatorial reforms but, though Cinna swore a solemn oath to Sulla that he would respect the revised constitution, he attempted to repeal it as soon as Sulla left Italy. However, after fighting had taken place in the forum, he was driven out of Rome by Octavius, who had him declared a public enemy and illegally replaced him as consul with L. Cornelius MERULA, the priest of Jupiter (*Flamen Dialis*). Cinna, with the support of CARBO (3), collected troops in Latium and Campania and won over a Roman army at Capua; MARIUS (1) and SERTORIUS joined him with their troops and they marched on Rome. POMPEIUS (5) Strabo vacillated and Cinna was able to besiege the city, which he starved into submission; the Senate surrendered and Octavius was killed wearing his consular insignia. Cinna and his colleagues massacred their aristocratic opponents, but Marius' men were stopped with difficulty from an indiscriminate slaughter. Cinna and Marius made themselves consuls for 86 without election. When Marius died in 86, Valerius FLACCUS (8) took his place as consul. Cinna worked during the next three years to restore peaceful government to Rome, enrolling new Italian citizens to the Roman tribes and organising a fresh census. He was consul in 85 and 84 with Carbo as his colleague, until he was killed in a mutiny by his troops in 84 when he was embarking for a campaign against the Liburni of Istria.

3, Lucius Cornelius (C1 BC), was the son of CINNA (2), a supporter of the rebellion in 77 BC of LEPIDUS (3), and pardoned through the influence of CAESAR (1) (who was married to his sister) by the Plautian Law. He was not entitled to stand for election until Caesar in 49 restored the right to the sons of those proscribed. He became praetor in 44, and after the murder of Caesar expressed approval of it: he was attacked two days later and saved by Lepidus. In November 44 he refused to govern the province that ANTONIUS (7) assigned him.

4, Gaius Helvius (C1 BC), was a Roman poet of the neoteric school and friend of CATULLUS (1); like him he was born in Cisalpine Gaul, near Brescia; he was a friend (not a pupil) of VALERIUS CATO. He went with Catullus to Bithynia in 57 BC in the retinue of the dilettante MEMMIUS (2): he may also have been there in 66 BC and brought to Rome the poet PARTHENIUS. Cinna wrote an epyllion, entitled *Zmyrna*, which Catullus praised, on the love affair of Myrrha with her father Cinyras, composed with such learned reference that it later needed a commentary (written by Lucius Crassicius) to be understood. He wrote a *Send-off for Pollio*, in which with much geographical lore he described the journey which Asinius POLLIO (1) was to make through Greece and the east in 56 BC: it too needed a commentary, written by HYGINUS (1). He also wrote love-poems and epigrams. He was the pro-Caesarian tribune of the *plebs* lynched by the mob in Rome after the funeral of Caesar in 44 BC in mistake for the conspirator L. Cornelius CINNA (3).

Civilis, Gaius Julius (C1 AD), was a Batavian of royal descent, the commander of an auxiliary unit in the Roman army, who was instigated by Antonius PRIMUS to rebel against VITELLIUS (1) in AD 69 in support of VESPASIAN. He had already been acquitted by GALBA (1) the previous year of a charge of rebelling, but now raised an army of Germans from both sides of the Rhine and unsuccessfully attacked the camp at Vetera. During the winter of 69–70 he extended the uprising and brought Gallic peoples, the Treveri and the Lingones (see CLASSICUS), into alliance with him and took the Roman bases of Novaesium and Vetera. He made his followers, including some Roman legionaries, swear allegiance to the 'Empire of the Gauls'. He was defeated in 70 near Vetera by an army led by CERIALIS, and retired towards his homeland. After further fighting he was captured and probably killed.

Classicus, Julius (C1 AD), was a Gallic rebel and supporter of CIVILIS' revolt. He was a member of a rich Treveran family, a Roman citizen, and commanded a squadron of Treveran cavalry in the Roman auxiliary forces. He joined Civilis' rebellion against Roman rule in AD 70, had the commander of a legion, Dillius Vocula, killed, and persuaded members of the Roman army on the Rhine frontier to break their oath of allegiance to VESPASIAN in favour of a new 'Empire of the Gauls'. His loyalty to Civilis did not waver: we do not know his fate.

Claudius 1. (10 BC–AD 54) The fourth emperor, named Tiberius Claudius Nero, reigned from January 41 until October 54. He was born at Lyons, the youngest son of DRUSUS (3), the emperor TIBERIUS' brother. His mother was ANTONIA (2), younger daughter of ANTONIUS (7); AUGUSTUS' wife LIVIA (2) was his paternal grandmother. As a child he was regarded by his family, especially by his mother and grandmother, as an imbecile: he limped and may have suffered from some form of paralysis. He lived in obscurity, overshadowed by his elder brother GERMANICUS, and held no public office other than augur until CALIGULA appointed him his colleague in a suffect consulship in AD 37. He was made emperor almost accidentally by the Praetorian Guard after Caligula's murder. He was fifty and, though lacking administrative experience, had a good knowledge of Roman history and tradition – he had been on close terms with the historian LIVY – and was deeply interested in questions of jurisdiction. He often heard cases in his chamber, and was notorious for the influence his wives and freedmen had over him. When he acceded he was married to his third wife, Valeria MESSALLINA, whom he recalled from an exile imposed by Caligula and who bore him two children, OCTAVIA (3) *c*.40 and BRITANNICUS *c*.42. He already had a daughter, Claudia Antonia, by his second wife Aelia Paetina. In 42 L. Arruntius Camillus SCRIBONIANUS vainly raised a rebellion against him in Dalmatia. Messallina was executed in 48 through the action of the freedman NARCISSUS in detecting a plot led by Gaius SILIUS, who had gone through a marriage ceremony with her. He finally married his niece AGRIPPINA (3) on the advice of PALLAS and his friend Lucius Vitellius. She was the widow of Cn. Domitius AHENOBARBUS (5) and already had a son, the future emperor NERO (1).

The administration of the Empire became less despotic and more bureaucratic in Claudius' reign. His 'cabinet' of freedmen ran an efficient civil service, which had replaced the republican system of administration by aristocratic amateurs: Claudius mistrusted senators for responsible posts. They were Narcissus, his secretary of state (*ab epistulis*), Pallas, his minister of finance (*a rationibus*), CALLISTUS, his secretary for petitions (*a libellis*) and Polybius, his patronage secretary (*a studiis*). They were open to bribery, becoming immensely rich, and their power, based mainly on the fact that they controlled the secrets of Empire, led to much resentment by the senators against Claudius. He in his turn worked hard to eliminate any who might have an equal or better claim to the throne: the early years of his reign were characterised by many executions, the rate of which eased off after he married Agrippina, directly descended from Augustus.

He successfully invaded Britain in 43, which gave the army back its self-esteem after Caligula's futile campaigns. Claudius visited his victorious army in the new province where he spent sixteen days, being present at the fall of Camulodunum (Colchester). On his return from Britain he held a triumph. He added the provinces of Thrace and Mauretania to the Empire. He expelled the Jews from Rome but repealed Caligula's anti-Jewish policy in Judaea and Alexandria. He held the Centennial Games in 47 to celebrate 800 years since Rome's foundation. He was an avid scholar and writer, but none of his writings have survived. He reformed the Latin alphabet by enacting the use of special letters to show long vowels.

He may have wished his son, first called Germanicus but after 43 Britannicus, to succeed him; however, he succumbed in 50 to Agrippina's pleas to adopt her son Nero, four years the older, and make him Britannicus' guardian. He also married Octavia to Nero. The death of Claudius ensued on 13 October 54 and was believed with reason to have been caused by a plot of Agrippina's to poison him with a dish of mushrooms, prepared by LOCUSTA. She was presumably fearful that Nero's succession would become less sure as Britannicus grew up. Claudius was the first emperor since Augustus to be deified, a measure which enhanced the prestige of Nero; SENECA (2), however, wrote a satire of the scene of Claudius' death and reception into heaven: the *Pumpkinification of Claudius* (*Apocolocyntosis*). Claudius had been an effective ruler, as is proved by ample documentary evidence, with a marked weakness for women and his freedmen ministers. See Suetonius, *Life of Claudius*; Tacitus, *Annals*, books 11f; B. Levick (1990) *Claudius*, New Haven: Yale University Press.

2. II Gothicus (reigned AD 268–270) The emperor Marcus Aurelius Claudius was a professional soldier of Illyrian origin who had served under GALLIENUS and succeeded him after his assassination. The senators were happy to support him in place of his predecessor, whom they had hated. He moved to besiege the usurper AUREOLUS at Milan. After the latter's surrender and death, Claudius met the advancing Alemanni near Lake Garda and defeated them. He made AURELIAN his cavalry commander. His main achievements were in the Balkans, where in 269 he defeated the Goths in two battles and earned his title *Gothicus*. The Goths had invaded the peninsula in a huge host and divided into two sections, intending to occupy the Balkans for good and to advance yet further south. Claudius thrust between the sections and routed one of them at Naissus (Niš) in southern Serbia and the other at Doberus in Macedonia. Many of the Goths surrendered and were settled by Claudius in vacant lands in the peninsula. He thus eliminated the Gothic threat for a hundred years. He also cleared the Aegean Sea of pirates. But he was unable to tackle the problems of the Gallic Empire of POSTUMUS and of the disruptive behaviour of queen ZENOBIA of Palmyra, which it fell to his successor Aurelian to solve. Claudius died of plague at Sirmium, near Belgrade, early in 270. See M. Grant (1985) *The Roman Emperors*, London: Weidenfeld & Nicolson.

3, Appius (C5 BC) A lawgiver and politician, he was a member of the board of ten men (*decemviri*) which according to some authorities replaced the consuls in 451 BC. Though himself a patrician he is said to have supported the plebeians in their demands for a fairer legal system; he tried to reach a compromise with them according to which they would give up the office of tribune in return for participation in the chief magistracies. He thus became unpopular with the patricians though his code survived. The rule of the ten lasted for two years. Claudius was the only member to survive for both years and in the second led a tyrannical regime. He then fell from power. He is said to have been killed by an enraged father, Verginius, for his designs on his daughter, Verginia, or to have committed suicide as a result of the scandal. It is impossible to disentangle legend from fact.

4, Appius, known as Caecus 'the Blind' (late C4 BC) We do not know when he went blind; he was elected censor in 312 BC even before he had been consul. He quarrelled violently with his colleague, who resigned, leaving him as sole censor, in which office he remained illegally for four years, the normal term being eighteen months. He carried out radical reforms with the aim of increasing the participation of the plebeians in the management of affairs. Thus he permitted plebeians and even freedmen's sons to become senators. It is possible that he allowed landless men to join the voting tribes and so changed the balance of voting in the Comitia in favour of the lower classes. However, he opposed the reform carried out by OGULNIUS. During his censorship he increased taxes so as to enable him to build the first aqueduct, the *Aqua Appia*, and the Appian Way, the road that led south from Rome to Capua. His reforms cannot have been unpopular because he was elected consul for 307 and again for 296 when he made war successfully against the Etruscans, and praetor for 295. He was also involved in war against the Samnites in central Italy. When PYRRHUS wished to make peace with Rome in 279 and claimed a large part of southern Italy, he sent Cineas to argue his case. But Claudius, fearing the loss of the lands he had won in his earlier wars, spoke so eloquently for a continuation of the war and a refusal to allow Pyrrhus any rights in Italy, that the Senate rejected the terms.

5. Caudex, Appius (C3 BC) As consul in 264 BC, he began the First Punic War by invading Sicily to assist the inhabitants of Messina to expel their Carthaginian garrison, which had recently saved them from a siege by the Greek Syracusans. After indecisive deliberations by the Senate and popular Assembly Claudius intervened, and when the Carthaginians struck back,

successfully led two legions to relieve a small party of Romans who were helping to defend the city against Greeks and Carthaginians. This action almost accidentally led to the outbreak of large-scale hostilities between Carthage, angry at being cut off from the Straits, and Rome.

6. Pulcher, Appius (died *c.*130 BC), was consistently hostile to SCIPIO (11) Aemilianus and supported the Gracchan reforms, marrying his daughter to Tiberius GRACCHUS (2). He was consul in 143 BC, when he won a victory over the Alpine nation of the Salassi. He took it upon himself to celebrate an unauthorised triumph in which he was aided by his daughter, a Vestal Virgin. He was appointed censor in 136 and became leader of the Senate. He served on the Gracchan agrarian commission until his death.

7. Pulcher, Appius (C1 BC), was a son of CLAUDIUS (6), an enemy of the dynast CINNA (2) and a supporter of SULLA (2); as praetor in 88 BC he was dismissed for disobeying a tribune, went into voluntary exile, and was expelled from the Senate by his nephew L. Marcius PHILIPPUS (2). He returned after Cinna's fall and was consul in 79, and governed Macedonia from 78 until 76, when he died there after some successful campaigning. He married twice: his first wife was the mother of the CLODIA who married METELLUS (8) Celer, the second that of Publius CLODIUS who was his third son.

8. Pulcher, Appius (died 48 BC), was the eldest son of CLAUDIUS (7). In the 80s BC he had the task of supporting the family during his father's exile. From 72 to 70 he served in the east as military tribune to his brother-in-law Lucius LUCULLUS (2). He was praetor in 57 when he supported his brother's opposition to CICERO (1)'s recall from exile. He governed Sardinia from 56 to 55 and was consul in 54 with L. Domitius AHENOBARBUS (6), with whom he tried corruptly to sell the consulship for the next year: POMPEIUS (2) denounced them. He governed Cilicia from 53 to 51. On his return he was prosecuted for extortion by DOLABELLA (4) but was acquitted with the help of Pompeius and Marcus BRUTUS (5) and was elected censor with PISO (6) in 50. He had married a Servilia and given his two daughters in marriage to Gnaeus POMPEIUS (3) and to M. Brutus. He dedicated his book on augury to Cicero, who had mixed feelings about him. He supported Pompeius in 49 and died in Greece the following year before the battle of Pharsalus.

9. Pulcher, Gaius (died 167 BC) In his consulship in 177 BC he sent home men of Latin status who were living in Rome, and fought a war in the north against the rebellious Ligurians in which he recaptured Mutina (Modena) and brought the Istrian War to a successful conclusion. He held a command in Greece in 171 and was censor in 169 with Tiberius GRACCHUS (2); the pair were austere and restrictive towards the equestrian *publicani* or tax-farmers, and freedmen, whose rights they limited. He died while serving on a commission to settle Macedonia.

10. Pulcher, Publius (C3 BC), was a disastrous commander in the First Punic War. He was consul in 249 when he commanded the Roman forces in Sicily. While blockading the port of Lilybaeum (Marsala) with Syracusan help, he attacked the Carthaginian fleet under the command of Adherbal which had been refitted and was concentrated at nearby Drepanum, but was routed by a sudden Punic sally which led to the capture of 93 of his 123 ships. He is said to have acted impiously before the battle, throwing the sacred chickens, which would not eat, into the sea. Claudius was fined for his failure and died not much later.

11. Quadrigarius, Quintus (C1 BC) An annalistic historian who wrote the history of Rome in twenty-three or more books from the sack of the city by the Gauls to the Sullan civil war. LIVY used his work as a major source. A few fragments of his history survive, enough to show that its style was simple and archaic.

12, Tiberius (died AD 92), was a former Greek slave from Smyrna who served the early emperors. He was freed by TIBERIUS and made a procurator or financial superintendent by CLAUDIUS (1). VESPASIAN made him his financial secretary (*libertus a rationibus*) with equestrian rank. DOMITIAN exiled him in AD 82 but later recalled him at the request of his son (see below). He died aged about ninety.

13. Etruscus, Tiberius, was a Roman patron of poets, son of CLAUDIUS (12) and his wife Tettia Etrusca. Besides winning his father's recall from exile *c.*AD 89, he supported the poets STATIUS, who dedicated his *Silvae* 3. 3 to him, and MARTIAL.

14. Pompeianus, Tiberius (C2 AD), was a general whose father was a Roman knight from Antioch. Claudius became a senator and was suffect consul *c.*AD 167 in which year, as governor of Lower Pannonia, he withstood an invasion of the Germanic Marcomanni and Quadi which was the prelude to the wars of MARCUS AURELIUS. In 169 the emperor made him marry his daughter LUCILLA, the widow of Lucius VERUS, against her will, and he held a second, ordinary consulship in 173. Marcus used Claudius' talent for generalship in his campaigns. He was inactive in the reign of COMMODUS and escaped complicity in his wife's plot of 182. In 193 PERTINAX and DIDIUS Julianus unsuccessfully tried to bring him back into the administration of the Empire.
See also NERO.

Cleander was a Praetorian Prefect under COMMODUS, appointed in 185 on the removal of Tigidius PERENNIS. He sold offices of state, including the consulship, but was removed in 189 when an appointee of his caused a famine in Rome by choking off the grain supply for his own profit.

Clemens, Titus Flavius (C1 AD), was the grandson of the emperor VESPASIAN's brother Flavius SABINUS (2), and married a kinswoman, DOMITIAN's niece Flavia Domitilla: Domitian adopted two of their sons as his heirs. After Clemens had held the consulate in AD 95 he was executed for treason and his wife was sent into exile: they were also accused of irreligion and may have been guilty of Jewish or Christian practices.

Clement 1. (late C1 AD) was a Roman Christian who wrote an extant letter to the church at Corinth, protesting at the removal of clerics. The letter, using martial images, is characterised by a concern for good order and accepts the benefit of Roman imperial rule. Other writings were falsely attributed to him.

2. of Alexandria (*c.*AD 150–*c.*211) was a Christian writer and apologist. Titus Flavius Clemens went to Alexandria in search of instruction in Christian doctrine. He succeeded Pantaenus *c.*190 as head of the catechetical school at Alexandria and remained there until the reign of Septimius SEVERUS (1) in 202 when he fled from persecution to Cappadocia. He was succeeded by ORIGEN (1). His surviving writings, which show deep knowledge of Greek literature and philosophy, are *A Call to the Greeks to Conversion*, which tries to show the superiority of Christian teachings to those of the Greek philosophers, *The Tutor*, a treatise on Christian morality, and the *Miscellanies* in eight books, further criticism of Greek philosophy. Other writings are fragmentary. Some later Christian authorities considered him doctrinally unsound.

Cleopatra 1. I (*c.*215–176 BC) Queen of Ptolemaic Egypt, the daughter of King ANTIOCHUS (1) III and Laodice, she married King PTOLEMY (1) V in 193. They had two sons and a daughter. When her husband died in 180 she ruled on behalf of her son PTOLEMY (2) VI until her death.

2. II (*c*.185–116 BC) was a queen of Egypt, daughter of CLEOPATRA (1). She was married to her brother PTOLEMY (2) VI *c*.175 BC. They and their brother PTOLEMY (4) VIII were co-rulers of Egypt from 171 until 164 during a war with ANTIOCHUS (2) IV of Syria in which Rome finally rescued Egypt. She became regent for her son Ptolemy VII in 145 on her husband's death, and married her other brother, Ptolemy VIII, in 144, whereupon he slew Ptolemy VII and made himself king. In 142 he married her younger daughter, his niece, CLEOPATRA (3) III, without divorcing his sister, and made his new wife joint ruler. Cleopatra II led a rebellion against Ptolemy in 132 and she remained hostile to him until a public reconciliation was declared in 124 BC. She had promised the throne of Egypt to her son-in-law DEMETRIUS (2) II, king of Syria, but in 125 Ptolemy had him assassinated. After this she ruled jointly with her brother and daughter until 116 when Ptolemy died, leaving the kingdom to Cleopatra III. She herself died shortly after; Ptolemy had murdered his son by her to promote the interests of his son by her daughter, Cleopatra III.

3. III (died 101 BC) was a queen of Egypt, daughter of CLEOPATRA (2). She was seduced by her uncle PTOLEMY (4) VIII in 142 BC and married him, even though he was still married to her mother. He made her joint ruler and played his two wives off against each other. When Ptolemy died in 116 BC Cleopatra inherited the throne and installed her elder son PTOLEMY (5) IX, though she preferred her second son. She led rebellions against Ptolemy IX in 110 and 108. In 107 she succeeded in banishing him to Cyprus and installing her second son as PTOLEMY (6) X. She possibly died at his hands, after having quarrelled continuously with him.

4. VII (69–30 BC) was the most famous queen of Egypt, the daughter of PTOLEMY (8) XII the Piper. On his death in 51, as a result of his will, she became joint ruler with her younger brother PTOLEMY (9) XIII. They supported POMPEIUS (2) in 49 in his war with CAESAR (1) and supplied him with ships and foodstuffs. In 48 Ptolemy's guardians Pothinus and Achillas expelled her and she fled to Syria, but when Caesar came to Egypt in pursuit of Pompeius, whom Ptolemy's men had murdered, she had herself smuggled into his presence in a roll of cloth. She made full use of her talents and became his mistress. Ptolemy was killed in the Alexandrian War (48 BC) while resisting Caesar, so Caesar made her other, younger brother, PTOLEMY (10) XIV, co-regent with her. After a two-month tour with her up the Nile, Caesar left Egypt in late spring 47, leaving a garrison of three legions, and in the summer Cleopatra bore him CAESARION. In 46 she joined Caesar in Rome and lived there in a villa he provided until his death in 44, after which she returned to Egypt. She is said to have poisoned her brother Ptolemy XIV and made Caesarion joint ruler in his place. In 42 she attempted to help the Caesarians but was foiled by CASSIUS (2) Longinus, who stole her troops. ANTONIUS (7) summoned her to Tarsus in 41 to account for her failure, and she persuaded him to kill her sister Arsinoë. She invited him to Alexandria where he spent the winter: she later bore him twins. She did not see him again until 37 when he invited her to Antioch and they formed a permanent liaison. He recognised her twins and named them Alexander Helios and Cleopatra Selene. She bore him another son in 36, Ptolemy Philadelphus. In 35 she restored his losses after his Parthian campaign, and he returned territories to Egypt that had been lost long before and granted her some she had never held.

As Octavian (see AUGUSTUS) was irked by Antonius' treatment of his sister OCTAVIA (1), Antonius' wife, he grew resentful of Cleopatra's power over Antonius and his propaganda painted her as a monster. In 32 he declared war on Egypt and Cleopatra. Antonius' forces were concentrated in Greece and Asia Minor, and Cleopatra sent them supplies. She moved her fleet to join his. After months of uncertainty during which Antonius was deserted by most of his principal Roman supporters, the naval battle of Actium was fought off the coast of western Greece, in which Antonius was defeated. There is no evidence for the story that Cleopatra began the rout by fleeing. The two with their most faithful supporters returned to Egypt, where Octavian pursued them. After Antonius' suicide, Cleopatra killed herself on 10 August 30, by applying asps to her body, fearing the threat of Octavian that he would parade her in his triumph. She was the last ancient ruler of independent Egypt. Octavian killed Caesarion but spared Antony's children by Cleopatra, whom Octavia took into her household. See R.D. Sullivan (1990) *Near Eastern Royalty and Rome*, Toronto: University of Toronto Press, 1990.

Clitomachus (*c.*187–109 BC) was a Carthaginian philosopher, originally named Hasdrubal; on migrating to Athens aged 24 he changed his name and became a pupil of Carneades the Sceptic who founded the New Academy. In 140 he founded his own school of philosophy in the Palladium, a precinct in Athens. In 129 he returned to the Academy, of which he became the head in 127. He left a large corpus of writings, none of which has survived. It was, however, influential in passing on the substance of Carneades' philosophical theories. He wrote *On Suspension of Judgment*, *On Philosophical Schools*, and a *Consolation* addressed to his fellow countrymen on the destruction of Carthage by the Romans in 146 BC. He dedicated works to the Roman poet LUCILIUS (1) and to L. Censorinus.

Clodia (C1 BC) was the name of the three sisters of Publius CLODIUS who, like him, preferred to adopt the plebeian version of their name. They were the daughters of Appius CLAUDIUS (7) Pulcher. The eldest, born *c.*97 BC, who *c.*79 married METELLUS (8) Celer, was the only offspring of Claudius' first marriage. She was widowed in 59. CICERO (1) refers to her often in his letters and in his speech in defence of M. Caelius RUFUS (1) (*Pro Caelio*) delivered in April 56. There he depicts her as a woman of no morals, ready to poison her husband and to commit incest with her brother.

Her two younger half-sisters were full sisters of Clodius, and married respectively Lucius LUCULLUS (2), – he divorced her on his return to Rome from the east in 65–64 (we do not know if she remarried) – and Quintus Marcius REX (2), who died in 63. In the early 50s a married Clodia had a love affair with the poet CATULLUS (1), which turned to hatred. See T.P. Wiseman (1985) *Catullus and his World*, Cambridge: Cambridge University Press.

Clodius Pulcher, Publius (*c.*92–52 BC), was the youngest of the three sons of Appius CLAUDIUS (7); a populist, he preferred this form of his name as being in accord with lower-class speech. His first political act was to incite the troops of his brother-in-law LUCULLUS (2) to mutiny in 68 BC. In May 61, having been denounced by CAESAR (1)'s mother Aurelia, he was put on trial for having disguised himself in female dress the previous December to attend the rites of the 'Good Goddess' (*Bona Dea*) which were forbidden to men. As a result, Caesar divorced his wife POMPEIA (1). CICERO (1) gave evidence against Clodius and earned his undying hatred. However, Clodius was acquitted by a corrupt jury which CRASSUS (3) had bribed. At some time he married the rich heiress FULVIA by whom he had a daughter, Claudia, later betrothed to Octavian (see AUGUSTUS). He was quaestor in Sicily in 60, and in 59 sought to be transferred into the plebs (the Claudii Pulchri were an ancient patrician family). In spite of opposition, he was formally adopted into the plebs at a ceremony presided over by Caesar, the *Pontifex Maximus* (chief priest of the Roman state). This enabled Clodius to be elected tribune the following year and to embark on a programme of legislation with a popular slant. He proposed providing the plebs with free food supplies, legalised the guilds of craftsmen, repealed the Aelian-Fufian Law which hindered meetings of the Popular Assembly, and had Cicero exiled for his execution of the fellow-conspirators of CATILINE. He bribed the consul GABINIUS (2) with the province of Syria so as to refrain from blocking the exile of Cicero; he likewise bribed PISO (6) with Macedonia. Clodius also had Cicero's friend CATO (2) despatched to Cyprus to arrange its annexation. He acted in hostility to POMPEIUS (2) by threatening to kill him and by allowing the son of the Armenian king TIGRANES (1) II to escape. He pillaged Cicero's property and destroyed his house in Rome. In 57 Cicero returned from exile with the support of Pompeius in spite of Clodius' efforts to prevent it. He was aedile in 56 but his disruptive powers were diminished by the conference of Lucca and the renewal of the 'Triumvirate'. He indulged in gang warfare with the followers of MILO and used the members of the guilds as his troopers. He stood for the praetorship for the year 52, but the election was postponed because of riots. He was murdered in an affray at Bovillae between his followers and Milo's on 18 January 52, before the elections could be held. His followers in Rome cremated his body in the Senate House, which was destroyed thereby. He was a populist and an opportunist and made no permanent alliances with the great men of the time. See H.H. Scullard (1982) *From the Gracchi to Nero*, London: Methuen.

Cluentius Habitus, Aulus, was a citizen of Larinum who in 76 BC charged Oppicianus, his stepfather, with trying to poison him. He won his case, though bribery was used freely on both sides. In 66 the son of Oppicianus charged Cluentius with murdering his father. CICERO (1) spoke for the defence (*Pro Cluentio*), and won his case.

Cluvius Rufus (C1 AD) was a Roman historian of the early imperial period, possibly a major source for the *Annals* of TACITUS (1). He was consul before 41, governed eastern Spain in 68, and in 69 vacillated between supporting OTHO and VITELLIUS (1).

Coelius 1. Caldus, Gaius, was a tribune of the *plebs* who in 107 BC enacted that a secret ballot should be applied in trials for treason. He was praetor in 99, consul in 94, and probably governor of Gaul in 90.

2. Antipater, Lucius (late C2 BC), was a Roman historian, jurist and rhetorician, and the teacher of Lucius Licinius CRASSUS (1). Fragments of his *History of the Second Punic War* survive. It was composed in seven books and relied on both Roman and Carthaginian sources: LIVY used it as a source. Drawing upon Hellenistic models, Coelius was the first to introduce to Rome the historical monograph, which was adopted by SALLUST and others.

Cogidubnus (or **Tog–**), Tiberius Claudius (reigned *c.*AD 43–75), was a British king of the Atrebates or a section of them, the Regni. He ruled his people under Roman suzerainty and appears to have been installed in power by CLAUDIUS (1), probably as a result of helping the invading Roman army. He may have been related to Verica, the last descendant of COMMIUS. His loyalty to Rome seems to have been recognised by the extension of his kingdom and by the donation by VESPASIAN of the magnificent palace at Fishbourne, where he spent his declining years. He is recorded by an inscription from Chichester as 'Great King of Britain', which shows him to have held senatorial and perhaps even praetorian status. After his death the kingdom was incorporated in the Roman province.

Columella, Lucius Junius Moderatus (born *c.*AD 16), was a Latin writer on agriculture and gardens. He was born at Gades (Cádiz) in Spain. He came from a rich family with lands in Spain and served as a military tribune in the Sixth Legion in Syria *c.*AD 36. Whether or not he intended to pursue a senatorial career, he settled to the life of a landowner and bought estates in central Italy on which he practised and wrote about agriculture. He left two works, *On Farming* (*De Re Rustica*) and *On Trees* (*De Arboribus*). The former was written between AD 60 and 65 and consists of twelve books, which deal systematically with the whole subject of running a farm. Book 10, about horticulture, is in verse. The latter is an independent work and the earlier of the two. He was influenced and moved by Virgil's *Georgics*, but does not match their poetry in his book 10. See K.D. White (1970) *Roman Farming*, London, Thames & Hudson.

Commius (C1 BC) was a chieftain of the Belgic Atrebates. CAESAR (1) raised him to the kingship of the nation in 57 BC. For a time he was loyal to Caesar and served him as a cavalry commander and as an envoy to Britain, where he was sent to pave the way for the incursion of 55. However, he joined VERCINGETORIX's rebellion in 52 and attempted to relieve Alesia. After its failure he joined Correus of the Bellovaci who resisted the Romans in 51; after their defeat LABIENUS (1) made an unsuccessful attempt to assassinate Commius, who received a head wound. After a skirmish with Volusenus, in which the latter was seriously wounded, Commius submitted to ANTONIUS (7) on condition that he should never again come into the presence of any Roman. Subsequently he fled to Britain with many followers and established himself in a kingdom with Calleva, Silchester, as its capital. He had two sons, TINCOMMIUS and Eppilius. See Caesar, *Gallic War*; S.S. Frere (1969) *Britannia*, London: Routledge.

Commodus (161–192 AD), the emperor, was born at Lanuvium, the elder surviving son of MARCUS AURELIUS and FAUSTINA (2). His full name was Lucius Aelius Aurelius Commodus. He was gradually advanced to the position of joint ruler with his father at the age of fifteen in 177, receiving the titles of *Caesar*, *Imperator* and *Augustus*. In the same year he married Bruttia Crispina, and accompanied his father in a campaign against the Marcomanni and Quadi on the upper Danube frontier. In 180 he inherited an Empire with safe frontiers, thanks to his father's untiring efforts. During his reign he maintained this situation by coercion and diplomacy. In Britain, however, the Caledonians overran the Antonine Wall in 183 but were repelled by Ulpius Marcellus, and a mutiny of the troops was suppressed by Helvius PERTINAX. Commodus organised a regular service of ships conveying African agricultural produce to Rome, and freed the tenants of Roman growers in that province from a form of serfdom.

At Rome in 182 his sister LUCILLA made a plot with Ummidius Quadratus to kill him and replace him with her stepson Pompeianus, for which she was banished to Capri and then executed. Commodus then inaugurated a reign of terror, which involved the exile and execution of his wife Crispina. He then ruled in conjunction with favourites and showed increasing hostility to the Senate. He took the praetorian prefect Tigidius PERENNIS as his chief adviser until 185, when he executed him on a trumped-up charge of treason and replaced him with

CLEANDER, a venal freedman whom he made praetorian prefect and his chief adviser. There was a story that Cleander sold twenty-five consulships in a day. In the last years of his reign Commodus was under the influence of his mistress MARCIA and his chamberlain Eclectus. In 189 he made Cleander the scapegoat for a famine engineered by a jealous official, and had him killed to appease the angry populace. He appointed a series of praetorian prefects under Marcia's influence, including Aemilius Laetus in 191. A financial crisis resulted from his raising the pay of the legionaries from 300 to 375 denarii, and from his various extravagances including games and shows in the arena: Commodus resorted to confiscating the property of the rich. The emperor renamed Rome *Colonia Commodiana*, 'Commodus' Colony', and imagined himself to be the reincarnation of Hercules: he amused himself by dressing up as Hercules and slaying animals in the arena with arrows or club. He intended to present himself to the people as consul and gladiator on 1 January 193, but was strangled in his bath the day before by an athlete, Narcissus, at the behest of Marcia, who was now losing his favour, Eclectus and Laetus. His memory was universally condemned, though Septimius SEVERUS (1) restored it and deified him in 195. He may be compared to NERO (1) or CALIGULA for his cruelty and ostentation and to DOMITIAN for the manner of his death and the succession, which was decided by his assassins. See M. Grant (1985) *The Roman Emperors*, London: Weidenfeld & Nicolson.

Constans (*c.*AD 320–350) was an emperor of the west. Flavius Julius Constans was the youngest son of CONSTANTINE (1) I and FAUSTA (2). He was created Caesar in 333 and on his father's death in 337 inherited Italy, Africa and Illyricum. In early 340 he fought and slew his elder brother CONSTANTINE (2) II, who had invaded northern Italy; as a result he took over Gaul, Spain and Britain and was thus in control of the whole western section of the Empire. He campaigned against the Sarmatians and Franks, whom he defeated in 342, and visited Britain in 343. In 350 he was overthrown and killed in Gaul by MAGNENTIUS.

Constantia was a sister of CONSTANTINE (1) I who married the emperor LICINIUS in AD 313 and begged for his life, with temporary success, after his defeat by Constantine in 324.

Constantine 1. I (*c.*AD 274–337) is the Roman emperor known to history as Constantine the Great. He was born out of wedlock at Niš in Serbia, then Upper Moesia, to CONSTANTIUS (1) Chlorus and his mistress Helena; he was given the name Flavius Valerius Constantinus. On his father's appointment as *Caesar* (subordinate emperor) in 293, Constantine became a courtier of the *Augustus* (senior emperor) DIOCLETIAN at Nicomedia. He was sent to serve as a staff officer under the other *Caesar*, GALERIUS, in his campaign in Armenia against the Persians, and distinguished himself. In 305 Diocletian and Maximian abdicated and Galerius and Constantius became the new *Augusti*. Galerius kept Constantine at his court as a hostage for his fellow *Augustus*' good behaviour; but the following year Constantius requested that his son should accompany him on an expedition to Britain and Galerius reluctantly agreed. Constantine supported his father's campaign in Scotland against the invading Picts. When Constantius died in York in July 306, Constantine, who had further distinguished himself in war against the Franks on the lower Rhine, was proclaimed emperor (*Augustus*) by the Roman armies of Gaul and Britain. He wrote to Galerius acknowledging that SEVERUS (3) had a better claim to be *Augustus* than he, but seeking the title of *Caesar*, to which Galerius reluctantly agreed. Constantine spent the next few years fighting wars in Britain and on the Rhine frontier. In March 307 he was visited by the former *Augustus* MAXIMIAN, who gave him in marriage his daughter FAUSTA (2), to whom Constantine had been betrothed since 293, and recognised him as the *Augustus* of the west. Meanwhile, in a coup, Maximian's son MAXENTIUS had seized Italy and Africa, and first Severus and then Galerius, the two *Augusti*, tried vainly to dislodge him. In 308 a conference was held at Carnuntum (in Austria near Haimburg) attended by Diocletian, Galerius and Maximian, which declared LICINIUS to be the *Augustus* of the West (Severus had been murdered by Maxentius), and demoted Constantine and MAXIMINUS (2) to the position of 'sons of the Augusti'. Constantine rejected the decision but sheltered Maximian when he was driven out of Rome by Maxentius whom he had tried to depose. Constantine was defending the Rhine frontier from the Germans in 310 when Maximian seized Massilia (Marseille) in an attempt to regain his position as emperor; Constantine defeated and captured his father-in-law and forced him to commit suicide.

In 311 Galerius died and Licinius sought an alliance with Constantine against Maximinus and Maxentius. In 312 Constantine invaded Maxentius' fiefdom of Italy and won victories at Turin and Verona before driving Maxentius' forces before him to Red Rocks (*Saxa Rubra*), a short distance from the gates of Rome. Here Constantine won a great victory aided, he claimed, by the Christian god. Maxentius was drowned attempting to cross the Tiber at the Milvian Bridge, after which the battle was named. Constantine thus gained possession of the whole western part of the Empire and was welcomed by the Senate as the new *Augustus*, in which position he replaced Maximinus, whom Licinius had recently destroyed. The Arch of Constantine was erected in the forum in commemoration of his victory. He abolished the Praetorian Guard, which had been so influential in making and unmaking emperors. Licinius, now the senior *Augustus* and sole ruler of the east, met Constantine at Milan in 313 and married his half-sister Constantia. At the same time the two rulers issued the Edict of Milan which guaranteed freedom of religion throughout the Empire. The effect of the edict was to give Christians the right to practise their religion openly. The relationship between the two *Augusti* then slowly disintegrated. They were in conflict in 316, when Constantine won a victory at Cibalae (near Belgrade) which gained him the Balkan peninsula excluding Thrace. They patched up their differences, and in 317 the two sons of Constantine, Crispus and the infant CONSTANTINE (2) II, as well as Licinius' son Licinius II, were made *Caesars*. In 323 trouble flared up again when Constantine entered Thrace in hostilities with the Goths and Licinius intervened to save his territory. Constantine beat him at the battle of Adrianople in 324 and took his European possessions; a sea battle was fought in the Hellespont and Licinius was briefly besieged in Byzantium, whence he escaped. Then Constantine crossed the Bosporus. Licinius was defeated at Chrysopolis and abdicated at Nicomedia on condition that his life was spared (his wife pleaded for him with her brother), but the next year Constantine executed him for plotting.

An exceedingly able emperor of great military prowess had united the Roman Empire under one ruler for the first time for many years. By this time the administration of the Empire was quite different from that of earlier centuries: the emperor was an autocrat and all pretence of partnership with senators or people had been abandoned. Constantine developed the reforming plans of Diocletian and created a new capital of the Empire in his new foundation of Constantinople, on the site of the Megarian colony of Byzantium in Thrace, which he began in 324 and consecrated four years later, and dedicated with both traditional and Christian rites in 330. Though it did not officially replace Rome, it was called 'New Rome' and had many of the features of Rome such as a senate and a food-dole. Apart from a few ancient Byzantine temples, however, the only places of worship permitted were Christian ones. Constantine also reformed the army: having abolished the Praetorian Guard he created a new field army with higher pay than the frontier troops. He employed a large number of Germans in his new corps and in the higher posts of command.

Besides being a man of great erudition, he was deeply superstitious, and came to believe he received better treatment from the Christian god than from any other. He encouraged the spread of Christianity and founded churches. He did much to maintain the unity of the Church and himself presided at the Council of Nicaea in 325 in an attempt to suppress the Arian heresy. The depth of his own Christianity is dubious, however, and he was as willing to deify his own father as Christ. He did not seek baptism until he was dying at Nicomedia. His reign was peaceful after the fall of Licinius, though in 332 he had to drive the Goths back from the Danube frontier. In 334 he settled 300,000 Sarmatians in Roman territory along the Danube to act as a source of manpower for future wars. He falsely claimed descent from CLAUDIUS (2) II Gothicus to enhance his position. Just before his death, war broke out with SAPOR II, king of Persia, which Constantine's last illness prevented him from concluding. In 326 he executed his wife Fausta and his eldest son Crispus, not Fausta's son but Minervina's, on the grounds of treason. After his death there was a massacre of his family (apart from his sons by Fausta, who succeeded him) which he may have ordered before his death. See T.B. Barnes (1982) *Constantine and Eusebius*, Cambridge MA: Harvard University Press; M. Grant (1985) *The Roman Emperors*, London: Weidenfeld & Nicolson; A.H.M. Jones (1962) *Constantine and the Conversion of Europe*, new rev. edn, New York: Collier Books; R. Lane Fox (1986) *Pagans and Christians*, Harmondsworth: Penguin; S.N.C. Lieu and D. Montserrat (eds) (1995) *Constantine: History, Historiography and Legend*, London and New York: Routledge.

2. II (AD 317–340) An emperor, the second son of CONSTANTINE (1), his first by FAUSTA (2). He was born at Arles in Gaul and was made *Caesar* a month later. On his father's death in 337 he became ruler of Gaul, Spain and Britain. He was defeated and killed at Aquilea (near Venice) after invading Italy against his brother, CONSTANS. See M. Grant (1985) *The Roman Emperors*, London: Weidenfeld & Nicolson.

Constantius 1. I (*c*.AD 250–306) was an emperor of the west. Of Illyrian stock, he was named Flavius Valerius Constantius; his nickname *Chlorus* ('Green') was not contemporary with him. After serving as an able general and governor, he was appointed *Caesar* (subordinate emperor) in the west by DIOCLETIAN in 293, under MAXIMIAN, his father-in-law: he had married Maximian's stepdaughter Theodora. He now dispensed with his mistress or first wife, HELENA, the mother of CONSTANTINE (1) I the Great. He was made ruler of Gaul, Spain and Britain, the last of which was then in the hands of the usurper CARAUSIUS. He seized the Channel port of Boulogne, but when ALLECTUS murdered and surplanted Carausius, Constantius took no action against him for three years. In 296, however, while Maximian guarded the Rhine frontier, Constantius invaded Britain and his pretorian prefect ASCLEPIODOTUS defeated and killed Allectus in Hampshire. He himself sailed up the Thames and secured London. In 298 Constantius defeated the Alemanni at Langres and strengthened the Rhine frontier.

Constantius became *Augustus* (senior emperor) of the west in 305 when

Diocletian and Maximian abdicated. He had shown sympathy for the Christians during Diocletian's persecution of 303 by his leniency and by ending the persecution in his territories at the earliest opportunity. However, his colleague GALERIUS held Constantine, the son of Constantius and Helena, a virtual hostage at his court in Nicomedia. The invasion of Britain by the Picts in 306 gave Constantius the opportunity to ask for his son's help in the war, which Galerius reluctantly allowed. After beating the Picts in a resounding victory, Constantius died at York on 25 July 306, and was succeeded by Constantine. See M. Grant (1985) *The Roman Emperors*, London: Weidenfeld & Nicolson.

2. II (*c.*AD 318–361) was the third son of CONSTANTINE (1), his second by FAUSTA (2); his full name was Flavius Julius Constantius. His father made him *Caesar* (subordinate emperor) in November 324, and on Constantine's death in 337 he became ruler of the east. His first task after the massacre of most of his male relatives was to settle the eastern frontier, where he fought a protracted war against SAPOR (2) II of Persia, defeating him decisively in 345. He then turned to face MAGNENTIUS, who had deposed and killed his brother CONSTANS in the west. He defeated him at Mursa in Pannonia in 351 and captured Italy and Gaul in the next two years; he made his cousins GALLUS (3) and JULIAN his Caesars in the east and west respectively, but executed the former in 354. Constantius was greatly influenced by the Arian bishops around him, and vainly tried to achieve a doctrinal settlement of the Church. Julian controlled Gaul and Britain, and was proclaimed *Augustus* in opposition to Constantius by his mutinous troops at Paris in 361. Constantius moved to put the rebellion down, but died in November of that year at Mopsucrenae in Cilicia. He was succeeded by Julian. See M. Grant (1985) *The Roman Emperors*, London: Weidenfeld & Nicolson.

Corbulo, Gnaeus Domitius (*c.*AD 5–66), was a distinguished general of the early imperial period, who probably served as suffect consul in AD 39. In 47 he was sent to govern Lower (northern) Germany, made a successful punitive expedition against the Frisii and fought the Chauci who were led by Gannascus. A strict disciplinarian, he made his troops dig a canal between the Maas and the Rhine. CLAUDIUS (1) ordered him to withdraw behind the Rhine and then posted him to the east as proconsul of Asia. After the death of Claudius, NERO (1) appointed him to a command against the Parthians, giving him the title of legate (governor) of Cappadocia and Galatia. He took the opportunity to reorganise the Roman armies of Syria and the east, and in 58 he advanced into Armenia where, after capturing the cities of Artaxata and Tigranocerta in 59, he installed the pro-Roman TIGRANES (4) as king. In 60 Corbulo was made governor of Syria. Tigranes rashly attacked Adiabene in Parthian Mesopotamia, and in 61 was driven out of his kingdom. Corbulo asked Nero for a new commander for the army in Armenia, and he sent Caesennius PAETUS (2). The latter was heavily defeated at Rhandeia in 62, and Nero gave Corbulo supreme command on the eastern front. He crossed the Euphrates in 63 and the Parthian nominee for the throne of Armenia, Tiridates, submitted to him, accepted Roman suzerainty and went to Rome to be crowned by Nero in person. Corbulo remained in the east until October 66 when Nero summoned him to Cenchreae in Greece where, afraid of Corbulo's power, he ordered him to commit suicide. His son-in-law Vinicianus had conspired against Nero, and this may have provided him with a pretext for the general's removal. Corbulo's daughter Domitia Longina married the emperor DOMITIAN in 70.

Cordus, Aulus Cremutius (C1 BC–AD), was a historian of the Augustan period who wrote an account of the Civil Wars to 18 BC or after. SENECA (2) stated that he 'proscribed the proscribers', so uncompromisingly republican a stance did he take. He was prosecuted for treason by a friend of SEJANUS in AD 25 in TIBERIUS' reign and, after making a spirited defence in which he compared LIVY's freedom to express republican sentiments with the illiberality of his own times, committed suicide. His works were burnt, but were in circulation in the reign of CALIGULA. They have not survived. See Tacitus, *Annals*, 4, 34.

Cornelia 1. (C2 BC) was a Roman matron, the second daughter of SCIPIO (7) Africanus. She married Tiberius Sempronius GRACCHUS (3) by whom she had twelve children. Three survived to be adults, her sons Tiberius and Gaius, and her daughter Sempronia who married SCIPIO (11) Aemilianus. After her husband's death in 154 BC she engaged tutors for her sons' education. She refused to remarry, despite an offer from the king of Egypt, PTOLEMY (4) VIII *Physcon*, and settled on her estate at Misenum after the death of her revolutionary sons. During their political careers she may have tried to check the extreme measures of Gaius, especially his attack on Marcus OCTAVIUS (4) for vetoing Tiberius' agrarian bill. A highly cultured woman with an interest in Greek literature, she was hospitable and a respected letter-writer.

2. (died 68 BC) was the daughter of Lucius Cornelius CINNA (2) and the first wife of Julius CAESAR (1), whom she married in 84 BC, and mother of his only legitimate child, JULIA (4).

3. was the daughter of Q. Cornelius METELLUS (11) Scipio. She was married first in 55 BC to P. Licinius CRASSUS (7), the younger son of the triumvir. After his death at Carrhae she married POMPEIUS (2) in 52 and accompanied him to Greece in 49 and thence, after his defeat at Pharsalus, to Egypt where she witnessed his murder. She returned to Italy and Caesar despatched her husband's ashes to her there.

Cornelius 1, Gaius, was a tribune in 67 BC when he was a colleague and supporter of GABINIUS (2); together they pressed for reforms which they failed to secure in the face of Optimate (aristocratic) opposition. They did, however, pass a law compelling the city praetor to abide by his edict in the administration of justice. Cornelius was prosecuted for treason in 66 for having ignored a fellow-tribune's veto the previous year, but was acquitted at his trial in 65 when CICERO (1) defended him. He was a client of POMPEIUS (2).

2. Severus (late C1 BC) was an epic poet and friend of OVID, who mentions his *Carmen Regale* or *Royal Poem* in his *Letters from the Black Sea.* We have a short passage on the death of CICERO (1), quoted by SENECA (2). QUINTILIAN admired the first book of his poem on the Sicilian War of 38 BC.
See also BALBUS, CETHEGUS, CINNA, DOLABELLA, GALLUS (4), LENTULUS, NEPOS (1), SCIPIO, SULLA, TACITUS (1).

Cornificius 1, Lucius (C1 BC), was a follower of Octavian (see AUGUSTUS) and the prosecutor of BRUTUS (5) in 43 BC for Caesar's murder. He took part as an admiral in the Sicilian War of 38 BC and in 36 commanded three legions which were cut off at Taormina. He saved them by marching them to join AGRIPPA (1) at Tyndaris. He was consul in 35 and *c.*33 was appointed governor of Africa. He won a triumph for his victories there and held it in December 32. He used an elephant to convey him home from banquets and rebuilt the temple of Diana on the Aventine from the booty he won.

2, Quintus, was a poet who married CATILINE's widow. Of senatorial family, he was quaestor in 48 BC when he recovered Illyricum for Caesar. In 46 he became governor of Cilicia, but was moved to Syria in the war against Caecilius BASSUS (1). In 44 Caesar appointed him governor of Old Africa. He refused to recognise the authority of the triumvirs, and would not give up his province to their nominee, Calvisius SABINUS (1). In 43 he was proscribed by the triumvirs who gave his province to T. Sextius, already governor of New Africa. The latter defeated and killed him in 41 at Utica, his troops deserting him. He was a friend of CATULLUS (1) and of CICERO (1), who corresponded with him. His poetry has not survived: we know of an epyllion named *Glaucus*.

3. The author of an extant rhetorical work in four books, *Ad Herennium*. Nothing is known of him.

Cornutus 1, Lucius Annaeus (born *c.*AD 20), was a Stoic philosopher and writer from Lepcis Magna in Libya, possibly a client of the Younger SENECA (2). He became a teacher of rhetoric and Stoic philosophy at Rome. LUCAN and PERSIUS were among his pupils: the latter dedicated to him his fifth satire, in which he pays a moving tribute to Cornutus. On his early death in AD 62 Persius bequeathed to Cornutus his library and a sum of money, the latter of which Cornutus refused. But he did edit Persius' satires for publication in collaboration with Caesius BASSUS (3). He was exiled by NERO (1) in the 60s, and his subsequent career is unclear. One work survives, a treatise on mythology in Greek with a Stoic slant, addressed to a small child, entitled *Summary of the Traditions of Greek Mythology*. He may also be the author of the play *Octavia* wrongly attributed to Seneca. His works on logic and rhetoric have not survived. Aulus GELLIUS (1) reports his commentaries on VIRGIL's *Aeneid*, criticising several carping comments on Virgil's diction. He also wrote a critique of Aristotle's *Categories*.

2. Tertullus, Gaius Julius (C1/2 AD), was a senator, born at Attaleia (Antalya) in Pamphylia. He was given praetorian rank in 70 by VESPASIAN, and, after serving as governor of Crete and Cyrene, was proconsul of southern Gaul in DOMITIAN's reign. In 98 he was appointed prefect of the treasury in company with his friend, the younger PLINY (2), and in 100 was suffect consul when Pliny was consul. He conducted a census in Aquitania in 109–110, was governor of Bithynia and Pontus *c.*112–115 (on the same terms as Pliny who had died there in 112) and was proconsul of Africa *c.*116–118.

Coruncanius 1, Gaius and Lucius, were ambassadors sent in 230 BC to Teuta, queen of the Illyrians, demanding that she pay compensation for some merchants killed by pirates in her kingdom. She refused to comply and the ambassadors were attacked, probably without meeting her. Lucius was killed and war broke out. See Polybius, *History*, 2, 8.

2, Tiberius, was a consul in 280 BC, originating from Tusculum. He led Roman attacks on the Etruscans, over whom he triumphed. He resisted the advance of PYRRHUS. He was the first Roman jurist to allow students to attend his legal consultations and so was the first teacher of Roman law. He was also the first plebeian to be *Pontifex Maximus* (chief priest), in 254 BC, and he died in 243.

Corvinus *see* MESSALLA (4).

Cossus, Aulus Cornelius (C5 BC), was a partly legendary figure who was said to have won one or two wars against Fidenae, a town in Latium. He won the *spolia opima* ('rich spoils', dedicated to Jupiter Feretrius by a commander who personally defeated and killed the enemy leader) against Lars Tolumnius of Veii. He placed the Etruscan's linen corselet in the temple of Jupiter and inscribed it with an account of his feat. Augustus read this inscription and put the date of the event in 428 BC when Cossus was consul. Historians including LIVY, however, regarded the correct date as 437 when Cossus was military tribune or, according to a few, 426 when he was Master of the Horse.

Cotta 1, Gaius Aurelius (died 73 BC), was a senator and orator who was exiled by Varius' court set up to investigate those who had supported the Italians in the Social War. He returned with SULLA (2) and was consul in 75, passing a law allowing the tribunes to stand for the higher offices, in spite of Sulla's having forbidden it. He was governor of Cisalpine Gaul the following year, but died suddenly after his return to Rome and so missed his triumph. CICERO (1) used him as a character in his dialogues *On the Orator* and *The Nature of the Gods*. In the latter Cotta defends Platonic philosophy.

2, Marcus Aurelius, was a general and senator, the younger brother of COTTA (1). Consul in 74 BC, he was put in charge of the defence of Bithynia against MITHRIDATES (3) VI, but speedily lost the province and was defeated in a naval battle off Chalcedon and besieged there. He was relieved by LUCULLUS (2), whose deputy he became, and besieged Heraclea. He took this Pontic city in 71 after a long siege, and was later accused by CARBO (5) of enriching himself from the spoils, and expelled from the Senate.

3, Lucius Aurelius (C1 BC), was a senator, the younger brother of COTTA (1) and COTTA (2). He was praetor in 70 BC when he carried the law bearing his name (*Lex Aurelia*) concerning juries, rescinding the enactment of SULLA (2) that only senators might serve on criminal juries. Instead he enacted that juries be composed equally of senators, equestrians and *tribuni aerarii* (a property class below the equestrians). In 66 he and L. Manlius Torquatus successfully prosecuted the consuls elect for the following year for bribery, and were elected to replace them. In 64 he held the post of censor and supported CICERO (1) in his campaign with CATILINE and in his exile. His sister Aurelia was CAESAR (1)'s mother, and after Caesar's assassination Cotta withdrew from public life. Cicero (*Letters to Atticus*, 12, 27) relates that his house was dirty, small and mean.

Cottius, Marcus Julius (C1 BC), the son of Donnus, was a Ligurian client-king of a region in the Alps. AUGUSTUS allowed him to continue to rule, nominally as prefect, the area around the Mont Cénis pass after the Roman conquest of the region. The little province was known as the *Alpes Cottiae*. The capital was at Segusio (Susa), where Cottius erected an arch in honour of the emperor in 6 BC. CLAUDIUS (1) restored the title of king to his son, on whose death NERO (1) annexed the country.

Crassus 1, Publius Canidius (died 30 BC), was a general and henchman of ANTONIUS (7). He first appears as a subordinate of LEPIDUS (4) in southern Gaul who in 43 BC worked to ally him with Antonius. He became suffect consul in 40 BC and went to the east with Antonius where in 36 he fought in the Caucasus region, subjugating the Iberians and Albanians before joining Antonius' expedition against Parthia. He may have governed Armenia for a time and brought his forces to support Antonius in 32 when the War of Actium was beginning. He led Antonius' land force in that campaign, deserting them after Antonius' defeat and flight to Egypt, and going himself to Egypt where Octavian (see AUGUSTUS) had him put to death.

2, Lucius Licinius (140–91 BC) An orator and advocate who learnt law from COELIUS (2), SCAEVOLA (3) and SCAEVOLA (4). He successfully prosecuted CARBO (1) who committed suicide. In company with Cn. Domitius AHENOBARBUS (1) he founded the colony of Narbo (Narbonne) in 118 BC and defended its privileges in the Senate; he took advantage of a quaestorship in Asia to pursue his studies. In his earlier career he supported popularist causes but in 106 used his oratorical skill for an Optimate cause in promoting CAEPIO (3)'s law designed to give senators a majority on criminal juries. He was elected consul for 95 with Q. Mucius SCAEVOLA (4); together they passed a law depriving foreigners of citizenship illegally gained, a measure which was one of the causes of the Social War. After successfully defending the younger Caepio on a charge of treason, he became allied to MARIUS (1) and was sent to govern Gaul. He was censor in 92 in company with Cn. Domitius AHENOBARBUS (2), with whom he agreed to the extent of banning the teaching of rhetoric in Latin, to prevent the rise to power of those who were not noble. In 91, however, Crassus supported the attempts of the tribune Livius DRUSUS (2) to enfranchise the Italians and to open political power to the equestrians. He spoke eloquently in the Senate in favour of Drusus' reforms against the consul L. Marcius PHILIPPUS (2), who called for Drusus' law to be declared invalid for having breached the constitution. Crassus died soon after making this speech, which was referred to as his swan song.

He was greatly admired by CICERO (1) who assumed the adult toga in the year of his death: Cicero makes him the principal speaker in his rhetorical work *On the Orator.* He is also important in the *Brutus*. See E. Badian (1964) *Studies in Greek and Roman History*, Oxford: Blackwell.

3, Marcus Licinius, known as Dives, 'the Rich' (*c.*115–53 BC), was a statesman, general, and member of the 'First Triumvirate'. Son of CRASSUS (6), he went to Spain in 87 BC to escape from the civil war provoked by CINNA (2), and after Cinna's death in 84 returned to Italy to join SULLA (2), under whom he fought against the Marian party in 83 and 82. He commanded the victorious right wing of Sulla's army at the battle of the Colline Gate of Rome. He profited greatly from the proscriptions of Sulla's enemies, buying their estates for nominal sums. He was praetor in 73 and the next year had to face the menace of a slave revolt in southern Italy. He raised an army of 40,000 men, and in 71 crushed SPARTACUS in Lucania, crucifying 6,000 of the surviving slaves, whose masters could not be identified, by the side of the Appian Way, which leads south from Rome. His rival POMPEIUS (2), who came in on the end of his campaign and also caught some of the fugitives, claimed credit for the victory, to the annoyance of Crassus. However, they shared office as consuls in 70 BC because Crassus lacked the courage to stand up to Pompeius' unconstitutional demand for an office for which he was not qualified, but joined forces with him in demanding power rather than opposing him: thus through caution he lost the chance to become the outright master of the political scene. Together they embarked on a reform of the Sullan constitution, and entrusted the reform of criminal court juries to L. Aurelius COTTA (3). They also passed a law restoring to the tribunes all their traditional powers, which Sulla had removed. Pompeius, however, had the best of the bargain, and through the newly restored tribunate managed to acquire important commands in the east and against the pirates. Crassus' activities henceforth were motivated by hostility to Pompeius.

Crassus had been sidelined, in spite of his fabulous displays of generosity to the populace, and he found himself needing to seek new alliances. In 67 he bought CAESAR (1)'s support by settling his debts, and used him to try to annex Egypt for Rome, but failed because CICERO (1), acting in Pompeius' cause, attacked the proposal. Crassus then turned to support the ambitions of CATILINE, and used his influence and money to save him from prosecution for plotting to kill the new consuls of 65. He was censor with Q. Lutatius CATULUS (3) in 65 and tried to enrol the Transpadane Gauls as citizens, but was opposed by his colleague. He still hoped to use Catiline as his tool against Pompeius, but when Catiline failed to secure election as consul, Crassus abandoned him and did not support his insurrection of late 63. He next tried to thwart Pompeius' distribution of land to his veterans by means of a bill proposed in 63 by the tribune P. Servilius Rullus, whereby there would be a redistribution of public land in Italy and the provinces. Cicero managed to have the bill thrown out by his speech *On the Agrarian Law*. Crassus left Rome when Pompeius returned, but quickly reappeared to play a part in the Senate's refusal to ratify his eastern settlement and pay off his veterans. He assisted Caesar to become a consul for 59, and when Caesar and Pompeius made an alliance to defeat senatorial obstruction of their plans, Crassus allowed himself to be reconciled to Pompeius by Caesar and to become the third man in the alliance, an unofficial triumvirate.

During Caesar's absence in Gaul, his former henchman CLODIUS, for his own purposes, succeeded in separating Crassus from both Pompeius and Cicero. Crassus had let his military talents lie dormant for several years, but he now wished to replace Pompeius in a commission to restore PTOLEMY (8) XII the Piper to the throne of Egypt. This came to nothing, but signalled disagreement among the triumvirs. Cicero did his best to separate Pompeius from the group, and Lucius AHENOBARBUS (6), as candidate for the consulship, proposed the recall of Caesar from Gaul.

In April 56 Crassus met Caesar in Ravenna, and after he had informed him how things stood in Rome, the three triumvirs met a few days later at Luca (Lucca) where they were joined by many senators. They patched up their differences and made decisions about the future: Crassus, after serving as consul for a second time with Pompeius, was to have an eastern command for five years. Late in 55 he set out for Syria with a large army to make war on the Parthians who had done nothing to provoke it: in 54 he won some successes, and in 53, after plundering the Temple in Jerusalem, he invaded Parthia. He allowed himself to be separated from his Armenian allies and so had little useful cavalry, but advanced to try to conquer Mesopotamia. He was caught near Carrhae (Harran) by an army of mounted archers under the Parthian general SUREN, which picked off the Roman legionaries piecemeal. The Roman infantry forced Crassus to surrender and he was killed at an interview with Suren. His severed head was used at the Parthian court in a performance of Euripides' *Bacchae*. Less than a third of the Roman force escaped back to Roman territory; the rest were held in captivity in Parthia.

Crassus was married to Tertulla, a woman of obscure family. He had two sons by whose marriages he allied himself to the powerful Metelli. See F.E. Adcock (1966) *Marcus Crassus, Millionnaire*, Cambridge: Heffer.

4, Marcus Licinius (late C1 BC), was the grandson of CRASSUS (3), the son of his elder son. As a young man after CAESAR (1)'s assassination in 44 he gave his support to Sextus POMPEIUS (4) and, after his fall, to ANTONIUS (7). He appears to have deserted Antonius before or during the campaign of Actium in 31 BC on the offer by Octavian (see AUGUSTUS) of a consulship which he held in 30. He was then appointed proconsul of Macedonia for two years and performed well, subduing Thrace and defeating the Dardani and the Bastarnae, whose king he killed with his own hands. He claimed a triumph and the title of *Imperator*, and went so far as to demand the *spolia opima* ('rich spoils') which were the right of a Roman general who performed the deed of personally slaying an enemy leader, a prize won only twice before since Romulus. Octavian, jealous of his own rights as universal ruler and conqueror, rebutted the claim to the *spolia opima* (see COSSUS) by asserting that Crassus would only have qualified for the honour had he been acting under his own auspices. Crassus was arbitrarily denied the title *Imperator*, which the emperors henceforth reserved for themselves, but was granted a triumph rather late, in July 27; nothing more is heard of him. He adopted a son who was consul in 14 BC. See R. Syme (1939) *The Roman Revolution*, Oxford: Clarendon Press.

5, Publius Licinius (C2 BC), was an influential politician and lawyer, the son-in-law of Appius CLAUDIUS (6) and father-in-law of Gaius GRACCHUS (1). His father was a Mucius Scaevola, his brother Publius Mucius Scaevola, consul in 133; he himself was adopted by a wealthy Crassus and so was known as Dives ('rich') Mucianus. He was an important member of the opposition to SCIPIO (11) Aemilianus and a supporter of the Gracchi and their agrarian reforms. As tribune in 145 he proposed a land reform bill which failed. He replaced Tiberius GRACCHUS (3) on the land commission and as a result of popularity thus gained was elected consul for 131 and *Pontifex Maximus* (chief priest). In 131 and 130 he campaigned against ARISTONICUS, the pretender to the throne of Pergamon, and was killed after suffering a defeat.

6, Publius Licinius (died 87 BC), was tribune *c*.105 when he proposed a law regulating private expenditure. He was consul in 97, when the Senate passed a resolution forbidding human sacrifice. Appointed proconsul of Further Spain, he subdued the Lusitani, and held a triumph in 93. After service in the Social War in Italy in 91 and 90 he was responsible as censor in 89 with Lucius CAESAR (5) for the enrolment of Italians into Roman citizenship which brought the war to a successful end. In 87 he supported SULLA (2), and when MARIUS (1) and CINNA (2) took Rome he committed suicide. His son, the future 'triumvir', escaped to Spain.

7, Publius Licinius (died 53 BC), was the younger son of CRASSUS (3). He saw military service under CAESAR (1) in Gaul, where he was cavalry commander in 58 and then legate. He acted firmly against ARIOVISTUS and subdued the Gauls of the west coast. In 56 he conquered the Aquitanians and returned to Rome to support his father's candidacy for the consulship of 55. In 55 he married CORNELIA (3), a daughter of METELLUS (11) Scipio. He accompanied his father in 54 on his eastern campaign and commanded the Gallic cavalry at the battle of Carrhae in 53. He killed himself as a result of the disastrous defeat and the loss of his men.

8, Titus Otacilius (C3 BC), after serving as praetor in 217, was appointed to command a Roman fleet in Sicilian waters whence he harrassed the African coast. He stood for the consulship for 214 but was foiled by his kinsman FABIUS (8) Maximus, and had to be content with a second praetorship. He commanded the fleet at the siege of Syracuse from 213 to 211, the year of his death.

Cratippus (C1 BC) was a philosopher of the Peripatetic School, a native of Mytilene and contemporary of CICERO (1), who held him in high esteem. Cicero sent his son to Athens to study under him. He became head of the Lyceum in 44 BC in succession to Andronicus of Rhodes.

Crispus *see* FAUSTA (2).

Culleo, Quintus Terentius (early C2 BC), was a senator who was captured in the Second Punic War and rescued by SCIPIO (7) Africanus in 201. He walked in Scipio's triumphal parade wearing a freedman's cap of liberty. He was much concerned with matters of citizenship: as tribune in 189 he passed a law enrolling the sons of freedmen in the country tribes, and as praetor in 187 he tried cases of Latins being unlawfully registered as citizens, and expelled a huge number from Rome. He also served on embassies to Africa in 195 and 171.

Cunobelinus (reigned *c.*AD 10–40) was a British king before the Roman occupation, the son of TASCIOVANUS, king of the Catuvellauni. Early in his reign, despite the treaty that CAESAR (1) had imposed on the Catuvellauni, he conquered the Trinovantes and moved his capital from Verulamium (St Albans) to Camulodunum (Colchester). He also conquered Kent and imported Roman goods; he issued coins with Latin superscriptions. He had at least three sons, CARATACUS, Togodumnus and Adminius: late in his reign he banished the last-named, who fled to the emperor CALIGULA in Gaul and suggested that a conquest of Britain would be easy. Cunobelinus was dead by the time of CLAUDIUS (1)'s invasion in 43. Shakespeare based the character of Cymbeline upon him.

Curio 1, Gaius Scribonius (early C1 BC) As a military tribune in 90 BC he went east with SULLA (2); he profited from Sulla's proscriptions in 82. He was consul in 76 and defended the Sullan constitution against the tribune Sicinius. He was proconsul of Macedonia in 75 where he fought successfully to extend the province northwards and earned a triumph in 73. No friend of CAESAR (1) or CICERO (1), he supported VERRES and CLODIUS and was the target of a pamphlet whose authorship Cicero later denied. He was appointed *Pontifex Maximus* (chief priest) in 57 and died in 53.

2, Gaius Scribonius (mid-C1 BC) Like his father, CURIO (1), he was friendly with CLODIUS. In 59 he was denounced by VETTIUS (3) for plotting against POMPEIUS (2), but survived; he was quaestor in 54 and worked against Caesar. But after being heavily bribed he turned to side with Caesar, and as tribune in 50, tried to force Pompeius to give up his commands at the same time as CAESAR (1). After his resolution in the Senate designed to prevent the Civil War was vetoed in December, he joined Caesar in 49. He occupied Sicily for Caesar and crossed to Africa. He was embroiled in a war first with the Pompeian general P. Attius Varus and then with king JUBA (1) I of Numidia. He won a battle near Utica over the former but was wiped out by the latter in the Bagradas valley. He married Clodius' widow, FULVIA, by whom he had a son whom Octavian (see AUGUSTUS) executed after the battle of Actium.

Cursor 1, Lucius Papirius (late C4 BC), was a general, dictator, and five times consul. He is credited by LIVY and other historians with the Roman victories in the Second Samnite War at Luceria in 320 BC and Satricum in 319, restoring the situation after the disastrous battle of the Caudine Forks in 321. He held five consulships between 326 and 313 and was dictator in 325 and 310. In the earlier dictatorship he accused his second-in-command, the Master of the Horse, FABIUS (7) Maximus Rullianus, of disobedience by engaging in battle without orders, and tried to have him executed. However, the two men, the greatest Roman leaders of the age, were equally revered in later times. He derived his surname, *Cursor*, from his prowess as a runner: he is also described by Livy as a Roman Alexander, with strict military discipline, great strength of body, and an enormous appetite for food and wine. In his first consulship he and his colleague LIBO Visulus passed a law outlawing slavery as a penalty for failure to pay debts.

2, Lucius (early C3 BC), was a son of CURSOR (1), and held two consulships: in 293, when he won a battle against the Samnites at Aquilonia, and in 272, when he conquered the peoples of southern

Italy, the Lucanians, the Bruttians, and the Tarentines, and drove PYRRHUS out of Italy. PLINY (1) the Elder reports that he put up Rome's first timepiece, a sundial.

Curtius *see* MONTANUS (1), RUFUS (2).

Cyprian (*c.*AD 200–258) was a Christian writer, Thascius Caecilius Cyprianus. The son of rich parents, he was baptised and elected bishop of Carthage in 248. He was an excellent administrator and met the problems posed by the persecutions instigated by DECIUS in 250 and by VALERIAN in 257 with courage and good sense. His writings consist of letters and tracts and show a mind which interpreted authority in the church on the analogy of the Roman state and Roman law. In 256 he split from Stephen the bishop of Rome on theological grounds because the latter readmitted the followers of NOVATIANUS. He was executed for his faith in 258. His deacon, Pontius, wrote his biography.

Cyrenius *see* QUIRINIUS.

D

Daia *see* MAXIMINUS (2).

Decebalus (C1–2 AD) was a Dacian king who in 85 invaded the Roman province of Moesia. After a five-year war DOMITIAN agreed to pay him an annual subsidy because, though Rome had won the war, the Romans needed his cooperation at a critical point on the frontier during the Germanic and Sarmatian uprising beyond the Danube. Later, in 101 and 102, he was attacked by TRAJAN and had to accept the status of a client king; in 105 he again invaded Moesia but was thrown back and lost his kingdom, which Trajan turned into a province. He was hunted but evaded his pursuers by suicide in 106.

Decius (reigned AD 249–251), an emperor, was born in 201 near Sirmium (Belgrade). A Pannonian by birth, with Italian connexions on his mother's side, Gaius Messius Quintus Decius governed Lower Moesia from AD 234 to 238 and was later appointed prefect of the City of Rome. When the emperor Philip the Arab (PHILIPPUS 1) in 249 sent him to restore order among the troops on the Danube frontier, he was forced by the soldiers to accept the imperial title. He invaded northern Italy and defeated Philip at Verona, killing him and his son. He adopted both the mien and the name of TRAJAN and determined to instil discipline in his troops. He wished to model the state on ancient republican virtues and practices, and supported senatorial authority and Roman cults while discouraging Christianity. In 250 he was brought back to the Danube frontier by an invasion of Goths and Carpi, and was defeated in Macedonia near Beroe. The next year, after refusing the Goths safe conduct back to the north, he attacked them on their march and was killed together with his son Herennius at Abrittus. He was succeeded by Trebonianus GALLUS (8). See M. Grant (1985) *The Roman Emperors*, London: Weidenfeld & Nicolson.
See MUS, SUBULO.

Deiotarus (C1 BC) was a Galatian king. As tetrarch ('ruler of a quarter') of western Galatia, he became an ally of Rome in the Third Mithridatic War and in recognition of his loyalty was given part of Pontus by POMPEIUS (2) in his eastern settlement in 63 BC. In 52 Pompeius obtained the Senate's approval for granting him the title of king, and in 51 he lent support to CICERO (1) in his post as governor of Cilicia. He naturally supported Pompeius in the Civil War and fled with him from Pharsalus, but then joined CAESAR (1)'s side. He gave help to Cn. Domitius CALVINUS (2) in his campaigns in Asia Minor and Syria in 48, and seized the rest of Galatia; after Caesar's five-day campaign against PHARNACES of Pontus, he was forced to give up the eastern half of Galatia to Mithridates of Pergamon. In 45 on Caesar's return to Rome he was accused by his grandson of having tried to murder Caesar while he was his guest. At his trial in 44 he was defended by Cicero (*Pro Rege Deiotaro*) but Caesar was assassinated before the end of the trial and no verdict was reached. Deiotarus bought back his confiscated territory for a large sum from ANTONIUS (7): in the subsequent civil war he began by supporting BRUTUS (5) but changed sides to the triumvirate just in time to escape with his kingdom intact; he died peacefully in 40 BC.

Dellius, Quintus (C1 BC), having changed sides three times in the Civil War, supported ANTONIUS (7) and wrote an account of his Parthian campaign which was drawn on by PLUTARCH in writing his *Life of Antonius*. He deserted Antonius just before the battle of Actium and earned from MESSALLA (4) the mocking description, 'the bare-back vaulter of the civil wars'. HORACE addressed an ode to him (2, 3).

Demetrius 1. I (187–150 BC) was the second son of SELEUCUS (1) IV and seized the throne of Syria in 162. He had been a hostage in Rome, from where he escaped, aided by POLYBIUS; he made his way home and overthrew his cousin ANTIOCHUS (3) V, an eleven-year-old child. Demetrius' reign had an auspicious start: he put an end to a rebellion in the east led by an insurgent general, Timarchus, and in 161 subdued the Jewish revolt of the Maccabees. The Roman senate recognised his title to the throne in 160: he took the title *Soter*, 'Saviour'. He wished for political reasons to marry his sister to ARIARATHES (2) V, king of Cappadocia, but that monarch refused, and Demetrius supported a pretender to his throne. Ariarathes' friend and ally, king ATTALUS (2) II of Pergamon, then stepped in to support a pretender to the Seleucid throne, Alexander BALAS, a man of obscure origin who claimed to be a son of ANTIOCHUS (2) IV. Balas had the support not only of Pergamon and Cappadocia but also of Rome, Egypt and the Jews. Demetrius was killed in battle by Balas in 150.

2. II (*c*.161–125 BC) was the eldest son of DEMETRIUS (1) I. On his father's death in 150 he took refuge in Crete, where he had gained the support of the king of Egypt, PTOLEMY (2) VI, whose eldest daughter Cleopatra Thea he married. After ejecting Alexander BALAS from the throne of Syria in 145 BC, he was forced a year later to share his throne with the general DIODOTUS Tryphon, who had first promoted the claims of the baby son of Balas, but then in 142 deposed the child and himself took power in Palestine where Demetrius was unpopular for his oppressive treatment of the Jews. In 140, however, in a campaign against the Parthians, Demetrius was captured and held prisoner by them for ten years. In 129, after a decisive victory over the Syrians, the Parthians released him and he regained his throne. Four years later, while undertaking an expedition against Egypt, he suffered the indignity of being replaced on his throne by yet another pretender, Alexander Zebina, supported by PTOLEMY (4) VIII. On his return to Syria, Demetrius, who had taken the title *Nicator*, 'Conqueror', was defeated near Damascus by Zebina, and fled to Tyre, where he was assassinated by Egyptian agents. He was succeeded by his eldest son Seleucus, who was murdered by his mother within a year.

3. (died 214 BC) was a ruler of Pharos, a small island state in the Adriatic (now Hvar), who gained his power by betraying Corcyra to Rome in 229 BC. At the battle of Sellasia in 222 he helped Antigonus III *Doson* of Macedonia against Cleomenes III of Sparta. In 220 he broke his treaty with Rome by ravaging the Greek coast and Aegean islands jointly with the Illyrian SCERDILAIDAS. Consequently in

219 Rome expelled him from Pharos and he took refuge with PHILIP (1) V of Macedonia, whom he encouraged in his opposition to the Romans. He became involved in Macedonian intervention in Messenia and was killed at Messene. See Polybius, *History*, 3, 19.

4. The Cynic (C1 AD) was a Greek philosopher of the Cynic school. He was acquainted with the anti-monarchist senator THRASEA Paetus and with SENECA (2), and was banished from Rome in AD 66 by NERO (1). He returned under VESPASIAN.

Dentatus, Manius Curius (C3 BC), was a plebeian statesman and general, consul in 290, 284, 275 and 274 BC, and censor in 272. During his first consulship he won a decisive victory over the Samnites, which brought a long and intermittent war to an end. In the same year he overcame the Sabines, and defeated the Senones in 284 and PYRRHUS in 275 in a battle fought near Beneventum. In 274 he defeated the Lucani. He triumphed twice, in 290 and in 275. He partly drained Lake Velinus and during his censorship started to build an aqueduct, the Anio Vetus, but died in 270 before it was complete. He had a reputation for frugality and incorruptibility.

Dexippus, Publius Herennius (C3 AD), was a Greek historian and general. According to an inscription on the base of a statue at Eleusis where he was a hereditary priest, he was a member of the ancient Eleusinian family of the Heralds. He was archon of Athens and is reputed to have beaten back an invasion of Greece by the Germanic Heruli in AD 269. He wrote three works of which fragments survive, an epitome of Arrian's history of the period after the death of Alexander the Great, a history of the wars between Rome and the Goths, preserved in the works of Zosimus, and a chronological history from earliest times to his own day, which was continued by Eunapius.

Didius, Titus (died 89 BC), was a tribune of the *plebs* in 103 BC, and unsuccessfully tried to prevent the prosecution of CAEPIO (3) by NORBANUS. He fought in Macedonia during his praetorship in 100 BC and won a triumph. In 98 as consul he was a proposer of the *lex Caecilia Didia*, a law to regulate the people's unfettered power to legislate, giving the Senate the ultimate decision in cases where the validity of legislation was contested. He held a command in Spain where he defeated the Celtiberians and gained a second triumph in 93. He was killed in the Social War.

Didius Julianus, Marcus (died AD 193), was an emperor who reigned for three months in 193. The son of a distinguished general, he was a rich senator and a jurist in the reign of HADRIAN. On the death of PERTINAX in March 193 the Praetorian Guard put the Empire up for auction to the highest bidder, and Didius eventually won, beating his father-in-law, the city prefect Flavius Sulpicianus, by offering 25,000 sesterces a man. He did not, however, pay the price he had offered, and rapidly became unpopular with the people and the provincial armies, many of which revolted against him. Septimius SEVERUS (1) was proclaimed emperor at Carnuntum on the Danube and PESCENNIUS NIGER in Syria. The former marched on Rome and received the support of the Praetorian Guard, whereupon the Senate condemned Didius to death. He was executed on 2 June in the same year. See M. Grant (1985) *The Roman Emperors*, London: Weidenfeld & Nicolson.

Dio (died 57 BC) was an Alexandrian philosopher of the Academic school, sent in 57 BC by the Alexandrians to Rome to oppose the restoration of PTOLEMY (8) XII the Piper, but murdered by Ptolemy's agents while he was staying with the senator T. Coponius.

Dio Cassius *see* CASSIUS (1) Dio.

Dio Chrysostom (*c.*AD 40–115) was a Greek rhetorician and popular philosopher born at Prusa in Bithynia. His real name was Dio (or Dion) Cocceianus: *Chrysostomos*, 'Golden mouth', was a nickname given him for his eloquence. He went to Rome to teach rhetoric, and was influenced by the Stoic philosopher Musonius RUFUS (3). He fell foul of DOMITIAN, who banished him; he spent the next years acting as a teacher wandering through Greece and the Balkans. NERVA (4) rehabilitated him though he continued on his travelling ministry of preaching Stoic-Cynic philosophy. He was a friend of TRAJAN and, after retiring to Bithynia, was prosecuted at Nicaea before PLINY (2) for mishandling a building contract. Eighty speeches attributed to Dio survive, though two were written by his pupil FAVORINUS. Dio modelled his style on those of Plato and Xenophon and avoided excessive archaism, writing in the atticist style fashionable in his day. The subject matter of his speeches is very varied, though the exposition of his philosophical belief is common. He touches on mythology, morality, literature, politics, and several of his speeches were delivered to the Assembly of Citizens at Prusa. See C.P. Jones (1978) *The Roman World of Dio Chrysostom*, Cambridge MA: Harvard University Press; for the text, Loeb edn. in 5 volumes.

Diocletian (*c.*AD 240–313) was an influential and important emperor. He was born Diocles near Salonae in Dalmatia, of obscure parents, and rose through the ranks to become commander of the bodyguard of the emperor NUMERIAN. When Numerian was murdered in November 284 near Nicomedia by his father-in-law, the praetorian prefect Arrius APER, the army elected Diocles to succeed him. The following spring, when Diocles had crushed him in a tough battle on the river Margus (Morava), CARINUS was assassinated by one of his officers, and Diocles was left in sole power. He ruled from his capital Nicomedia in Bithynia under the name Gaius Aurelius Valerius Diocletianus. A revolt occurred in Gaul and he sent his trusted friend MAXIMIAN to tackle the rebellious peasants known as the Bacaudae. In 286 he made Maximian the *Augustus* of the west, and in 293 he reformed the administration of the Empire and established a system of four rulers, two *Augusti*, to each of whom he appointed a deputy with the title *Caesar*: GALERIUS in the east and CONSTANTIUS (1) I in the west. This was partly to solve the problem of the succession, which had bedevilled the Empire for years, and partly to provide a more efficient defence of the frontiers. Before he made this arrangement he and Maximian had to fight several frontier wars, against the Alemanni in 288, the Sarmatians in 289 and 292, and the Persians over Armenia in 290. He placed his nominee Tiridates III on the throne of Armenia, the latter's conversion to Christianity distancing him from both Persia and Rome. He vigorously suppressed a revolt in Egypt in 293. In Britain CARAUSIUS had set up his own miniature empire and taken the title *Augustus*; he was recognised in 290 but replaced in 293 by ALLECTUS, who was overthrown in 296. In 297 Diocletian himself suppressed a serious revolt at Alexandria led by an imperial pretender named Achilleus aided by Domitius Domitianus. In 298 Galerius won a decisive victory over a new Persian king, Narses, who had expelled Tiridates. The eastern frontier was extended and secured. Thus Diocletian had achieved a stability that had eluded his predecessors. In 303 he visited Rome for the first time to celebrate twenty years of power. The next year he was extremely ill and on 1 May 305 he retired from his post and forced Maximian to do likewise, so that the Caesars were elevated to the rank of *Augustus*, and two new Caesars were appointed, Flavius Valerius SEVERUS (3) in the west and MAXIMINUS (2) Daia in the East. Diocletian retired to his hometown of

Salonae (Split), where he built himself an enormous palace, which partly survives to this day. In 308 he and Maximian took part in a conference at Carnuntum (in Austria near Haimburg) at which he tried to re-establish order among his successors. He died disillusioned by their quarrels.

The reign of Diocletian marks a turning point, heralding a period of much greater stability. His tetrarchy did not prove permanent, though henceforth there would always be more than one emperor at a time. He reformed both the civil and military structures of the Empire, at first treating them as one, but later in his career separating the officials (*praesides*) who carried out civil administration. The four emperors had something of a roving commission and were not tied down closely to particular areas, and even between himself and Maximian there was a sort of hierarchy: he referred to himself as 'Jupiter' but to his colleague as 'Hercules'. He was devoted to the ancient religion of Rome and persecuted the Christians in 303, probably under pressure from Galerius. He divided the Empire into thirteen large units named dioceses (*dioikeseis*), each governed by a *vicarius*, from which three major proconsular provinces, Achaea, Africa and Asia were excluded. Each emperor had his staff or *comitatus* (companions); they moved around as circumstances required, and the major seats of government were Nicomedia in Bithynia (Asia Minor), Sirmium near Belgrade, and Trier in western Germany. Rome was of lesser importance, and senators were mostly excluded from administrative posts. The massive increase in the size of the army and the enormous building programme of fortifications on the frontiers caused a rise in taxation: both land and people were taxed, and many people contributed in kind. There was rampant inflation, which he tried to curb by an unsuccessful attempt to set maximum prices. His attempt to impose a single currency on the empire also failed. The reforms which were begun by Diocletian were developed by CONSTANTINE (1) I, but the crushing burden of taxation grew and with it economic decline. See A.H.M. Jones (1964) *Later Roman Empire*, Oxford: Blackwell; T.D. Barnes (1982) *The New Empire of Diocletian and Constantine*, Cambridge MA: Harvard University Press; S. Williams (1985) *Diocletian and the Roman Recovery*, London: Batsford; M. Grant (1985) *The Roman Emperors*, London: Weidenfeld & Nicolson.

Diodotus Tryphon (C2 BC) was a king of the Seleucid kingdom of Syria. As a general of the army he had promoted the claims of the infant son of Alexander BALAS, but then in 142 he deposed and killed the child and himself seized power in Palestine where DEMETRIUS (2) II was unpopular for his oppressive treatment of the Jews. However, internal strife led in 143 BC to the establishment of Hasmonean rule, and in 138 Diodotus was attacked and defeated in Antioch by ANTIOCHUS (5) VII of Side. Diodotus committed suicide.

Dionysius of Halicarnassus (C1 BC) was a Greek historian and literary critic from Halicarnassus in southwestern Asia Minor who moved to Rome in about 30 BC where he taught rhetoric and became a great enthusiast for all things Roman. Much of his work survives: his *Roman Antiquities*, of whose twenty books we have the first ten, began publication in 7 BC. The work is basically historical but has a strong moralising slant and contains the fruit of careful research and is a valuable source. He was an important and seminal writer on literature with developed theories of his own. The following works survive: *On the Arrangement of Words*, which is a unique ancient discussion of the effects of word order on the sound of language; *Commentaries on the Ancient Orators*, mainly about the Attic orators and displaying hostility to the Asianic as opposed to the Attic style; *On Thucydides*; *Letters to Ammaeus* about Demosthenes and Thucydides; a *Letter to Cn. Pompeius* on Plato; and fragments of a work on *Imitation*. See E. Gabba (1991) *Dionysius and the History of Archaic Rome*, Berkeley: University of California Press.

Dioscorides, Pedianius (C1 AD), was a physician from Anazarbus in Cilicia. As an army doctor in NERO (1)'s reign he studied the use of drugs and herbs extensively for their healing properties and wrote in Greek two books which superseded all previous work on the subject: *On Medical Material*, and *Simple Drugs*. Of these the former deals in five books with the medicinal properties of about 600 plants, thirty-five animal derivatives and a large number of minerals. His approach was rational, thorough and free from prejudice, and modern plant names owe much to his work. His influence on medicine and botany lasted down to modern times, and his works were translated into Latin and Arabic.

Divitiacus 1. (*c*.100 BC) was a king of the Belgic Suessiones and the most powerful king in Gaul. He also ruled part of Britain. See CAESAR (1), *Gallic War*, 2, 4. 7.

2. (C1 BC) was a Druid and magistrate of the Gallic Aedui who preferred Roman domination to that of the Germans and sought Roman help in 61 BC after the invasion led by ARIOVISTUS. Though this was not forthcoming, he supported CAESAR (1) in 58 against Ariovistus and DUMNORIX, his own brother. The following year he successfully pleaded with Caesar to excuse the Bellovaci who had abandoned their alliance with the Aedui and, with disastrous consequences, joined a Belgic rebellion. See CAESAR (1), *Gallic War*, 2.

Dolabella 1, Gnaeus Cornelius (C1 BC), was a senator who served in Sulla's army and was a consul in 81 BC. He governed Macedonia and held a triumph in 78.

2, Gnaeus Cornelius (C1 BC), was a senator who was praetor in 81 BC and governed Cilicia in 80 and 79: he thereby enriched himself with the help of VERRES, his legate, who gave evidence against him in his trial for extortion; he was convicted and went into exile.

3, Publius Cornelius (C3 BC), was a consul of 283 BC when he defeated an army of Gallic Boii and Etruscans near Lake Vadimo in the war that led to the Roman annexation of Etruria.

4, Publius Cornelius (*c*.80–43 BC), prosecuted Appius CLAUDIUS (8) in 50 BC for extortion, after marrying CICERO (1)'s daughter Tullia while her father was absent in Greece. His first wife had been a Fabia by whom he had a son. He joined the Caesarians in the Civil War, and after a naval command in the Adriatic he fought at Pharsalus in 48 and later at Thapsus and Munda. Born a patrician, he had himself adopted as a plebeian in 47 so as to be elected tribune: his aim was to propose a law to cancel debts – he was himself heavily in debt – and his proposal led to riots (see RUFUS 1). He was opposed in the matter by ANTONIUS (7). Tullia died in 45 after bearing him two sons who died in infancy. Against Antonius' advice CAESAR (1) designated him consul for the remainder of 44 BC while he himself went to the Balkans: upon Caesar's assassination Dolabella claimed the vacant post and sided with the murderers to the extent that he suppressed the worship of Caesar as a god. However he received funds from Antonius and was allotted the province of Syria for 43. He departed in October to secure the province and the dissaffected legions in Egypt. On his way there, in January 43, he attacked and seized Smyrna where he found the governor of Asia, TREBONIUS, a close friend of his former father-in-law Cicero, and murdered him for denying him access to Smyrna. When the news reached Rome, the Senate declared Dolabella a public enemy. He had by now reached his province but was forestalled by CASSIUS (3) in securing the army and was besieged in Laodicea. There he was defeated, and he ordered a soldier to kill him.

5, Publius Cornelius (C1 AD), the grandson of DOLABELLA (4), was a suffect consul in AD 10 and governor of Dalmatia from AD 14 to 20. He was proconsul of Africa in 23 and in 24 brought the war against the Numidian TACFARINAS to a successful end.

Domitia *see* DOMITIAN.

Domitian (AD 51–96) was the third and last Flavian emperor. Titus Flavius Domitianus was the second son of the emperor VESPASIAN and his wife Flavia Domitilla. When he was seventeen, in July 69, his father Vespasian became the fourth claimant to imperial power in a year by raising his standard in Syria with the support of the governors and troops of Syria and Egypt: others quickly joined the rising which soon became a powerful movement. Domitian was in Rome with his uncle Flavius SABINUS (2), commander of the urban cohorts: together they took refuge in the Capitol, which VITELLIUS (1) besieged. Domitian escaped and a few days later, after the fall of Vitellius, the Senate gave him the title *Caesar*; he shared power with MUCIANUS until in summer 70 Vespasian arrived. Thenceforth, until the premature death of his elder brother TITUS, Domitian remained in obscurity as neither his father nor his brother gave him any responsibility, though he held two full and three suffect consulships. In September 81 Titus died without an heir and Domitian succeeded unchallenged. He was a marked contrast to his popular brother, with whom he had had an uneasy relationship: somewhat like TIBERIUS (whom he admired) he was gloomy and unapproachable; he did not trust the Senate and controlled its membership by taking the office of censor permanently from 84 to his death. He was consul ten times during his reign – to enhance his prestige rather than for the powers of the office. He compelled the senators to vote as he wished. He used a much smaller body to advise him, a privy council (the *consilium principis*) on which a few select senators and an equal number of equestrians sat. Having inherited a fairly prosperous treasury, he kept the legions sweet by raising their annual pay from 300 to 400 denarii, and gave lavish doles to the urban poor, but made no extraordinary gifts to the military and slightly reduced the size of the army. He engaged in lavish building works, including the restoration of Jupiter's temple on the Capitol and the building of his extravagant Alban villa. He left the coinage purer than he found it.

He was a highly efficient administrator and the Empire ran smoothly under his control. The provinces were well governed though taxes were high and efficiently collected. He used his powers as censor to suppress immorality, and in 83 punished three Vestal Virgins with death for unchastity. He similarly punished their leader, Cornelia, in 90, by burying her alive – the traditional penalty. He had married Domitia Longina, daughter of CORBULO, in 70 but their children, a son and a daughter, did not live long, and he divorced and banished her on the pretext of her adultery with the actor Paris; he later took her back. The hypocrisy of one who insisted on a high standard of public morality whilst himself practising lechery, including his adulterous liaison with his niece FLAVIA JULIA, was criticised by the philosophers who formed a second opposition besides that of the senators. He twice expelled philosophers from Italy, in 89 and 95. He encouraged flattery and insisted on receiving divine honours and being called 'Lord God'. He wore the triumphal dress of a Roman general and himself held a triumph for his victory over the Dacians in 89.

He was popular with the armies and keen to improve the frontiers: in 83 he won a victory in Germany over the Chatti, leading to the completion of a fortified frontier between the Main and the Neckar rivers. He fought campaigns against the Dacians in the mid-80s: DECEBALUS their king had finally to be bought off with a subvention; the attacks of the Germanic Marcomanni and Quadi proved difficult to repel though Domitian himself took the field against them and was defeated. He nevertheless fortified the Danube frontier and celebrated his triumph, taking the title Germanicus. During his reign AGRICOLA made great strides towards the conquest of Britain, but was recalled in 85 with his work unfinished, perhaps because Domitian was jealous of his success.

He became more tyrannical as his reign wore on, and his last three years have been described as a reign of terror. After 88, the year of SATURNINUS (1)'s rebellion in Upper Germany, he reintroduced treason trials, which Titus had abolished: many senators were executed or exiled and informers were encouraged. There were other conspiracies against him after this, though some were more imagined by him than real: one victim was his kinsman T. Flavius CLEMENS, husband of his niece DOMITILLA; he killed him in 95. He had adopted their sons as his heirs, naming them Domitian and Vespasian. He was assassinated on 18 September 96 in a palace plot approved by his wife and led by the two commanders of the Praetorian Guard: the deed was done by Stephanus, a freedman of Clemens. Only the army grieved. His memory was condemned by the Senate and his name erased from monuments. See M. Grant (1985) *The Roman Emperors*, London: Weidenfeld & Nicolson; E.T. Salmon (1968) *A History of the Roman World*, London: Methuen; P. Southern (1997) *Domitian, Tragic Tyrant*, London and New York: Routledge.

Domitilla, Flavia (C1 AD), was a daughter of Flavius Liberalis. She married VESPASIAN, but died before he became emperor, and was the mother of his three children, TITUS, DOMITIAN and Domitilla. Domitilla junior also died before her father became emperor, and was the mother of a third Domitilla, whose two sons by T. Flavius CLEMENS were adopted by the emperor Domitian. In 95 she and her husband were accused of atheism, i.e. false religion, and she was exiled while her husband was put to death: some have suggested that the cult they followed was Judaism or Christianity.

Donatus 1, Aelius (C4 AD), was a Latin grammarian and literary commentator. He wrote two grammatical treatises: the *Lesser Art of Grammar*, dealing with the parts of speech, and the *Greater Art*, dealing with more sophisticated points including questions of style. He also wrote a commentary on the plays of TERENCE, which survives in a mutilated form and omits the *Self-Torturer*. Of his commentary on VIRGIL only the preface and the *Life* survive, though Servius' commentary owed much to Donatus' work. He was the teacher of Jerome, the Christian scholar who translated the *Bible* into Latin.

2. Magnus (*c.*AD 312) was a bishop of Carthage who founded the puritanical Donatist Christian heresy in North Africa.

Drusus 1, Marcus Livius (died 109 BC), probably a descendant of Lucius Aemilius PAULLUS (2), was a tribune of the *plebs* in 122 BC. In collaboration with the consul FANNIUS he opposed Gaius GRACCHUS (1)'s plans to extend the citizenship and tried to outflank his reforms by proposing his own: that twelve new colonies of citizens should be planted, that allotments of land under Tiberius

GRACCHUS (4)'s law should be rent-free, and that Latins be exempted from corporal punishment. Thus he secured Gracchus' failure to be re-elected as tribune for 121, though he refused to carry out his own proposals. He was consul in 112 and then governed Macedonia where he fought the Scordisci and reached the Danube: he held a triumph in 110. He was then elected censor with SCAURUS (2), but died in office. He had a son, DRUSUS (2), and a daughter, LIVIA (1).

2, Marcus Livius (died 91 BC), was the son of DRUSUS (1). Originally a close friend of CAEPIO (4), who married and then divorced his sister LIVIA (1), he was a member of the group of young men patronised by Lucius CRASSUS (2), who influenced him greatly. After holding the quaestorship and aedileship, he became tribune of the *plebs* in 91 BC in which post, with the encouragement of the leader of the Senate, SCAURUS (2), he proposed a series of measures unpopular with the Senate and the equestrians (see RUFUS 4). By including them in a single measure he managed to push them through the assembly of the people. After debasing the coinage, he proposed to reform the courts by enrolling 300 equestrians into the Senate and drawing all criminal juries from the enlarged Senate; the poor would be assisted by the founding of colonies and distribution of land, and the citizenship would be extended to all Italians. L. Marcius PHILIPPUS (2) led the opposition on behalf of the landed senators and Caepio, now hostile, spoke for the equestrians: they had his bill declared a nullity as carried against the auspices. CRASSUS (2) defended him but died and Drusus' position had become untenable. He was assassinated in late 91 by an unknown hand, but the outcome was the Social War and the commission proposed by Q. Varius. He provided a home for the children of his dead sister Livia, including CATO (5) of Utica and SERVILIA, mother of BRUTUS (5), and himself adopted a member of the Claudian family (M. Livius Claudianus) who became the father of AUGUSTUS' wife, LIVIA (2).

3, Nero Claudius (38–9 BC), was the second son of Tiberius Claudius NERO (3) and LIVIA (2), younger brother of the emperor TIBERIUS. Livia was pregnant with him when she was divorced by Nero and married Octavian (see AUGUSTUS) in 38 BC. Named Decimus Claudius Nero, he moved to Octavian's house in 33 on his father's death and the name change to Nero Claudius Drusus was effected, in recognition of his mother Livia's family. He was appointed quaestor in 18 BC, Augustus having enacted that he might stand for magistracies five years earlier than the law allowed. He served in his brother Tiberius' army on the northern frontier in 15 BC and helped subdue the territory of Raetia (modern Switzerland). In 13 Augustus appointed him to rule the three Gallic provinces which were on the brink of revolt. Having settled their grievances, he held a census and dedicated an altar to Rome and Augustus at Lyons, the capital. He was then entrusted with the conquest of Germany for the purpose of establishing a new frontier for the Empire on the river Elbe. He advanced into Germany in four successive campaigns from 12 to 9 BC. In 12 he won the alliance of the Batavi and Frisii on his western flank and made a notable use of ships in his campaign, digging a canal to link the Rhine and the lakes of Holland and the North Sea. He sailed into the river Ems and challenged the Chauci, but had to withdraw with Frisian help. He was praetor in 11, but hastened back to Germany and made a more southerly march along the river Lippe to the land of the Cherusci. In 10, now proconsul, he advanced against the yet more southerly Chatti. In 9 he was consul: he advanced to the Elbe in a southeasterly direction, making war upon the Chatti, Suebi, Marcomanni and Cherusci; while on this campaign he fell from his horse and died a month later. Tiberius reached him during his last illness. His achievements in Germany were spectacular but did not last: the territory he invaded was soon free again. The Senate, however, conferred the title Germanicus on him and his children: he had married the younger ANTONIA (3), daughter of ANTONIUS (7), who bore him three children, GERMANICUS, LIVIA (3) (Livilla), and the emperor CLAUDIUS (1). He was brilliant and popular and undoubtedly a serious loss to Augustus.

4. Julius Caesar (13 BC–AD 23) was the son of the emperor TIBERIUS and his first wife Vipsania AGRIPPINA (1), daughter of AGRIPPA (1). Drusus Julius Caesar married his cousin, the sister of GERMANICUS, LIVIA (3) Julia, known as Livilla. In AD 14 while serving in Pannonia he suppressed a mutiny of the soldiers caused by dissatisfaction with their conditions of service, was consul in 15, and governed Illyricum from 17 to 20, winning a triumph for his military successes. He held a consulship in partnership with his father in 21 and, Germanicus now being dead, was made his father's destined successor the next year by the award of the power of a tribune for life. But having borne him a son, Tiberius Gemellus (see CAESAR [10]) and a daughter, Livia Julia, his wife had been seduced by the praetorian prefect SEJANUS and, with his complicity, now poisoned Drusus. The murder was successfully concealed from the emperor until it was denounced by ANTONIA (2) in 31.

5. Julius Caesar (AD 7–33) was the second surviving son of GERMANICUS and AGRIPPINA (2). As a possible successor to TIBERIUS, he fell victim to SEJANUS, who arrested him in 30 during Tiberius' retirement to Capri. However, even after Sejanus' death he was kept in custody, where he died. He married AEMILIA (1) LEPIDA, who appears to have been partly responsible for his downfall.

Duilius, Gaius (C3 BC), was a general during the First Punic War. When consul in 260 BC he defeated the Carthaginian fleet off Mylae in Sicily with the newly built Roman fleet, and liberated Segesta. This first Roman naval victory was won through Duilius' foresight in equipping his new ships with grappling irons and boarding bridges, although his men lacked experience of such warfare. It earned him the first naval triumph, his deed being commemorated by an inscription on a column placed in the forum and decorated with the sawn-off beaks of captured enemy ships. Duilius used the booty from the battle to erect a temple to Janus in the vegetable market.

Dumnorix (died 54 BC) was a chief of the Aedui, younger brother of DIVITIACUS (2); unlike his brother he opposed the Romans, and when chief magistrate in 61 BC he plotted with his father-in-law the Helvetian Orgetorix to allow the Helvetii to migrate to western Gaul. Caesar prevented the migration and spared Dumnorix only at his brother's earnest entreaty. Caesar continued to mistrust him and ordered him to accompany him in 54 in his invasion of Britain: Dumnorix tried to flee but was killed in the act.

E

Egnatius 1, Gellius (early C3 BC), was a Samnite general who organised opposition to Rome in the Third Samnite War by uniting Samnite, Etruscan and Gallic forces. He defeated SCIPIO (1) Barbatus at Camerinum in 296 but was killed at the battle of Sentinum in 295 when Rome, despite the loss of her general P. Decius MUS (2), won control of central Italy. See FABIUS (7) Maximus Rullianus.

2, Gnaeus In his praetorship *c.*145 BC he governed Macedonia and began the Egnatian Way which linked the Adriatic ports of western Macedonia with Thessalonica, Thrace and Byzantium.

3. Rufus, Marcus (died 19 BC), during his aedileship *c.*26 formed a private fire brigade with his slaves and others, which brought him immense popularity. He offered himself as candidate for the consulship in 19 which AUGUSTUS had declined, but the sole remaining consul, SATURNINUS (3), declared that even if the people elected him, he would veto the election. Shortly after this he was arrested and executed on a charge of plotting against the emperor's life.

Elagabalus (Heliogabalus) (*c.*AD 203–222) was born at Emesa in Syria, the son of an equestrian, Varius Marcellus, from Apamea. In 217, on the assassination of CARACALLA, his grandmother, JULIA (11) Maesa, sister of the empress JULIA (10) Domna, being banished from the imperial court by the new emperor MACRINUS, took him and his cousin SEVERUS (2) Alexander from Rome back to Emesa. The next year, when he was fourteen, he became *Augustus* (emperor) through the wiles of his grandmother and the deceit of his mother, JULIA (12) Soaemias, in claiming that he was Caracalla's bastard son. His original name was Varius Avitus Bassianus and he was hereditary priest of the sun god, Elah-Gabal, in Emesa. He was popular with the legions stationed in Syria on account of his beauty and the gorgeous ceremonies over which he presided. Julia Maesa organised his proclamation as *Augustus* with the name Marcus Aurelius Antoninus Elagabalus; a battle was fought on 2 June 218 near Antioch between his supporters and those of Macrinus, in which the latter was killed, much of his army having gone over to the handsome boy. Elagabalus spent the winter at Nicomedia in Bithynia and reached Rome in 219. The only consistent policy of the new emperor was the spread of the worship of his god, and he brought from Emesa the sacred black stone of the cult to the Palatine and 'married' it to the Carthaginian goddess Tanit whose image he also imported to Rome. He built two fine temples for his god and enthusiastically carried out the cult with barbarous cruelty and immorality. His grandmother was the only check on his excesses: she instituted her own female Senate, which held debates on matters of etiquette. The reign was increasingly unpopular, and in 221 his grandmother sought to save him by persuading him to adopt his fourteen-year-old cousin Severus Alexander as his heir. But in 222 he twice tried to murder his cousin: the Praetorian Guard, bribed by JULIA (13) Mamaea, Severus' mother, mutinied and killed the emperor and his mother. See M. Grant (1985) *The Roman Emperors*, London: Weidenfeld & Nicolson.

Ennius, Quintus (239–169 BC), was a poet born at Rudiae in Calabria and a native speaker of Messapian (an Illyrian tongue) rather than Latin. He must have come early under the influence of Greek culture and the Greek language, which was spoken close by at Tarentum. Also nearby was the Messapian town of Brundisium, which had recently been created a Latin colony and where the youthful Ennius may have become acquainted with Latin. He joined the Roman army in the Second Punic War and became a centurion: when serving in Sardinia in 204 BC he was noticed by CATO (4) who took him to Rome. In Rome he lectured on poetry and translated Greek plays into Latin for the stage, as had Livius ANDRONICUS. In 189 he accompanied the general M. Fulvius NOBILIOR on a campaign in Aetolia; three years later his son who was then on an official board to found a colony, obtained Roman citizenship for Ennius. He spent the rest of his life in Rome, where he taught Latin and Greek grammar to the sons of the nobility and received the patronage of the Scipios and perhaps of Servius Sulpicius GALBA (4); he was befriended by CAECILIUS (7) Statius. His nephew was the poet PACUVIUS of Brundisium.

His most original and seminal work was a great epic poem in Latin hexameters, named *Annals* (*Annales*), which tells the story of Rome from Aeneas' flight from Troy down to the Punic Wars. About 600 lines of this work survive in fragments; the work probably ran to 20,000 lines. It was highly influential on the development of the Latin epic and didactic style, and inspired VIRGIL in his composition of the *Aeneid*, in which the metrical structure of the hexameter line is only marginally different. Ennius was still working on this poem when he died at the age of seventy. It became a schoolbook and was a core text in Roman schools until the Aeneid replaced it. He also translated or rather adapted a range of Greek plays for the Latin stage: of the known titles three are from Aeschylus and twelve from Euripides. Fragments of his *Medea* show the extent to which Ennius was prepared to depart from the original and include explanation in his text. They also show how lofty and grandiose was his style (as distinct from that of Euripides), a quality CICERO (1) admired. He wrote 'satire', which differed greatly from the genre inaugurated by LUCILIUS (1), and celebrated the exploits of SCIPIO (7) Africanus in a poem. His *Hedyphagetica* translated a Greek poem on food by Archestratus, and he wrote a prose work based on Euhemerus' novel *The Sacred Record*, which is quoted extensively by LACTANTIUS.

Ennius' great contribution to the development of Latin literature was his adaptation of Greek metres, the epic hexameter and the elegiac, to use in Latin in place of the traditional metres of Saturnian verse. He referred to himself as a Latin Homer for the innovation he achieved in the composition of his *Annals*. See O. Skutsch (1985) *The Annals of Quintus Ennius*, Oxford: Clarendon Press.

Epaphroditus 1. (died AD 95) was a freedman minister of NERO (1) and DOMITIAN. As secretary to the former he assisted in the discovery of PISO (2)'s plot and accompanied him in his flight in AD 68. He was appointed state secretary by Domitian and served him faithfully until his fall from grace when he was executed for having helped Nero to die. Epictetus was his slave in youth and was treated generously by him.

2. (*c.*AD 18–*c.*97) was a literary critic from Alexandria: as a slave he was educated by his master, Archias, and after obtaining his freedom he migrated to Rome where he taught and wrote commentaries (no longer extant) on Homer, Hesiod and Callimachus.

Eprius Marcellus, Titus Clodius (died AD 79), was an orator and governor of Asia. He was of lowly origin from Capua but emerged to become praetor in AD 48, after which he governed Lycia: he was prosecuted by the Lycians for extortion in 57 and was acquitted through his oratory and bribery. He governed Cyprus and then held a suffect consulship in 62. He joined the persecution of the Stoic opposition to NERO (1) and accused THRASEA Paetus in 66, being richly rewarded for his condemnation. He threw in his lot with VESPASIAN and attacked the Stoic opposition, notably HEVIDIUS (1) Priscus. Vespasian appointed him proconsul of Asia from 70 to 73 and to a second suffect consulship in 74. In 79, however, he was accused by TITUS of plotting with CAECINA (3) Alienus against Vespasian, and forced to kill himself.

Eumenes II Soter ('Saviour') (reigned 197–159 BC) was a king of Pergamon who maintained the alliance with Rome of his father ATTALUS (1) I. He was active in promoting diplomatic hostility between the Romans and the Seleucid king ANTIOCHUS (1) III in the years from 196 to 192, and in the war which followed he assisted the Romans in 191 with a fleet at the battle of Cape Corycus, and in 190 suffered a short siege of Pergamon. The Romans then crossed into Asia Minor and in 189 fought a decisive battle at Magnesia in which Eumenes distinguished himself. The settlement made at Apamea in 188 brought him a large expansion of his territory, including Gallipoli and most of Seleucid Asia Minor. He persuaded the Romans to send Cn. Manlius VULSO in 189 to clear the Galatians from the territories near the sea. The Romans withdrew their forces from Asia Minor in 188; however with Roman diplomatic support Eumenes made war on PRUSIAS I of Bithynia from 186 to 183, and then on Pontus from 183 to 179, when he and his allies decisively defeated its king, Pharnaces I. In 172 Eumenes visited Rome to denounce PERSEUS, king of Macedonia, and so instigated the Third Macedonian War which ended at the battle of Pydna in 169. The war at first went badly for the Romans and they became suspicious of Eumenes' loyalty to them and transferred their support to Eumenes' brother ATTALUS (2), who succeeded him. Eumenes' long reign saw the establishment of the famous library at Pergamon, which was transferred by CLEOPATRA (4) to Alexandria. He also added many fine buildings to the city including the great altar of Zeus.

Eumenius (*c.*AD 264–312) was a rhetorician born at Augustodunum (Autun) in Gaul who was appointed his private secretary by the emperor CONSTANTIUS (1) I. In 296 he obtained a new appointment as head of a college, the Scholae Maenianae, at Augustodunum and restored it from its war-damaged state with his own funds, as he reported in an extant speech, *For the Restoration of the Schools*, which he made there a couple of years later, in which he delivered eulogies of the four contemporary emperors.

Eunus was a Syrian slave who, with a Cilician named Cleon, led a revolt of slaves at Enna in Sicily in 136 BC (the First Servile War); calling himself Antiochus, he raised a large army and defeated several Roman commanders. He conciliated the natives and was at first opposed by inferior Roman troops. By 133 the Romans were recovering and in

132 Eunus was beaten and captured by Rupilius. He died in captivity.

Eurycles, Gaius Julius (late C1 BC), was the son of Lachares, a pirate whom ANTONIUS (7) executed. After receiving his support in the campaign of Actium in 31, Octavian (see AUGUSTUS) gave him Roman citizenship and appointed him client king of Sparta and district. His rule became oppressive and, after travelling to Judaea and Cappadocia in 7 BC, he provoked such disturbances that after two inquiries into his conduct Augustus exiled him. His son Laco, who founded games in his memory, succeeded him as king of Sparta.

Eusebius (*c.*AD 260–339) was a Greek historian and apologist of the Christian Church who was bishop of Caesarea in Palestine *c.*314. He was a prolific writer. He seems to have been adopted by one Pamphilus (martyred in 310), and through his influence had access to the library of ORIGEN (1). He supported ARIUS though he deserted him at the council of Nicaea (325) and signed the Nicene Creed, a decision he greatly regretted. He attended the council of Tyre in 335 and opposed ATHANASIUS. He was influential with CONSTANTINE (1) the Great, whose 'life' he wrote in the form of a panegyric after his death in 337. He was a fervent opponent of traditional Greek philosophy (writing *Preparation for the Gospel* and *Divine Revelation* for this purpose: his particular target was PORPHYRY), and tried to prove that the doctrines of Plato originated in the Bible. He also tried to prove to the Jews, in the *Proof of the Gospel*, of which half survives, that prophecies in their scriptures related to JESUS. He composed careful chronological tables of historical and pseudo-historical events from Abraham's time to his own. His *Ecclesiastical History* was his greatest work and covered the history of the church until his own day. He also wrote a history of the world from the beginnings to his own time, based on the work of JULIUS AFRICANUS (2), entitled *Chronicon*; he also wrote *The Martyrs of Palestine* and *Theophany*. His *Onomasticon* was a gazetteer to the geography of Palestine, and *Against Hierocles* was an attack on those who would compare Jesus with APOLLONIUS (4) of Tyana. See T.D. Barnes (1981) *Constantine and Eusebius*, Cambridge MA: Harvard University Press; D.S. Wallace-Hadrill (1982) *Eusebius of Caesarea*, Cambridge MA: Harvard University Press; R.M. Grant (1980) *Eusebius as Church Historian*, Oxford: Oxford University Press.

Eutropius (C4 AD) was a Latin historian who served in JULIAN's eastern campaign in AD 363 and under Valens. He wrote a *Survey of Roman History* from the foundation of Rome to the reign of JOVIAN (AD 364). His main sources were LIVY, SUETONIUS (2), an unknown 'Imperial History', and his own memory of events. In spite of its brevity the work is balanced and useful.

F

Fabianus, Papirius (C1 AD), was a philosopher who was a teacher of SENECA (2). Seneca gives rich illustrations of his speeches in his *Controversies*, book 2.

Fabius 1. Ambustus, Marcus (C4 BC), a patrician, was consul three times, in 360, 356 and 354 BC. In an attempt to reassert Rome's influence after the Gallic War, he overcame the Hernici in 356 and the people of Tibur (Tivoli) in 354, and held a triumph in the latter year. But he was defeated by the army of Tarquinia. When he was dictator in 351, he unsuccessfully opposed a move by the plebeians to be allowed to stand for the consulship again.

2. Ambustus, Quintus (C4 BC), was a tribune who held consular authority in 391 BC, was sent as ambassador to Clusium in 391 or 390, and to whom was assigned responsibility for provoking the Gauls into their attack on Rome at the battle of the Allia. He was said to have murdered a Gallic chieftain with whom he was negotiating, and escaped prosecution because of the influence of his father who was *Pontifex Maximus* (chief priest). LIVY (6, 1) implies that he was prosecuted after the withdrawal of the Gauls and died before he could be tried.

3. Buteo, Marcus (C3 BC), was consul in 245 BC and censor in 241. He was probably one of the delegates at Carthage in March 218 who unsuccessfully demanded the surrender of Hannibal. He was dictator in 216 and recruited senators to make up for the senators who had fallen.

4. Justus, Lucius (late C1 AD), was a Roman general and friend of PLINY (2) the Younger. He served as general during TRAJAN's reign, was suffect consul in 102 and proconsul of Syria in about 109. TACITUS (1) dedicated his critical work *Dialogue on Orators* to him.

5. Maximus Aemilianus, Quintus (*c.*186–130 BC), was a general of the second century BC. Born Lucius Aemilius Paullus, he was adopted by a son (or grandson) of Verrucosus (FABIUS 8): he was praetor in Sicily in 149 and consul in 145. He then served in Spain where he fought against VIRIATHUS. He was a legate to his younger brother SCIPIO (11) Aemilianus at the siege of Numantia in 134.

6. Maximus Allobrogicus, Quintus (late C2 BC), was the son of FABIUS (1). He was praetor *c.*124 BC and held a command in Spain; after his consulship in 121 he was successful in his proconsulship in Gaul, where he defeated the Arverni and Allobroges on the Rhone and, after holding a triumph, built the first triumphal arch in Rome, the Fornix Fabianus.

7. Maximus Rullianus, Quintus (C4 BC), was an important general who held five consulships between 322 and 295 BC, was censor in 310 and dictator in 315 and possibly again in 313. He was the colleague of P. Decius MUS (2) in his last four consulships. He was an active and successful commander against the Samnites, the Etruscans and the Gauls, over each of whom he celebrated a triumph. He first defeated the Samnites in 325 when he was impeached by the dictator PAPIRIUS (1) Cursor for attacking without orders. He lost a battle at the hands of the Samnites at Lautulae in 315 but led a successful expedition against the Etruscans in 310; he decisively defeated a combined army of Samnites, Etruscans, Umbrians and Gauls at Sentinum in 295. This victory enabled Rome to conquer the whole of Italy. See W.V. Harris (1971) *Rome in Etruria and Umbria*, Oxford: Clarendon Press.

8. Maximus Verrucosus, Quintus (C3 BC), was a distinguished general and statesman known as *Cunctator*, 'the Delayer', because of his cautious tactics in the war with HANNIBAL; a great-grandson of FABIUS (1). He held his first consulship in 233 BC and soon afterwards celebrated a triumph over the Ligurians. He was censor in 230 and again consul in 228, 215, 214 and 209, and was appointed dictator in the war against Hannibal in 221 and again after the defeat at Lake Trasimene in 217. His delaying policy was so unpopular that he quarrelled with his second-in-command, MINUCIUS (3) Rufus, and resigned the dictatorship: the Romans were disastrously routed at Cannae in 216 and he was recalled, his cautious policy being perforce adopted for the next ten years, while Fabius held various posts. In 213 he served as legate to his own son who was consul. In 209 he recovered Tarentum, which Hannibal had taken in 212, by subverting its inhabitants. In 205 he opposed SCIPIO (7) Africanus' plan to invade Africa, which ultimately led to Roman victory, and died in 203. He held the priesthood (*pontifex*) for the last twelve years of his life and was also an augur: he used these religious and prophetic positions to further his policies. See Plutarch, *Life of Fabius*; H.H. Scullard (1973) *Roman Politics*, Oxford: Clarendon Press; J.F. Lazenby (1978) *Hannibal's War*, Warminster: Aris & Phillips.

9. Maximus, Paullus (died AD 14), was a consular of the Augustan period and a friend of AUGUSTUS. He was the son of the Caesarian Q. Fabius Maximus, consul in 45 BC, who died in that year. Paullus, named after his ancestor L. Aemilius PAULLUS (2) Macedonicus, was consul in 11 BC, proconsul of Asia, and in 3 BC legate of Eastern Spain. He was a man of great distinction and a friend of HORACE and of OVID, who both address him in their poems. TACITUS (1) (*Annals*, 1, 5) reports a rumour that he accompanied Augustus on his last visit to AGRIPPA (2) Postumus.

10. Pictor, Quintus (C3 BC), was a Roman historian and senator. A patrician and member of the ancient Fabian clan, he fought in the Second Punic War and consulted the Delphic oracle after the Roman defeat at Cannae. He was the first Roman to compose history in Greek, motivated by desire for a wider audience and attracted by the Greek tradition of historiography as opposed to the dull annalistic Roman chronicles. In fact he created the Roman tradition of senatorial history. Little of his work survives, but it is clear that he attached the origins of Rome to the Homeric myths by assigning the ancestry of the Romans to Aeneas of Troy. He also included an account of the history of Rome down to his own times, which was used as a source by the later historians, POLYBIUS, LIVY and DIONYSIUS of Halicarnassus. See A.D. Momigliano (1990) *The Classical Foundations of Ancient Historiography*, Berkeley: University of California Press.

11. Rusticus (C1 AD) was a Roman historian from Spain who composed a history, which has not survived, of his own times, showing hostility to NERO (1) and partiality to SENECA (2), his fellow-countryman and patron. TACITUS (1) admired his style and may have used his work as a source.

Fabricius Luscinus, Gaius (early C3 BC), was a statesman, consul in 282 and 278, who proved a brilliant diplomat in his successful negotiations with the Tarentines in 284 and with PYRRHUS, king of Epirus, in 280 and 278. He is said to have rejected bribes and offers from traitors to poison the king. He was also a successful general, winning triumphs in 282 over the Tarentines, and over the Bruttii, Samnites and Lucanians, from whom he liberated Thurii. He was censor in 275, when he is said to have sternly opposed growing luxury among the Romans. He thus became famous for his austerity of character and incorruptibility, though this picture may be more legend than fact.

Falco, Quintus Pompeius (C2 AD), was a general and provincial governor from Sicily. In 101–2 he commanded a legion in the First Dacian War and was procurator of Pamphylia and then of Judaea, being appointed consul in 108. He governed Lower Moesia *c.*117, and after TRAJAN's death was appointed by HADRIAN governor of Britain, where he remained until 122 and may have begun the Wall. He then governed Asia as proconsul until 124. He was a friend and correspondent of PLINY (2) the Younger, married a daughter of SENECIO, and *c.*140 showed MARCUS AURELIUS his fruit trees.

Fannia, a daughter of THRASEA Paetus, married *c.*AD 55 HELVIDIUS (1) Priscus, a notable opponent of the imperial regime of VESPASIAN, as his second wife. She must have shared his political views and the exile he consequently suffered.

Fannius, Gaius (late C2 BC), was a Roman historian; he had military experience at Carthage in 146 and in Spain in 141. He served as tribune and praetor and with Gaius GRACCHUS (1)'s help was elected consul for 122, when he turned his coat and spoke out against Gaius Gracchus' Italian legislation. His *History,* which treated of the events of his own time, was admired by CICERO (1), BRUTUS (5) and SALLUST, but only fragments survive.

Fausta 1. The daughter of SULLA (2); she was born *c.*88 BC and for a time was the ward of LUCULLUS (2). She was married in 72 to Gaius MEMMIUS (2) and in 54 to T. Annius MILO. She was said to have committed adultery with the historian SALLUST.

2. was the daughter of MAXIMIAN and wife of the emperor CONSTANTINE (1) I. After a long engagement she was married to Constantine in AD 307 and received the title *Augusta* in 325. She developed a close relationship with her mother-in-law HELENA: both were Christians. In the following year, arising from a scandal which is unclear to us, she and her stepson Crispus, Constantine's eldest son, were executed by her husband.

Faustina 1, Annia Galeria ('Faustina the Elder') (died AD 141), was the daughter of M. Annius VERUS and aunt of the emperor MARCUS AURELIUS. She married the emperor ANTONINUS Pius *c.*110. She bore him two sons and two daughters, the most conspicuous being FAUSTINA (2) the Younger. She received the title *Augusta* in 138 on her husband's accession and on her death was deified and eventually shared with her husband a temple in the Roman Forum, part of which still stands. Antoninus named a charity for poor girls after her.

2, Annia Galeria ('Faustina the Younger') (*c.*AD 130–175), was the wife of the emperor MARCUS AURELIUS and younger daughter of FAUSTINA (1) and ANTONINUS Pius. HADRIAN wished her to marry Lucius VERUS, the son of his intended successor, but after the emperor's death in AD 138 she was betrothed by her father the emperor to Marcus Aurelius, whom she married in 145. She bore him thirteen children and was given the title *Augusta* in 146 after the birth of the first of her children, a daughter. Other children were LUCILLA, born in 148, and the future emperor COMMODUS, born in 161. Her vivacious character was in contrast to her husband's austerity and she was even accused, probably falsely, of treacherously supporting the revolt of AVIDIUS CASSIUS. She accompanied her husband on his campaigns on the northern and eastern frontiers between 170 and 175 and died in Cappadocia. Her husband, who had given her the title 'Mother of the Camp' in 174, deified her and founded a charity for poor girls in her name.

Favorinus (*c.*AD 80–*c.*150) was a teacher of philosophy and rhetoric from Arles in Provence. A congenital eunuch, he received a Greek education at Marseille, proceeding to Rome where he became a pupil and friend of DIO CHRYSOSTOM of Prusa. He travelled in Greece and Asia Minor, teaching and displaying his oratorical powers. He became a friend of the historical writer PLUTARCH and taught HERODES (2) Atticus, FRONTO, and Aulus GELLIUS (1). HADRIAN became his patron and promoted him to the equestrian rank but he was replaced *c.*130 in the emperor's favour by his rival, POLEMO (2), and went into exile in Chios. He was restored to favour by the emperor ANTONINUS Pius. The titles of about thirty of his works are known though little survives. Two speeches (37 and 64) ascribed to Dio are probably Favorinus' work. Other titles include: *On Fleeing*, *The Corinthian*, *On Fate* and *Memoirs*. See G.W. Bowersock (1969) *Greek Sophists in the Roman Empire*, Oxford: Clarendon Press.

Felix, Marcus Antonius (or Claudius) (C1 AD), was a Greek freedman and provincial governor. As the freed slave of ANTONIA (2) her son, the emperor CLAUDIUS (1) knew him and appointed him and his brother PALLAS to administrative posts. In 52 he was sent to govern Samaria and, after the trial of Ventidius Cumanus, became procurator of the whole of Judaea. He retained this post until 60 and had to deal with unrest and rioting between Jews (probably diaspora Jews) and Greeks in Caesarea, the administrative capital. The Jews complained of him to NERO (1), who acquitted him. Shortly after taking office he married DRUSILLA, the daughter of king Marcus AGRIPPA (3) I, after persuading her to leave her husband, king Azizus of Emesa. He had previously been married to a granddaughter of ANTONIUS (7) and CLEOPATRA (4). He sat in judgment on PAUL, whom he refused to release (*Acts of the Apostles*, 23, 24), probably thinking him too dangerous. TACITUS (1) (*Annals*, 12, 54) condemns his cruelty and lust.

Fenestella (C1 BC and AD) was a Roman historian and antiquarian, fragments of whose writings survive: he wrote the history of Rome in twenty-two books as well as works on political and social matters. He was used as a source by PLINY (1) the Elder.

Festus 1, Sextus Pompeius (C2 AD), was a scholar who wrote an abridgment in twenty books of the lexographical work of VERRIUS FLACCUS, *On the Meanings of Words*, the second half of which survives.

2, Porcius (died AD 62), was a procurator (governor) of Judaea, in which he succeeded FELIX *c.*60. He had to deal with a discontented province, Jewish terrorists and a messianic prophet, and was involved in the quarrel of the Jews and AGRIPPA (4) II. He sent PAUL to Rome for trial before the emperor NERO (1) (*Acts of the Apostles*, 24, 25). He died in office.

Figulus, Publius Nigidius (C1 BC), was a scholar and mystic: GELLIUS (1) described him as the most learned of Romans apart from VARRO (3). He held the praetorship in 58 BC, was a friend of CICERO (1), and sided with POMPEIUS (2) in the Civil War. In 48 he was captured at the battle of Pharsalus and banished by CAESAR (1), to die in exile in 45. He was a student of Pythagorean philosophy and tried to revive it by his writings, from which he derived a reputation as a magician. He also wrote on grammar, religion (*On the Gods*), and natural science. Fragments of his work survive, edited by A. Swoboda. See E. Rawson (1985) *Intellectual Life in the Late Roman Republic*, London: Duckworth.

Fimbria, Gaius Flavius (early C1 BC), was one of the most violent partisans of MARIUS (1) and CINNA (2), and killed several of Cinna's opponents in the civil war of 87 BC. The next year he was sent to Asia as legate to Valerius FLACCUS (8), who dismissed him for insubordination; Fimbria then persuaded his troops to kill their general Flaccus at Nicomedia and took the command himself. He invaded the province of Asia, plundered the Greek cities, and pursued war against MITHRIDATES (3) VI, whom he drove out of the province and nearly captured, being foiled by LUCULLUS (2) who, following SULLA (1)'s policy, allowed him to escape by sea. In 85 Sulla approached Fimbria at Thyatira with superior forces, forced him to suicide, and took over his two legions.

Firmicus Maternus, Julius (C4 AD), was a Syracusan astrologer. At first a Stoic, he was later converted to Christianity. He wrote *c.*337 a work in Greek on astrology in eight books entitled *Learning*. He later wrote an intolerant polemic against polytheistic religions.

Flaccus, Q. Horatius *see* HORACE.

Flaccus 1, Aulus Avillius (early C1 AD), was a noble friend of the imperial family and of the praetorian commander MACRO. He prosecuted AGRIPPINA (2) the Elder in AD 29, which led to her banishment. He was prefect of Egypt from 32 to 38, where he gained a reputation for being anti-Jewish. The leader of the Alexandrian Jews, PHILO (2), wrote a polemic against him, *Against Flaccus*. In 38 he was recalled by CALIGULA and tried and condemned to banishment to Andros, where he was subsequently murdered on the emperor's orders. His fate was probably implicated with those of his friend Macro and Gemellus (CAESAR 10), and may be connected with Philo's embassy to Caligula.

2, Quintus Fulvius (late C3 BC), was a distinguished general of the second Punic War. He was four times consul, the first time in 237 BC when he campaigned against the Gauls; he was again consul in 224, his colleague being Manlius TORQUATUS (2), when he defeated the Boii; he then held two praetorships, in 215 and 214, and was Master of the Horse in 213. He fought successfully against Hanno when he was consul in 212, capturing his camp near Beneventum, and he took Capua as proconsul in 211 after a harrowing siege. In 210 he was campaigning in Campania and held a dictatorship to run the elections. His last consulship was in 209 after which he served again as proconsul, crushing resistance among the Lucanians in southern Italy. He opposed SCIPIO (7) Africanus' expedition to Africa in 204 and died shortly afterwards.

3, Quintus Fulvius (early C2 BC), was a son of FLACCUS (2) above. While praetor in 182 BC he continued the war on the Celtiberians in Spain which Tiberius GRACCHUS (2) brought to a successful conclusion in 179. He held the consulship in 179, when he fought in Liguria, and was censor in 174. In 173 he made amends for desecrating Hera's temple at Croton by founding the temple of Equestrian Fortune. He killed himself in 172.

4, Marcus Fulvius (late C2 BC), was a supporter of Tiberius GRACCHUS (4)'s reforms. He was appointed to serve on the late Tiberius Gracchus' land commission in 130 BC and unsuccessfully proposed that the Italian allies be given Roman citizenship so as to obtain rights to public land. Elected consul for 125, he was forestalled from carrying out his proposal by the opposition of the Senate, which sent him to the aid of Massilia (Marseille) against the Ligurians. As a result of his success in this war he held a triumph in 123. In 122, however, he lowered himself to the office of tribune along with Gaius GRACCHUS (1) in order once again to reintroduce this and other radical policies. This led to their deaths the following year at the hands of a senatorial posse, led by the consul OPIMIUS, which was appointed to tackle the perceived threat, when the reformers, now out of office, resorted to violence. See D. Stockton (1979) *The Gracchi*, Oxford: Clarendon Press.

5, Gaius Valerius, *see* VALERIUS FLACCUS.

6, Lucius Valerius (died 180 BC), governed Sicily as praetor in 199 and was the colleague of CATO (4) (whose patron he was) in the consulship in 195 and in 184 in the office of censor. He defeated Celtic incursions in 195 and subdued the Insubres in 194, and fought in Greece in 191 at Cato's side in the second battle of Thermopylae. Appointed to a board of three to establish colonies in Cisalpine Gaul, he founded Bononia (Bologna) and reinforced Cremona and Placentia.

7, Lucius Valerius (early C1 BC), was a supporter first of MARIUS (1) and later of SULLA (2). Though prosecuted in 101 BC for corruption in his praetorship, he held the consulship in 100 as Marius' colleague – he was accused by Rutilius RUFUS (4) as being more Marius' slave than colleague – when he assisted Marius in tackling the excesses of SATURNINUS (2). He was censor in 97 with Marcus ANTONIUS (5) and enrolled many Italians into the citizenship. In 86 he became leader of the Senate and tried to conciliate Sulla, whom he eventually joined. As *interrex* he won him indemnity from prosecution from the proscriptions of his enemies and the position of dictator, himself becoming his Master of the Horse (second-in-command). His subsequent history is unknown.

8, Lucius Valerius (early C1 BC), governed Asia as propraetor and was suffect consul in 86 BC after Marius' death. He led an army against MITHRIDATES (3) VI, and on arrival in Bithynia was assassinated at Nicomedia in a mutiny of his troops led by FIMBRIA.

9, Lucius Valerius (C1 BC), a son of FLACCUS (8), was serving under his father in 86, and on his father's murder fled to his uncle in Gaul. He followed a military career in Cilicia, Spain and Crete, and was city praetor in 63 BC when he supported CICERO (1)'s action against Catiline's conspiracy. Cicero repaid him by defending him against a charge of corruption during his governorship of Asia (62–61) in a speech which has mostly survived. After serving in Macedonia as legate under PISO (6), he returned to Rome and died in 54.

Flamininus, Titus Quinctius (*c.*228–174 BC), was a general, statesman and philhellene. After serving at Tarentum he held the consulship in 198 when only thirty; and was sent to fight PHILIP (1) V in the Second Macedonian War. He won the support of the Greeks and in 197 defeated the king decisively at Cynoscephalae in Thessaly. After the imposition of harsh terms on Philip, Flamininus attended the Isthmian Games in 196 where he announced to the assembled Greeks that henceforth they would enjoy autonomy. In 195 he forced NABIS, the tyrant of Sparta, to give up Argos and in 194, after seeing to the application of the settlement with Macedonia, he withdrew Roman troops from Greece to the plaudits of the inhabitants. But the Romans could not stay permanently out of Greece (in 193 and 192 he overthrew Nabis of Sparta) and in 190 war broke out with ANTIOCHUS (1) III. The latter had been invited into Greece by the Aetolians, whom Flamininus met on a diplomatic mission which received a hostile response, though he succeeded in persuading the Greek cities to refuse cooperation with Antiochus; he also kept Philip in the pro-Roman camp. He persuaded the Greek states to accept a truce. He held the censorship in 189 when he and his colleague MARCELLUS (5) restored citizenship rights to the Campanians. In 183 he went to Bithynia on an embassy to king PRUSIAS (1) I to demand the surrender of HANNIBAL. Plutarch wrote a life of Flamininus, which survives. See E. Badian (1970) *Titus Quinctius Flamininus: Philhellenism and Realpolitik*, Cincinnati: Cincinnati University Press; E.S. Gruen (1984) *The Hellenistic World and the Coming of Rome*, Berkeley: University of California Press.

Flaminius, Gaius (late C3 BC), was a 'new man'. As tribune of the *plebs* in 232 BC he carried a land law in the teeth of bitter opposition from the Senate to distribute newly acquired public land, confiscated from the Senones along the east coast of central Italy, in small lots to the poor citizenry of Rome. He was praetor in 227 when he governed Sicily and won commendation from the islanders. He held his first consulship in 223 when he led an army across the Po to defeat the Gallic Insubres and receive the honour of a triumph by popular demand. In 221 he was second-in-command (Master of the Horse) when his enemy FABIUS (8) Maximus was dictator, and when censor in 220 he constructed the road that is named after him, the *Via Flaminia*, from Rome to Ariminum (Rimini) and the *Circus Flaminius* in Rome. He was the only senator to support the Claudian Law of 218, which regulated the senators' commercial opportunities. He was re-elected consul for 217, when his army was ambushed by Hannibal at Lake Trasimene, and he died a heroic death in battle. The Roman sources, pro-senatorial and aristocratic in tendency, vilified him and adversely coloured the record of his achievements. See J.F. Lazenby (1978) *Hannibal's War*, Warminster: Aris & Phillips.

Flavia Julia (died *c.*AD 90) was a daughter of the emperor TITUS and his first wife Arrecina Tertulla. She married her cousin Flavius SABINUS (3), who was later put to death for treason. She then became the mistress of his killer, her uncle, the emperor DOMITIAN, with whom she lived until her death, caused by an abortion which he forced on her, when he accorded her divine honours.

Flavius, Gnaeus (late C4 BC), was a legal expert and politician, whose father, having been a freedman of Appius CLAUDIUS (4) the Blind, obtained or was given a copy of the latter's work on *Legal Procedures*. This he (the son) published with or without its author's permission, thus opening up to ordinary citizens legal business, which had previously been the monopoly of the priests. The act made Flavius popular and he was elected to the tribunate and the consulship despite his low birth. He was curule aedile in 304 and posted the calendar of court-days on which litigation was permissible.

Flavius *see* CLEMENS, SABINUS (2, 3).

Florianus, Marcus Annius (reigned AD 276), perhaps half-brother of the emperor TACITUS (2), had been the prefect of his Praetorian Guard. In mid-276, after Tacitus' death at Tyana, he seized power as his successor. He won wide recognition but was opposed by PROBUS (1), who was in control of Syria and Egypt. Probus overthrew him, after a couple of months' rule, at Tarsus in Asia Minor, not by confronting him but by avoiding battle and so demoralising his troops that they murdered Florianus in the autumn of that year.

Florus 1, Gessius (C1 AD), was of Greek origin from Clazomenae, married to Cleopatra, a friend of POPPAEA. He was appointed by NERO (1) in 64 to rule Judaea as its procurator. The floodgate of Jewish anger at Roman oppression broke during his brief and cruel period of office. In 66 there was rioting in Caesarea and Jerusalem as a result of Roman interference in the Jewish cult, and the Roman garrison of Masada was massacred. The stronghold of Jerusalem was besieged and taken by the rebels. Florus summoned the aid of the governor of Syria, who brought an army, but failed to act because winter was at hand: Nero then appointed VESPASIAN as commander of three legions, charged with the task of putting down the insurrection.

2, Publius Annius (C1–2 AD), was a Roman poet and rhetorician. He wrote a partially extant dialogue entitled *Virgil: Orator or Poet?*, in which he gives biographical facts about himself: born in Africa, he took part in a competition in Rome organised by DOMITIAN, and left Italy for Spain where he established a rhetorical school at Tarraco. If he is the same person as HADRIAN's friend he must have returned to Italy and become familiar with that emperor. A small selection of his poetry survives: twenty-six lines *On the Quality of Life*, a few lines on *Roses*, and epigrammatic lampoons of Hadrian addressed to that emperor.

3, Lucius Annaeus, *or* Julius (mid-C2 AD), was a Roman historical writer, often identified with FLORUS (2). He was the author of an extant epitome of Roman history down to the time of AUGUSTUS, entitled *An Abridgment of All the Wars of 700 Years*, mainly derived from LIVY and SALLUST, with material from CAESAR (1) and reminiscences of LUCAN and SENECA (2). The tone is highly patriotic. He claims to be writing not much less than 200 years after the time of Augustus.

4, Julius, *see* SACROVIR.

Fonteius, Marcus (C1 BC), was a Roman politician. He switched sides from CINNA (2) to SULLA (2), fought in Spain and Macedonia, and was propraetor of Transalpine Gaul (Provence). On his return in 72 BC he was accused of extortion and defended by CICERO (1). We do not know the outcome of the trial.

Frontinus, Sextus Julius (C1 AD), was a general and writer on strategy and engineering. Born perhaps in Gaul *c.*AD 30, he was urban praetor in 70 and was involved in the suppression of CIVILIS' rebellion. After being suffect consul *c.*73, he governed Britain until 78; he extended the province, which was still restricted to the south of the island, by subduing the Silurians of South Wales and establishing a legion at Exeter. He held a further suffect consulship in 98 and was distinguished by holding a full consulship with TRAJAN in 100. NERVA (4) put him in charge of Rome's water supplies in 97 as a result of which he wrote a treatise *On Rome's Water Supply* in two volumes which survives. He also wrote *Strategems* in four volumes which survive, a manual for the would-be successful general with illustrations from history; two volumes on land surveying, now mostly lost; and a book *On Warfare*, also lost but used as a source by Vegetius. Some doubt is cast on the authenticity of his *Strategems*. See A.T. Hodge (1992) *Roman Aqueducts*, London: Duckworth.

Fronto, Marcus Cornelius (*c.*AD 100–*c.*170), was an orator and teacher, born at Cirta in Numidia, who went to Rome for the standard education in rhetoric of his day. He was sufficiently noble to enter the political career at Rome, and was suffect consul in 143. He had already been appointed by ANTONINUS Pius tutor to MARCUS AURELIUS and Lucius VERUS, and remained close to the imperial family until his death. Part of his correspondence with Marcus Aurelius was discovered in the nineteenth century, and reveals something of the domestic life of the imperial family as well as delving into topics of rhetoric and language. His disapproval of Marcus' adherence to Stoicism, which he himself deprecated, and his criticism of the unfeeling coldness of upper-class Roman society, especially at court, are clear from the letters. He also wrote of literature, preferring the earlier authors, CATO (4) the Censor, PLAUTUS, ENNIUS and SALLUST. He was lukewarm towards CICERO (1), whom he accuses of using banal diction in his speeches, though he admired the letters, and he condemned outright the more recent Silver Latin writers LUCAN and SENECA (2).

Except for some fragments, his speeches have not survived. A learned man, he attempted to open up the Latin language to new influences and to a more varied syntax and richer vocabulary than Cicero had used, and breathed new life into it. The new style was named the *elocutio novella* and was also used by GELLIUS (1) and APULEIUS. He was opposed to Christianity, and in a lost speech used by MINUCIUS (2) Felix he accused the Christians of ritual incest and murder. We do not know how this speech was connected with Marcus' persecution of Christians. See M.D. Brock (1911) *Studies in Fronto and his Age*, Cambridge: Cambridge University Press.

Fulvia (died 40 BC) was an influential and ambitious woman, the daughter of Marcus Fulvius Bambalio and Sempronia. She inherited fortunes from both parents, and married successively Publius CLODIUS, CURIO (2) and ANTONIUS (7). By her first husband she had a son, Publius, and a daughter, Claudia, who was married in 43 to Octavian (see AUGUSTUS) but abandoned untouched when Octavian quarrelled with Antonius in 41. To Curio she bore a son whom Octavian executed after the battle of Actium. She was widowed again in 49 and at some date thereafter married Antonius, to whom she bore two sons, Marcus and Iullus (see ANTONIUS 8, ANTONIUS 3). After playing a part in the campaign of Perusia (Perugia) in 41 BC, she fled to Antonius in Greece but received a cold reception from him, and died at Sicyon, leaving her husband free to marry OCTAVIA (2).

Fundanius, Gaius (late C1 BC), was a writer of comedy and a protégé of MAECENAS; HORACE admired him and put into his mouth the account of the dinner party of Nasidienus in *Satires*, 2. 8. See also *Sat.*, 1. 10, 40ff.

Fundanus, Gaius Minicius (early C2 AD), held a suffect consulship in AD 107 and was proconsul of Asia in 122 where he received a reply (rescript) to a letter written by his predecessor to HADRIAN about the legal position of Christians: they were not to be condemned merely on the grounds of their religion. He was a friend of PLINY (2) the Younger and of PLUTARCH.

Furius 1, Aulus, of Antium (early C1 BC), was a Roman poet who, under the influence of ENNIUS, wrote a historical epic in eleven books entitled *Annals*, of which six lines survive. He was a friend of CATULUS (3) and influenced the work of VIRGIL.

2. Philus, Lucius (C2 BC), was a scholar and politician; a member of the circle of friends of SCIPIO (11) Aemilianus. He was consul in 136 BC and, when the Senate refused to accept a treaty made with the people of the Spanish city of Numantia in 137, he sent the maker of the treaty, MANCINUS, back to Numantia.

See also BIBACULUS, TIMESITHEUS.

Furnius 1, Gaius (C1 BC), was an orator and politician and a supporter of ANTONIUS (7). He was a protégé of CICERO (1) who joined CAESAR (1) and in 44 BC was a legate of PLANCUS (1) in Gaul. During the Perusine War of 41 BC he tried to hold Sentinum but was defeated by SALVIDIENUS RUFUS; he escaped from Perusia. In 35 he acted as governor of Asia for Antonius. He was among the followers of Antonius whom Octavian spared after the battle of Actium on the plea of his son FURNIUS (2) and granted him the rank of a consular in 29.

2, Gaius, was a son of FURNIUS (1). He used his influence with Octavian (see AUGUSTUS) to secure his father's life after Actium, and was consul in 17 BC.

Fuscus, Cornelius (mid-C1 AD), chose an equestrian career though being of senatorial family and supported GALBA (1) in AD 68, for which he was appointed procurator of Illyricum. In 69 he threw in his lot with VESPASIAN and helped his generals invade Italy. DOMITIAN made him commander of the Praetorian Guard and sent him in 85 to Moesia to withstand a Dacian invasion of the province led by DECEBALUS. After successfully restoring the position, the following year he unsuccesfully invaded Dacia and was killed in the rout of his army.

G

Gabinius 1, Aulus (C2 BC), was a politician who was of humble origins, his grandfather being a freed slave. He served in Macedonia and Greece from 148 to 146 BC; as tribune in 139 he passed a law introducing the secret ballot at elections for officers of state.

2, Aulus (C1 BC), was a Roman politician and supporter of POMPEIUS (2) and later CAESAR (1), probably a grandson of GABINIUS (1). He married Lollia, a daughter of PALICANUS. As tribune in 67 BC he transferred Bithynia and the army commanded by LUCULLUS (2) to GLABRIO (3) and carried a law granting Pompeius an unlimited and overriding command against the pirates who plagued the waters of the Mediterranean. From 66 to 63 he acted as legate to Pompeius in his eastern command, and was consul in 58 when he resisted CICERO (1)'s appeal for assistance against CLODIUS. From 57 to 54 he governed Syria, the bribe with which Clodius had obtained his compliance. He reorganised Judaea and installed ANTIPATER (2) in power with HYRCANUS (2) as high priest. In 55 for a huge bribe he restored PTOLEMY (12) the Piper to the throne of Egypt and he took the side of the provincials against the Roman tax-gatherers. On his return to Rome he was therefore prosecuted on three counts: being acquitted of treason, he was defended reluctantly by Cicero on a charge of extortion, found guilty, and went into exile; a charge of electoral bribery by SULLA (3) was dropped. Caesar recalled him to public life in 49 and appointed him as his legate in Illyricum, where he died at Salonae (Split) in 47.

Gaetulicus *see* LENTULUS (5).

Gaius (mid-C2 AD) was the first name of a Roman jurist and prolific writer on Roman law who wrote an elementary legal treatise in four books named the *Institutes* (*Institutionum Commentarii Quattuor*), probably published *c.*162. The work, of striking clarity and economy, is not cited by his contemporaries or by the writers of subsequent times much before the fifth century AD. His work was, however, admired and used by the emperor Justinian who brought it up to date and established it as authoritative. It is the most substantial classical work on Roman law to have survived, its text (as revised by Justinian's experts) having been discovered at Verona in 1816 by Niebuhr. Gaius also wrote *Everyday Matters*, which expands the often brief and incomplete statements of the *Institutes*, and voluminous commentaries on the praetors' edicts (*The Provincial Edict* and *The City Praetor's Edict*) which formed the basis of much of the private civil law, and on the ancient *Law of the Twelve Tables* of Roman civil law. It appears unlikely that Gaius, though a Roman citizen, ever held an official post. After studying at Rome in the Sabinian law school, he seems to have lived and worked in the east, perhaps in Beirut or Smyrna. His works were cited more than 500 times by the compilers of Justinian's code, and his classifications were fundamental to the European legal systems until the early nineteenth century. See A.M. (Tony) Honoré (1962) *Gaius, a Biography*, Oxford: Clarendon Press.

Galba 1, Servius Sulpicius (*c.*3 BC–AD 69), was emperor for six months in AD 68–69. He was the son of Gaius Sulpicius Galba and his wife Mummia. His father's second wife, Livia Ocellina, adopted him and he became a valued friend of all the emperors from AUGUSTUS to CLAUDIUS (1). Having been praetor in AD 20 and governor of Aquitania, he held the consulship in AD 33; CALIGULA appointed him legate of Upper Germany after the rebellion of LENTULUS (5). In 45 Claudius appointed him as proconsul of Africa and in 60 NERO (1) recalled him from retirement to put him in charge of the province of Hispania Tarraconensis in eastern Spain, where he remained until 68. In March of that year VINDEX, governor of Gaul, rebelled and invited Galba to become emperor, but he refrained from action except to allow his troops to declare him 'legate of the Senate and People of Rome'. Meanwhile Vindex's revolt was crushed by Verginius RUFUS (5), and the army in general and the Praetorian Guard in particular, led by its commander NYMPHIDIUS SABINUS, rejected the rule of the unstable Nero. Sabinus invited Galba to become emperor and in his name promised the soldiers a huge bribe. Galba took the title *Caesar* and the Senate confirmed his appointment; Nero killed himself on 9 June and Galba set out for Rome in the company of OTHO, governor of Lusitania. Sabinus, who now claimed the imperial title, was killed by his troops, and Galba arrived at Rome in October.

Galba proceeded to disappoint everybody, refusing to pay the soldiers their bribe, massacring a party of marines, and preferring to adopt L. Calpurnius PISO (9) as his son and heir rather than Otho, who rebelled. Galba had a number of Nero's freedmen and advisers executed and replaced Verginius Rufus as governor of Upper Germany, thus weakening control over the powerful armies of the Rhine frontier. In January 69 these forces refused to swear loyalty to Galba and proclaimed VITELLIUS (1), while the Praetorian Guard, under Otho's influence, seized Galba and Piso and killed them on 15 January. He was honest and able but lacked diplomatic skills and was mean and austere. TACITUS (1)'s judgment on him was 'generally considered capable of holding power, had he not actually done so'. See Tacitus' *Histories*, 1; M. Grant (1985) *The Roman Emperors*, London: Weidenfeld & Nicolson; K. Wellesley (1975) *The Long Year, AD 69*, London: Elek.

2, Gaius Sulpicius (C2 BC), was a son of GALBA (3) who allied himself by marriage to the Gracchi, taking as his wife Licinia, elder daughter of Publius CRASSUS (5) in 143: her sister married Gaius GRACCHUS (1). He may have served on the Gracchan land commissions in Italy and Africa. In 110 he was found guilty of corruption in the war with JUGURTHA by the commission established by MAMILIUS (1): his defence speech was greatly admired in CICERO (1)'s time.

3. Maximus, Publius Sulpicius (C3–2 BC) A soldier, statesman and diplomat who was elected consul for 211 BC without serving in the lower posts, and successfully defended Rome against a surprise attack by HANNIBAL. He held a proconsular command in Greece from 210 to 206 when he fought PHILIP (1) V of Macedonia (the First Macedonian War) with scant success, though he took Aegina in a naval assault. He was elected dictator in 203, probably to supervise the holding of elections. He held a second consulship in 200 when he commanded Roman armies in the Second Macedonian War: he attacked Macedonia from the west and won the support of the Aetolians, but retired to Illyria for the winter. In 197 he served as legate to FLAMININUS, on a board of ten commissioners appointed to settle Greece in 196, and as an ambassador to ANTIOCHUS (1) III in 193.

4, Servius Sulpicius (C2 BC), was praetor in Further Spain in 151 and 150 BC when, with the support of Lucius LUCULLUS (1), he killed a group of Lusitani who were suing for peace, for which he was prosecuted in 149. CATO (4) the Censor, now in his nineties, spoke up for the oppressed provincials but to no avail: Galba paraded his family in mourning before the Assembly and gained acquittal. He was consul in 144.

5, Servius Sulpicius (C1 BC), was a supporter of CAESAR (1) who became one of his assassins. He fought in Gaul from 62 to 56 BC as a legate under Pomptinus and Caesar, and was praetor in 54. He failed to be elected consul in 50. After joining the plot to assassinate Caesar in 44, he fought against ANTONIUS (7) in 43 at the battle of Forum Gallorum and was outlawed as a murderer of Caesar by the Law of PEDIUS (1). He sent an account of the battle to CICERO (1).

Galen (AD 129–*c.*199) was a Greek physician, anatomist, and writer on medicine and philosophy. He was born at Pergamon in Asia Minor, the son of Nicon, a rich well educated architect, who gave him an excellent education in rhetoric, philosophy and mathematics. When he was sixteen his father, under the influence of dreams, transferred him to the study of medicine in the precinct of the god Asclepius at Pergamon (which contained a facility for dream-cures), and after his father's death he pursued his medical studies at Smyrna, Corinth and Alexandria. He returned to Pergamon in 157 to become doctor to the gladiatorial school, but finding this work distasteful he moved in 162 to Rome, where he quickly established a fine reputation and was in demand among the highest society. After four years, however, he had made enemies within his profession through his outspoken criticism, and withdrew to Pergamon, where he remained until 169 when the emperor MARCUS AURELIUS summoned him back to Rome, perhaps on account of the last illness of his co-emperor Lucius VERUS, to be court physician: he remained in this post during the reigns of Marcus' son COMMODUS and of Septimius SEVERUS (1). He is generally said to have died in 199, but the date is uncertain and he may have survived well into the next century.

Galen, who was deeply religious and a monotheist, wrote copiously about both medicine and philosophy. He conducted practical experiments to prove his hypotheses, such as his work on the spinal cord. He drew on all four existing schools of medicine for ideas and created a body of medical knowledge and opinion which became universally accepted and remained authoritative for more than 1,500 years. He chiefly admired Plato for his philosophy and his account of creation, and in medicine Hippocrates (insofar as the Hippocratic writings can be attributed to anybody), but was also greatly influenced by Aristotle, and in anatomy and physiology by Herophilus and Erasistratus. His approach to medicine was teleological and he sought to discover the functions and purpose of the various organs of the body; once this work had been done he found no need for further research. In his early writings he concentrated on philosophy: these works are nearly all lost, but the medical treatises are driven by his religious and philosophical ideas. He refers to Christianity and Judaism among other 'philosophies' in his writings, tending to lump them together, and criticising their irrational nature. He admired the fortitude shown by Christians meeting death in the arena. He knew the Greek writer Lucian, whom he considered to be a literary fraud. Many of his prolific medical writings survive: 350 authentic titles are known. About 100 genuine works and fragments survive: much material still awaits editing. He made important discoveries in the field of neurology and the cardiovascular system. He accepted the theory of the four humours and produced a synthesis of earlier discoveries regarding pharmacology and diet. Some of his works have come down to us in Arabic.

Galen's achievement in extending, fixing and codifying medical knowledge and in establishing an unchallenged body of scientific teaching and practice in the medical field was enormous, and it was not until the seventeenth century that his work was seriously questioned and revised. See G. Sarton (1954) *Galen of Pergamon*, Lawrence: University of Kansas Press; G.W. Bowersock (1969) *The Sophists in the Roman Empire*, Oxford: Clarendon Press.

Galerius (*c.*AD 250–311) The emperor Gaius Galerius Valerius Maximianus was born at Serdica (in modern Bulgaria) to a peasant family, and was uneducated: he joined the army and rose to be DIOCLETIAN's right-hand man. After a distinguished career under AURELIAN and PROBUS (1), he was elevated by Diocletian in 293 to the title of *Caesar*, became Diocletian's deputy in the east and divorced his wife to marry the emperor's daughter Valeria. He fought the Sarmatians on the Danube frontier in 294 and the Carpi in 295, defeating them and settling some of them in Pannonia. Next he made Thessalonica his base for war against the Persian king Narses, whose forces Galerius met at Carrhae in 297 where he was defeated. The following year, with reinforcements from the Balkans, he again moved against the Persians and won a decisive victory. Diocletian prevented him from extending the empire beyond Mesopotamia, where a fortified frontier was constructed and the instability of the previous forty years was rectified. It is thought that Galerius was behind the persecution of Christians which began with an imperial edict in February 303; he took the place of Diocletian on his abdication as *Augustus* or senior emperor of the east in May 305. He became the senior *Augustus* the following year on the death of CONSTANTIUS (1), and opposed the advancement of the latter's son CONSTANTINE (1), whom he had held at his court in Nicomedia as a virtual hostage in 305 to prevent his father Constantius from opposing him. He therefore promoted his nephew MAXIMINUS (2) Daia as his *Caesar* or deputy, and elevated his loyal follower Flavius SEVERUS (3) as *Augustus* of the west. However, he reluctantly accepted Constantine, who had been proclaimed emperor by his troops at York, as *Caesar* of the west. In 306 Galerius' son-in-law MAXENTIUS rebelled with his father Maximian's support and set himself up as emperor at Rome, controlling Italy, Spain and Africa.

In 307 Galerius ordered Severus to move against the usurper, but Severus was defeated and executed. Galerius himself then unsuccessfully invaded Italy. In 308 he called a conference at Carnuntum near the present Vienna and summoned Diocletian out of retirement to lend it his authority: LICINIUS was appointed *Augustus* of the west, Maxentius was declared a public enemy, and Constantine and Maximinus Daia were to be degraded as mere 'Sons of the Augusti', honorary titles in place of the position of deputy emperor which the title *Caesar* now conveyed. Both understandably refused the titles offered and proclaimed themselves emperors. Galerius, impotent to influence events in the west, continued to rule the east until his death, and left Maximinus as his ill established heir. Shortly before his death Galerius had rescinded the edict of persecution against the Christians and had issued a new edict granting them a measure of tolerance. His opposition to Constantine may have been motivated by anti-Christian feeling. See M. Grant (1985) *The Roman Emperors*, London: Weidenfeld & Nicolson.

Gallienus (*c.*AD 218–268), the son of VALERIAN, was taken into partnership by his father upon the latter's accession as emperor in 253 and created *Augustus* to defend the Rhine and the western part of the empire while his father faced the Persians. His full name was Publius Licinius Egnatius Gallienus. From 254 to 260 he fought a series of successful battles against the Germans, finally driving back an invasion of Italy by the Alemanni at Milan. In 259 the Goths took and briefly held Byzantium, engaging in piracy and naval warfare. Gallienus was unable to do anything to help his father in 260 when he was captured by the Persian king SAPOR (1) I, an event which destabilised the empire and left Gallienus with invasions and usurpers to deal with. These latter were somewhat humorously called the 'thirty tyrants' by the fourth-century *Historia Augusta*. In the previous year (259) POSTUMUS had set himself up as emperor of Gaul, killing Gallienus' son, and had added Spain and Britain to his realm. Gallienus was unable to shift him, and by 264 had tacitly recognised his position as ruler of the west. His strongest ally was Publius Septimius ODAENATHUS, the Roman client ruler of Palmyra in Syria, who did much to hold the line in the east while Gallienus put down the rebellions of Ingenuus in Moesia and Regalianus in Pannonia. In 260 Odaenathus diverted Sapor from invading Asia Minor by himself striking deep into Mesopotamia, and in 264 he recovered Mesopotamia and put down a conspiracy in Syria of two Roman officers, Macrianus and Ballista, who attempted to replace Gallienus with the two sons of Macrianus (see MACRIANUS, QUIETUS (2)). Gallienus consequently gave him the title *Dux Orientis* (General of the East) and recognised him as king of Palmyra; in 267 however, Odaethanus was assassinated before he could repel an attack by Goths and Heruli on Greece, which a local commander, DEXIPPUS, dealt with. In 268 Gallienus faced an insurrection in northern Italy by an officer named M. Acilius AUREOLUS who was declared emperor at Milan, where Gallienus besieged him. There his own staff, angered by his tolerance and Greek sympathies, assassinated him and replaced him with an Illyrian like themselves, CLAUDIUS (2) II. Gallienus was hated by the senate of his day, but conducted a military reform, including the enhancement of the role of cavalry, which enabled his successors to build an army capable of defending the fissiparous structure of the empire. See M. Grant (1985) *The Roman Emperors*, London: Weidenfeld & Nicolson.

Gallio, Lucius Annaeus Novatus (died AD 65), born at Corduba in Spain, was the eldest son of M. Annaeus SENECA (1) and brother of the philosopher Lucius Annaeus SENECA (2). However, he was adopted by the orator and senator L. Junius Gallio, whose name he took. He was exiled in AD 41 and recalled in 49 with his brother. He was *c.*52 proconsul of Achaea, Greece, when he dismissed a charge brought by the Jews at Corinth against PAUL (*Acts of the Apostles*, 18). He was suffect consul *c.*55 and survived his brother's fall, but in 65 was forced by NERO (1) to commit suicide.

Gallus 1, Aelius, was a prefect of Egypt under AUGUSTUS. At the emperor's command he led an unsuccessful expedition against Arabia Felix in the years 25 and 24 BC. He was a friend of STRABO, the writer on geography, and probably adopted the son of Seius Strabo, commander of the Praetorian Guard, the notorious SEJANUS. He also wrote on medicine.

2, Gaius Asinius (41 BC–AD 33), was a Roman politician, the son of C. Asinius POLLIO (1). In 12 BC he married AGRIPPA (1)'s daughter Vipsania when TIBERIUS was forced by AUGUSTUS to divorce her, and so earned the future emperor's hatred. He had five sons by her. Admired by Augustus, he held the consulship in 8 BC and governed Asia as proconsul in 6. At the accession of Tiberius in AD 14 he spoke offensively of the new emperor, who nursed his resentment and, in 30, when Gallus was seventy-one, threw him into prison where he languished for three years, finally starving himself to death. Gallus was the author of a work on CICERO (1), *A Comparison of Cicero and my Father*, which was critical of the former, and to which the emperor CLAUDIUS (1) wrote a rejoinder.

3, Flavius Claudius Constantius (C4 AD), was the son of Julius Constantius and Galla, and the half-brother of JULIAN. He was born in Etruria in AD 325. Having survived the massacre of CONSTANTINE (1)'s kinsmen in 337, he was brought up with Julian in exile in Cappadocia from which CONSTANTIUS (2) II recalled him in 351 and appointed him *Caesar* of the east. He had a brief and bloody reign based at Antioch from 351 to 354, where he resisted Persian incursions and a Jewish rebellion. He was then recalled and executed. He had married the sister of Constantius, Constantina.

4, Gaius Cornelius (*c*.69–26 BC), was a prefect of Egypt and a poet, born at Fréjus in southern Gaul, perhaps of Gallic blood. He was a friend of Octavian (see AUGUSTUS), VIRGIL and PARTHENIUS, who dedicated to him an extant collection of obscure legends for Gallus to use as subject matter for poetry. He was a friend of C. Asinius POLLIO (1) and probably served on his staff in Gaul in 41, when he seems to have used his influence to spare Virgil's farm near Mantua from the confiscation of land for veterans in that year. He spent the next few years in the east with ANTONIUS (7); but in 30 BC as aide-de-camp (*praefectus fabrum*) of Octavian's army, he took over Antonius' four legions in Cyrenaica, occupied Paraetonium on the coast west of Alexandria, defeated Antonius and captured CLEOPATRA (4). His work in planning a forum in Egypt was commemorated on an obelisk that was later moved to Rome. Octavian appointed him the first prefect or governor of Egypt, a new role in which he answered to the emperor alone. He did useful work in subduing Egyptian rebellions (including one in the Thebaid in 29) and moving south beyond the first cataract to meet the king of the Ethiopians at Philae, and receive him into the protection of Rome. He established a buffer zone between the two countries and appointed its ruler. He then behaved arrogantly, setting up inscriptions of his exploits and statues of himself at many places, for which Augustus recalled him *c*.27 and renounced his friendship. He became liable to prosecution, perhaps for treason, and committed suicide. As a poet he was greatly admired by his contemporaries, Virgil above all. OVID in the next generation considered him the greatest composer of Latin elegiac poetry, but only a few indifferent lines of his work have survived.

He wrote four books of love-elegies entitled *Loves* (*Amores*): he addressed them, under the pseudonym Lycoris, to his mistress Volumnia or Cytheris, an actress who had once been involved with Antonius; he also wrote miniature epics (epyllia). Virgil wrote on the unrequited love of Gallus in his tenth *Eclogue*, and seems to have included in the poem a few lines reminiscent of Gallus' own lines. See D.D. Ross (1975) *Backgrounds to Augustan Poetry: Gallus, Elegy and Rome*, Cambridge: Cambridge University Press.

5, Aulus Didius (C1 AD), was suffect consul in 39 and governor of Moesia *c*.46, when he made an expedition to the Crimea. There he installed Cotys as client king of the Bosporus, which included the Crimea and adjacent territories around Lake Maiotis. For this success CLAUDIUS (1) awarded him triumphal decorations. He held further governorships, the proconsulship of Asia, and the governorship of Britain from 52 to 58, where he retrieved a difficult situation left by his predecessor, OSTORIUS SCAPULA, tackled the continuing resistance of the Silures, and founded a legionary fortress at Usk for the Twentieth Legion. He adopted Fabricius VEIENTO as his son.

6, Gaius Lucretius (C2 BC), in 171 BC as praetor led a fleet against the Macedonian king PERSEUS. His behaviour towards Greek allies of Rome was high-handed and on his return he was convicted of extortion and fined.

7, Gaius Sulpicius (C2 BC) After serving as city praetor in 169, while serving as military tribune in the army of Aemilius PAULLUS (2) in 168, he predicted, or explained, a lunar eclipse before the battle of Pydna. He met with Paullus' anger in 167 for laxness in guarding the captive king Perseus. He was consul in 166 when he held a triumph over the Ligurians, and led an embassy to Pergamon in 164, working against king EUMENES II and encouraging the Greeks of the Achaean Confederacy to rebel, for which POLYBIUS condemned him.

8, Gaius Vibius Trebonianus (mid-C3 AD), was emperor from AD 251 till 253. Under his predecessor DECIUS, Gallus was military governor of Moesia in the Balkans, and in 251 was proclaimed emperor by his troops when Decius was killed at Abrittus near the lower Danube, in battle with the Goths under Kniva. In 252 he bought peace with the Gothic invaders but in the following year they invaded Moesia again. The Persians also attacked the province of Syria. Gallus had gone to Rome to receive the Senate's recognition, and meanwhile the new commander of the army in Moesia, M. Aemilius AEMILIANUS, had defeated and expelled the Goths, and was proclaimed emperor by his troops. Gallus by this time had lost his troops' support and was murdered together with his son and colleague Volusianus during a battle at Interamna near Rome. See M. Grant (1985) *The Roman Emperors*, London: Weidenfeld & Nicolson.

See also ROSCIUS (2).

Gellius 1, Aulus (*c.*AD 130–*c.*180), was a Latin writer, born in Rome, where he studied under Sulpicius Apollinaris and knew FRONTO and FAVORINUS. He went to Athens for further study where he visited HERODES (2) ATTICUS. As a young man he practised law as a private arbitrator in Rome and he married and had a family.

His great work is the *Attic Nights* in twenty books, of which nineteen survive: a collection of notes and aphorisms on literary and other topics, written in his later years but the fruit of many years of collecting. It was originally composed with the aim of educating and entertaining his children. Its greatest value for us lies in its wealth of quotations from earlier authors, which often allow a glimpse of otherwise unknown works. He had a marked preference for the archaic writers, but not to the exclusion of great names such as CICERO (1) and VIRGIL. The book has much charm, and though its organization is somewhat haphazard, the individual chapters are carefully constructed. His work was esteemed by later generations, including the Middle Ages, which accounts for its preservation. Only book 8 is missing, though we have its chapter headings. The work owes its title to Gellius' having begun his collection of material during the winter nights he spent in Athens in his youth, as his preface confirms. See L.A. Holford-Strevens (1988) *Aulus Gellius*, London: Duckworth.

2, Gnaeus (late C2 BC), was an annalist of whose work some fragments survive.

He wrote a history of Rome from the beginnings to 146 BC in about forty books, of which fragments remain, in greater detail than his predecessors. DIONYSIUS of Halicarnassus used his work as a source.

3, Lucius (*c*.136–51 BC), was praetor in 94 with jurisdiction over non-citizens. The following year he acted as proconsul of a province in the east. He fought in the Social War under POMPEIUS (5) Strabo and was consul in 72, when he was defeated by SPARTACUS. With his colleague Cornelius LENTULUS (3) he had a law passed allowing commanders to confer Roman citizenship on soldiers distinguished for bravery. He was censor with Lentulus in 70, when they purged the Senate of sixty-four corrupt members. He was POMPEIUS (2)'s legate in 67 in the war with the pirates, supported CICERO (1) against CATILINE, and adopted a Valerius Messalla as his son.

Gemellus *see* CAESAR (10).

Genucius, Lucius (C4 BC), was a tribune of the *plebs* to whom are attributed three laws passed in 342 BC, one forbidding temporary loans being made at interest to relieve the pressure of social difficulties, another forbidding office-holders to be re-elected within ten years, and the third prescribing the election of at least one plebeian to the consulship. The authenticity of the two latter enactments is doubtful.

Germanicus, Julius Caesar (15 BC–AD 19), born Nero Claudius Germanicus on the 24 May 15, was the adopted son and heir presumptive of his uncle the emperor TIBERIUS. His parents were the elder DRUSUS (3), brother of Tiberius and stepson of AUGUSTUS, and ANTONIA (3), daughter of ANTONIUS (7). He was adopted by Tiberius on Augustus' order in AD 4, and thus became a member of the Julian family and an acceptable heir to Augustus, who also adopted Tiberius at the same time. In his twenties he was brought into the public eye and promoted in line with Augustus' wishes by being given military commands under Tiberius in Pannonia from AD 7–9, and in Germany in 11. He held his first consulship in 12, and in 14, while proconsul of the provinces of Gaul and Germany, he coped with a mutiny of the army in lower Germany caused by unrest at Tiberius' accession. He solved the problem by granting the main demands of the disaffected men; he then led the troops into a full-scale invasion of Germany, which gained considerable success until Tiberius recalled him. During these campaigns he attacked the Marsi, Chatti and Cherusci, and was opposed by the German leader ARMINIUS. In 15 he reached the *Teutoburgiensis Saltus*, where Quinctilius VARUS had been defeated six years earlier, and buried the Roman dead, but after a further battle with the Cherusci he was harrassed on his return journey and suffered severe losses. A naval expedition in 16 through the wetlands of the Netherlands, using the canal built by Drusus, led to victories over Arminius but also to severe storm damage on the return journey. Tiberius, reviewing the situation, believed that the gains did not justify the losses, renounced the conquest of Germany, and summoned Germanicus to a triumph in Rome in May 17. Germanicus was impetuous and headstrong, and there was undoubtedly a lack of sympathy between him and the emperor.

He held a second consulship in 18 and was at the same time appointed to a new command in the east: he was to have overriding powers over all the Roman governors of the eastern provinces (except Egypt, which was the emperor's personal domain). At Nicopolis in western Greece he ceremonially crowned a new king of Armenia, ARTAXIAS (2), son of POLEMO (1) the former Pontic king, and declared Cappadocia and Commagene, hitherto client kingdoms, Roman provinces. He made a tour of Egypt in 19, largely to see the antiquities, but thereby offended Tiberius, whose permission for the visit he should have asked. After returning to Syria he quarrelled with the proconsul, Gnaeus Calpurnius PISO (4), whom Tiberius trusted and had appointed to keep a check on Germanicus, for altering some of the arrangements he had made, and ordered him to leave the province. However he himself fell ill shortly after and died at Antioch on 10 October, convinced that Piso had poisoned him. He had been very popular on account of his dashing style and military success, and was mourned with extravagant demonstrations. His ashes, conveyed to Rome by his widow, were placed in the mausoleum of Augustus.

He had married AGRIPPINA (2), the daughter of AGRIPPA (1), and JULIA (5), the daughter of Augustus, by whom he had nine children including the future emperor CALIGULA and AGRIPPINA (3), the mother of the emperor NERO (1). He was also a writer, and translated Aratus' *Phaenomena* into Latin. See R. Seager (1972) *Tiberius*, London: Eyre Methuen.

Geta 1, Gnaeus Hosidius (C1 AD), in 42 succeeded SUETONIUS (1) Paulinus as governor of Mauretania where he was involved in war with the Moor Sabalus. He later served on the staff of Aulus PLAUTIUS (1) in the invasion of Britain, and fought in the battle of the Medway. He was suffect consul *c.*AD 47, when he proposed the senatorial decree regarding urban conservation that bore his name.

2, Hosidius (C2 AD) A tragedian who wrote a 'cento' version of Euripides' play *Medea* using hexameter lines from VIRGIL, with the choral lyrics taken from final halves of lines. The work survives in the *Anthologia Latina*.

3, Lucius (later Publius) Septimius (AD 189–212), was the younger son of Septimius SEVERUS (1). His father granted him the title *Caesar* in 198 and *Augustus* in 209. He acted as governor of Britain in 209 and saw to the supply-line while his father and brother CARACALLA fought in Scotland to subjugate the Caledonii who the previous year had taken York and Chester. When Severus died in February 211 at York, his sons gave up the lands north of Hadrian's Wall for good. The brothers, who were named jointly to succeed to the purple, then returned to Rome, but were unable to collaborate despite the efforts of their mother, JULIA (10) Domna, to reconcile them. A plan to divide the empire between them failed to mature. Geta was assassinated by Caracalla.

Glabrio 1, Manius Acilius (early C2 BC), as a 'new man' in 201 BC was tribune of the *plebs* and aedile in 197. With the support of SCIPIO (7) Africanus he was elected praetor for 196 when he put down a rebellion of slaves in Etruria. As consul in 191 he defeated ANTIOCHUS (1) III at Thermopylae. He held a triumph in 190 and stood for the censorship but desisted when accused of accepting bribes.

2, Manius Acilius (late C2 BC), was a legislator, grandson of GLABRIO (1). As tribune of the *plebs* in 122 he passed a law to alter the procedure in extortion cases, enacting that the juries should consist entirely of men of the equestrian class. He was an augur, a friend and colleague of Gaius GRACCHUS (1), and he married a daughter of the jurist Q. Mucius SCAEVOLA (3).

3, Manius Acilius (C1 BC), was the son of GLABRIO (2), who in 70 BC when he was praetor in charge of the court for recovery of stolen property, presided at the trial of VERRES. As consul with C. Calpurnius PISO (1) in 67, he quarrelled publicly with the praetor LUCCEIUS and introduced the law bearing their names (*Lex Acilia Calpurnia de ambitu*) against corrupt canvassing at elections, rendering anyone found guilty ineligible for further election. The following year he was proconsul of Cilicia with command in the war against MITHRIDATES (3) VI, but proved ineffective and was succeeded by POMPEIUS (2) under the Manilian law. CICERO (1) accused him of laziness, but he held a priesthood and may have been censor in 64.

4, Manius Acilius (C1 AD), was a senator who held the consulship with the future emperor TRAJAN in AD 91. For some reason he was condemned in the same year to fight in a gladiatorial show and was exiled: he was condemned to death in 95. He may have been implicated in Christianity and may be connected with the catacomb of Priscilla.

Glaphyra 1, *see* ARCHELAUS (5).

2. was the daughter of ARCHELAUS (5), king of Cappadocia: she had three husbands, first Alexander, a son of HEROD (1) the Great, next King JUBA II, and thirdly ARCHELAUS (6), a half-brother of her first husband and the ruler (ethnarch) of Judaea from 4 BC to AD 6.

Glaucia, Gaius Servilius (died 100 BC), was an outspoken politician of the popular party: in 102 the censor METELLUS (5) Numidicus wished to expel him and SATURNINUS (2), whose partisan he was, from the senate, but was foiled by the mob they raised in their defence. In 101, when he was tribune, Glaucia passed a law to restore to the equestrian order membership of the juries in the court which tried cases of extortion. He was praetor in 100 but was prevented from standing for the consulship of 99 by the intemperate action of the tribune Saturninus, who organised a gang to murder his competitor MEMMIUS (1). MARIUS (1), to prevent further bloodshed, penned Saturninus and Glaucia in the Capitol, where they surrendered to Marius, who placed them for safety in the Senate House. Their enemies tore the roof off and pelted them to death with the tiles.

Gnipho, Marcus Antonius (C1 BC), was a Latin writer and teacher of rhetoric. He ran a school, and CICERO (1) attended his lectures on rhetoric in 66 BC while he was praetor; a work in two books entitled *On the Latin Language* is attributed to him.

Gordian The name of three emperors of the third century AD. They were father, son, and grandson: their full name was in each case Marcus Antonius Gordianus.

I (*c.*AD 159–238) was a rich and reputable man, the proconsul of Africa under MAXIMINUS (1) the Thracian. In 238, at the age of seventy-nine, he was invited to become emperor by some disaffected young noblemen who had rebelled at Thysdrus in Africa in opposition to the emperor's taxation policy. He decided to associate his son, GORDIAN II, with his power, and the Senate recognised their joint rule. The governor of the neighbouring province of Numidia, however, Capelianus, remained faithful to Maximinus, and advanced on Carthage. Gordian II led some irregular troops against Capelianus' legionaries, and was killed in battle, whereupon his father killed himself after a reign of twenty-two days.

II *see* GORDIAN I.

III (reigned AD 238–244) was the grandson of GORDIAN I by his mother Maecia Faustina. He 'reigned' for six years: he was thirteen at the time of his accession in 238. He was first appointed *Caesar* to quell the unpopularity of BALBINUS and Pupienus; then, when they were murdered by the Praetorian Guard, he was proclaimed emperor by the Guard. But his mother held the reins of government until 241 when the commander of the Praetorian Guard, TIMESITHEUS, whose daughter he married, supplanted her. In 242 he led the army against the Persians who had attacked the empire the previous year; the Romans made useful headway until the death of Timesitheus late in 243. Gordian appointed an Arab named PHILIPPUS (1) as the new prefect of the Guard: in February 244 at Zaitha the latter connived at the murder of Gordian by the soldiers who were suffering from shortage of food and despised their youthful emperor. See M. Grant (1985) *The Roman Emperors*, London: Weidenfeld & Nicolson.

Gordius (C2 BC) was a Cappadocian nobleman who acted as an agent of MITHRIDATES (3) VI of Pontus and murdered king ARIARATHES (3) VI of Cappadocia.

Gorgias (mid-C1 BC) was a Greek teacher of rhetoric from Athens. He wrote four books on figures of speech which Rutilius RUFUS (4) abridged into an extant Latin version in one book. He appears to have favoured the Asianist style. See CICERO (1), *Ad Fam.*, 16. 21, 6.

Gracchus 1, Gaius Sempronius (154–121 BC), was a politician and social reformer, the younger brother of GRACCHUS (4). He served on the land commission established under his brother's legislation in 133 when he was only twenty-one. He was an able orator and saw himself as his brother's avenger. In 134 he was in Spain where he served under his cousin SCIPIO (11) Aemilianus in the campaign at Numantia. In 126 he unsuccessfully opposed a proposal of the tribune Iunius Pennus to rid Rome of non-citizen settlers, and was sent to Sardinia as quaestor. He abandoned this post in 124 before the end of his governor's extended term of office, and had to answer to the censors for his action. He was elected tribune of the *plebs* for 123 BC and again for the following year: during this period he undertook a heavy programme of legislation the order of which we do not fully know: at his mother's instigation he dropped a proposal to ban magistrates who had been deposed by the Assembly of the People from holding any further office (an attack on OCTAVIUS [4]). He passed a retrospective measure to pronounce illegal courts which assumed the power to inflict capital punishment but were not authorised by the People; and Popillius LAENAS (3), who had executed the supporters of Tiberius Gracchus after trying them in 132 in a tribunal set up by the Senate, was himself impeached and exiled. He then renewed his brother's agrarian legislation, removing limitations imposed on the commission by Scipio Aemilianus. He also passed a bill to found new colonies of Roman citizens in Italy and thus allow more of the urban poor as well as some richer people to start a new and more productive life. He enacted the supply of grain at subsidised prices, influenced by shortages of imported cereals. By this law the state would bulk-buy grain and store it in state-owned granaries to sell it at a steady and inexorbitant price to the public. This *annona* was an innovation at Rome but was already established in the Greek world. He passed laws to improve military service, regulating the minimum age to seventeen and providing soldiers with free clothing; and to build roads in Italy: these measures were undoubtedly popular with the commons.

An attempt to radically change the franchise and admit the Latins to the citizenship failed, however, and Gaius determined to widen his support by wooing the equestrian order which was composed of many rich though non-political members of society. He therefore transferred the juries in the courts that dealt with extortion from the Senate to equestrians, thus removing a source of senatorial corruption and partisanship. He also gave the equestrians control of the taxation of the rich new province of Asia by enacting that the censors should auction contracts for the collection of the tithes of that province. Thus the power of the equestrians over provincial governors was increased and the freedom of the senators to abuse their powers was checked.

Gaius had a smooth ride in his first year as tribune, but in 122, though he had the support of the ex-consul M. Fulvius FLACCUS (4), another tribune of aristocratic background, M. Livius DRUSUS (1), aided by Gaius' former friend FANNIUS, tried to undermine his influence with the people by proposing measures even more popular than his. He enacted that twelve more colonies should be founded, that the allotments given out by the land commission should be free of rent, and that it should be illegal to scourge men with Latin rights, even on military service. It was Drusus and Fannius who upset Gaius' plan to extend the franchise to Latins. The commission set up to carry out Drusus' enactments took little action, but Gaius' popularity had begun to wane. During his second year of office he left Rome for over two months to supervise the foundation of Junonia, a colony on the site of Carthage, and in his absence his enemies did their best to discredit his policies. Consequently he failed to be re-elected to the tribuneship for 121, and when the law for the foundation of Junonia was attacked in the new year, he appeared in the forum with a bodyguard to oppose the changes, and a riot ensued in which a servant of the consul OPIMIUS was killed. The consul was furious and persuaded the Senate for the first time to pass the resolution *That the Consuls See that the State Suffer no Harm* (later called the Ultimate Decree). The reformers took their stand on the Aventine Hill where the followers of Opimius, fortified by the Senate's support, overwhelmed and killed them. Opimius then proceeded to round up and kill without trial 3,000 more supporters of the Gracchan reforms. See D. Stockton (1979) *The Gracchi*, Oxford: Clarendon Press.

2, Tiberius Sempronius (late C3 BC), was a general in the war against HANNIBAL. After the battle of Cannae in 216 BC, when he was aedile, he commanded two legions consisting of freed slaves. The following year he was consul and prevented Hannibal from taking Cumae. In 214 as proconsul he stopped Hanno at Beneventum from marching up from the south to join Hannibal. After a second consulship in 213, he was killed in action the following year in battle with Hannibal's brother MAGO at Campi Veteres in Lucania. The Carthaginians honoured him with a splendid funeral.

3, Tiberius Sempronius (early C2 BC), was a general and statesman, nephew of GRACCHUS (2). He was closely allied to the Scipionic family, marrying CORNELIA (1), daughter of SCIPIO (7) Africanus; he accompanied the two Scipio brothers, Africanus and Asiagenus, to the east in 190 and conducted negotiations with PHILIP (1) V of Macedonia; in 184, as tribune, he saved the latter from condemnation for corruption. He was sent to Greece as an ambassador in 185 and was aedile in 182. In 180, as praetor, he was posted to Spain as Q. Fulvius FLACCUS (3)'s successor in the war against the Celtiberians, which he brought to a successful conclusion in 179, partly through his generous dealings with the Spaniards: he founded the town of Gracchuris. As consul in 177 he ruthlessly suppressed a rebellion in Sardinia. Censor in 169, he was active to restrain the tax-farmers (*publicani*) and to limit the rights granted to freed slaves: he was noted for his austerity. He died in 154 after begetting twelve children, of whom three survived: two sons, GRACCHUS (1) and GRACCHUS (4), and a daughter, Sempronia, who married and may have murdered SCIPIO (11). See A.E. Bernstein (1978) *Tiberius Sempronius Gracchus: Tradition and Apostacy*, Ithaca NY: Cornell University Press; D.C. Earl (1963) *Tiberius Gracchus*, Brussels: Collection Latomus 66.

4, Tiberius Sempronius (*c*.164–133 BC), was a politician and social reformer, the eldest surviving son of GRACCHUS (3) and of CORNELIA (1). He was an augur at the age of ten, and served as military tribune at Carthage under his cousin SCIPIO (11) Aemilianus in 146 BC. In 137 he was quaestor in Spain under Hostilius MANCINUS, whose army was trapped near Numantia; Tiberius then used his father's good name to negotiate a treaty which saved the army, though later the Senate, on Scipio's advice, repudiated it. Undoubtedly this treachery by Scipio and the Senate was a factor in Tiberius' disillusionment with the establishment of the time: but he must have gained popularity from his action in Spain and he had powerful support for a radical reform. He married Claudia, a daughter of Appius CLAUDIUS (6) Pulcher, the doyen of the Senate, and, when he was elected tribune of the *plebs* in 133, he was backed by Claudius, the consul Publius SCAEVOLA (2), the latter's brother P. Licinius CRASSUS (5) Mucianus, Marcus Fulvius FLACCUS (4), C. Papirius CARBO (1) and C. Porcius CATO (1). His aim was to solve the land problem – in Italy land (the *latifundia* or 'broad estates') was now mainly in the hands of a few large often-absent landowners, who grazed sheep on it or farmed it with slave gangs to the exclusion of the free peasant farmers – by legislation he revived the old rule (under the Licinian Rogations; see STOLO) that nobody might hold more than 500 *iugera* of public land (120 hectares, 300 acres) and that illegally held land should be reclaimed from the occupants and distributed to poor citizens, probably in small allotments of thirty *iugera* or less: as a palliative he proposed that 250 *iugera* per son up to 1,000 *iugera* might additionally be left in the hands of the landowners. He exempted the rich public land in Campania from his provisions. The purpose of his proposed legislation was to relieve the poverty of citizens, many of whom had been displaced from their holdings and drifted into unemployment in Rome, and, by increasing the number of men with property, to extend the field of recruitment to the army.

Tiberius had serious difficulties in passing his proposals, as there was much opposition from the Senate, which consisted of the richest landowners. He decided to put the matter straight to the Assembly of the People, which alone had the right to pass laws, though traditionally the Senate had priority in the consideration of proposals. But a fellow tribune, Marcus OCTAVIUS (4), vetoed Gracchus' agrarian bill, and Tiberius, after many appeals to him to change his mind, moved in the Assembly the removal of Octavius from the tribuneship: the people passed this proposal, elected another tribune, and passed the agrarian law of Tiberius Gracchus. They also set up a commission of three, which he had proposed, consisting of himself, his younger brother Gaius (see GRACCHUS (1)) and Claudius, to supervise the confiscations and redistribution of the public land: the commissioners were thus linked by family ties, and were probably subject to annual reappointment. Tiberius lacked funds to finance his work, including initial sums for the poor farmers to get started, and the Senate, which controlled the state treasury, refused his appeal for such support. At this time news reached him of the bequest of his kingdom made by ATTALUS (3) III of Pergamon to Rome, and he made a move to introduce a bill to the Assembly authorising the use of some of this wealth for his purposes. In doing so he finally alienated the Senate, which claimed the prerogative of making all decisions regarding foreign policy and finance, though his move to procure the money from Pergamon was successful.

He decided to stand for a second tribuneship (for 132) to protect his legislation, though such re-election was without precedent in the previous two centuries. The elections were held at harvest time and Tiberius may have proposed new legislation, acceptable to the city proletariat, to make his candidature welcome to the Assembly, as the country people would not attend. The elections were postponed through a dispute as to which tribune should preside. The next day, at an assembly on the Capitol, a brawl took place and, after the meeting ended, the chief priest (*Pontifex Maximus*) SCIPIO (12) Nasica led a mob from the Senate to the Capitol, where they clubbed to death Tiberius and 300 of his supporters. His whole approach to reform had been too radical and un-Roman in its contempt for 'ancestral custom' (*mos maiorum*): his legislation survived, however, and the work of the commission continued. See D.C. Earl (1963) *Tiberius Gracchus*, Brussels: Collection Latomus; D. Stockton (1979) *The Gracchi*, Oxford: Clarendon Press.

Graecinus, Julius (C1 AD), entered the Senate under TIBERIUS and reached the rank of praetor: COLUMELLA cites his work on viticulture. It seems likely he was the father of Cn. Julius AGRICOLA: if so, he was executed *c.*AD 40.

Granius Licinianus (C2 AD) was an annalist who adapted material from LIVY's history as well as from SALLUST's works. The surviving text covers periods from 165 to 162, 105, and 86 to 77 BC. Granius' main interest was in strange tales and prodigies. He also wrote a (lost) treatise on dining etiquette.

Grattius Faliscus (late C1 BC) was a Latin poet contemporary with AUGUSTUS and OVID. A single poem of his, the *Hunting to Hounds* (*Cynegetica*) survives to line 541: it deals with a variety of themes and contains some interesting digressions, owing something to the influence of VIRGIL's *Georgics*. Nothing is known of his life or his connection with Falerii.

Gregory **1.** (*c.*AD 213–*c.*275) was a Greek Christian preacher of Neocaesarea in Pontus. He was born in Pontus in a noble family and studied law in Beirut; in the neighbouring city of Caesarea in Palestine he met ORIGEN (1), who converted him to Christianity and wrote a *Panegyric* about him. He returned to Pontus where he became a successful preacher and bishop of his native town. His biography was composed by GREGORY (3) of Nyssa a hundred years later, and contained much fanciful material based on folk-memory: hence he is also known as the 'Miracle-worker' (*Thaumaturgus*). See R. Lane Fox (1986) *Pagans and Christians*, Harmondsworth: Penguin.

2. of Nazianzus (*c.*AD 330–389) was a Greek Christian bishop and writer. His father was the bishop of Nazianzus in Cappadocia; he was sent to Athens to be educated, where he formed a close friendship with BASIL of Caesarea. Both appear to have learnt rhetoric from LIBANIUS. He was influenced by the writings of ORIGEN (1) and in company with Basil became a monk: under Basil's influence he took Christian orders and became bishop of Sasima. He resided at Constantinople from 379 to 381, when he assisted the emperor Theodosius I to expel the Arian Christians. He was created bishop of Constantinople in 381 and presided at the church council of that year and became acquainted with Jerome, the translator of the *Bible* into Latin, but resigned as a result of the general discontent with his policies and retired to Cappadocia to write. He was in debt to classical literature for the style of his writings: he composed speeches and letters and a verse autobiography. He also attacked the late emperor JULIAN who had revived 'paganism'.

3. of Nyssa (*c.*AD 332–*c.*395) was a Greek Christian bishop and theological writer. He was the younger brother of BASIL of Caesarea and was born in Cappadocia. Basil made him bishop of Nyssa in 371, and from 379 to 380 he was in Constantinople where he assisted the emperor Theodosius I in expelling the Arian Christians. He wrote copiously and displayed in his writings, many of which survive, a close knowledge of the 'pagan' philosophers, especially Plato and PLOTINUS, and owed a deep debt to ORIGEN (1). He was a central figure in Christian theological writing. He wrote the *Life* of his sister Macrina, in which he expounded important theological and philosophical insights.

H

Hadrian (AD 76–138), an emperor who reigned from 117 to 138, was born on 24 January 76 in Spain, probably at the colony of Italica in the province of Baetica. He was the son of P. Aelius Hadrianus Afer and Domitia Paulina; his full name was Publius Aelius Hadrianus. His family had been settled in Spain for 200 years, having originated from Hadria in Picenum. He was related by marriage to the future emperor TRAJAN: his grandfather had married Trajan's aunt. When his father died in 85, Hadrian became the ward of Trajan and ATTIANUS. He spent the next six years in Rome, but at the age of fifteen returned to Spain to join the army. In 93 Trajan summoned him to Rome and arranged for him to be military tribune in the Second Legion Adiutrix at Aquincum (Budapest) in Pannonia in 95 and in the Fifth Macedonica in Moesia in 96. In 97, being sent to Upper Germany to congratulate Trajan, then consul and governor of the province, on his adoption by the emperor NERVA (4), he remained there with the Twenty-Second Primigenia as a tribune under his brother-in-law Julius Ursus SERVIANUS. Trajan became emperor in 98, and in 99 he returned to Rome with his ward, to whom in 100 he married his great-niece Vibia SABINA with the warm approval of his wife PLOTINA, who seems to have been a strong supporter of Hadrian's succession. He then pursued a career that was mostly military but included the main civil posts and priesthoods: he was quaestor in 101, on campaign in Dacia from 101 to 102, tribune of the *plebs* in 105, in Dacia again from 105 to 107 when he commanded a legion, praetor in 106 and governor of Lower Pannonia in 107. He held a suffect consulship in June 108. In 111 he was elected archon at Athens, a city he loved and beautified (in his youth he had been nicknamed *Graeculus* ('little Greek') for his devotion to Greek culture), and from 113 he assisted Trajan in his Parthian campaigns. In 117 Trajan appointed him governor of Syria, strategically important for the Parthian war, but in August of that year, having left the war owing to an illness, Trajan died childless at Selinus in Cilicia: Hadrian was nearby at Antioch and announced on 9 August that he had been adopted by Trajan and on the 11th that he was dead. There were many who were ready to discredit his claim of adoption, but Hadrian had certainly been held in high honour by his predecessor and had previously received many marks of favour. The army proclaimed him emperor and, after he wrote to it promising to respect its rights, the Senate reluctantly confirmed his succession.

Hadrian was greatly aware of the dangers to the empire of threats of rebellion in Mauretania, Britain, Dacia and Moesia, and he set about repairing the situation, withdrawing from most of Trajan's eastern conquests (namely Armenia, Assyria and Mesopotamia) except Arabia, and removing the governor of Judaea, LUSIUS Quietus, from his post. He spent much of his life touring the frontier provinces and regulating the armies. He was consul in 118 and returned to Rome in July after pacifying the Danube frontier: he found the Senate disaffected by the executions of four senators of consular rank, perhaps instigated by the praetorian prefect Attianus. The men thus removed were Lusius Quietus, A. Cornelius Palma Frontonianus, L. Publilius Celsus, and C. Avidius NIGRINUS. Hadrian claimed that he had not authorised the executions and sought general favour by his remissions of taxes, lavish gladiatorial shows and generous distributions of largesse to the commons. Hadrian held a triumph in Trajan's name for his eastern victories. In 121 he dedicated to Venus and Rome a new temple in the Roman forum which he himself had designed. In the same year he went to the German frontier to commission a new frontier defence-work, the *limes*, which ran from the Rhine to the Danube; thence he proceeded to Britain in 122, where he instituted the building of Hadrian's Wall. For some obscure reason he dismissed from his service SUETONIUS (2) Tranquillus, his secretary of state, and the prefect Septicius. He then crossed to Gaul on his way to Spain and founded a temple at Nîmes for Plotina, who died in 123. He spent the winter at Tarragona, where he proclaimed that his title was henceforth to be simply Hadrianus Augustus. A rebellion was put down at this time in Mauretania, which he did not, however, visit. He sailed in 123 from Spain to the east, calling at Cyrenaica to found the city of Hadrianopolis for refugees from Palestine, and proceeding to the border with Parthia to sign a treaty of peace. He toured Asia Minor and in 124 reached Greece: in these eastern provinces he encouraged building programmes, and in Athens in particular his patronage beautified the city. He was initiated into the mysteries of Eleusis. In 125 he returned via Sicily to Rome; he stayed in Italy until spring 128, and divided the country into four provinces to be governed by ex-consuls. Having accepted the title *Pater Patriae* (*Father of the Fatherland*) he set out for Africa, where he established a defence-work in Mauretania; he visited Rome en route for Greece, where he passed the winter of 128–9 in Athens. Here he gave orders for the restoration of the temple of Olympian Zeus and was awarded the title 'Olympian', being worshipped in Greece and the east in the cult of Zeus Panhellenios.

He spent 129 in Asia Minor and Syria, and visited Palmyra before proceeding to Egypt via Arabia and Judaea. In the latter province he refounded Jerusalem as Colonia Aelia Capitolina, and set up a temple to Jupiter on the site of the Jewish temple; he also forbade the practice of circumcision, thus enraging the Jews and provoking their final revolt in 132. In Egypt in 130 he toured the ancient sites and lost his favourite ANTINOUS through drowning in the Nile. He founded the city of Antinoöpolis and instituted a cult in his honour. In 131 Hadrian proceeded to Athens via Lycia in southern Asia Minor: he established in the city a council of all the Greek states, the *Panhellenion*, and dedicated the temple of Zeus he had restored. In 132 the Jewish revolt under BAR KOCHBA began and lasted until 135: Hadrian recalled Sextus Julius Severus from Britain to tackle the insurgents, who initially had much success. Hadrian himself spent some time in the east, principally at Antioch, because of the revolt: but in 134 he returned to Rome suffering illness, and lived at his immense new villa near Tivoli (Tibur). Hadrian settled Judaea by expelling the Jews from their country and founding his temple to Jupiter: he posted two Roman legions there to ensure calm.

In 136 Hadrian planned the succession: being childless himself, he determined to follow the precedent set by Augustus and choose his heir by adoption. First he adopted L. Ceionius Commodus, a consul of 136 who took the name Lucius AELIUS (3); he died, however, on the first day of 138. The elderly statesman Julius SERVIANUS, who had married Hadrian's elder sister, Paullina, may have expressed misgivings and suggested the better claims of his grandson Fuscus: the emperor had them both killed, perhaps by suicide. Hadrian now chose a relation of his wife, ANTONINUS Pius, whom he adopted and caused to adopt MARCUS AURELIUS and L. Aelius' son Lucius VERUS. Hadrian died at Baiae aged 63 on 10 July 138, uttering the famous lines addressed to his soul, *Animula Vagula Blandula*. He was buried in one of his greatest edifices, the mausoleum which is now known as the Castel Sant' Angelo on the Tiber bank, and was deified, though many senators were loth to vote for the honour, such was his unpopularity at Rome.

His cautious policy of secure frontiers, though a departure from Trajan's expansionist approach, had given the empire a long period of peace and security. He had been energetic in his building programme, his oversight of the provinces, and his general administration. He was a legal and financial reformer who published an authoritative text of the praetor's perpetual edict which henceforth could only be amended by an emperor. He extended Latin rights to councillors in all Italian cities. His reform of tax collection brought in the revenues to pay for his building programme and charities. At Rome he restored the Pantheon of AGRIPPA (1), built a temple in honour of Trajan and Plotina, and rebuilt much of the city and Ostia. At Athens he built a 'new town' next to the ancient market-place of the Classical city. See A.R. Birley (1977) *The Roman Emperor Hadrian*, Northumberland: Barcombe Publications; and (1997) *The Restless Emperor*, London: Routledge.

Hamilcar (died 229 BC) was a Carthaginian general, the father of HANNIBAL: he had the surname Barca, 'lightning'. He served as fleet commander in the First Punic War, first in 247 BC when he attacked the coast of Bruttium, then in Sicily, where he held an outpost near Palermo in the west of the island against all attempts of the Romans to eject him, and conducted raids along the south-west coast of Italy. He seized Mount Eryx but could not raise the siege of Drepanon. He gave up his command at the end of the war in 241 after negotiating a peace treaty. There ensued a revolt of mercenary troops in the Carthaginian army which in 240 Hamilcar was appointed to suppress, taking over command from his enemy HANNO (2): the remorseless struggle, a 'truceless war', lasted until 237 and cost many lives and atrocities. In the end he collaborated with Hanno to capture Utica. He was then sent to Spain, where he took his three small sons, Hannibal, HASDRUBAL (2) and MAGO. He married a daughter to HASDRUBAL (1). He made Cádiz his base and extended operations throughout southern Spain, founding Alicante. He eventually provoked the Romans in 231 to send a fact-finding mission: he told the envoys that he was trying to secure funds to pay the war indemnity imposed by Rome after the First Punic War. He was drowned while retreating from Helice.

Hannibal (247–*c*.182 BC) was a Carthaginian general, the greatest and most successful enemy of republican Rome. The eldest son of HAMILCAR, at the age of nine he was made to swear an oath of undying enmity to Rome by his father and taken to Spain, where he remained after his father's death in 229. He remained there while his brother-in-law HASDRUBAL (1) held the command, and succeeded him after his assassination in 221, at the age of twenty-two, being elected by the army and confirmed in the post by the Carthaginian assembly. He then pursued an aggressive policy to expand the empire of Carthage in Spain. He challenged Rome over her alliance with Saguntum on the eastern coast of Spain, and despite Roman protests took Saguntum in 219 after an eight-month siege. This had been a deliberate provocation of Rome, which demanded his surrender for punishment, and Hannibal without further delay began his march into Italy to attack Rome at her heart, thus precipitating the Second Punic War (218–201 BC). Hannibal's war aim seems to have been to weaken Rome and destroy her empire rather than to take the city, as the outcome shows. His army consisted largely of foreign mercenaries. He set out from New Carthage (Cartagena) in May 218 with 90,000 infantry, 12,000 cavalry and some elephants, forced his way through northern Spain to the Pyrenees, where he awaited the expected arrival of a Roman force under P. Cornelius SCIPIO (6) until September, and then advanced through Gaul, where he evaded Scipio, to the Alps, which he crossed during autumn in foul weather, losing many men and most of his elephants. His route took him up the valley of the Isère, over one of the higher passes, perhaps the Col du Clapier, and down into Italy (then Cisalpine Gaul) near Turin, which he reached in late October with a much reduced force of 26,000 men. Scipio had meanwhile returned to Cisalpine Gaul by the coast and met Hannibal's force on the river Ticino: a cavalry battle took place which revealed Hannibal's great superiority in that quarter and sent Scipio in retreat to Piacenza. In December, with his colleague Sempronius Longus, Scipio attacked Hannibal across the swollen river Trebbia but was caught off-guard in the rear and lost three quarters of his army. The Romans then retired from Gaul and the local people flocked to join Hannibal. The following May he advanced with a refreshed force over the Apennines, where he again evaded a Roman army (losing an eye when he crossed the marshes of the Arno), ravaged Etruria and drew the Roman force under Gaius FLAMINIUS to follow him to Lake Trasimene. Here he caught the consul's force in an ambush and wiped it out.

Hannibal now moved to southern Italy as the towns of central Italy remained faithful to Rome, but he fared no better in the south and was shadowed and harried by a fresh Roman force under the dictator FABIUS (8) Maximus, who avoided confronting Hannibal in open battle. In 216 thc Romans lost patience with Fabius' delaying tactics and appointed two consuls to meet Hannibal head on, L. Aemilius PAULLUS (1) and M. Terentius VARRO (1). He offered them battle with their 54,000 men in an open plain near Cannae; he had himself not more than 45,000 men. His tactics were superior, rolling up and surrounding the Romans in a ring of iron, and he defeated them so soundly that only 14,000 escaped from the field: Hannibal lost 6,000. He could have driven his men on that night to take Rome, which was undefended, but preferred to spare his troops. Hannibal sent his Italian prisoners to their homes but kept the Romans prisoner: however, they were not ransomed. The towns of southern Italy now began to waver, and Capua through starvation surrendered to Hannibal, who used it as his principal base. The strategy of Fabius was reinstated after Cannae, and the next three years were barren for Hannibal in Italy. He was handicapped by his failure to capture a port until 212, when he took Tarentum by treachery. While his forces were massed at Tarentum the consul Q. Fulvius FLACCUS (2) mobilised the largest force he could and advanced into Campania where he invested Capua: Hannibal, unable to break his stranglehold, in 211 advanced on Rome itself, but failed to prevent the loss of Capua. Hannibal was thus penned more and more in the extreme south of Italy and in 209 lost Tarentum to Fabius Maximus. However, he had one further brilliant success, catching and defeating both consuls that year by an ambush near Venusia, killing Claudius MARCELLUS (3) and fatally wounding his colleague T. Quinctius Crispinus.

Hannibal's forces were now weakening, and he was desperately in need of reinforcement: in Spain, where he had left his brother HASDRUBAL (2) in charge, P. Cornelius SCIPIO (7) Africanus had taken the Carthaginian capital, New Carthage, and in 208 defeated Hasdrubal at Bailen. In 207 Hasdrubal was ordered to abandon Spain and go to his brother's rescue. But communications between the two were difficult and though Hasdrubal got safely as far as northern Italy and recruited many Gauls, the Romans captured his messengers and he was caught on the river Metaurus, south of Rimini, where after facing both consuls he was defeated and killed. After this setback the Senate allowed Hannibal to retire to Bruttium, where he lingered until 203, though he lost Locri to Scipio in 205. However in 203, after Scipio had invaded Africa and inflicted a defeat upon the Carthaginian and Numidian forces on the river Bagradas, Hannibal was recalled to Africa to defend his city. His return interrupted a treaty (whose terms had already been agreed by both Carthage and Rome) for Spain to be ceded, the Punic navy to be reduced to twenty ships, and an indemnity of 5,000 talents to be paid to Rome. He brought back a trained and toughened army which gave the Carthaginian 'hawks' hope of futher resistance to Rome, and the negotiations were annulled. After landing at Lepcis, Hannibal met Scipio in summer 202 near Zama Regia, south of Carthage: here he was shown that Scipio had learnt all that Hannibal could teach him. The Numidian cavalry was now on the Roman side and Hannibal's army was rolled up as he had rolled the Romans up at Cannae. After frightful carnage, Hannibal surrendered and accepted worse terms than had been offered in 203: in future, Carthage would not be allowed to make war without first obtaining Rome's permission.

Thus peace was made, and Hannibal settled down to political life in Carthage, becoming sufet (chief magistrate) in 196, when he brought in a constitutional reform to extend the franchise and a financial reform to enable the indemnity of 10,000 talents to be paid without further taxing the people. His deep enmity for Rome had not ceased, however, and he plotted against Rome with the Seleucid king ANTIOCHUS (1) III of Syria, to whom he fled in 195 when his enemies denounced him to the Roman Senate. He encouraged Antiochus to take on the Romans, and was with him when he invaded Greece in 192. Hannibal was put in charge of a Syrian fleet in 190, and was defeated by the Rhodians under Eudamus at sea near Side. After Antiochus' defeat at the battle of Magnesia and the subsequent traeaty of 188, Hannibal was forced to flee again, first to Crete and later to Bithynia where he supported king PRUSIAS (1) I in 184 in a war against EUMENES (2) II of Pergamon. A year or two later he was again in danger when FLAMININUS persuaded Prusias to hand him over to the Romans: when flight proved impossible, he took poison and died.

Though his career ended in apparent failure, Hannibal was nevertheless one of the most attractive men of action of the ancient world. He was able to command though thick and thin the loyalty of an army composed mainly of foreign mercenary troops, and to extract a brilliant performance from them; both his tenacity and humanity were admirable. He was a uniquely powerful strategist and tactician, learning from studying Alexander the Great and Pyrrhus. He developed the combination of infantry and cavalry warfare to a perfection which was displayed at Cannae. However, some of his principal assumptions in waging the Second Punic War were misguided, and he underestimated the loyalty of the Italians to

Rome and overestimated his own power to enlist the support of the Gauls. He was also wrong about the ability or readiness of the Carthaginian state to reinforce and supply him, and Hasdrubal's chances of relieving him. His political activity, though brief, was that of a determined reformer. We must guard against a historical tradition, based on Roman sources, which does him less than justice. See Polybius, *History*, books 9–11; E. Bradford (1981) *Hannibal*, London: Macmillan; J.F. Lazenby (1978) *Hannibal's War*, Warminster: Aris & Phillips.

Hanno (late C3 BC) was an influential Carthaginian, hostile to the Barca family and to HANNIBAL. He gained the title 'the Great' from his military exploits in Africa of which we have no record. He caused a revolt of mercenary soldiers in 240 BC by refusing to pay them, and suffered defeat at their hands. He was replaced in command by HAMILCAR Barca. In 218 he opposed Hannibal's actions at Saguntum and seems to have proposed his surrender to the Romans (see HANNIBAL). The same year he was defeated in Spain by a Roman force, and in 216 sought a peace with Rome after Cannae; he negotiated the treaty after Zama in 202. He appears to have been the leader of the landed nobility at Carthage who wished to pursue trade in Africa rather than war in Europe.

Harpocration, Valerius (C2 AD), was a Greek lexicographer from Alexandria. He may have been a tutor of the emperor VERUS; he composed a work in dictionary form entitled *Lexicon of the Ten Orators*, which partly survives. It is meant as a reference work for readers and quotes in alphabetical order words and phrases, including names, drawn not only from the orators but also from a wide variety of ancient Greek writers, together with explanations: we derive from it much information about Athenian forensic practice, commerce, religion and constitutional law. His *Collection of Flowers* is lost: it probably resembled APULEIUS' *Florida*.

Hasdrubal 1. (died 221 BC) was a Carthaginian general, the son-in-law of HAMILCAR Barca. In 237 BC he went to Spain with Barca, returning to put down a rebellion of Numidia. In 229 on the death of his father-in-law, Hasdrubal was appointed Carthaginian commander in Spain where he used his talent for diplomacy rather than warfare to accomplish his goals, and won over many Spanish peoples to Carthage. His first wife being dead, he married a Spanish princess and he founded New Carthage (Cartagena) on the eastern coast to be the capital of Carthaginian Spain. In 226 he made a treaty with the Romans agreeing that the river Ebro should be the boundary between their two provinces. He was assassinated by a Celtic slave.

2. (*c.*245–207 BC) was a Carthaginian general, the second son of HAMILCAR Barca, and HANNIBAL's younger brother. He was taken by his father to Spain in 237 and became commander of the Carthaginian army in Spain in 218 when Hannibal left for Italy. He made a raid into northern Spain and harried the Roman army which had defeated HANNO (2). He made a further attempt to invade Spain north of the Ebro in 217 but was defeated at sea off the river-mouth. In 215 he suffered defeat at the hands of SCIPIO (1) and SCIPIO (6) at Dertosa near the mouth of the river Ebro. In 214 he was recalled to Africa to deal with the revolt of SYPHAX. He returned to Spain, and in 212 led one of three armies in pursuit of the Scipios, routing Gnaeus Cornelius Scipio Calvus in 211 at Ilorci. He was however himself defeated in 208 by Gnaeus' nephew Publius SCIPIO (7) Africanus at Bailen (Baecula) just north of the upper Guadalquivir, but escaped with most of his army: knowing of the growing crisis of Hannibal's position in Italy, he determined to reinforce him; he therefore made a dash for the north, crossed the Pyrenees and marched in a manner rivalling his brother's expedition in 218 through Gaul, where he gained many recruits, over the Alps and into Cisalpine Gaul and northern Italy, which he reached in 207. As he marched southwards in Umbria down the Via Flaminia, he was confronted by both consuls, C. Claudius NERO (2) and M. Livius SALINATOR: he tried to withdraw up the valley of the river Metaurus but was caught, defeated, and died fighting. His head was thrown into Hannibal's camp.

3. (died 202 BC) was a Carthaginian general, the son of Gisgo. He was in command of an army operating in Spain from 214 BC. He took part in 211 in the movement of three Punic armies to destroy the Scipios: with HANNIBAL's brother MAGO (2) he defeated and killed Publius SCIPIO (6), the father of Africanus, and aided HASDRUBAL (2) to overcome Scipio's brother Gnaeus SCIPIO (1). In 207 he was driven from his base at Jaen to Cádiz, and in 206 was decisively defeated together with Mago at Ilipa, on the Guadalquivir north of Seville, by SCIPIO (7) Africanus. He then fled to Numidia and allied himself with SYPHAX, king of the Masaesylii, to whom he married his daughter SOPHONISBA, thus winning his support for Carthage. In 204 Hasdrubal was commander-in-chief of the Punic armies in Africa and relieved Utica, which Scipio had been besieging. In spring the next year Scipio avenged himself by capturing and burning the joint camp of Hasdrubal and Syphax: they recovered their strength and met him again at the battle of the Great Plains, where they were defeated. In 202, shortly before Zama, Hasdrubal was accused of treason and killed himself.

4. (C2 BC) was a Carthaginian general who commanded the Carthaginian campaign against the Numidian king Masinissa, Rome's ally, and was defeated in 150, for which he was condemned to death at Carthage. But he rejected the sentence and gathered a rebel force to resist: when the Romans renewed war in 149 (the Third Punic War) he was recalled as commander and waged a guerrilla war against them until 148, when he was penned in Carthage. A bitter siege followed, during which Hasdrubal was responsible for atrocities to Roman prisoners and Carthaginian civilians who opposed his policy of resistance; finally he tried to negotiate with SCIPIO (11) Aemilianus that the city should be spared, but failed. In 146 he surrendered and became a prisoner for the rest of his life. His wife killed herself and their children, and Carthage was razed to the ground.

Haterius, Quintus (*c.*54 BC–AD 26), was an orator of senatorial rank, suffect consul in 5 BC. In speaking his delivery was so rapid that Augustus remarked that he needed a brake. Tacitus wrote his obituary in *Annals*, 4. 61, suggesting that his eloquence could not survive his death.

Hecaton (C2 BC) was a Stoic philosopher from Rhodes. He was a pupil of PANAETIUS and wrote on ethics: his works have not survived, though CICERO (1) reproduced some of his arguments in his philosophical works.

Helena (*c.*AD 255–*c.*327) The first consort of the emperor CONSTANTIUS (1) I and the mother of CONSTANTINE (1) I the Great. Born in Bithynia in humble circumstances, said to be an innkeeper's daughter, she became the mistress or wife of Constantius and bore his best known son Constantine at Niš *c.*AD 273. However, in 292 Constantius rejected her so that he might marry Theodora, daughter of MAXIMIAN, who gave him six children: Helena returned to court only after the accession of her son in 306. She was baptised in 312 when Christianity was officially tolerated, and proved a strong Christian influence on her son. With her daughter-in-law FAUSTA (2) she was given *c.*325 the title

Augusta. In 326 she visited Jerusalem and Bethlehem, sought for and claimed to have found the sites of events described in the *Gospels*, and founded churches there. The claim that she found the cross on which JESUS was crucified rests on no contemporary evidence. She died at about eighty and was buried at Rome in a mausoleum.

Heliodorus (C1–2 AD) A Greek medical writer: Juvenal refers to him (*Sat.*, 6. 373). He was a member of the Pneumatic school of medicine. His works only survive in references and fragments; the chief one was *Surgery*; he also wrote on *Bandages*, *Bleeding*, *Dislocations*, *Joints* and *Weights and Measures*.

Heliogabalus *see* ELAGABALUS.

Helvidius 1, Priscus (C1 AD), was a philosopher and senator of humble origins, the son of a regular soldier from Cluviae in Samnium who reached the rank of *primuspilus*, he was tribune of the *plebs* in AD 56. He was a student of the Stoic school of philosophy and in *c.*55 married as his second wife FANNIA, the daughter of the Stoic THRASEA Paetus. He did not conceal his opposition in the Senate to NERO (1)'s tyranny and so was banished by Nero in 66, after his father-in-law's condemnation and suicide, which he witnessed. GALBA (1) recalled him in 68 and he proceeded to impeach Thrasea's prosecutor, EPRIUS Marcellus, though he soon dropped the case. As praetor in 70 he incurred the anger of VESPASIAN (normally very tolerant) by his rudeness, despite previous friendship. He subsequently pursued a war of words against the emperor and was finally banished again by 75. Vespasian later ordered his execution which, although the order was countermanded, was carried out. He almost certainly did not advocate republicanism and his quarrel with Vespasian seems to have been increasingly personal. See Tacitus, *Histories*, 4. 5; Cassius Dio, *Roman History*, 66. 12.

2. was the son of HELVIDIUS (1) by his first marriage. He was consul during DOMITIAN's reign but was executed by that emperor *c.*AD 93. He was a friend of both TACITUS (1) and PLINY (2) the Younger.

Herennius *see* DEXIPPUS, MODESTINUS.

Hermas (late C1 AD) was a Christian mystic and writer, probably the Hermas greeted by PAUL in his *Letter to the Romans*, 16. 14. He may have been a Christian Jew captured in the Jewish war of AD 70 and sold as a slave to an Italian woman named Rhoda. He wrote *The Shepherd*, an extant account of a series of dreams he claimed to have had in the locality of Cumae: he was familiar with apocryphal Jewish texts as well as traditional Roman mystical practices. His strange story narrowly failed to be included in the Christian canon of Scriptures.

Hermogenes 1. (early C2 BC) was a Greek architect from Priene or Alabanda in Caria. He built two temples, that of Dionysus on Teos and that of Artemis Leucophryene at Magnesia on the Maeander. The Roman architect VITRUVIUS wrote of these temples and drew on them for his principles of proportion; his measurements of them, however, seem to have been inaccurate. He attributes to Hermogenes the rejection of the Doric order for temple design in favour of the Ionic. STRABO admired the Magnesian temple: the strong Roman interest in his work influenced the architecture of the Augustan age.

2. (C2 AD) was a Greek rhetorician and writer on style from Tarsus. He was considered to be an infant prodigy and was admired for his eloquence by MARCUS AURELIUS; he turned later to writing on the subject, and produced a number of textbooks. Two extant works are genuinely his: *Issues* and *Styles*. He used classical Greek orators such as Demosthenes as his models. His book on *Issues* restates the doctrines of Hermagoras. His *Styles* proposes seven distinct types of style: clarity, grandeur, rapidity, beauty, character, fidelity and effectiveness. This classification descends from DIONYSIUS of Halicarnassus and from Theophrastus. It is similar to a scheme proposed in *The Art of Rhetoric* wrongly attributed to the contemporary writer ARISTIDES. Other works attributed to Hermogenes are spurious: *Invention* and *The Method of Effective Speaking*. He was much studied in the Byzantine period.

Hermogenianus, Aurelius (late C3 AD), was a jurist or legal expert of the time of Diocletian who held the post of Master of Petitions in AD 293 and 294 and was subsequently Maximian's Master of Petitions. He published *c.*300 *Epitomes of Law* in six books summarising the classical legal texts which was excerpted in Justinian's *Digests of Law*. He may also be the author of a compilation of Roman imperial law under the title *Codex Hermogenianus*. It seems probable that he was the Aurelius Hermogenianus who served as prefect of the Praetorian Guard under CONSTANTIUS (1) Chlorus. He was an important and original thinker about the law, having a fine analytical mind, and he began the process of finding and enunciating the basic principles which underlie the law from which solutions to particular legal problems may deduced.

Herod 1. (the Great) (*c.*73–4 BC) was a ruler of Judaea and adjacent lands, the son of the Idumaean ANTIPATER (2) whom in 47 BC Caesar appointed procurator (governor) of Judaea and gave Roman citizenship. In the same settlement Herod was made governor of Galilee and a Roman citizen. ANTONIUS (7) shortly after gave him and his brother Phasael the title of tetrarchs ('rulers of a quarter'). In 43 BC Herod succeeded his father as ethnarch of Judaea. In 40, however, when the Parthians invaded Syria and Asia Minor and removed the Hasmonean HYRCANUS (2) from the throne of Judaea, replacing him with his nephew Mattathias ANTIGONUS, son of ARISTOBULUS (2), Herod took refuge in Rome where he ingratiated himself with ANTONIUS (7) and Octavian (see AUGUSTUS), and became a close friend of AGRIPPA (1). He consequently obtained the title king of Judaea from the Senate. He returned in 37 when Antonius' general C. Sosius recaptured Jerusalem from Antigonus. He had married as his second wife Miriamne, a member of the Hasmonean family and granddaughter of both Hyrcanus and Aristobulus, thus reconciling the two branches of the family. He supported Octavian in the Actium campaign in 31 (but see MALCHUS), and was consequently confirmed in power with a larger territory, gaining the cities Pompeius had freed in 63 including the site of Caesarea (see below). Augustus later added much of the tetrarchy of Ituraea in Lebanon to his kingdom.

Herod was not eligible to hold the Jewish high priesthood, as his predecessors the Hasmoneans had, but he reserved the right to appoint one, and encouraged the growth of a priestly caste. He abandoned the practice of life-long high priesthoods, and reduced the powers of Sanhedrin or priestly council in favour of a royal council, which included non-Jews. He carried out a policy of high taxation, using the proceeds to build a new port named Caesarea on the coast and to rebuild the temple of Jerusalem, which was done on a lavish scale and in accordance with Jewish law. He also gave Jerusalem a theatre and an amphitheatre, and rebuilt Samaria which he renamed Sebaste after Augustus' Greek title (*Sebastos*). He developed the resources of his kingdom and was generous in giving to Greek causes including the Olympic Games and the city of Athens. He was strongly philhellenic, having been educated in Greek culture and philosophy by NICOLAUS of Damascus, and he educated his sons likewise. He enhanced his power by fortifying his kingdom with a string of forts including one in Jerusalem, the Antonia, and another at Masada. He used foreign servants and a secret police to maintain his position, and won the favour of Augustus for his success in keeping his difficult kingdom in order. He maintained his favourable image with the emperor by his own occasional visits to Rome and by the support he enjoyed from Agrippa and Nicolaus of Damascus.

He was, however, far from popular with his Jewish subjects, and towards the end of his life the Pharisees, who had supported him, turned against him. The orthodox Jews detested him for his Hellenism (he remained a polytheist) and his preference for Jews of the diaspora. He also lost the favour of Augustus by attacking Nabataea in 9 BC and by his cruelty to his own family. He had ten wives and a large number of children; he killed his favourite wife Mariamne in 29 for intriguing against him. He killed two of her sons, Alexander and Aristobulus, in 7, fearing their growing popularity, and, five days before his own death in 4 BC, he killed his eldest son, Antipater, whom he accused of plotting against him. Herod's death led to serious civil disturbance, which brought about Roman intervention in the kingdom and its division into tetrarchies (quarter-kingdoms) under three of his sons, HEROD (2) Antipas, PHILIP (2) and ARCHELAUS (4). There is no historical evidence of a 'massacre of the innocents'. See Josephus, *The Jewish War*; A.H.M. Jones (1938) *The Herods of Judaea*, Oxford: Clarendon Press.

2. Antipas (ruled 4 BC–AD 39) was a ruler of Galilee and Peraea, son of HEROD (1) by a Samaritan woman, Malthace. In his father's will he was named as a successor and confirmed by AUGUSTUS as tetrarch from 4 BC. He founded the city of Tiberias on Lake Galilee and restored the town of Sepphoris. He divorced his wife *c.*AD 33, a daughter of the Arab king ARETAS (2) IV, who four years later avenged his daughter's dishonour by seizing Peraea from Antipas. In her place Antipas married his niece Herodias, the former wife of his brother Philip (not the tetrarch), who had divorced her husband. He arrested JOHN the Baptist in 34 and held him in the fortress of Machaira, either because he criticised Antipas' matrimonial affairs (a woman had no right to divorce her husband) or simply because he feared his popular influence. He was probably not involved in the trial of the Galilean JESUS in AD 36 (despite Luke's *Gospel*, 23, 6ff). In 39 Antipas went to Rome to ask the emperor Gaius (CALIGULA) to make him king; the emperor was, however, influenced by his friend AGRIPPA (3) I, whom he appointed tetrarch in Antipas' place, sending the latter into exile in Spain on a charge of treason invented by Agrippa. See Josephus, *The Jewish War*; A.H.M. Jones (1938) *The Herods of Judaea*, Oxford: Clarendon Press.

Herodes Atticus 1, Tiberius Claudius (died *c.*AD 137), was an Athenian of the early second century AD, the son of Hipparchus, a very wealthy man who fell under Domitian's anger: the son recovered part of his fortune during Nerva's reign. Trajan appointed him suffect consul *c.*AD 104 and procurator (governor) of Judaea in 107. Hadrian, noted for his love of Athens, granted him a second suffect consulship after 128. He spent much time in Athens, where he was chief priest of the imperial cult. He was honoured with a special seat in the Theatre of Dionysus.

2, Lucius Vibullius Hipparchus Tiberius Claudius (AD 101–177), was the son of HERODES ATTICUS (1). A philosopher, writer and statesman, he was a generous patron of many Greek cities in giving sums of money for building projects. He practised as a sophist and, as a friend of Hadrian, was invited to teach the children of the imperial family including MARCUS AURELIUS and Lucius VERUS. He was appointed consul in 143. Some of his relationships were stormy: he quarrelled with FRONTO, another imperial tutor, and with the two brothers Quintilius, who were Roman commissioners in Greece in the 150s. In 174 some Athenians complained to MARCUS AURELIUS that he was tyrannical, and the emperor reconciled the parties. His buildings included the Odeon in Athens beneath the Acropolis as a memorial to his wife Regilla, part of which survives, and the stone seating in the stadium of Delphi. He was a fine public speaker, with an elegance of style said to recall that of Critias. Of his writings a Latin translation of a story survives in the works of GELLIUS (1) and a speech to the Athenian Council which may be his. His biography was written by Philostratus in *Lives of the Sophists*. See W. Ameling (1983) *Herodes Atticus*, Hildesheim and New York: G. Olms.

Herodian (C3 AD) was a historian from Syria who wrote in Greek a *History of the Roman Empire* from MARCUS AURELIUS in eight books which is extant: it is unreliable and tends to moralise, though it improves as it approaches his own time. It ends with the reign of GORDIAN III, covering AD 180–238. Its author may have been an imperial freedman and civil servant in Rome.

Hiempsal 1. (C2 BC) was a prince of Numidia in North Africa. He was the elder son of king Micipsa, who left his kingdom at his death in 118 BC to be equally divided between his two sons, Hiempsal and ADHERBAL, and his nephew JUGURTHA, whom he had adopted. Jugurtha, the eldest and ablest of the three, picked a quarrel with Hiempsal and assassinated him. See Sallust, *Jugurthine War*, 10–13.

2. (reigned 106–*c*.60 BC) A Numidian king, the son of Gauda the half-brother of JUGURTHA, whom he succeeded as king in 106 BC. In 81 he was deposed by his kinsman Iarbas with the support of Cn. Domitius AHENOBARBUS (3), a Marian; however, in the same year POMPEIUS (2), while turning Marians out of office in the provinces, restored him to power. He wrote in the Punic language works on anthropology and ethnology which were quoted by SALLUST; he died *c*.60 BC and was succeeded by his son JUBA I.

Hilarion (*c*.AD 291–371) was a Christian hermit and monastic innovator from Gaza in Palestine. Born a 'pagan', he was educated in rhetoric in Alexandria but in 306, probably under the influence of ANTONY, he took to the life of a hermit in the desert near Gaza. There he stayed for most of his life, living most frugally and helping all comers with their problems; at the end of his life, in his seventies, he went on a tour encompassing Libya, Sicily and finally Cyprus, where he died in 371. Jerome wrote his *Life*.

Hippalus (early C1 AD) was a Greek navigator and merchant who is said to have discovered how to use the seasonal winds such as the south-west monsoon to reach the coast of India across the Arabian Sea. The gentler south-east monsoon gave him the opportunity of a return journey. An African cape and part of the Arabian Sea were named after him, as was the south-west monsoon. There exists an ancient account of the subject in Greek, *Navigation [Periplus] of the Red Sea*. See V. Begley and R.D. De Puma (1991) *Rome and India: The Ancient Sea Trade*, Madison: University of Wisconsin Press.

Hippolytus (*c*.AD 170–*c*.236) was a Christian writer and bishop of Portus (Ostia). He wrote against heresies and opposed the current expectation that the world was about to end. Books 1 and 4–10 of his *Refutation of All Heresies* are extant and preserve fragments of the works of Greek Presocratic philosophers including Heraclitus, which Hippolytus quotes because he sees them as a source of Christian heresies. A statue of him, preserved at Rome, provides a list of his works and a table for reckoning the date of Easter. He wrote an extant *Chronicle* of events from the creation to AD 234, a *Commentary on Daniel*, and a book, *The Universe*. He developed a doctrine of the Logos (Word of God) and accused Callistus, the bishop of Rome, of heresy for not accepting it. He suffered in the persecution of the Church under the emperor MAXIMINUS (1) and died in exile in Sardinia.

Hirtius, Aulus (died 43 BC), was a Caesarian officer in the Gallic and civil wars who wrote the eighth book of CAESAR (1)'s *Gallic War* and the *War at Alexandria*. He fought in Spain in the civil war, was praetor in 46, and governed Transalpine Gaul in 45. As consul in 43 he sided with Octavian (AUGUSTUS) and was killed, with his colleague PANSA, at the battle of Mutina. His correspondence with CICERO (1) is lost.

Horace (Quintus Horatius Flaccus) (65–8 BC), a Latin poet, was born 8 December 65 at Venusia (Venosa) in Apulia, the son of a freedman. His father, originally a slave of Italian stock, possibly enslaved in the Social Wars, was a smallholder and a tax collector, charged with the collection of auction-tax. He seems to have been quite wealthy, and decided that the local school was not good enough for his son, whom he took to Rome. There he sent him to the best schools, including that of ORBILIUS, and protected from evil influences by acting personally as his *paedagogus* or escort, a task normally performed by a slave. He could even afford to send his son to Athens to complete his liberal education in Greek philosophy and literature. While Horace was there, the civil war of 44 BC broke out between the supporters of Julius CAESAR (1) and his assassins. Horace joined the latter faction and enrolled as a military tribune in BRUTUS (5)'s army, which was defeated at Philippi in 42. He fled from the field, as he later admitted, shamefully discarding his shield. The position of military tribune which he had held was normally the preserve of men of equestrian rank or youthful aspirants to the Senate, and the defeat cost Horace much: the farm in Apulia was confiscated and he had to sue for pardon. He was permitted to return to Italy, unlike many other republicans, and had enough money left to buy himself a post as archivist to the quaestors of the treasury.

It was at this period of his life that Horace first started to compose poetry, which came to the attention of VIRGIL and VARIUS Rufus. They introduced him in 39 BC to MAECENAS, the minister of AUGUSTUS and a great patron of literature, who in 38 made him a member of his close circle of literary friends. Later, *c.*34, he gave him an estate in the Sabine country about 25km north of Tibur (Tivoli), which gave him the financial status of an equestrian and enabled him to write free from concern about his livelihood. He was thus able to decline Augustus' offer of the post of his private secretary; he was, however, on affable terms with the emperor, who later seems to have taken over the role of his patron. Horace was delighted with his Sabine retreat, and divided his time between it and the city. He left a description of himself: short of stature, with dark eyes and prematurely grey hair, and inclined to stoutness; his health was poor and in later life he cultivated frugal habits to cope with this weakness. He never married. Maecenas left a request to Augustus in his will: 'be mindful of Horatius Flaccus as of me'. Maecenas died in the summer of 8 BC, followed by Horace himself on 27 November. Horace was buried beside Maecenas. His biography was written by SUETONIUS (2) in his *Lives of the Poets*.

Horace's poetic works are remarkably varied, and include both lyrical and satirical poems in several metres. His earliest work was the book of *Epodes*, completed and published in 30 BC, consisting of seventeen iambic or iambo-dactylic poems mainly on satirical themes: eight are invectives against unidentifiable people. They are based on the example of the Greek poets Archilochus and Hipponax, and their mockery and bitterness may well reflect Horace's feelings in the aftermath of Philippi and the loss of his property. Some of these poems offer the Romans advice and warning; some are poems on love affairs. Indeed, the polish and sophistication of the *Epodes* owe more to Hellenistic predecessors than to the early Greek poets.

During the thirties BC Horace was also writing his two books of *Satires* in hexameter verse which he also called 'chats' (*sermones*). His chief model for this kind of composition was LUCILIUS (1), even though ENNIUS and PACUVIUS had also written satires. These were also published in 30: they are composed in a loose, conversational style which is nearly prose, and range far and wide in their subject matter. Book 1 contains ten satires of which only one has a date: number 5, the *Journey to Brundisium*, has a dramatic date in 37 BC. The 'voice' in book 1 is Horace himself, and the audience learns of his feelings, opinions and experiences in a number of situations. The first three satires are diatribes, the next three autobiographical, satires 7–9 recount anecdotes, and 10 is a consideration of Horace's own satiric art. Book 2, with eight satires, is of similar length to book 1: it consists of a series of dialogues (except one) with a strong parallelism between the themes of first four and the last four poems.

In 23 BC Horace published three books of *Odes* (*Songs*), and about ten years later yet another. Original as were his *Satires*, the achievement of the *Odes* is unique in Latin literature. His models were the early Greek lyric poets such as Alcaeus, Sappho, Pindar and Anacreon, but he also owed a debt to the Alexandrian poets for his polished style, to the Greek writers of epigram, and to his Roman predecessor CATULLUS (1). The range of theme and style in the eighty-eight poems in the first three books is enormous: from resonant poems on great national and moral themes to the much more frequent and congenial poems on love, friendship, philosophical reflection, drinking and partying, and hymns to gods which dwell on mythological stories and divine exploits but are not intended to be performed in worship. The whole work is introduced by a dedication to Maecenas and ends with a final august claim to literary immortality. The poems are complex, subtle, carefully crafted, sometimes teasing or ironic (especially regarding himself) and metrically ingenious and effective. The development of thought in an ode is often concealed at first and the goal only hinted at; Horace will take his audience on a path which moves unpredictably along the lines he has chosen; word-order is difficult and complex but liberates the poet to produce original effects. He succeeded in composing poetry of great technical skill, which appealed to a wide spectrum of taste. There is, however, a contrast between his poetry and that of the previous two centuries. Horace does not strive for a unity of atmosphere in each ode but is happy, especially in longer poems, to travel long distances from the tone or mood presented at the outset and to shift his focus of attention in surprising ways. Here his work shows a marked contrast with the love poetry of Catullus and PROPERTIUS. The order of the poems is carefully arranged to place serious and important poems near the beginnings and ends of the books and to achieve balance by interspersing the lighter poems among the more weighty. The metres of the *Odes* are varied: Sapphics, Alcaics, Asclepiads both greater and lesser, and a few isolated poems in other metres.

Augustus commissioned Horace (now regarded as a 'poet laureate') to compose a hymn, the *Carmen Saeculare* or *Centenary Hymn*, for performance by twenty-seven boys and the same number of girls at the Centenary Games to be held in 17. At the same time he encouraged him to write the fourth book of the *Odes* containing fifteen poems, which he dedicated to a friend, Paullus FABIUS (9) Maximus. The collection contains a few poems of political import requested by Augustus, celebrating victories won by imperial generals TIBERIUS and DRUSUS (3); and the tone is generally more serious than in the first three books.

The last literary compositions of Horace were the *Epistles*, which revert to the style and themes of the *Satires*. The *Epistles* are in the form of letters in hexameter verse addressed to various people, but without the pretence that real letters are being sent on real occasions. That the recipients of the twenty epistles of book 1 are sometimes recognisable is not the point: the form allows Horace to handle many different topics in a personal and subjective way. The first book is full of humorous and colourful stories and portraits, though the style is somewhat more refined than in the *Satires*. Book 1 is hard to date but cannot have been published before 20 BC. Book 2 contains two very long epistles, addressed to Augustus and Florus, and cannot be earlier than 15. The first, to Augustus, voices a complaint against contemporary taste, which prefers the works of earlier Latin writers to present-day writing, and seeks to exalt the latter. To Florus, a friend of Tiberius, he writes that he prefers to study philosophy rather than continue to involve himself with lyric poetry. The *Art of Poetry* (not Horace's title), which is really an epistle like those in this group, is addressed to Lucius PISO (7), consul of 15 BC, and his two sons. It is nearly 500 lines long, and follows the tradition of Aristotle's teachings about literature. Horace treats his subject with humour and skill but says nothing new or profound about the kind of poetry he himself wrote, concentrating for the most part on epic and drama. He is said to have based his discussion on a series of maxims drawn from a manual by the Hellenistic Greek critic, Neoptolemus of Parium, on each of which Horace comments in turn. It contains a number of well known and oft quoted phrases (the 'purple patch', 'Homer nods', *ridiculus mus* for bathos, *in medias res* for plunging abruptly into a new subject) and was very inflential on later European literature. See E. Fraenkel (1957) *Horace*, Oxford: Clarendon Press; C.O. Brink (1971) *Horace on Poetry*, Cambridge: Cambridge University Press; R.O.A.M. Lyne (1980) *The Latin Love Poets*, Oxford: Clarendon Press; N. Rudd (1980) *The Satires of Horace*, Cambridge: Cambridge University Press; G. Williams (1968) *Tradition and Originality in Roman Poetry*, Oxford: Clarendon Press; P. Levi (1997) *Horace, a Life*, London: Duckworth.

Hortensius 1, Quintus (C3 BC), was a plebeian hero. The plebeians, oppressed by the debts they owed to their patrician creditors, seceded *c*.287 BC from Rome to the Janiculum, a hill across the Tiber – their last such secession. Hortensius was elected dictator and was commissioned to bring the strife to an end. He passed two laws: by the first the plebeian assembly was given the power to pass laws binding on the whole state without the need for the senate to ratify them. His other law allowed lawsuits to take place on market days, so that the peasants would be able to participate in them. The relevance of his measures to the debt problem is not obvious. He was the only dictator to die in office.

2. Hortalus, Quintus (114–50 BC), was a Roman advocate, descended from HORTENSIUS (1). He was a childhood friend of LUCULLUS (2) and SISENNA, and was involved in the Social War in Italy (91–

87 BC). He cultivated oratory, developing a florid Asianic style of speaking, enjoying success during the domination of CINNA (2) and CARBO (5). He went over to SULLA (2) on the latter's return to Italy in 83 and was the leading forensic orator of the 70s. He married a daughter of CATULUS (2). He resorted to large-scale bribery in the courts and was only checked when CICERO (1) successfully prosecuted his friend, the corrupt governor of Sicily VERRES in 70 BC, the year before Hortensius' consulship. He championed the cause of the *Optimates* or aristocratic party as against the *Populares*, and continued to play a part in politics and at the bar. He opposed POMPEIUS (2)'s special commands from 67 to 62. He later spoke alongside his former rival, CICERO (1), in several cases such as those of RABIRIUS (2), Publius SULLA (3) and SESTIUS, but as the junior partner. He gradually retired from public life and devoted himself to good living, his gardens and fishponds: Cicero rated him a *piscinarius* or idle plutocrat at this time. Cicero warmed to him after his death and wrote glowingly of him in his *Brutus* and *Hortensius*; he had been touched by Hortensius' support for his application to become an augur in the state religion. None of his speeches survives. His only son was executed by ANTONIUS (7) after the battle of Philippi.

Hostius (C2 BC) was a Roman epic poet whose *Istrian War* (*Bellum Histricum*) in at least two books commemorated the victory of Gaius SEMPRONIUS Tuditanus (to whom he was related) over the Illyrian Iapyges in Istria in 129 BC. A few fragments survive.

Hyginus 1, Gaius Julius (C1 BC), was a scholar from Spain or Alexandria who was brought as a slave to Rome by Julius CAESAR (1), freed by AUGUSTUS, and appointed to be librarian of his Palatine Library. He studied under ALEXANDER (7) Polyhistor and himself taught OVID, who addressed him in poem 14 of *Sorrows* (*Tristia*), book 3. We know the titles of his works, which are all lost: *Agriculture*, *A Commentary on Virgil* cited by GELLIUS (1) and Servius, *Trojan Families*, *The Origins and Sites of Italian Towns*, *The Lives and Histories of Famous Men* with examples, *The Properties of the Gods* and *The Household Gods*.

2. (*c.*AD 100) A Roman writer on surveying who wrote treatises, still extant, on *Boundaries*, *Categories of Land* (including their designation on maps), and *Land Disputes*. The author refers also to a lost work of his on imperial decisions relating to land.

3. Two works in Latin were traditionally ascribed to a Hyginus who, as he knew no Greek, cannot be HYGINUS (1): *Genealogies*, a handbook on mythology derived from Greek sources by one ignorant of that language, of which the manuscript was lost in the Renaissance after it had been edited by Micyllus of Basel under the title *Fabulae*. It seems that we have an abridgment of the original work. The other is a work on astronomy, which may be by the same man.

4. A Roman writer on land-division and allocation, of unknown date, often referred to as *Gromaticus*, 'the surveyor'. An incomplete treatise, *The Fortifications of Camps*, has wrongly been attributed to him.

Hyrcanus 1, Johanan (John) (ruled 135–104 BC), was a ruler and high priest of Judaea, the third son of the Hasmonean Simon Maccabaeus. After military exploits against the Syrians, he succeeded his murdered father in 135, and held office until his death. After initial opposition from the Seleucid king of Syria, ANTIOCHUS (5) VII, who besieged Jerusalem, Hyrcanus made peace with him and an alliance against the Parthians. He renewed Hasmonean treaties with Rome. He annexed Samaria and Idumaea to the Jewish state and forcibly converted his

Idumaean subjects to Judaism. His elder son ARISTOBULUS (1) succeeded him briefly, to be followed by his younger son ALEXANDER (1) Jannaeus. The increasing Hellenism of these reigns caused dissension among the Jewish people, especially the Pharisees. See W.D. Davies and L. Finkelstein (1989) *The Cambridge History of Judaism*, vol. 2, Cambridge: Cambridge University Press; R.D. Sullivan (1990) *Near Eastern Royalty and Rome, 100–30 BC*, Toronto: University of Toronto Press.

2. (C1 BC) was a high priest of the Jews, son of ALEXANDER (1) Jannaeus and ALEXANDRA Salome. He succeeded to the office in 76 BC which he exercised while his mother was in power: when she died in 67 her sons quarrelled over the succession to political power and his brother ARISTOBULUS (2) expelled and replaced Hyrcanus. He took refuge with ANTIPATER (2) of Idumaea, and in 63 POMPEIUS (2) restored him as high priest and made him ethnarch, namely ruler of Judaea under Roman suzerainty. In 57, however, GABINIUS (2), governor of Syria, gave the ethnarchy to Antipater, leaving Hyrcanus with the priesthood. In 47 Hyrcanus gave assistance to Julius CAESAR (1) when he was embroiled at Alexandria, and was rewarded with reappointment as ethnarch. The Parthian invasion in 40, however, led to Hyrcanus' removal from office and exile in Babylonia: his enemies mutilated him to render him unfit to serve as priest again. In 36 HEROD (1) invited him back to Judaea, but had him executed in 30 BC on a charge of treason. See W.D. Davies and L. Finkelstein (1989) *The Cambridge History of Judaism*, vol. 2, Cambridge: Cambridge University Press; R.D. Sullivan (1990) *Near Eastern Royalty and Rome, 100–30 BC*, Toronto: University of Toronto Press.

I

Iarbas *see* HIEMPSAL (2).

Ignatius (*c.*AD 35–*c.*107) was a Christian bishop of Antioch. He was arrested under the emperor TRAJAN in 107 and dispatched to Rome for trial; on the way he visited POLYCARP at Smyrna and wrote the surviving *Ignatian Epistles*, which warned against Judaism and Docetism and encouraged the churches of Asia Minor. He was said to be a disciple of John (the disciple of JESUS) and was the second Christian bishop of his see. His martyrdom is confirmed by statements of POLYCARP and ORIGEN (1).

Innocentius (C4 AD) was a land-surveyor, though the book attributed to him, *Casae Litterarum* or *Estates by Letter*, is by a writer of some two centuries later in date. In it thirty-nine different types of farm or estate are categorised by a letter of the Latin or Greek alphabet. The language of the treatise shows development into Vulgar Latin.

Irenaeus (*c.*AD 130–202) was a Greek Christian apologist and theologian from Smyrna, later bishop of Lugdunum (Lyons) in Gaul. In his youth he came under the influence of POLYCARP. He wrote two works, *Against Heresies*, which has survived in Latin, Syriac and Armenian translations and opposes Gnostic and especially Valentinian teachings, and a brief *Proof of Apostolic Preaching*, extant in an Armenian translation. He intervened with the Roman church in 177 for the Montanists of Lyons, where he was a presbyter under Pothinus, and on whose martyrdom in that year he was elected its bishop. In 190 he defended the Quartodecimans, an Asian Christian sect who observed Easter at the Passover. He was possibly a victim of the Severan persecution. He was an important bridge between eastern Christianity and the west. See H. Chadwick (1986) *The Early Church*, Harmondsworth: Penguin; R.M. Grant (1997) *Irenaeus of Lyons*, London: Routledge.

Isauricus 1, Publius Servilius Vatia (134–44 BC), was a supporter of SULLA (2). A grandson of METELLUS (4) Macedonicus, he was granted a triumph by Sulla in 88 BC for his achievements in Sardinia; he lost the consulship of 87 to CINNA (2). He gave Sulla valiant support in his campaigns in Italy in the Civil War of 83–81, and was rewarded with the consulship of 79. Proconsul for four years in Lycia and Cilicia (CAESAR 1 was on his staff briefly in 78), he rooted out piracy there and in Pamphylia and fixed the borders of Cilicia. He captured the town of Old Isaura and took its name. He held another triumph on his return home, and was elected censor in 55 with Marcus MESSALLA (2) as his colleague.

2, Publius Servilius (died *c.*40 BC), was the son of ISAURICUS (1). He began his political career as praetor in 54 under the wing of CATO (5), but joined the supporters of CAESAR (1), whose colleague he was in the consulship of 48. He collaborated in 47 with Marcus ANTONIUS (7), Master of the Horse in Caesar's dictatorship, in dealing with an armed insurrection by some disgruntled debtors, young nobles led by Caelius RUFUS (1) and DOLABELLA (4). He then became proconsul of Asia, and corresponded with CICERO (1), but publicly quarrelled with him in 43. He had married Junia, a daughter of SERVILIA, and in 43 betrothed his daughter to Octavian (AUGUSTUS), who jilted her. In compensation, he was awarded the consulship of 41, but failed to assist Octavian in the Perusine War.

Isidorus (early C1 AD) was a Parthian from Charax at the head of the Persian Gulf who wrote in Greek on geography. PLINY (1) the Elder quotes his work on the staging posts along the way between Parthia and Syria, and his work on pearl fisheries of the Gulf.

J

Jannaeus *see* ALEXANDER (1).

Javolenus Priscus, Gaius (or Lucius) Octavius Tidius Tossianus (late C1 AD), was a Roman jurist and administrator. He commanded two legions and held the post of *iuridicus* (second in rank to the governor) in Britain. He was appointed suffect consul in 86 and in 90 governed Upper Germany. A year or two later he governed Syria and *c.*96 was proconsul of Africa. TRAJAN promoted him to membership of his privy council. He was head of the Sabinian law school and wrote abridgments with brief comments of works of Antistius LABEO (his *Posthumous Works*), CASSIUS (3) Longinus, and Plautius. He also published fifteen books of *Letters* on legal problems, which have not survived but are quoted extensively by the compilers of Justinian's *Digest.* He was known by the Younger PLINY (2) (see *Letters*, 6, 15). He taught JULIANUS.

Jesus (*c.*10 BC–AD 36) was a Jewish religious teacher and charismatic from Nazareth in Galilee. Born during the reign of HEROD (1) the Great, he began a preaching mission *c.*AD 34 (see JOHN), and taught in the synagogues. The facts of his life are difficult to recapture owing to the nature of the sources, but he was rejected by his family (who had high expectations of him) and his fellow-townsmen of Nazareth, and spent much of this time in the countryside of Galilee, especially at Capernaum. Galilee at that time was ruled by the tetrarch HEROD (2) Antipas and was separate from Judaea. After the death of John he left Galilee for a time. According to imaginative accounts of his life written some decades later, the *Gospels*, he preached that a new dispensation, the 'Kingdom of Heaven', was imminent. The image of him presented in the *Gospels* is that of a prophet, healer, exorcist and miracle-worker, proclaiming the imminent arrival of the new kingdom, and challenging his hearers to confront their unreadiness for the coming age. This he did within the framework of traditional Judaism, especially as it was practised by the Pharisees, but he offered more liberal interpretations of the Judaic law, which led to conflict with the established religious authorities. But he became extremely popular and gathered a number of disciples and hearers, including many women, though he was apparently unmarried. His association with people such as notorious wrongdoers and hated tax-gatherers, regarded as agents of Rome, was considered scandalous by his critics, the scribes and Pharisees.

He may have expected a divine intervention (the 'Day of the Lord'), when God would miraculously expel the Romans and establish a purified Jewish state in Judaea, with Jesus himself as its ruler. He went with his disciples to Jerusalem before the Passover in 36 and, according to the first three *Gospels*, entered the city in a 'triumphal' procession, 'cleansed' the Temple by driving out the traders, and predicted its destruction. John's *Gospel*, however, regards him as already a wanted man at the time of his coming to Jerusalem, and dates the Temple cleansing much earlier. He was arrested in a garden outside the city by the high priest's men or a unit of Roman soldiers led by a military tribune. The high priest Caiaphas and an informal group of members of his council, the Sanhedrin, delivered him to the Roman prefect of Judaea, Pontius PILATE, for trial and execution as a troublemaker and potential rebel. They feared the wrath of the Romans if they allowed Jesus' apparent threats to go unchecked: he was also suspect as the leader of a band of Galileans, who had a reputation for rebelliousness. For claiming to be king of the Jews and thus a rebel against Rome, he was crucified, the normal Roman punishment for unenfranchised criminals, probably on 30 March 36, the day before the Passover (see the *Gospel of John*). None of his disciples was made to share his punishment, which suggests that the authorities were satisfied they had dealt with the threat he posed. A claim was made in the *Gospels* that he rose from the dead and appeared to his followers in several places before ascending, like Elijah, into the sky. There was also an expectation of his imminent return as a glorious judge and king; there is, however, much discrepancy in the four *Gospels* over the details of events during Jesus' last days. His brother James, who had previously been aloof from Jesus' mission, became the leader of Jesus' Jewish followers, and the Jerusalem branch of the movement continued as a Jewish sect (the Nazarenes or Ebionites) until HADRIAN expelled the Jews from Judaea in 134.

No contemporary account of Jesus exists: apart from a brief and sympathetic allusion to him (contaminated by a Christian interpolator) by JOSEPHUS, writing in the *Jewish Antiquities* fifty years later (18. 3, 3), the earliest documents about him are Christian. Various members of early Christian communities, already separated from Judaism, wrote accounts of him: such are the four *Gospels* and the *Acts of the Apostles*, written from *c.*AD 70 onwards. They were not written by or for historians, but to spread a religious ideology. Other testimonies and open letters, often of pseudonymous authorship and anti-Jewish in tone, were composed within forty years or so of his death. Thus in considering his life it is very difficult to disentangle fact from myth. His historical importance lies in the effect of the spreading of a redemptive creed centred upon his life and death, based on the accounts of these given in the *Gospels*, and on the conversion of non-Jews by PAUL and others, which competed with and eventually, after the conversion of CONSTANTINE (1) I, largely replaced the other religious cults and philosophies of the later Roman empire. The century following the splitting of the now largely gentile Church from Judaism, a change brought about by Paul and other Christian missionaries and accelerated by the fall of Jerusalem to TITUS in 70, saw great developments in the nature of Christianity. Subsequently the Church was organised, like a parallel state, along territorial lines based on Roman administrative districts, and incorporated much Greek philosophy into its theology. Paradoxically, much of the culture of the classical world was later preserved through the strength of the Roman and Byzantine Churches, though Christians also censored and destroyed much that was valuable, such as documents concerning Epicurean and other philosophy, comic plays, and erotic poetry such as Sappho's lyrics.

See also ATHANASIUS, BASIL, CLEMENT, EUSEBIUS, GREGORY, HERMAS, JUSTIN, ORIGEN (1).

See E.J. Bickerman (1986) *Studies in Jewish and Christian History*, Leiden: E.J. Brill; R. Lane Fox (1991) *The Unauthorised*

Version, Harmondsworth: Penguin; and (1986) *Pagans and Christians*, Harmondsworth: Penguin; G. Vermes (1983) *Jesus the Jew*, 2nd edn (and other titles) London: SCM Press; M. Grant (1977) *Jesus*, London: Weidenfeld & Nicolson; H. Chadwick (1986) *The Early Church*, 2nd edn, Harmondsworth: Penguin; E.P. Sanders (1993) *The Historical Figure of Jesus*, London: Allen Lane; A.N. Wilson (1992) *Jesus*, London: Sinclair-Stevenson.

John the Baptist (died AD 34) was a Jewish prophet and preacher and, according to the Christian *Gospels*, a cousin of JESUS of Nazareth, whom John is said to have baptised in the river Jordan *c.*AD 34. He began preaching a call to repentance *c.*AD 29, and gathered a large following including sinners and outcasts of society, but fell foul of HEROD (2) Antipas in 34 by denouncing him for marrying Herodias, his brother PHILIP (2)'s former wife. He was arrested, perhaps because Herod feared his popularity, and executed at the request of Herodias' daughter Salome. There were reports that he rose from the dead. His follower Apollos carried his message to the Jewish diaspora, and was confronted by PAUL. See Josephus, *Jewish Antiquities*, 18. 5, 2.

Josephus, Titus (?) Flavius (AD 37–*c.*100), was a Jewish historian and apologist for Rome. The son of Matthias, he was of a noble family, a member of the priesthood, and a kinsman of the Hasmoneans. Our knowledge of him derives entirely from his own writings. In his youth he studied the three 'philosophical' schools of the Jews, finally rejecting the Sadducees and Essenes for the Pharisees. He spent three years in the wilderness with an Essene hermit named Banos. In 56 he embarked on education as a Pharisee, and in 64 was one of a delegation sent to Rome to try to obtain the release of certain Jewish priests who had been sent there for trial by the procurator FELIX some years before. He obtained the help of NERO (1)'s wife POPPAEA and succeeded in his mission: but he was greatly impressed by the power of Rome and formed the conviction that God favoured the Romans for the present and it would be pointless to resist them. On his return home, therefore, he argued against rebellion, but was nevertheless made commander of Galilee for the rebels on the outbreak of war in 66. In the war his attitude was ambiguous: he was besieged in Jotapata and in 67, after evading a suicide pact of the leaders, he was captured by the Romans and saved himself by prophesying that VESPASIAN would become emperor, which happened in 69. He stayed with TITUS during the siege of Jerusalem and failed in his attempts to persuade the besieged to surrender. At the storming of the city he saved the lives of a number of his friends. He was granted land in Judaea and accompanied Titus to Rome where the emperor made him a Roman citizen and gave him a pension and a house in the capital.

Following Roman custom and taking the name Flavius in honour of the new emperor, Josephus settled in Rome and wrote four works, the *Jewish War*, first in Aramaic for the Jews of Mesopotamia. He then, between AD 75 and 79, wrote a Greek version in seven books. This work covered the period between 170 BC and AD 70 and is an invaluable historical source, more especially for the period of his own lifetime. He appears to have had access to the campaign logs (*commentarii*) of Vespasian and Titus as well as consulting others who had witnessed the events described: and he was himself a witness of many. He included an account of the Roman triumph over the Jews. At the outset he knew little Greek and was aided in his work by Greek assistants. The work was later translated into Latin and Old Slavonic. His *Jewish Antiquities* in twenty books, finished in 93, is a further history of the Jews from the 'creation' to AD 66. This was essentially aimed at Greek-speaking readers, Jewish and gentile, modelled on DIONYSIUS of Halicarnassus' *Roman Antiquities*, and depended on a variety of sources. The first ten books are based on the Hebrew scriptures. His account of Maccabean times is fuller than in his earlier work. He paraphrased the letter of Aristeas, which purports to describe the process of translating the Septuagint, and he adapted the Second Book of Esdras and the First of Maccabees, drawing heavily on the works of NICOLAUS of Damascus for the last seventy-five years BC. He added to the latter work a brief *Autobiography*, in which he defends himself against the charge, asserted by JUSTUS of Tiberias among others, of having caused the Jewish rebellion. He also wrote two books entitled *Against Apion* (see APION), defending the Jews against attacks by Greeks and asserting the antiquity of Judaism in comparison to Hellenic culture. He was notoriously inaccurate in giving statistical evidence. His works were of great interest to Christians of all periods, and were preserved by the Church; but his favourable reference to JESUS in the *Antiquities* was later embroidered by a Christian interpolator. References in his last two works prove he lived until at least AD 93. See T. Rajak (1983) *Josephus, the Historian and his Society*, London: Duckworth; P. Bilde (1988) *Flavius Josephus: Between Jerusalem and Rome*, Sheffield: JSOT; S.J.D. Cohen (1979) *Josephus in Galilee and Rome*, Leiden: E.J. Brill; G.A. Williamson (tr) (1981) *Josephus: The Jewish War*, rev. E.M. Smallwood, Harmondsworth: Penguin.

Jovian (AD 331–364) was born Flavius Jovianus of Danubian parents at Singidunum (Belgrade). He had been household praetor to the emperor JULIAN and served on his campaign in Persia. When Julian was killed in June 363 Jovian was elected emperor by the army, and to extricate the army from its exposed position he made an unpopular treaty with the Persians by which he surrendered DIOCLETIAN's conquests to the east of the river Tigris as well as Nisibis and Singara. He overturned Julian's religious reforms in favour of Christianity, but died in February 364 at Dadastana in Asia Minor while travelling to Constantinople. See M. Grant (1985) *The Roman Emperors*, London: Weidenfeld & Nicolson.

Juba 1. I (reigned 60–46 BC) was a king of Numidia, the son and successor of HIEMPSAL (2), and is known from pro-Caesarian writers for his arrogance and cruelty. In his youth he went on an embassy to Rome where he was slighted by Julius CAESAR (1). He nursed resentment against him and supported POMPEIUS (2) in the Civil War. When CURIO (2) as Caesar's legate entered Africa in 49 BC and determined to annex his kingdom, Juba opposed him and wiped out his force in the battle of the Bagradas in which Curio was killed. After the battle of Pharsalus in August 48, he embarked on a policy of annexing the province of Africa, encouraged as he claimed by METELLUS (11) Scipio. CATO (5) refused to admit him to Utica; he was attacked by SITTIUS and King BOCCHUS II but was able to unite with the republican Metellus Scipio to oppose Caesar at the battle of Thapsus in 46. He escaped after their defeat and subsequently, lacking any support, killed himself in a suicide pact with Marcus PETREIUS. See D. Braund (1984) *Rome and the Friendly King*, London: Croom Helm.

2. II (died *c.*AD 23) A king of Mauretania, the son of JUBA (1). CAESAR (1) captured him as a small child after the battle of Thapsus in 46 BC and had him led in his triumphal procession. In 30 BC Octavian (see AUGUSTUS), who had kept him at his court and given him Roman citizenship, made him client king of Numidia. He later married him to Cleopatra Selene, daughter of ANTONIUS (7) and CLEOPATRA (4) VII. In 25 BC, however, Augustus annexed Numidia to the province of Africa and gave Juba in exchange Mauretania and part of Gaetulia. The Gaetuli, who rebelled *c.*AD 6, were reduced with help from the Roman governor of Africa, Cossus LENTULUS (1). During Juba's reign Augustus founded twelve Roman colonies on the coast including Tingis (Tangier). In AD 17 Juba assisted in the defeat of the rebel TACFARINAS. After Cleopatra's death he married GLAPHYRA (2). He was succeeded by his son by his first marriage, PTOLEMY (12).

He was a man of great learning who wrote in Greek books on historical, geographical, literary, artistic and botanical subjects, none of which has survived, which were used as sources by among others PLINY (1) the Elder and PLUTARCH. He encouraged the spread of Greek and Roman culture in Mauretania. He established fine artistic collections housed at his two capital cities of Caesarea (previously Iol) on the coast and Volubilis in the Atlas Mountains. He encouraged the development of a dye, Gaetulian purple. He sent an expedition to explore the Canary Islands. See D. Braund (1984) *Rome and the Friendly King*, London: Croom Helm.

Judas Maccabaeus (died 160 BC) was a Jewish revolutionary of the Hasmonean family, the son of Mattathias. He and his brothers led the revolt in 167 BC against the Seleucid attempt to take over the Temple and citadel at Jerusalem and exclude the Jews from their holy place. With a band of loyal followers, they drove out the 'pagan' cult, then fled into the desert, where they gained strength. When his father died in 166, Judas took command and gradually restored Jewish worship in the cities of Judaea. After recapturing Jerusalem and rededicating the Temple in 164, he made an alliance with Rome. He continued a political struggle with the Jewish hellenisers, and was killed in battle in 160. His brothers succeeded in driving out the hellenisers. See E.J. Bickerman (1988) *The Jews in the Greek Age*, Cambridge MA: Harvard University Press; W.D. Davies and L. Finkelstein (1989) *The Cambridge History of Judaism*, vol. 2, Cambridge: Cambridge University Press, 1989.

Jugurtha (*c.*150–104 BC) was a king of Numidia. He was the illegitimate son of Mastanabal and a grandson of MASINISSA. He lost his father at an early age and was brought up by his uncle, king MICIPSA, together with Micipsa's own sons, ADHERBAL and HIEMPSAL (1). He served in the Roman army in 133 at the siege of Numantia in Spain under SCIPIO (11) Aemilianus, patron of Numidian royalty, and made such a great impression on the Roman that he recommended Micipsa to adopt him. On the death of Micipsa in 118, Jugurtha inherited a third of the kingdom along with his 'brothers', but on their objection to the arrangement he murdered Hiempsal and made war on Adherbal. Adherbal was defeated and fled to Rome, where he asked the help of the Senate. A Roman commissioner, Lucius OPIMIUS, divided Numidia up and awarded the poorer western half to Jugurtha. But he was not satisfied, and in 112 attacked Adherbal again, besieging him in Cirta (Constantine). Despite two embassies from the Senate, one of which was led by the president of the Senate, M. Aemilius SCAURUS (2), Jugurtha persisted in the siege, and on taking the town killed Adherbal and a number of Italian residents who had assisted in its defence. The Roman people, instigated by Gaius MEMMIUS (1), were outraged by Jugurtha's action and the Senate determined to intervene. An army was sent the following year (111) under the ineffective L. Calpurnius BESTIA who, after bribery or persuasion by Jugurtha's Roman friends, concluded a peace with Jugurtha which the Senate disavowed. In the turmoil that followed, Jugurtha was invited to Rome under safe conduct to reveal who his supporters were, but was prevented from speaking in the Assembly by the interdiction of the tribune C. Baebius. After arranging the assassination by BOMILCAR of Massiva, his cousin and rival for the throne of Numidia, who was then a refugee in Rome, Jugurtha returned home.

The war was therefore resumed and a large army was dispatched under the consul for 110, Sp. Postumius ALBINUS (4), who left it to his brother Aulus to lead a disastrous winter campaign: his army was routed and forced to go under the yoke. The natural outrage in Rome led to the creation of a commission under MAMILIUS (1) to enquire into corruption among the nobles, and the dispatch of a further army under the new consul, Q. Caecilius METELLUS (5), who won military successes over Jugurtha, but could not deliver a decisive blow. Gaius MARIUS (1) used his reputation gained as senior legate in Metellus' campaign to obtain the consulship of 107, and after opening up military service to the lowest class of citizens, took a new army to Numidia but failed to win the war. This was only achieved in 105 when SULLA (2) persuaded Jugurtha's father-in-law BOCCHUS (1), king of Mauretania, to surrender him in exchange for the title 'friend of the Roman People'. Jugurtha was paraded in Marius' undeserved triumph and then, on 1 January 104, put to death. The main impact of the war was its effect on Roman politics and the development of the Roman army, destined to become a force in politics, rather than any change to the scene in Africa. See Sallust, *Jugurthine War*; R. Syme (1964) *Sallust*, Berkeley: University of California Press; T. F. Carney (1970) *A Biography of Gaius Marius*, Chicago: Argonaut.

Julia 1. was the wife of Gaius MARIUS (1), whom she married in 113 BC. She bore a son, Gaius MARIUS (2). Her funeral oration was spoken by her nephew, Julius CAESAR (1).

2. was the daughter of L. Julius CAESAR (5) and mother of Marcus ANTONIUS (7).

3. was CAESAR (1)'s sister, the wife of M. Atius Balbus and the grandmother of AUGUSTUS.

4. was CAESAR (1)'s daughter by CORNELIA (2); she married POMPEIUS (2), who loved her deeply, and died in childbirth in 54 BC.

5. (39 BC–AD 14) was the only legitimate child of the emperor AUGUSTUS. Her mother was SCRIBONIA, but she was brought up by her father and stepmother, LIVIA (2). She was married in 25 to her cousin MARCELLUS (7) and, after his early death in 23, to M. Vipsanius AGRIPPA (1) in 21. She bore him five children, Gaius CAESAR (3) and Lucius CAESAR (8), JULIA (6), AGRIPPINA (1) and AGRIPPA (2) Postumus. She was finally married in 11 BC to TIBERIUS, who detested her, and after she had borne him a son who died in infancy, retired in 6 BC to Rhodes without her. In 2 BC she was banished by Augustus, probably for a plot involving Iullus ANTONIUS (3), to the island of Pandataria. Her mother accompanied her into exile. She was later transferred to Rhegium where she died in the year of her father's death. See H.H. Scullard (1982) *From the Gracchi to Nero*, London: Methuen.

6. (18 BC–AD 28) was the daughter of JULIA (5): she married *c.*4 BC Lucius Aemilius PAULLUS (4), and after his execution for conspiracy was banished by her grandfather for immoral conduct with Decimus Junius SILANUS and others; she was recalled but in AD 8 finally exiled for the rest of her life on the isle of Trimerus in the Adriatic (see OVID). Her daughter, Aemilia Lepida, married Marcus Junius SILANUS.

7. Drusilla (AD 17–38) was the second daughter of GERMANICUS and AGRIPPINA (2), and was married first to CASSIUS (5) Longinus, consul in 30, and second to M. Aemilius LEPIDUS (7). She was believed to have had incestuous relations with her brother CALIGULA, who made her husband

and then herself his heir and deified her after her death.

8. Livilla (born AD 18) was the youngest child of GERMANICUS and AGRIPPINA (2). She was married to Marcus Vinicius in 33 and was honoured by her brother the emperor Gaius (CALIGULA) until he banished her for adultery with her brother-in-law LEPIDUS (7) and implication in the plot of LENTULUS (6) Gaetulicus to kill Caligula. She was brought back to Rome by CLAUDIUS (1) but later accused by his wife MESSALLINA of adultery with SENECA (2); she was once more banished and later murdered.

9. Balbilla (C2 AD), a friend of HADRIAN and his wife SABINA, accompanied them on their trip to the Colossi of Memnon in Egypt in November AD 130. There she wrote and inscribed four extant elegiac poems. On her mother's side she was a member of the royal family of Commagene.

10. Domna (died AD 217) was the wife of the emperor Septimius SEVERUS (1), whom she married in 187. She was a Syrian: her father, Julius Bassianus, was a priest of the sun god Elagabalus at Emesa. She bore CARACALLA and GETA (3) and in 193 was granted the title *Augusta*, and two years later 'Mother of the Camp'. From about 200 she lost her influence to the praetorian prefect Plautianus, but regained it when Caracalla had him killed in 205. She was well educated and was unofficially known as 'the Philosopher'. She encouraged GALEN and PHILOSTRATUS, inspiring the latter to write his *Life of Apollonius of Tyana*. She tried in vain to save Geta from his brother, but flourished in Caracalla's court, acting as supervisor of his correspondence. She brought a number of Greek and Roman scholars of law, science and literature to the court, including Galen, Philostratus, Diogenes Laërtius, AELIANUS, Oppian, PAPINIANUS, PAULUS and ULPIANUS. She committed suicide in 217 at Antioch on hearing of Caracalla's murder. JULIA (11) Maesa was her sister. See M. Grant (1985) *The Roman Emperors*, London: Weidenfeld & Nicolson.

11. Maesa (died 226 AD) was the daughter of Julius Bassianus of Emesa and sister of JULIA (10) Domna. She married C. Julius Avitus Alexianus, a distinguished Syrian who attained the rank of consul, and bore JULIA (12) Soaemias Bassiana and JULIA (13) Avita Mamaea. After the assassination of CARACALLA in 217 she returned to Emesa but was involved in the coup in 218 which raised her grandson ELAGABALUS to the purple: she accompanied him to Rome where he gave her the title of *Augusta* and named her 'Mother of the Army and the Senate'. In 221 she persuaded her unpopular grandson to adopt his cousin SEVERUS (2) Alexander, and in the following year, in collusion with Julia Mamaea, bribed the Praetorian Guard to overthrow Elagabalus and replace him with Severus Alexander.

12. Soaemias Bassiana (died AD 222) was the elder daughter of the Syrian C. Julius AVITUS Alexianus and JULIA (11) Maesa: *c.*AD 200 she married a Syrian equestrian, Sextus Varius Marcellus, and in 204 bore the future emperor ELAGABALUS. When he was fourteen she conspired with her mother to assassinate MACRINUS and set Elagabalus on the imperial throne, pretending that he was the illegitimate son of CARACALLA. She was murdered at the time of her son's deposition and death.

13. Avita Mamaea (C3 AD) was the younger daughter of C. Julius Avitus Alexianus and JULIA (11) Maesa. Her second husband was the Syrian procurator Gessius Marcianus, to whom she bore the future emperor SEVERUS (2) Alexander. Her son gave her the title *Augusta* on his accession in AD 222 and gave her a prominent place in his court. She was murdered with him in 235 by mutinous troops.

See also FLAVIA JULIA.

Julian (AD 331–363) Flavius Claudius Julianus was born at Constantinople, the son of Julius Constantius, a half-brother of the emperor CONSTANTINE (1) I the Great, and his wife Basilina. He was brought up a Christian: after his father was assassinated in 337 his cousin CONSTANTIUS (2) II placed him and GALLUS (3), his half-brother, in a secluded castle in Cappadocia, where they received a Christian education. But Julian also read widely in classical literature under the influence of his tutor the eunuch Mardonius, and formed a secret passion for the old religion. In 351, when his brother Gallus was made *Caesar* (deputy emperor), he went to Ephesus to study under the Neoplatonist philosopher Maximus, and was initiated as a theurgist ('priest') in the rites of that discipline. He went on to further study in Athens, keeping his conversion secret: in November 355, however, he became a public figure when Constantius II summoned him to Milan, married him to his sister Helena, and appointed him *Caesar* with jurisdiction over Gaul and Britain; he thus replaced Gallus who had been executed the previous year. His administration was exemplary, and he reduced the rate of taxation by a prudent reform. He also proved to be an excellent general, winning victories over the Germans: the Alemanni in 356, and the Franks between that year and 359. He was popular with his troops, whose hardships he was content to share, to such an extent that they mutinied when in 360 his best units were ordered to join the emperor's forces in the east. The result of the mutiny was that his army proclaimed Julian emperor (*Augustus*) and in 361 marched with him towards Constantinople. Constantius, however, died in late 361 and the expected conflict was thus averted.

On entering the capital in December 361, Julian, who had openly declared his commitment to the ancestral religion on becoming emperor, decreed the toleration of all religions. At the same time he encouraged the restoration of the old religious cults, appointing priests, rebuilding damaged temples and making funds available for public charity; he removed the state financial support of Christianity and the immunity from taxation of the clergy. Though he did not actively persecute Christianity, Julian sought to marginalise it. He even forbade Christians to teach classical literature. He also planned the restoration of the Jewish Temple in Jerusalem in line with his other measures to revive past religious practices. He reduced the size of the imperial civil service, reformed the organisation of the official postal service, and improved the effectiveness of municipal government by restoring revenues and ensuring the proper election of councils. After six months in Constantinople, Julian moved to Antioch, his springboard for a proposed attack on the Persian empire under King SAPOR II. The people of that mainly Christian city openly showed their opposition to him during his stay and the city council undermined his efforts to relieve a famine. He wrote a satirical defence of his position entitled *The Beard-hater* (i.e. 'the hater of philosophers'). He left Antioch in March 362 at the head of his army and won a victory over SAPOR (2) II's army near Ctesiphon. But he had little success thereafter, his army was harried by Persian flying battalions, and in June 363 he was killed in a skirmish. His wife had died in 360 and he left no heir. The throne was seized by his second-in-command JOVIAN. His friend LIBANIUS delivered his funeral oration.

Julian was a scholar and an ascetic. He was a talented administrator with much financial ability. His writings, many of which survive, show his learning and literary skill. We have about eighty of his letters, some of which give us a picture of the man and his life. He was a satirist, and his *Banquet* is a comic description of Constantine's arrival among the gods of Olympus. Only fragments of his treatise *Against the Galileans*, which opposes

Christianity, survive. There are also eight *Speeches*. Julian's personal commitment seems to have been to the single universal god of the Neoplatonists as taught by Iamblichus. His public stance in favour of a dying polytheistic cult-system seems to have been his chosen means of reducing the influence of Christianity, which later saw him as the 'Apostate'. Though his early death brought the ultimate failure of his policy, he was an extremely diligent and conscientious ruler. See G.W. Bowersock (1978) *Julian the Apostate*, London: Duckworth; R. Browning (1975) *The Emperor Julian*, London: Weidenfeld & Nicolson; S.N.C. Lieu (1986) *The Emperor Julian, Panegyric and Polemic*, Liverpool: Liverpool University Press; R.B.E. Smith (1995) *Julian's Gods*, London: Routledge; M. Grant (1985) *The Roman Emperors*, London: Weidenfeld & Nicolson.

Julianus, Publius Salvius (died *c.*AD 169) Lucius Octavius Cornelius Publius Salvius Julianus Aemilianus was a lawyer of African (Tunisian) extraction from Hadrumetum. He studied under JAVOLENUS Priscus; as quaestor, at HADRIAN's invitation, he revised the praetors' edicts, which were then voted into permanent form as a code of civil law by the Senate in AD 131. He became both an eminent lawyer and a successful state official, being praetor and in 148 consul. He governed Lower Germany in the next years and held further governorships, of Nearer Spain from 161 to 164, and Africa in 167 and 168. He headed the famous Sabidian law school, was a member of Hadrian's privy council, and wrote a vast legal source book, the *Digests*, in ninety books, probably in the decade of the 50s when he held no office. The work was original and highly influential: his approach to legal problems was practical and pragmatic, and he was prepared to admit anomalies. His work was recognised as a primary source by Justinian, whose Code contains many extracts from it. See H.F. Jolowicz and B. Nicholas (1972) *Historical Introduction to the Study of Roman Law*, Cambridge: Cambridge University Press.

Julius Africanus 1. (C1 AD) was a public speaker from Gaul: QUINTILIAN knew him and praised his talent. He quotes from a speech of Julius congratulating NERO (1) on escaping from his mother's 'plot' in AD 59. See Quintilian, *Institutions*, 8. 5, 15.

2. (C3 AD) was a Greek Christian writer from Aelia Capitolina (Jerusalem). He was a member of an embassy to the emperor ELAGABALUS in 220, which gained official status for Emmaeus as the city of Emmaeus Nicopolis. He stayed in Rome, where he formed a library in the Pantheon for the emperor SEVERUS (2) Alexander. He made a chronological comparison between biblical and classical events, and published his findings in five books entitled *Chronographies*, which EUSEBIUS used as a source. He wrote an encyclopaedia in twenty-four books entitled *Amulets* (*Kestoi*), largely about magic: fragments of both these works survive. Two letters are also extant: one to ORIGEN (1) challenging the authenticity of the Apocryphal story of Susannah, the other to one Aristides, attempting to reconcile the conflicting genealogies of JESUS given in the *Gospels*. See F.C.R. Thee (1984) *Julius Africanus and the Early Christian View of Magic*, Tübingen: Mohr.

Junia Calvina (C1 AD) was the daughter of Marcus Junius Silanus Torquatus: in AD 48 her husband Vitellius accused her of incest with her brother Lucius, for which she was banished from Italy in 49. NERO (1) recalled her after the death of his mother AGRIPPINA (3), who was said to have encouraged the incest.

Justin (*c.*AD 100–*c.*165), born at Shechem in Samaria, was a Christian teacher and apologist. He spent his youth travelling in search of a satisfactory philosophy and studied in turn the Stoic, Peripatetic, Pythagorean and finally Platonist creeds. He was converted to Christianity *c.*130 by an old man at Ephesus, more from his admiration of the unflinching bravery of the Christians under persecution than for intellectual reasons. He moved to Rome in mid-life and founded a small school for Christians. He wrote *c.*155 an *Apology*, a defence of Christianity which he addressed to the emperor ANTONINUS Pius, trying to show him that it was an honourable creed and worthy of respect; he wrote a second *c.*162 to MARCUS AURELIUS complaining about the persecution of Christians. His *Dialogue with Trypho* defends Christianity against Judaism. His approach to theology was essentially philosophical, a tendency which was to grow among later theologians. He is said to have been denounced by a Cynic philosopher named Crescens and to have been executed after a trial by the City prefect Quintus Junius Rusticus. See L.W. Barnard (1967) *Justin Martyr*, Cambridge: Cambridge University Press.

Justus (C1 AD) was a Jewish historian from Tiberias in Galilee. We know of him through JOSEPHUS' *Autobiography*, which gives a hostile view of him, arising mainly from his opposition to Josephus' command of Galilee against the Romans in AD 66. He was one of those who began the revolt of Tiberias, and he later took refuge with AGRIPPA (4) II who protected him against punishment. He acted as Agrippa's secretary, and after his death published his *History of the Jewish Kings*, which may have contained the account of the Jewish War condemned by Josephus for inaccuracy.

Juvenal (Decimus Junius Juvenalis) (*c.*AD 55–*c.*130), a satirical poet about whose life virtually nothing is known, was from Aquinum in Latium. A tomb inscription at Aquinum, now lost, if indeed his, suggests that he was a Roman knight and imperial servant as well as a local magistrate, and had served in the army as a military tribune. Three epigrams addressed to him by his friend MARTIAL tell us that he was skilled in oratory, and suggest he had a career as a lawyer after the usual rhetorical education. There was a story that he was banished from Italy for writing a lampoon on an influential courtier, the actor Paris: if this happened in DOMITIAN's time, it would account for his evident loathing of that emperor. Some have claimed that he spent his exile in Egypt, from his obvious knowledge of that country. His material wealth is a matter of dispute: exile would have entailed loss of property; yet he does not dedicate his work to a patron, which suggests that he lived in relative affluence, as would be expected of a Roman knight. It is said that HADRIAN helped him by giving him a small property. However, his published poetry cannot be taken as any kind of guide to his life, as the voices which speak through it are artificial creations of his imagination. The few references to datable events indicate that his work was written between *c.*AD 110 and 130.

Over these twenty years he published his sixteen poems in five books, and there were notable stylistic and thematic developments as his work progressed. His first book, published *c.*110, consists of poems 1–5; its tone is angry and indignantly critical of the Roman society described. In *Satire 1* he sets forth his programme: instead of the popular contemporary themes of poetry, hackneyed themes from myth, he will handle real life and show up the hypocrisy and scandalous behaviour of the times, naming only the dead and sparing the living. In *Satire 2* he also satirises hypocrisy, taking as his target those whose private lives belie their philosophical pretensions. *Satire 3* gives a picture of life in contemporary Rome, and includes Juvenal's praise of a friend who is taking his leave of the city. Umbricius is fleeing a place where the honest poor man has no chance of making a living and Greek men and fashions are dominant. Those who succeed are unworthy: the foreigner, the bully, the thief. Moreover, life in the overcrowded slum is dangerous and only the rich can hope for safety and prosperity. He satirises the court and administration in *Satire 4*, where a huge turbot, which cannot be held on any dish, is presented to Domitian, and the privy council is summoned to solve the difficulty. In *Satire 5* Juvenal discusses the humiliation of poor clients at the dinner parties of their patrons.

The second book, published *c.*116, consists of one long poem, *Satire 6*, which, though it begins calmly, turns into a bitter invective on the affectation and immorality of Roman women. In the remaining books there follows a change of tone from anger to irony and even cynicism: Book 3, published *c.*119, contains *Satires* 7–9. Of these, 7 discusses the fall from public esteem of the literary professions, especially teaching, and 8 is an attack on those who consider themselves noble from their ancestry, which Juvenal sees as exacerbating the vice of those who are already lacking in virtue. Book 4, which marks a new attitude of detached amusement instead of the previous sardonic style, gives no hint of its date: it contains three satires, 10–12. Of these, 10 exposes the folly of human prayer, whether for wealth, power, eloquence, longevity, beauty, or anything except to have a sound mind in a healthy body. *Satire 11* attacks gluttony and 12 attacks those who seek to profit from the wills of the rich. Book 5, Juvenal's last, dated *c.*127, pursues the tone of cynical detachment: it consists of three further complete poems, 13–15, and an unfinished satire, 16. In 13, Juvenal warns a friend who has been cheated of 10,000 sesterces against seeking vengeance. He claims that the fraud's conscience will punish him sufficiently. The fourteenth satire is about education and the importance of parental example in the upbringing of a child. In 15 Juvenal takes his reader to Egypt and describes a quarrel between two towns which results in the capture of a man who is killed and eaten by his enemies. He holds this example up as the reverse of the sympathy and understanding which should guide mankind, and distinguish them from animals. In 16 he attacks the impunity of the military in their dealings with civilians.

Juvenal has never been surpassed as a satirist of behaviour: he wrote roughly at the time when TACITUS (1) was writing his historical works, and the two shared striking rhetorical and epigrammatic powers and the ability to expose the vices of their society with graphic punch. Juvenal imported something of the grandeur of the epic style into satire, and was the last great Roman poet to exploit all the possibilities of hexameter verse. His grand style owes much to epic and to tragedy and yet has a range of diction extending to everyday speech, foreign words and even a few obscenities. His epigrammatic shots are often quotable (such as *facit indignatio versum*, 'my anger inspires my poetry', *mens sano in corpore sano*, 'a healthy mind in a healthy body', and *quis custodiet ipsos custodies*, 'who will guard the guards?'), and his poetry contains elements reminiscent of comedy and mime, pastoral poetry, and even philosophy. He shows some philosophical attitudes, but is not a philosopher (he shows a tendency to Epicurean views in his later poems). The unifying factor in his work is its constant rhetorical power.

His works were neglected for two centuries after his time, and he was relatively unknown until his rediscovery in the fourth century by LACTANTIUS, who mentions his name, and Ausonius, who imitates him. Thereafter he attained great popularity: in the late fourth century his poems were edited and a commentary was written. See N. Rudd (1986) *Themes in Roman Satire*, London: Duckworth; S.H. Braund (1988) *Beyond Anger: A Study of Juvenal's 3rd Book of Satires*,

Cambridge: Cambridge University Press; W.S. Anderson (1982) *Essays on Roman Satire*, Princeton: Princeton University Press.

Juvencus, Gaius Vettius (C4 AD) was a Christian priest and poet of the fourth century from Eliberri in Baetica, Spain. He was the first to try to tell the stories of the Christian scriptures in classical Latin hexameter verse: he rendered the *Gospels* in this way *c.*325 under the title *The Four Gospels*, and was praised by Jerome, translator of the *Bible* into Latin, for his efforts. His work, which shows the influence of VIRGIL, survives.

Juventius 1. Laterensis, Marcus (C1 BC), was a member of a Tusculan family of consular rank: after military service in Bithynia he was quaestor (financial manager) in Crete and Cyrene. He gave up his candidacy for the tribuneship in 59 because it would have meant taking an oath to preserve CAESAR (1)'s land law. He stood for the post of curule aedile for 55 but was defeated by Gnaeus PLANCIUS, whom he then prosecuted for bribery, asserting that a mere equestrian could not defeat a member of the senatorial class without bribery. But CICERO (1) defended Plancius, who was acquitted. Juventius held the praetorship in 51 but seems to have kept a low profile during the Civil War. When he was LEPIDUS (4)'s legate in 43 he killed himself in his despair when Lepidus joined ANTONIUS (7). The senate later honoured him for his noble death.

2. *see* CELSUS (2).

L

Labeo, Marcus Antistius (died *c.*AD 11), was a jurist or legal expert whose father had been one of CAESAR (1)'s assassins and had committed suicide in 42 BC after the republican defeat at Philippi. Labeo, a republican by conviction and a former pupil of CICERO (1), was appointed by AUGUSTUS to a commission in 18 BC to revise the membership of the Senate, but offended the emperor by his proposal to include LEPIDUS (4). He held the praetorship but declined the consulship which Augustus offered him late (in AD 5) and which passed to his rival CAPITO (2). Thus, like AQUILLIUS (3) Gallus before him, he deserted political life for the law. Taught by C. Trebatius Testa, Labeo not only mastered the law, but also grammar, literature, philosophy and dialectics: he had an excellent knowledge of early Latin literature. He was an innovator in legal thinking but also preserved in his voluminous writings a massive corpus of republican legal material, which he was now, because of the fall of republican institutions, unable to develop. He used to spend half the year teaching his law students in Rome and the other half in the country writing. It was said that he wrote 400 volumes, though only some fragments survive in quotations. His rivalry with Capito is said by the historian Sextus POMPONIUS (2) to have been the cause of the foundation of the two great law schools, later known as the Sabinian and the Proculian: Labeo inspired the latter, which represented his own characteristics of principle and consistency. The following titles of his works are known: *Reliable Decisions* (*Pithana*), *Replies*, *Letters*, *The Pontifex's Law*, *A Commentary on the Praetor's Edict*, and *Posthumous Works*, which JAVOLENUS Priscus edited and published. ULPIANUS quotes him freely, but only the first and last of these works were available to Justinian's commissioners.

Laberius, Decimus (C1 BC), was an equestrian who composed scripts for mimes in the southern Italian manner. We know of forty-three titles of his works; some 178 lines survive suggesting themes such as mythological burlesque, sexual adventures, false identities, and other common comic situations. Women acted in his plays, a precedent in Rome. In 46 BC, at the celebrations following CAESAR (1)'s triumphs, Laberius was requested by the dictator to act a mime of his own composition in competition with PUBLILIUS SYRUS for an enormous fee. To satirise Syrus, Laberius played the part of a Syrian slave, and spoke a prologue, which drew attention to the new illiberal regime.

Labienus 1, Quintus (died 39 BC), was a general, the son of LABIENUS (2). CASSIUS (2) sent him to Parthia in the winter of 43 BC to ask for help against the triumvirs.

He was left high and dry in Parthia by the defeat of his side at Philippi in 42, but gained the support of Pacorus, the crown prince, who led a Parthian army to attack Syria and overthrow Decidius Saxa, the governor appointed by ANTONIUS (7). Saxa's army joined Labienus, who led it into Asia Minor and overwhelmed the southern part as far as Caria. He issued coins styling himself *Q. Labienus, Commander of Parthia*. In 39, however, he was opposed by Antonius' general VENTIDIUS who drove the Parthians out in three battles and in the last, at Gindarus, killed Labienus and Pacorus.

2, Titus (*c*.100–45 BC), was a general and politician from Cingulum in Picenum, CAESAR (1)'s most effective and senior assistant in the conquest of Gaul. He assisted Caesar by prosecuting RABIRIUS (1), reviving an old law (*Lex Domitia*) which provided for the priesthoods, including that of *Pontifex Maximus*, to be elected by a section of the Popular Assembly (Caesar consequently became *Pontifex Maximus* by lavish bribery of the qualified tribes), and proposed that POMPEIUS (2), still in the east, be given special honours for his achievements. In 58 he was appointed Caesar's legate in Gaul and remained with him until 51, often commanding independently of Caesar in important campaigns. A cruel and arrogant man, he deserted Caesar for Pompeius in 49 at the outbreak of the Civil War. He seems to have had ties with Pompeius through his origin in Picenum. In the Civil War he fought at Pharsalus and, in the campaign in Africa, he was in command of the republican forces twice when Caesar was in the utmost peril; he assisted Pompeius' two sons in Spain and was killed at the decisive battle of Munda in November 45.

3, Titus (late C1 BC) An orator and historian; his relationship to the above, if any, is unknown. He remained a republican and Pompeian, and his books, including a pamphlet attacking Bathyllus, a disreputable actor whom MAECENAS loved, were formally burnt by decree of the Senate; CALIGULA, however, restored them. In speaking, his invective was so violent that he was nicknamed 'Rabienus', i.e. 'rabid'. He refused to survive the destruction of his books.

Lactantius (*c*.AD 240–320) Lucius Caelius Firmianus, a Latin Christian writer and poet, was a north African; 'Lactantius' appears to have been an alias, perhaps a *nom de plume*. He studied under the Numidian philosopher ARNOBIUS, later a Christian apologist but still 'pagan' when Lactantius was young. By Diocletian's imperial command Lactantius became, in the 290s, an official teacher of rhetoric at Nicomedia, then capital of the empire, and adopted Christianity sometime before 303 when the persecution began that caused him to lose his post. In 305 he left Nicomedia for the west, and *c*.313 he was invited by CONSTANTINE (1) I to be the tutor of his eldest son Crispus in Gaul (see FAUSTA 2).

One poem survives, the *Phoenix*; the rest is prose, mostly written in polished Ciceronian Latin, consisting mainly of Christian apologetics. As he realised he could not use the Christian scriptures to refute 'pagan' arguments, his use of the methods of philosophy, for which he had little talent, renders his works of small interest for any contribution to our knowledge of Christian development. His Christian writings which survive are *God's Craftsmanship*, using the human body and its construction as evidence for divine providence, *Divine Institutions*, written between 303 and 313, purporting to refute all possible attacks on Christian doctrine, of which he also produced an abridgment, the *Epitome*. In this work, however, he shows considerable knowledge of classical Latin literature, especially of CICERO (1) and the poets, including ENNIUS. *The Wrath of God*, *c*.314, argues that anger must be a characteristic of God's nature. *The Deaths of*

Persecutors, *c*.318, purports to prove that those who persecuted the Church always came to a bad end. He was popular in Renaissance times for his combination of Christianity and classical learning. See R.M. Ogilvie (1978) *The Library of Lactantius*, Oxford: Clarendon Press.

Laelius 1, Gaius (C3–2 BC), was a 'new man' and close friend of Publius Cornelius SCIPIO (7) Africanus, under whom he served in his Spanish campaign of 210 to 206 BC, when he commanded a fleet. He accompanied him to Sicily in 205, and to Africa from 204 to 202, where he defeated SYPHAX, took Cirta, and commanded cavalry at the battle of Zama. He was helped by Scipio to become quaestor in 202, plebeian aedile in 197, praetor in 196 and consul in 190 in partnership with Scipio's brother Lucius SCIPIO (4). The following year he took Gaul as his province and served in 174 on an embassy to PERSEUS, king of Macedonia, and to some Transalpine Gallic nations in 170. While POLYBIUS was in detention in Rome in the 60s, Laelius was a valuable source of information to him about Scipio.

2, Gaius (*c*.190–*c*.125 BC), son of LAELIUS (1), he was well enough educated to be able to participate in philosophical debate with contemporary Greek philosophers and was involved with the embassy of philosophers who were sent from Athens to the Senate in 155 BC, especially with Diogenes the Stoic, and later with the Stoic PANAETIUS. He thus acquired the nickname *Sapiens*, 'the Philosopher'. He was tribune in 151, served in Africa under SCIPIO (11) Aemilianus in 147 and 146 in the Third Punic War, when he commanded the storming of Carthage. He was praetor in 145, when he conducted operations against VIRIATHUS in Spain, and at home he spoke successfully against the proposal of a tribune, C. Licinius Crassus, to make the priesthoods subject to election by the people. He was appointed augur and in 140 held the consulship. He was aware of the agrarian problem and supported a proposal for an agrarian reform bill, but backed off and assisted the consuls of 132 in prosecuting the supporters of Tiberius GRACCHUS (4). A year later he spoke against the proposal of the tribune C. Papirius CARBO (1) to permit tribunes to be re-elected for a further term.

Laelius was a fine orator as well as being a leading member of the 'Scipionic Circle'. He wrote poetry and was one of those philhellene Romans of the second century who did much to introduce Greek culture to Rome. He was a friend of PACUVIUS and LUCILIUS (1). CICERO (1) was aware of his contribution to philosophy and oratory, and introduced him as a character in his dialogues *Laelius on Friendship*, *Old Age*, and *The Republic*. See A.E. Astin (1967) *Scipio Aemilianus*, Oxford: Clarendon Press.

Laenas 1, Gaius Popillius (C2 BC), was praetor in 175 and consul in 172 when he defended his brother Marcus (consul the previous year), accused of enslaving the Ligurian Statielli whom he had needlessly attacked. In 170 he went to Greece under the consul Aulus Hostilius Mancinus and worked as a diplomat as well as a soldier. In 168 he led a mission to the Seleucid king ANTIOCHUS (2) IV who was invading Egypt: the ambassadors met the king near Alexandria, and Laenas gave him a letter from the Senate, demanding his immediate withdrawal from Egypt. When Antiochus promised to consider the matter, Laenas drew a circle in the sand round him with his staff and forbade him to leave it until he had given his reply. The king was alarmed by this aggressive behaviour, and consented.

2, Marcus Popillius, *see* LAENAS (1).

3, Publius Popillius (C2 BC), was a Roman politician, a son of LAENAS (1). During his consulship in 132 BC he severely punished the associates of the reformer Tiberius GRACCHUS (4), as a result of which the tribune Gaius GRACCHUS (1) passed a law in 123 which caused him to be exiled. Lucius Calpurnius BESTIA subsequently passed a law allowing his return after OPIMIUS had been legally vindicated. During his consulship Laenas built the Popillian Way, a road in north-east Italy.

Laevinus, Marcus Valerius (*c.*267–200 BC), was a Roman politician and military man. He was praetor in 227 and, being invalidly elected consul for 220, did not serve. He was praetor again in 215 and consul in 210. In 214 he was sent against PHILIP (1) V with a fleet, and in 212 won the support of the Aetolian League and ATTALUS (1) I of Pergamon in the First Macedonian War. During his consulship he operated in Sicily, where he recaptured Acragas (Agrigento) and finished off the work of MARCELLUS (3). He remained there as governor for two more years and restored the Sicilian grain farming industry. In 208 he made an expedition to North Africa and mauled a Carthaginian fleet. He led a commission in 205 which brought the sacred stone of Cybele, the 'Great Mother' (a simple black stone) from Pessinus in Asia Minor to Rome.

Laevius (early C1 BC) was a lyric poet of whose poetry only fragments survive, though we have several titles. Little is known of him: his last name was probably Melissus. He was an innovator and experimenter in metre, and seems to have modelled himself on Anacreon and Hellenistic poetry. He wrote lighthearted lyric poems with a general title *Love-Games*, in six or more books, with subtitles from mythology such as *The Phoenix*, *Adonis*, *Helen* and *Ino*. The fragments suggest a romantic and sometimes fantastic handling of well known myths. He experimented with diction and metre, inventing new compound words, Greek borrowings, special meanings, and diminutives. He varied his use of metre and produced anapaestic dimeters, anacreontic metres such as iambic dimeters, and scazons, sometimes even switching between them within a poem. He had an influence on VARRO (3), who used a similarly large range of metres in his *Menippean Satires*. He was largely ignored by his successors, and interest in him was only revived in the second century AD by writers such as GELLIUS (1), APULEIUS, FRONTO and Septimius Serenus. He was a pioneer of Alexandrian innovation in Roman poetry.

Lateranus, Sextius Sextinus *see* STOLO.

Lenaeus, Pompeius (C1 BC), was a freedman of POMPEIUS (2) who opened a school in Rome and translated for Pompeius a work of MITHRIDATES (3) VI, king of Pontus, on drugs and poisons. After Pompeius' death Lenaeus attacked SALLUST for describing Pompeius as a shameless hypocrite.

Lentulus *N.B.*: there is insufficient evidence to establish the family relationships of most of the Cornelii Lentuli.

1, Cossus Cornelius (C1 BC/C1 AD), was a son of Gnaeus; he was consul in 1 BC and proconsul of Africa in AD 5 and 6 in succession to his kinsman Lucius. He fought a successful war against the Gaetuli of North Africa. TIBERIUS made him city prefect. His son was LENTULUS (6).

2, Gnaeus Cornelius (died 184 BC), was consul in 201. He wished to prolong the Second Punic War but the Popular Assembly voted down his plan to succeed SCIPIO (7) Africanus as commanding general. He served on a board of ten appointed to make a peace treaty with PHILIP (1) V of Macedonia in 196 after the Roman victory in the Second Macedonian War.

3, Gnaeus Cornelius, known as Clodianus (early C1 BC), was a plebeian, probably a Claudius Marcellus, who was adopted into the family of the patrician Cornelii Lentuli. He supported SULLA (2) and was with him in his march on Rome. He was consul in 72 BC and with his colleague Lucius GELLIUS (3) tried to stop VERRES' extortions in Sicily. They were defeated by SPARTACUS when they tried to put down his rebellion in southern Italy. Together with Gellius he acted as censor in 70: they purged the Senate of sixty-four corrupt members. He was a legate of POMPEIUS (2) in his war against the pirates (67), and supported MANILIUS (1)'s law.

4, Gnaeus Cornelius, known as Marcellinus (C1 BC) As his name implies, his father was a Claudius Marcellus, adopted into the Lentulan family with the forename Publius. His wife was SCRIBONIA, whose third husband was AUGUSTUS. He supported CICERO (1)'s prosecution of VERRES, having himself strong ties with Sicily. He was a legate of POMPEIUS (2) in his war with the pirates in 67, and was sent to Cyrenaica where he imposed a settlement. He was among the prosecutors of CLODIUS in 61. He was praetor in 60 and proconsul of Syria in 59 and the following year; he was consul in 56 and used his oratorical skills against the three 'triumvirs' in conference at Lucca and against their decision to restore PTOLEMY (8) XII the Piper to the throne of Egypt.

5, Gnaeus Cornelius (died AD 25), was a son of Gnaeus (possibly LENTULUS 4). He was known as 'the Augur', to differentiate him from a slightly older man of the same name, probably a kinsman, who was consul in 18 BC. AUGUSTUS gave him a donation to help him from poverty into a senatorial career and he multiplied it to a vast sum, gaining a capital of 400,000,000 sestertii. He was consul in 14 BC and subsequently governed Moesia, winning a victory over the Getae for which he received triumphal decorations. In 3 BC he was made governor of Asia. He was friendly with TIBERIUS, went to Pannonia with DRUSUS (4) in AD 14, and left Tiberius his fortune in his will. According to CASSIUS (1) Dio, he was accused of treason in AD 24.

6, Gnaeus Cornelius, known as Gaetulicus (died AD 39), was a senator and poet, son of LENTULUS (1), and was called Gaetulicus from his father's military exploits in North Africa. He was consul in AD 26 and governed Upper Germany as legate from 30 to 39; he was popular with the troops on account of his weak discipline. He married his daughter to SEJANUS' son: in 34, after Sejanus' fall and death in 31, Gaetulicus was unsuccessfully attacked as his associate. He and Marcus Aemilius LEPIDUS (7) organised a conspiracy in 39 to kill CALIGULA at Mogontiacum (Mainz) and replace him with Lepidus; the plot was reported to the emperor: both were executed. MARTIAL admired his erotic poetry.

7, Lucius Cornelius (late C3 BC), was sent to Spain in 206 BC during the Second Punic War with Lucius Manlius Acidinus to serve with proconsular powers in place of SCIPIO (7) Africanus, though they had never held public office. Lentulus remained there until 201 and, having put down the rebellion of Indibilis and Mandonius, claimed a triumph, which was rejected because he had held no public office before his command in Spain. Instead he was granted an ovation. He was consul in 199 BC, when he was active in northern Italy against the insurgent Gauls, and had to continue operations the next year. The Senate sent him on a diplomatic mission in 196 to Lysimacheia to negotiate with ANTIOCHUS (1) III, who had invaded Thrace and looked likely to push on into Europe and to support Egyptian territorial claims.

8, Lucius Cornelius, known as Crus ('leg') (died 48 BC), was a republican senator, younger brother of LENTULUS (9), chief prosecutor of CLODIUS in 61, praetor in 58, when he supported CICERO (1) and became friendly with him; after which he served in Spain, where he became a close friend of BALBUS (1). He was consul in 49; though he was greatly in debt and eminently bribable, CAESAR (1) failed to secure his support: the Senate appointed him governor of Asia, whence he marched to Dyrrhachium with two legions. There Balbus tried to win him over to Caesar with a generous offer, but he stuck to POMPEIUS (2)'s side. Like Pompeius he fled to Egypt after the battle of Pharsalus and was killed there by the Egyptian king's servants the day after Pompeius' death. Cicero and others described him as lazy, venal and pretentious.

9, Publius Cornelius, known as Sura (executed 63 BC), was a supporter of SULLA (2) in his march on Rome; he was a failure as Sulla's quaestor in 81 but was elected praetor in 75 and put in charge of the court which heard claims for restitution of illegally seized property. He was consul in 71 but was expelled from the Senate for corruption by the censors in 70. He was elected to a further praetorship in 63, which restored his status as a senator, during which he attached himself to CATILINE. He was appointed by the conspirators to lead the party in Rome. The plan to kill CICERO (1) misfired, for Cicero received evidence of the plotters' intentions from a delegation of Gallic Allobriges, with whom Lentulus had foolishly opened negotiations and whom Cicero persuaded to extract written details of the plot. Lentulus was arrested, dismissed from office, imprisoned and strangled on 5 December 63 on the instructions of the consul, Cicero, and with the Senate's approval.

10, Publius Cornelius, known as Spinther ('choker') (executed 48 BC) The elder brother of LENTULUS (8), quaestor *c.*74 BC, he spent lavishly in his aedileship in 63, supported CICERO (1) against CLODIUS, spent freely in 60 when city praetor, and was an ally of Cicero again in his consulship of 57, moving his immediate recall and assisting in recovering his confiscated property. He was commissioned by the Senate to restore the king of Egypt, PTOLEMY (8) XII the Piper, to the throne from which the Egyptians had expelled him. He was expected to perform this task during his proconsulship of Cilicia in Asia Minor in 56, but was unable to do so. He remained in Cilicia until 53, and won victories for which he was granted a triumph in 51. In 49 he joined the republican cause and was one of those who laid claim to CAESAR (1)'s priesthood, the office of *Pontifex Maximus*. He fled from Asculum, where he commanded the garrison, but fell into Caesar's hands at Corfinium: he was released, but returned to POMPEIUS (2)'s side and fought at the battle of Pharsalus, after which he was captured and executed by Caesar.

Lepidus 1, Manius Aemilius (early C1 AD) His paternal grandfather was the triumvir LEPIDUS (4), his mother's father was Faustus Sulla, his mother's mother was POMPEIUS (2)'s daughter. He held the consulship in AD 11, and was proconsul of Asia in 21 and 22, after unsuccessfully defending his sister Aemilia Lepida in 20 when she was charged by her divorced husband QUIRINIUS of trying to poison him twenty years earlier. He was father-in-law to the emperor GALBA (1).

2, Marcus Aemilius (died 152 BC), was a patrician statesman who in 200 BC participated in an embassy in which he gave PHILIP (1) V king of Macedonia an ultimatum bidding him not to attack the Greek states, which Philip rejected. His career then developed: aedile in 193, he governed Sicily in 191 when he held the praetorship, and was consul in 187 having been defeated at the polls the two previous years. He was bitter about the hostility of Marcus NOBILIOR, whom he blamed for these setbacks, and tried to prevent his triumph for successes in Ambracia. Lepidus spent the next year or two in Liguria fighting a bitter and unsatisfactory war against the native people. He also built the Via Aemilia from Placentia

(Piacenza) to Rimini, by which he gave his name to the Italian province of Emilia Romagna. In 183 he was again in Cisalpine Gaul, acting as a commissioner to found Roman colonies at Mutina (Modena) and Parma. He was appointed chief priest (*Pontifex Maximus*) in 180, and in 179 held the censorship as colleague of his old enemy Nobilior, with whom he celebrated a public reconciliation (see METELLUS 3). They reformed the Comitia Centuriata, and Lepidus built the Basilica which bore his name. He held a second consulship in 175 when he again pursued the war in Liguria, and two years later returned as a commissioner to distribute land in Gaul and Liguria to individual Romans. He was Leader of the Senate from 179 until his death in 152.

3, Marcus Aemilius (died 77 BC), was a decendant of LEPIDUS (2) and the father of the triumvir LEPIDUS (4). He began his career by serving as the legate of POMPEIUS (5) Strabo and was aedile during the ascendancy of CINNA (2) (86–84 BC). He joined SULLA (2) on his return to Italy and profited from Sulla's proscriptions of his enemies: he divorced his wife, a kinswoman of the populist SATURNINUS (2), a cause of embarrassment to him in his new alliance. He was praetor in Sicily in 80 and was elected consul for 78 with the support of POMPEIUS (2), quickly breaking with his colleague CATULUS (3) by attempting to reform Sulla's pro-senatorial constitution even before his death (Sulla had opposed his election but had not abandoned his retirement to intervene). There was trouble in Etruria where dispossessed locals attacked Sulla's veterans who had been settled on their land: when both consuls were sent to put down the rising, Lepidus took the side of the dispossessed. The Senate in alarm made the two consuls swear an oath not to indulge in civil war. For 77 he was allotted Gaul, with which he had ancestral connections, as his province, and sent his legate, Marcus Junius BRUTUS (4) to raise troops in Transalpine Gaul. He was also in touch with the rebel SERTORIUS in Spain. He marched on Rome with men from Etruria without waiting for Brutus; the 'Ultimate Decree' was passed by the Senate and he was defeated by Catulus, now proconsul, at the Milvian Bridge. Lepidus escaped to Sardinia, was again defeated by a legate, Triarius, and died there. The remnant of his army, under PERPERNA (3), escaped to Spain and Sertorius.

4, Marcus Aemilius (89–13 BC), was the Roman triumvir of the Civil War period, the younger son of LEPIDUS (3); his elder brother was L. Aemilius PAULLUS (3). He threw in his lot with CAESAR (1) and married Junia, a daughter of SERVILIA, Caesar's mistress. He was praetor and Caesar's city prefect in 49 BC: he proposed Caesar's dictatorship and the enabling legislation after which in 48 he governed Nearer Spain. While in the province he had to help his neighbour, the rapacious CASSIUS (5) Longinus, to put down a rebellion in Further Spain and held a triumph on his return to Rome. He was Caesar's colleague as consul in 46 and became Caesar's deputy during his dictatorship from 46 to 44. He supervised affairs in the City during Caesar's absence in Spain in 46. He entertained Caesar to dinner on the eve of his assassination.

He acted as a close supporter of ANTONIUS (7) after Caesar's death, commanding a legion near Rome which he was ready to use to avenge Caesar, but was dissuaded from doing so by HIRTIUS and Antonius; with Antonius' help he was elected chief priest (*Pontifex Maximus*) in place of Caesar. In summer 44 he reconciled Sextus POMPEIUS (4) to the Senate. In 43 he took over the provinces of Narbonese Gaul and Nearer Spain which Caesar had assigned him. He supported Antonius in his dispute with the Senate, and later, in May 43, joined forces with him, playing a double game, writing to CICERO (1) of his loyalty to the republican constitution. The Senate pronounced him *hostis*, public enemy. In October 43 he met Antonius and Octavian (see AUGUSTUS), who had crushed opposition in Rome, at Bononia (Bologna) where the triumvirate of the three leaders was established. As his share of the empire he was to rule Spain and Gaul: his elder brother Paullus was to be proscribed for his cooperation with the Senate in naming Lepidus *hostis*. After holding a second triumph for victories he claimed to have won in Spain, he was again consul in 42 and was left to take care of Italy during the campaign of Philippi. He was then demoted by his two partners and deprived of his provinces because he had, they claimed, collaborated with the independent Sextus Pompeius. He was defeated by Lucius ANTONIUS (4), the consul of 41, as the latter marched on Rome.

At the conference of Brundisium in September 40, Lepidus' inferior position was clear: after the empire had effectively been split between his colleagues, he was given Africa, riven with strife, as an afterthought. He became even less important when the treaty of Puteoli was struck with Sextus Pompeius. Excluded from the conference of Tarentum in 37, he remained in Africa until 36, when Octavian summoned his help against Sextus Pompeius in Sicily. With a powerful army he fought a successful campaign and then laid claim to Sicily, for which Octavian, having won over the loyalty of Lepidus' troops, arrested him and removed him from the triumvirate. Lepidus, still chief priest of the Roman state, was kept confined at Circeii until his death in 13 BC, when Augustus himself took the priesthood.

5, Marcus Aemilius (died 30 BC), was a son of LEPIDUS (4). He plotted to kill Octavian (see AUGUSTUS) in 30 BC upon his return to Rome after Actium, perhaps to avenge his father's humiliation. MAECENAS discovered the plot and suppressed it. Lepidus and his wife Servilia, formerly Octavian's wife, killed themselves.

6, Marcus Aemilius (died AD 33), was the elder son of Paullus Aemilius Lepidus. He held the consulship in AD 6 after which he was a legate to TIBERIUS in his suppression of the Pannonian rebellion, being honoured with the triumphal decorations in AD 9, and probably governing Dalmatia until *c*.12. He governed Nearer Spain in 14, and in 21 yielded the proconsulship of Africa to Junius BLAESUS. The following year he saw to the repair of the Aemilian Basilica (see LEPIDUS 2). In 14 AD the dying AUGUSTUS was said to have remarked that Lepidus was capable of holding power but would scorn it. His daughter was AEMILIA LEPIDA (1).

7, Marcus Aemilius (died AD 39), was the son of LEPIDUS (6) and the last member of the family. He married CALIGULA's sister JULIA (7) Drusilla and was promised the right of succession by that emperor. However, he was implicated in the plot of LENTULUS (6) Gaetulicus, which aimed to kill Caligula and install Lepidus as emperor, and executed.

8, Paullus Aemilius (C1 BC), was a son of L. Aemilius PAULLUS (3) who, though he was proscribed in 43, survived to serve Octavian (AUGUSTUS) in his war with Sextus POMPEIUS (4) in Sicily in 38. He held a suffect consulship in 34 and governed a province the following year. In 22 he was censor but quarrelled with his colleague PLANCUS (1) and resigned. PROPERTIUS wrote him an elegy, 4. 11, on the death of his wife Cornelia, a daughter of SCRIBONIA, by whom he had two sons. The younger, PAULLUS (4), married Augustus' granddaughter JULIA (6). He finished restoring the Aemilian Basilica in the forum, which his father had begun.

Libanius (AD 314–393) was a Greek teacher of rhetoric from Antioch, of a rich and influential provincial family, well educated locally and then at Athens where he spent four years from 336 studying. He then became a teacher of rhetoric at Constantinople, moving in 346 to Nicomedia. The emperor CONSTANTIUS (2) II offered him a post as professor of rhetoric at Athens, which he declined, but in 354 he accepted an appointment to a chair of rhetoric at Antioch, where he lived until his death in 393. He had many distinguished pupils including some Christians. Probable students of his were BASIL of Caesarea, GREGORY (2) of Nazianzus, John Chrysostom, Theodore of Mopsuestia and the historian AMMIANUS MARCELLINUS. He became a friend of the emperor JULIAN, whom he probably met in Antioch. He remained a 'pagan' all his life, in spite of which Theodosius I consulted him and gave him the honorary title of Praetorian Prefect.

He left a large extant oeuvre. Sixty-four speeches and more than 1,600 letters survive, as well as school exercises in rhetoric which he wrote for his pupils. From his writings much is to be learnt about the public and private life of his day: educational and cultural matters are also richly treated. One of the speeches includes an autobiography composed nineteen years before his death, and another is his funeral oration for the emperor Julian, whose death was a great blow to him. He also wrote a speech in praise of Antioch. He wrote in Greek, in a painstaking, even pedantic style. See H.W.G. Liebenschuetz (1972) *Antioch*, Oxford: Clarendon Press; N.G. Wilson (1963) *Scholars of Byzantium*, London: Duckworth.

Libo Volusus, Gaius Poetelius (C4 BC), was a plebeian politician who triumphed over the Gauls and Tiburtines as consul in 360. In 358, as a tribune, he introduced a law against election bribery which may have increased with the opening of the consulship to plebeians a few years earlier. He held further consulships in 346 and 320. It is uncertain whether he or his son passed a law in 326 as a colleague of L. Papirius CURSOR (1) to prevent imprisonment for debt. His son was dictator in 313, the year VARRO (3) dates the law.

Licinius (*c.*AD 265–325) was an emperor of Dacian peasant extraction, and was named Valerius Licinianus Licinius. He owed his advancement to the emperor GALERIUS, a man of similar background to himself. At the conference of Carnuntum in November 308, Galerius appointed Licinius to be his fellow *Augustus* or senior emperor in place of SEVERUS (3), with jurisdiction over the western provinces. However, CONSTANTINE (1) and MAXENTIUS were already in possession of most of the west, and Licinius had to content himself by taking Dalmatia, Pannonia and Noricum, realising that his western rivals were too strong for him. In 311, on the death of Galerius, he moved to replace him as emperor of the east, and acquired his European territories, making an agreement with MAXIMINUS (2) Daia that the latter should rule in Asia. In 312 Licinius approached CONSTANTINE (1) to form an alliance to balance that of Maximinus and Maxentius, ruler of Italy, and during their conference at Milan in early 313 married Constantine's half-sister CONSTANTIA. He now controlled the whole of the Balkans and part of central Europe. But Maximinus invaded Europe and fought Licinius in spring 313 at Adrianople in Thrace: Licinius defeated him and took his territory, declaring himself *Augustus* of the eastern Empire. Meanwhile Constantine had overcome Maxentius and was sole ruler of the western Empire. As part of his pact with Constantine, Licinius proclaimed religious toleration and the restoration of confiscated Christian property throughout the empire. The two *Augusti*, however, were soon quarrelling and war broke out in 316: Constantine won two limited victories in Pannonia and captured and executed Valens, whom Licinius had made his fellow ruler. Peace was restored in early 317, Licinius ceding his European lands apart from the Thracian diocese.

Shortly after, on 1 March, he made his little son Licinius II *Caesar*: simultaneously Constantine gave the same title to his own sons.

Constantine's continuous presence in the Balkans irked Licinius, who revived the persecution of the Christians. The conflict came to a head when, in his campaign against the invading Goths in 323, Constantine usurped Licinius' role and entered his territory: Licinius reacted, and a decisive battle was fought in July 324 between the two emperors at Adrianople. Licinius took refuge in Byzantium, where he appointed his cavalry commander Martinianus emperor. When Byzantium was taken they escaped, but were defeated at Chrysopolis. Licinius surrendered and abdicated in favour of Constantine. His life was spared by the prayers of his wife, Constantia, and he was confined with Martinianus at Thessalonica. They were both put to death the following year for plotting against Constantine, and Licinius' son was likewise killed the following year. See T.D. Barnes (1982) *Constantine and Eusebius*, Cambridge MA: Harvard University Press.

See also CALVUS, CRASSUS, LUCULLUS, MACER (3), MUCIANUS, MURENA, STOLO, SURA.

Ligarius (C1 BC) was the name of three brothers from Sabinum whose loyalty wavered between CAESAR (1) and POMPEIUS (2). The best known, Quintus, appointed in 50 BC legate to the governor of Africa, C. Considius Longus, surrendered the province in 49 to the Pompeian P. Attius Varus and supported him in resisting the Senate's appointee, L. Aelius Tubero; in 46 Caesar captured him at Hadrumetum. His two brothers, however, had supported Caesar, and used their influence and that of CICERO (1) in his cause, despite the opposition of Tubero's son Quintus TUBERO, who prosecuted him unsuccessfully for helping King JUBA (1) in Africa. However, he joined the conspiracy against Caesar in 44. His brothers were killed in the proscriptions of 42.

Livia 1. (C2–1 BC) was a sister of M. Livius DRUSUS (2), married first to Q. Servilius CAEPIO (4), to whom she bore *c.*100 Servilia, mother of BRUTUS (5), CAESAR (1)'s assassin; and secondly to M. Porcius Cato, to whom *c.*95 she bore CATO (5) of Utica. After her death her brother brought up her children by both marriages.

2. (58 BC–AD 29) was the second wife of AUGUSTUS. Livia Drusilla was the daughter of Livius Drusus Claudianus, a member of the Claudian family who had been adopted by M. Livius DRUSUS (2), and who was killed at the battle of Philippi. At about the same time she married a republican kinsman of hers, Tiberius Claudius NERO (4), to whom she bore two sons, TIBERIUS, the future emperor, in 42, and DRUSUS (4) Julius Caesar in 38. Encumbered by the infant Tiberius, she joined her husband in his flight from Perusia to Campania and Sicily in 40. She then accompanied him to join ANTONIUS (7) in Greece, but after the Pact of Misenum in 39 they went back to Rome, and in January 38, when she was already pregnant with Drusus, Octavian (see AUGUSTUS) persuaded her husband to divorce her so that he might himself marry her. Previously he had been married to SCRIBONIA, many years his senior and the mother of JULIA (5), his only child, but he found her troublesome and divorced her in 39. Octavian appears to have made a love match with Livia, but also one calculated to enhance his life and produce deep stability of affection. The college of priests was consulted as to the legitimacy of the arrangement, and gave approval. They were married on 17 January.

She served her new husband well, not only as a dutiful wife and mother to her sons, who eventually became involved in Augustus' dynastic plans, but in a role that was more prominent than Roman women had previously played. She was extremely intelligent and perceptive, and was his best and most loyal adviser in all things of which she had experience. She also supported his desire to return to an old-fashioned morality, and brought up her stepdaughter Julia, who naturally lived in her father's house, perhaps too strictly. The marriage lasted fifty-two years, and in his will he adopted her into his family as *Julia Augusta*, in consequence of which she was also involved in his cult. Her relationship with her son Tiberius was ambiguous. Some sources accuse her of promoting his accession to the imperial throne by any means at her disposal, including (implausibly) the murders of several of Augustus' proposed heirs: OCTAVIA (2)'s son MARCELLUS (7); the three sons of AGRIPPA (1) and Julia; Gaius CAESAR (3) and Lucius CAESAR (8); AGRIPPA (2) Postumus; and even her own grandson, Tiberius' heir GERMANICUS. There is evidence of a rift between them after his accession, and even a suggestion that Tiberius retired to Capri in 26 BC to get away from her influence. On her death he refused to execute her will or deify her (these duties were later performed respectively by CALIGULA and CLAUDIUS 1). Caligula, who lived with her in his formative years, described her as a cunning intriguer, 'Odysseus in a dress'. She did, however, plead for mercy to be shown to conspirators, e.g. CINNA (1) and Munatia PLANCINA.

3. (*c.*13 BC–AD 31) was a member of the imperial family, officially Livia Julia, also known as Livilla, daughter of DRUSUS (3) Julius Caesar and his wife ANTONIA (3) the Younger. She married first Gaius CAESAR (3), the eldest son of AGRIPPA (1) who died in AD 4, and thereafter DRUSUS (4) Julius Caesar, son of Tiberius, to whom she bore a son, Gemellus (more correctly Tiberius Julius CAESAR 10 Nero) and a daughter, Livia Julia, who married RUBELLIUS (1) Blandus. She helped SEJANUS, the praetorian prefect, with whom she was infatuated, to poison her husband in AD 23, and two years later Sejanus asked Tiberius' permission to marry her, which was refused. In 31, after the fall of Sejanus, the manner of his son's death and the adultery of Livia with Sejanus were reported to Tiberius and he had Livia executed.
See also JULIA (8).

Livius *see* ANDRONICUS, LIVY, SALINATOR.

Livy (Titus Livius) (*c.*59 BC–AD 17) was a historian born at Patavium (Padua), at that time in Cisalpine Gaul; he also died there, by now the richest city of northern Italy on account of its flourishing woollen industry. He received a good education in philosophy and rhetoric, including a good command of Greek, and after composing some philosophical dialogues, he spent most of his life from 27 BC in Rome researching and writing his history of Rome, which he entitled *From the City's Foundation* (*Ab Urbe Condita*). Through his reputation as a writer (he gave public readings of his history) he became well acquainted with the emperor AUGUSTUS, who gave him moral but not financial support as he had plentiful private means. He was therefore for all his patriotism not an official historian; Augustus even called him a Pompeian for his conservative, republican sentiments, and Livy may well at first have approved of the principate only as a temporary expedient. Patavium was an old-fashioned, puritanical sort of place, and C. Asinius POLLIO (1) may have been referring to the obvious moralistic agenda of Livy's history when he derided Livy for 'patavinity' or 'paduanity'. A tomb inscription from Padua appears to refer to Livy: according to it he was married to Cassia Prima and had two children; to his son he wrote a letter recommending CICERO (1) and Demosthenes as models for composition, and his son wrote a lost work on geography. His daughter is known to have married a rhetorician, Lucius Magius. Livy was friendly with the future emperor CLAUDIUS (1) and encouraged him in his historical writings.

Livy's history consisted of 142 books, of which only thirty-five still survive mostly intact. The work covered the period from the supposed foundation of Rome in 753 BC to 9 BC and seems to have been divided, though not rigorously, into tens or 'decades', fives or 'pentads', and perhaps even fifteens, according to subject matter. The surviving books are the first ten, which describe the early legends and history of Rome down to 294 BC; and books 21–45 (219 to the battle of Pydna in 168 BC), which recount the war with HANNIBAL and subsequent events centred on King PHILIP (1) V of Macedonia, ANTIOCHUS (1) III, and the reign of PERSEUS of Macedonia. Some fragments of other books have come down: a palimpsest of part of book 91, some quotations and, because the whole work was available throughout antiquity, summaries (*periochae*) which give us a fair idea of what most of the lost books contained and an epitome on papyrus from Oxyrhynchus of books 37–40 and 48–55. Furthermore, several later Roman historians made use of Livy as a source for their own works: FLORUS (3), GRANIUS, EUTROPIUS, Festus Cassiodorus and Obsequens. As regards the dates of composition of the various sections of the history, internal evidence offers some clues, though it is possible that Livy added passages later to his original draft: thus he appears to have written the first five books by 25 BC; book 28 was written after AGRIPPA (1)'s campaign in Spain in 19 BC; book 59, with a reference to Augustus' views on marriage, after 18 BC; and books 121–142 were published, as is inferred from a note in the summaries, after the death of Augustus in AD 14.

Livy was essentially a sedentary historian who consulted sources both recent and ancient, but had no personal experience of the events he wrote about or the geography involved. He only occasionally refers to places or monuments he has seen, and he makes no use of source material other than literature. He reworked what he found in the works of annalists and chroniclers, mostly Romans, some of whom were subject to family or partisan bias, in a way that was rather uncritical. He put speeches into the mouths of historical characters, not that he knew what they really said, but to enliven his narrative with an exposition of the motives and feelings a character could have been credited with. He was a fine stylist, using a greater range of vocabulary than Cicero and CAESAR (1), including a frequently poetical diction and turn of phrase in the first two books appropriate to the legendary stories of early Rome, and he had a talent for imaginative description. He avoided the contortions of SALLUST's Thucydidean style. The critic QUINTILIAN, in writing of Livy's style, described it as having a 'milky richness', referring to the density, variety and rhetorical flow of his narrative.

Livy only occasionally names his sources, usually when he is unsure of actual events. His most notable and reliable source was POLYBIUS whom he used copiously as a source for events in the east, though he had some difficulty in reconciling Polybius' Greek chronology, based on the Olympiads, with Roman dating. Other sources he used included early historians like FABIUS (10) Pictor, L. Calpurnius PISO (5) Frugi, and CATO (4) the Censor; and late republican annalists VALERIUS Antias, C. Licinius MACER (3) and CLAUDIUS (11) Quadrigarius. He wrote at least two prefaces to his history: the first, at the beginning of book 1, deplores the disastrous nature of recent events, which included a series of civil wars, and expresses his pleasure in recounting the brave deeds of early times, while not pressing the literal truth of the foundation stories. He enunciates a theory of historiography as being a 'medicine of the mind' and emphasises what he sees as its moral purpose, offering examples both to be recommended and to serve as warnings of what to avoid. However, his work is largely free of overt moralising. There was a second preface at the beginning of book 6. See P.G. Walsh (1972) *Livy, his Historical Aims and Methods*, Cambridge: Cambridge University Press; (1974) *Livy*, Oxford: Clarendon Press; T. Luce (1977) *Livy, the Composition of his History*, Princeton: Princeton University Press; A.J. Woodman (1988) *Rhetoric in Classical Historiography*, London: Croom Helm; T.A. Dorey (1971) *Livy*, London: Routledge.

Locusta (mid-C1 AD) was a female poisoner whose services NERO (1)'s mother AGRIPPINA (3) used to poison her husband the emperor CLAUDIUS (1), and similarly Nero himself made her concoct a poison for Claudius' son BRITANNICUS. GALBA (1) executed her in AD 68. See Suetonius, *Nero*, 33.

Lollia Paulina was the granddaughter of Marcus LOLLIUS. She inherited from him a huge fortune and impressed the Elder PLINY (1) with her wonderful jewels. CALIGULA wished to marry her in AD 38 and forced her husband Publius Memmius Regulus to divorce her. But he divorced her himself in 39, and she survived to be considered by CLAUDIUS (1) in 48 as a possible spouse. Her successful rival, AGRIPPINA (3), had her banished with forfeiture of her fortune, claiming she had illegally consulted an astrologer. She committed suicide in exile.

Lollianus was a Greek novelist of unknown date or place. Fragments of his only work, *A Phoenician Story*, in a second-century AD papyrus, have revealed the first Greek picaresque novel with a background of low life, like that of PETRONIUS (1)'s *Satyricon*. The novel consisted of at least three books, of which some five modest fragments are extant.

Lollius, Marcus (died AD 2), was a 'new man' and supporter of AUGUSTUS. He was governor of Galatia in 25 BC, consul in 21 and proconsul of Macedonia in 18. He was governor of Gaul in 17 and 16 BC, when he was defeated by German raiders who captured the standard of the Fifth Legion: TIBERIUS had to be dispatched to rectify the situation. Lollius amassed a huge fortune in plunder from the provinces he ruled. In 1 BC Augustus entrusted him with the task of overseeing Gaius CAESAR (3) on his mission to the east: in Rhodes he poisoned the mind of Gaius against Tiberius, whom he had hated since 16 BC. However, Lollius fell into disgrace, accused in AD 2 of receiving bribes from king PHRAATES (2) of Parthia, and committed suicide. HORACE dedicated *Ode* 4. 9 to him, addressing him with ambiguous praise; VELLEIUS PATERCULUS (a partisan of Tiberius) described him in the blackest terms as greedy and corrupt. See LOLLIA PAULINA.
See also PALICANUS, URBICUS.

Longinus *see* CASSIUS Longinus.

Lucan (AD 39–65) was an epic poet from Cordoba in Spain. The son of a Roman equestrian, Marcus Annaeus Mela, brother of the younger SENECA (2), he was named Marcus Annaeus Lucanus. In 40 his father migrated with him to Rome where he studied rhetoric and, under L. Annaeus Cornutus, Stoic philosophy, and proved his proficiency in those subjects. He moved to Athens to undertake advanced study, from where the emperor NERO (1), having heard of his talent, invited him to his court and promoted him to the augurate and a quaestorship. He wrote a poem in praise of Nero on the occasion of the first Neronian games, with which he won a prize. But later Nero's favour turned to resentment of Lucan's superior talent, for the emperor himself claimed distinction as a poet and musician. Two years later Lucan published and read aloud to an audience the first three books of his epic poem *The Civil War*, which was strongly republican in sentiment, and Nero forbade him to give any more public readings or to plead in court. In the early months of 65 Lucan joined Calpurnius PISO (2)'s conspiracy, which was detected: he was ordered to end his life. He opened his veins on 30 April and died reciting lines from his poem. After his death a story was put about that he tried to gain a pardon by betraying his accomplices in the plot, including his mother.

His greatest work, the only one surviving in its entirety, is the epic *The Civil War* (*De Bello Civili*) in ten books, the last of which he did not finish. (The title *Pharsalia* is incorrect and arose from a misunderstanding of 9. 985.) It tells of the war between CAESAR (1) and POMPEIUS (2), which began in 49 BC when the former invaded Italy, and makes Pompeius and the republican Stoic CATO (5) its heroes; Caesar is the villain and destroyer of Rome's liberties. Lucan used the relevant books of LIVY's history, now lost, as his main source, but was content to report events inaccurately (setting CICERO 1, for example, at Pharsalus on the eve of the battle) and select material to support his pro-republican thesis. He was also responding to Virgil's *Aeneid*, which gave an account of the origin of Rome as, ironically, his own poem described the fall of Roman freedom. He alludes frequently to Virgil's epic and uses many of its techniques, though often with a perverse exaggeration, and he breaks the convention of epic objectivity by allowing his own feelings to intrude too much in commenting on the narrative. The full extent of Lucan's rhetorical powers are marshalled to storm the reader's attention: digressions, excessively long speeches, hyperbole and use of paradox all add up to a work of baroque intensity. The gods are replaced in the epic by a grim sense of fate, accompanied by omens and portents, and he conveys a gloomy preoccupation with death and suicide. In *The Civil War* Lucan echoes the melodramatic and sensational quality of his uncle's tragedies. His versification, however, is monotonous and inflexible compared with Virgil's.

Lucan wrote much more of which only fragments survive: we know of *A Journey to the Underworld*, *Orpheus*, *Trojan Matters*, and epigrams, and an address to his wife, Polla Argentaria. His epic was admired by STATIUS, though QUINTILIAN thought him worthier of imitation by orators than by poets. He was very popular in the Middle Ages, and Dante distinguished him as one of the four supreme poets. He pleased Goethe, and was an inspiration to Shelley and Macaulay. See F.M. Ahl (1976) *Lucan, an Introduction*, Ithaca: Cornell University Press; M.P.O. Morford (1967) *The Poet Lucan*, Oxford: Blackwell; J.M. Masters (1992) *Poetry and Civil War in Lucan's Bellum Civile*, Cambridge: Cambridge University Press.

Lucceius, Lucius (C1 BC), was a rich man and a friend of POMPEIUS (2). He was city praetor in 67 BC when, in a quarrel, the consul GLABRIO (3) broke his official chair. He foiled CAESAR (1) in 64 when the latter, in charge of the murder court, encouraged prosecution of SULLA (1)'s supporters who had killed citizens in the proscriptions, by prosecuting CATILINE, who was Caesar's crony. Consequently he supported CICERO (1) in his election as consul for 63 and in his subsequent campaign against Catiline. In 60, however, he assisted the election campaign of Caesar (now allied with Pompeius), paying all Caesar's election expenses, on a joint ticket for the consulship of 59, but was himself defeated by BIBULUS (1), who had the support of the conservatives. In the 50s he embarked on a career as a historian with a lost account of the period from the Social War (90 BC) to his own time. Cicero tried unsuccessfully to persuade him to compose a favourable account of his consulship and campaign against Catiline. Lucceius was a close adviser of Pompeius in 49, survived the battle of Pharsalus, was pardoned by Caesar, and wrote Cicero a letter of consolation on the death of his daughter in 45.

Lucilius 1, Gaius (*c.*180–102 BC) A satirical poet who was born at Suessa Aurunca in northern Campania; though his family was of senatorial rank and very wealthy, he remained in the equestrian class and devoted his adult life to his art. His brother's daughter Lucilia married POMPEIUS (5) Strabo and was POMPEIUS (2)'s mother. He served in Spain on the staff of his friend SCIPIO (11) Aemilianus at the siege of Numantia in 134 BC and was also friendly with Gaius LAELIUS (2), Junius Congus and Rutilius RUFUS (3). He probably visited Athens and other parts of Greece, as did other literary figures of the time. He died at Naples.

As a close friend of Scipio's he may be considered to have been a member of the 'Scipionic Circle', though the informality of such a group must be recognised. He drew on Archilochus as a model for the matter of his satires, and ENNIUS as a model for his metrical style. He began by writing the books later numbered 26–30, perhaps in the late 130s and early 120s, in a variety of traditional metres, the septenarius and other dramatic metres, though by book 30 he had adopted the hexameter as his vehicle of satire. He attacked his enemies, naming them fearlessly, as had Aristophanes, and included much detail about himself and his feelings, so that he is the most self-revealing Roman poet before CATULLUS (1). He then wrote in hexameters books 1–21. Book 1 contains an assembly of the gods and an attack on Cornelius Lentulus Lupus; book 2 a parody of the trial of Q. Mucius SCAEVOLA (3) for extortion as governor of Asia on the accusation of ALBUCIUS; book 3 a *Journey to Sicily* which HORACE imitated in his *Journey to Brundisium*; book 5 a reproach to a friend for failing to visit Lucilius when he was sick; and book 6 Scipio's encounter with a bore. Other books contain material on sexual activity, language and grammar, style, philosophy and personal attacks, especially on powerful men whom Lucilius considered to have demeaned themselves. He attacked extravagance of dress and eating and upheld a strict standard of morality. He even attacked tragedy.

Fragments only of his work survive, extending to 1,400 lines; some fragments are quite long, many are brief and difficult to place. His style was often chatty and sometimes careless, and he freely included Greek words and technical terms; he could be obscene and vituperative, but often wrote powerful and imaginative poetry. He inspired Horace in the composition of his *Satires*, and was admired by the generation of PERSIUS and JUVENAL. He firmly established the loosely flowing hexameter metre as the best for Roman satirical composition. See N. Rudd (1986) *Themes in Roman Satire*, London: Duckworth; M. Coffey (1989) *Roman Satire*, Bristol: Bristol Classical Press.

2, Gaius, known as the Younger (C1 AD), was a poet and philosopher of equestrian rank from Campania, born in humble circumstances, who was befriended by SENECA (2) the Younger on account of his talents and interests in philosophy and literature, and became a Roman knight through good connexions and his own efforts. He entered the equestrian career and rose to be procurator in turn of the Graian Alps, Epirus (or Macedonia), Africa and Sicily. Despite his success as an equestrian officer of state, he cherished the memory of several people who perished at the hands of the powerful: LENTULUS (6) Gaetulicus, executed for a plot against CALIGULA, and those killed by the empress MESSALLINA and the freedman of CLAUDIUS (1), NARCISSUS. It was to him that Seneca dedicated his *Moral Letters*, written in his retirement, though not all of them were genuinely part of a correspondence, in which he discussed many matters of interest to Lucilius of a philosophical, linguistic or literary nature. He was also the addressee of Seneca's *Natural Investigations* and the philosophical *On Providence*. Seneca saw Lucilius both as a fine philosopher in his own right and a fitting recipient of his ideas and teaching. Lucilius wrote poetry, and a few of his lines are quoted by Seneca. He wrote a Greek epigram preserved in an inscription at Sinuessa.

Lucilla (AD 150–182) was a daughter of the emperor MARCUS AURELIUS and his wife FAUSTINA (2) the Younger. Annia Aurelia Galeria Lucilla was the eldest daughter to survive her parents. In 161 she was engaged to her father's partner in power Lucius VERUS and married him at Ephesus in 164, whereupon she was proclaimed *Augusta* ('empress'), but was widowed in 169. The emperor then caused her to marry Tiberius CLAUDIUS (14) Pompeianus against her will. She had children by both husbands. She was hostile to the reign of her brother the emperor COMMODUS, and in 182 plotted against him, intending to replace him with her stepson, but was arrested and banished to Capri. She was put to death there.

Lucillius (C1 AD) was a Greek satirical poet who in NERO (1)'s reign composed some hundred epigrams which have survived in the *Greek Anthology*. His work shows him to have been cultivated and witty: he often satirises types for their foibles or professional idiosyncracies. He enjoyed any unexpected turn of events. He developed the pointed, witty, unexpected climax at the end of the epigram, and in this respect was an inspiration to MARTIAL.

Lucretius (*c.*97–*c.*53 BC) was a didactic poet, the author of the Latin poem *The Nature of Things* (*De Rerum Natura*). His name was Titus Lucretius Carus but nothing more is known for certain about him or his life. He set himself the task of expounding in hexameter poetry the tenets of Epicurean philosophy, despite the fact that Epicurus himself had rejected the medium of poetry as a serious vehicle for philosophical exposition. He therefore used the precedent set by the early Greek philosophers Empedocles and Parmenides, especially the former's lost poem *On Nature*, in composing didactic poetry to expound natural philosophy, while criticising their doctrines. The chief source that Lucretius used for the material in the poem will have been the works of Epicurus, most of which are lost: his title, however, recalls that of Epicurus' mostly lost treatise *On Nature*, and there is a significant resemblance to his extant *Letter to Herodotus*. Lucretius' principal aim in writing his poem was an evangelical one: to save humankind from irrational fear of the gods and of death, by carefully explaining the true nature of the universe we live in, its material quality (namely that the 'soul' is mortal as is the body), and the absence from this world of the supernatural (he conceded the existence of 'gods' which are unconcerned with mankind and inhabit spaces set between the 'worlds'). In dedicating the poem to Gaius MEMMIUS (2) (a politician and former praetor exiled in 52 BC for corrupt practices who chose thereafter to live in Athens and was appealed to by CICERO (1) not to destroy the remnant of Epicurus' house there) Lucretius may have taken a shot in the dark and given more offence than he intended: the poem is clear in condemning political involvement such as brought Memmius to grief, though his fall probably occurred after Lucretius' death. Cicero knew the poem well and admired it: in a letter of 54 BC to his brother he praised its skilful composition. It is hard to gauge Lucretius' social position; and a story, originating from SUETONIUS (2) via the Christian scholar Jerome, that he was the victim of a love-potion administered by his wife, can scarcely be true. According to it, the philtre drove him mad and he composed the poem, which Cicero is said to have edited, in moments of lucidity, but eventually killed himself.

The poem, our best evidence for the Epicurean physical system (despite Lucretius' real purpose, defined above), is in six books, each exceeding 1,000 lines in length. The books are all introduced by a prologue, and all end with a section which is differentiated from the main body of the book. The argument in each book is carefully signposted: in its general effect his poem is a diatribe, that is, a philosophical, almost religious plea supported by the devices of rhetoric. There is consequently a strong element of satire in Lucretius' handling of his material, arising from his evident indignation with the deceptions he saw peddled around him. His style is somewhat rugged as compared with the sophistication of contemporary poets like CATULLUS, and owes much to earlier poets such as ENNIUS and PACUVIUS, with a strong use of alliteration and assonance, archaic forms and invented compound words. The hexameter verse is even sometimes clumsy and monotonous, but is carried along by the power of the argument. The achievement of Lucretius in expounding the atomic theory of natural philosophy in a tongue whose deficiencies he felt all too keenly, and to do it with conviction and passion, was astonishing. What is missing from the poem, however, is an exposition and discussion of the Epicurean ethical system.

Lucretius adopts the goddess Venus as the dramatic addressee of his introductory prologue in book 1, conceiving her as a life force. He then describes the physical nature of the universe in terms of the atomic theory. Nothing can come of nothing: the atoms, of various shapes and sizes, are the only stable and unchanging things, and shifts in their relative positions in the void account for the impermanence of the visible world. After refuting the systems described by earlier philosophers, Empedocles, Heraclitus and Anaxagoras, he demonstrates the infinity of the universe in terms of the void and the atoms it contains. Book 2 develops his description of the atomic system and discusses the motion of the atoms, avoiding the absolute determinism of Democritus by postulating an unpredictable swerve in the motion of the atoms, and differentiating between primary qualities which are inherent in the atoms and secondary ones like colour, temperature and smell, which are incidental and arise from the combination of atoms. There are many other worlds in the universe besides this one, and all are susceptible to birth and death. In book 3, after a poem in praise of Epicurus, he discusses the soul, arguing that it is made of fine, light atoms, and is consequently mortal together with the body. He also shows how disease of the body is paralleled by disease of the mind and advances a series of 'proofs' of the mortality of the soul: hence it is foolish and unwarranted to fear death. Book 4 restarts the poem with a prologue closely similar to that of book 1 and the remaining books deal in detail with matters arising from the basic premises set out previously. The book then discusses perception and other psychological issues such as sensation and thought processes. He considers the fallibility of the senses but argues against scepticism. He ends the book with a condemnation of the passion of love. In book 5, after another encomium of Epicurus, he returns to the theme of the impermanence of the world and offers a rational account of its beginning and early development, discussing the origins of life ranging from the botanical to the human. He then describes the manner of humankind's creation and progress to civilisation. Book 6 treats of various phenomena of the atmosphere, such as weather systems and storms, and of the earth, such as volcanoes, earthquakes and the Nile; he moves on to disease and plague and ends with a graphic account of the Athenian plague described in Thucydides' *History*. There is some doubt as to whether the poem as we have it is complete: the end is quite abrupt and it is possible that there is corruption in the text. Besides the division into two broad sections suggested above, the poem may alternatively be considered as divided into three parts, the first two books referring to the atomic theory, the middle two to humankind, and the last pair to the broad sweep of the whole world.

Besides being admired by Cicero, Lucretius' poem was praised by VIRGIL, STATIUS and OVID, but was ignored in the later Empire and the Middle Ages and, like the works of Catullus, was only preserved by chance through a single manuscript. In the Renaissance Lucretius was recognised as an important thinker for his rationalism, and Milton imitated him in his *Paradise Lost*. The work was influential among political philosophers such as Hobbes and Rousseau in offering them an account of the development of human society devoid of religious dogma. See D.R. Dudley (1965) *Lucretius*, London: Routledge; E.J. Kenney, 'Lucretius', *Greece and Rome New Surveys*, 11, 1977, Oxford: Clarendon Press; D. West (1969) *The Imagery and Poetry of Lucretius*, Edinburgh: Edinburgh University Press; D. Clay (1983) *Lucretius and Epicurus*, Ithaca: Cornell University Press; C. Segal (1990) *Lucretius on Death and Anxiety*, Princeton: Princeton University Press.

Lucullus 1, Lucius Licinius (mid-C2 BC) As consul in 151 he overreached himself by using force to enlist soldiers and officers for his campaign in Spain, and with his colleague ALBINUS (2) was imprisoned for a time by the tribunes. In Spain he made an unprovoked attack on the Vaccaei and massacred many of the inhabitants of Cauca, which had surrendered, thus stiffening the opposition of the Spaniards to Rome. The next year he went to the aid of GALBA (4) against the Lusitani and inflicted a severe defeat on them. Galba massacred their leaders who sued for peace. The upshot was the revolt of VIRIATHUS.

2, Lucius Licinius (*c.*118–56 BC), was a grandson of LUCULLUS (1); his maternal uncle was METELLUS (5) Numidicus, whose son METELLUS (7) Pius he supported in pleading for the recall of the former from exile. He was a staunch supporter of SULLA (2) in the Social War which began in 91 BC and gained his entire trust: in 88 when he was quaestor he was the only one of Sulla's officers to support him in his march on Rome. In 86 Sulla took him to the east on his military staff for his campaign (the First Mithridatic War) against MITHRIDATES (3) VI of Pontus and trained him in the manner of fighting there. Sulla entrusted him with the difficult task of collecting ships and cash from the eastern allies, and near Pergamon, according to Sulla's instructions, he allowed Mithridates to escape the clutches of Gaius FIMBRIA. Lucullus' naval force later conveyed Sulla across the Hellespont to negotiate from strength with Mithridates at Dardanus. In 79 Lucullus held the aedileship in company with his brother, and put on lavish games for the people. As praetor the following year, Sulla being dead, he acted as guardian to his children and his literary executor. In 77 he was propraetor of Africa, which he ruled effectively, and held the consulship in 74, when he supplied POMPEIUS (2), who was fighting in Spain. He intrigued in Rome with CETHEGUS (3) to enable Marcus ANTONIUS (6) Creticus to obtain an unlimited command against the pirates of the Mediterranean, and himself to have the command against Mithridates as governor of Asia and Bithynia.

The neighbouring kingdom of Bithynia had become Roman territory early in 74 on the death of NICOMEDES IV: Mithridates saw this as a new threat to his independence and anticipated Roman action by occupying Bithynia himself. The resulting Third Mithridatic War involved both Lucullus and his fellow consul of 74, M. Aurelius COTTA (2): the latter was defeated at sea and besieged in Chalcedon; Mithridates invaded Asia but was unable to take Cyzicus, while Lucullus concentrated his forces, relieved Cyzicus and drove the army of Mithridates in turmoil into Bithynia. He then tried to trap the king there but was failed by the slowness of his naval wing; Mithridates' fleet escaped but was crippled by a storm in the Black Sea. Lucullus spent the summer of 73 ineffectively trying to subdue Pontus, but the next year, with the assistance of DEIOTARUS, a Galatian prince, he defeated Mithridates' cavalry and massacred his infantry near Cabira. Mithridates fled for refuge to his kinsman, TIGRANES (1) II of Armenia. While his army completed the reduction of Pontus, Lucullus returned to his province of Asia, which was in a financial crisis. Sulla had imposed a fine of 20,000 talents on the province, and the provincials had borrowed from Roman businessmen at a crippling rate of interest: they now owed the financiers six times the original amount of the fine. Lucullus imposed a settlement which was more favourable to the provincials, scaling down their debt to 40,000, than to the Roman moneylenders, who were to be paid a reduced sum by instalments over four years. In 69, after requesting the Senate to annex Pontus, Lucullus invaded Armenia with a mediocre force and won a devastating victory, capturing and plundering Tigranocerta, the new capital. He forced Tigranes to surrender the large territories he had annexed in eastern Asia Minor and Syria. However, Tigranes retreated east to Artaxarta, his former capital, and in 68 Lucullus pursued him. But his army mutinied and the Senate refused him more troops, even depriving him of his provinces: there was great resentment at Rome arising from his settlement of the Asian debt crisis. He spent the winter in Nisibis: his brother-in-law Publius CLODIUS was active at that time in urging the troops to rebel against Lucullus. Moreover, Pompeius' new command against the pirates deprived him of any source of fresh soldiers. As his army mostly melted away, Lucullus returned to Pontus but had to watch Mithridates and Tigranes recover their kingdoms. After the defeat of his legate TRIARIUS at Zela, the situation was hopeless (ironically the Senate now approved the creation of a province in Pontus) and Lucullus (65 BC) had to surrender his command to Pompeius under the Manilian law. On returning home he divorced his wife CLODIA, a sister of his enemy P. Clodius, and married Servilia, a half-sister of CATO (5). He had to wait until 63 for his triumph. He failed miserably in his further political interventions, against CAESAR (1) and Pompeius. He was immensely rich and lived the last few years of his life in proverbial luxury (his gardens were famous), dying insane. He was a writer and patron of literature, and an Epicurean. See E.S. Gruen (1974) *The Last Generation of the Roman Republic*, Berkeley: University of California Press; A. Keaveney (1992) *Lucullus: A Life*, London: Routledge.

Lusius Quietus (died AD 118) was a Moorish commander who served Domitian at the head of a cavalry corps until he was dismissed for unspecified misconduct. He volunteered for service with his cavalry under TRAJAN in the conquest of Dacia (102) and fought well. In 114 he accompanied Trajan to Mesopotamia, where he took Singara without a fight and saved the emperor's army from being cut off on the Persian Gulf. He ruthlessly suppressed a Jewish rebellion in Mesopotamia in 116, and was sent thence to govern Judaea, where he pursued the same harsh policy. Trajan rewarded his service by making him a senator with praetorian rank and conferring on him a suffect consulship. After Trajan's death in 117, HADRIAN recalled Quietus from Judaea and deprived him of his command.

He executed him in 118 for participating in a conspiracy against the emperor.

Lycophron, whose real identity is unknown, was the writer of an extant poem in Greek entitled *Alexandra*. He may have adopted the name ironically to recall a predecessor's combination of tragic composition and comic redaction. His work is datable to the early second century BC from a reference to the victory of FLAMININUS over PHILIP (1) V at the battle of Cynoscephalae in 197 BC. The poem purports to be a prophecy uttered by Cassandra, a daughter of king Priam of Troy, and is both powerful and deeply obscure. It contains a prediction of the future power of Rome, and runs to 1,474 iambic lines.

Lycortas (C2 BC) was an Achaean statesman and soldier from Megalopolis. He was a friend of PHILOPOEMEN and supported his policy of a unified Peloponnese in the Achaean Confederacy and the enforced adhesion of Sparta, Messene and Elis. He held at different times both the post of *Hipparch*, 'Master of the Horse', and 'General', i.e. leader of the Confederacy; he fought in the war against NABIS, tyrant of Sparta, and in 189 appeared in Rome as ambassador of the Confederacy to defend its policy against Sparta and Messene. After further negotiations with the Romans, he supported Philopoemen's attempt to coerce Sparta and Messene back into the Confederacy in 182, and replaced him as general after his death, readmitting the seceding states to membership of the Confederacy. But his policy was attacked by CALLICRATES, who favoured a pro-Roman line, and he was unable to maintain Achaean neutrality in the Third Macedonian War. His son was the historian POLYBIUS.

Lygdamus (C1 BC) was a Roman elegiac poet whose six elegies have come down to us at the beginning of the third book of elegies attributed to TIBULLUS. The poems are stylistically competent but slight in content. The identity of Lygdamus is unknown: he seems to try to identify himself (5, 18) with OVID. Some have suggested implausibly that Lygdamus was a pen-name of Ovid in his youth. His association with Tibullus and Ovid suggests that he was a member of MESSALLA (4)'s circle of patronage. He has also been identified with PROPERTIUS' freedman Lygdamus.

M

Macer 1, Aemilius (died AD 16), was a didactic poet of the Augustan period from Verona; OVID mentions having heard him recite. Fragments of his works survive: *Snake-bites* (*Theriaca*) and *The Generation of Birds* were based on the writings of Bolus and Nicander in Greek.

2, Lucius Clodius (died AD 68) As a military legate in the province of Africa in 68, Macer stopped the supply of grain from the province to Rome. On the fall of NERO (1) that year he refused to recognise any authority but the Senate's, and established himself as an independent governor, enrolling a legion (*The First Macrian Liberator*) and minting coins. The emperor GALBA (1) had him assassinated in October of that year.

3, Gaius Licinius (died 66 BC), was tribune in 73, praetor in 68, and, convicted of extortion in 66, committed suicide. He wrote a history of Rome along annalistic lines in at least sixteen books. His work, which has not survived, was well researched and dealt with the early myths in a rational way. LIVY and DIONYSIUS of Halicarnassus used it as a source.

Macrianus, Titus Fulvius Junius (died AD 261), was an emperor elevated to the purple by his father, Titus Fulvius Macrianus, a staff officer of VALERIAN. On the capture of Valerian by the Persians in AD 260, the father himself declined the office on account of his age and lameness, but nominated his sons Macrianus and QUIETUS (2) to joint power. Macrianus accompanied his father to Thrace to attack GALLIENUS, but both were killed in battle there by Gallienus' general AUREOLUS. See M. Grant (1985) *The Roman Emperors*, London: Weidenfeld & Nicolson.

Macrinus, Marcus Opellius (AD 164–218), was an emperor from Mauretania. While prefect of the Praetorian Guard in April 217, Macrinus hatched a plot and assassinated the emperor CARACALLA in Syria as he was about to attack the Parthian empire. Macrinus was proclaimed *Augustus* by the army, the first non-senator to become emperor. His brief reign was a failure: he lost the support of the army by his lack of generalship, losing two battles against the Parthian king ARTABANUS (5) and ceding Mesopotamia, and he became unpopular by reducing the legions' pay and leaving the troops from Europe in Syria. JULIA (11) Maesa caused his deposition by falsely claiming that her grandson Bassianus was the natural son of Caracalla: he was proclaimed as the emperor ELAGABALUS and Macrinus was overthrown in a battle fought near Antioch in June 218; he and his son were captured and executed. See M. Grant (1985) *The Roman Emperors*, London: Weidenfeld & Nicolson.

Macro, Quintus Naevius Cordus Sutorius (died AD 38), born at Alba Fucens, was a prefect of the Praetorian Guard under TIBERIUS. As Commander of the Watch he was employed by Tiberius in the overthrow of SEJANUS and was appointed the latter's successor. He exercised influence in the absence of the emperor from Rome comparable to that wielded by Sejanus, and he assisted in CALIGULA's succession. The new emperor appointed him prefect of Egypt in AD 38 but, unable to tolerate the existence of one to whom he owed so much, ordered him to kill himself before he could assume his post.

Maecenas, Gaius (*c*.64–8 BC) was a patron of the arts and in this and other matters the agent of the emperor AUGUSTUS. Maecenas was of Etruscan blood and ancient family: HORACE (*Odes*, 1, 1) hails him as descended from kings. He may have been born in Arretium (Arrezzo); he is sometimes referred to by the Arretine name of his mother's family, Cilnius. At Rome, as a member of the equestrian class, he was ineligible for high public office, and served Octavian (see AUGUSTUS) in capacities such as diplomacy and the organisation of public opinion. He was rich (gaining wealth from confiscations) and seemed indolent: his services to Augustus were more personal than public and his preference was for the arts and good living. He fought for Octavian in the Philippi campaign, conducted the arrangement of his marriage with SCRIBONIA, took part in the negotiations leading to the pacts of Brundisium and Tarentum, the latter in 37 BC when he was accompanied by a retinue of poets including Horace and VIRGIL. He acted as Octavian's personal envoy to ANTONIUS (7) in 38, and on two occasions acted as Octavian's deputy in Rome and Italy, in the years 36–33 and during the Actium campaign, 31–29. The latter period saw trouble with mutinous veterans which Octavian himself temporarily returned to quell, and Maecenas put down a plot by executing its instigator, M. Aemilius LEPIDUS (5), son of the triumvir. In the 20s relations between the emperor and Maecenas cooled: AGRIPPA (1) hated him; Maecenas' wife Terentia, Augustus' mistress, caused friction; and when Maecenas in 23 secretly warned his brother-in-law, the consul Terentius Varro Murena, that he was suspected of plotting against the emperor, Augustus could not forgive him for the indiscretion. However, on his death he left all he had to the emperor.

He was also a writer, though only a few fragments of his works have survived. His works included prose dialogues and verse, the latter in the manner of CATULLUS (1). His style appears to have been affected and precious. His greatest contribution to literature was his patronage of Virgil, Horace and PROPERTIUS and his influence on them to present the Augustan regime in a favourable light. See A. Wallace-Hadrill (1989) *Patronage in Ancient Society*, London: Routledge.

Maecianus, Lucius Volusius (mid-C2 AD), was a legal writer and teacher, probably from Ostia, and probably a pupil of P. Salvius JULIANUS. An equestrian, he held administrative posts, secretary for petitions and prefect of the grain supply, under ANTONINUS Pius, and was a tutor of MARCUS AURELIUS, whom he failed to impress. Antoninus made him a member of his privy council. In 160 he was appointed to govern Egypt. We know from the *Digests* of a number of lengthy and original lost legal works: *Trusts*, in 16 books; *Trials of Public Importance*, in 14 books; and, in Greek, *The Rhodian Sea Law*. He also wrote a short treatise for Marcus Aurelius on measurement and fractions, *Assis Distributio*, which survives.

Maelius, Spurius (mid-C5 BC), a possibly legendary character, was a rich member of the plebeian order who *c*.440 BC relieved a famine by buying grain from Etruria at his own expense and selling it cheaply to his fellow citizens. The story arose that he was accused by the patricians of aspiring to become a tyrant, was summoned to appear before the dictator CINCINNATUS, and on refusing was stabbed to death by C. Servilius AHALA in the forum. His property was confiscated and his house razed: its site was named *Aequimaelium*.

Maenius, Gaius (late C4 BC), was a consul in 338 BC who, in commemoration of his victory over the Latin and Antiate forces, fixed the beaks of captured enemy ships to the speakers' platform in the forum, which was thenceforth known as *Rostra* ('beaks'). The balcony (*Maenianum*) of the Basilica Porcia and the *Columna Maenia*, a column attached to the Comitia, also commemorate his work in remodelling the Roman forum. He was censor in 318 and dictator in 314.

Magnentius, Flavius Magnus (died AD 353), of Gallic descent and nominally a Christian, was a usurper of the imperial power in the west. He had been a distinguished general under CONSTANS, whom he overthrew and killed in a coup in January 350 at Augustodunum (Autun). He came into conflict with the eastern emperor CONSTANTIUS (2) II, whose forces defeated him in the great battle of Mursa in Pannonia in September 351. He lost Italy the following year and in 353 committed suicide on losing Gaul.

Magnus (C4 AD) was a historian of JULIAN's campaign against the Persians in AD 363. A native of Carrhae (Harran), he may have been a tribune in Julian's army. A summary and some fragments of his work are extant. See J. Matthews (1989) *The Roman Empire of Ammianus Marcellinus*, London: Duckworth.

Mago (late C3 BC), the youngest brother of HANNIBAL, was a Carthaginian general. After fighting in Hannibal's Italian campaign, he was sent to Spain to join HASDRUBAL (2) in 215, where he waged a successful campaign against Roman forces in which two SCIPIOs, Gnaeus (1) and Publius (6), were killed in 211. In 206, however, Mago was defeated by SCIPIO (7) Africanus at Ilipa and transferred his attention to the Balearic Islands: in 205 he sailed to Genoa. He recruited troops there and in 203 suffered a defeat, and was severely wounded, at the hands of the Romans in Cisalpine Gaul. He was summoned back to Carthage to assist in its defence and re-embarked his troops, but died on the voyage home.

Maharbal (C3 BC) The commander of HANNIBAL's cavalry in Italy in the early years of his campaign there. He is credited by LIVY with reproaching Hannibal, saying that he knew how to win a victory but not to use it, when the latter refused to march on Rome immediately after winning the battle of Cannae.

Malchus or **Malichus** (reigned *c.*57–30 BC) was a Nabataean king who assisted CAESAR (1) with cavalry in the Alexandrian War. In 40 as an ally of Parthia he refused refuge to HEROD (1) and later was fined by VENTIDIUS for having helped Parthia. ANTONIUS (7) gave part of his territory to CLEOPATRA (4) of Egypt. Herod attacked him in 31 on Antonius' orders and defeated him.

Mamilius the name of an important family from Tusculum.

1. Limetanus, Gaius, was a tribune of 109 BC who then established three courts, manned by equestrian juries, to try those accused of collaborating with JUGURTHA; one was presided over by SCAURUS (2). The targets were mostly men who had opposed the Gracchi. He also passed a law to settle the boundaries of public land, needed as a result of Gracchan agrarian laws, from which he gained his last name which means 'the boundary-maker'.

2, Lucius, was granted Roman citizenship in 458 BC because, as dictator of Tusculum, he had two years before freed the Capitol from its occupation by a Sabine, Appius Herdonius, and thus saved the Republic in a crisis.

Mamurra (C1 BC) was CAESAR (1)'s chief of engineers (*magister fabrum*) in his campaign in Gaul, where he enriched himself enormously. Mamurra was of equestrian stock from Formiae and may have been related to the architectural writer VITRUVIUS. CATULLUS (1) lampooned him mercilessly, calling him *Mentula*, 'Prick', and suggested he was sexually involved with Caesar. He is said to have been the first Roman to line the walls of his house with marble and to have the columns made of solid marble.

Mancinus, Gaius Hostilius (C2 BC), while fighting in Spain as consul in 137 BC, was defeated and his army trapped near Numantia. His quaestor Tiberius GRACCHUS (4) used his father's good name to extricate the army with the promise of terms, but SCIPIO (11) Aemilianus persuaded the Senate to reject the treaty. Mancinus agreed to be surrendered to the Numantines to be punished for this breach of faith, but they would not touch him, and he returned to take up his office again.

Mani (AD 216–277) was a Babylonian religious teacher who founded the developed form of Gnosticism known as Manichaeism. Born an Aramaic speaker, he came to believe at the age of 24 that he was the Holy Spirit promised to his disciples by JESUS of Nazareth. He left the Mandaean sect and travelled in India; returning thence he was well received at the court of the Sassanian royal family and became a friend of King SAPOR (1) I. He spent the whole of Sapor's reign from 240 until 272 in preaching his new religion, which owed elements to a number of sources including Christianity, Zoroastrianism, and the doctrine of transmigration of souls. He taught that there is an ethical struggle between good and evil, rather than the natural struggle of light and dark. His followers practised an ascetic life, avoiding worldly activities and possessions. Those who succeeded in achieving such asceticism were considered to be 'elect' and destined for redemption and to be delivered from the cycle of transmigration; those who fell short could be 'hearers', likely to transmigrate into bodies capable of being 'elect'. The cult became very popular: Roman emperors such as DIOCLETIAN tried to suppress it, but the cult had a wide vogue in the Roman Empire, and Augustine was a 'hearer' for nine years. It extended to China in the east. On the death of Sapor, his successor Bahram I had Mani executed in 277 at the instigation of the Zoroastrians. A number of texts survive including a catechism in Coptic, and biographical material about Mani is preserved in a Greek codex in Cologne. See S.N.C. Lieu (1985) *Manichaeism in the Later Roman Empire and Mediaeval China*, Manchester: Manchester University Press.

Manilius 1, Gaius (C1 BC), while a tribune of 66 BC proposed the Manilian Law, supported by CICERO (1) in an extant speech, which gave POMPEIUS (2) a special command against MITHRIDATES (3) VI of Pontus and TIGRANES (1) II of Armenia. Pompeius thereby received overriding powers in the provinces of Asia Minor. When Manilius' term of office expired he was accused of corruption by C. Calpurnius PISO (1) but the case did not come to court. He was, however, condemned for treason in early 65.

2, Manius (C2 BC), was proconsul of Spain in 155 or 154 BC, when he lost a campaign against the Lusitani. As consul in 149, in company with his colleague L. Marcius Censorinus, he besieged Carthage in the Third Punic War, engaging in such duplicity in his dealings with the besieged that he had to be rescued from disaster by the intervention of SCIPIO (11) Aemilianus. In 133 he persuaded Tiberius GRACCHUS (4) to agree to senatorial arbitration in his quarrel with Marcus OCTAVIUS (4). CICERO (1) introduces him as a character and friend of Scipio Aemilianus in his philosophical work *The Republic*, and refers to him in *Brutus* (108). He wrote seminal books on the law, including legal opinions and formulas for contracts and other documents: a few passages survive. He is referred to by POMPONIUS (2) and the *Digests*.

3, Marcus (C1 AD), was the Stoic author of an incomplete didactic poem on astrology in five books entitled *Astronomy*, written in the final years of AUGUSTUS' reign and that of TIBERIUS. We know nothing of his life. His text survives in a corrupt state and shows considerable literary merit. The chief literary influences on him were LUCRETIUS (whom he attacks violently while echoing his poetry), VIRGIL's *Georgics*, and CICERO (1)'s *Scipio's Dream*. The sources of his subject matter are uncertain: they include Aratus, the body of writings designated 'Hermetic' and deriving from the devotees of the Egyptian god Thoth, and the works of POSIDONIUS. His work is no more a technical treatise than is Virgil's *Georgics*, and there are serious omissions from a complete treatment of the subject, such as the lack of reference to the influence of planets upon humankind. He had a sure command of composition of the hexameter, and attracted the attention of the greatest modern critics, Scaliger, Bentley and Housman. As a poet he bears comparison with his great contemporary, OVID.

Manlius, Marcus (died *c.*385 BC), as consul in 392 BC defeated the Aequi and won an ovation. Legends then accrued to his name, including the story that he saved the Capitol from the Gauls during their invasion in 390 after he had been woken by the sacred geese; assisted the plebeians by relieving debt; and was accused and put to death for aspiring to become tyrant. He was surnamed Capitolinus for reasons we do not know.
See also TORQUATUS, VULSO (1).

Marcellinus (C2 AD) was a writer on anatomy: his work *Pulses* is extant.
See also AMMIANUS.

Marcellus 1, Gaius Claudius (died 40 BC), was the cousin of MARCELLUS (2) and first husband of OCTAVIA (1), Octavian's (see AUGUSTUS) sister: he was consul in 50 BC and supported POMPEIUS (2)'s efforts to force CAESAR (1) to return to Italy and face trial, and to build up a force against him. The next year he remained in Italy, met Caesar and begged for pardon, which was granted. He took no further part in events, leaving a son, MARCELLUS (7), who through his mother became part of AUGUSTUS' dynastic plans, and two daughters, the elder of whom married firstly AGRIPPA (1) and then, on divorce so that he could marry JULIA (5), Iullus ANTONIUS (3).

2, Gaius Claudius, was a cousin of MARCELLUS (1) and younger brother of MARCELLUS (6), consul in 49 BC and a resolute supporter of POMPEIUS (2), with whom he fled to Greece and in 48 became the joint commander of his Rhodian fleet.

3, Marcus Claudius (*c.*271–208 BC), was a general in the Second Punic War, five times consul. After service in the first Punic War he rose to be consul in 222 BC, when he and his colleague SCIPIO (1) Calvus defeated the Insubrian Gauls. He personally won the *spolia opima* ('rich spoils'), which were the prize of victory in single combat over an enemy leader, and a triumph. He relieved Clastidium and captured Mediolanum (Milan). He supported the delaying strategy of FABIUS (8) Maximus in opposing HANNIBAL in Italy, and in 216 he foiled an attack on Nola. He was appointed suffect consul in 215 but resigned in favour of Fabius when the augurs pronounced his election invalid, and was later elected consul for 214. During both these years he continued actively to oppose Hannibal's attempts to take Nola, and himself seized Casilinum. In autumn 214 he was posted to Sicily, where he brutally sacked Leontini, and in 213 began a two-year blockade and siege of Syracuse, which ended with its betrayal and pillage, involving the death of Archimedes. He took Agrigentum in 211 and then returned home, consul for the fourth time, to an ovation. He campaigned in Italy in 209, abandoning the Fabian strategy and being punished with defeat. In 208 he held his fifth consulship and was killed along with his colleague Crispinus, having been ambushed near Venusia. His piety is attested by his dedications of temples at Rome, but his exploits were doubtless enhanced by later writers. See J.F. Lazenby (1978) *Hannibal's War*, Warminster: Aris and Phillips.

4, Marcus Claudius (died 177 BC), was the eldest son of MARCELLUS (3) who, as tribune in 204 BC, investigated allegations against SCIPIO (7) Africanus and PLEMINIUS. As consul in 196 he defeated the Gallic Insubres and Cenomani near Comum but was worsted by the Boii; he served as legate under Merula, of whose command he wrote critical letters, in 193 in Cisalpine Gaul. He was censor with FLAMININUS in 189 and restored enfranchisement to the people of Campania. He was a *pontifex* from 196 to his death.

5, Marcus Claudius (died 148 BC), was a son of MARCELLUS (4), to whose priesthood he succeeded in 177. He was praetor in 169 when he and a colleague replaced the consuls in recruiting troops, and then he governed the whole of Spain for a year. He held the consulship in 166 and 155, winning triumphs for his campaigns in Cisalpine Gaul and again in 152 when he led an army in Spain. After a further successful campaign he recommended the Senate to make peace, but was rebuffed, the party for prolonging the war being led by SCIPIO (11) Aemilianus. Marcellus was drowned in 148 while conducting an embassy to MASINISSA.

6, Marcus Claudius (died 45 BC), was consul in 51 BC. He proposed resolutions to force CAESAR (1) to return to Rome on 1 March 50 from his command in Gaul. The tribunes vetoed his proposals, but he in turn overturned VATINIUS' law which authorised Caesar to make Como a Roman colony, and flogged a citizen of Comum to defy Caesar. He retired to Lesbos after the battle of Pharsalus and lived at Mytilene until 46 when Caesar pardoned him: he was murdered at Piraeus in May 45 on his way back to Rome. CICERO (1) admired him and wrote a speech (*For Marcellus*) in thanks for his pardon.

7, Marcus Claudius (42–23 BC), was AUGUSTUS' chosen heir, the son of MARCELLUS (1) and of OCTAVIA (1), Augustus' sister. He was betrothed at three years of age briefly to a daughter of Sextus POMPEIUS (4); in 25 BC Augustus took him to Spain on military service and in the same year married him to his own daughter JULIA (5). He also enacted an accelerated official career for Marcellus, allowing him (despite the tacit opposition of AGRIPPA 1, who retired to Mytilene) to reach the consulship ten years early. In 23 Marcellus, as aedile, put on lavish games to impress the Roman people, but he died towards the end of the same year at the resort of Baiae, to the consternation of Augustus, who named a theatre after him and had him buried in the mausoleum he had built for himself. VIRGIL commemorated him in the *Aeneid* (6. 860).

8, Ulpius (C2 AD), was a jurist of equestrian rank and a teacher of law at Rome who also served on the privy councils of the emperors ANTONINUS Pius and MARCUS AURELIUS. Besides teaching law, he wrote several books. His thirty-one books of *Digests* (abstracts of legal cases and decisions) were begun *c.*160; he also wrote five books on *The Consul's Duties*, a book of *Legal Opinions* (*Responsa*) and a commentary on the Julio-Papian Law. He annotated the *Digests* of JULIANUS in a critical spirit, while his own work was used and commented on by ULPIANUS and SCAEVOLA (1). His writings, which are lost, were quoted extensively and with approval by later legal writers, and there are more than 120 citations of his work in Justinian's *Digests*.

9, Victorius (suffect consul AD 105), was a public speaker and man of letters: QUINTILIAN dedicated to him his *Teaching of Oratory* and STATIUS the fourth book of his *Silvae*.

See also EPRIUS.

Marcia (died AD 193), a freedman's daughter, was the mistress of Ummidius Quadratus, a great-nephew of MARCUS AURELIUS. After his execution, she became the mistress of Marcus' son COMMODUS, who treated her like a wife, even though she was married to his chamberlain Eclectus. In 192 she administered poison to the emperor in a plot in which Eclectus and the Prefect of the Praetorian Guard Laetus were involved. She was murdered the next year by the emperor DIDIUS Julianus. She was a supporter of the Christians.

Marcius (C3 BC) was a prophet whose oracular verses were 'discovered' in 213 BC: they predicted the battle of Cannae and declared that the Romans must found a cult and games in honour of Apollo if they were to be rid of HANNIBAL. After an official consultation of the Sibylline Books, the first such games were held the following year. The prophecies of Marcius are reported by several historians including LIVY, PLINY (1) the Elder, and AMMIANUS MARCELLINUS.

See also PHILIPPUS, REX.

Marcus Aurelius (AD 121–180) was the successor of the emperor ANTONINUS Pius. He was born Marcus Annius Verus at Rome, the son of Annius Verus whose sister was the elder FAUSTINA (1), wife of Antoninus Pius. His father's family had a Spanish origin like that of HADRIAN, while through his mother, Domitia Lucilla, he inherited a large tile factory near Rome. He received his education from tutors, among them HERODES ATTICUS (2) and M. Cornelius FRONTO. He came early to the notice of Hadrian, who nicknamed him *Verissimus*, 'Most True', the superlative form of his own name Verus. In 136 at the age of fifteen Marcus was betrothed by Hadrian to Aelia, the daughter of his designated heir Lucius AELIUS (3). After the death of the latter on 1 January 138, Hadrian caused Antoninus, now his own adopted son and heir, to adopt Marcus along with Lucius Aelius, his brother-in-law elect. Marcus was now known as M. Aelius Aurelius Verus Caesar, and Lucius as L. Aelius VERUS. In fact Antoninus married Marcus to his own daughter FAUSTINA (2) the Younger in 145. He promoted him to the consulship, with himself as colleague, in 140, and when Faustina had produced a daughter in 146, he received tribunician power and a proconsular command: of the two adopted sons of the emperor, Marcus, the elder by ten years, was clearly the senior in rank. He adopted Stoicism as a 'religion' in about 146 and gave up the study of rhetoric he had received from Fronto, whose influence was now replaced by that of Rusticus. He had a very close, happy relationship with Antoninus.

When he became emperor on the death of Antoninus in March 161 as Marcus Aurelius Antoninus, he asked the Senate to make his adoptive brother Lucius Verus his partner and equal in power. Lucius was betrothed to Marcus' daughter Lucilla, now aged fifteen. Marcus now had to confront problems that Antoninus' inertia had done nothing to correct. Wars broke out on the frontiers that demanded the presence of the ruler. A rebellion in Britain and German incursions across the borders were dealt with, but in the east the Parthians under Vologeses III invaded Armenia in 162 and twice defeated Roman forces. L. Verus was sent in 162 with a strong force to rectify the situation. He proceeded slowly, arriving in 163, but Statius Priscus won back Armenia, and AVIDIUS CASSIUS, to secure the frontier of Syria, invaded Mesopotamia, which was brought under Roman influence: a Roman garrison was stationed at Carrhae. Thus Cassius, nominally under the command of Verus, had achieved a useful strengthening of the eastern frontier. In 165 Verus returned with his troops to Italy, but the men had been infected with the most destructive plague ancient Rome ever suffered. In 167 a German invasion of the Danube lands and North Italy took place in which the Sarmatian Iazyges were also involved. The Marcomanni and Quadi penetrated Italy as far as Aquileia. The emperor acted decisively, hastily raising two new legions from all classes including gladiators and slaves, and freed Italy of the threat.

In 169 Verus died, which enhanced Marcus' authority. He raised as much money as he could by selling imperial heirlooms and devaluing the currency, and prepared for war on the Danube front, in which he was engaged from 169 to 175. He cleared the Germans from the Roman territories of the Danube basin, and was on the point of extending the Empire and joining Dacia to Pannonia by the conquest of the Iazyges, when in 175 Avidius Cassius rebelled in Syria and declared himself emperor. To combat this insubordination, Marcus made a speedy but ineffective treaty with the Germans, settling tribesmen south of the Danube with a duty to defend the river frontier, and hastened to Syria. When he arrived, Cassius had already been murdered, but he took firm steps to put down the insurrection in both Egypt and Syria, returning home in 176 via Greece (where he gave generous donations to educational establishments) to celebrate a triumph. In 177 the Germans again attacked Pannonia, and Marcus made dispositions for the succession, breaking the felicitous tradition of nominating the best man by adoption, by making his own son COMMODUS his partner in office: he granted to Commodus the titles *Caesar* and *Augustus* and powers of an emperor. He himself in 178 went back to the frontier and defeated the Marcomanni. He again cleared the Roman territories of invaders, and was about to move the frontier north to the Carpathian mountains when he suddenly died in Vindobona (Vienna) on 17 March 180. He was commemorated at Rome by a sculpted column and by the bronze statue which still stands on the Capitoline Hill. He was succeeded, as he had planned, by Commodus.

Besides defending the imperial frontiers, Marcus carried out social legislation. He improved the judicial system in Italy by appointing circuit judges. He appointed permanent officials to supervise the distribution of food, the treasury and the care of children: freeborn children had to be registered. The civil service worked smoothly and benignly and the Senate was respected and given scope for initiative. However, the long wars and the plague caused a decline in population and in the economic situation of the Empire, bankruptcies became a problem, and there was stagnation and economic downturn. More than 200 years had now passed since AUGUSTUS had established the principate and given Rome strong government. AD 180 marks the end of a 'second series' of highly beneficent and successful rulers which started with NERVA (4) and TRAJAN. This was the stablest period in Rome's long history. A more despotic monarchy was to follow and, in the next century, a chaotic and dangerous loss of control.

Marcus Aurelius is unique among Roman emperors in having left writings which are still influential. His *Letters to Fronto* are limited in their appeal, but the *Meditations* remain a monument to his good qualities. They seem to have been notebooks made on his campaigns, written up without substantial change after his death. Though the thinking they express is not original, their message is often profound and forceful, owing much to the Stoic philosophy he fervently believed in, as it had been reformed by the work of POSIDONIUS. See A. Birley (1987) *Marcus Aurelius*, London: Eyre and Spottiswoode, rev. edn London: Batsford, 1993; M. Grant (1994) *The Antonines*, London: Routledge.

Mariccus (C1 AD) was a Celtic rebel against Roman rule in Gaul, who by claiming to be divine and championing the cause of Gallic freedom gathered a large following, but was overthrown by VITELLIUS (1) in AD 69.

Marius 1, Gaius (*c*.157–86 BC), was a general and statesman from Arpinum, a 'new man' of equestrian family who rose to be consul seven times. He served at the siege of Numantia in 133 BC under SCIPIO (11) Aemilianus, with whose support he was later elected to be a military tribune. He became quaestor *c*.123 and, with the help of the family of the Metelli, was elected tribune of the *plebs* in 119. During his tribunate he proposed a law, which the Metelli opposed, to make voting in the *Comitia* (elections) secret. He threatened METELLUS (2) Delmaticus for his opposition, thus earning the hostility of that family, which cost him the aedileship. He stood for the praetorship for 115, and though accused of corruption, he became city praetor. The next year he served as proconsul in Further Spain and proved his aptitude for guerrilla combat. On his return he married a patrician woman, JULIA (1), the aunt of Julius CAESAR (1). In 109 the consul, METELLUS (5) Numidicus, chose Marius as his senior deputy for the campaign against JUGURTHA, which had only moderate success. Marius decided to stand for the consulship and requested Metellus' consent, but was met with an insult. He was now the leader of the popular party and succeeded in invoking support among the equestrian order and a wide constituency in Italy and Africa so as to win the election for 107. Once in post, he had a law passed by which he took over Metellus' command; he also abolished the system of recruiting soldiers from the propertied classes only, and enrolled a large volunteer army from the proletariate, the poorest class of citizens, who owned no property. The war continued fruitlessly for two years until Marius' quaestor SULLA (2) captured Jugurtha through diplomacy and guile (see BOCCHUS 1), and so ended the war.

The threat of a German invasion of Italy and the defeat of the Romans under CAEPIO (3) by the Cimbri near Orange united the Romans behind Marius: they consequently elected him consul each year from 104 to 101. He held his triumph over Jugurtha on 1 January 104: he inherited from his enemy Rutilius RUFUS (5) an improved army, and proceeded to improve it yet more by drill, better equipment, and organisation. In 102 he met and routed the Teutones and their allies near Aix-en-Provence, and in 101 he and his colleague of the previous year, CATULUS (2), decisively defeated the Cimbri at Vercellae near Rovigo in the valley of the Po. The two men held a joint triumph; Marius stood for his sixth consulship in 100 and defeated Metellus Numidicus with the support of many nobles as well as that of equestrians and the common people. He was now at the peak of his prestige, but he had an ambiguous relationship with the ambitious and violent tribune Lucius SATURNINUS (2), who had supported him in 103 by legislating for the provision of land for his veterans from the Jugurthine War. In 100 he repeated the legislation for the veterans of Marius' German campaign, and led a move to exile Marius' enemy, Metellus. The support that Marius commanded at that time was wide-ranging, including most of the powerful interests in Rome, but he now proceeded to lose two important strands of support, the party of Saturninus, who plotted revolution in company with the praetor, Gaius GLAUCIA, and the established nobility, who resented Marius' refusal to countenance the recall of Metellus. He was firm against the former when they went too far and organised the assassination of Gaius MEMMIUS (1), a candidate for the next year's consulship, and he united the urban mob with the aristocrats to crush their growing power, passing the 'Ultimate Decree' to save the republic. As consul he used his veterans to pen them on the Capitol. Granting them a place of safety in the Senate House, he abandoned them to the mob, which proceeded to kill them.

Marius was dissatisfied with his ambiguous position, and when he could no longer resist Metellus' recall he gave up further political advancement and went east to meet MITHRIDATES (3) VI of Pontus. A law of Saturninus passed in 100 had by implication appointed Marius to settle the menace the pirates and Mithridates posed but, lacking an official post, all Marius could do was to warn him sternly. He returned to Rome: he had been elected an augur in his absence for the tough line he had taken with Mithridates, and he spent the next years defending old friends whom his enemies attacked in the courts, AQUILLIUS (2), NORBANUS (1) and T. Matrinus, whose citizenship Marius had procured. In 92 Marius prosecuted Rutilius Rufus with equestrian support, and in 91 he opposed the proposals of M. Livius DRUSUS (2) to grant citizenship to a wide range of Italian allies of Rome. In 90, after severe defeats suffered by Roman armies in the Social War, Marius did much to restore the situation by taking over command from a dead general, Rutilius Lupus, but himself received no official command and retired from the war. In 88, when the Senate appointed SULLA (2) commander against Mithridates, Marius was nominated in his place by the tribune Publius SULPICIUS (1) Rufus, who passed the required legislation through the Assembly. Sulla escaped from Rome to his legions in Campania, and promptly marched north and seized Rome. Marius fled to Cercina, a colony of his veterans in North Africa, and in 87 returned to Etruria and with many of his veterans joined Lucius CINNA (2) in sacking Ostia and storming Rome. Marius proceeded to take murderous vengeance on all who had failed to support him, and many nobles were butchered by his men. He and Cinna appointed themselves consuls for 86, and Marius was voted to replace Sulla as commander in the east. He died of pleurisy, however, early in his last consulship before he could depart.

A brilliant general while in his prime, Marius was a controversial figure who deliberately took on the old Roman nobility at their own game of intrigue and alliance without particular success. Despite his spectacular career, he failed to appreciate what power army reform could now give a successful and popular commander. He had in any case no clear policy for political reform and was reactive to the march of events. See T.F. Carney (1970) *A Biography of Gaius Marius*, Chicago: Argonaut.

2, Gaius (*c.*110–82 BC), was the son of MARIUS (1) and JULIA (1). To his mother's dismay he was elected consul with Cn. Papirius CARBO (5) for 82 BC, when he was defeated by SULLA (2) and besieged in Praeneste. There he killed himself after its reduction by Q. Lucretius Ofella.

3. Graditanus, Marcus (died 82 BC), was the nephew of MARIUS (1), being a son of his sister, and adopted by one of his brothers. When he was tribune in 87 he was a supporter of CINNA (2), and prosecuted Quintus CATULUS (2), who had deserted Gaius Marius for SULLA (2): Catulus committed suicide. He was praetor twice, in 85 and 84, and announced as if his own idea a new procedure, which had been devised by the praetors and tribunes, for authenticating the coinage: for this he was voted special honours by the plebeian assembly, but was prevented from standing for the consulship. He was proscribed in 82 by Sulla and murdered by his brother-in-law CATILINE over the tomb of Catulus at the request of Catulus' son.

4. Maximus, Lucius (consul AD 223), was a Roman historian who wrote a lost continuation of SUETONIUS (2)'s *Lives of the Caesars*. He imitated both the method and the approach of his predecessor, including much sensational material of dubious authenticity. He wrote the lives of the emperors from NERVA (4) to ELAGABALUS, and was quoted by the author of the *Augustan History*. AMMIANUS MARCELLINUS disapproved of Marius' work and criticised those who read him. He is usually identified with the legate of Septimius SEVERUS (1) who besieged PESCENNIUS NIGER in Byzantium in 193, was City Prefect in 217, governed Africa, Asia and Syria, and held two consulships.

Maroboduus (died AD 37) was a king of the Suebic (west German) Marcomanni who persuaded his nation to migrate *c.*9 BC into Bohemia. He made himself king of a powerful confederacy extending to the north and west of the Bohemian frontier. In AD 6 TIBERIUS began an enveloping movement against him with twelve legions when a revolt broke out in Illyricum and Pannonia. Tiberius negotiated peace, granting Maroboduus the title of King and Friend of the Roman People, and withdrew to settle the revolt. ARMINIUS, leader of the Cherusci, was hostile to him and in AD 17 attacked and defeated him: only a change of sides by Arminius' uncle Inguiomerus saved him from destruction. However, in 19 the Marcomanni led by Catualda drove Maroboduus out of his kingdom. He took refuge in Italy and spent the rest of his life interned at Ravenna.

Martial (*c.*AD 40–*c.*104) was a Latin poet, the master of the epigram. Marcus Valerius Martialis was born and brought up at Bilbilis in north central Spain and moved in AD 64 to Rome where he may have studied law; he lived briefly under the patronage of other Spaniards, the younger SENECA (2) and LUCAN, besides other patrons, PISO (2), Vivius Crispus and Memmius Regulus. But in spring 65 on the discovery of Piso's plot against NERO (1), Piso, Seneca and Lucan perished. Martial acquired, perhaps through Seneca's generosity, a small property in the country at Nomentum. After fifteen years at Rome, Martial began publication with a short *Book of Epigrams* (its modern title is *Book of the Shows*) celebrating the opening of the Flavian Amphitheatre (the Colosseum) in 80. From that time he assiduously courted the favour of the Flavian emperors TITUS and DOMITIAN, the latter with abject flattery: his reward was the 'three-children privilege', an immunity from taxation normally granted to fathers, which he never was. He was also awarded an honorary military tribuneship giving him equestrian rank. He must have gained a name by circulating and reading poems before that time, and in the next few years published two practical works. These were books of short poems on gifts (in the form of amusing descriptions of the presents to be written on their labels), entitled *Xenia* (*Gifts to Hosts*) and *Apophoreta* (*Presents to Take Away*) for the parties held at the midwinter festival of Saturnalia. Between 86 and 102 he published twelve full-length books of epigrams of great variety in a number of metres, the third being composed during a long stay at Imola and the last after his retirement to Bilbilis in 98. All these works survive.

Martial's model in writing the epigram was CATULLUS (1), whose work he knew well and to whom he refers, and like him he adopted the elegiac, hendecasyllabic, and scazon metres as his chief vehicles for writing humorous and realistic verses. There was also an influence of OVID in his elegiac poems. There is no moralising in Martial's work, but there is great variety of subject matter and purpose from the satirical to the complimentary, the sentimental to the scurrilous. Martial developed the technique of ending his epigrams with a point or twist which surprises the reader and adds a memorable quality to the poem (cf. LUCILLIUS). Few of the poems exceed thirty or forty lines, and Martial was at his best in setting a scene in swift brushstrokes or quoting a dialogue with economic brevity. He also wrote poems more like the traditional Greek epigram: dedications, epitaphs, and celebrations of people, places and events. He had a fertile imagination, a ready wit, felicity of language and genuine affection for his friends; he was also capable of vulgarity and obscenity. His poems throw valuable light on the social life of his period. There is evidence that his poetry became very popular, and was read eagerly throughout the empire.

Though he makes much of his poverty, Martial had influential friends including many of the writers of the day, among them PLINY (2) the Younger, who paid for his journey back to Spain, QUINTILIAN, JUVENAL, to whom he addresses an epigram, FRONTINUS and SILIUS Italicus. He changed his approach after the fall of Domitian, dropping the flattery and indecency of his earlier work. He cannot have made much money out of his writing, such was the nature of publishing, and always depended on the good will of others: even after his return to Spain he lived in accommodation provided by a patroness, Marcella. In his retirement he missed Rome and its life deeply, realising how greatly it had fed his muse with its variety and vigour: he saw that he had cut himself off from the source of his inspiration. See J.P. Sullivan (1991) *Martial: The Unexpected Classic*, Cambridge: Cambridge University Press.

Martialis, Quintus Gargilius (C3 AD), was a Latin writer on gardens. Parts of three of his works on gardens and tree cultivation are extant and reveal a stylish writer who was well acquainted with his subject (much of what is preserved is about trees), through personal experience as well as from reading earlier authorities. He knew, and criticised, the work of COLUMELLA. See W.F. Jashemski (1979) *The Gardens of Pompeii, Herculaneum, and the Villas Destroyed by Vesuvius*, New Rochelle: Caratzas Bros.

Martinianus *see* LICINIUS.

Masinissa (238–148 BC) was a king of Numidia (whom POLYBIUS knew as Massanasses), the son of Gaia, king of the eastern Numidian Massyli. He was brought up at Carthage; *c.*213 he and his father, in alliance with Carthage, defeated SYPHAX, king of western Numidia. He then joined the Carthaginian army in Spain where he campaigned from 211 to 206. He then changed sides in the war and, at a meeting near Cádiz, offered his support to SCIPIO (7) Africanus. Masinissa's father died about this time and he went to Africa to claim his kingdom, which had been usurped by his nephew Massiva. Meanwhile Syphax allied himself with Carthage and overran eastern Numidia, so that Masinissa had to flee his kingdom. After many adventures, he joined the Roman army that invaded Africa in 204. He was active in the war against Carthage and attacked and defeated Syphax in the battle of the 'Great Plains', taking Cirta (see SOPHONISBA), now Constantine, the capital of his kingdom, which he made his own capital. Scipio then publicly declared him king of Numidia; his cavalry played a decisive part in the battle of Zama in 202, which brought the Second Punic War to an end.

In the years that followed, Masinissa

applied constant pressure, military and diplomatic, to Carthage and eventually (in 150) goaded her into making war on him. He won the war and so precipitated the Third Punic War, in the middle of which he died, leaving his kingdom to his sons, MICIPSA, Gulussa and Mastanabal. He was successful in both the military and the diplomatic spheres, understanding the power of Rome and seeing how to manipulate it to his own advantage: he was a useful ally of Rome who did not seriously threaten Roman interests in the region. He was a man of great culture who encouraged the spread of Punic arts and civilisation among his subjects so that they survived the collapse of Carthage in 146.

Massa, Baebius (late C1 AD), was a favourite of DOMITIAN and an informer, prosecuted by PLINY (2) the Younger in AD 93 for plundering the province of Baetica (southern Spain) of which he had been governor.

Maternus (late C2 AD) was a mutineer in the Roman army stationed in Germany *c.*AD 185, unreliably stated by HERODIAN to have led an attack on Rome and to have tried to assassinate COMMODUS.

Matidia Salonia (*c.*AD 65–119) was a niece of TRAJAN and mother-in-law of HADRIAN: the daughter of Trajan's sister Marciana, she was close to Trajan and his wife PLOTINA and accompanied them when they travelled around the empire. She married L. Vibius Sabinus, by whom she had two daughters, one of whom, Vibia SABINA, married Hadrian. The other, Matidia the Younger, remained unmarried.

Matius 1, Gnaeus (early C1 BC), was a poet and translator of the *Iliad* into Latin hexameter verse, and the writer of *mimiambi* (dramatic short poems in the limping iambic metre) along the lines of those by the Greek poet Herodas. His works, now lost, were admired by Aulus GELLIUS (1) and VARRO (3).

2, Gaius (mid-C1 BC), was an equestrian writer on the cultivation of trees and on gastronomy and a friend of Octavian (see AUGUSTUS). He may be identical with CICERO (1)'s friend of the same name who assisted him in his dealings with CAESAR (1) in 49–48 BC and who in July 44 was Octavian's partner in arranging the games in memory of Caesar. See his correspondence with Cicero about Caesar (*Ad Fam.*, 11. 27, 28).

Maxentius, Marcus Aurelius Valerius (*c.*AD 283–312), reigned as emperor from 306 to 312, holding power in Italy, Spain and Africa. The son of MAXIMIAN and Eutropia, he was aggrieved to be passed over by DIOCLETIAN and Maximian in 305, when they abdicated in favour of GALERIUS and CONSTANTIUS (1) I. On the death of the latter, Flavius Valerius SEVERUS (3) was proclaimed *Augustus* (emperor) and CONSTANTINE (1) was likewise proclaimed by the army in Britain. The Praetorian Guard at Rome and the people of the City, aggrieved at their loss of status, then proclaimed Maxentius emperor (*Augustus*). He recalled his father from retirement in Lucania to help him, and proclaimed them both *Augusti*. They repelled an attack by Severus, whom they caught and executed at Ravenna, and another by Galerius. Maxentius' father struck an alliance with Constantine by marrying his daughter FAUSTA (2) to Constantine, but in 308 quarrelled with Maxentius, whom he tried to depose before taking refuge with Constantine. At the conference of Carnuntum in November 308, Diocletian, Maximian and Galerius combined to declare Maxentius a public enemy. However, his next problem was a famine at Rome caused by a revolt in the province of Africa (Rome's breadbasket) under its governor Domitius Alexander, which was put down by forces under Maxentius' praetorian prefect. In 310

Maximian again made a bid to be emperor but was checked by Constantine, whose ties with Maxentius' family were broken. In 312 Constantine invaded Italy and killed the prefect of the Praetorian Guard at Verona; he defeated Maxentius' army at Red Rocks (*Saxa Rubra*) near Rome: the emperor himself was drowned in the Tiber at the Milvian Bridge. See T.D. Barnes (1982) *Constantine and Eusebius*, Cambridge MA: Harvard University Press; M. Grant (1985) *The Roman Emperors*, London: Weidenfeld & Nicolson.

Maximian (*c.*AD 250–310) was an emperor who ruled in the western half of the empire from 285 until 305. Marcus Aurelius Valerius Maximianus, of humble origins, from Sirmium in Pannonia, was a fellow officer of DIOCLETIAN. After a successful military career, he was promoted by his comrade in 285 to the rank of *Caesar* or deputy emperor, with responsibility for the government of the western empire, his capital being Milan. Nine months later, after his successes against a peasant rebellion in Gaul and a German invasion, Diocletian made him his colleague and gave him the title *Augustus*. Maximian failed, however, to regain Britain from CARAUSIUS and was preoccupied for several years in defending the Rhine and Danube frontiers. In 293 Diocletian, who still wielded superior power, imposed a deputy on him with the title of *Caesar*, namely his Praetorian Prefect CONSTANTIUS (1), to whom he had already married his daughter Theodora. While Constantius recovered Britain, Maximian held the Rhine frontier, and in 296 went to Africa to quell a rising in Mauretania. He visited Rome where he held a triumph in 299 and began the building of the Baths of Diocletian. In 303 he and Diocletian celebrated a joint triumph in Rome. He strictly enforced laws against the Christians in Italy, Spain and Africa.

In May 305, on the instruction of and in company with Diocletian, he abdicated and retired to Lucania. The following year his son MAXENTIUS was proclaimed emperor and recalled Maximian to be his colleague. Maximian used his military and diplomatic skills, beating the attack of SEVERUS (3) and winning the friendship of CONSTANTINE (1), to whom he married his daughter FAUSTA (2). In April 308 he turned on his son, whom he failed to depose, and fled to Gaul, where he lived for a time with Constantine. He attended the conference of Carnuntum where he was compelled by Diocletian and GALERIUS to abdicate again. Some time later he rebelled against Constantine, proclaimed himself *Augustus* a third time, was captured, and in 310 killed himself in confinement at Massilia. He was deified by Maxentius and the Senate. See A.H.M. Jones (1964) *The Later Roman Emperors*, Oxford: Blackwell; T.D. Barnes (1982) *The New Empire of Diocletian and Constantine*, Cambridge MA: Harvard University Press; S. Williams (1985) *Diocletian and the Roman Recovery*, London: Batsford; M. Grant (1985) *The Roman Emperors*, London: Weidenfeld & Nicolson.

Maximinus 1. (reigned AD 235–238) was an emperor of humble Thracian origins, known therefore as *Thrax*, 'the Thracian'. Gaius Julius Verus Maximinus was a successful career soldier who had come to the attention of Septimius SEVERUS (1) for his great size and strength. In March 235 at Mogontiacum (Mainz) he was made emperor by the army in a mutiny against SEVERUS (2) Alexander, whom he ordered to be killed together with his mother JULIA (13) Mamaea. He lacked political foresight and remained with the army on the frontier while opposition to his expensive campaigning grew in Rome. He won a victory near Würtemburg in Germany and fought on the Danube frontier for a further two years until in

238 the Senate, which hated and feared him, appointed BALBINUS and Pupienus to oppose him and elected GORDIAN (1) I to replace him. He invaded Italy but was held up by the need to besiege Aquilea, which resisted stoutly: his army became disillusioned and killed him and his son, the *Caesar* Maximus. See M. Grant (1985) *The Roman Emperors*, London: Weidenfeld & Nicolson.

2. (*c.*AD 270–313) was an emperor in the east, originally named Daia, known during his reign as Gaius Galerius Valerius Maximinus; he was the nephew of GALERIUS, to whom he owed rapid promotion in the army and the title *Caesar* (deputy emperor) in 305 when Galerius became *Augustus* on the retirement of DIOCLETIAN. He governed Syria and Egypt in this capacity but was angered in 308 when Galerius preferred to make LICINIUS the next *Augustus* of the west, rather than himself. Like CONSTANTINE (1), he refused to be a simple 'Son of Augustus' and made his troops hail him as *Augustus*; the following year Galerius recognised his claim. In May 311 Galerius died and Maximinus was now senior *Augustus* and occupied Asia Minor, but he refrained from advancing further, which would have involved fighting Licinius. He made an alliance with MAXENTIUS to strengthen himself against the powerful alliance of Constantine and Licinius. The situation changed after the overthrow of Maxentius in October 312, and Maximinus took the initiative and invaded Europe, seizing Byzantium: he was defeated decisively by Licinius in April 313 near Adrianople and fled before him to Tarsus, where he killed himself.

Maximinus was a devoted follower of traditional religion and applied pressure to the Christian community in his territory, punishing recalcitrant Christians with hard labour in the mines, mutilation, and some executions, especially in Egypt. He also reformed the priesthoods to be hierarchic like the Christian ministries. He published anti-Christian propaganda, citing evidence given by Christians in confessions to incest. See M. Grant, *The Roman Emperors*, London: Weidenfeld & Nicolson, 1985.

Maximus **1,** Spurius Carvilius (C3 BC), was a conqueror of the Samnites: he was consul in 293 and 272 BC and censor in 289. He dedicated a statue made from Samnite armour in the temple of Jupiter on the Capitol.

2. (*c.*AD 125–185) was a Greek sophist or lecturer from Tyre. Forty-one of his lectures on various subjects are extant: not an original thinker, he was unacquainted with the works of any philosopher except Plato. He was well read in other Greek literature and wrote in an easy, graceful style, with many quotations, mainly from Plato and Homer. His lectures, delivered in Rome during the reign of COMMODUS, are bland, moralising, uncontroversial homilies.

3. (died AD 370) was a Greek Neoplatonist philosopher from Ephesus and a teacher of the emperor JULIAN. He was trained in the tradition of Iamblichus and was interested in the mystical and magical side of Neoplatonism. He also produced critical studies of Aristotle's writings on logic, including a lost commentary on the *Categories*. Once he had become emperor in 361, Julian invited Maximus to join his court at Constantinople: he remained with the emperor from then until his death. He was well received by JOVIAN's successor Valens, an Arian Christian, until he was imprisoned in 364. After his release, gained by Themistius, he plotted to kill Valens and was put to death.
See also FABIUS (5)–(9).

Mela, Pomponius (mid-C1 AD), was a geographer from Tingentera in southern Spain who wrote an extant Latin work in three books entitled *Chorography* ('study of places'): its date is proved by reference to Claudius' invasion of Britain in AD 43.

The method of his study was to start from the Straits of Gibraltar and to describe in order the lands bordering the Mediterranean and Black Seas from northern Africa via Egypt, Syria, Asia Minor, Scythia, the Balkans, Italy, southern Gaul, Spain, and the islands of the Mediterranean. He then covered the Atlantic coastlands from Spain to Germany, Scandinavia and eastern Asia; finally, in a wider sweep, he took in the British Isles, India and south Asia, the Red Sea, and eastern and western Africa. He neglected central Europe and central Asia. He introduced the work with a description of the divisions of the globe into five climatic zones and of the ocean, seas and three continents. He was uninterested in mathematical relations or distances, but was keen on human customs, myths and history. See STRABO.

Melito (died AD 190) was a bishop of Sardis who wrote in Greek a defence of Christianity, of which fragments survive, which he addressed to MARCUS AURELIUS, and a highly rhetorical sermon on the eucharist which is wholly or partly extant in five languages.

Memmius 1, Gaius (late C2 BC), was a Roman politician who, as tribune in 111 BC, attacked the nobles for their corrupt dealings with JUGURTHA; when he summoned Jugurtha to Rome to give evidence, his colleague Baebius forbade the hearing. He was active on the prosecuting side when the commission of MAMILIUS (1) Limetanus, set up in 109, tried those accused of corruptly assisting Jugurtha. He was praetor *c.*105, after which he was prosecuted for extortion in his province: he gained acquittal despite the hostile witness of his enemy Marcus SCAURUS (2). He stood for the consulship for 99 BC but was murdered by a gang organised by his fellow-candidate GLAUCIA (1).

2, Gaius (mid-C1 BC), was a politician, poet and literary patron. He married *c.*72 FAUSTA (1), daughter of SULLA (2) and ward of LUCULLUS (2); however, he conceived a passionate hatred for the Lucullan family. He was tribune in 66 when he prosecuted Marcus Lucullus and succeeded in delaying the triumph of Lucius for a year. As praetor in 58 he assisted L. Domitius AHENOBARBUS (6) against CAESAR (1); the next year he governed Bithynia and Pontus: he took with him, as members of his civilian staff or as friends, CATULLUS (1), Gaius CINNA (4) and PARTHENIUS. In 54, after divorcing Fausta, who married MILO, he was a candidate for the consulship with the support of both POMPEIUS (2) and Caesar: he failed to be elected as he was implicated in an electoral scandal, which he himself revealed (see CLAUDIUS 8). He was found guilty in 52 of electoral corruption and exiled: he went to live in Athens. In 50 he hoped to be allowed to return home, but we have no evidence that he did. He died a year or two later. He may have turned to Epicurean philosophy: the poet LUCRETIUS dedicated his poem *The Nature of the Universe* to him. He was an orator and poet, and corresponded with CICERO (1).

3. Regulus, Publius (C1 AD), was a provincial governor from southern Gaul, favoured by TIBERIUS who made him his quaestor; he held a suffect consulship in AD 31 when he organised the fall of SEJANUS. He then governed Moesia, Macedonia and Achaia. In 38 the new emperor CALIGULA forced him to bring his wife LOLLIA Paulina to Rome so that he himself might marry her: Memmius had to play the part of her father. He governed Asia *c.*48 and served both CLAUDIUS (1) and NERO (1).

Menelaus (late C1 AD), a Greek mathematician and astronomer from Alexandria, made observations at Rome in AD 98 as mentioned by PTOLEMY (13). PLUTARCH also mentions him in his book about the moon's face. Menelaus wrote an extant mathematical work, in three books, on spherical geometry, *The Sphere*, transmitted through an Arabic translation, probably mostly original. Lost works included a chord-table and an elementary geometry. See T.L. Heath (1921) *A History of Greek Mathematics*, Oxford: Clarendon Press.

Menodorus (or **Menas**) (C1 BC) was an adventurer and naval commander who, after a career as a pirate, joined forces with Sextus POMPEIUS (4) and in 40 BC took Sardinia from Octavian (see AUGUSTUS) for him. He warned Pompeius in 39 not to collaborate with ANTONIUS (7) and Octavian in the Pact of Misenum, and even urged him to kill them treacherously at a banquet. The following year he deserted Pompeius for Octavian and returned Sardinia to him. Being raised to equestrian rank he fought a naval campaign against Pompeius under the command of Calvisius SABINUS (1). He briefly flirted with Pompeius again in 36 BC but quickly returned to Octavian, in whose campaign in Illyricum he was killed while besieging Siscia.

Merula, Lucius Cornelius (early C1 BC), was priest of Jupiter (*Flamen Dialis*); see CINNA (2).

Mesomedes (mid-C2 AD) was a Cretan poet and freedman-courtier of HADRIAN. Fourteen of his poems survive on various subjects and in various metres; four of these are set to music. See M.L. West (1992) *Ancient Greek Music*, Oxford: Clarendon Press.

Messalla 1, Manius Valerius Maximus (consul 263 BC), successfully fought the Carthaginians and their ally Hieron II, tyrant of Syracuse, in the Etna region of Sicily during his year of office. He caused Hieron to change sides, and was given the honorific name Messal(l)a for his relief of the Greek city of Messina. He held a triumph and had a painting of his exploit placed on a wall of the senate-house.

2, Marcus Valerius (*c.*102–*c.*50 BC), was an advocate and friend of CICERO (1), known as *Niger*, 'black' to distinguish him from his cousin MESSALLA (3) Rufus. He was a protégé of SULLA (2), who made him a priest (*pontifex*), but was expelled by the censors from the Senate in 70 BC. He was elected city praetor for 64, he reached the consulship in 61 and served in 59 on the land commission appointed by CAESAR (1). He was censor in 55 and 54, and in the latter year took action after the Tiber had flooded. He held interregna three times in the later fifties because of unsatisfactory elections.

3, Marcus Valerius (100–26 BC), was a politician and historical writer, known as *Rufus*, 'red', to distinguish him from his cousin MESSALLA (2). SULLA (2) married his sister and made him augur. He was consul for the latter part of 53 after electoral scandals had delayed the poll. He was convicted in 51 of bribery and fined: his uncle HORTENSIUS (2) got him off another charge of bribery. In the civil war he supported CAESAR (1), fighting in Africa and Spain. He then settled down to write books on the state religion and the ancient families, which served as a source for later historians, but have not survived.

4. Corvinus, Marcus Valerius (64 BC–AD 8), was a statesman, orator and patron of literature. The second son of MESSALLA (2), he fought with distinction at Philippi in 42 BC in the forces of CASSIUS (2) on the republican side. He then joined ANTONIUS (7), with whom he stayed for several years but *c.*37, growing disgusted by Antonius' conduct, he returned to Italy and joined the followers of Octavian (see AUGUSTUS). He waged war on Sextus POMPEIUS (4) for Octavian in 36 and fought in Illyricum in 35–34, conquered the Salassian Alps in 33 and was rewarded by Octavian with the consulship of 31 which had been assigned to Antonius: in that year he fought in the Actium campaign. He was sent to Syria, which he ruled for a couple of years, then in 28 he governed Gaul, where he subdued the Aquitanians and held a triumph in 27. A year later AUGUSTUS appointed him city prefect, a post which sat ill with his republican sympathies, and he resigned within days of his appointment. His claim that he did not understand how to act in the post saved him from a rift with the emperor. He held no further military or provincial posts but was made an augur and an Arval Brother, and was appointed to manage Rome's water supply; he also repaired much of the Latin Way, the road leading south-east from Rome. In 2 BC he was chosen, as a relatively independent man of great prestige, to propose the title *Father of the Fatherland* (*Pater Patriae*) for the emperor.

He was a fine public speaker and a writer of both prose (memoirs, grammatical and philosophical treatises) and verse, though nothing survives but some titles. He gathered a circle of literary protégés second only to that of MAECENAS, which included TIBULLUS, LYGDAMUS, OVID and Messalla's niece SULPICIA (1); he was also a friend of HORACE. A panegyric of him, which survives, was dedicated to him by its anonymous author. PLUTARCH states that he married TERENTIA, the widow of SALLUST and former wife of CICERO (1), who would have been some sixteen years his senior.

5, Marcus Valerius, also known as Messallinus (consul 3 BC), was a soldier and orator, the son of MESSALLA (4). TIBULLUS, his father's protégé, celebrated his election *c.*21 BC as a guardian of the Sibylline Books. He took part as governor (legate) of Illyricum in the frontier campaign of TIBERIUS in AD 6 and was entrusted by him with the task of quelling a rebellion in Pannonia and Dalmatia: he received triumphal decorations for his success. OVID addressed poems to him from his exile in Tomis. He is recorded as speaking several times in the Senate during Tiberius' reign in favour of proposals to gratify the emperor.

Messallina, Valeria (died AD 48), was the third wife of the emperor Claudius. Descended from AUGUSTUS' sister OCTAVIA (1) through both her father (M. Valerius Messalla Barbatus) and mother (Domitia Lepida), she married Claudius in AD 39. She bore him two children, BRITANNICUS and OCTAVIA (2), but her promiscuity became notorious (JUVENAL painted a gruesome picture of her behaviour in *Satires* 6 and 10). In 48 she arranged to go through a wedding ceremony with the consul designate, Gaius SILIUS: for this outrage NARCISSUS, the emperor's secretary, contrived her death while Claudius was recovering from the news: with the encouragement of her mother she committed suicide, assisted by an officer.

Metella, Caecilia (died 81 BC), was a daughter of L. Caecilius METELLUS (2) Delmaticus: her first husband was M. Aemilius SCAURUS (2) whom she bore three children; a widow *c.*89, she married SULLA (2) to whom she bore twins, Faustus Sulla and FAUSTA (1), later MILO's wife. In 81 Metella fell seriously ill with a disease which it was thought he had given her; however, he had her removed from his house and divorced her, to escape becoming ritually contaminated.

Metellus 1, Lucius Caecilius (died 221 BC), was a general who, the year after his consulship in 251, defeated the Carthaginians defending Panormus in Sicily and captured several elephants. He was consul again in 247 and was made *Pontifex Maximus* in 243. There was a tradition that in 241 he was blinded rescuing the image of Pallas from the burning temple of Vesta. He was made dictator for the purpose of holding elections in 224.

2, Lucius Caecilius, known as Delmaticus (late C2 BC), offended MARIUS (1) when, as consul in 119, he opposed his proposal to reform the elections. He conquered Dalmatia in 118 and triumphed the following year, adopting his honorific name. He was elected chief priest (*Pontifex Maximus*), and as such in 114 tried three vestal virgins accused of immorality, acquitting two. He was censor in 115. METELLA was his daughter.

3, Quintus Caecilius (C3–2 BC), the son of METELLUS (1), was a statesman and general. He was among those who brought to Rome news of the victory on the Metaurus over HASDRUBAL (2) in summer 207. He was deputy to the dictator of that year, M. Livius SALINATOR, and was elected consul for 206, during which he won Lucania from HANNIBAL. In the years that followed he became a firm supporter of SCIPIO (7) Africanus, taking his side against Fabius in the affair of PLEMINIUS. He acted as commissioner to assist in settling Scipio's veteran troops in 201. He was sent twice to Greece as an ambassador, in 185 and 183. He brought an end to the quarrel of the censors LEPIDUS (2) and NOBILIOR in 179. He won a fine reputation as a public speaker. He quarrelled with the poet NAEVIUS.

4, Quintus Caecilius, known as Macedonicus (died 115 BC), was a statesman and general, son of METELLUS (3). He served under Aemilius PAULLUS (2) and was in the embassy which brought news of the victory of Pydna over Macedonia in 168 BC to the Senate. He was praetor in 148 when he was sent to Macedonia and put an end to the career of the pretender Andriscus. In 146, after organising Macedonia into a Roman province, he had to put down a rebellion by the Achaean Confederacy. He returned to a triumph and the assumption of his honorific title. He then stood three times for the consulship, succeeding at last in 143. He was sent to Spain to suppress a rebellion by the Celtiberians, in which he succeeded everywhere but at Numantia and Termantia. In 135 Q. Furius Philus, as governor of Hither (eastern) Spain, took Metellus together with his enemy Quintus Pompeius as his legates. In 133 he opposed the proposed reforms of Tiberius GRACCHUS (4), and in 131, as censor with Pompeius, he spoke in favour of compulsory marriage to raise the birth-rate: he himself had four sons, three of whom he lived to see as consuls, and three daughters. At this time he enclosed with a portico the precinct containing the temples of Jupiter Stator and Juno Regina. In 121 he joined the attack on Gaius GRACCHUS (1). See A.E. Astin (1967) *Scipio Aemilianus*, Oxford: Clarendon Press.

5, Quintus Caecilius, known as Numidicus (died 91 BC) A politician and general, nephew of METELLUS (4) and brother of METELLUS (2) above, he was consul in 109 BC when he led a successful campaign against JUGURTHA, winning two battles and taking some towns. He did not, however, make much headway against the guerrillas. He insulted his successful legate Gaius MARIUS (1) when the latter asked for permission to return to Rome to stand for the consulship. The latter persisted and intrigued against him, so as to gain the consulship for 107. Marius had a law passed to confer Metellus' command on himself, but Metellus left Africa before his enemy's arrival. On his return to Rome he was prosecuted but acquitted and, when popular favour allowed it, he celebrated a triumph and took his honorific title. He was censor in 102 when he tried unsuccessfully to eject SATURNINUS (2) and GLAUCIA from the Senate. He was prevented from doing so by the other censor, his cousin Metellus Caprarius. He stood for the consulship of 100 against Marius but failed and in 100 went into exile because he was the only senator to refuse to swear an oath to observe Saturninus' new laws. After the death of Saturninus, Marius did his best to prevent his return, but in 98 the Senate voted to restore him. His return to Rome was celebrated by his large and influential clan, but he took no more part in politics. See E.S. Gruen (1968) *Roman Politics and the Roman Criminal Courts*, Cambridge MA: Harvard University Press.

6, Quintus Caecilius, known as Balearicus (consul 123 BC), was the son of METELLUS (4). In 123 and 122 he conquered the Balearic Islands and settled them with Italian colonists. He held a triumph in 121 and was censor the following year.

7, Quintus Caecilius, known as Pius (died *c.*63 BC), acquired his honorific title ('the dutiful') from his attempts to win the restoration of his father (see METELLUS 5) from exile in 100 BC. As praetor *c.*89 he enrolled Italians into Roman citizenship under the law of Plautius and Papirius, including his friend ARCHIAS (2). In 88 he defeated and killed the Marsian rebel POPPAEDIUS Silo. In 87 he went in exile to Africa after failing to defend Rome against CINNA (2). After the death of Cinna he returned to Italy in 83 and supported SULLA (2), thus lending him the approval of the aristocratic class. He conquered much of northern Italy for Sulla. He was rewarded with a consulship with Sulla himself in 80, the office of chief priest (*Pontifex Maximus*), and a command in western (Further) Spain against SERTORIUS where, after an unsuccessful campaign, he gave support to the campaign of POMPEIUS (2), who became governor of eastern (Hither) Spain in 77. He had some successes during the next two years and stayed in Spain until 71, when he returned to a triumph. See E.S. Gruen (1974) *The Last Generation of the Roman Republic*, Berkeley: University of California Press.

8, Quintus Caecilius, known as Celer ('swift') (died 59 BC), was a Roman politician and general, son of Q. Metellus Nepos (consul of 98) and brother of METELLUS (9) Nepos (consul of 57). He and his brother were adopted by their father's cousin Q. Metellus Celer (tribune in 90): their half-sister was MUCIA Tertia, POMPEIUS (2)'s wife. Celer married CLODIA, eldest daughter of Appius CLAUDIUS (7) and half-sister of Publius CLODIUS. In 66 he was a legate (deputy commander) to Pompeius in the east. In 63 BC, when city praetor and augur, he put an end to the trial of RABIRIUS (1). In the same year he was appointed by the consul CICERO (1) to a command, jointly with Gaius ANTONIUS (1), of the forces sent to put down CATILINE, and was made governor of Cisalpine Gaul. As consul in 60 he cooperated with CATO (5) and LUCULLUS (2) against Pompeius, who on his return from the east had divorced Mucia, but he died before he could set out for his province of Transalpine Gaul, leaving its conquest to CAESAR (1).

9, Quintus Caecilius, known as Nepos (died *c.*55 BC), was a Roman politician and general, full brother of Celer (see METELLUS 8), and like him adopted by Q. Metellus Celer. During POMPEIUS (2)'s campaigns in the east from 67 to 63 he acted as his legate. In 62 held the tribunate when he attacked CICERO (1) and endeavoured to upset his plans to deal with CATILINE by combining with CAESAR (1) to propose that the command against Catiline should be awarded to Pompeius. But he and Caesar were suspended from office, and Nepos fled to his old commander Pompeius, still in the east. He was elected praetor for 60, held a governorship, and was consul in 57, when he supported Pompeius and CLODIUS, but acquiesced in Cicero's return from exile. He received Hither (eastern) Spain as his province in 56, and stopped on the way there at Lucca, where the conference of the 'triumvirs' was taking place. He died soon after returning from Spain.

10, Quintus Caecilius, known as Creticus ('of Crete') (died *c.*52 BC) The grandson of METELLUS (4), he was praetor in 73 and assisted VERRES at his trial in 70. He was consul in 69 with HORTENSIUS (2), who let him take his province of Crete: Metellus had much success in defeating the pirates with whom the island was infested, and took his honorific title from his exploits. He had a brush with POMPEIUS (2) who, under the Gabinian law, had equal power and tried to take his command from him, and insulted his representative, but Pompeius had to leave abruptly to fulfil his duties under the Manilian law. Metellus finished the conquest and organised the provincial status of the island and returned home to triumph, but was prevented by Pompeius' supporters from doing so until 62.

11, Quintus Caecilius, known as Pius Scipio (C1 BC), was the son of P. Cornelius Scipio Nasica and adopted (perhaps in his will) by METELLUS (7) Pius. He held an interregnum before consuls could be elected in 53 BC though he was no longer a patrician. He stood for the consulship of 52, but the elections were invalidated through his open bribery and POMPEIUS (2) became sole consul. Pompeius then married his daughter Cornelia (previously married to CRASSUS 7), secured his acquittal on a charge of corrupt electioneering, and in July chose him as his colleague. In January 49 he proposed the decree outlawing CAESAR (1), and went to Syria as its proconsul. In 48 he took his two legions to support Pompeius in the Pharsalus campaign, where he was given command of the centre. He escaped to Africa where he organised resistance to Caesar, and killed himself after losing the battle of Thapsus: his death was memorable for his courage in telling his enemies, when they found him dying, 'the commander is well'.

Micipsa (reigned 148–118 BC) was a king of Numidia, successor of MASINISSA and uncle of JUGURTHA.

Milo, Titus Annius (died 48 BC), was a politician from Lanuvium, where his family held a hereditary priesthood. He was friendly with CICERO (1) and as tribune in 57 BC actively supported his recall from exile. He married in 54 FAUSTA (1), a daughter of SULLA (2) and the divorced wife of Gaius MEMMIUS (2). During the next five years he and SESTIUS engaged in gang warfare with the partisans of CLODIUS in the streets of Rome, with various attempts to resort to prosecutions for assault on both sides: the magistrates could do nothing to suppress the violence without a senatorial 'Ultimate Decree'. Both Milo and Clodius stood for office for 52, Milo for the consulship, for which he put on games costing 1,000,000 sesterces: but no elections took place on account of the disorder and in January 52 Milo's men killed Clodius near Bovillae. POMPEIUS (2) had supported Clodius' attempts to prevent the elections, but was now made sole consul to restore order (Clodius' followers burnt down the Senate House): he passed new laws to regulate the conduct of elections and to punish assault and battery to prevent further violence. Milo was prosecuted under this law and Pompeius so guarded the courthouse with troops that Cicero felt intimidated from completing his defence speech. Milo was banished and went to Massilia (Marseille) where he ironically thanked Cicero for enabling him to enjoy the fine mullets. Cicero afterwards published a finished version of his speech. Milo returned to Italy in 48 without CAESAR (1)'s permission and assisted the praetor M. Caelius RUFUS (1) in his scheme to raise a rebellion among the poor of Italy: he was captured by the praetor PEDIUS (1) and executed at Cosa.

Minucius 1. Esquilinus Augurinus, Lucius (C5 BC), was an early Roman politician about whose life little is known for certain, though many tales were woven in later times. He was consul in 458 BC and was a member of the Second Decemvirate in 450, which, if it existed, had the duty of drawing up a set of provisions for the civil law; he consequently went into exile with its other members *c.*448. A patrician, he was in later times said to have been allowed to become a plebeian, to explain the fact that the Minucii were plebeians. Fictitious stories relate that he was rescued from defeat at the hands of the Aequi by CINCINNATUS, and became a commissioner for dispensing cheap grain and a public benefactor for relieving the Romans of famine.

2. Felix, Marcus (early C3 AD), was the writer of an extant dialogue in Latin between a Christian named Octavius and a traditional Roman polytheist, Caecilius Natalis of Cirta in Africa. Octavius bases his arguments on the Stoicism of CICERO (1) and SENECA (2) and on the *Defence* (*Apologeticus*) of his contemporary, TERTULLIAN; while Caecilius uses an anti-Christian treatise by FRONTO.

3. Rufus, Marcus (died 216 BC), was a general in the war with HANNIBAL. After helping to conquer Istria during his consulship in 221 BC, he held a dictatorship in 218 when a bad omen prevented him from choosing FLAMINIUS as his deputy. After the disastrous Roman defeat at Lake Trasimene in 217 he was elected by the Assembly to be the deputy (*Master of the Horse*) to the dictator Quintus FABIUS (8) Maximus, but was disloyal to his superior, refusing to refrain from attack, and won a victory over Hannibal at Gerunium. The Assembly then appears to have made his power equal to that of Fabius, and he claimed to be a fellow dictator with him: however, according to a critical source, he was later rescued by Fabius from being ensnared by Hannibal. He fell at Cannae.

4, Marcus (late C2 BC), was consul in 110. He was proconsul of Macedonia in 109, winning several victories and triumphing in 106. He built a colonnade in Rome, the *Porticus Minucia*, used in imperial times as the centre for distributing cheap grain to the commons. He was the patron of the Ligurians and settled a border dispute for Genoa.

Mithridates the name of six kings of Pontus, a kingdom in northern Anatolia.

1. IV Philopator Philadelphus ('Father- and Brother-loving') (155–151 BC) was the second son of Mithridates III. He succeeded his brother Pharnaces, whose aggressive policy he modified. He developed friendship with Rome and aided Pergamon against Bithynia.

2. V Euergetes ('Benefactor') (151–120 BC) was probably a son of Pharnaces I. He continued the policy of his predecessor of friendship to Rome and lent support to her during the Third Punic War (149–146) and in the war with ARISTONICUS (2) of Pergamon; he was rewarded with Phrygia. He increased his influence by invading Cappadocia and marrying his daughter Laodice to its king ARIARATHES (3) VI. He was keen on Greek ways and attempted to hellenize his kingdom. He gave financial support to Delos and Athens and was honoured by those states: Apollo was the object of his special devotion and he portrayed the god on coinage. He was murdered at Sinope in 120, perhaps by members of his family: his wife Laodice, a Seleucid princess, perhaps through a forged will, claimed the succession for herself and her younger son.

3. VI Eupator Dionysus, also known as The Great (reigned 120–63 BC) His first task was to gain the throne despite his mother's intrigues. He was twelve at the time of his father's murder: having fled from the court, he lay low for some years, then raised a force and captured Sinope, his mother's capital, and killed his mother and brother. He then set about the conquest of the Crimean peninsula and other parts of the northern coastlands of the Black Sea, which furnished him with wealth and troops. He extended his power and influence in Asia Minor, causing in 116 the assassination of his brother-in-law ARIARATHES (3) VI of Cappadocia by means of his agent, a Cappadocian nobleman named GORDIUS. He then worked through his nephew, ARIARATHES (4) VII, whom he replaced in 101 with his own eight-year-old son ARIARATHES (6) IX. He also took over Inner Paphlagonia, using NICOMEDES III of Bithynia as his ally. Though warned by Gaius MARIUS (1) in 99 that he risked falling foul of Rome, yet irritated by SULLA (2)'s intervention in Cappadocia in 95, when he installed ARIOBARZANES (1) as king, Mithridates exploited Rome's weakness during the Social War in Italy (91–87), and took over Cappadocia and Bithynia.

In 89, after the intervention of the commission under Marcus AQUILLIUS (2), who ordered Mithridates to withdraw from Cappadocia and Bithynia, which he did, the First Mithridatic War broke out. Aquillius persuaded NICOMEDES IV to attack Pontus, with disastrous results. Aquillius divided his small force into three and was routed and killed. Mithridates sought to secure as much of Asia Minor as he could, calling himself the 'Deliverer' and winning much support from the local people on account of the exactions of the Roman tax-gatherers. In the province of Asia in late 88 he ordered the cities to round up the Italian community, consisting of 80,000 people, and massacre them. Rhodes resisted his fleet but Athens invited him (see ARISTION) and he sent a force commanded by his general ARCHELAUS (1) to invade Greece. Sulla responded by moving into Greece in 87 with five legions: he blockaded the Piraeus and Athens, and won significant victories at Chaeronea and Orchomenus. He then moved into Asia where Mithridates had lost his popularity and inflamed hostility by taking reprisals. Mithridates was forced to capitulate at Dardanus in 85 on the terms which Sulla dictated, and was confined to his own kingdom of Pontus: he had to pay an indemnity of 2,000 talents and surrender seventy warships; he was to be recognised as a 'Friend and Ally of Rome'. In 83 Sulla's legate L. Murena, against orders, provoked Mithridates with incursions into his territory: fighting took place in which Mithridates repelled the invader (the Second Mithridatic War). During the next few years Mithridates consolidated his hold on Pontus and his territories to the north of the Black Sea and prepared for war, enlisting the aid of the pirates.

In 75 Nicomedes IV of Bithynia died, leaving his kingdom to the Roman Senate, and the next year the Senate decided to accept the gift. Mithridates, unwilling to see Rome in command of the straits and the balance of power disturbed, made an alliance with SERTORIUS, the Spanish leader, and in spring 73 invaded Bithynia, thus starting the Third Mithridatic War. He was unable to take Cyzicus, however, and the Roman commander, LUCULLUS (2), governor of Cilicia and Asia, cut him off from his supplies. During bitter fighting he forced Mithridates to retreat, and finally in 72 to take refuge in Armenia with his son-in-law TIGRANES (1) II, whose new capital of Tigranocerta Lucullus in 69 briefly captured. By 70 Lucullus had conquered the whole of Pontus. Mithridates was unable to return to his kingdom until 68, when a Roman army mutiny against Lucullus relieved the pressure on him. Even so, he had a hard time defeating the Roman garrison under Triarius in 67. But POMPEIUS (2) succeeded Lucullus in 66 and with superior forces defeated Mithridates at Nicopolis. Mithridates' only recourse was to flee to the Crimea where he seized his lands from his rebellious son Machares and conceived the ambitious plan to invade Italy by a land offensive from the north. But this was too much for his subjects who, led by his eldest son PHARNACES II, rebelled. At the age of 69 Mithridates had himself killed by his bodyguard, having proved unable to dispatch himself by poison, so inured was he by his constant taking of antidotes.

Mithridates was Rome's most dangerous enemy in the last century BC, but suffered from defects which made his task impossible: he was too cruel to win unwavering support from his subjects and allies, and he was an indifferent general. He was passionate in his opposition to Rome and saw himself as pro-Greek and a liberator of Rome's Greek subjects: he liked to see himself as an Alexander-like figure. But for all his talents (he could, for example, speak twenty languages) and energy, in taking on the might of Rome he set himself a task that was beyond his ability or resources. See B.C. McGing (1986) *The Foreign Policy of Mithridates VI Eupator*, Leiden: E.J. Brill.

4. of Pergamon was an adventurer who raised a force which assisted in the rescue of CAESAR (1) while he was besieged at Alexandria in 48 BC. He was rewarded by Caesar with the kingdom of the Crimean Bosporos, though Caesar was unable to install him and he lost his kingdom to Asander. See POLEMO (1).

Modestinus, Herennius (C3 AD), was a jurist from Pontus, a pupil of ULPIANUS. In AD 223 he was appointed the secretary for petitions (*a libellis*) to the emperor SEVERUS (2) Alexander. In this post he wrote authoritative rescripts, answers to petitioners' requests, on behalf of the emperor. In 226 he became the commander of the Rome police (*Praefectus Vigilum*). He later acted as an advocate, giving legal opinions (*responsa*) of which one is dated to 239. He was a prolific writer of books to be used as aids to teaching, producing a work in nine books entitled *Distinctions*; another, *Guidelines*, in ten; *Pandects* in twelve; nineteen books of *Opinions*; and others, including a substantial discussion of the grounds for exemption from guardianship. He wrote in Greek about Roman law and tried to accommodate the practice of the provinces in his writing. His work was highly influential in later times and he was one of the five authorities recognised in the Law of Citations of 426: Justinian's compilers included at least 300 quotations of his writings.

Montanus 1, Curtius (C1 AD), was a satirical poet who was prosecuted in NERO (1)'s time for his outspoken attacks: he was ordered to be entrusted to his father's care and not to hold public office. He (or his father) spoke violently against M. Aquilius REGULUS (2) in the Senate in AD 70. He was an adviser of DOMITIAN and PLINY (2) the Younger corresponded with him.

2. (later C2 AD) was a Christian reformer from Phrygia in Asia Minor. He enrolled two prophetesses into his movement, Prisca and Maximilla, who *c.*172 gave ecstatic predictions of the forthcoming end of the world and the arrival of a New Jerusalem near the village of Pepuza. He was a strong proponent of the efficacy of martyrdom, as spectacular as possible. The heresy of Montanism became established in parts of Phrygia despite opposition from orthodox Christianity, and developed its own hierarchy: it lasted there until the eighth century. It spread briefly to Africa, where TERTULLIAN was an adherent.

Mucia Tertia (C1 BC) was a daughter of the lawyer Q. Mucius SCAEVOLA (4) and half-sister of the two Metelli, Celer and Nepos (see METELLUS 8, METELLUS 9). She married POMPEIUS (2) *c.*80 and bore him his two sons, Gnaeus and Sextus, and a daughter. She was divorced on Pompeius' return from his long sojourn in the east in 62 for her adultery with CAESAR (1). She subsequently married M. Aemilius SCAURUS (3), to whom she bore a son. In 39 she attempted to reconcile Octavian (see AUGUSTUS) and her son Sextus POMPEIUS (4), and in 31 after Actium she obtained a pardon for her son SCAURUS (4).

Mucianus, Gaius Licinius (C1 AD), served under CORBULO in Armenia in 58, held three suffect consulships, in 64, 70 and 72, and governed Syria in 67. In 69 he supported OTHO as emperor, and on his death urged VESPASIAN to take the purple.

He then marched at the head of an army through Asia Minor and the Balkans, where he gathered the powerful Danube armies to his standard, to win Rome for Vespasian, foiling an invasion by the Dacians on the way. He tried to prevent Antonius PRIMUS' rash advance into danger near Cremona and reached Rome a few days after Primus had occupied it. Here he displaced the youthful DOMITIAN, Vespasian's younger son, and sent packing the huge provincial army which was roaming the city. He also reduced the number of Praetorian guardsmen to what it had been before VITELLIUS (1) increased it. He urged Vespasian to expel the philosophers from Rome. He wrote a book on strange geographical phenomena, which his protégé PLINY (1) the Elder used as a source.

Mucius *see* SCAEVOLA.

Mummius, Lucius (mid-C2 BC), as praetor in 153 commanded an army in western Iberia and as proconsul the next year fought against the Lusitani, and held a triumph in 152. He was consul in 146 when he succeeded METELLUS (2) Macedonicus in Macedonia and led his army against the Achaean Confederacy, when he sacked and destroyed the ancient city of Corinth. With the help of a commission of senators he reorganised the administration of Greece and asked advice of the historian POLYBIUS. He carted off fabulous wealth from Corinth and elsewhere, which he gave to his friends or exhibited in Rome. He held a triumph and became a friend of SCIPIO (11) Aemilianus, with whom he was censor in 142, when he mitigated Scipio's enthusiasm to purge the state of immorality.

Munatius *see* PLANCUS.

Murcus, Lucius Staius (mid-C1 BC), was a military man of Italian origin, perhaps from Sulmo. He served as a legate to CAESAR (1) in Gaul and was praetor in 45; appointed proconsul of Syria in 44 after Caesar's death, he took over the siege of Apamea by Q. Caecilius BASSUS on the surrender of which he was hailed as *Imperator.* But on the arrival of CASSIUS (3) in 43, the armies of Syria, Bithynia (under Q. Marcius Crispus) and Bassus' own force all agreed to join Cassius and follow him in the republican cause, and Cassius appointed Murcus to command the fleet. In 42 he had some successes and with the help of AHENOBARBUS (4) he won command of the Straits and defeated CALVINUS (2), who was trying to transport two legions to Macedonia for the Philippi campaign. He later joined Sextus POMPEIUS (4), whose confidence he lost: Pompeius killed him *c.*40.

Murena, Lucius Licinius (C1 BC), served under his father, SULLA (2)'s legate, in the 80s in the province of Asia. After a quaestorship in 75 he served under LUCULLUS (2) in Asia Minor, was city praetor in 65 and governor of Transalpine Gaul in 64. He stood for the consulship for 62 and was elected, but was accused by CATO (5) and the defeated candidate Servius SULPICIUS (2) Rufus of bribing the electorate. He was defended at his trial by an array of talent including CICERO (1), whose speech is extant. He was acquitted, perhaps unfairly. His last known act was to carry with his colleague Silanus a law for the promulgation of proposed bills.

Mus 1, Publius Decius (C4 BC), while consul in 340, in a battle against the Latins and Campanians at Veseris in Campania, deliberately rode his horse into the enemy and died fighting, having vowed himself and his foe to the gods of the Underworld. It was believed that his act won the day for the Romans. The story may, however, be fictitious and owe its existence to the exploit of his son.

2, Publius Decius (C4–3 BC), was four times consul and censor, and is said, like his father, MUS (1), to have vowed himself to the infernal gods in battle at Sentinum in 295 and died fighting, thus bringing victory to his side. He was closely associated with FABIUS (7) Maximus Rullianus, his colleague in three consulships and the censorship.

3, Publius Decius (C3 BC) was the son of MUS (2). As consul in 279, he was defeated and killed by PYRRHUS in battle at Asculum Satrianum.

N

Nabis (reigned 207–192 BC) was a king of Sparta. His father's name Demaratus suggests possible descent from the Eurypontid king Demaratus. In 207 he succeeded Machanidas as guardian of the young king Pelops, on whose death that year he seized the throne. He engaged the support of a guard of mercenary soldiers and the Cretan pirates. He may have been maligned by the tradition that he tried in a brutal manner to reimpose the reforms of Cleomenes III. He was sole king and conducted an active foreign policy of opposition to the Achaean Confederacy: he raided Megalopolis in 204, he failed to take Messene in 201, and was defeated by the Achaean general PHILOPOEMEN in 200. In the Second Macedonian War which followed he at first supported PHILIP (1) V who betrayed Argos to him, but then attempted to change sides: however, FLAMININUS in 195 accused him of tyranny and compelled him to renounce his claim to Argos and the ports of Laconia. He tried to regain his lost ports in 193 with the help of Aetolia but was defeated by Flamininus and Philopoemen. The following year he was murdered by the Aetolians as they took over at Sparta. See P. Cartledge and A.J.S. Spawforth (1989) *Hellenistic and Roman Sparta*, London: Routledge.

Naevius, Gnaeus (*c.*270–201 BC), was an epic poet and dramatist from Campania who served on the Roman side in the First Punic War (264–241): it was about this war that he wrote his epic, *The Poem of the Punic War*, in the Saturnian metre. Only fragments of Naevius' works have survived. His stage plays, both tragedies made from Greek myth and Roman material, known as *fabulae praetextae*, and comedies based on the Attic New Comedy, are known mainly from their titles. His stage activity began in 235 and at some point he offended the powerful family of the Metelli who, according to an inference from PLAUTUS, had him imprisoned some time before his exile in 204. He treated Attic themes in his comedies with some freedom, having his characters' monologues and even dialogues accompanied by instrumental music, like Plautus, and he mixed an Italian element into the Greek settings of these plays. We know of six titles of tragedies on Greek mythical themes, two of which are also titles of plays by Livius ANDRONICUS, and he wrote Roman tragedies on Romulus and on the victory of M. Claudius MARCELLUS (3) over the Gauls at Clastidium in 222. The latter play suggests patronage of the poet by the family of the Claudii Marcelli: it may have been performed at the funeral of Marcellus in 208 or at the dedication of the temple he had vowed to Venus.

His greatest work in the eyes of Roman posterity was his epic, which a hundred years later was divided into seven books by Octavius Lampadio. It contained a long digression describing the foundation myths and early history of the two protagonists, Rome and Carthage, and, somewhat like VIRGIL's *Aeneid*, suggests that the war had a cosmic significance. Virgil took a number of phrases from the poem in composing the *Aeneid*. CICERO (1) states that ENNIUS found fault with the poem (see Cicero, *Brutus*, 72), but it continued to raise interest until HORACE's time. Naevius died in exile, at Utica in Carthaginian territory.

Narcissus (died AD 54) was a Greek freedman of the emperor CLAUDIUS (1) who served him as his secretary of state (*praepositus ab epistulis*) and became very powerful in the imperial administration. He enriched himself with a vast fortune, 400,000,000 sesterces, greater than that of CRASSUS (3) a century earlier. He gave considerable support to the career of the future emperor VESPASIAN. Claudius depended on him heavily, and in 43 sent him to the embarkation port for his army of invasion of Britain, where Narcissus suppressed a mutiny and organised the operation. In 48 he was instrumental in the overthrow and death of Claudius' unfaithful wife MESSALLINA, for which he earned the status of a quaestor. However, he lost the contest of selecting Claudius' next wife, his candidate being rejected in favour of AGRIPPINA (3), the choice of his rival PALLAS. In 52 Narcissus was entrusted with the drainage of the Fucine Lake, which he mishandled, and he failed to secure BRITANNICUS' place in the succession. Agrippina made him kill himself after she had murdered Claudius.

Nemesianus, Marcus Aurelius Olympius (late C3 AD), was a Latin pastoral poet from Carthage. He composed four eclogues in 319 lines on country themes, owing much to VIRGIL's *Eclogues* and Theocritus' *Idylls*, sometimes lifting whole lines from the former; strong, too, is the influence of CALPURNIUS SICULUS, once thought to be the author of these poems. He also wrote a poem, *Hunting to Hounds* (*Cynegetica*), of which some 325 lines are extant. He may have imitated the work of GRATTIUS, though he changed the order of topics in Grattius' poem of the same name. He discusses the preliminaries, the hounds, horses and their treatment, and the other equipment, but stops just short of the actual day's hunting. Little is known of his life, though he is said to have won poetic contests and to have wished to write an epic on the deeds of the imperial brothers NUMERIAN and CARINUS (AD 283–4). His language and prosody are largely classical, but his originality is slender.

Nepos 1, Cornelius (*c.*110–24 BC), was a biographer from Cisalpine Gaul whence he moved to Rome *c.*65 but kept out of political life. Nepos was on friendly terms with CICERO (1), ATTICUS and CATULLUS (1), the last of whom dedicated to him his first book of polymetric poetry. He wrote *The Lives of Famous Men* which he first published in 34 BC in sixteen books. It contained at least 400 lives grouped in categories, comparing Romans with foreigners; a second enlarged edition appeared in 27. A part of this work is extant: the lives of CATO (4) the Censor, of Atticus, and of a number of foreign leaders. His other work is lost: a history of the world in three books, referred to by Catullus (poem 1), five books of stories ('examples'), a geographical treatise, extended biographies of Cicero and Cato, and some light verse. He was a populariser, made little first-hand use of the sources he cites, and is of slight historical value. See T.P. Wiseman (1979) *Clio's Cosmetics*, Leicester: Leicester University Press; J. Geiger (1985) *Cornelius Nepos and Ancient Political Biography*, Stuttgart: Franz Steiner.

2, Aulus Platorius (early C2 AD), was a friend of HADRIAN. He was appointed to govern Thrace in 117 and held the consulship in 119. He then served as governor of Lower Germany before being moved to Britain in 122 with the Sixth Legion (*Victrix*) which he commanded. Hadrian seems to have accompanied him to the province and entrusted him with the construction of Hadrian's Wall, much of which he completed, including several forts and milecastles.

Neratius Priscus, Lucius (early C2 AD), was a jurist from Saepinum in Samnite country. After a suffect consulship in AD 97 and a spell as prefect of the treasury of Saturn, he governed Pannonia and returned to Rome to a legal career. He became the last head, with his junior partner, CELSUS (2), of the Proculian school of law. Hadrian appointed him a member of his privy council. He wrote several works that are lost, seven books of *Notes* (*Membranae*), *Rules* (*Regulae*), i.e. guidelines, and three books of legal opinions (*Responsa*). PAULUS wrote a commentary on his work and he was cited frequently in the *Digests* and other legal compilations. He leant towards Stoic philosophical views.

Nero 1. (AD 37–68), the last of the Julio-Claudian emperors, reigned from October 54 until June 68. He was born at Antium, Lucius Domitius Ahenobarbus, son of Gnaeus AHENOBARBUS (5) and of AGRIPPINA (3), the daughter of GERMANICUS, which gave him a firm link with the imperial family. His chance of gaining power came when his widowed mother became the fourth wife of her uncle the emperor CLAUDIUS (1) in 48. She had SENECA (2) recalled from exile to become her son's tutor and persuaded Claudius to betroth him to his daughter OCTAVIA (3). In 50, when Nero was thirteen, he was adopted by Claudius as his eldest son, under the adoptive name Tiberius Claudius Nero Caesar: the names Drusus and Germanicus were also added. Stories were put about to strengthen his claim to membership of the family and his descent from AUGUSTUS was emphasised. Claudius was willing to advance him before his own son BRITANNICUS, and in 51 created him Leader of Youth (cf. CAESAR 3): he was married to Octavia in 53. On 13 October 54 Claudius died, probably murdered by Agrippina, and Nero, aged sixteen, was escorted by BURRUS, commander of the Guard, to the Praetorian camp. The Senate then voted him the powers he needed as emperor.

The emperor TRAJAN considered the first five years of Nero's reign a golden age for the excellence of the quality of the administration. Nero made a speech (written by Seneca) to the Senate promising to rule according to Augustus' example; he issued coinage bearing a mark of senatorial authority and showing his mother's head with his own, but in reality he cold-shouldered her and put his trust in Seneca and Burrus. He also had his 'father' Claudius deified, made a show of declining to apply the death penalty, and was hailed as 'Apollo' for his support of the arts. He also appointed excellent provincial governors. However, Nero's hands were soon stained with crimes, first the murder of Britannicus in 55, when Agrippina, irked by Nero's neglect, showed some sympathy for her stepson: after the murder she withdrew from court. In 59 Nero fell in love with POPPAEA Sabina, the wife of a courtier, OTHO, and wished to divorce Octavia, who was barren. Agrippina opposed the divorce and, despite her attempts to insinuate herself into her son's favour, was murdered: the first attempt to cause her death in an apparent sailing accident misfired, so Nero had her stabbed to death in her house. In 62 Burrus died, Seneca retired, and Nero was unfettered: he divorced and later murdered Octavia and married Poppaea, who in 63 bore him a daughter who died four months later. TIGELLINUS, one of the two new commanders of the Praetorian Guard, was a baneful influence and encouraged the worst side of Nero.

Nero's interest in the arts and athletics took off in 59 when he celebrated the Juvenalian Games in honour of his first shave, at which senators competed and he himself sang and played music. In 60 he established the five-yearly Neronian Games; in 61 he founded a gymnasium at Rome, and gave out free oil to the participants. His musical and poetic compositions seem to have been mediocre and banal, though his interest in the arts was genuine. In June 64 there broke out in Rome a great fire which lasted nine days and devastated much of the city. Although Nero provided emergency shelter and helped in the reconstruction of the ruined areas, he increased his already considerable unpopularity by taking over a large area which had been occupied by private buildings for a new palace and gardens for his own use, the 'Golden House'. Rumours spread that he had sung and played the cithara during the fire, though he was not in Rome at the time. It was commonly believed that he started the fire, and so he invented the story that the newly arisen sect of Christians had done so, and punished some of them by burning them alive.

He took little interest in military or provincial affairs, though the destruction caused by Boudicca's revolt in Britain, the wars on the eastern frontier with Parthia, and the huge loss of property in the fire at Rome brought about a debasement of the currency. His unpopularity was mainly with the upper class who resented his ostentatious behaviour and ineffective rule: the Roman poor loved him for the games and shows he put on. A conspiracy to remove him and replace him with a noble, C. Calpurnius PISO (2), was made after the fire but detected in 65 and led to many executions, the principal victims being Piso, Seneca, the poet LUCAN, and Faenius Rufus. As Nero's suspicions grew, he cast his net wider and ordered the deaths of PETRONIUS (1), OSTORIUS SCAPULA, and a number of Stoics who were critical of his monarchy including THRASEA Paetus and Barea SORANUS. Poppaea died in 65 from a kick he gave her while she was pregnant. In 66 he remarried, taking the cultured Statilia Messallina (whose fifth husband he was) as his last wife. The same year he crowned TIRIDATES (3) in Rome as his vassal king of Armenia, but had to face a serious rebellion in Judaea, which had reached the end of its tether after suffering a series of harsh governors. Nero sent the general MUCIANUS to govern Syria and chose VESPASIAN to crush the Jewish revolt.

By this time (autumn 66) he was in Greece, where he stayed to enjoy an orgy of adulation until 68, leaving a Greek freedman, Helios, in charge at Rome. He had summoned the successful general CORBULO from the eastern frontier to meet him near Corinth, and out of fear or jealousy ordered him to kill himself forthwith. Likewise the brothers Scribonii, who had each governed a region of Germany, were forced to suicide. While he was in Greece Nero toured the artistic and athletic contests, winning every first prize; he collected works of art, started the construction of the Corinthian Canal, and proclaimed the province free of Roman taxation and administration: his speech is preserved. In January 68, however, Helios came to Greece to warn Nero that his throne was in danger and he was needed urgently at home: a famine had broken out, perhaps because Nero had interfered in the grain supply. In March VINDEX, governor of Gaul, led a rising which was crushed by the governor of Upper Germany. In Spain the elderly governor GALBA (1) declared himself the appointee, not of Nero, but of the Senate and People. In Africa the governor MACER (2) rebelled and stopped the grain ships from sailing to Rome. Nero, who had no military experience at all, was unable to organise resistance to these acts of insubordination, and the Praetorian Guard deserted him, offered a huge bribe on Galba's behalf by their commander, NYMPHIDIUS SABINUS. The Senate, also in favour of Galba, then declared Nero a public enemy. In despair he fled, and committed suicide (9 June 68) at the villa of his freedman, Phaon: his last and oft repeated words were *qualis artifex pereo*, 'what an artist I die'. He died hated by most Romans and the Jews and Christians, but dear to many Greeks, after a life of self-indulgence, cruelty and self-deception. See M. Grant (1985) *The Roman Emperors*, London: Weidenfeld & Nicolson; M.T. Griffin (1984) *Nero, the End of a Dynasty*, London: Batsford.

2, Gaius Claudius (late C3 BC), was a military commander in the Second Punic War. As praetor he besieged Capua in 214–3 BC, and later served in Spain, keeping the territory north of the river Ebro in his hands until SCIPIO (7) Africanus arrived in 210. He then returned to Italy where he fought under Marcus MARCELLUS (3) in 209. In 207 he held the consulship in partnership with Livius SALINATOR, his personal enemy. He led the Roman forces fighting HANNIBAL in southern Italy, but returned northwards by forced marches when he heard of HASDRUBAL (2)'s approach and with his colleague defeated him on the river Metaurus: he then marched south again and tossed Hasdrubal's severed head into his brother Hannibal's camp. He was censor with Salinator in 204, and served on the embassy to PHILIP (1) V of Macedonia in 200 which delivered an ultimatum to make him indemnify the Rhodians and ATTALUS (1) and leave the Greek states in peace.

3, Tiberius Claudius (died 33 BC) As quaestor he commanded CAESAR (1)'s navy in the Alexandrian War (48 BC); in 46 he settled Caesar's veteran troops in southern Gaul. He deserted the Caesarian cause in 44 when he proposed a motion that Caesar's assassins should be rewarded. He was praetor in 41, when he opposed Octavian (see AUGUSTUS) and supported Lucius ANTONIUS (4) at Perusia. He tried to raise a rebellion of slaves in Campania and joined Sextus POMPEIUS (4) in Sicily, taking his wife LIVIA (2) and his baby son TIBERIUS. After quarrelling with Pompeius he moved to Greece to join ANTONIUS (7) in 40 and returned to Rome in 39 after the Pact of Misenum. In January 38 Octavian persuaded him to divorce Livia so that he could himself marry her, even though she was then carrying Nero's second son, DRUSUS (3), who was born the following April.

4, Julius Caesar (*c*.AD 6–31), was the eldest son of GERMANICUS and, after the death of DRUSUS (4) in AD 23, TIBERIUS' heir. However, in 29 SEJANUS denounced him and his mother AGRIPPINA (2) to Tiberius, now living in retirement, who then requested the Senate to banish him to the island of Pontia where he was later murdered.

Nerva 1, Lucius Cocceius (C1 BC), was a brother of NERVA (2), whom Octavian sent in 41 BC to Syria to negotiate with ANTONIUS (7). He returned to Italy in Antonius' company the next year and was in the team which negotiated the Pact of Brundisium. He went from Rome to Brundisium in 37 to negotiate the Pact of Tarentum: HORACE accompanied him (see Horace, *Satires*, 1. 5).

2, Marcus Cocceius (C1 BC), a brother of NERVA (1), supported Lucius ANTONIUS (4) in 41 BC in the siege of Perusia. Forgiven by Octavian (see AUGUSTUS), he was proconsul of Asia *c*.37 and consul in 36. He was one of the officials at the Secular Games in 17.

3, Marcus Cocceius (died AD 33), was a jurist and a close friend of the emperor TIBERIUS, with whom he went to Capri in AD 26 when he retired there. He appears to have been a grandson of NERVA (2). He was suffect consul and in 24 was appointed to manage Rome's water supply. He was head of the law school founded by LABEO and his son Marcus succeeded him. Nerva is said to have starved himself to death in disgust at Tiberius' tyrannical behaviour.

4, Marcus Cocceius (*c.*AD 30–98), reigned as emperor for sixteen months between the assassination of DOMITIAN in mid-September 96 and his own death in late January 98. The grandson of NERVA (3), he was born at Narnia in Umbria. The Senate in an unprecedented show of authority elected him to succeed Domitian, as being a senior ex-consul (he had held the post twice, with imperial colleagues, in 71 and 90), though he had little administrative experience. NERO (1) had admired him as a poet and had given him triumphal decorations after the suppression of PISO (2)'s conspiracy. He had not played any overt part in the death of Domitian: the only people to regret his passing were the soldiers. Nerva had much to commend him: he was affable, of high birth, eloquent, experienced in senatorial affairs, though he had never governed a province. He was voted the title *Father of the Fatherland*, and adopted moderate and republican measures and slogans: he put an end to treason trials, recalled exiles and returned confiscated property. The Senate damned Domitian's memory and his name was erased from inscriptions; his acts were also annulled, though Nerva seems to have retained much of Domitian's legislation. He distributed generous bonuses to the troops and gifts to the people of Rome; he also instituted a system of poor relief, in particular for those living in the Italian countryside. He relieved Italian towns of the cost of the postal service, built granaries, and repaired the aqueducts. His generosity, however, led to a financial crisis, and a committee of senators was appointed to consider economies.

Nerva was, however, in poor health and had no heir. In 97 a dark mood prevailed, especially as anger in the armies about Domitian's death had not diminished. The Praetorian Guard, encouraged by their commander Casperius Aelianus, demanded the execution of Petronius Secundus, their other commander, who had kept them in check while the Senate chose the successor. Nerva reluctantly complied: a series of executions of those considered responsible ensued. There was some opposition to his government, indicated by an abortive plot formed by C. Calpurnius Crassus. In October Nerva showed a resolute spirit by adopting as his son and co-ruler the governor of Upper Germany, TRAJAN, one of the most distinguished generals in the empire, whom he gave the title *Germanicus* and invested with all the powers of an emperor. Trajan had to wait only three months to succeed. See R. Syme (1958) *Tacitus*, Oxford: Clarendon Press; M. Grant (1985) *The Roman Emperors*, London: Weidenfeld & Nicolson.

Nicolaus (born *c.*64 BC) was a Greek historian and biographer from Damascus, an adviser and friend of HEROD (1) the Great. He studied philosophy and joined the Peripatetics, taught the children of ANTONIUS (7) and CLEOPATRA (4), and joined Herod's court *c.*14 BC. Herod used him as a diplomat as well as his own instructor in philosophy and rhetoric, and sent him to Rome to plead for him when he offended AUGUSTUS in 7 BC. He also assisted ARCHELAUS (4) to inherit most of his father's kingdom. His greatest work was a *History of the World* down to 4 BC in 144 books: we have some acquaintance with this through excerpts and translations, especially the first seven books: his account of Herod, for which he used the king's own memoirs, was preserved by JOSEPHUS. His chief sources and models were the Greek historians Ephorus, Ctesias, Xanthus, Hellanicus and POSIDONIUS. He also wrote a *Life of Augustus* down to *c.*20 BC, which he based on the emperor's autobiography: the earlier part is preserved in fragments and excerpts. He also wrote his autobiography, placing much emphasis on his education. His tragedies and comedies are lost; his philosophical works are known through fragments and works in Aramaic and Arabic.

Nicomedes The name of four kings of Bithynia, a kingdom in northwestern Anatolia.

II (reigned 149–*c.*127 BC) He succeeded his father PRUSIAS (2) II after encompassing his death with the help of ATTALUS (2) II of Pergamon and the connivance of the Romans. He won the favour of the Greek cities and was an ally of Rome, assisting in the war against ARISTONICUS, the pretender to the throne of Pergamon, from 133 to 129. He was disappointed by the refusal of the Romans to extend his frontiers in Phrygia.

III (reigned *c.*127–*c.*94 BC) was the son of the above, generous in his munificence to Greek cities from which he earned the title Benefactor (*Euergetes*). MARIUS (1) asked him for troops for his war against the Cimbri in 104, but Nicomedes claimed that very many Bithynians had been enslaved by the Roman tax-gatherers. The Senate then put an end to such enslavement for debt of citizens of allied states. He intrigued with MITHRIDATES (3) VI of Pontus, hoping to share Paphlagonia with him, and intervened in Cappadocia, marrying the queen mother Laodice in the hope of extending his rule there, but was prevented by Roman action.

IV (reigned *c.*94–*c.*74 BC) The last king of Bithynia, son of the above, he was expelled from his kingdom *c.*92 by MITHRIDATES (3) VI, who preferred to support his brother Socrates. Rome, represented by Manius AQUILLIUS (2), restored him a couple of years later and, by demanding a large fee, persuaded him to attack Pontus, thus precipitating the First Mithridatic War, a disaster for Bithynia, during which he lived in exile. He was restored by SULLA (2) in 85 but found his kingdom, now an ally of Rome, little more than a dependency. When CAESAR (1) carried out a mission in 81 to ask him to supply ships for a siege of Mytilene, the two were said to have become lovers. At his death he bequeathed his kingdom to the Roman Senate, as he had no children.

Nigrinus, Gaius Avidius (early C2 AD), was an influential statesman under TRAJAN. After a suffect consulship in 110 and a spell as military governor of the normally senatorial province of Achaia (Greece) he was appointed legate (governor) of Dacia, which had recently been conquered. In 118 he was executed on the order of the Senate at Faventia for plotting against HADRIAN, whose chosen successor he had appeared to be. His stepson was Lucius AELIUS (3), originally L. Ceionius Commodus, who married his daughter and was later adopted by Hadrian as his son and heir. See QUIETUS (1).

Nobilior, Marcus Fulvius (early C2 BC), was active in Further (Western) Spain as praetor in 193 and proconsul in 192, when he subdued Oretania and Carpetania. As consul in 189 he defeated the Aetolians and stormed and pillaged Ambracia, putting an end to the power of the Aetolian League. In 188 he besieged Same on Cephallenia and intervened between the Achaean Confederacy and Sparta. In 187 he returned to Rome for a triumph, which was unsuccessfully opposed by M. Aemilius LEPIDUS (2), who regarded Nobilior as reponsible for his own political failures; in 179 they were publicly reconciled and held the censorship together when they reformed the electoral system. He founded a temple of Hercules and the Muses, which he decorated with statues he had pillaged from Ambracia. He wrote a commentary on the Roman calendar; he was a friend and patron of the poet ENNIUS, who celebrated his victories in his *Annals*, and wrote a play for him entitled *Ambracia*. However, he fell foul of the Elder CATO (4). See H.H. Scullard

(1973) *Roman Politics, 220–150 BC*, Oxford: Clarendon Press.

Nonius Marcellus (early C4 AD) was the writer of a compendious encyclopaedia in Latin about the Latin language and literature: the work consists of twenty books, all extant except book 16. The first twelve books are concerned with grammar and semantics, the remainder with various subjects from everyday life, excluding religion. He illustrates his points by quotation, mainly from republican writers and other sources, including GELLIUS (1). He is our main source for VARRO (3)'s poetry.

Norbanus, Gaius (died 82 BC), was a 'new man'. He was elected tribune in 103 BC when he supported SATURNINUS (2) and successfully prosecuted CAEPIO (3) for his failings as governor of Narbonese Gaul. To do this he had forcibly to resist the attempted veto of the proceedings by his colleagues Titus DIDIUS and Aurelius Cotta. In 95 he was prosecuted for treason (*maiestas*) by SULPICIUS (1) Rufus for his part in Caepio's trial, but was successfully defended by Marcus ANTONIUS (5), whose quaestor he had been. He was praetor in 91 and governed Sicily safely during the Social War of 90–89, defeating an Italian attack on Rhegion. In 83 he was chosen consul as representing the new men in collaboration with the aristocrat SCIPIO (4) Asiagenes. In that year and the next he undertook the leadership of opposition to SULLA (2) and was defeated several times by him and METELLUS (7) Pius. He took refuge in Rhodes, where he killed himself.

Novatianus (mid-C2 AD) was a Christian schismatic, a presbyter at Rome who was consecrated bishop of Rome in opposition to Cornelius. He founded a schismatic church known as the *Catharoi* ('pure ones'), which lasted for several hundred years. He wrote several extant works in Latin: *The Trinity*, *Public Shows*, *The Advantage of Chastity* and *The Jewish Diet*. He had a fine sense of Latin style. He may have been martyred under VALERIAN.

Novius (early C1 BC) was a playwright, the author of at least forty-four Atellan farces which he and his contemporary Lucius POMPONIUS (1) turned into a literary genre. More than a hundred lines survive.

Numerian (reigned AD 283–4) The emperor Marcus Aurelius Numerianus was the younger son of CARUS, who created him *Caesar* at his accession in 282. Leaving his elder son CARINUS behind to administer the western provinces, Carus took Numerian on his expedition against Persia. After the murder of Carus by Arrius APER, prefect of the Praetorian Guard, in July 283, Numerian took the title *Augustus*. He withdrew the army from Persia but was himself murdered by Aper in Bithynia as he made for Nicomedia. The army elected DIOCLETIAN to be the new emperor, who immediately executed Aper, thus raising the question of his own possible implication in the assassination.

Nymphidius Sabinus, Gaius (died AD 68), was a prefect of the Praetorian Guard under NERO (1). He claimed to be the bastard son of CALIGULA, and had a military career in Pannonia before joining the Praetorian Guard as a tribune. He was active in the suppression of PISO (2)'s conspiracy, for which Nero honoured him with consular decorations and promoted him to be joint prefect of the Guard with TIGELLINUS. In 68 he supported GALBA (1), made inordinate promises to the troops on his behalf, and forced his colleague to resign, hoping to become sole commander of the Guard for life: however, when Galba refused to acknowledge Nymphidius' promises, the troops deserted and killed him.

O

Octavia 1. was the half-sister of AUGUSTUS by his father's first marriage with Ancharia. She married Sextus Appuleius, to whom she bore two sons, Sextus and Marcus, who reached the consulship early.

2. (64–11 BC) was the daughter of Gaius OCTAVIUS (1) and Atia, and the elder sister of the emperor AUGUSTUS. She was married to C. Claudius MARCELLUS (1), by whom she had a son, Marcus MARCELLUS (7), and two daughters. In 40 BC, on the death of her husband, her brother married her to ANTONIUS (7) to seal the pact of Brundisium; she bore him two daughters (ANTONIA 1, ANTONIA 2). She passed the next two winters in Athens with her husband, and in 37 helped to negotiate the treaty of Tarentum; but Antonius sent her back from Corcyra and would not take her with him on the campaigns of the next two years. When he requested troops from Octavian in 35, Octavia was sent to him at Athens with a small force of men, but he refused to see her and sent her back to Rome. She remained in Antony's house there against Octavian's will and brought up his children by FULVIA along with all her own, even when he had divorced her in 32; after Actium and Antonius' death she sheltered his children by CLEOPATRA (4). She was widely admired and loved for her qualities of courage and humanity.

3. (AD 40–62) Claudia Octavia, daughter of the emperor CLAUDIUS (1) by his third wife MESSALLINA, was betrothed in her childhood to L. Junius SILANUS, and after his fall was married to NERO (1) in 53 at the urging of his mother Agrippina. Nero hated her and in 62 tried to prove her adulterous: that failing, he divorced her for being childless so that he might marry POPPAEA. He banished her to Campania where she was guarded by soldiers. A rumour of her return to favour with him was greeted with popular acclaim: Nero angrily dispatched her to the island of Pandateria, accusing her of treason and adultery, and had her murdered there. An extant play, a *fabula praetexta* in 983 lines, about the fate of Octavia and named after her, vilifying Nero and implicitly praising SENECA (2) for his vainly wholesome advice, was written in a style similar to Seneca's by an unknown author some time after AD 68.

Octavian A modern name applied by historians to C. Julius Caesar, the adopted son and great-nephew of CAESAR (1), originally before his adoption Gaius Octavius, who in 27 BC styled himself *Augustus*, and through his constitutional and other reforms became recognised as the first Roman emperor. See AUGUSTUS.

Octavius 1, Gaius (died 58 BC), the father of the emperor AUGUSTUS, was a rich man of equestrian stock from Velitrae, praetor in 61 and governor of Macedonia from 60 until he died while returning home. His second wife ATIA was the daughter of Julius CAESAR (1)'s sister. See OCTAVIA (1), OCTAVIA (2).

2, Gnaeus (C2 BC), was a general and diplomat, sent to Greece in 170 BC by Aulus Hostilius Mancinus to reassure the cities of Roman benevolence. He commanded a fleet while praetor in 168 against King PERSEUS of Macedonia, whose surrender he received after the battle of Pydna. The next year he held a triumph and built a colonnade (the Porticus Octavia) to commemorate his victory. He was consul in 165 and was sent in 163 to Syria with a mission to weaken the Seleucid kingdom during a time of weakness caused by the accession to the throne of a child, ANTIOCHUS (3) V, by destroying its fleet and incapacitating its elephants. He was, however, murdered by an angry mob in Laodicea in 162.

3, Gnaeus (early C1 BC), was a politician elected consul for 87 with CINNA (2) as his colleague. He unsuccessfully resisted Cinna's repeal of SULLA (1)'s legislation.

4, Marcus (C2 BC), was a tribune of the *plebs* who in 133 BC opposed Tiberius GRACCHUS (4) by vetoing his agrarian legislation: Gracchus then proposed his removal from the tribuneship in the Assembly of the People, which passed the measure. The legality of Octavius' deposition was disputed but not disproved. Gaius GRACCHUS (1) moved a bill in 123 effectively to exclude Octavius from politics, but withdrew it at his mother CORNELIA (1)'s request.

Odaenathus, Publius Septimius (C3 AD), was a king of Palmyra and ally of Rome. Active for several years already in asserting Palmyran trading rights against Persian intervention, Odaenathus took the title of king when the emperor VALERIAN was captured by the Persians in 260. He opposed the Persian invasion of Asia Minor by attacking Mesopotamia with his Arab forces, and inflicted a severe defeat on the Persian king, SAPOR (1) I. In 264 he recovered Mesopotamia and Armenia but failed to take the Persian capital, Ctesiphon. In Syria he put down a conspiracy of two Roman officers, Macrianus and Ballista, who attempted to replace GALLIENUS with the two sons of Macrianus (see MACRIANUS, QUIETUS); he killed one, the pretender Quietus, at Emesa. He was rewarded by Gallienus with the title *Dux et Corrector totius Orientis* (General and Governor of the entire East) and was recognised as king of Palmyra. He and his eldest son were killed in a family quarrel in 267, and his widow ZENOBIA effectively became his successor.

Ogulnius Gallus, Quintus (C3 BC), as tribune in 300 BC, with the help of his brother Gnaeus, secured the passing of a law to give plebeians access to the two highest priesthoods, those of *pontifex* and *augur*, in such a way that plebeians had superiority to or equality with patricians. His measure was bitterly opposed by the patricians led by Appius CLAUDIUS (4) the Blind. He and his brother were aediles in 296 when they fined moneylenders who charged excessive interest, and used some of the money to erect the statue of Romulus and Remus suckled by the wolf. In 292 he was sent to Epidaurus to bring the cult and the cult-serpent to Rome which had been ravaged by plague. In 273 he went on an embassy to the court of Ptolemy II at Alexandria. He was consul in 269.

Onasander (C1 AD) was a Greek writer on the art of generalship: his work, which survives, was popular during the Renaissance. He dedicated it to Quintus Veranius, governor of Britain 57–8.

Opimius, Lucius (C2 BC), as consul in 121 BC was the first to persuade the Senate to pass the 'Ultimate Decree' which he interpreted as giving the consuls extraordinary powers to bring an end to a threat to the security of the state. As his colleague FABIUS (6) Maximus was away in Gaul, he had a free hand to suppress the movement of Gaius GRACCHUS (1) whom he violently killed together with M. Fulvius FLACCUS (4) and a large number of other citizens. He created a special court to try those he regarded as rebels and sentenced some 3,000 men to death. As a symbol of his duty done he restored the temple of Concord. He was prosecuted in 120 by P. Decius SUBULO but was acquitted thanks to the pleading of CARBO (1), thus gaining legitimacy for his use of the 'Ultimate Decree'. He was appointed *c.*116 to preside over a commission to settle the Numidian problem by assigning JUGURTHA and ADHERBAL their respective shares of the kingdom. He was tried for corruption in this post by the court established by MAMILIUS (1), went into exile, and died at Dyrrhachium.

Oppius 1, Gaius, was a tribune of the *plebs* in 215 BC during the war with Hannibal. He proposed and carried a law forbidding women to wear bright clothes, ride in a carriage and pair, or own more than half an ounce of gold. LIVY gives an account (34. 1ff) of the debate about its repeal in 195, and indicates the vehement opposition of the Elder CATO (4).

2, Gaius (C1 BC), was an equestrian who acted as CAESAR (1)'s financial adviser (see BALBUS 1) and wrote letters to CICERO (1) for Caesar. He supported Octavian (see AUGUSTUS) after Caesar's death and wrote a pamphlet denying that CAESARION was Caesar's natural son. He also wrote a lost biography of SCIPIO (7) Africanus and perhaps those of Caesar and CASSIUS (2).

Orbilius Pupillus, Lucius (C1 BC), was a schoolmaster and grammarian who moved from Beneventum to Rome at the age of fifty in 63 BC. He was the teacher of HORACE, who recalls the beatings he administered to his pupils while teaching them the *Odyssey* of ANDRONICUS (1). He was critical of the educational conditions he found at Rome though Horace presents him as a bad-tempered martinet. His statue was erected at Beneventum.

Oribasius (C4 AD) was a Greek physician and medical writer from Pergamon who studied in Alexandria under Zeno of Cyprus. While working in Ephesus he became the personal doctor of JULIAN, who in 355 took him to Gaul. He stayed with Julian through his proclamation as emperor and until his death in 363: he was banished by JOVIAN and lived abroad among the Goths until Valens recalled him. He lived to a great age. He was not an original scholar: his chief interest as a writer is as a transmitter of accurate information about medical documents and writers from the earliest times in a vast work named *Medical Collections*. Of its seventy books, twenty-five survive, and some of the rest is known from epitomes made by Oribasius himself. He also compiled a lost book of excerpts from GALEN. He formed part of an anti-Christian movement led by Julian to exalt the classical past and its achievements. His works were translated into Latin, Aramaic and Arabic.

Origen 1. (*c.*AD 185–254) was a Greek Christian writer (a 'Church Father') from Alexandria, whose full name was Origenes Adamantius. Of Christian parentage and upbringing, he was taught first by his father Leonides, who died in 202 as a result of persecution, and then by CLEMENT (2) in the catechetical school of Alexandria. He became head of this school in 203 and studied Neoplatonism and other philosophies under AMMONIUS SACCAS or another Ammonius. EUSEBIUS (book 6 of whose *Ecclesiastical History* is our main source for Origen's life) declares that he had himself castrated in obedience to *Matthew's Gospel* (19, 12), but

Epiphanius cast doubt on the report. He left Alexandria in 215, when CARACALLA ordered a pogrom of Christians there, and went to Caesarea in Palestine, where he preached and wrote. Demetrius, bishop of Alexandria, recalled him, and Origen's influence grew: in 230 while in Greece he was ordained priest by the bishops of Jerusalem and Caesarea but Demetrius objected, defrocked him, and in 232 had him banished from Alexandria. He returned to Caesarea, where he founded a school and devoted himself to his writing; he also travelled widely. He fell victim to torture in the persecution of DECIUS. He died as a result of his sufferings, aged sixty-nine, at Tyre.

There was a *Panegyric* to him written by GREGORY (1) the Miracle-worker, whom he had converted. Eusebius and Pamphilus wrote a *Defence of Origen*, which Rufinus of Aquilea translated into Latin.

Only a fraction of Origen's extensive writing is extant. He did much original work on the criticism and exegesis (explanation) of biblical texts. He had an enormous influence on subsequent Christian theology. Those of his works which survive in Greek are *Against Celsus*, a treatise in eight books defending Christian beliefs against the attacks of the anti-Christian Platonist CELSUS (3); three devotional works, *Prayer* (*c.*231), *An Exhortation to Martyrdom* (*c.*235) and *The Pasch*; and large fragments of a doctrinal work, *First Principles* (*De Principiis*), written before 215, which is complete in the garbled Latin translation of Rufinus. His commentaries on the *Gospel of Matthew* and the *Gospel of John* also survive in Greek. Moreover GREGORY (3) and BASIL compiled extracts of Origen's writings which they published under the title *Philocalia*. He also wrote much that is lost or fragmentary, including an edition of the Hebrew Scriptures in several versions, the original Hebrew, and three translations into Greek, entitled *Hexapla* ('sixfold'), which took him twelve years to compile; commentaries on scriptures both Hebrew and Christian; and a work on the *Resurrection* which gave offence to Methodius. Origen was ultimately rejected by his fellow-believers because of his readiness to speculate and his openness to Greek philosophical theories, and though he left a following he was condemned for heresy by the Council of Constantinople in 553. See H. Chadwick (1966) *Early Christian Thought and the Classical Tradition*, Oxford: Clarendon Press; E.A. Clark (1992) *The Origenist Controversy*, Princeton: Princeton University Press; R. Lane Fox (1986) *Pagans and Christians*, Harmondsworth: Penguin.

2. (C3 AD) was a Neoplatonist philosopher who, like his contemporary ORIGEN (1), studied under AMMONIUS SACCAS. PORPHYRY states that he wrote two works that are lost, *About the Spirits*, and *That the King is the Only Creator.* Unlike PLOTINUS and Numenius, he identified 'supreme being' with 'creator'.

Orodes II (reigned *c.*55–37 BC) was a king of Parthia, the son of Phraates III and brother of Mithridates III, against whom he fought long to secure the throne and whom he took and killed in 55. When in 53 CRASSUS (3) invaded Parthia in order to capture Mesopotamia, Orodes struck at Armenia whence Crassus hoped to supply himself with cavalry, while his vassal the general SUREN led a large force of mounted archers to annihilate the Roman infantry in the desert at Carrhae (Harran). For this success Orodes shortly afterwards executed Suren. He sent his son Pacorus in 51 to invade Syria, but CASSIUS (2) expelled him. During the Roman civil wars, Orodes supported POMPEIUS (2) and later the Republicans, even sending troops to the battle of Philippi, and in 40 he again sent Pacorus assisted by LABIENUS (1) to invade Syria, this time successfully. The Parthian forces made deep inroads into the Roman Empire as far as Caria in Asia Minor: in 39, however, they met with opposition from VENTIDIUS, a general appointed by ANTONIUS (7), who drove the Parthians out and killed Pacorus. Orodes then chose as his successor PHRAATES (1) IV, who killed him shortly after his abdication.

Ostorius Scapula, Publius (C1 AD), after a suffect consulship was appointed legate (governor) of Britain in 47 in succession to Aulus PLAUTIUS (1). His time in Britain was passed in struggling with the peoples then inhabiting Wales. After settling a revolt of the Iceni in 47 by force of arms, he defeated the Deceangli of north-east Wales and then, after disarming the inhabitants of the province and establishing *c.*49 a colony of veterans at Colchester, he advanced against the Silures of south Wales and the Ordovices of north-west Wales who were led by CARATACUS. He won a victory, probably at Caersws, which led to Caratacus' flight to the Brigantes who handed him over to Rome. But the Silures remained a threat and were tough opponents: in 49 he founded a fortress at Gloucester for the Twentieth Legion. He died in 52, worn out by his efforts to overcome Silurian opposition. He had been awarded triumphal decorations by CLAUDIUS (1).

Otho, Marcus Salvius (AD 32–69), was emperor for three months in 69. He was a patrician (his father had received the status from CLAUDIUS 1) and a friend of NERO (1), who fell in love with Otho's wife POPPAEA SABINA and consequently sent Otho away to govern Lusitania in 58, where he remained until Nero died in 68. He was the first governor to support the claim of GALBA (1), and expected to be named his heir. When Galba named PISO (9) as his heir (10 January 69), Otho played on the disappointment of the Praetorian Guard and persuaded its members, on 15 January, to kill Galba and proclaim himself emperor. The Senate and many of the imperial armies approved his succession, but those on the German frontier had already appointed VITELLIUS (1) to the purple and now marched to Italy in his support. They reached the Po valley in force where Otho's generals met them with a much inferior army at Bedriacum near Cremona. Upon its defeat he killed himself on 16 April. See M. Grant (1985) *The Roman Emperors*, London: Weidenfeld & Nicolson; K. Wellesley (1975) *The Long Year, AD 69*, London: Elek.

Ovid (Publius Ovidius Naso) (43 BC–AD 17), the most elegant and productive of Roman poets, was born on 20 March 43 at Sulmo. His father, of an old and respected equestrian family, sent his two sons, of whom Publius was the younger, to Rome to prepare for a senatorial career. He was an outstanding pupil of the rhetoricians ARELLIUS FUSCUS and PORCIUS (1) Latro. After the death of his brother in 24 he made a tour of Greece with a friend, the poet Pompeius Macer, and on his return began his ascent of the senatorial ladder by holding minor legal appointments. He quickly gave up this career, however, to devote himself to writing poetry, encouraged by his patron MESSALLA (4) who noticed him at the outset of his poetic career. This association brought him into contact and friendship with GALLUS (4) and TIBULLUS; he was also a close friend of PROPERTIUS. We know about his life and poetic development from his own autobiographical works, written in exile, included in the *Sorrows* (*Tristia*) and *Letters from the Black Sea* (*Epistulae ex Ponto*). He married three times: he divorced his first wife, had a daughter by his second wife, who subsequently died; his third wife, who was a member of the family of Paullus FABIUS (9) Maximus, worked assiduously for him during his exile. He wrote easily and fluently, always in the elegiac metre except in his *Metamorphoses* ('changes of shape') and his lost play, *Medea*. Much of his early poetry was wittily erotic: he enjoyed describing amatory encounters, often dressing them in the cloak of myth.

He entitled his first work *Love Affairs* (*Amores*), which he originally published *c.*16 BC in five books, but later re-edited to three. He departed from the serious and often ironical approach of Propertius by adapting the character of his protagonist to a more knowing and worldly stance, thus responding with humour and even parody to the work of his fellow elegists. He gave readings of his poems and thus gained a reputation that helped to sell his books. His *Heroines* (*Heroides*) were written after the first edition of the *Amores* (*c.*13) and purported to be imaginary letters from the famous heroines of Greek myth to the men who had abandoned them: they are in effect dramatic monologues, ingenious and highly rhetorical in style, reflecting Ovid's education. Number 15, with the poetess Sappho as its heroine, is probably by another hand. His friend Sabinus wrote the heroes' replies. His elegant and witty *Art of Love*, of which he published the first two books in 1 BC, adopted the guise of a treatise on the acquisition of a lover. The third book, published a little later as a sequel, turned the tables on the first two, which were addressed to the male sex, as it advised girls how to get a man. Before publishing the third book, he brought out a poem on *Cosmetics* (*Medicamina Faciei Femineae*), of which the first hundred lines survive and reveal Ovid's ability to contend with Nicander in making poetry of pharmacy. *Remedies for Love* purported to be a recantation of the thesis of the *Art*, seeming to give advice how to rid oneself of an unwanted passion, but its tone is as teasing as that of the earlier poem. Myth was now to become Ovid's main preoccupation, and in the years before his banishment he wrote two works. *The Calendar* (*Fasti*) tells the stories behind the festivals of the Roman year, and his masterpiece, the *Metamorphoses*, largely concerned with Greek myths, is vast and epic in scale and style. It is described as a *carmen perpetuum*, a continuous poem, and has as its unifying element the use of metamorphosis, a change of shape from one creature to another, which occurs in every story. Unlike a traditional epic it tells many tales, seeming thus to satisfy the Callimachean criterion of the miniature ideal, while prolonging the work to epic proportions. The transitions from tale to tale are handled with great skill, and the whole work flows like a mighty river.

He had just completed the *Metamorphoses* in AD 8 when he was informed of his banishment to Tomis (Constança) on the Black Sea coast of Romania. As a protest he symbolically burnt a copy of the *Metamorphoses*, but other copies existed: he had completed and eventually published the first six books of *The Calendar*, about the festivals from January to June, but he never completed the second half. He had somehow incurred the bitter resentment of the emperor AUGUSTUS, but the reason for his exile is unknown to us beyond Ovid's own statement that it was caused by a 'poem and an error'. The poem was the *Art of Love* (*Ars Amatoria*), but it had been published ten years before. The error may have been his implication in some misbehaviour of the emperor's notorious granddaughter JULIA (6), who was banished to an island in the same year, AD 8. He clearly, however, offended against the puritanical morality which Augustus was attempting to impose on the upper class of Romans. Ovid was allowed to keep his rights as a Roman citizen and his property, which his wife, who was not allowed to accompany him, administered, as well as acting as his literary agent and advocate. While at Tomis, Ovid wrote between AD 9 and 12 five books of the *Sorrows*, partly autobiographical, partly descriptive of his new surroundings and partly (book 2) an appeal to the emperor for mercy. He also wrote four books of *Letters from the Black Sea*, verse letters addressed by name to friends in Rome. Both these collections, in which he reverts to the elegiac metre, are effectively pleas for his sentence to be annulled, though book 4 of the *Letters* seems to have been published after his death. He wrote an elaborate curse poem, *Ibis*, to an unidentified man he hated and named after the bird chosen for its filthy way of life, which he published *c.*AD 11. We do not know the date of his lost play *Medea*, but his affinity with the Greek tragedian Euripides (who wrote the extant *Medea*) is clear from the *Heroines* and numerous stories in the *Metamorphoses*. He also owed a debt to the Hellenistic poet Callimachus, whose aetiological works are reflected in *The Calendar*, and whose power of invective is reflected in the *Ibis*. In his poems he complained bitterly of the harsh conditions of the tiny frontier town where he was forced to live, but he went on composing and he learnt the local language, Getic. His sentence was never remitted, not even after the death of Augustus in AD 14.

Ovid was a brilliant poet who offered a refreshing departure from the gravity of his Roman predecessors and the pessimism of much Greek poetry. The exuberance and *joie-de-vivre* of his pre-exile poetry are strikingly attractive and his frequent reworking of ideas and phrases are an interesting characteristic. As he proceeded, he engaged in an ever deeper exploration of human emotions and passions. His work was extremely popular during his lifetime and remained so for the rest of Antiquity, though QUINTILIAN criticised him for self-indulgent excess in his composition. He was treasured throughout the later Middle Ages and well into the Renaissance: he was a favourite of both Chaucer and Shakespeare. A moralised and Christianised version of some of his poems was current in the fourteenth century, and Renaissance painters mined him for subject matter. He continues to influence poetry and art. See L.P. Wilkinson (1955) *Ovid Recalled*, Cambridge: Cambridge University Press; H. Fraenkel (1945) *Ovid, A Poet Between Two Worlds*, Berkeley and Los Angeles: University of California Press; S. Mack (1988) *Ovid*, New Haven: Yale University Press; R.O.A.M. Lyne (1980) *The Latin Love Poets*, Oxford: Clarendon Press.

P

Pacorus *see* ORODES.

Pacuvius, Marcus (*c.*220–130 BC), was a tragic playwright and stage painter from Brundisium, the nephew of Quintus ENNIUS. He spent most of his life and career in Rome and knew L. Aemilius PAULLUS (2) or his sons, as well as Gaius LAELIUS (2). We know of thirteen titles of tragedies in the Greek tradition and a Roman *praetexta* on the life of Paullus. He is also said to have composed satires and a comedy, *Pseudo*. A painting of his was reported by PLINY (1) the Elder in the temple of Hercules in the cattle market. He ended his life in Tarentum and his modest epitaph is quoted by GELLIUS (1).

His tragedies are partly based on those of Euripides (the *Antiopa*) or Sophocles and partly on later Greek plays: they were not translations but adaptations. We have some fragments amounting to about 400 lines of his tragedies, mainly from citations by later commentators such as CICERO (1). Pacuvius was an innovator in grammar and in diction, borrowing Greek words or building new Latin compounds from simple words. Some of his plays were still being performed in the first century AD, and Cicero considered him the greatest composer of tragedy in Latin, surpassing those by ACCIUS. See W. R. Beare (1964) *The Roman Stage*, 3rd edn, London: Methuen.

Paetus 1, Publius Autronius (C1 BC), a supporter of CATILINE, was convicted of bribery after winning the consular election for 65 BC and declared ineligible for the post: he plotted to kill CICERO (1) in 63, was convicted of assault and went into exile in Epirus.

2, Lucius Caesennius (C1 AD), was appointed by NERO (1) as governor of Cappadocia: in this office he capitulated in 61 to the Parthians in Armenia: he was dismissed from his post. Nine years later VESPASIAN, his relation by marriage, appointed him to govern Syria, in which post he annexed Commagene in 73.
See also THRASEA.

Palicanus, Marcus Lollius (C1 BC), was a supporter of POMPEIUS (2) from Picenum of lowly background who aspired to power: he was tribune in 71 when he paved the way for Pompeius' consulship the next year, working to undo SULLA (1)'s reforms by restoring the role of the tribunes and the composition of juries. His daughter was married to GABINIUS (2). He supported the victims of VERRES. He reached the praetorship in 69 thanks to Pompeius, but was foiled of the consulship by Gaius PISO (1).

Pallas, Marcus Antonius (died AD 62), was a Greek freedman of ANTONIA (2), the brother of FELIX, and became the financial secretary of her son, the emperor CLAUDIUS (1). He enriched himself enormously in his post and became widely hated for his arrogance. He was close to AGRIPPINA (3), the mother of NERO (1), and was reputed to be her lover. He persuaded Claudius to marry her and to adopt Nero as his son. When the Senate decreed praetorian decorations and an honorarium for him, he accepted the honour but declined the money, which brought him a public commendation for his modest life. But after Nero's accession he lost his influence and resigned his post on the understanding that no questions were asked about his accounts. Nero later killed him to get his wealth.

Pamphila (C1 AD) was a Greek writer of anecdotal history from Epidaurus: she worked in the reign of NERO (1), and of her thirty-six books entitled *Historical Notes* some ten extracts are preserved by Diogenes Laërtius and Aulus GELLIUS (1). Her work may have been summarised by FAVORINUS.

Panaetius (*c.*185–109 BC) was a Greek Stoic philosopher from Rhodes, the son of Nicagoras. Of noble and priestly birth (he was priest of Poseidon at Lindos), he studied under Crates at Pergamon and later at Athens under Diogenes and Antipater. He moved to Rome *c.*140, where he became a member of the circle of SCIPIO (11) Aemilianus. He travelled *c.*144 in the east with Scipio and made his home alternately in Rome and Athens. In 129 he became the head of the Stoic school at Athens in succession to Antipater; POSIDONIUS was his pupil. He had much influence, and CICERO (1) based his major ethical treatise, *Duties*, on Panaetius' lost work of the same name. He represents a mildly reformist element in the development of Stoic thought: he was open to ideas taken from the works of Plato and Aristotle and rejected astrology and prophecy, though he accepted the traditional Stoic doctrine of Providence. He seems to have been more concerned with the practical morality of active Roman citizens than the ideal of the Stoic sage. Some fragments of his works survive.

Pansa, Gaius Vibius (C1 BC) After serving under CAESAR (1) in Gaul, in 51 he acted as tribune in support of Caesar, who appointed him to govern Bithynia in 47 and Cisalpine Gaul in 45. He designated Pansa consul for 43 with HIRTIUS: while in the post, in March 43 Pansa was wounded by the forces of ANTONIUS (7) near Mutina and after the battle of Mutina died of his injury.

Papinianus, Aemilius (*c.*AD 150–212) (Papinian), was a jurist and legal expert in the service of the emperor Septimius SEVERUS (1). He probably came from Emesa in Syria and may have been related to JULIA (10) Domna, the wife of Severus; he was assessor to the praetorian prefect, and from 194 to 202 he acted as the emperor's secretary (*a libellis*) with the role of replying to petitions presented to his master. In 205 he succeeded Fulvius PLAUTIANUS as Praetorian Prefect. He wrote authoritatively on legal topics both officially and unofficially. His *Legal Cases* (*Quaestiones*) in thirty-seven books was finished before 198; between 206 and 212 he published *Opinions* (*Responsa*) in nineteen books. His style is concise and difficult, but his grasp and reasoning are powerful: he has a strong sense of the need for equity to underpin the rules of law. His works were very influential and CONSTANTINE (1) I refused to accept that PAULUS and ULPIANUS might have superior authority. Moreover, the Law of Citations of 426 enacted that Papinianus' opinion should have pre-eminence when other authorities differed. CARACALLA dismissed him from his post on his accession in 211, and allowed the praetorians to murder him for refusing to support his killing of his brother GETA (3) in 212.

Papirius *see* CARBO, CURSOR.

Papius Mutilus, Gaius (early C1 BC), was a Samnite general who in the Social War commanded the southern force of the rebel allies which, after successful fighting in Campania, was defeated in 90 BC by Lucius CAESAR (5) and by SULLA (2) in 89. During Sulla's eastern campaigns he accepted Roman citizenship but was proscribed by Sulla on his return in 83, and killed himself.

Parthenius (C1 BC) was a Greek scholar and poet from Nicaea in Bithynia, captured in the Third Mithridatic War and brought to Italy *c.*65. He was freed and lived in Rome, where he introduced the neoteric poets, CATULLUS (1), CALVUS and CINNA (4), who may have been responsible for bringing him to Italy, to the works and poetic techniques of Callimachus and Euphorion. He was taken to Bithynia by MEMMIUS (2) along with Catullus and Cinna in 57 when he was its governor. In his later years he moved to Naples where he wrote and taught. Most of his poetry, highly regarded by the ancients, is lost except for fragments found on papyri: a strong influence of Euphorion is detectable in it. In elegiacs he wrote three books in praise of his wife Arete; he also wrote hexameters. However, a prose collection of outline versions of love stories (*Erotic Experiences*), morbid and grotesque, is extant: it was dedicated to Cornelius GALLUS (4) with the intention that he would versify the stories. Parthenius also extended VIRGIL's knowledge of Greek literature, who in his turn imitated the style of his description of the death of Byblis.

Pasiteles (first half C1 BC) was a Greek sculptor and writer on sculpture from southern Italy who obtained Roman citizenship in 90 BC. None of his works survives: he wrote in five volumes *Notable Artistic Works throughout the World*, which was known to PLINY (1) the Elder. He made an ivory statue of Jupiter for the temple of METELLUS (4) Macedonicus. He was famous for his metalwork and for his studies from nature (Pliny tells a story that he was almost killed by a panther when sketching a lion). He founded a workshop from which two works are extant, an athlete signed by his pupil Stephanus, and a pair of figures, Electra and Orestes, signed by Stephanus' pupil Menelaus. Pasiteles seems to mark a change in the adaptation of Greek sculpture to Roman taste.

Paternus, Publius Taruttienus (died AD 182), served under the emperor MARCUS AURELIUS as his principal private secretary (*praepositus ab epistulis Latinis*) and had a legal background. During the war with the Marcomanni he led an embassy to the Cotini. He was appointed Praetorian Prefect in the late 170s and had a success on the northern front in 179, but in 182 was removed from his post by Tigidius PERENNIS, the favourite of COMMODUS, and soon put to death for plotting against the emperor.

Paul (died *c.*AD 64) was the chief spreader and arguably the originator of Christianity. Originally named Saul, a Greek-speaking Jew from Tarsus, or a Greek-speaking Cilician converted to Judaism, by trade a tent-maker, he claimed to be a Pharisee by training. Though in Jerusalem at the time of JESUS' crucifixion, he claimed not to have met him in the flesh. As a result of a mystical experience he had in AD 37, he underwent a spiritual conversion and now not only claimed that Jesus was the Messiah (Greek: *Christ*) and Son of God, but also regarded him as the redeemer of mankind from divine punishment. He later took upon himself a mission to convert the Jews of the diaspora and even the gentiles to his new creed, which combined faith in Jesus as saviour with novel interpretations of the Hebrew scriptures.

After this conversion, he spent two years in Damascus and Arabia, formulating his new faith. In 39 he returned for a short visit to Jerusalem, where Barnabas persuaded some members of the Nazarene movement (Jewish followers of Jesus) to accept his claim to be a convert, though others rejected it. He then spent some five years in and around his native Tarsus. He passed a year (*c.*44–5) in Antioch with Barnabas before setting out on his first missionary journey to Cyprus and Asia Minor. He associated with the governor, Sergius Paulus, whose name he adopted. On his return to Antioch he was confronted with a controversy raised by his admission of gentiles to the Christian community, as to whether they should be obliged to conform to Jewish practices such as the food laws and circumcision. He consequently went to Jerusalem (spring 49) where he met some prominent followers of Jesus. Paul went on two more missionary journeys to Asia Minor and Greece (see GALLIO), where to prove his loyalty he collected much money to give to the Nazarenes in Jerusalem. He claimed to have been born with Roman citizenship, but in fact may possibly have purchased it with some of this money. By his own account he suffered terrible hardships on his journeys, as well as frequent persecution in the cities he passed through; on his third journey he spent three years in Ephesus. On a visit to Jerusalem in 58 he was arrested, mainly to protect him from the Jews, who were outraged because they believed he had taken a gentile into the inner part of the Temple. He was then arraigned before the high priest and held in custody by the governor FELIX in the capital, Caesarea. Two years later his case came up for trial by the new governor, FESTUS (2), who decided to send him to Jerusalem for trial, but Paul, by virtue of his Roman citizenship, appealed from the governor to the emperor. He was consequently sent to Rome, where, after shipwreck on Malta, he arrived in spring 62: here he was kept for a further two years under house arrest and later in prison. There are conflicting traditions about his death: one suggests that he perished in NERO (1)'s persecution of Christians after the fire of Rome in 64, but there was a different tradition that he was freed and travelled to the west as far as Spain.

A tormented and moody character, he was a powerful speaker and writer, and during the decade *c.*54–*c.*64 wrote letters (later included in the canon of the New Testament) to various communities of Christians: two each to the *Thessalonians* and the *Corinthians*, one each to the *Galatians*, the *Romans* and the *Philippians*, and possibly others. Letters in his style were also composed by others and passed off as his. His influence on the fundamental doctrine of the new and ever more gentile Christian movement was profound: he was largely responsible for the breach between Christians and Jews. Most of the other Christian scriptures, which were composed later by various hands, reflect Paul's teachings. They include the three synoptic *Gospels* and the *Acts of the Apostles*, the latter containing a detailed though unreliable account of Paul's career. See E.P. Sanders (1991) *Paul*, Oxford: Oxford University Press; M. Grant (1976) *Saint Paul*, London: Weidenfeld & Nicolson; A.F. Segal (1990) *Paul the Convert*, New Haven: Yale University Press; H. Maccoby (1986) *The Mythmaker*, London: Weidenfeld & Nicolson; R. Lane Fox (1991) *The Unauthorised Version*, Harmondsworth: Penguin; F.F. Bruce (1977) *Paul, Apostle of the Free Spirit*, Exeter: Paternoster; R. Wallace and W. Williams (1998) *The Three Worlds of Paul of Tarsus*, London: Routledge; and (1993) *The Acts of the Apostles: A Companion*, London: Bristol Classical Press.

Paullus 1, Lucius Aemilius (died 216 BC), was a general in the Second Punic War. His first consulship was in 219, when with his colleague SALINATOR he drove DEMETRIUS (3) out of Pharos (Hvar) in Illyria and held a triumph. In 218 he went to Carthage on an embassy at the outbreak of war. He was killed at the battle of Cannae during his second consulship, having (despite POLYBIUS' statement to the contrary) approved the decision to meet Hannibal in a pitched battle. His daughter Aemilia Tertia married P. Cornelius SCIPIO (7) Africanus.

2. Macedonicus, Lucius Aemilius (228–160 BC), son of PAULLUS (1), was a distinguished general. He governed western Spain, including modern Portugal, from 191, when he was praetor, to 189, and despite a setback he conquered the Lusitani. In 189 he was sent to Asia Minor as one of a commission of ten who reached a settlement at Apamea after the defeat of ANTIOCHUS (1) III at Magnesia, and opposed the granting of a triumph to VULSO (1). He was elected consul for 182: during that year and 181 he subdued much of Liguria and held a triumph. He acted as a patron of the Spanish provincials in 171 in their complaints against extortionate governors. He held a second consulship in 168 when he successfully ended the Third Macedonian War with his victory over PERSEUS at Pydna. At the Senate's behest he imposed a tough settlement on Greece, and sacked Epirus. His booty was sufficient to relieve the Romans of direct taxation, but he kept only Perseus' library for himself. His two young sons by his second wife died at the time of his triumph: the two by his first wife Papiria had been adopted as Q. FABIUS (5) Maximus Aemilianus and P. Cornelius SCIPIO (11) Aemilianus. His daughter married a son of CATO (4) the Censor. Paullus was censor in 164 and died in relative poverty. He was a philhellene and educated his sons in Greek as well as Latin culture, and probably assisted TERENCE in his career as a writer.

3, Lucius Aemilius (C1 BC), was the elder brother of the triumvir LEPIDUS (4). In 63 he brought a prosecution against CATILINE for violent behaviour, and was himself accused in 59 by Vettius while governor of Macedonia of plotting to murder POMPEIUS (2). In 56 during his aedileship he began the restoration of the Aemilian Basilica for which CAESAR (1) gave him 1,500 talents in 50, when he was consul, as a bribe to prevent him from obstructing Caesar's ambitions. By nature a conservative, after Caesar's murder he supported the Senate, on behalf of which he negotiated with Sextus POMPEIUS (4). In 43 he had supported the declaration of his brother Lepidus a public enemy, for which the new triumvirs proscribed him in 42. He was, however, permitted to get away to join BRUTUS (5) in Asia: he lived quietly at Miletus and was pardoned after the battle of Philippi.

4, Lucius Aemilius (C1 BC/AD), the younger son of Paullus Aemilius LEPIDUS (8), married JULIA (6), the granddaughter of AUGUSTUS, and was consul in AD 1. Some time after this the emperor executed him for conspiracy. Julia herself was disgraced in AD 8 and their daughter Aemilia Lepida's engagement to CLAUDIUS (1) was annulled.

Paulus, Julius (early C3 AD), was a jurist, writer, and teacher of law in the reign of Septimius SEVERUS (1). A pupil of Cervidius SCAEVOLA (1), he began his career as an advocate, but in 205 he became the emperor's secretary for legal affairs (*a cognitionibus*). He sat as a legal adviser on Severus' privy council and published accounts of cases heard by the emperor. He remained influential until the reign of ELAGABALUS, who married his daughter and made him Praetorian Prefect. A year later, however, in 220, the emperor divorced Paula and banished Paulus. In 222 he was recalled by the new emperor, SEVERUS (2) Alexander, who restored his dignities. He may have shared the prefecture with Ulpianus. He was a voluminous writer, producing more than 300 books. He wrote seventy-eight on *The [Praetor's] Edict*, sixteen on the *Civil Law* of SABINUS (4), twenty-six of *Legal Cases*, twenty-three of *Opinions*; he also wrote commentaries on earlier legal works, on legislation, and on other legal topics. A compilation of some of his writings was published about seventy years after his death under the title *Paulus' Thoughts*. He was one of the legal authorities recognised by the Law of Citations of 426, and was frequently cited in the *Digests* of Justinian.

Pedius 1, Quintus (C1 BC), was a nephew of CAESAR (1), the son of his eldest sister Julia and a Campanian equestrian. He served as one of Caesar's legates in the Gallic campaign and was a natural supporter after he crossed the Rubicon. He held the praetorship in 48 when he crushed MILO's attempted rebellion. As governor of eastern Spain in 46 and 45 he took part in the campaign of Munda, and earned a triumph. After Caesar's murder he inherited an eighth of his estate, which he resigned to Octavian (AUGUSTUS). He was consul in the latter half of 43 with Octavian, and passed a law for the punishment of Caesar's assassins. He was left in Rome by Octavian to begin the work of eliminating the proscribed while the latter met ANTONIUS (7) and LEPIDUS (4) at Bononia, but died in November 43 of a breakdown caused by his dreadful task.

2, Sextus (mid-C2 AD), was a jurist who is known from quotations and references to his work by PAULUS and ULPIANUS. He may be the Sextus Pedius Hirrutus who was suffect consul in 158. He wrote with authority lost works on *The Praetor's Edict*, *The Curule Aediles' Edict*, and *Stipulations*.

Perennis, Sextus Tigidius (died AD 185), was Praetorian Prefect, first as the colleague of Taruttienus PATERNUS until 182, and then by himself, under the emperor COMMODUS. During the latter period he was effectively ruling the Empire single-handed, but became unpopular by appointing men of equestrian rank rather than senators to the command of legions. Commodus finally allowed a mutinous army to kill him and he was replaced by CLEANDER.

Perperna 1, Marcus (died 129 BC), as praetor *c.*132 won a decisive victory over the slaves of Sicily at Henna for which he was granted an ovation. As consul in 130 he was sent to Asia where he succeeded CRASSUS (5) and captured ARISTONICUS of Pergamon. He died at Pergamon.

2, Marcus (*c.*148–49 BC), was a son of PERPERNA (1). He was consul in 92 and censor with PHILIPPUS (2) in 86: they enrolled the first Italians to be enfranchised as citizens.

3. Veiento, Marcus (died 72 BC), was a son of PERPERNA (2). As praetor in 82, after declining to join SULLA (2), he abandoned Sicily to POMPEIUS (2). In 77 he joined LEPIDUS (3) in Gaul, was associated in his rebellion and fled with him to Sardinia. He took Lepidus' army to Spain where he joined SERTORIUS. Later he grew jealous of Sertorius' success and in 73 assassinated him; a year later he was overwhelmed by Pompeius, to whom he offered the correspondence of Sertorius which would have incriminated several leading Romans. But Pompeius refused to read it and executed Perperna.

Perseus (reigned 179–168 BC) was the last king of independent Macedonia. He was the elder of the two sons of PHILIP (1) V and acceded at the age of thirty-three. He opposed his younger brother Demetrius' pro-Roman stance and claim to the throne (there was a false rumour that Perseus was a slave's son), and after plotting against him for two years engineered his execution in 180. He did, however, fight against the Aetolians in his father's alliance with Rome, and renewed the treaty after his accession. He strengthened the power and influence of his kingdom by dynastic marriage: he took Laodice, daughter of SELEUCUS IV, as his wife, and married his sister to PRUSIAS (2) II of Bithynia. He won the friendship of Rhodes and conquered Dolopia in Thessaly; he interfered in conflicts in Aetolia and Thessaly and visited Delphi with an armed force, restoring Macedonia to the leadership of the council of states centred on Delphi. His energetic policy, however, was at the expense of Pergamon, whose king, EUMENES (2) II, complained in 172 to Rome. In the following winter he met Q. Marcius PHILIPPUS (4), who tricked him into thinking that Rome would not attack him before he had time to negotiate. However, he faced up to the coming conflict (the Third Macedonian War) and won a frontier skirmish in 171. He tried to rally support in Greece with little success. His one ally, Genthius, an Illyrian king, collapsed before the Romans as they attacked from the west, and Perseus met L. Aemilius PAULLUS (2) at Pydna on the Thermaic Gulf in June 168. After being routed he burnt his archives and fled to Samothrace, where he was captured. He marched in Paullus' triumph and died two years later in confinement at Alba Fucens.

Persius Flaccus, Aulus (AD 34–62), was a satirical poet, born of a wealthy equestrian family at Volaterrae. His father died when he was six; his mother had him educated at Rome under the Stoic philosopher L. Annaeus CORNUTUS (1) and the grammarian Remmius Palaemon. He became associated with the Stoic opposition to the imperial system, probably through his kinship with ARRIA (2), wife of THRASEA Paetus: LUCAN, Thrasea and Caesius BASSUS (3) were his friends. When he died in November 62 he left his poetry, consisting of six satires amounting in all to 650 hexameter lines with a brief introduction in limping iambics, to Cornutus, who gave them to Bassus to edit for publication.

The poems are scarcely political but owe much to HORACE's *Satires* in being personal and self-critical. They are, however, much more bitter in tone than Horace's Epicurean chat; their style is dense and difficult ('the taste of bitten nails') and the Stoic standpoint is uncompromising. They were much admired by Lucan, who called them truly poetic, and Martial, who admired their distillation. There are hints of an attack on NERO (1) in Satire 1, where poetry thought to resemble the emperor's own is pilloried, and in 4 where the young statesman is criticised for seeking public approval rather than virtue of character. The poems, which were unrevised on Persius' death, do not present a consistent 'voice' or straightforward argumentation: he shifts around, using language that is tortuous and obscure, and dark metaphors, often taken from anatomy. He also makes use of the vigorous, colloquial language of common people and seems to be highly self-conscious in his manner of composition. The rhythmic quality and the striking sound effects of his poetry are, however, most skilful. John Donne thought highly of his work. See J.C. Bramble (1974) *Persius and the Programmatic Satire*, Cambridge: Cambridge University Press; N. Rudd (1986) *Themes in Roman Satire*, London: Duckworth.

Pertinax, Publius Helvius (AD 126–193), was an emperor who was born in Liguria, a freedman's son who worked as a schoolteacher before applying to become a centurion. Having failed, he went to Syria, held a succession of equestrian posts in the 160s, and was put in command of the North Sea fleet. He held procuratorships, the last in Dacia, and was promoted to the Senate by MARCUS AURELIUS; he was consul in 175. He governed Moesia, Dacia and Syria. Dismissed by COMMODUS' protégé the prefect Tigidius PERENNIS, he lived in retirement from 182 to 185, when he was sent to govern Britain, where he suppressed a mutiny of the soldiers. He served as prefect of the food supply in Italy and as proconsul of the province of

Africa. He held a second consulship in 192 when he was appointed city prefect of Rome. He had foreknowledge of the plot to assassinate Commodus, and though reluctant was voted to succeed him by the Senate on the last evening of the year. On 1 January the Praetorian Prefect Laetus proclaimed him emperor to the guards. His amazing rise to power had reached its zenith: he ruled for three months and was murdered in late March at the instigation of Laetus by the praetorian troops, who were tired of his strict discipline. He had proved unable to solve the financial problems of the empire, had sold public offices, and lost the support both of the Senate and the praetorians. There had been two conspiracies against him, and the guardsmen had tried to replace him with the consul Falco. Three months after the death of Pertinax he was honoured by the incoming emperor, Septimius SEVERUS (1), who deified him and took his name. See M. Grant (1985) *The Roman Emperors*, London: Weidenfeld & Nicolson.

Pescennius Niger Justus, Gaius (died AD 194), was an emperor who, after the murder of PERTINAX, ruled in parts of the eastern Empire for a year from April 193. He was an Italian with popular support in Rome who had served as a senior centurion before holding a command in Egypt, and was raised to the Senate by COMMODUS. He held the consulship in 190 with Septimius SEVERUS (1) as his colleague. He governed Syria from 191 and was proclaimed emperor by his troops in opposition to DIDIUS JULIANUS. He fought vainly against Severus, who cut him off from Italy: Pescennius seized Byzantium, which he attempted to make his base of operations, but was defeated in a series of battles and fled to Antioch. He faced Severus' troops for the last time at Issus, where he was routed. He fled again but was captured and executed as he made for Parthia. See M. Grant (1985) *The Roman Emperors*, London: Weidenfeld & Nicolson.

Petreius, Marcus (*c.*115–46 BC) As legate (deputy) for the consul Gaius ANTONIUS (1), he defeated CATILINE's forces at Pistoria in Etruria in 63 BC. In 55 he was appointed by POMPEIUS (2) to govern Western Spain as his legate, where he remained until the battle of Ilerda in 49, when his forces, combined with those of AFRANIUS (2), governor of Eastern Spain, were defeated by CAESAR (1). He tried to prevent the armies from surrendering after the battle, but escaped to Greece before sailing to Africa in 48 with CATO (5). There he had some success before the defeat in 46 at Thapsus, after which he made a suicide pact with king JUBA (1) of Numidia: he first killed the king and then himself.

Petronius 1. (C1 AD) was a writer and senator of the Neronian period. There is some doubt about the identification of NERO (1)'s courtier Gaius Petronius (or Titus/Publius Petronius Niger) with the author whose *cognomen* Arbiter (which may, however, be a nickname) and *praenomen* Titus are found in the manuscript of the *Satyrica*. The senator, suffect consul in 62 and previously an energetic governor of Bithynia, is paradoxically described by Tacitus as carefree, indolent and amoral, which nevertheless accords with the style and subject matter of the novel, also known as (*sc. Libri*) *Satyricôn*. The courtier (as *arbiter elegantiae*: 'expert on good taste') guided Nero's explorations of art and entertainment until 66 when he was forced through TIGELLINUS' jealousy to commit suicide. This he did in a manner calculated to cause maximum damage to the emperor by denouncing his profligacies in his will, breaking his most precious vase, which Nero coveted, and his signet-ring, so that it might not be used to endanger the innocent.

Only a fragment survives of the *Satyrica* (lit. 'satyr tales', but with an allusion to 'satire'), but it is substantial, consisting of much of three books, and includes the whole episode of *Trimalchio's Dinner* (book 15). The style and setting are consistent with the Neronian period. The novel is picaresque (of low life) and in the Menippean genre, with frequent snatches of poetry interspersed in the prose tale. The work must have been long: the chief characters are the homosexuals Encolpius (the first-person narrator) and his youthful companion Giton, and the setting is southern Italy. There is a strong element of parody in the work. The easy infidelities of Giton satirise the hard-pressed fidelity of heterosexual couples in traditional Greek romances. Encolpius' impotence is attributed to the wrath of Priapus rather as Poseidon's anger bears on Odysseus in the *Odyssey*, and a woman named Circe crops up. In the *Dinner* scene, which takes place in the house of a rich freedman at Puteoli, there is much satire of the *nouveaux riches*: yet Encolpius' snobbery is nearly as revolting as Trimalchio's ignorant ostentation. The narrative, in a parody of Plato's *Symposium*, contains a number of tales told by guests; some of the language foreshadows Vulgar Latin. Other incidental tales resemble Hellenistic Milesian tales, such as the story of the *Widow of Ephesus* and the *Boy from Pergamon*. The two longest poems, introduced as being compositions of a character in the story, the poet Eumolpus, satirise contemporary poetry: a *Sack of Troy* in iambic trimeters suggests an extract from a tragedy by SENECA (2), and a *Civil War* restores to the treatment the supernatural apparatus which LUCAN omitted in his poem of the same name. The state of the text of the *Satyrica* is poor and contains some interpolations. A few other lyric and elegiac poems, some of which may be by Petronius, have also survived independently. See J.P. Sullivan (1968) *The Satyricon of Petronius*, London: Faber; T. Hägg (1983) *The Novel in Antiquity*, Oxford: Blackwell; N.W. Slater (1990) *Reading Petronius*, Baltimore: Johns Hopkins University Press.

2. Turpillianus, Publius (died AD 68), after holding a consulship in 61, succeeded SUETONIUS (1) Paulinus as governor of Britain; in 63 he was put in charge of Rome's water supply. He assisted NERO (1) in suppressing the plot of Gaius PISO (2). Nero appointed him to oppose the rebels of 68, but he vacillated and GALBA (1) executed him.

Phaedrus, Gaius Julius (*c.*15 BC–*c.*AD 50) The versifier of Aesop's fables in Latin. He was born a slave in Thrace and was brought to Rome where he became a slave in AUGUSTUS' household, and obtained his freedom. He wrote five books of fables, in iambic verse, which he failed to finish: by some reference in his work he gave offence to SEJANUS, the prefect of TIBERIUS, and was punished. His work, which is mentioned by no Roman critic or author before MARTIAL, became popular in the late Empire and the Middle Ages. He made the fable into an independent genre, basing his stories on the Aesopian collection, on Hellenistic tales, and his own experience. He is at his best when he sticks to the original versions of the stories; he also sometimes successfully exploits the possibilities of satire of contemporary life. He showed talent in using everyday urban speech, and is a worthy successor of the earlier writers of comedy in the same metre. Retorts against critics in his poems suggest that his work was sometimes the butt of detractors.

Pharnaces II (ruled 63–47 BC) was the son of MITHRIDATES (3) VI of Pontus. He led the rebellion that brought about his father's death and was rewarded by POMPEIUS (2) with the kingdom of Bosporus in the Crimea. In 48 he took advantage of the Roman Civil War to seize Colchis, Lesser Armenia, Cappadocia and part of Pontus: he defeated a Roman army under CALVINUS (2) at Nicopolis. The following year, in a lightning campaign, CAESAR (1) defeated him at Zela (which Caesar reported with *veni, vidi, vici*, 'I came, I saw, I conquered') and he returned to Bosporus, where he was killed in an insurrection by Asander.

Philip 1. V (238–179 BC) was a king of Macedonia, the son of DEMETRIUS (2) II and adopted son of Antigonus III (*Doson*). He succeeded the latter in summer 221 BC at the age of seventeen, and quickly made an impression of energy and strength. After campaigning against the Illyrians (see SCERDILAIDAS) he met Aratus of Sicyon, and at his instigation led the forces of the Hellenic Confederacy in the Social War against Aetolia and her allies, Sparta and Elis. The war was successfully ended in 217 by the Peace of Naupactus, which gave Philip the opportunity to strike to the north and take over Illyria and the Dalmatian coast from the Romans who were embroiled in the Second Punic War. He was instigated to embark on this First Macedonian War by the exiled DEMETRIUS (3) of Pharos. He made a treaty with HANNIBAL in 215, to little effect, and lost his Adriatic fleet in 214 when LAEVINUS brought a Roman force to Apollonia, but was more successful by land. He then turned to the Peloponnese, where he dealt harshly with Messene and alienated the Achaean Confederacy. In 212 the balance of power swung against him as Rome allied herself with Aetolia and Pergamon; he now supported the Achaeans in their war with Sparta and showed skill in resisting Aetolian and Roman aggression. The Romans retired in 207 and Philip sacked Thermum, the capital of Aetolia. The war finally fizzled out when the Aetolians made peace in 206 and, at the Peace of Phoenice in 205, Rome accepted terms granting Philip access to the Adriatic.

Philip now turned to the Aegean, where he employed a pirate, Dicaearchus, as his admiral in an attack on shipping and on the possessions in Asia Minor of the youthful Egyptian king, PTOLEMY (1) V. The extent of the involvement of ANTIOCHUS (1) III, with whom he made a treaty in 203, is uncertain. He turned the Greeks against him by the cruelty of his treatment of prisoners and captured cities. Rhodes, a formidable sea power, and ATTALUS (1) I of Pergamon defeated him at the battles of Chios and Lade in 201, though suffering heavy casualties themselves. Attalus and the Rhodians requested help from the Roman Senate, which was now free of the war with Hannibal. In 200 Philip attacked Athens and the Thracian Chersonese, learning of the Roman ultimatum and declaration of war while at Abydos. In the Second Macedonian War Philip fought the Romans in Macedonia and Thessaly, but was defeated decisively by FLAMININUS at Cynoscephalae in 197. The Romans dictated terms: he was confined to Macedonia, and obliged to pay an indemnity of 1,000 talents, surrender his fleet, and give hostages including his younger son, Demetrius. Philip realised how weak he now was and cooperated with Rome in her dealings with the Greeks, assisting her against NABIS of Sparta in 195 and against the alliance of Antiochus with the Aetolians in 192 and the years following. He helped the Scipios to cross his kingdom with their forces in 190, for which his debt to Rome was remitted and his son restored. In the next five years he gave his attention to the prosperity of Macedonia, but after 185, suspecting that Rome would interfere again, he asserted his supremacy in the Balkans where he worked by force and diplomacy. In 180 the differences between his sons over Demetrius' friendship with Rome, which fostered in him hopes of succeeding to power, flared up and Philip reluctantly executed Demetrius for treason. He died at Amphipolis the following year while trying to engineer further disruption in Illyria. Like Philip II he was a brilliant general, but was unable to maintain a consistent policy and was faced with a rising power he could not match. See E.S. Gruen (1984) *The Hellenistic World and the Coming of Rome*, Berkeley: University of California Press.

2. (died AD 34) was a tetrarch (ruler) of a territory to the east of the Sea of Galilee, including Golan, the north-eastern section of the kingdom of his father HEROD (1) the Great. He founded the city of Caesarea Philippi at the foot of Mt Hermon as his capital. JOSEPHUS praised his successful administration.

Philippus 1, Marcus Julius, 'Philip the Arab' (reigned AD 244–9), was an emperor of Arab blood from Shahba in Syria. Shortly after his appointment as prefect of the Praetorian Guard by GORDIAN III, Philippus seized the throne, conniving at the murder of his young predecessor. He made peace with the Persians, and in a long campaign culminating in 247 drove the invading Carpi back over the Danube. On 21 April 248 he celebrated the thousandth birthday of Rome. The next year DECIUS, a commander with a good record in a recent war against the Goths, whom Philippus had sent to restore order on the Danube frontier, was proclaimed emperor by the troops there and in the autumn defeated and killed the emperor at Verona. See M. Grant (1985) *The Roman Emperors*, London: Weidenfeld & Nicolson.

2, Lucius Marcius (early C1 BC), was a politician and orator, a grandson both of PHILIPPUS (4) and of Appius CLAUDIUS (6) Pulcher. Tribune *c.*104, he was elected consul for 91 after a previous attempt. He led opposition to the proposals of M. Livius DRUSUS (2) to reform the structure of the Senate and grant the Italians citizen status, and later, after being appointed an augur, he had the new law invalidated as passed against the auspices. In 86 he held the censorship in company with PERPERNA (2), and despite earlier opposition registered newly enfranchised Italians. He joined in the defence of the youthful POMPEIUS (2), who was accused of corrupt practices which his father had actually perpetrated, and joined SULLA (2) on his return to Italy and reduced Sardinia for him. After Sulla's death he opposed LEPIDUS (3) and proposed Pompeius' special command against SERTORIUS. He tried to persuade the Senate to annex Egypt in conformity with the will of PTOLEMY (7) XI who died in 80: though unsuccessful, he gained the admiration of the young CICERO (1).

3, Lucius Marcius (mid-C1 BC), was the stepfather of Octavian (AUGUSTUS); the son of PHILIPPUS (2). He governed Syria from 61 to 59 BC and was consul in 56. Inactive in the Civil Wars, he and his wife Atia tried in March 44 to talk Octavian out of accepting his inheritance from his uncle, Julius CAESAR (1), but Philippus later helped him settle the legacies. The following January the Senate sent him on an embassy to ANTONIUS (7) in Cisalpine Gaul: the terms he brought back angered CICERO (1).

4, Quintus Marcius (C2 BC), was consul in 186. With his colleague ALBINUS (3) he suppressed the rites of Dionysus (*Bacchanalia*), and was defeated in battle by the Ligurians. He was sent in 183 to Greece as an ambassador and gave a hostile report of the Achaean Confederacy. In 172 he returned to Greece to gather support for Rome's war against PERSEUS (the Third Macedonian War): he tricked Perseus by promising that Rome would not attack him until he had sent an embassy to negotiate with the Senate. As consul in 169 he led an army into Macedonia, but had to retreat through failure of supplies into Greece, where he refused reinforcements offered by POLYBIUS on behalf of the Achaean Confederacy. In 164 he was censor with PAULLUS (2). The *History* by his critic Polybius is responsible for his poor reputation.

Philo 1, Quintus Publilius (C4 BC), was a plebeian constitutional reformer. In 352 he served on a commission to settle a debt crisis. As consul or perhaps dictator in 339 he passed laws to ensure that when censors were appointed one must always be a plebeian, to prevent patrician obstruction in the Centuriate Assembly, and to enact that laws passed by the Plebeian Assembly were binding on the whole state. He held four consulships (in 339, 327, 320 and 315) and in 336 was the first plebeian to be praetor. In his first consulship he triumphed over the Latins, and when censor in 332 he enrolled two new voting tribes and granted citizenship to Latins. He took Naples in 327 after a siege and negotiated peace, the first with a Greek city. In 326 he again triumphed, this time as the first proconsul. He was involved in the recovery of Roman fortunes after the defeat at the Caudine Forks, participated in southward expansion, and worked in partnership with the popular leaders such as Appius CLAUDIUS (4) and CURSOR (1). See T.R.S. Broughton (1951–2) *The Magistrates of the Roman Republic*, New York: American Philological Association.

2. (159–83 BC) was a Greek philosopher from Larissa, the last head of Plato's Academy. He studied at Larissa under Callicles, a pupil of Carneades, and at twenty-four went to Athens to study under Clitomachus, whom he succeeded as head in 109. He migrated to Rome in 88 and taught there: his pupils included CICERO (1) and CATULUS (3). Cicero refers to his teachings in his *Former Academics* and in his *Lucullus*, and we know something of it from an account in the works of John of Stobi. We know nothing, however, of his writings, not even the titles. He was challenged for the headship of the Academy by his pupil ANTIOCHUS (16) of Ascalon, who seized it, condemning his old master for being too sceptical and himself turning to dogmatic ideas of a Stoic type: he wrote a work, the *Sosus*, against Philo. Philo appears to have had little influence on later Platonism. See H. Tarrant (1985) *Scepticism or Platonism?*, Cambridge: Cambridge University Press.

3. (*c*.30 BC–AD 50) was a Jewish scholar from Alexandria. He wrote extensively on Jewish culture, had an influence on Christian theology and Greek philosophy (the Neoplatonist thinkers), and was a leading figure in the contemporary Jewish life of Alexandria. His brother was Alexander the Alabarch, whose sons were Tiberius Julius ALEXANDER (3), and Marcus Julius Alexander who married BERENICE (2). In AD 40, at the age of seventy, Philo led an embassy to Rome to plead with the emperor Gaius (CALIGULA) not to defile the Temple by placing his image there nor force Jews to engage in emperor-worship. The embassy failed: Philo returned to Alexandria and Caligula was murdered shortly afterwards. Much of his writing survives: his main work was an elaborate treatise on the *Pentateuch*; he wrote a *Life of Moses*, *Contemplative Life*, and works on the persecution of the Jews: *Against Flaccus* (FLACCUS 1, the governor of Egypt who favoured the Greeks) and *The Embassy to Gaius*. He was a Greek-speaker and imbued with Greek philosophical terminology; his knowledge of the Hebrew Scriptures was gained through the Greek version, the Septuagint; he may not have known the Hebrew language. Most of his surviving works were preserved by their inclusion in ORIGEN (1)'s library at Caesarea to which EUSEBIUS also contributed. His writings on philosophy, while deeply influenced by Plato, are founded upon Jewish theology. He seems to have influenced the writers of *The Gospel of John* and the *Epistle to the Hebrews*. See Dorothy I. Sly (1996) *Philo's Alexandria*, London: Routledge; E.R. Goodenough (1962) *An Introduction to Philo Judaeus*, 2nd edn, Oxford: Blackwell.

4, Herennius (*c*.AD 70–*c*.160) was a Greek historian of Phoenicia from Byblos. EUSEBIUS preserved a considerable amount of his history by quoting it in his *Prepara-*

tion for the Gospel. Philo gives an account of Phoenician religion which owes something to Euhemerus, accounting for the gods as being originally heroes of past times. How much of his work is derived from genuine Phoenician sources is uncertain: he claimed to have translated a considerable amount from an ancient Phoenician author named Sanchuniathon, and some of his work is in agreement with material found in texts from Ugarit. He also wrote on grammar and synonyms, on cities, on bibliography, and a work on the reign of the emperor HADRIAN.

Philodemus (*c*.110–*c*.37 BC) was a Greek poet and Epicurean philosopher from Gadara in Syria, educated at Athens, who *c*.75 moved to Italy where he enjoyed the friendship and protection of the Piso family. He passed much time in a villa at Herculaneum probably owned by PISO (6) Caesoninus, and there taught and wrote about Greek literature and philosophy: his library of some 1,200 papyrus scrolls, preserved by a lucky chance, has been discovered there. His poems are of erotic character, and some thirty-five are preserved in the *Greek Anthology*; they were admired by CICERO (1) and imitated or alluded to by HORACE, VIRGIL, PROPERTIUS and OVID. In old age he was associated with a group of young men around the Epicurean Siro, namely Virgil, Horace, Plotius Tucca, VARIUS Rufus, and VARUS. He composed books for the Piso family on philosophy and the history of philosophy. He also wrote works of literary criticism, psychology and aesthetics, and elaborated a theory of art which bypassed moral philosophy and logic. His prose works did not survive antiquity, but now, rediscovered in the villa, they are being slowly deciphered despite their charred and damaged state. See J. Annas (1992) *Hellenistic Philosophy of Mind*, Berkeley: University of California Press; M. Gigante (1995) *Philodemus in Italy*, Ann Arbor: University of Michigan Press; D. Obbink (1995) *Philodemus and Poetry: Poetic Theory and Practice*, Oxford: Oxford University Press.

Philopappus (C2 AD) was a Commagenian prince of Seleucid descent whose name was Gaius Julius Antiochus Epiphanes: the title *Philopappus* ('loving his grandfather') refers to his grandfather ANTIOCHUS (15) IV, the last king of independent Commagene. Suffect consul at Rome in AD 109, he settled at Athens, where he was a citizen and was elected archon: as a benefactor of his adopted city he was allowed to build a splendid memorial, still visible, on Museum Hill.

Philopoemen (*c*.253–182 BC) was a general and statesman of the Achaean Confederacy, the son of Craugis of Megalopolis in Arcadia. In 223 he took part in the defence of Megalopolis when it was attacked by King Cleomenes III of Sparta. After playing a major role in the battle of Sellasia in 222 he went to Crete, where he became captain of a force of mercenary soldiers. He returned to the Peloponnese *c*.209 and was elected cavalry commander of the Achaean Confederacy and 'general', the title of the chief magistrate, for the following two years: during this time he reformed the army. He led the Achaeans successfully at the battle of Mantinea against Sparta in 207, when he overthrew the tyrant Machanidas. From 202 to 199 he opposed the Spartan king NABIS, first as a citizen and later as general, joining forces with the Romans to do so; but he then returned to Crete for six years. In 193, after the Romans had withdrawn, he began a further period as general and, after the assassination of Nabis, he brought Sparta into the Confederacy despite the opposition of the Roman general FLAMININUS. In 191 he annexed Messene and Elis to the Confederacy, and was general from 191 to 188, when he annulled the constitution, destroyed the walls, and abolished the military system of Sparta. He did this despite the opposition of the Roman Senate, whose right to oversee the Confederacy Philopoemen consistently rejected. He held office for two further years, 187–6 and 183–2, and during the last he was captured in the rebellion of Messene, and killed by poison. POLYBIUS the historian, who wrote a lost biography of him, played a leading part in his funeral. Philopoemen was the last great independent statesman of Greece. Effectively, his heir as leader of the Confederacy was CALLICRATES, who, however, yielded to Roman authority.

Philostratus, Lucius Flavius (died *c.*AD 245), was a Greek biographer; his family originated from Lemnos, though he lived mostly in Athens. The empress JULIA (10) Domna asked him to write for her the life of APOLLONIUS (4) of Tyana. He also wrote biographies of Sophists (providing useful information about the 'Second Sophistic') and probably works entitled *Athletic Training*, *Erotic Letters* and *Hero-cults*, this last being a dialogue on the heroes of the Trojan War. These works are extant. Two other members of the family of Philostratus wrote surviving works which describe paintings, both of which are named *Pictures*.

Phraates 1. IV (reigned *c.*38–2 BC) murdered his father ORODES II and a large number of noblemen to gain the throne of Parthia. In 36 his general Monaeses beat off an invasion of Media Atropatene by a Roman army under ANTONIUS (7), inflicting heavy losses on the retreating Romans in Armenia. His position as king was endangered from 31 by the claim of TIRIDATES (1), who drove him off the throne: Phraates retaliated the next year, however, though Tiridates captured one of his sons, whom he took into exile in Syria. In 26 Tiridates again invaded Parthia with Roman connivance, but was finally expelled in May 25. Phraates had promised to restore the Roman standards and prisoners taken in 53 from CRASSUS (3) at the battle of Carrhae (Harran) in return for Roman assistance in the civil war (which had not been forthcoming). In 20, in response to a show of Roman force by TIBERIUS in Armenia, Phraates returned the standards and prisoners, and regained his son who had been a hostage of the Romans since 31. He later sent four sons to Rome; whether for their safety or as hostages is uncertain. He was assassinated in a palace plot led by his wife Musa, a former slave given him by AUGUSTUS, in favour of her son, PHRAATES (2) V.

2. V (reigned BC 2–AD 4) was a king of Parthia, also known as Phraataces, the son of PHRAATES (1) by the Italian former slave Musa, who killed her husband to gain the throne for her son. He began by being tough with the Romans by expelling Artavasdes, the appointee of AUGUSTUS to the throne of the buffer state of Armenia, and replacing him with his own nominee TIGRANES (3) IV. In 1 BC Augustus sent his adopted son Gaius CAESAR (3) with a strong force; Phraates agreed to meet him on the Euphrates and made a treaty giving Rome a free hand in Armenia. In AD 2 he married his mother, and was deposed in AD 4 by the Parthian nobles, who installed Orodes III as king. A succession of short-lived reigns ensued.

Pilate, Pontius (C1 AD), was the equestrian prefect of Judaea from AD 26 to 36 under TIBERIUS. He showed insensitivity to Jewish feelings by introducing into Jerusalem images of the emperor on the military standards, and Tiberius ordered him to remove from his residence shields depicting human images: he used excessive violence in suppressing the riots brought about by these provocations. He used troops against Jews protesting against the use of Temple monies to build an aqueduct. His part in the trial of JESUS in 36 is hard to assess from the conflicting evidence of the *Gospels*, though elements of the normal Roman trial procedure are preserved by the version given in the *Gospel of John*. Late in 36 he was arrested by VITELLIUS (2), governor of Syria, and sent to Rome for trial for his massacre of Samaritans on their holy Mount Gerizim. He reached Rome in 37 after Tiberius' death. His further history is unknown. See G.A. Williamson (1981) *Josephus: The Jewish War*, rev. E.M. Smallwood, Harmondsworth: Penguin.

Piso 1, Gaius Calpurnius (consul 67 BC), although himself acquitted of electoral bribery before his election as praetor in 72, passed a law together with his colleague in the consulship, GLABRIO (3), against such corruption, and for such behaviour disqualified the Pompeian Lollius PALICANUS from standing for the consulship. He was inimical to POMPEIUS (2) and opposed Pompeius' adherents, the tribunes GABINIUS (2), MANILIUS (1) and CORNELIUS (1). He governed both provinces of Gaul as proconsul from 66 to 64 and subdued the Allobroges. He also intervened in Transpadane Gaul to check trouble there, for which he was later prosecuted by CAESAR (1) and successfully defended by CICERO (1). He supported the latter in his consulship against the conspiracy of CATILINE, but is not heard of after 59.

2, Gaius Calpurnius (died AD 65), was the ineffectual leader of a conspiracy against NERO (1). CALIGULA, who took a fancy to his wife Livia Orestilla and forced her to leave him, banished him *c.*40, after accusing him of committing adultery with her. CLAUDIUS (1) made him a suffect consul. A fine orator and a very rich man, he was very popular for assisting all manner of people, and was considered courteous and affable. He was the proposed replacement for Nero in the plot of 65, which included many senators and the joint commander of the Praetorian Guard, Faenius Rufus. When it was betrayed, he committed suicide.

3, Gnaeus Calpurnius (C1 BC), having served under POMPEIUS (2) in 49, joined the republican cause in Africa. He supported the assassins of CAESAR (1) in 44, obtained a pardon, but left public life until AUGUSTUS nominated him as his colleague in the consulship for 23: his acceptance marked acquiescence in the regime he and his like had hitherto spurned. He was entrusted with important state papers on finance and military dispositions during Augustus' illness that spring.

4, Gnaeus Calpurnius (died AD 20), the son of PISO (3), was consul in AD 7, and governed eastern Spain and Africa, the latter as proconsul. He had an affinity with TIBERIUS, his friend and colleague in the consulship, with his critical, independent temperament and republican sympathies. The emperor appointed him to govern Syria in AD 17 when GERMANICUS was making his eastern tour of duty, to assist the young heir to the principate on his journey. Germanicus reached Syria in 19 and quickly quarrelled with him for changing some arrangements. He then broke off relations with him and ordered him to leave the province. Shortly after this Germanicus fell ill and died: his wife and friends claimed that Piso had poisoned him, and there was much popular indignation against Piso and his wife PLANCINA. The next year the Senate tried Piso for conspiring to kill Germanicus: he rebutted the accusation but was found guilty of re-entering his province by force, and took his own life.

5, Lucius Calpurnius, known as *Frugi* (C2 BC), was tribune in 149 when he passed a law establishing the first senatorial standing committee (*quaestio*) to judge cases of extortion of property from provincials by Roman governors. In his consulship in 133 he fought against the slaves in Sicily and was censor in 120. He wrote a history of Rome to his own time in seven books in annalistic form, which were used as a reliable source by later historians. GELLIUS (1) admired the work and quotes from it the only major surviving fragment. Piso was deeply aware of the decline in Roman morals in tune with the teachings of CATO (4) the Censor, whom he must have heard in his youth. His extra name, meaning 'honest' became hereditary.

6, Lucius Calpurnius, known as Caesoninus (died *c.*33 BC) His daughter married CAESAR (1) in 59; swiftly promoted thereby to be consul in 58 BC with GABINIUS (2), he supported CLODIUS' attack on CICERO (1). He governed Macedonia as proconsul from 57 to 55 thanks to a law proposed by Clodius. Cicero spoke vehemently and dishonestly in the Senate against Piso's conduct in his governorship, first in the speech *The Consular Provinces* and, after Piso's return, *Against Piso*. Piso defended himself in the Senate and the case was never brought to trial. Though reluctant, he was elected censor for 50 and worked to prevent the civil war between Caesar and the Pompeians, striving to mitigate the hostility of his colleague CLAUDIUS (8) towards Caesar. After this he dropped out of public life and devoted himself to Epicurean philosophy with the help of PHILODEMUS, whom he lodged in his seaside villa at Herculaneum where his library has been discovered. After Caesar's assassination he tried once more to prevent civil war, serving on an embassy from the Senate to ANTONIUS (7). There is evidence that he lived until at least 33.

7, Lucius Calpurnius (48 BC–AD 32), son of PISO (6), was a patron of literature. He was consul in 15 BC and governed the province of Galatia as the emperor's legate; from there he was dispatched *c.*13 BC with his army to Thrace to put down an insurrection, which he achieved in three years and for which he was awarded triumphal decorations. He was subsequently sent to govern Asia as proconsul, and perhaps Syria later. At some time before the death of AUGUSTUS he was appointed prefect of the city of Rome, the first of many such imperial prefects, a post he held for twenty years until his death. A man of great culture, he knew the poet HORACE, who dedicated his poem *The Art of Poetry* to his two sons. He also acted as patron of the poet ANTIPATER (4) of Thessalonica.

8, Lucius Calpurnius (died AD 24), was the younger brother of PISO (4), called the Augur to distinguish him from PISO (7). He was consul in 1 BC and then governor of Asia. TACITUS (1) reports that in AD 16, because of his quarrel with URGULANIA, a friend of LIVIA (3), whom he prosecuted for a debt, he spoke in the Senate against the corruption of the courts and threatened to leave public life: the emperor TIBERIUS saved the situation by settling the debt. In 20 he defended his brother against the charge of murdering GERMANICUS; he was accused of treason in 24 but died before the trial opened.

9. Frugi Licinianus, Lucius Calpurnius (AD 38–69), was a son of Marcus Crassus Frugi. His eldest brother, Cn. Pompeius Magnus, married Antonia, daughter of the emperor CLAUDIUS (1), who had him executed in 46. Another brother, Marcus Crassus, was compelled to commit suicide by NERO (1). GALBA (1) recalled Piso from exile to make him his heir and partner and adopted him in January 69: both were killed in the forum five days later. He left a wife, Verania, known to PLINY (2) the Younger.

10, Calpurnius (C2 AD), was a poet known to PLINY (2) the Younger. He wrote a lost poem in elegiacs on the *Constellations*. It is likely that he was the consul of AD 111.

11. Frugi, Marcus Pupius (early C1 BC), was originally Calpurnius Piso, but was adopted by the elderly Marcus Pupius. He married the widow of CINNA (1), but in 83 as quaestor went over to SULLA (2) and divorced his wife. He was a clever speaker and a friend of CICERO (1). He governed Spain as proconsul from 71 to 69 and gained a triumph. Between 67 and 62 he served POMPEIUS (2) in a military role as legate, and received the consulship for 61, in which he disappointed his leader. He failed in his attempt to win senatorial approval for Pompeius' settlement of the east, was friendly to CLODIUS and thereby annoyed Cicero, especially as he slighted him in calling his relative PISO (1) to speak first in the Senate. In revenge, Cicero thwarted his wish to govern Syria. He seems to have died soon after.

Plancina, Munatia (died AD 33), was a daughter of PLANCUS (1) and wife of PISO (4), governor of Syria in AD 19 when GERMANICUS and AGRIPPINA (2) returned from Egypt: Germanicus died in October at Antioch in Piso's province and Agrippina accused Piso of poisoning her husband. In 20, after a trial, her husband was compelled to kill himself, but Plancina was spared through the intervention of her friend the dowager empress LIVIA (2). She was again accused in 33 after Livia's death, and committed suicide.

Plancius, Gnaeus (C1 BC), was the son of an equestrian tax-collector from Atina. He was quaestor in Macedonia in 58 BC when he assisted CICERO (1) during his exile. He was prosecuted for electoral bribery after his election as curule aedile for 54. Cicero and HORTENSIUS (2) both defended him: Cicero's speech (*For Plancius*) is extant. In the civil war he fought on POMPEIUS (2)'s side and failed to obtain a pardon from CAESAR (1) in spite of entreating Cicero's help.

Plancus 1, Lucius Munatius (C1 BC), was of senatorial family, which came originally from Tibur, and he served under CAESAR (1) in Gaul and later. He governed the newly conquered 'Comata' province of Gaul as proconsul from 44 to 42, founded the colonies of Lyons and Augst (near Basel) and invaded Raetia. Despite protestations of loyalty to the Republic made in his correspondence with CICERO (1), he deserted Decimus BRUTUS (2) for ANTONIUS (7) and LEPIDUS (4). In the proscriptions of 43 he did not prevent his own brother L. Plotius Plancus from being condemned and killed. He held a triumph for his Gallic victory in December 43 and was consul in 42 with Lepidus as his colleague: he then restored the temple of Saturn with cash raised from his booty. In the war of Perusia in 40 he commanded a force for Antonius but let down ANTONIUS (4) and, deserting his men, fled with FULVIA to Greece to join her husband Antonius. Antonius appointed him governor of Asia from 40 to 37 (he abandoned his post and fled during the invasion of Pacorus) and, in 35, during his campaign against the Parthians, governor of Syria as his deputy. He had a change of mind in 32 before the Actium campaign and, though he had earlier fawned on CLEOPATRA (4), claimed to find her participation in the war unacceptable: he fled to Octavian (AUGUSTUS) with his nephew Marcus TITIUS. He was welcomed: he revealed that Antonius had deposited his will with the Vestal Virgins, and in 27 was allowed to propose for Octavian the new title *Augustus*. He was censor in 22 with Paullus Aemilius LEPIDUS (8), but the two quarrelled and resigned quickly, achieving nothing. He was the last non-emperor to have a priestly cult, and that was in Caria. He was buried at Gaeta where he had built a mausoleum: the inscription is extant. He wrote elegantly to CICERO (1), HORACE addressed him in an ode (1, 7), but POLLIO (1) hated him. He left a son, Lucius, and a daughter, PLANCINA.

2, Titus Munatius, known as Bursa (C1 BC), was a close relative, perhaps brother, of PLANCUS (1), a supporter of CLODIUS against MILO, whom he as tribune in 52 tried to punish. He helped POMPEIUS (2) to delay the holding of elections. After he left office he was prosecuted by CICERO

(1) for assault and condemned to exile despite Pompeius' help. CAESAR (1) gave him support during this time and restored him in 49. In 43 he fought on the side of ANTONIUS (7) at Mutina but was expelled from Pollentia by AQUILA.

Plautianus, Gaius Fulvius (died AD 205), from Lepcis Magna, was a kinsman of Septimius SEVERUS (1). He was appointed prefect of the Praetorian Guard in 196 after serving as commander of the city police (*vigiles*). A close associate of the emperor, he was his companion (*comes*) on his campaigns, and his daughter Fulvia Plautilla married the emperor's son CARACALLA in 202. He was made a senator and in 203 held the consulship. However, Caracalla soon became disillusioned with his marriage and brought about his murder in 205. Fulvia was banished and in 212 executed by her husband.

Plautius 1, Aulus (died *c.*AD 65), was the conqueror of Britain and its first Roman governor. Suffect consul in 29, he was governor of Pannonia in 42 during the revolt of SCRIBONIANUS in Dalmatia, when he was steadfast in his loyalty to CLAUDIUS (1). In 43 he led the force that Claudius sent to subdue Britain, landing at Richborough and advancing to the Medway where, with the help of the legionary commander VESPASIAN, he decisively defeated the British forces under CARATACUS in a two-day battle which involved fording the river. He welcomed Claudius and arranged his triumphant entry to Camulodunum (Colchester), the capital of the Trinovantes. He conquered the whole of south-eastern Britain, made the Regni and Iceni into client kingdoms, and established a treaty with CARTIMANDUA, queen of the Brigantes. He left Britain in 47 and was awarded an ovation, the last ever given to anybody other than an emperor. He tried his wife in 57 for entertaining foreign religious beliefs, and acquitted her. See G. Webster and D.R. Dudley (1965) *The Roman Conquest of Britain*, London: Batsford; S.S. Frere (1967) *Britannia*, London, Routledge; J.G.F. Hind (1989) in *Britannia*, vol. 20, 1–21.

2. Hypsaeus, Publius (C1 BC), was a supporter of POMPEIUS (2), his quaestor in his campaigns in the east. He was a candidate for the consulship of 52 with Pompeius' support, but after the elections were postponed through the violence and corrupt practices of the candidates, he authorised an attack on the house of LEPIDUS (4) the *interrex*, whose function it was to arrange new elections. Pompeius was then elected sole consul: however, he abandoned Plautius to a charge of electoral corruption, for which he was condemned.

3. Silvanus, Marcus (C1 BC), was a tribune of the *plebs* in 89 BC who legislated with CARBO (2) to extend the citizenship to qualified Italians. This enactment was particularly useful to the Greek cities of southern Italy. He also reformed the jury system in criminal trials by changing their composition so as to be dominated by senators. Q. Varius was thus convicted under a law he had passed as tribune, which had established an equestrian court to try those accused of aiding Italian rebels.

4. Silvanus, Marcus (consul 2 BC), was the proconsul of Asia in AD 4 and 5 and governed Galatia the following year when he defeated the Isaurians. He fought under TIBERIUS in the Pannonian war and received triumphal decorations in AD 9. His daughter Urgulanilla was the first wife of CLAUDIUS (1).

5. Silvanus, Tiberius (C1 AD), was the son of L. Aelius Lamia, the consul of AD 3. He was adopted by PLAUTIUS (4) and so was known as Plautius Aelianus. He commanded a legion in the invasion of Britain under PLAUTIUS (1) and was suffect consul in 45. He was proconsul of Asia at some date in the fifties and governed Moesia as NERO (1)'s legate during much of the 60s. He secured the lower Danube frontier by moving a host of local people from the north to the south bank of the river. He lost a large number of his troops *c.*63 to CORBULO for his campaign against Parthia, yet nevertheless stopped a Sarmatian revolt, relieved the siege of Chersonesus in the Crimea, and sent a plentiful supply of grain to Rome. Recalled *c.*67, he was ignored by Nero but honoured by VESPASIAN, who gave him triumphal decorations and made him consul for 74. In 70 Vespasian appointed him to govern eastern Spain, but recalled him soon after to be city prefect. An inscription at Tibur records his career.

Plautus, Titus Maccius (*c.*254–*c.*184 BC), was a writer of comedies in Latin, perhaps from Sarsina in Umbria. He is reported to have migrated to Rome, worked at a trade in the theatre, made some money thereby, and then lost it when his business collapsed. Whatever the truth of that, he wrote verse comedies (*fabulae palliatae*) based on the now mostly lost poetic comedies of Greek New and Middle Comedy. He won huge success: his extant plays are the first substantial surviving written works in Latin and were popular enough to have been preserved entire. The metres in which he wrote his dialogues were a compromise between the Greek quantitative metrical patterns and the natural stress patterns of popular Latin speech. It is impossible to determine how many plays he wrote: twenty-one certainly genuine plays are extant (of which one is a fragment), backed by the authority of VARRO (3). There are a further thirty named plays of which we have fragments or quotations, but we cannot say, and Varro was unsure, whether these were genuine works of Plautus. GELLIUS (1) states that many of the 130 comedies he was said to have written were not authentic. Even his name is doubtful, and 'Maccius' may be a corruption of 'Maccus', the clown's name in the Atellan farces, and 'Plautus', meaning 'flat-foot' suggests a character in mime.

His technique was to adapt rather than simply translate his models, and he added much more music in the form of songs (*cantica*), rather like operatic arias, than had been usual in the New Comedy. Few of his plays can be dated, except the *Stichus*, first produced at the Plebeian Games in 200 BC, and the *Pseudolus* of 191 at the Megalensian Games when Cybele's temple was dedicated. As to which Greek plays were the sources of Plautus' plays, the prologues, which sometimes give us this information, are our best evidence. Plautus often changed a play's name, sometimes to Latinise it, and sometimes we cannot be sure what Plautus' name for a play was. The plays appealed to their Italian audiences as presenting them with a glimpse of Greek sophistication and outrageous behaviour, which would have been well outside their normal experience. Plautus also introduced Italian elements and abandoned Greek stage conventions, as he thought fit. His plays lack the refinement of characterisation and plot found in the New Comedy, and much of the humour consists of jokes and verbal tricks. Stock characters are also more prominent in his plays, and there may be an influence of the *Atellan* farces of the countryside, which were constructed around such characters.

His extant plays are *Amphitruo*, his only play to be based on myth, and for that reason considered to be from a Middle Comedy original: the character of Alcmena in it is nobly drawn; *The Donkey Play* (*Asinaria*) derived from *Onagos* by the unknown Demophilus; the *Pot of Gold* (*Aulularia*) with the brilliantly drawn portrait of a poor man, Euclio; *Bacchides*, loosely based on Menander's *Twice a Deceiver*; *The Prisoners* (*Captivi*), without a love story but genuinely moving and based on dramatic irony arising from unsuspected relationships; *Casina*, based in Diphilus' play *The Lot-drawers* (*Kleroumenoi*); *The Casket* (*Cistellaria*), produced before 201 BC, which was based on a play by Menander and lacks Plautus' characteristic humour; *The Weevil* (*Curculio*); *Epidicus*; *The Menaechmi Brothers*, a comedy of errors about twins separated in infancy, which is ambiguous about its Greek setting and contains many overtly Roman references; *The Merchant* (*Mercator*), based on *The Merchant* (*Emporos*) of Philemon; *The Boastful Soldier* (*Miles Gloriosus*), based on a play named *Alazon*, showing the humiliation of the stock character of the title; *The Ghost Story* (*Mostellaria*), probably based on one of several plays entitled *Phasma* (*The Ghost*) around a fiction of a haunted house; *The Persian* (*Persa*), about the deception of a pimp; *The Little Carthaginian* (*Poenulus*), after a Greek play *Karchedonios*, a melodramatic tale of loss and rediscovery; *Pseudolus*, after a cunning slave with a significant name; *The Rope* (*Rudens*), Plautus' most romantic play, about a shipwrecked pimp, a rescued girl, and tokens which prove her true identity as a free Athenian entitled to marry her lover; *Stichus*, derived from Menander's *Brothers*, a play with little plot, named after a slave who leads the revels in the last scene; *Three Quid* (*Trinummus*), based on Philemon's *The Treasure*, in which a venal sycophant, bought for a trifling sum, is amusingly exposed; *The Ill Humoured Man* (*Truculentus*), which Plautus himself is said to have admired along with *Pseudolus*, is a story of roguery and trickery on the part of a cynical courtesan; and finally *The Travelling-bag* (*Vidularia*), a fragmentary play derived from a Greek original, the *Schedia*, perhaps by Diphilus. TERENCE said that Plautus also wrote *The Flatterer* (*Colax*) and *Those Who Die Together* (*Commorientes*).

The continued popularity of his plays, which were regularly performed for centuries after his death, is attested by the high opinion shown by CICERO (1), VARRO (3) and others, and they were much admired and produced from the Renaissance to the seventeenth century in many parts of Europe. His influence on European drama was profound: for example, pieces such as Shakespeare's *Comedy of Errors* and many of Moliere's plays are deeply Plautine. See G.E. Duckworth (1952) *The Nature of Roman Comedy*, Princeton: Princeton University Press; W. Beare (1964) *The Roman Stage*, London: Methuen; E. Segal (1987) *Roman Laughter*, 2nd edn, Oxford: Oxford University Press; N. Slater (1987) *Plautus in Performance: The Theatre of the Mind*, Princeton: Princeton University Press.

Pleminius, Quintus (late C3 BC), was a praetorian legate put in charge of the garrison of Locri in southern Italy by SCIPIO (7) Africanus after he had retaken it in 205 BC in the Second Punic War. Pleminius plundered the city, including the temple of Persephone. He tortured and killed some Locrians and two Roman military tribunes who had protested to Scipio, when the latter held an enquiry. The next year, after the Locrians complained to the Senate, Pleminius was sent by a commission of enquiry to Rome where he died while waiting to be tried for his crimes.

Pliny 1. (*c.*AD 23–79) (Gaius Plinius Secundus) was an equestrian administrator, historian, and writer on natural phenomena from Novum Comum (Como), known as the Elder to distinguish him from his nephew PLINY (2). He served in the army in Germany for twelve years under the command and patronage of Quintus Pomponius Secundus, consul of 41, whose biography he wrote and whose last name he took. This service included a cavalry command on which experience he later based a book. He returned *c.*58 to write and to practise law, staying in the background during NERO (1)'s reign. In VESPASIAN's reign, however (he had served in Germany with TITUS), with the support of his patron MUCIANUS, he gained an appointment as procurator of Eastern Spain (*c*.71–73). Other important posts followed. Greatly respected for his learning and integrity, he was enrolled in the emperor's privy council and given the post of commander of the fleet at Misenum. He was there when Vesuvius erupted in August 79: his interest in the phenomenon and his desire to assist victims of the disaster, towards which he sailed and landed at Stabiae (Castellammare di Stabia), and his poor health (he was probably asthmatic), led to his death on the beach there from asphyxiation by fumes. His nephew wrote an account of his last hours derived from those who had been with him. He did not marry, and his heir was his sister's son, whom he had adopted, PLINY (2) the Younger.

Of his copious literary production only one work has survived, the *Natural History*, a vast encyclopaedic work in thirty-seven books dedicated to his friend the emperor Titus, on science, art, technology, medicine, agriculture, metalworking and other matters, including many interesting digressions. He was at his best when writing of the concrete and drawing upon his own experience: abstract ideas and philosophical theories were not his strength, though such material contains interesting remarks and sometimes baffling imagery. His approach to research has been proved to be somewhat offhand and careless, and his work is consequently often unreliable. He knew nothing of economics or sociology, but in the sphere in which he had knowledge he left us an invaluable account of great achievements of which we should otherwise have been ignorant. The work had a great influence in mediaeval times.

His nephew (who was amazed by his industry) reports his other, lost works: a *History of Rome from the End of Aufidius Bassus* (see BASSUS 2) in thirty-one books, published in 77 and covering *c*.AD 44–71, which TACITUS (1) may have used as a source; *Campaigns in Germany* in twenty books, written in the early 60s and used by Tacitus for his *Annals* and *Germany*; *Doubtful Diction*, in eight books, compiled in 67 when he was engaged in the law, in which he tries to reconcile analogy and anomaly; *The Student* in three books (six rolls), a collection of points eloquently made in debates destined for those learning oratory; and the two early works mentioned above, the monograph on throwing the cavalry-spear and the biography of Pomponius. See J.F. Healy (1991) *Pliny the Elder:* Natural History, *a Selection*, Harmondsworth: Penguin.

2. the Younger (AD 61–*c*.112) was a lawyer, administrator and writer, the son of Caecilius Clio, a landowner of Como, who died while Pliny was a child. He and his mother then lived with her brother (see PLINY 1) who adopted him: henceforth he was known as Gaius Plinius Caecilius Secundus. He inherited fortunes from both his father and his uncle. Having studied rhetoric under QUINTILIAN and Nicetes, he was a military tribune in Syria *c*.81 and was admitted to the Senate *c*.90 thanks to support from family friends, Verginius RUFUS (5) and Julius FRONTINUS. He was praetor *c*.93 and consul in 100; he also held important public administrative posts, Prefect of the Military Treasury *c*.94–96 and Prefect of the Treasury of Saturn *c*.98–100. A few years later he was put in charge of the management of the river Tiber. He was a distinguished advocate and led in cases regarding wills and in prosecutions of corrupt provincial governors. He married three times, but had no children, though through the good offices of Julius SERVIANUS he was granted the tax immunity of those who had three children. He was trusted by the emperor TRAJAN, who *c*.110 appointed him to a special post as governor (*legatus Augusti*) of the normally senatorial province of Bithynia, which had suffered incompetent administration. He died in this office.

His extant writings consist of *Letters* in ten books, the last being his correspondence with Trajan about his duties in Bithynia, and a *Panegyric* of the emperor Trajan delivered in the Senate on the occasion of his election to the consulship and afterwards expanded. He published the *Letters* at intervals in the first decade of the second century, and edited them carefully to make them accessible to the public and to make himself appear in the best light possible. The general effect is that of a self-conscious stylist. Though the starting point of many letters is an everyday event, Pliny will enlarge upon it, often moralising about an issue, and seeks to present the reader with a picture of the activities and experiences of a public figure, which many people would not have otherwise known of. He writes to friends who are often no more than names to us, but he publishes none of their replies, unlike the case of the correspondence of CICERO (1); his most famous correspondent was TACITUS (1), with whom he was once, to his great delight, confused at the theatre. The letters are rhetorical and somewhat mannered in style, concentrate each on a single theme, and examples, when offered, usually come in threes. The arrangement of the letters in each book is artful and deliberate. Pliny shows a liberal attitude to moral questions such as the correct treatment of slaves. He expresses the commonly felt abhorrence of DOMITIAN and his tyrannical reign. His tenth book, in which Trajan's replies are also given, is historically important and shows us the problems faced by a provincial governor operating in special circumstances. The style here is different, as Pliny could not revise the letters, which were published after his death. A long letter (10. 96) and its detailed reply are our first documents that derive from a non-Christian source about the activities of Christians and the attitude of the Roman government to them. Pliny also wrote poems in the style of his friend MARTIAL, but the few that have reached us are of poor quality. See R. Syme (1958) *Tacitus*, Oxford: Clarendon Press; G.O. Hutchinson (1988) *Latin Literature from Seneca to Juvenal*, Oxford: Clarendon Press; A.N. Sherwin-White (1966) *The Letters of Pliny*, Oxford: Clarendon Press.

Plotina (died AD 123) was the wife of the emperor TRAJAN. Born in Nîmes, she was already married to him in 98 when he took the purple. She accepted the title *Augusta* in 113. Childless, she supported the claim of HADRIAN to be her husband's successor: she arranged the supposed adoption of Hadrian by the dying Trajan at Selinus in 117. She even chose Hadrian's wife, Vibia SABINA. She was interested in Epicurean philosophy and supported the 'Garden' at Athens. On her death Hadrian commemorated her at Nîmes with a basilica.

Plotinus (AD 205–269–70) was a Greek philosopher from Lycopolis in Egypt, the founder of Neoplatonism. His life is known to us from a memoir by his pupil PORPHYRY: he began attending lectures given by AMMONIUS SACCAS at Alexandria *c*.233, and in 242 accompanied the unsuccessful expedition of GORDIAN III to Mesopotamia against Persia in the hope of learning about oriental philosophy. He went to Rome in 244, where he founded a school and taught philosophy until *c*.262 when he retired to Campania, where he died. At the age of fifty he started writing philosophical essays generated by discussions with his pupils, which Porphyry collected by subject into six groups of nine (the *Enneads*). They are difficult reading and were unrevised by Plotinus, whose eyesight was poor.

In the works of Plotinus we have the largest and most complete ancient philosophical system after that of Aristotle. His idealist philosophy is focused on the concept of the One (cf. Parmenides) which he identifies with Plato's 'Good'. All existence depends upon the One and all values derive from it. All reality may be compared by analogy with a series of concentric circles set around the One, resulting from its expansion. Each circle depends logically on the one inside it, its 'cause': matter exists on the edge of the outermost circle. There are three grades of reality, starting from the One and proceeding outwards: Mind, Soul and Nature. As you move outwards, you find lessening unity and increasing individuality. Mind contains the Platonic forms, which it perceives beyond the realm of change and time: here the known and the knower are only distinguished logically. Soul apprehends its objects of perception in a chronological sequence and as distinct from each other. Nature resembles the World-soul of the Stoics: the perceived physical world is, according to Plotinus, a faint dream perceived by Nature. Man may momentarily attain 'ecstasy' and union with the One by a supreme effort of intellectual activity. It is here that Plotinus shows affinity with oriental mysticism. He also contributed in important ways to psychology in the areas of memory, perception and consciousness; to aesthetics, and to ethics. He makes no mention of Christianity, though later Christian thinkers used his ideas. He was opposed to Gnosticism. See R.T. Wallis (1972) *Neoplatonism*, London: Duckworth; J.M. Rist (1967) *Plotinus: The Road to Reality*, Cambridge: Cambridge University Press; A.H. Armstrong (1940) *The Architecture of the Intelligible Universe in the Philosophy of Plotinus*, Cambridge: Cambridge University Press.

Plutarch (*c.*AD 46–*c.*121) was a Greek biographer and moral philosopher from Chaeronea in Boeotia, where he lived most of his life, though he travelled as far as Egypt. In the reign of DOMITIAN he lectured on philosophy in Rome and acquired influential friends there, his patron the ex-consul L. Mestrius Florus, whose name he took on acquiring Roman citizenship as L. Mestrius Plutarchus, C. Minicius FUNDANUS, Q. Sosius SENECIO, and the Syrian-Athenian PHILOPAPPUS: like Philopappus he was a lover of Athens. He was appointed *c.*90 to be a priest of the shrine at Delphi, whose influence he enhanced, and he was later commemorated there with a bust dedicated by the Delphians and Chaeroneans. He was a pious believer in the gods and in the collaboration between Rome and her teacher Greece. He may have held a procuratorship in Achaea, though the evidence for this is weak. Towards the end of his life he was a magistrate at Chaeronea.

Plutarch was a prolific writer and produced over 200 books. Of these, most of the biographies and many miscellaneous works survive: fifty *Lives* consisting of twenty-three pairs of 'parallel' lives of famous Greeks and Romans such as Alexander and CAESAR (1), Theseus and Romulus, including nineteen 'comparisons', and four other lives including those of two emperors, GALBA (1) and OTHO. These biographies are not straightforward accounts of men's lives on historical lines: they were written with a moral purpose, to present useful patterns of behaviour for readers to follow, or examples of what to avoid. Plutarch is keen to record certain features of his subjects' lives, their education, entry into public life, points of climax, changes of fortune, and later years. He was glad to introduce anecdotes, especially those with the effect of revealing character. Consequently, the usefulness of the *Lives* for historians is limited.

The rest of his works, loosely entitled *Moralia* or *Moral Essays*, are very mixed in subject-matter: there are rhetorical eulogies of great cities and pleas for good behaviour; there is advice for the young, advice on marriage, and a consolation written for his wife on their daughter's death. He wrote nine books of witty and learned *Table Talk*. He was a Platonist, though his manner of composition can appear more Aristotelian: his dialogues tend to long speeches and he is often himself a participant. He was interested in prophecy, and set four dialogues, in which he expounds his philosophical and religious views, in Delphi. His aim appears to have been to reconcile Plato's monotheism with the traditional Greek cults to which he was devoted. Though he was well versed in Roman history, his knowledge of Latin may have been weak and he shows little acquaintance with Latin literature. He wrote essays critical of Stoic and Epicurean philosophy. In *Herodotus' Spitefulness* he attacked the historian for his hostile account of Thebes in the Persian Wars. Several spurious works were included in his collected works, and some of these are important in their own right: on education, on fate in Platonic thought, and on music. He has always been a popular writer, with a graceful, flowing style, and he greatly appealed to Byzantine teachers. He was influential on Montaigne and Francis Bacon and was an important source of plots for Shakespeare. He was translated into French by Amyot in the sixteenth century, and a little later into English. See C.P. Jones (1971) *Plutarch and Rome*, Oxford: Clarendon Press; D.A. Russell (1973) *Plutarch*, London: Duckworth. Many of Plutarch's works are translated in the Penguin Classics series.

Polemo 1. (reigned 37–8 BC) was a king of Pontus and the Crimea, the son of Zeno, a rich rhetorician of Laodicea on the Lycus in the province of Asia. He appears to have gained Roman support and citizenship by leading (with his father) the defence of the city against the Parthian invasion of 40 BC. ANTONIUS (7) appointed him prefect (governor) of part of Cilicia and Lycaonia in 39, but in 37 ceded it to CLEOPATRA (4) and sent him instead to rule Pontus as its king. He accompanied Antonius on his expedition via Armenia against Parthia in 36 and was captured: he was ransomed and in 35 he assisted at the negotiations between Antonius and his former captor ARTAVASDES (2) of Media Atropatene (Azerbaijan). In 34 Antonius added Lesser Armenia to his kingdom, which he lost, however, in 31 after supporting Antonius in the Actium campaign. Octavian (AUGUSTUS) allowed him to keep Pontus and added the Bosporan kingdom (Crimea), which AGRIPPA (1) helped him to seize. He was killed in 8 BC by rebels in the Crimea and succeeded in Pontus by his widow, Pythodoris. His son was ARTAXIAS (2).

2, Marcus Antonius (*c.*AD 88–144), was a sophist and physiognomist from Laodicea distantly related to POLEMO (1): in 130 he was selected to deliver the opening speech of HADRIAN's temple of Olympian Zeus at Athens. He published speeches of which two are extant, imaginary pleas delivered by the fathers of two heroes of the battle of Marathon asking for their sons to be awarded a prize for valour. He also published a work on physiognomy known from translations into Latin and Arabic.

Pollio 1, Gaius Asinius (76 BC–AD 5), was a politician, historian and literary figure. In his life, which spanned the late republic and early principate, he knew Rome's greatest writers and statesmen. CATULLUS (1) praised him in poem 12. He knew Cornelius GALLUS (4), who was on his staff in 41 when he rescued VIRGIL's farm from confiscation while he was settling veterans in northern Italy as ANTONIUS (7)'s legate. HORACE wrote him an ode (2. 1) in which he contrasted Pollio's serious historical writing with his own playful verse. He himself, in the last decade of the republic, had written tragedies based on myth. Virgil addressed his fourth *Eclogue* to him. There is, however, some dispute as to how far he was Virgil's patron. He founded Rome's first public library from the booty he won in Illyria. He criticised the writings of CICERO (1), whose style and character he had found objectionable, and of CAESAR (1); he found fault with SALLUST's antiquated style, and accused LIVY of 'paduanity'. He was the first Roman writer to hold recitals at which he read aloud his works. He was also a powerful orator in the plain Atticist style, and a poet; but his style was harsh, outdated and graceless, and his oratory was contrasted with that of MESSALLA (4).

Son of a landowner in the territory of the Marrucini on the Adriatic coast due east of Rome, he occupied Sicily for Caesar in 48, and after a praetorship in 45 held a command in Spain in 44–3; he joined Antonius after Caesar's murder. He was consul in 40, when he actively promoted the treaty of Brundisium between Antonius and Octavian. The following year, as governor of Macedonia, he fought in Illyria against the Parthini, for which he won a triumph. He then went into retirement and wrote an account of the Civil Wars (*Historiae*) from 60 to 42 (the battle of Philippi) in seventeen books, which was used as a source by later historians including PLUTARCH and APPIAN. None of his work has survived. His son was Asinius GALLUS (2).

2, Publius Vedius (died 15 BC), was the son of a freedman from Beneventum. He amassed a large fortune, gaining equestrian status and serving AUGUSTUS in the province of Asia; he had a reputation for cruelty, punishing slaves by throwing them to his moray eels. He left much of his property to the emperor, whose friendship he enjoyed, including his villa Pausilypon (Posilipo on the ridge between Puteoli and Naples) and his house in Rome, which Augustus demolished to build the Arcade of Livia.

Polyaenus (C2 AD) was a Macedonian rhetorician who wrote an extant work on military practice entitled *Strategems* that he dedicated to MARCUS AURELIUS and Lucius VERUS. His purpose was to help them plan their campaign against the Parthians (AD 162–6). It is a strange mixture of fact and fiction, but the main purpose is didactic and examples of military successes are taken from Greek and Roman history. It shows signs of the haste with which it was compiled.

Polybius (*c*.200–*c*.118 BC) was a Greek historian of Rome. He was the son of LYCORTAS of Megalopolis, and in 180 carried the ashes of PHILOPOEMEN to burial. Hence in his youth he was at the centre of the politics of the Achaean Confederacy, in which he quickly rose to prominence: he was sent to Alexandria as an envoy in 180, and ten years later was elected hipparch ('master of the horse') of the Confederacy. After the Roman victory over Macedonia in 168 at Pydna, Polybius was one of a thousand Achaean noblemen deported to Italy for having failed to assist Aemilius PAULLUS (2). Whereas the other captives were scattered throughout Etruria, Polybius was kept in Rome and befriended by SCIPIO (11) Aemilianus (the son of Paullus) and became attached to the 'Scipionic Circle'. Scipio took him in 151 to Spain and Africa, where he met MASINISSA. In 150 the hostages were released, and in 146 he was again in Africa and witnessed the destruction of Carthage. He took part in a voyage of exploration on the Atlantic and then returned to Greece where he helped the Romans to organise the province of Macedonia. He subsequently visited Alexandria and Sardis. In 133 he was present at the siege and fall of Numantia.

Most of his writings are lost, including his biography of Philopoemen, a book on military tactics, an account of the siege of Numantia, and a treatise on the equatorial region of the earth. Substantial parts of his *Histories* (in forty books) survive, however, including the whole of books 1–5. The work covered the period 220–168 and set out to show how Rome conquered so much of the known world in so short a time, and the nature of her constitution. There is an introductory section from the First Punic War, the end of Timaeus'

History in 264–220, and the first thirty books were published *c.*150. He later added ten more books to continue the period to 146 and included, in book 34, a geographical conspectus. Some books are entirely lost, some are known from epitomes, and there exist quotations of others of varying lengths. His method involved a temporal progression by Olympiads, and a geographical progression from west to east in four blocks (Rome and the west, Greece and Macedonia, Asia, and Egypt). His approach was pragmatic, and he used carefully collected and assessed primary evidence, interviewing eyewitnesses, visiting sites of important actions, studying public and private records; he had access to Roman official documents through his association with Scipio. He was particularly interested in political and military history, and described the Roman constitution as a mixture of monarchic, oligarchic and democratic features. He was keen to account for actions by determining their causes in the broadest way. Not without bias himself, he criticised other historians for their bias and inaccuracy; however, he was a writer of integrity who strove to record faithfully what was actually done and said. He was used as a source by LIVY. See F.W. Walbank (1972) *Polybius*, Berkeley: University of California Press; S. Hornblower (ed.) (1994) *Greek Historiography*, Oxford: Clarendon Press.

Polycarp (*c.*AD 70–*c.*155) was a Christian bishop of Smyrna and a correspondent of IGNATIUS. He wrote a *Letter to the Philippians*, which is extant, warning its readers against the sin of apostasy: some consider it on internal grounds to be a conflation of two letters. In about 154 he visited the Roman Church to persuade its members that Easter should be celebrated at the time of the Jewish Passover, as was the custom in Asia. He is said to have been arrested a year later at a religious festival and burnt to death for refusing to renounce Christianity: an extant but interpolated letter from the church of Smyrna to that of Philomelium in Phrygia describes his death. See W.H.C. Frend (1965) *Martyrdom and Persecution in the Early Church*, Oxford: Blackwell.

Pompeia 1. (married 67 BC) was a granddaughter of SULLA (2) and of Q. Pompeius Rufus, and was the second wife of CAESAR (1). Caesar recognised her noncomplicity in the scandal of the Good Goddess festival in 62, but nevertheless divorced her, declaring that Caesar's wife must be above suspicion.

2. *See* PLOTINA.

Pompeius 1, Quintus (consul 141 BC), was a politician and 'new man' of obscure background who was a client of SCIPIO (11) Aemilianus but gained the consulship by the strength of his oratory and probably against Scipio's will. He took command at the siege of Numantia in Spain, where he held his predecessor METELLUS (4) Macedonicus responsible for his failure: however, he negotiated a treaty with the Numantines in 140 that he repudiated when his successor arrived, with the Senate's approval. Metellus, his enemy, prosecuted him unsuccessfully for extortion, and in 136 both men served as legates under Lucius FURIUS (2) Philus in Spain. In 131 they were again associated in the censorship. Pompeius took the lead in opposing the reforms of Tiberius GRACCHUS (4).

2. Magnus, Gnaeus (106–48 BC), is known in English as Pompey. A general and politician from Picenum, and a great-nephew of LUCILIUS (1), he served under his father, the consul POMPEIUS (5) Strabo, at the siege of Asculum in 89 in the Social War and took part in his triumph. Charged with illegal possession of booty, he was defended by leading advocates including Antistius, whose daughter he married. In 86 he met the Stoic POSIDONIUS on his visit to Rome, who had a profound influence on him. He was a legate in the army of CINNA (2) in 84, which mutinied and killed Cinna. In spring 83 he chose to join the rising star of SULLA (2) and lent him valuable support with a private army of three legions of his Picentine clients. In 82 he supported METELLUS (7) Pius in a campaign in Gaul and northern Italy against Marian supporters; he then turned south to assist Sulla by besieging CARRINAS in Spoleto. Though he let the latter go, Pompeius ambushed a large force under Censorinus, and shortly afterwards massacred the army that the consul CARBO (5) had abandoned at Clusium when he fled. He reached Rome soon after the battle of the Colline Gate and was persuaded by Sulla to divorce the now-orphaned Antistia and marry his own stepdaughter, Aemilia, already pregnant by her present husband.

There was a severe food shortage in Rome in 82, and Sulla made haste to liberate the main sources of grain: he sent Pompeius to recover Sicily and Africa. With the rank of propraetor and with an army of six legions, he sailed for Sicily and caught Carbo near Lilybaeum: he interrogated and executed him despite his having thrice been consul and having defended Pompeius at his trial in 87. Then in a forty-day campaign he destroyed a large Marian force under AHENOBARBUS (3) near Utica, and with the help of BOGUD drove King Iarbas out of Numidia, replacing him with HIEMPSAL (2). Despite the disapproval of Sulla, Pompeius, not yet a senator, held a triumph in March 81 and adopted the *cognomen* Magnus, 'the Great' in imitation of Alexander the Great: he was, however, called 'The Young Butcher' by Helvius for his enthusiasm in slaughtering his fellow-citizens. Aemilia having died in childbirth, Pompeius took MUCIA TERTIA, the daughter of SCAEVOLA (4), as his third wife (the mother of his three children) in 80. In 79 he again offended Sulla by his outspoken support of the candidacy of LEPIDUS (2) for the consulship of 78. In 77, when Lepidus 'went off the rails', Pompeius was awarded a special command by the Senate to deal with him by force. He killed BRUTUS (4) at Regium (Reggio Emilia), and by defeating Lepidus at Cosa forced him to sail to Sardinia, where he died. Later in the year Pompeius was sent to Spain with proconsular powers as governor of the Hither or Eastern province to assist METELLUS (6) Pius against SERTORIUS. The latter foiled Pompeius' attempt to join up with Metellus by defeating him at the battle of Lauro (76) but the next year Pompeius heavily defeated an enemy army near Valentia, took the city, and formed a link with Metellus in the south. His life was endangered in a defeat on the Sucro, and a battle near the Turia was inconclusive. Pompeius showed his mettle by hanging on despite adversity, and his strategy of attrition eventually succeeded with the murder of Sertorius in 73. He took a further year of tough campaigning to subdue PERPERNA (3), the last Marian leader.

On his return to Italy in spring 71 he gave support to CRASSUS (3) in mopping up the followers of SPARTACUS, and gained his support for his extraordinary bid for the consulship of 70 with Crassus as his colleague. Although he was too young, not yet a senator, and had not held the qualifying posts, his reputation and widespread support among the equestrians and the people won him the office and a second triumph, held jointly with Metellus. He and Crassus then legislated to reverse Sulla's revision of the tribunes' powers and restore the censorship. He stayed in Rome until 67, when the law of GABINIUS (2) gave him a special and overriding command against the pirates for three years, a task which he accomplished in three months: he then stayed in the east consolidating his work. In 66 a further task was assigned to him by a special law passed by MANILIUS (1): to finish the war against MITHRIDATES (3) VI with command of a province which included Bithynia, Pontus and Cilicia, and overriding powers in the whole of Asia Minor.

Displacing the unhappy LUCULLUS (2), he made a pact with Phraates III, the Parthian king, and sent Mithridates an ultimatum, which was rejected. He besieged the king's forces at Dasteira (Nicopolis) and after he broke out, ambushed and defeated him, so that Mithridates fled to the Crimea. Pompeius next invaded Armenia and imposed a fine of 6,000 talents on King TIGRANES (1) II; he also deprived him of his possessions in Asia Minor. He left AFRANIUS (2) in charge of Armenia and first settled the affairs of the Caucasus and wintered at Amisus. During 64 he blockaded Mithridates in the Crimea and then turned his attention to the rump of the Seleucid empire in Syria, where he created a new province and settled the dispute between the brothers ARISTOBULUS (2) and HYRCANUS (2) for control of Judaea, installing the latter as ruling high priest after a three-month siege of Jerusalem (63), but stripping Judaea of its non-Jewish territories.

After spending the winter of 63–2 in organising the new eastern provinces, Pompeius returned to Rome, triumphed, and disbanded his army. Though he had doubled the provincial revenues, he lacked support for his much needed legislation to give his veterans land and to ratify his settlement of the east. The conservative majority in the Senate distrusted him and CATO (5) worked hard to obstruct him. He divorced Mucia for adultery with CAESAR (1), but in 60 the latter came to his rescue, reconciled him with Crassus, and formed the unofficial pact known as the 'first triumvirate'. In 59 Caesar was consul and Pompeius married his daughter JULIA (4) in a love-match despite a thirty-year difference of age. Caesar saw to the passing of Pompeius' legislation. But Pompeius had lost his popularity (there appears to have been an unsuccessful plot to kill him) and CLODIUS was a thorn in his flesh. In 57 he secured appointment to manage the supply of grain for five years with the powers of a proconsul. He also assisted CICERO (1)'s return from exile. During two years of political inactivity (59–8), Pompeius had encouraged a circle of writers and artists, and concerned himself with the construction and decoration of his new theatre in the Campus Martius. He met Caesar and Crassus at Lucca in spring 56 when they agreed to continue their alliance for five more years: he and Crassus were designated consuls for 55, and he was to govern both Spanish provinces for the five years. He did this through subordinate officers (legates) and himself resided at his house outside Rome. The triumvirate, however, was destroyed by two blows: the death of Julia in childbirth in 54, and Crassus' death in Mesopotamia in 53. The year 52 began in chaos without consuls, and when MILO murdered Clodius in January the Senate appointed Pompeius sole consul with powers to clean up politics. He organised Milo's trial, passed new legislation against violence and bribery and, to prevent the latter, enacted a law providing for a five-year gap between a magistracy and a governorship, and making candidates stand for election in person. These measures threatened Caesar's position, as did the extension of Pompeius' command in Spain for a further five years. Pompeius, rejecting a further marriage alliance with Caesar, now married Cornelia, the daughter of METELLUS (11) Scipio, making her father his colleague for the rest of the year. In 51 he tried to avoid offending Caesar, but others wished to recall him and precipitate his fall. An attempt in spring 50 by the tribune CURIO (2) to force both men to give up their commands simultaneously failed, and towards the end of the year the consul MARCELLUS (1), with the consuls elect, offered him the command against Caesar. In January 49 the Senate passed the 'Ultimate Decree' against the threat from Caesar. Pompeius saw that he had insufficient troops at hand to defend Italy, and in any case preferred to fight Caesar abroad, where a victory would be his rather than the

Senate's. In March he transported his troops to Macedonia and spent the summer collecting a formidable army from all the eastern provinces. In spring 48 he mauled Caesar at Dyrrhachium, but on 9 August was routed in a pitched battle at Pharsalus in Central Greece despite having superior forces. After fetching his wife from Lesbos he fled to Egypt, which he reached on 28 September: as he landed he was stabbed to death on the order of a minister of PTOLEMY (9) XIII.

The career of this determined and ambitious man had brought him great successes, but the nobility long considered him an outsider; nor could he remain a man of the people. He suffered from the problem faced by Roman conquerors of his time that once his term of office was up he lacked a role and was vulnerable to his enemies. He was a subtle general, better at strategy than tactics, and his persistence in the face of adversity was a great strength. In youth he was capable of ruthless cruelty to his enemies, but the mature man showed much humanity and led an exemplary life. His fourth and fifth marriages were very happy. He was a patron of the arts, and his theatre was a great achievement. He managed his political dealings with subtlety, and supported the Roman constitution while allowing it to be strained to breaking point for his own ends. Comparison of his career with that of AUGUSTUS is justified, and Augustus recognised an affinity with him. See J. Leach (1978) *Pompey the Great*, London: Croom Helm; R. Seager (1979) *Pompey: A Political Biography*, Oxford: Blackwell, 1979; P.A.L. Greenhalgh (1980) *Pompey: The Roman Alexander*, London: Weidenfeld & Nicolson; and (1981) *Pompey: The Republican Prince*, London: Weidenfeld & Nicolson.

3. Magnus, Gnaeus (79–45 BC), was the elder son of POMPEIUS (2) and MUCIA TERTIA. He married *c.*54 Claudia, a daughter of Appius CLAUDIUS (8) Pulcher. In 49 his father appointed him commander of a fleet of sixty Egyptian ships in the Adriatic under BIBULUS (1) to prevent CAESAR (1) from crossing with his army to Epirus, and he destroyed Caesar's transport ships before the Dyrrhachium campaign. In 47 he seized the Balearic Islands and then moved to Spain, where his brother POMPEIUS (4) and LABIENUS (2) joined him after the battle of Thapsus. He raised thirteen legions but on the arrival of Caesar was forced southwards to Munda where early in 45 he was soundly defeated and afterwards executed.

4. Magnus Pius, Sextus (*c.*67–35 BC) A general and Republican leader, the younger son of POMPEIUS (2) and MUCIA TERTIA. He joined his father's flight from Lesbos to Egypt in 48, and after his father's death he made his way to Africa and thence, after escaping after the battle of Thapsus in 46, to Spain, where he held Corduba during the Munda campaign. He continued the fight, raised an army of Pompeians, and harrassed the governors of Further Spain whom CAESAR (1) appointed, Carrinas and POLLIO (1). In 44 LEPIDUS (4) reconciled him with the Senate and he moved to Massilia (Marseilles) with his forces. The next year in April the Senate appointed him admiral of the fleet, to conduct war against ANTONIUS (7), but in August he was declared outlaw by the law of PEDIUS (1): he seized Sicily, to which he conveyed many of those proscribed by the triumvirs. He instigated a blockade of Italy and in 42 drove off SALVIDIENUS RUFUS, who tried to dislodge him, and in 40 made an alliance with Antonius against Octavian (AUGUSTUS). His lieutenant the ex-pirate MENODORUS seized Sardinia and warned Pompeius against Antonius, but at Misenum in 39 Pompeius made a pact with the triumvirs by which he was to keep Sicily and Sardinia, gain Corsica and Achaea, and hold a consulship, if he guaranteed to give up his blockade of Italy. Octavian, who controlled Italy, felt most threatened by him, and in 38 accused him of breaking faith and attacked him unsuccessfully in two sea-battles, near Cumae and off Messana. In 36 AGRIPPA (1) defeated him at Mylae, but he beat Octavian at Tauromenium (Taormina). Lepidus invaded Sicily and won the battle of Naulochus. Pompeius fled with a small fleet to Asia, where he was eventually killed by the ungrateful TITIUS, whose father Pompeius had saved.

5. Strabo, Gnaeus (died 87 BC), was a general from Picenum, the father of POMPEIUS (2). He was tribune in 104 when he successfully prosecuted an ex-censor, Q. Fabius Maximus Eburnus. He was deeply involved in the Social War between Rome and her Italian allies, and brought the war to a close in the northern sector by defeating T. Lafrenius in 90, and in 89, when he was consul, by reducing Asculum in Picenum by siege. As consul he legislated to extend Latin rights to Cisalpine Gaul, and he granted citizenship to certain Spanish cavalrymen on the battlefield. He held a triumph and returned to his army. When his kinsman the ex-consul Q. Pompeius Rufus was sent by SULLA (2) to replace him, he allowed his men to murder Rufus. In 87 he received a call from the Senate to defend Rome against CINNA (2), and marched his troops to Rome, where after a brief fight he suggested to Cinna that he hold a joint consulship with him in 86. He died shortly afterwards in an epidemic, and his unpopularity was shown by the abuse of his corpse. His son inherited his large following in Picenum.
See also TROGUS.

Pomponius 1, Lucius (early C1 BC), was a Latin playwright from Bononia (Bologna), the author of at least seventy Atellan farces of which 200 lines are preserved. He may also have written satyr plays entitled *Atalante*, *Styphos* and *Ariadne*.
See also NOVIUS.

2, Sextus (C2 AD), was a lawyer, legal teacher, and writer. He wrote over 300 books, half of them commissioned by HADRIAN as a commentary, which ULPIANUS used, on the city praetor's edict, but he held no public office. His *Enchiridion* or elementary handbook on law, of which a long extract was borrowed by the compilers of Justinian's *Digests*, contained much information on the history of the Roman constitution and of the legal profession. He also wrote commentaries on SCAEVOLA (4)'s works and on SABINUS (4)'s *Civil Law*, *Letters* and *Diverse Readings*, and many books on legal cases. He may have been associated with the legal writer GAIUS. Apart from numerous extracts in the *Digests*, his work has not survived.

3. Proculus, Titus (C2 AD), was a provincial governor, related by marriage to MARCUS AURELIUS. He was promoted to patrician status before his marriage to the emperor's cousin Annia Fundania Faustina. After a suffect consulship in 151 he governed Lower Moesia and Nearer Spain and was appointed proconsul of Asia. He was deputy to the emperor in his wars on the Danube frontier, and held a full consulship in 176.

4. Secundus, Publius (died after AD 51), accused of treason in AD 31, survived seven years in prison: he governed Crete and Cyrene and held a suffect consulship in 44. While governor of Upper Germany he put down a revolt of the Chatti in 50, for which he was awarded triumphal decorations. PLINY (1) the Elder admired him and wrote his biography (lost). Secundus also wrote a lost play entitled *Aeneas*, which received a hostile reception from the audience.

Pontius *see* AQUILA, PILATE.

Poplicola 1, Publius Valerius (late C6 BC), is a shadowy figure, more legend than history, associated with the fall of the monarchy in 509 and the foundation of the republic. He was credited erroneously with establishing the right of appeal against magistrates. His reality is, however, borne out by the discovery of an inscription at Satricum of *c.*500 BC, recording a dedication to Mars by his companions.

2, Publius Valerius Potitus (C5 BC), was consul in 449 with Marcus Horatius Barbatus. LIVY (3. 55) attributes to them three laws, of which one strengthened the power of the popular assemblies by making its enactments binding on the whole people including the Senate, one upheld the right of appeal against the decisions of magistrates, and the last protected the tribunes of the *plebs* from injury. However, the first of these enactments is also attributed to PHILO (1) and to HORTENSIUS (1), both much later, and the Valerian-Horatian Law may have been less radical. The tradition of this legislation is tied up with the fall of the Second Decemvirate, the historicity of which is extremely doubtful. Equally dubious is the story that Poplicola was granted a triumph for his victories over the neighbouring Aequi and Volsci by the Popular Assembly and not by the Senate.

Poppaea Sabina (died AD 65) was the second wife of the emperor NERO (1). The daughter of Titus Ollius, she was named after her mother's father Poppaeus Sabinus, consul in AD 9. She first married Rufrius Crispinus, a prefect of the Praetorian Guard, to whom she bore a son, later killed by Nero. Her second husband was the future emperor OTHO, a close friend of Nero's, and when Nero made her his mistress in 58 he appointed Otho governor of Lusitania to be rid of him. She is reported to have urged Nero to kill his mother AGRIPPINA (3), which he accomplished in 59, and in 62 to divorce his wife OCTAVIA (3) so that he could marry her. She bore a short-lived daughter, Claudia, in 63 and received the title *Augusta*. She enabled Pompeii, her native town, to become a colony, and built herself a palace at Oplontis nearby. She assisted JOSEPHUS in his mission to free some Jewish priests in 64, but in the same year persuaded Nero to make FLORUS (1) governor of Judaea. When she was pregnant in 65, Nero is said to have given her a kick, which killed her. She was accorded divine honours.

Poppaedius Silo, Quintus (early C1 BC), was a Marsian leader and able Italian commander in the Social War between Rome and her Italian subjects. In northern Italy in 90 BC he defeated and killed Q. Servilius CAEPIO (4), and the next year the consul L. Porcius Cato. However, the other consul of 89, POMPEIUS (5) Strabo, defeated him and drove him out of Corfinium, the headquarters of the Italians. He retired south to retake Bovianum Vetus and recover his strength. In 88 he was defeated and killed by Quintus METELLUS (7) Pius. He had been a friend of M. Livius DRUSUS (2), at whose house the young Marcus CATO (5) conceived a hatred of him.

Porcia (C1 BC) was a daughter of Marcus Porcius CATO (5) who married BIBULUS (1) and, after being widowed in 48, married Marcus BRUTUS (5) in 45. A firm republican, she was a participant in the conference of CAESAR (1)'s assassins at Antium in June 44. She returned to Rome while her husband went to Greece. She committed suicide in the summer of 43 as her health failed.

Porcius 1. Latro, Marcus (late C1 BC), was a rhetorician from Spain and an intimate friend of the Elder SENECA (1), who in his *Controversies* described Latro's character and capacity for hard work, quoting at length from his speeches, e.g. *Contr.*, 2. 7. Seneca reports that OVID admired his work and used his ideas, while MESSALLA (4) was critical of him. He preferred teaching rhetoric to practising at the bar. He committed suicide *c.*AD 4.

2. Licinus (late C2 BC) was a Roman historian of literature who wrote in verse: a few lines survive, two referring to the arrival of the Muse in Latium during the Second Punic War, and a dozen to TERENCE. GELLIUS (1) quotes an elegiac epigram by him which marks the beginning of Hellenistic influence on poetry at Rome.
See also CATO, FESTUS (2).

Porphyry (AD 234–*c*.305) was a hellenised Neoplatonist scholar from Tyre. Originally named Malchus ('king'), he adopted the Greek name Porphyrius ('purple'). He studied at Athens under CASSIUS (7) Longinus, after which he moved in 263 to Rome and became a disciple of PLOTINUS, whose *Enneads* he edited and whose extant biography he wrote. He was scarcely an original thinker, but because of his wide interests and habit of quoting his sources, his works, many of which have survived in whole or part, offer useful information from earlier authorities. Seventy-seven titles are known, a few predating his conversion to Plotinism: we have considerable fragments of *Philosophy from Oracles*, giving information about ritual; also of *Statues*, and a *History of Philosophy* of which only the *Life of Pythagoras* survives complete. His works on Plotinian thought include *Subjects for Reflexion*, an extant random collection of Plotinian propositions. *On Abstinence*, a plea for vegetarianism in four books (written because of the apostasy of his friend Firmus Castricius), survives whole, as do two letters, *To Anebo*, a critical discussion of religious ritual, rejecting animal sacrifice, and *To Marcella*, his wife, giving moral advice. Some fragments of his polemic in fifteen books *Against Christians* survive, though the work was officially destroyed in 448: the critical method he employs in it is based on historical arguments. He also proved the *Book of Zoroaster* to be a forgery. He wrote many commentaries on the classical philosophers: a short commentary on Aristotle's *Categories* survives complete and there are fragments of a longer one. His *Introduction to Aristotle's Categories* was widely used in the Middle Ages as a textbook on logic. Other philosophical commentaries on Plato, Theophrastus and PLOTINUS are lost. He wrote an influential commentary on PTOLEMY (13)'s incomplete *Harmonics* and another on his astrological *Tetrabiblos*. He also wrote a treatise on the quickening of the embryo; *The Cave of the Nymphs in the Odyssey*, an extant allegorising interpretation of its subject; *Homeric Enquiries*, a landmark study of Homer; and other works about language. See R.T. Wallis (1972) *Neoplatonism*, London: Duckworth.

Posidonius (*c*.135–*c*.51 BC) was a Greek Stoic philosopher, historian and scientist from Apamea in Syria. He studied philosophy under PANAETIUS in Athens and settled in Rhodes, where he acquired citizenship and set up a school. He travelled extensively for scientific research in Italy, Gaul and Spain, and in late 87 BC served on an embassy to Rome to represent the Rhodians and had dealings with MARIUS (1), whom he came to detest. Thereafter several noted Romans visited him, including CICERO (1), who studied at the school, and POMPEIUS (2), whom Posidonius admired and whose eulogy he wrote.

He wrote *Histories* in fifty-two books starting from 146 BC, the close of POLYBIUS, to the dictatorship of SULLA (2) in 85, possibly incomplete, of which we have some brief quotations by the Greek writer Athenaeus of Naucratis. The work, which was centred on the development of Rome, rested on a moralistic theory of historical explanation. As he accepted a unitary theory of history and considered character so important in determining events, Posidonius showed a special interest in ethnology, national characteristics, and in the relationships between the ruling class and the ruled. He decried the Gracchi, Marius, the equestrians, and the Greek independence movement, and praised the Roman nobility, the Empire, and above all Pompeius. To satisfy himself of his view of the world he did much observation and research of a 'scientific' nature, and wrote extensively about his findings. Though little of his work has survived, we know of works on astronomy, mathematics, geography, meteorology, seismology, zoology, botany and anthropology: some thirty titles are known. He invented a theory connecting the tides and the phases of the moon and a means to measure the circumference of the earth: he constructed a globe and made a map. His book *Oceans* explored the effects of ocean currents on climate, the connection between astronomic observations and the geographical climatic zones, and human geography.

His stoicism was orthodox, though he believed that philosophical ideas were capable of development in the light of fresh criticism. He reacted against the ethical teachings of Chrysippus and preferred to recognise the irrational, natural forces in the mind: the main arguments of his *Emotions* can be recovered from GALEN. He also wrote on logic and natural philosophy, poetry and rhetoric. He had an enormous influence both on his contemporaries and on posterity until the dark ages, and was more appreciated and studied for his work in history and the sciences than for his philosophical system. However, when Cicero asked him to write a history of his consulship, Posidonius tactfully declined. See A.A. Long (1971) *Problems in Stoicism*, London: Athlone Press; L. Edelstein and I.G. Kidd (1988) *Posidonius*, 2 vols, Fragments and Commentary, Cambridge: Cambridge University Press.

Postumius 1. Megellus, Lucius (C4–3 BC), was a general in the wars against the Samnites. He was consul thrice, and triumphed in each consulship (305, 294 and 291); in the last he stormed Venusia and brought the war to a successful conclusion. In 282 he was sent to Tarentum to demand restitution, but was insulted, an outcome which led to the war with PYRRHUS.

2. Tubertus, Aulus (C5 BC), was a dictator who defeated the Aequi and perhaps the Volsci at the pass on the Algidus in June 432 or 431.

Postumus, Marcus Cassianius Latinius (died AD 268), was an emperor of Gaul, Spain and Britain. Originally appointed in 259 by GALLIENUS as governor of the German provinces, he quarrelled in 260 with Silvanus, the Praetorian Prefect, and Saloninus, the emperor's son, and besieged them in Cologne, which he took; he killed them and was recognised as emperor by the legions of Germany. He made his capital at Trier. In 261 he repulsed an invasion by the Franks and Alemanni. In 263 Gallienus attacked his empire but received a serious wound and had to withdraw: he then accepted Postumus as *de facto* ruler of the west. In 268 Postumus faced a rebellion by his subordinate Laelianus, who took refuge in Maintz: Postumus seized Maintz and executed Laelianus, but when he forbade his men to sack the town, they killed him. His Gallic realm outlived him and was ruled by Victorinus and TETRICUS until 274. See M. Grant (1985) *The Roman Emperors*, London: Weidenfeld & Nicolson.

Prasutagus *see* BOUDICCA.

Primus, Marcus Antonius (C1 AD), was a general from Toulouse in Narbonese Gaul, described by TACITUS (1) as outspoken and turbulent but a useful ally in war. In 61 he was found guilty of forging a will and exiled; he was recalled in 68 by GALBA (1) and put in command of the Seventh Legion in Pannonia. The following summer, after the fall of OTHO, he declared for VESPASIAN, won over the rest of the Danubian armies and defeated VITELLIUS (1) at Bedriacum near Cremona in northern Italy. He allowed his troops to sack Cremona, for which he was held blameworthy. In December 69 he took Rome, where he held supreme power for a while: he yielded to MUCIANUS on his arrival and faded from the scene. He retired peacefully to his native city.

Proaeresius (AD 276–367) was a Greek rhetorician from Cappadocia who became professor of the subject at Athens, where he taught BASIL, GREGORY (3) and the emperor JULIAN. He spent some time in Gaul at the court of the emperor CONSTANS and was offered and refused a chair of rhetoric at Rome. He resigned his chair in 362 when Julian forbade Christians to teach, even though he was exempted from the rule, and resumed it after Julian's death.

Probus 1, Marcus Aurelius (*c.*AD 232–282), was an emperor from Sirmium who, having served successfully on the German frontier under AURELIAN, rose from being commander in the east to the purple in autumn 276 after challenging and beating FLORIANUS at Tarsus by declining battle and waiting for his troops to remove him. In his six-year reign he showed respect for the Senate and proved to be an able general, driving Franks and Alemanni out of Gaul, and defeating the Vandals and Burgundians who came to their aid by meeting them separately. Then in 278 he went on to Raetia and Illyricum, whence he expelled the Vandals. In 280 he went east to Antioch and Egypt, suppressing the rebellion of Saturninus and putting down the brigands of Isauria. He had to give up plans to tackle Persia because of rebellions in Gaul and Britain: he suppressed the revolts of Proculus and Bonosus centred on Cologne, and in late 281 held a triumph in Rome. The next year, however, he lost the support of his weary troops and, when CARUS in Raetia made a bid for the throne, his troops killed him at Sirmium. See M. Grant (1985) *The Roman Emperors*, London: Weidenfeld & Nicolson.

2, Marcus Valerius (C1 AD), was a Latin grammarian from Beirut who settled in Rome in the Flavian period. He collected texts of earlier authors such as PLAUTUS, TERENCE, SALLUST and VIRGIL, to which he added punctuation and critical marks: he published little, however, and communicated mostly orally. His notes on earlier Latin usage survived him and were known to Aulus GELLIUS (1) and other commentators. As a result of his fame certain other works were wrongly attributed to him.

Proculus, Sempronius (C1 AD), was a Roman legal writer and teacher who wrote eleven books of 'letters' on legal subjects from which the compilers of Justinian's *Digests* took thirty-four extracts. He also wrote notes for LABEO's works. He founded the Proculian law school, the rival of the Cassian or Sabinian school (see CASSIUS 3).

Propertius, Sextus (*c.*50–*c.*2 BC), was an elegiac poet from Assisi in Umbria. He came from wealthy equestrian stock, though his father died while Sextus was young, and the family estate suffered during the triumvirs' confiscations of land in 41 BC after the battle of Philippi. Yet he was affluent enough to receive a good education and settle in Rome, where he eventually became a member of the circle patronised by MAECENAS. But he retained his political independence, showed his sympathy for those defeated by Octavian (AUGUSTUS) at Perugia in 41, and appears to have been financially independent of his patron, unlike VIRGIL and HORACE. He departs from Augustan seriousness by referring to love as military service and to his own lot as one of enthralment to his mistress, as opposed to the normal equestrian career of service to the state.

He published four books of poetry, which show development both in theme and range. His first book, published *c.*28, which MARTIAL called *Cynthia Monobiblos* ('Cynthia's book') introduces his first and greatest passion, his love for a woman he significantly names Cynthia (the name conjures up Delian Apollo and shows a link with the Alexandrian poet Callimachus), whose real name APULEIUS reports as Hostia. What her social status was we do not know, but her existence is beyond doubt. Book 1 is devoted to poems about his affair with Cynthia, and the theme threads through the next two books, but in book 4 only two poems refer to her, and in one she speaks from beyond the grave. Book 2, 1, in which he declines the role of a heroic poet, introduces his friendship with Maecenas: by book 4, however, Maecenas has left the scene. Many elegies in book 1 are addressed to Propertius' friends, in particular Tullus and Gallus, though some are addressed to Cynthia herself. Book 2 was published in 26 and consists mainly of love poems; in book 3, published in 23, he makes a claim to be the Roman Callimachus, showing the importance he attached to learned allusions and his wish to write works offering an explanation of some mythical or historical event. In fact the poems in book 4, published *c.*16, are more successfully Callimachean, and several explain the origin of some such event. Three of his finest and most original poems are to be found in this last book, the two in which Cynthia reappears, and one in which Cornelia, wife of Paullus Aemilius LEPIDUS (8), speaks from the grave to justify her life. Propertius is a difficult poet, partly because his text contains many dubious readings, but mainly because of his allusive style requiring a close knowledge of Greek myth. Yet his ability to examine his love affair from so many interesting angles, and his talent for creating vivid images with great economy, make him an important and worthwhile poet. His influence on Ezra Pound's work is noteworthy. See M. Hubbard (1974) *Propertius*, London: Duckworth; R.O.A.M. Lyne (1980) *The Latin Love Poets*, Oxford: Clarendon Press.

Prusias 1. I (reigned *c.*230–182 BC) known as *Cholos* 'The Lame', the son of Ziaëlas and grandson of Nicomedes I, was a king of Bithynia. In 220 he made war on Byzantium and in 216 he defeated the invading Galatians. He made a marriage alliance with King PHILIP (1) V of Macedonia and supported him in his wars against Pergamon. During the First Macedonian War in 208 he attacked Pergamon when its king, ATTALUS (1) I, was engaged in Greece on the side of Rome against Macedonia, and was included as an ally of Macedonia in the treaty of Phoenice in 205. In 202 Philip gave him Cius and Myrlea on the south coast of the Sea of Marmora, which he renamed respectively Prusias and Apamea. He took parts of Mysia and Phrygia from Pergamon in 198 and attacked Heraclea on the Black Sea, from which he took Cierus, renaming it Prusias-on-the-Hypius, and Tieum on the Black Sea. In 191, when war broke out between Rome and ANTIOCHUS (1) III, he remained neutral, having received assurances from the Scipios who conducted the Roman campaign. He gave refuge *c.*188 to the fugitive HANNIBAL, whose services he used as his admiral. In 188 he began a war with EUMENES II of Pergamon, which he lost in 183, when he was forced to return territory he had earlier taken from Attalus. FLAMININUS then demanded the surrender of Hannibal, who preferred to kill himself. Prusias was succeeded by his son, PRUSIAS (2) II. See E.S. Gruen (1984) *The Hellenistic World and the Coming of Rome*, Berkeley: University of California Press.

2. II (reigned 182–149 BC) known as *Cynegetes* 'The Hunter', the son of PRUSIAS (1), was a king of Bithynia. He refrained from conflict with Rome and in

181 joined EUMENES II of Pergamon in an attack on king Pharnaces I of Pontus. He married a sister of PERSEUS, king of Macedonia, but did not help him against Rome. In 168, after the fall of Perseus, he went to Rome to plead with the Senate: his abject attitude to the Romans earned him the contempt of the Greeks. He made war on Pergamon (156–154) against the orders of Rome and was defeated. Rome imposed an indemnity and Prusias sent his eldest son NICOMEDES (II) to Rome to plead for release. Nicomedes, however, rebelled, believing that his father meant to kill him if he failed, and replace him with a half-brother. He returned to Bithynia and with help from ATTALUS (2) II of Pergamon caused his father to flee to Nicomedia where the citizens, who had no love for Prusias, were permitted to stone him. See E.S. Gruen (1984) *The Hellenistic World and the Coming of Rome*, Berkeley: University of California Press.

Ptolemy (Ptolemaeus) The name of all the Macedonian kings of Egypt.

1. V Epiphanes ('revealed') (210–180 BC) became king at the age of six and was a tool in the hands of the ministers Sosibius and Agathocles. The result was a sustained attack from both outside Egypt and within: in the Fifth Syrian War he was attacked by ANTIOCHUS (1) III and PHILIP (1) V and lost his territories in the Aegean and Asia Minor, and in 200 after the battle of Phanium, Palestine was also lost. In 197 Ptolemy came of age and was crowned Pharaoh at Memphis by the ancient Egyptian ritual, an occasion commemorated in the inscription on the Rosetta Stone. He made peace with Antiochus in 195 and two years later married his daughter CLEOPATRA (1) I. He won back Upper Egypt in 186. See E.S. Gruen (1984) *The Hellenistic World and the Coming of Rome*, Berkeley: University of California Press; P. Green (1990) *Alexander to Actium: The Historical Evolution of the Hellenistic Age*, Berkeley: University of California Press.

2. VI Philometor ('mother-loving') (*c.*191–145 BC) succeeded in 180 at the age of about twelve and ruled jointly with his mother CLEOPATRA (1) I until her death in 176; the following year he married his sister CLEOPATRA (2) II. In 170 ANTIOCHUS (2) IV began the Sixth Syrian War: he invaded Egypt twice and was crowned as its king in 168, but abandoned his claim on the orders of the Roman Senate. From 169 to 164 Egypt was ruled by a triumvirate consisting of Ptolemy, his sister-queen, and his younger brother known as PTOLEMY (4) VIII, but in 164 he was driven out by his brother and went to Rome to seek support, which he received from CATO (4). He was restored the following year by the intervention of the Alexandrians, and ruled uneasily, cruelly suppressing frequent rebellions, until he was killed in Syria, fighting against Alexander BALAS. See E.S. Gruen (1984) *The Hellenistic World and the Coming of Rome*, Berkeley: University of California Press.

3. VII Neos Philopator ('new father-loving'), a son of PTOLEMY (2), reigned briefly with his father in 145 and for a short time after that: he was murdered by his uncle, PTOLEMY (4), who succeeded him.

4. VIII Euergetes II ('benefactor') (*c.*182–116 BC) was the younger brother of PTOLEMY (2), known familiarly as Pot-Belly (*Physcon*); after ruling jointly with his brother and sister CLEOPATRA (2) II between 169 and 164 he expelled PTOLEMY (2) VI but the following year had himself to leave Alexandria and take up rule over Cyrene. The Roman Senate, despite his appeal, gave him no material help: however, in 154 he willed his possessions to Rome. In 145 he returned to succeed his brother, eliminated his nephew PTOLEMY (3) and married his brother's widow, his own sister CLEOPATRA (2)

II. He later took his niece, Cleopatra's daughter CLEOPATRA (3) III, as a junior wife. About this time the Senate sent SCIPIO (11) Aemilianus to investigate the state of Ptolemy's kingdom. In 132 Cleopatra III rebelled and tried to replace Euergetes with the Seleucid king of Syria, DEMETRIUS (2) II. A long internal war followed: Euergetes finally had Demetrius assassinated in 125, and a public reconciliation between the dynasts took place the following year: the three then ruled jointly until his death. Euergetes' reign was characterised by its brutality and vindictiveness towards Alexandria, which had supported his brother.

5. IX Soter II ('saviour') (142–80 BC), the elder son of PTOLEMY (4), was known as Chickpea (*Lathyrus*); his mother, CLEOPATRA (3) III, was a dominant force during much of his reign. He married two of his sisters, Cleopatra IV, who bore Berenice IV, and Cleopatra V Selene, who bore two sons. His mother inherited the kingdom in 116 and appointed him to rule jointly with her and his aunt, though the latter died soon after. However, his mother preferred her younger son, PTOLEMY (6). After several rebellions, Cleopatra III succeeded in driving Chickpea out in 107: he became king of Cyprus. There Chickpea became involved in the affairs of Palestine and won a victory over the Jews. He returned to power in Egypt in 88 when the Alexandrians drove Alexander out, and ruled until his death.

6. X Alexander (reigned 107–88 BC) was the younger brother of PTOLEMY (5) IX. Formerly governor of Cyprus, he joined their mother CLEOPATRA (3) III on the throne of Egypt. Alexander and his mother quarrelled constantly, and when she died in 101 he was believed to have killed her. Alexander married his brother's daughter, Cleopatra Berenice, making her joint ruler. The Alexandrians drove him out in 88, and restored Ptolemy IX.

7. XI Alexander II (*c.*100–80 BC) was a son of PTOLEMY (5) who was installed in power by SULLA (2) with his stepmother Cleopatra Berenice as his wife and partner in power. He murdered her within days and was himself murdered by the Alexandrians: thus the legitimate line descending from Alexander the Great's general Ptolemy was extinguished. He willed his kingdom to Rome but, despite the efforts of Lucius PHILIPPUS (2), the Romans did not take it.

8. XII Neos Dionysos ('new Dionysus') (ruled 80–51 BC), popularly known as the Piper (*Auletes*), was an illegitimate son of PTOLEMY (5). He was chosen as king by the Alexandrians and married his sister Cleopatra Tryphaena. In 58, however, the Alexandrians drove him into exile because of his pro-Roman policy but, after three years spent in Rome trying to rouse support, he was restored by the governor of Syria, GABINIUS (2). For this he had to pay Gabinius a huge bribe which, together with other expenditure to gain Roman support, crippled the Egyptian economy. He left his kingdom to his two oldest children, CLEOPATRA (4) VII and PTOLEMY (9) XIII. See E.S. Gruen (1984) *The Hellenistic World and the Coming of Rome*, Berkeley: University of California Press.

9. XIII (63–47 BC) was the elder son of PTOLEMY (8). He ruled jointly until 47 with his older sister CLEOPATRA (4) VII, whom he married. He had POMPEIUS (2) murdered in 48 when he arrived in Egypt fleeing from CAESAR (1), in order to gratify the latter, but instead greatly offended him: he was defeated in the war that ensued and was drowned in the Nile.

10. XIV (59–44 BC) was the younger son of PTOLEMY (8) and replaced his elder brother as king in 47 and married his sister CLEOPATRA (4) VII. Three years later she had him assassinated.

11. XV, *see* CAESARION.

12. (reigned AD 23–40) was a king of Mauretania, son of JUBA (2) II and of Cleopatra Selene, through whom he was descended from the Ptolemies of Egypt. He lent aid to the Romans in their war against TACFARINAS, for which he was rewarded by the Senate with the title of 'Ally and Friend of the Roman People' and a sceptre and robe which he displayed on coinage. He was summoned to Rome by his cousin the emperor CALIGULA, who executed him and seized his kingdom.

13. (*c.*AD 100–*c.*170) was a Greek writer on mathematics, astronomy, geography and music. Claudius Ptolemaeus was born at Ptolemaïs in Egypt, and lived and worked in Alexandria where he became head of the Museum. His writings on astronomy and geography were very influential for centuries to come, and his work on trigonometry was seminal. He did original research in a number of areas, but adopted as axiomatic Hipparchus' theory of a geocentric universe, which he refined in detail. His greatest work, known to us by its Arabic title as the *Almagest* (*Megistê Syntaxis*, 'the greatest collection'), was the *Mathematical Collection* in thirteen books, which covers the whole subject of astronomy and related mathematical tables and computations. Between 127 and 147, Ptolemy made the meticulous observations on which this work was based: in it he describes the nature of the visible universe, the theory and practice of trigonometry, his theories regarding the sun, the moon, eclipses, the fixed stars, and the planets. Though many of the works of earlier writers perished, mainly because of the success of Ptolemy's work, we can still evaluate their contributions to science. He reformed and clarified his predecessors' work and left a lucid, complete and authoritative account of the subject with the mathematical structure required to validate it. This work remained the standard textbook on the subject for 1,300 years. His other works on astronomy were the *Hypotheses of the Planets* in two books, containing instructions for building a planetarium, including the exposition of a theory that the heavenly bodies were fixed upon contiguous concentric spheres. This theory was widely accepted in the Middle Ages. His *Planispherium* described the theory of construction of the astrolabe; *Analemma* (preserved in Latin) described the mathematics underpinning sundials; *Handy Tables* expanded the tables given in the *Almagest*; *Phases of the Fixed Stars*, of which the second book survives, gave the risings and settings of certain bright stars. His earliest work, *The Canobic Inscription*, a list of astronomic constants, is repeated and corrected in the *Almagest.*

Of equal importance was his *Geography*, in eight books, perhaps with an atlas appended, in which he tried to collect the information to make maps of the entire known world. Unfortunately his work is blemished by a number of serious errors, including an underestimate of the earth's circumference and an elongation of the Mediterranean Sea. However, the method it rests on is fundamentally sound and it was a remarkable achievement, which had enormous influence on notions of geography until the age of exploration. He aimed to define the positions of a list of places in terms of latitude and longitude, and gave information about their principal features. He also wrote *Influences* on astrology, to complement the *Almagest*, in four books; *Optics*, four of whose five books are mostly extant in a Latin translation from Arabic: it deals with vision, colour, mirrors and reflection of light, and refraction, and is a considerable advance on the work of Euclid. His work on musical theory, entitled *Harmonics*, follows not uncritically the mathematical theories of the Pythagoreans, and at the same time employs practical methods and tests theory by perception. His book includes invaluable information about the octave, tones and the contemporary tuning of instruments, and describes his experiments and apparatus he used. One philosophical work, a short treatise on epistemology entitled *Judgment and Decision*, is also attributed to his pen.

Some of his lost works are reported by other writers: *Dimension*, proving that there are only three dimensions; *Mechanics*; and *The Elements*. See G.J. Toomer (1984) *Ptolemy's Almagest*, London: Duckworth; G. Grasshoff (1990) *The History of Ptolemy's Star Catalogue*, New York and London: Springer-Verlag; A. Barker (1989) *Greek Musical Writings*, II, Cambridge: Cambridge University Press.

Publilius *see* PHILO (1), VOLERO.

Publilius Syrus (C1 BC) was a Latin writer of mimes, originally a slave from Antioch in Syria (whence his name). He was brought to Rome *c*.50 BC. His intelligence and quickness of wit led to his freedom, and his former master gave him instruction. He competed in a mime contest in games organised by CAESAR (1) in 46, and beat all comers at improvisation of mimes. A collection of maxims purporting to be his, but mostly dating from at least a century after his time, exists under the title *Publilius Syrus' Sayings* (*Sententiae*): some fourteen, quoted by GELLIUS (1) are genuine. The terseness and moral point of these maxims was admired in ancient times, and they were given to schoolboys to copy out.

Pupienus *see* BALBINUS.

Pupius *see* PISO (11).

Pyrrhus (319–272 BC), a son of Aeacides and a cousin of Alexander the Great, was the most famous Molossian king of Epirus. As a youth he was exiled from his kingdom, over which he had reigned as a minor from 307 to 302, when Cassander seized it, and he took refuge with Demetrius the Besieger: he was present at the battle of Ipsus in 301 and was sent by Demetrius as a hostage to Ptolemy I, king of Egypt, whose stepdaughter Antigone he married. In 295 he won back his kingdom with the help of Ptolemy and Agathocles of Syracuse, and ruled jointly with his kinsman Neoptolemus whom he soon liquidated. He tried to gain the throne of Macedonia, but in 294 Demetrius seized it, though Pyrrhus won territory at the expense of that kingdom, namely southern Illyria, Parauaea and Tymphaea: he also took Ambracia, Amphilochia and Acarnania. On Antigone's death he remarried, wedding a daughter of Agathocles, and was given Corcyra and Leucas as her dowry. He took other wives in addition, the daughters of the Illyrian rulers of Paeonia and Dardania. In 291 war broke out between Pyrrhus and Demetrius, and in 287 the latter was forced to flee. Pyrrhus declared himself king of Macedonia and occupied half Macedonia and Thessaly, but three years later in 284, Lysimachus, the ruler of Thrace, now freed from the threat posed by Demetrius in Asia Minor, drove him out of Macedonia and established himself as king, and Pyrrhus turned his attention to the west.

Invited by the Tarentines in 281 to help them against Rome, he transported a force of 25,000 men, 3,000 cavalry and twenty elephants to Italy and in 280 defeated the consul Laevinus at Heraclea, sustaining such huge losses as to coin the phrase 'Pyrrhic victory'. He marched on Rome with a large force of Italians and Greek inhabitants of southern Italy, and after failing to negotiate peace won another battle in 279 at Ausculum, again sustaining heavy casualties. He then diverted his attention to Sicily where he answered an appeal from Syracuse and Messina for aid against the Carthaginians. Though he won some early successes, he quarrelled with his allies and was defeated at Lilybaeum. In 276 he withdrew from Sicily with little to show for his pains, and in 275 was crushed near Malventum (henceforth renamed 'Beneventum') by the consul M. Curius DENTATUS. He retired to Epirus with a third of those he had led out, and left a small garrison in Tarentum. He attacked Macedonia successfully in 273, drove out Antigonus Gonatas, and resumed his kingship, but became unpopular when he pillaged the royal tombs at Aegae. He invaded the Peloponnese, attacked Sparta unsuccessfully, and was killed in a riot at Argos by a roof-tile that a woman threw at him.

Despite his foreign adventures he did much for Epirus, completing its hellenisation and building among other structures the great theatre at Dodona.

Q

Quadratus 1. Bassus, Gaius Julius (died AD 118), was a general and provincial governor from Pergamon, where his ancestors were royal. He governed Judaea as legate *c.*102–105, was suffect consul in 105, and served as a general under TRAJAN in his Second Dacian War, in which he won triumphal decorations. He was successively governor of Cappadocia (*c.*107–110), Syria (115–117) and Dacia, where he died shortly after taking up his post.

2, Gaius Asinius (early C3 AD), was a Greek historian of Rome and Parthia: his *A Thousand Years* related Rome's history from the foundation to the time of SEVERUS (2) Alexander in fifteen books in Ionic Greek, and that of Parthia in nine books: only fragments of these works survive.

Quietus 1, Titus Avidius (late C1 AD), was a provincial governor from Faventia who served as proconsul of Achaea and was suffect consul in 93. He governed Britain as the emperor TRAJAN's legate *c.*98. A Stoic, he was a friend of THRASEA Paetus, PLINY (2) the Younger, and PLUTARCH. NIGRINUS was his nephew.

2, Fulvius Julius (died AD 261), was an emperor, the younger son of MACRIANUS. In 260 his father was created emperor by his troops, and made his two sons his partners in power. Quietus was left in Syria with the Praetorian Prefect Ballista while Macrianus went to Europe with his elder son to confirm his rule there. The following year Quietus was besieged in Emesa by ODONAETHUS of Palmyra and killed.

3. *See* LUSIUS.

Quinctilius *see* VARUS.

Quinctius Capitolinus Barbatus, Titus (C5 BC), was a statesman whose career is obscure and, as reported by LIVY, anachronistic. He may have held a series of consulships between 471 and 439 and won a triumph in 468 for capturing Antium, and was said to have rescued the consul of 464 with the help of Latin troops when he was trapped by the Aequi. *See also* CINCINNATUS, FLAMININUS.

Quintilian (*c.*AD 34–*c.*100) was a rhetorician and literary critic from Calgurris in Spain: his full name was Marcus Fabius Quintilianus. He was educated at Rome, perhaps firstly by the grammarian Remmius Palaemon and then by Domitius AFER. He returned to Spain, probably *c.*57, but was brought back to Rome in 68 by the emperor GALBA (1) and became a successful teacher of rhetoric, which he combined with the profession of advocacy for twenty years. During VESPASIAN's reign he was the first teacher of rhetoric to be paid a regular salary from the treasury. He taught distinguished pupils including PLINY (2) the Younger, possibly TACITUS (1), and the emperor DOMITIAN's heirs, Vespasianus and Domitianus; for this work he was awarded consular status. He retired *c.*88 from regular teaching, a rich man, to write his classic textbook *The Teaching of Oratory* (*Institutio Oratoria*), which he published *c.*96 before the death of Domitian (it contains flattery of him). He married: his wife died at eighteen years of age leaving him two sons, each of whom died in childhood to his great grief.

His only surviving work is the *Teaching of Oratory* in twelve books, dedicated to Victorius MARCELLUS (9), an exhaustive treatise covering the education of the complete orator from infancy to maturity. In it he discusses with great sensitivity and wisdom the upbringing of the small child, doubtless from his experience with his own sons, and proceeds to more formal education, placing much emphasis on grammar. He describes his ideal teacher before going on to the technicalities of rhetorical training and a dissection of language and style. He includes judgments passed on the famous writers of the past, both Latin and Greek, some of which are memorable. He also describes the desired appearance and dress of the orator, his gestures and delivery, and the character of the ideal orator, following the example of CICERO (1): he finally declares that oratory is capable of being a supreme moral force for good. The style in which the work is written is practical and straightforward, a little ponderous and certainly subordinated to its content. He was keener to follow the ideas and style of the Ciceronian age than those of his own time, which he considered debased, and he had a considerable effect on later times, notably the writers of the Renaissance.

His lost works include *The Causes of the Corruption of Eloquence*; defence speeches for Naevius Arpinianus, Queen BERENICE (2) and a woman accused of forgery; and two unauthorised publications of his lectures on rhetoric. See G.A. Kennedy (1969) *Quintilian*, New York: Twayne; T.A. Dorey (ed.) (1975) *Empire and Aftermath: Silver Latin*, II, London: Routledge.

Quintillus (died AD 270) was an emperor, the younger brother of CLAUDIUS (2) II, who left him in command of an army at Aquilea in northern Italy. On the report of Claudius' death early in 270, his troops elected him emperor and he was recognised by the Senate, but committed suicide when his men deserted him for AURELIAN.

Quintus (C2 AD) was a teacher of medicine and anatomy at Rome of the Hippocratic school, contemporary with HADRIAN. He indirectly influenced GALEN, whose teachers attended Quintus' school. For an unknown reason he was expelled from Rome and died at Pergamon.

Quirinius, Publius Sulpicius (consul 12 BC), a native of Lanuvium, in 15 BC defeated the Marmaridae, an African nation south of Cyrene. After his consulship, probably as governor of Galatia and Pamphylia, he fought a successful war against the Homanades, brigands living in the south of Galatia. He visited TIBERIUS during his exile in Rhodes, and was appointed to succeed Marcus LOLLIUS as supervisor of Gaius CAESAR (3) in his eastern expedition of AD 1. As legate (imperial governor) of Syria in AD 6 he incorporated Judaea as a sub-province under a prefect, after ARCHELAUS (6) had been removed from the ethnarchy, and organised a tax assessment of the territory. He crushed the rebellion consequently led by Judas the Galilean. The tax assessment is referred to in the *Gospel of Luke*, where he is referred to as Cyrenius, though the knowledge of it shown there is very inaccurate. Quirinius married Aemilia Lepida and lived in great wealth until his death in AD 21: Tiberius granted him a public funeral.

R

Rabirius 1, Gaius (C1 BC), was an equestrian who in 100 BC took a prominent part in the attack on and murder of the tribune SATURNINUS (2); thirty-seven years later, in 63 when he had become a senator, he was accused by the popular party, instigated by CAESAR (1), of activity hostile to the state, and found guilty by an ancient and obsolete procedure before two judges, one of whom was Caesar. He appealed to the *Comitia Centuriata*, and at the hearing was defended by CICERO (1) in an extant speech, LABIENUS (2) acting as prosecutor. The aim of the prosecution was to discredit the efficacy of the senatorial 'Ultimate Decree' which was considered to give consuls unfettered authority to act in times of crisis. Within a few months Cicero was to use it against CATILINE's conspiracy, and this may have been a shot across his bows. The praetor, METELLUS (8) Celer, closed the session of the *Comitia* before the trial could be finished, by lowering the flag on the Janiculum hill: the point had been made.

2. Postumus, Gaius (C1 BC), was an equestrian banker, the nephew of RABIRIUS (1) and son of C. Curtius the banker; his uncle adopted him by will. He invested money widely throughout the empire, but had trouble collecting a huge debt from PTOLEMY (12) XII the Piper, to whom he had lent the sum he needed to bribe his way to recover his throne, and went to live in Alexandria where the king appointed him his treasurer. Rabirius requisitioned the king's revenues and supplies until he was imprisoned and escaped from Egypt. He was prosecuted in 54 for receiving part of the bribe taken by GABINIUS (2) from Ptolemy, and acquitted thanks to an extant speech by CICERO (1), who appealed to the feelings of the equestrians on the jury and declared his client to have lost all his wealth. With the help of CAESAR (1) he recovered, became a Caesarian senator, and in 47 was proconsul of Syria; he aspired to the consulship in 45, and after Caesar's murder worked to raise funds for Octavian (AUGUSTUS).

3, Gaius (C1 BC), was an epic poet contemporary with Virgil, of whose work five lines, describing the fall of ANTONIUS (7), survive. Though OVID and VELLEIUS admired his work, QUINTILIAN considered him second-rate.

Regulus 1, Marcus Atilius (C3 BC) During his consulship of 267 in the First Punic War, having conquered the Sallentini of Calabria and captured Brundisium, he held a joint triumph with his colleague. He held a second, suffect consulship in 256, when with his colleague Manlius Vulso he won a crushing naval victory off Ecnomus near Licata, and landed in Africa with a considerable force and took

Tunis. He offered the Carthaginians terms too harsh for them to be able to contemplate, and in spring 255 was brought to battle on unfavourable ground by the Spartan mercenary commander XANTHIPPUS, defeated, and captured. He died in captivity. A legend arose about him according to which he was sent while a captive to negotiate an exchange of prisoners, under oath to return to Carthage if he failed, and having spoken against the proposal to the Senate, voluntarily returned and was tortured to death. It may have been invented to cover up the torture inflicted by his widow on two Carthaginian prisoners to avenge his death. HORACE used the tale effectively in *Odes*, 3. 5.

2, Marcus Aquilius (C1 AD), was an informer and legacy-hunter during the reigns of NERO (1) and DOMITIAN. Though a patron whom MARTIAL clearly admired, he was detested by PLINY (2) the Younger, who called him 'the most evil thing on two legs'. He restored his family's wealth after his father's exile by winning three convictions for treason (*maiestas*) in Nero's reign, for which he was rewarded with a priesthood and 7,000,000 sesterces. He published two works which are lost: his prosecution speech of ARULENUS Rusticus whom he described as a 'Stoic ape', and a panegyric on his own deceased son, of which he had 1,000 copies circulated. Herennius SENECIO condemned him as a 'bad man, unskilled in speaking', the opposite of the Catonian definition of a good orator.

Rex 1, Quintus Marcius (praetor 144 BC), began the Marcian Aqueduct during his praetorship, the first to make substantial use of arches, which he commemorated with coins bearing the image of king Ancus Marcius, his supposed ancestor.

2, Quintus Marcius (C1 BC), was consul in 68, and was sent to govern Cilicia in 67, but delayed his departure for fear of trouble in Cisalpine Gaul. Once in Cilicia he declined, at the instigation of CLODIUS, to assist Lucius LUCULLUS (2), whose brother-in-law each man was (Rex had married one of the CLODIA sisters), and on the appointment of POMPEIUS (2) to his eastern command in 66 his army deserted him to join Pompeius. In 63 he was outside Rome, vainly expecting to triumph, when he was ordered to use his proconsular power against CATILINE's army in Etruria. He died soon after.

Roscius 1, Sextus (early C1 BC), was the name of two Roman citizens, father and son, from Ameria. In 80 the father was murdered at Rome. His son was accused of the murder, while two of his kinsmen, with the help of SULLA (1)'s freedman CHRYSOGONUS, plotted to steal his property by entering his name on the list of those Sulla had proscribed: at the auction of the property nobody dared to bid against Sulla's favourite. CICERO (1) in his first major court speech, of which we have an edited version, defended Roscius against the murder charge and implicated Chrysogenus in the plot. The speech had strong political implications and Sulla, who was still consul at the time, recognising the force of the argument, made no hostile move when Roscius was acquitted.

2. Gallus, Quintus (died 62 BC), was a stage actor from Solonium near Lanuvium. A free citizen, he was raised by SULLA (2) to equestrian rank. He was handsome but had a squint and so appeared masked on the stage, in both comedies and tragedies. He is mentioned by several writers and his name became a byword for histrionic genius. CICERO (1) knew him well and represented him in court when he was sued by Fannius Chaerea. He earned great wealth by his work.

3. Otho, Lucius (C1 BC), was a tribune in 67 when he opposed the proposals of his colleague Aulus GABINIUS (2) to send POMPEIUS (2) against the pirates, and sought to win the equestrians over to the Senate by restoring their privilege of occupying the first fourteen rows in the theatre. Four years later CICERO (1) spoke up for him against popular vilification arising from his reform.

Rubellius 1. Blandus, Gaius (C1 AD), was a 'new man' senator who was suffect consul in AD 18, and in 33 married TIBERIUS' granddaughter Livia Julia.

2. Plautus (C1 AD) was a son of RUBELLIUS (1) who embraced Stoicism. As a kinsman of the imperial family he was, according to TACITUS (1), considered in 55 as a possible husband for NERO (1)'s mother AGRIPPINA (3). In 60 Nero, afraid of him as a possible rival, advised him to leave Italy, and he went to live in the province of Asia, where in 62 he was forced, at the instigation of TIGELLINUS, to commit suicide.

Rufus 1, Marcus Caelius (*c.*88–48 BC), was a senator from Interamna. He trained as an advocate under CICERO (1) and CRASSUS (3), and successfully prosecuted ANTONIUS (1) Hybrida in 59 for extortion in his province. He was prosecuted in 56 for his part in the murder of some Alexandrian ambassadors who had come to Rome to oppose the restoration of PTOLEMY (8) XII the Piper. He was acquitted with the help of Crassus and Cicero, whose extant speech suggested that Rufus was the victim of a revenge plot by CLODIA (the widow of METELLUS 8), whose lover he had been. He was tribune in 52 (when he supported MILO during his trial), aedile in 50, served in CAESAR (1)'s forces in Spain, and was praetor in 48. He tried to pass laws to relieve debt in opposition to his colleagues and was removed from office. He then led a rebellion, which Milo joined, only to be killed. He corresponded with Cicero, and his extant letters (*Ad Fam.*, 8) are lively and interesting. See T.P. Wiseman (1985) *Catullus and his World*, Cambridge: Cambridge University Press.

2, Curtius (C1 AD), was a 'new man' senator and protégé of TIBERIUS, said to be the son of a gladiator. He was suffect consul in 43, and in 47 was CLAUDIUS (1)'s legate in Upper Germany where he used troops to mine for silver and was awarded triumphal decorations. Many years later TACITUS (1) reports that he became proconsul of Africa, a post that had been predicted for him in a vision years earlier, and died while in office.

The same man was almost certainly the author of a history of the reign of Alexander the Great in ten books, of which the first two are lost and the rest, though extant, have gaps. His ultimate main source was Cleitarchus, though there is a strand shared with ARRIAN: he is useful for preserving the Cleitarchan tradition of Alexander and of Macedonian customs, though he dressed up his narrative in rhetorical showmanship, offering the reader unsubstantiated motives and moralising, and added many speeches. He delights in romanticising the story with sensational detail; he gives little information as to his sources, but does not invent 'facts'. Despite his view that Alexander's character deteriorated dramatically, he finished the work with an encomium of the king. See A.B. Bosworth (1988) *From Arrian to Alexander*, Oxford: Clarendon Press.

3, Gaius Musonius (*c.*AD 25–*c.*100), was a Stoic philosopher of equestrian rank from Volsinii, who was banished from Rome several times for his anti-imperial attitude. He accompanied RUBELLIUS (2) Plautus in 60 when NERO (1) banished him to Asia Minor. He returned on the death of his friend, but fell under suspicion in 65 on the discovery of PISO (2)'s plot and was exiled to Gyaros. After returning again in 68 he offended VESPASIAN the following year by seeming to try to undermine his army's loyalty. TITUS allowed him to return. He had a wide circle of adherents among the Roman nobility and taught Epictetus and DIO

CHRYSOSTOM, though no writings are known.

4, Publius Rutilius (*c.*160–*c.*90 BC) was a politician, lawyer and historian. A pupil of PANAETIUS and a Stoic, he studied law under SCAEVOLA (2) and public speaking under Sulpicius GALBA (4), and served at the siege of Numantia under SCIPIO (11) Aemilianus. He was defeated in the consular election for 115 by SCAURUS (2), and had to wait ten more years for the post. He and his opponent vainly prosecuted each other for electoral bribery. He served in Numidia in the army of METELLUS (5) Numidicus in 109 and 108, and in spite of success in the field he gained the undying hatred of his fellow legate MARIUS (1). In his consulship (105) he instituted army reforms, including new drills, and restored Roman morale after their crushing defeat by the Cimbri at Orange. In 94 he went to Asia as a legate of the consul SCAEVOLA (4), assisted in the reorganisation of the province, and ruled it alone for three months in 93, giving much offence to the Roman equestrian businessmen there, whom he controlled strictly. They unjustly prosecuted him for extortion in 92 with Marius' support, and though he compared himself to Socrates in his defence speech, the equestrian jury found him guilty. The provincials of Asia were grateful to him, however, and so he went into exile at Smyrna, of which he became an honoured citizen. There he wrote his influential (lost) history which was well known to SALLUST. CICERO (1) met him in Smyrna. The upshot of his trial was the reforms proposed by DRUSUS (2). See E. Badian (1972) *Publicans and Sinners*, Oxford: Blackwell; M.C. Alexander (1990) *Trials in the Late Roman Republic, 149–50 BC*, Toronto: University of Toronto Press.

5, Lucius Verginius (died AD 97), was a statesman and general from Milan, whose first consulship was in AD 63. In 67 NERO (1) appointed him governor of Upper Germany, and the following year he suppressed the rebellion of VINDEX at the battle of Vesontio (Besançon), though he had first tried to negotiate a settlement. Being of republican sentiment, he rejected an offer from his troops to make him emperor in 68, but was nevertheless suspect to GALBA (1), who removed him from his command. In 69 OTHO gave Rufus a second (suffect) consulship, and he was once more offered imperial power after Otho's murder. He lived quietly through the Flavian era, taking a third consulship in 97 with the emperor NERVA (4) as his colleague. He was the guardian of the Younger PLINY (2), who admired him greatly. The historian TACITUS (1) delivered his funeral oration. Pliny quotes his epitaph (9. 19).

6. of Ephesus (later C1 AD) was a physician and medical writer. After studying at Alexandria, he practised in his home city, also visiting other centres of medical learning in Cos and Caria. Being of the Hippocratic tradition, he took a pragmatic approach to medical practice and to treating patients: he avoided reliance on theories, and insisted on the importance of anatomical study. Many of his works survive, including treatises on diet and pathology. His work, which was praised by GALEN, had greater influence in the east than the west. His works surviving in whole or part are *The Nomenclature of the Parts of the Human Body*, *Medical Questions*, *The Pathology of the Kidneys and Bladder*, *Satyriasis and Gonorrhoea*, *The Treatment of Jaundice* (from Latin and Arabic versions), and *Gout* (from a Latin version). Fragments of works from Arabic versions, on diet, paediatrics and melancholia, are also known. He showed unusual interest in curing slaves and old people. See G.E.R. Lloyd (1933) *Science, Folklore and Ideology*, Cambridge: Cambridge University Press.

See also CLUVIUS, SALVIDIENUS, SULPICIUS, VALGIUS.

Rullus, Publius Servilius (tribune 63 BC), proposed to the People's Assembly a radical land bill, supported by CRASSUS (3) and CAESAR (1), with the aim of redistributing public land in Italy and the provinces. The bill may have been meant to forestall measures of POMPEIUS (2), who was expected back from the east. CICERO (1) put a stop to the bill with three largely extant speeches *On the Land Bill.*

Rupilius, Publius (died *c.*131 BC), from Praeneste, a friend of SCIPIO (11) Aemilianus, was consul in 132 when he and his colleague Popillius LAENAS (3) presided over a court of inquiry (*quaestio*) to punish the followers of Tiberius GRACCHUS (4), whose land commission nevertheless continued to act. Rupilius was, however, summoned to Sicily to deal with the rebellion of slaves, after which he held a commission of senators to reorganise the administration of the province under a law named after him.

Rutilius Gallicus, Publius (late C1 AD) The poet STATIUS, in a poem (*Silvae*, 1, 4) composed to mark his recovery from sickness, gives much information about his career. He came from Turin; during NERO (1)'s reign he ruled Galatia as CORBULO's legate for six years. He was suffect consul in 71 (or 72). He held a census in Africa in 73 and governed Lower Germany as the emperor's legate from 76 to 79, during which he defeated the Bructeri and captured Veleda, a priestess who had promoted the rebellion of CIVILIS. He was proconsul of Asia *c.*82, and held a second consulship in 85. He died *c.*92 while prefect of the city of Rome.

S

Sabina, Vibia (AD 88–*c*.137), was the daughter of L.Vibius Sabinus and MATIDIA and a great-niece of TRAJAN, whose wife PLOTINA selected Sabina for marriage to HADRIAN in 100. Their childless union was variously described as miserable or just satisfactory: Hadrian's biographer says that he declared that if he had not been emperor he would have divorced her for her unpleasant character. On the other hand Hadrian dismissed from their posts SUETONIUS (2), the Praetorian Prefect Septicius Clarus, and others for being too familiar with her. She received the title *Augusta* in 128, and accompanied Hadrian to Egypt in 130, when JULIA (9) Balbilla carved a poem praising her beauty on a statue of Memnon. The manner of her death is unknown, despite rumours that Hadrian poisoned her. He accorded her divine honours.

Sabinus 1, Gaius Calvisius (C1 BC), in 48 served in the army of CAESAR (1) in Greece, and in 45 governed Africa. He was praetor in 44 and tried to defend Caesar when he was assassinated. He was foiled of the province of Africa in late 44 when CORNIFICIUS (2) forestalled him. After his consulship of 39 he acted as Octavian's (see AUGUSTUS) admiral against Sextus POMPEIUS (4), and in 36 pacified Italy. He governed Spain in 30 and held a triumph the following year. He was rewarded for his steadfast loyalty and hard work with a couple of priesthoods.

2, Flavius (*c*.AD 6–69), was the emperor VESPASIAN's elder brother who, like him, embarked on a senatorial career. Having been present at the invasion of Britain, he was suffect consul *c*.47 and governed Moesia as CLAUDIUS (1)'s legate *c*.53–60; he also held the important post of city prefect of Rome, possibly more than once. He was dismissed by GALBA (1) but reinstated by OTHO, who was anxious to conciliate Vespasian, as city prefect commanding the urban cohorts. In December 69, as Vespasian's representative in Rome, he was negotiating with VITELLIUS (1) for his abdication when some troops loyal to Vitellius seized him and, after besieging him in the Capitol, killed him in front of Vitellius, who vainly tried to save him.

3, Titus Flavius (C1 AD), a grandson of SABINUS (1), was suffect consul in 69. He married FLAVIA JULIA, a daughter of the emperor TITUS and later DOMITIAN's mistress. He was appointed to be Domitian's colleague as consul in 82, but was executed after the herald had proclaimed him emperor instead of consul.

4, Masurius (early C1 AD), was a writer and teacher of law, born in Verona. A citizen of humble circumstances, he maintained himself by fees and gifts from his pupils, among whom was Gaius CASSIUS

(3) Longinus, and over a long career he achieved the highest distinction as a legal expert, gaining equestrian status when he was nearly fifty. TIBERIUS accorded him the privilege, previously only granted to senators, of giving legal opinions on the authority of the emperor. He wrote important legal handbooks which have not survived: the chief one, a standard systematic work, *Civil Law*, in three books, was simply known as 'Sabinus'; others were *The City Prefect's Edict*, *Theft* and *Opinions*; he also published correspondence. His works were the subject of commentaries by later jurists, Sextus POMPONIUS (2), PAULUS and ULPIANUS. His pupil Cassius Longinus founded a school for lawyers in which Sabinus himself also taught, and which came to be known as the Sabinian or Cassian school: it was a real school and survived until *c*.190; later heads of the school were JAVOLENUS and JULIANUS.

Sacrovir, Julius (C1 AD), was a Gallic rebel against the Roman occupation of his country. An Aeduan of citizen rank, he conspired in AD 21 with the Treveran Julius Florus to rebel against Rome, prompted by debt and the high interest rates charged by the Roman businessmen. Though he seized the town of Augustodunum (Autun) with a large army of Gauls, he was defeated by Gaius Silius, the governor of Upper Germany, and killed himself.

Salinator, Marcus Livius (254–*c*.200 BC), was consul in 219 with PAULLUS (1), when they triumphed over the DEMETRIUS (3) of Pharos. He was accused of lining his pocket, convicted, fined, and went into exile. He thus avoided service in the Second Punic War, and felt betrayed by the treachery of his father-in-law, Pacuvius of Capua, who joined the Carthaginian side. The consuls of 210 prevailed on him to come back, but he did not join senatorial debate for the next two years, until he had to speak for a friend in jeopardy. Elected once more consul for 207, he was reconciled for the republic's sake to his colleague Claudius NERO (2), who had given evidence against him at his trial, and he defeated HASDRUBAL (2) on the river Metaurus. He held a second triumph, and between 206 and 204 as proconsul he managed the war in Etruria and Gaul. He was censor in 204 with Nero as his colleague again: their former enmity reasserted itself. The poet Livius ANDRONICUS was his freedman and taught his children.

Sallust (86–34 BC) (Gaius Sallustius Crispus) was a Roman historian from Amiternum in the Sabine country. He was a member of the local gentry but a 'new man' in Roman politics. In 52 as a tribune he acted against MILO and CICERO (1), for which the censors expelled him from the Senate in 50 (though he was actually charged with immoral conduct). Subsequently he joined CAESAR (1) who gave him a legionary command in 49. He was elected praetor for 46 and served his year in Caesar's African campaign, following which he governed as proconsul Caesar's new conquests in Africa ('New Africa') to the west of the old Roman province. On his return to Rome he was accused of extortion (and was probably guilty) but escaped condemnation thanks to Caesar's influence. Having no prospect of further office, and being disgusted with the 'triumvirate', he then retired from public life to write history. He married TERENTIA, the divorced wife of CICERO (1), which might account for his hostility to him.

He began with a couple of monographs (see COELIUS 2), *Catiline's Conspiracy* and *The War with Jugurtha*. For the former, written *c*.42, he drew on the testimony of Cicero, though he played down the primacy of his role in the suppression of the plot. As a historian he was a moraliser, painting a picture of the deterioration and corruption of Roman nobility for which the destruction of Carthage and the civil strife between

SULLA (2) and his enemies was mainly to blame, and which came to infect the whole body politic. His interest in the subject of CATILINE's conspiracy was aroused by the 'novelty both of the crime and of the danger to which it exposed the state': thus he acknowledged Cicero's correct handling of the crisis. However, he makes Caesar and CATO (5) the heroes of the day, and presents their speeches in the Senate at excessive length: yet the two men represented very different qualities. He wrote *The War with Jugurtha c.*40, choosing the theme for the length and intensity of the struggle and uncertainty of its outcome and because it marked the first challenge to the arrogance of the nobles. The events of the military campaigns are presented patchily, but the accompanying political background is handled more firmly. Individuals are shown declining morally from good beginnings, men such as the 'new man' MARIUS (1), Sulla, JUGURTHA himself, and METELLUS (5) Numidicus, the last of whom, however, Sallust clearly admired. The work is divided up by speeches and digressions, and the geography and chronology are not always accurate. Next he embarked on a more ambitious work, the *Histories*, of which five books are known, perhaps continuing the work of SISENNA: the narrative starts from 78. Only a few speeches and letters survive from this enterprise, in which he again pictured the decline of the state with particular condemnation of POMPEIUS (2). Other works of later date, an *Invective against Cicero*, and *Letters to Caesar in Old Age*, were wrongly attributed to Sallust.

Sallust modelled his style on those of the Athenian historian Thucydides and of Marcus CATO (4) the Censor. It displays a terseness, obscurity, and archaic quality quite in line with the style of those authors. It also shows strong characterisation and powerful speeches, unusual diction, and Greek borrowings. The rapid, frequently epigrammatic style that Sallust thus adopted was very influential on later Roman historians, especially TACITUS (1). On the other hand Sallust lacked Thucydides' profundity and objectivity, and in his introductory statements he often expresses commonplace ideas and an uncritical morality. His prejudices must reflect the frustrations of an unsuccessful 'new man'. See D.C. Earl (1961) *The Political Thought of Sallust*, Cambridge: Cambridge University Press; R. Syme (1964) *Sallust*, Berkeley: University of California Press.

Sallustius 1. Crispus, Gaius (died AD 20), was the great-nephew of SALLUST, whom the latter adopted. He remained an equestrian and succeeded MAECENAS in the role of AUGUSTUS' private adviser. On the death of Augustus in AD 14 he was cognizant of the murder of AGRIPPA (2) Postumus which Tiberius must have approved. In 16 he arrested a slave who was claiming to be Agrippa. He was immensely rich, owning copper mines in the Graian Alps, and constructed the magnificent Gardens of Sallust on the Quirinal in Rome. TACITUS (1) describes his life of studied refinement as bringing elaborate wealth almost to the point of decadence. His heir, his adopted son C. Sallustius Passienus Crispus, married AGRIPPINA (4), the mother of NERO (1).

2. (C4 AD) was the writer of *The Gods and the World*, an extant Neoplatonic work. He was probably Flavius Sallustius, consul in 363 and a friend of the emperor JULIAN, and wrote his book in support of the emperor's anti-Christian stance.

Salvidienus Rufus, Quintus (died 40 BC), was an equestrian of obscure origin who was studying in Apollonia under ATHENODORUS (2) with Octavian (see AUGUSTUS) and AGRIPPA (1) in spring 44 when news came of CAESAR (1)'s assassination. For a time Octavian invested great trust in him (he was somewhat older than Octavian), and he proved a successful general. In 42 Sextus POMPEIUS (4) defeated him in a sea-battle near Rhegium (Reggio Calabria). In 41 he failed to reach his province in Spain, though he had six legions: ANTONIUS (7)'s men under POLLIO (1) blocked his way through northern Italy. He returned to face the recalcitrant Lucius ANTONIUS (4) at Perusia, on his way destroying the town of Sentinum. He prevented the Antonian relief army reaching Perusia, and after its fall was appointed by Octavian in 40 to govern Gaul, and designated to be consul the next year despite his equestrian status. However, later in 40 when Antonius was besieging Brundisium, Salvidienus offered to bring his army to assist him. After the pact of Brundisium had been forged, Antonius reported the fact to Octavian, who denounced Salvidienus to the Senate, which voted to declare him a public enemy. He died either by suicide or execution.

Sapor The Romanised form of the Persian *Shabuhr*, the name of several Iranian kings of the Sassanid house.

1. I (reigned AD 240–272) was the son of ARTAXERXES I, who founded the Sassanid house and made Sapor co-regent in the last year of his life. Like his father, he was aggressive towards Rome, his western neighbour, taking full advantage of her prolonged weakness with his opportunistic incursions. He took the title 'King of Kings of Iran and non-Iran' and claimed the ownership of all lands that Persia had ever lost to the Greeks and Romans. He engaged in three great campaigns against Rome: 242–4, when he overran Mesopotamia, culminating in the battle of Misiche (244) when GORDIAN (3) III was defeated and killed. The Romans then tried to buy him off, but *c.*252 he took over Armenia and drove out its last king. He next attacked Syria, taking Antioch for the first time, and in 259 began a further campaign into Asia Minor which led to his capture of the emperor VALERIAN in 260 near Edessa. He seized Syria, captured the passes over the Taurus Mountains, destroyed Tarsus, and took Caesarea in Cappadocia. P. Septimius ODAENATHUS, king of Palmyra, fought a major counter-offensive between 262 and 266, in which he ejected Sapor from Roman territory. Sapor had an inscription made of his achievements entitled, after the manner of the emperor AUGUSTUS, *The Deeds of the Divine Sapor* (*Res Gestae Divi Saporis*) with a carving showing Valerian kneeling before him, which he set up at Naqshi-i Rustam. He supported the religious movement of his contemporary, MANI, and built lavishly using Roman prisoners for labour.

2. II (reigned AD 309–379) ascended the throne in childhood. In 336 he invaded Armenia, but was expelled by Hannibalian, a nephew of CONSTANTINE (1) I. In the following years he kept up constant pressure on Nisibis, which he besieged three times. He was defeated in 345 by CONSTANTIUS (2) II. In 362 his army was defeated by that of JULIAN near Ctesiphon, but next year he killed Julian in a skirmish. JOVIAN made large concessions of territory to him.

Saturninus 1, Lucius Antonius (late C1 AD), was an insurgent against DOMITIAN. He was a 'new man' who attained to a suffect consulship *c.*82. Appointed governor of Upper Germany, he plotted with the Germans to overthrow the emperor for reasons we do not know. He struck on 1 January 89 at Mogontiacum (Maintz) and fought a battle near the Rhine with the army of Lower Germany under Lippius Maximus, in which he was defeated and killed. His German allies were prevented from helping him by a thaw of the ice on the river. Domitian, on hearing of the revolt, hurried to the province: he was deeply shocked by the event and thenceforth his suspicions of those around him were roused and executions ensued.

2, Lucius Appuleius (died 100 BC), was the quaestor in charge of the grain supply at Ostia in 104 when his sudden dismissal to be replaced by SCAURUS (2) changed his views to extreme radicalism. As tribune in 103 he passed a law to grant land allotments to the veterans of MARIUS (1)'s African army. In 101 he organised a mob to break up a meeting of the tribal assembly where he was being accused of insulting the ambassadors of MITHRIDATES (3) VI. Thanks to gang violence, he was re-elected tribune for 100. Either then or in 103 he proposed a law to distribute cheap grain in the teeth of his colleagues' opposition, and a law to establish a court to hear cases of 'debasing the majesty of the State', directed against the aristocratic faction in the Senate. In the years between his two tribuneships he united with Gaius Servilius GLAUCIA to stir up the mob. The censor METELLUS (5) Numidicus tried to expel the two from the Senate, but was thwarted by his colleague. In 100 Marius was consul, Glaucia praetor, and Saturninus tribune. He proposed measures to settle Marius' veterans in Gaul and to grant Marius the power to give citizenship to non-Roman colonists; he also legislated for the raising of troops and seeking of support from client states to clear the pirates from the eastern seas (Marius would be their commander). He attached to the bill an oath of obedience, which all senators had to swear on pain of exile, and passed it by means of violence. Though Marius softened the oath, Metellus refused to take it and departed into exile. Saturninus, however, had forfeited the support of the urban mob by his measures for extending the citizenship. He had already been elected tribune for a third time for 99, and supported the candidacy of Glaucia for the consulship of that year. Marius now turned on his allies and declared Glaucia's candidacy illegal. Saturninus organised the murder of Gaius MEMMIUS (1), a rival of Glaucia's, and also had a law steamrollered through the plebeian assembly to make Glaucia's candidacy legal. A riot ensued during which M. Scaurus, leader of the Senate, had the 'Ultimate Decree' passed. Marius, as consul, used an improvised force to pen the conspirators in the Capitol. They surrendered on an official promise of safety, and were transferred to the Senate House, where the mob climbed on the roof, tore it off, and killed them by pelting them with tiles. The Senate declared Saturninus' legislation null and void as having been carried by violence, though Marius' men probably received their land.

3, Gaius Sentius (late C1 BC), was a senator related to AUGUSTUS' wife SCRIBONIA. In Augustus' absence in the east in 20 BC, Saturninus was elected consul for the next year without a colleague. He refused to accept the candidacy of EGNATIUS (3) Rufus for the vacant consulship, declaring that he would not accept him even if the people elected him. He then had Egnatius arrested and put to death for plotting against the emperor. He resigned before the end of his year, and later held various posts, proconsul of Africa (*c.*14), governor of Syria from 9 to 6 BC, legate to TIBERIUS in Germany in AD 4 and 5, and commander of the Rhine army, which he led in 6 AD in concert with Tiberius' other forces against the German king MAROBODUUS in Bohemia. He was rewarded with triumphal decorations. His two sons were both consuls in AD 4.

Scaevola 1, Quintus Cervidius (late C2 AD), was a jurist, teacher and writer on legal matters from Carthage; his wife came from an important family in Nîmes. He was MARCUS AURELIUS' principal legal adviser and was appointed Chief of Police (*Praefectus Vigilum*) at Rome from 175 to 177. He taught the lawyers PAULUS and Tryphoninus. He published a work entitled *Various Questions* in twenty books, six books of *Opinions* and forty of *Abstracts* (*Digesta*). There is some overlap between these collections and it is conjectured that whereas the *Opinions* were published by Scaevola during his lifetime, the *Abstracts* were collected and published after his death, perhaps by his pupil Tryphoninus, who added notes. Many of the cases, which were taken from his vast practice, were concerned with the eastern provinces, and sometimes the facts are reported in Greek. The *Opinions* are sometimes very terse and carry annotation by his successors. Scaevola, who also added notes to the *Abstracts* of MARCELLUS (8) and JULIANUS, was admired by MODESTINUS, and though he fell into disrepute, he was quoted more than 300 times in the Code of Justinian.

2, Publius Mucius (C2 BC), a brother of CRASSUS (5) whom he succeeded in 130 as chief priest of the Roman state (*Pontifex Maximus*), was a politician and jurist. In his tribuneship of 141 he set up a court to try a corrupt former praetor, L. Hostilius Tubulus. He was praetor in 136 and, as consul in 133, being hostile to SCIPIO (11) Aemilianus and a legal expert, he lent support and advice to Tiberius GRACCHUS (4), declining to suppress him by force as certain senators wished. However, when SCIPIO (12) Nasica killed Gracchus, Scaevola refused to condemn Scipio's act. He continued a family tradition of legal expertise, which he passed on to his son SCAEVOLA (4), and was responsible for the publication of the *Great Annals* (*Annales Maximi*) of the Roman State, which was a record of postholders and events.

3, Quintus Mucius (C2–1 BC), was a politician and jurist, known as the Augur to distinguish him from his younger namesake SCAEVOLA (4). He was tribune in 128 and aedile in 125. He was a Stoic and his daughter married Acilius GLABRIO (2). He governed the province of Asia as praetor and proconsul in 121–0 and returned to a charge of extortion, of which he was acquitted: his accuser, Titus ALBUCIUS, was satirised by LUCILIUS (1) for his prosecution. Scaevola held the consulship in 117; in 100 he was an opponent of SATURNINUS (2). He taught law to his son-in-law Lucius CRASSUS (2) and to CICERO (1), who admired him greatly to the extent of introducing him as a speaker in his works *On the Orator*, *Laelius on Friendship* and *The Republic*. He died *c.*87.

4, Quintus Mucius (C2–1 BC), a son of SCAEVOLA (2), was the leading lawyer of his age. CICERO (1) in his *Orator* (1. 180) describes a case in which a will was disputed: Scaevola upheld the strict wording of the will against Lucius CRASSUS (5)'s pleas for greater weight to be given to equity and the writer's presumed intention. He was tribune in 106, aedile in 104 and consul in 95, his colleague being Lucius Crassus. During their year of office they passed a law to create a court to investigate false claims to Roman citizenship, and thus expel a mass of Italians who had joined the gangs of SATURNINUS (2) five years earlier. The measure was to cause distress, however, and led to the Social War. In 94 Scaevola governed the province of Asia as proconsul, and worked hard to reorganise a province which had fallen on hard times thanks to the tax-gatherers unleashed by the reforms of Gaius GRACCHUS (1). After publishing a model edict for the province, Scaevola returned home, leaving his legate Rutilius RUFUS (5) to finish his term of office and in 92 face the prosecution organised by the angry equestrian financiers at home. Scaevola was too well connected (MARIUS 1 was a distant relative) to be included in the prosecution. In 89 he was elected chief priest (*Pontifex Maximus*). After the death of Marius in 86, Gaius FIMBRIA threatened to prosecute him, but CINNA (2) protected him. He continued to live in Rome during the rule of Cinna and CARBO (5), urging restraint in the face of SULLA (2), but was killed by the Marian BRUTUS (3) Damasippus before he could join Sulla. Scaevola was the greatest legal writer and teacher of republican times. He published a lost work in eighteen books entitled *Civil Law*, which was being studied and commented on 200 years later, e.g. by POMPONIUS (2). He also worked on legal distinctions and wrote a book of definitions (*Horoi*) and studied classification, though he failed to produce a systematised code of law. He lectured on law to many leading men, including Cicero, Servius SULPICIUS (2) Rufus and AQUILLIUS (3) Gallus.

Scaurus 1, Mamercus Aemilius (early C1 AD), son of SCAURUS (4), suffect consul in AD 2, was an orator, advocate and poet. He married Aemilia Lepida, widow of QUIRINIUS, who bore him a son. Notorious for his immoral life, he was prosecuted for treason under TIBERIUS, who disliked him, in 32 and 34, and the second time committed suicide, accompanied by his wife.

2, Marcus Aemilius (*c*.155–89 BC), was a politician and advocate. His family was patrician but had fallen on hard times and he had to work as hard as a 'new man' for election to senatorial posts. Supported by the powerful clan of the Metelli – he married CAECILIA Metella, daughter of METELLUS (2) Delmaticus, who bore him two children – he was elected consul for 115, with a Metellus as his colleague. In doing so he defeated Rutilius RUFUS (4), and the two vainly engaged in mutual prosecution for bribery of the electorate. During his consulship he humiliated the praetor Decius SUBULO who had prosecuted the victorious OPIMIUS, won a victory over the Ligurians for which he earned a triumph, and began the great Aemilian Way through Cisalpine Gaul. He was made leader (*princeps*) of the Senate by the censors (one his father-in-law), perhaps unfairly, as there were patricians alive senior to him. He became the effective leader of the Metelli in the Senate and presided over the court to investigate senatorial corruption set up by the tribune MAMILIUS (1) Limetanus, despite his having led an embassy in 112 to negotiate with JUGURTHA. He had also served as legate to BESTIA in his unsuccessful campaign against Jugurtha in 111. He was a censor in 109 but had to resign when his colleague, M. Livius DRUSUS (1) died. In 104 he took over the management of the supply of cheap grain from SATURNINUS (2), and in 100 proposed the emergency 'Ultimate Decree' of the Senate against Saturninus and his mob. He went *c*.95 as head of an embassy to the province of Asia, which was suffering under the rapacity of Roman governors and businessmen: this seems to have led to SCAEVOLA (4)'s humane governorship. In 92 and again in 90 he was targeted by CAEPIO (4), who was hostile to M. Livius DRUSUS (2), whom Scaurus was now supporting in his attempt to conciliate the Italians, but escaped prosecution. In 90 the tribune Q. Varius, who had created a court to punish those who had negotiated with the Italians, summoned Scaurus before it, but Scaurus delivered a withering speech, which silenced him (see PLAUTIUS 3). He died a rich man, having earned his wealth through business rather than extortion: his methods may not always have been honest and he took a bribe from Jugurtha, but he was never convicted of a crime. A powerful man who, according to CICERO (1), 'almost ruled the world with his nod', he wrote an autobiography which failed to survive long. SALLUST described him as a disreputable power-seeker. See E. Badian (1964) *Studies in Greek and Roman History*, Oxford: Blackwell; E.S. Gruen (1968) *Roman Politics and the Roman Criminal Courts, 149–78 BC*, Cambridge MA: Harvard University Press.

3, Marcus Aemilius (C1 BC), became a stepson of SULLA (2) when his mother, Caecilia METELLA, remarried after the death of his father, SCAURUS (2). In 65, while serving under POMPEIUS (2) as quaestor, he fought a war in the Arab kingdom of Nabataea for any booty he could gain, which he dressed up as a victory on coinage he minted in 58 when he was an aedile. He had inherited a fortune from his father, which he spent on games to support his candidacy for the praetorship of 56. As city praetor he presided at the trial of SESTIUS for violent behaviour. As governor of Sardinia in 55 he robbed the provincials, for which he was tried in 54 but acquitted thanks to speeches by CICERO (1) and other leading men. In 54 he stood for the next year's consulship but, like all the other candidates, was found guilty of bribing the electorate. Once again, Cicero spoke for him, but the hostility of Pompeius, whose divorced wife MUCIA TERTIA Scaurus had married, tilted the balance, and he left Italy to live in exile.

4, Marcus Aemilius (C1 BC) A son of SCAURUS (3) by MUCIA TERTIA, he joined and supported his stepbrother Sextus POMPEIUS (4) throughout his campaigns. After the fall of Sextus he joined ANTONIUS (7), and after Actium surrendered to Octavian (AUGUSTUS), when he was pardoned. He may have played some part in politics, but did not reach the consulship.

Scerdilaidas (C3 BC) was a king of the Ardiaei of southern Illyria, probably the son of King Pleuratus and younger brother of King Agron. In 231 BC Agron died and his widow Teuta acted as regent for her stepson Pinnes: meanwhile Scerdilaidas led the army in an attack on Epirus. A year later Teuta was defeated by Roman forces in alliance with DEMETRIUS (3) of Pharos, who became the effective ruler and a 'friend and ally' of Rome, and the Illyrian kingdom was much reduced in size. We do not know what part Scerdilaidas took in these events. Subsequently, in 220, he joined Demetrius and the Aetolians in a naval attack on Pylos and the Aegean islands, but then switched sides and joined the Hellenic Confederacy led by PHILIP (1) V. In 219 Demetrius was expelled from Pharos by Rome and took refuge with Philip. After this Scerdilaidas seems to have cooperated with the Romans, and in 217–16 he warned them of Philip's aggressive preparations and received ten Roman ships to defend his coast. In 213–12 he was attacked by Philip, who took Lissus. At some time he discarded Pinnes and took the kingship, and in 211 he allied himself with Rome and Aetolia. He died sometime before the Peace of Phoenice in 205 and was succeeded by his son, Pleuratus. See J.J. Wilkes (1992) *The Illyrians*, Oxford: Blackwell.

Scipio 1, Gnaeus Cornelius, known as Calvus ('the bald') (died 211 BC), the son of SCIPIO (3) and elder brother of Publius SCIPIO (6), was a general in the Second Punic War. In his consulship in 222 BC he and his colleague MARCELLUS (3) were occupied against the Gauls of the Po valley and took Mediolanum (Milan) from the Insubres. In 218, his brother Publius the consul sent him to Spain to keep the Carthaginians there in play, to prevent them reinforcing HANNIBAL, now in the foothills of the Alps. Probably holding proconsular power, he based his army at Emporiae (Ampurias), and won considerable victories in Spain, conquering much territory north of the Ebro. In 217 he won a decisive battle over the Punic fleet in the mouth of that river. He next sailed south, raiding the coast to establish bases. His brother then joined him and they set up camp near Saguntum. In 215 they defeated HASDRUBAL (2), who was trying to lead reinforcements to Hannibal in Italy, at Ibera on the Ebro, and thus temporarily stopped his design. By 212 they had captured Saguntum and the next year, far from their base, in the face of a massive Carthaginian offensive on three fronts, they split their forces. Both were defeated, Publius was killed, and Calvus, who had sought to retreat, was caught and slain with his men at Ilourgeia (Ilorci) near Cartagena (New Carthage).

2, Lucius Cornelius, known as Barbatus ('bearded') (early C3 BC), was a general in the Third Samnite War, the first known member of the powerful family of the Scipios. We know something of him from the verse epitaph carved on his sarcophagus found in the tomb of the Scipios. He was consul in 298, censor *c.*280, took two places in Samnium, and 'subdued all Lucania', a very improbable claim. But in 296 he was heavily defeated at Camerinum in Umbria by a coalition led by the Samnite Gellius EGNATIUS (1).

3, Lucius Cornelius (mid-C3 BC), son of SCIPIO (2), was a successful admiral. He was consul in 259 and censor the following year. During his consulship in the First Punic War he fought in Corsica and Sardinia with mixed success, trying to prevent the Carthaginian fleet from establishing a base there. He took Aleria in Corsica but could not capture Olbia in Sardinia. However, he held a triumph and founded a temple of thanksgiving to the storm-winds near the Capena gate of Rome.

4, Lucius Cornelius, known as Asiagenes ('Asiatic') (C3–2 BC), was a son of SCIPIO (6) and younger brother of SCIPIO (7) Africanus. He served under his brother in several campaigns, and was considered far inferior to him in generalship. Between 207 and 202 BC he served as an officer (legatus) in his brother's army in Spain, Sicily and Africa: in 207 he took the Spanish town of Orongis. In 193 as praetor he operated again in Sicily. He was legate of Manius Acilius GLABRIO (1) in 191 in Greece and reported the victory over ANTIOCHUS (1) III at Thermopylae to the Senate. As consul in 190 he continued the campaign against Antiochus with his elder brother serving as his legate (though in fact the real commander). He made a truce with the Aetolians and transported his army to Asia Minor, where he decisively defeated Antiochus at Magnesia in December (his brother was sick and took no part). Having made a provisional peace treaty with Antiochus, he returned and in 188 held his triumph and adopted his extra name. In 187, however, he was charged before the Senate on the authority of CATO (4) the Censor with diverting a sum of 500 talents from the king's indemnity to give his troops a bonus. His brother, however, intervened and seized Lucius' accounts, so making himself answerable. The attack was transferred to the Assembly of the People, but Africanus' speech overwhelmed the tribunes bringing the action. In 184, an attempt to arrest and impeach Scipio was vetoed by Tiberius Sempronius GRACCHUS (3), but Cato with his colleague Valerius FLACCUS (6) expelled him from the Senate and equestrian order.

5, Lucius Cornelius (early C2 BC), the second son of SCIPIO (7), was taken prisoner before the battle of Thermopylae by ANTIOCHUS (1) III and released shortly before the battle of Magnesia. He was elected to the office of praetor for 174, but the election was held to be invalid and he was expelled from the Senate by the censors.

6, Publius Cornelius (died 211 BC), the son of SCIPIO (3) and younger brother of SCIPIO (1), was a general in the Second Punic War. Elected consul for 218, when the war began in March, he was ordered to take an army to Spain to confront HANNIBAL there, but was delayed by a rising in Cisalpine Gaul so that he failed to reach the Rhône before September. By this time Hannibal had already crossed the river well to the north. He divided his forces, sending part under his brother Gnaeus to Spain, while he himself returned to Cisalpine Gaul, where he suffered a defeat and was wounded in a cavalry skirmish on the river Ticino near Pavia. Having then retreated to Placentia (Piacenza), he joined forces with his colleague Tiberius Sempronius Longus, and in December they suffered a catastrophic defeat on the river Trebbia, losing more than half their army. The next year (217) he was sent as proconsul to join his elder brother in Spain, and together they established a base at Saguntum. In 215 the brothers defeated HASDRUBAL (2), who had been reinforced with African troops, near Dertosa; they moved south and wintered in the valley of the Guadalquivir. However, Hasdrubal was again heavily reinforced and in 211 caught the brothers unprepared and separated, far from their base, and defeated and killed them one by one: Publius was trapped by MAGO (2) and HASDRUBAL (3), and died fighting. His son was SCIPIO (7) Africanus.

7, Publius Cornelius, known as Africanus (236–183 BC), was a son of SCIPIO (6) and the elder brother of SCIPIO (4). He was the greatest Roman general of the Second Punic War. He was present at the battle of the Ticino in 218 when he saved his wounded father's life. He was a military tribune (legionary officer) at the disastrous defeat of Cannae in 216 and played a major part in restoring the morale of the survivors at Canusium. After serving as aedile in 213, he was voted unanimously by the people in 210 to the military command in Spain as proconsul despite not having held a senior post. He at once resumed his father's bold policy of taking the war to the enemy. In 209 he captured New Carthage (Cartagena), the enemy's chief base and depôt, by a brilliant stroke, sending his men wading across a lagoon which, he had been told, became shallow enough at low tide, to take the undefended walls. After spending the winter conciliating the inhabitants of Spain, he marched his army, swollen by Spanish recruits, towards HASDRUBAL (2)'s at Baecula (Bailen), attacked his camp, and fought a battle by unorthodox tactics, dividing his infantry so as to attack Hasdrubal's flanks. He won a complete victory, and was named *Imperator* by his troops. Hasdrubal escaped with the remnant of his army and elephants (later reinforced by troops from the army of MAGO 2) northwards towards the Pyrenees, hoping to reach Italy and reinforce his brother HANNIBAL. Scipio decided to refrain from pursuit and concentrate on the other two Carthaginian armies left in Spain. After further successes, in 206 he faced the armies of Mago and HASDRUBAL (3) son of Gisgo, at Ilipa near Seville: he crushed them there in two battles. The generals fled and Spain was freed from Punic power. Scipio sailed to Numidia for abortive discussions with SYPHAX, king of the Numidian Masaesylii. During the mopping-up operations Scipio fell ill and troops in camp on the Sucro mutinied: he recovered, executed the ringleaders and won back the loyalty of the rest. Near Cádiz he secretly met MASINISSA, exiled ruler of a small principality in eastern Numidia, and won his allegiance to Rome. He founded the colony of Italica near Seville.

On returning to Rome, though underage and unqualified, Scipio was elected consul for 205 and proposed to take the war to Africa. Against the opposition of the veteran ex-consuls Quintus FABIUS (8) MAXIMUS the Delayer and Quintus Fulvius FLACCUS (2), he was appointed to the province of Sicily and given permission to invade Africa should the opportunity arise. However, he was not granted the power to recruit troops, and had to rely on volunteers. After training his army in Sicily, on his way back he took the southern Italian town of Locri from Hannibal and installed the vicious PLEMINIUS as governor there, for which he was later severely criticised in the Senate. He invaded Africa in 204 with about 35,000 men, holding the rank of proconsul, besieged the town of Utica, and built a winter camp on a headland nearby, his enemies Syphax and Hasdrubal lying a little way to the south. The following spring he succeeded in attacking and burning their camps and killed many Carthaginian troops. He won a further crushing victory over Hasdrubal and Syphax on the 'Great Plains' in the valley of the Bagradas, installed Masinissa at Cirta on the throne of Numidia, and seized Tunis. Though he lost some sixty transport ships while trying to prevent a Carthaginian attack on his fleet at Utica, the Carthaginians indicated their readiness to come to terms. An armistice was made and the Senate agreed a peace treaty, which the Carthaginians accepted, though they recalled Hannibal and Mago against the terms of the treaty. Hannibal returned to Africa next spring (202), landing at Lepcis: a party of Carthaginians were ready to break the treaty, and soon after the Carthaginians attacked Roman ships and mauled some ambassadors Scipio sent to protest. Hannibal advanced from the south and though he had a large force of elephants, Scipio was now equipped with Masinissa's excellent cavalry. The battle of Zama Regia (19 October) proved at first to be an infantry stalemate, but the Roman and Numidian cavalry attacked the Punic rear and Scipio finished Hannibal's force the same way he had crushed the Romans at Cannae. Scipio earned a triumph and the title 'Africanus'.

Scipio was elected censor in 199 and became leader of the Senate (*princeps senatus*), an extraordinary position for such a young man and one in which he was confirmed by his successors in the censorship. In 195 he vainly tried to defend Hannibal against Carthaginian accusations before the Senate of meddling in eastern affairs. He was elected to a second consulship in 194 when, afraid of an invasion by ANTIOCHUS (1) III, he opposed the decision to withdraw Roman forces from Greece. He wished to be appointed to succeed FLAMININUS as Roman commander in Greece, but the Senate refused: he had to content himself with a campaign in Cisalpine Gaul. The Senate sent him in 193 to North Africa to negotiate a settlement between Carthage and Masinissa, but the task was not to his liking and came to nought. In 190 his brother Lucius SCIPIO (4) Asiagenes, the consul, was sent to settle matters with Antiochus, and Africanus volunteered to accompany him as his legate, though in fact he was effectively the commander. He rejected a bribe from Antiochus to grant favourable terms of peace, but received his son Lucius SCIPIO (5), a prisoner of war, back from the king. After crossing to Asia with his brother, Scipio fell ill and took no part in the battle of Magnesia, but was invited by his brother to conduct negotiations with Antiochus.

At home the Scipionic family and their associates now came under persistent attack from opponents led by M. Porcius CATO (4), who prosecuted various members of the family in the courts for corruption, though details of the trials are lost. In 187, however, he accused Lucius Scipio Asiagenes in the Assembly of misappropriating some of the war indemnity paid by Antiochus, though Africanus with a speech put a speedy end to proceedings. In 184 Cato as censor expelled Lucius from the Senate and equestrian order: Africanus, taking it as a personal insult, left Rome for a self-imposed exile at Liternum in Campania, where he died the next year. A mighty figure, Publius Scipio was at his grandest in the context of the war in which he showed great resourcefulness, flair and imagination. He was a humane man who handled his subordinates well and won the affection of his troops and even, by generous dealings, of some enemies. He was a philhellene but at the same time a great patriot. His reform of the Roman army, turning it into a semi-professional force capable of use far across the sea, was portentous. He had a strong sense of his own divine destiny, perhaps seeing himself as specially blessed by Jupiter, but showed no ambition to exceed the powers of a consul and general of the republic, and in no way threatened the power of his fellow noblemen. He found peacetime politics frustrating, was less successful in political life, and became the victim of the jealousy of lesser men. See H.H. Scullard (1970) *Scipio Africanus:*

Soldier and Politician, London: Thames & Hudson.

8, Publius Cornelius, known as Nasica (C3–2 BC), was a son of SCIPIO (1), who, in 204 BC, as a result of his excellent character, was granted the honour of receiving on its arrival at Ostia a sacred stone from Pessinus said to represent the Phrygian goddess Cybele (the 'Great Mother'). This ceremony was the origin of the Megalensian Games. As praetor in 194 he served in Spain where he defeated a force of Lusitani near Ilipa. After defeat in the consular election for 191 he was elected for 190, when he finished the work of subduing the Boii, who lived around Bologna in Cisalpine Gaul, for which he held a triumph. He failed to be elected censor, a mark of the decline of his family, but served on a commission (183–1) which established the Latin colony of Aquilea. In 171 he acted as patron on behalf of Spanish provincials who complained to the Senate about the behaviour of their Roman governors. The name 'Nasica', used to distinguish this branch of the family, means 'long-nosed'.

9, Publius Cornelius (C2 BC), the eldest son of SCIPIO (7), was elected augur in 180. Poor health prevented his career from further progress. He wrote some short speeches (admired by CICERO 1) and a historical work in Greek, which have not survived, and adopted SCIPIO (11) Aemilianus as his son.

10, Publius Cornelius, known as Nasica Corculum (C2 BC), was a Roman politician and lawyer, the son of SCIPIO (9) and son-in-law of SCIPIO (7). He fought with distinction under the command of PAULLUS (2) at the battle of Pydna in 168 BC, and wrote to a king a letter about the battle which was used as a source by PLUTARCH (*Aemilius Paullus*, 15ff). After his election as consul for 162 he was recalled from his duties and was made to resign because of irregularities in his election. As censor in 159, he and his colleague purged the forum of statues which had been placed there without permission. In his second consulship (155) he served in Dalmatia, where he brought the war to a successful conclusion and earned a triumph. In 154 he succeeded in preventing on moral grounds the building of a permanent theatre at Rome as was proposed by the censors; he also opposed CATO (4)'s oft-repeated demand to declare war on Carthage again. In 152 on an embassy to Africa, he persuaded MASINISSA to give up some Carthaginian land he had occupied. In 150 he was sent to Greece to investigate the pretender Andriscus and tried to rouse opposition to him: this led to the successful expedition of METELLUS (4) Macedonicus. He became Leader of the Senate (*princeps senatus*) in 147 and chief priest (*Pontifex Maximus*) in 150. He was given his nickname Corculum for his sagacity: he was a renowned orator and upholder of public morality.

11. Aemilianus Africanus, Publius Cornelius (*c.*185–129 BC), was a Roman statesman, general and patron of arts and philosophy. He was the second son of Lucius Aemilius PAULLUS (2), and was adopted by SCIPIO (9) in childhood on his mother Papiria's death. He served under his natural father at the battle of Pydna in 168 and became acquainted with POLYBIUS, who was a hostage in Italy, whom he kept with him as his tutor in Greek matters, friend, and ultimately travelling companion. In 151 the Macedonians sent an envoy to him asking for his help in their current predicament, but he preferred to serve in Spain as a legate under Lucius LUCULLUS (1) on a tough assignment that few would volunteer for. In this service he won a mural crown for leading a scaling party in a siege, a high distinction. When Lucullus sent him to Numidia to request war elephants from MASINISSA, he was a spectator at a battle between Carthaginians and Numidians and unsuccessfully lent his diplomatic services in the subsequent negotiations. He served again with great success in Africa in 149–8, acting as an officer (military tribune) in the army of the consul Manius MANILIUS (2), winning the prestigious grassy crown for raising a siege and persuading a Carthaginian general to change sides. He was the executor of Masinissa's will, and after his death in 149 he divided the kingdom among his three sons. He returned to Rome to be a candidate for the aedileship of 147, but was elected consul by popular acclaim, though he was not qualified for the office. The Senate was pressured into allowing special legislation to be passed, though the issue was contentious, and he was given the task of finishing the Third Punic War. He went to Africa and, supported by his friend and subordinate LAELIUS (2), restored discipline to the army, and blockaded Carthage by land and sea, constructing for the latter purpose a huge mole. In 146 his troops entered the city, which was defended step by step. He ordered its complete destruction, which he supervised in person, and sold its citizens into slavery. He organised Africa into a province, assisted by a commission from the Senate, and put on lavish games there. On his return to Rome he held a magnificent triumph. The Senate also granted him the title 'Africanus', first given to his adoptive grandfather.

About this time (the dates are uncertain) he travelled to the east on official business at the head of a roving embassy, with the Stoic philosopher PANAETIUS in his retinue, and may have reached the frontiers of Parthia. In Egypt he investigated the state of the kingdom of PTOLEMY (4) VIII, and probably advised the Senate on policy in the east. He was elected censor in 142 with Lucius MUMMIUS as his colleague: his desire to carry out a purge of morally corrupt senators was mitigated by Mummius. In 136 Scipio led a movement in the Senate to reject an agreement made by his brother-in-law Tiberius GRACCHUS (4) on behalf of C. Hostilius MANCINUS with the people of Numantia in north-central Spain. He became heavily involved in the Numantine problem, which represented the last desperate throw by the Celtiberians for their independence, and was elected consul for 134, again without seeking the office, to put an end to the affair. A special enabling bill had to be passed, as second consulships were still illegal. As manpower was scarce, he raised an army mostly from his own clients, and invested Numantia with circumvallations for nine months and starved it into submission. He sold those of the survivors who were still alive into slavery and laid the site waste. He returned home in 132 to a second triumph, but found that politics had been transformed by the agrarian legislation of Tiberius Gracchus, which he opposed vehemently. In late summer Gracchus was killed in a riot, and Scipio by approving it incurred serious unpopularity. Three years later in 129, to appease the angry Italian tenants of public land, he proposed a decree of the Senate which transferred to the consuls the chief powers of the Gracchan land commissioners, a measure which crippled Tiberius Gracchus' legislation. A short time later Scipio died and the circumstances of his death were considered suspect: his wife Sempronia and his wife's mother, CORNELIA (1), a sister of his adoptive father, came under suspicion, as did Gaius CARBO (1). They were not however prosecuted, and his funeral oration, given by Laelius, spoke of a natural death. He had no children.

Scipio Aemilianus was a man of great moral stature and courage, which endeared him to many Romans of his time, including CATO (4) the Censor, whose ardent plea for the destruction of Carthage he fulfilled. He was a rounded and cultured figure, interested in literature (he was the youthful patron of TERENCE) and philosophy, open to Greek ideas and yet full of admiration for the achievements of Rome and the virtues of her constitution. He was politically conservative, and merciless to his city's enemies, though he formed some staunch friendships with foreigners such as Masinissa and ATTALUS (2) II of Pergamon. CICERO (1) greatly admired him and introduced him as the central character in his *Republic*, his *Old Age* and his *Laelius on Friendship*, which portrays the close friendship of Scipio and Laelius. He envisaged him at the centre of a circle of intellectual aristocrats and their clients. See A.E. Astin (1967) *Scipio Aemilianus*, Oxford: Clarendon Press.

12, Publius Cornelius, known as Nasica Serapio (died 132 BC), was the son of SCIPIO (10). He served as consul in 138 with BRUTUS (1) Callaicus, and was arrested for a short time with his colleague by tribunes who complained of their handling of a military levy. In 133 he led the body of men, many of senatorial rank, who killed his kinsman Tiberius GRACCHUS (4), a controversial act for which he was not punished, but appointed by the Senate to lead a mission to the province of Asia, on which he died at Pergamon.

Scribonia (*c.*80 BC–16 AD) was the wife of Octavian (see AUGUSTUS) whom he married (her third husband) in 40 BC to win over Sextus POMPEIUS (4): she had been married twice before, was at least seventeen years his senior, and bore him his only child, JULIA (5). She was a sister of SCRIBONIUS LIBO. Octavian divorced her the following year to marry LIVIA (2). Scribonia went into exile with her daughter in 2 BC.

Scribonianus, Lucius Arruntius Camillus (died AD 42), adopted son of the wealthy Lucius ARRUNTIUS (2), was consul in 32. He was appointed legate of Dalmatia under CALIGULA and in 42, under pressure from a number of dissatisfied senators, he persuaded the two legions at his command to support him in a bid to restore republican rule. They quickly deserted him, however, and he was murdered. Several of his accomplices were tried and executed. The legions were honoured for their loyalty. See ARRIA (1).

Scribonius *see* CURIO.

Scribonius Libo (*c.*90–*c.*21 BC) A supporter of POMPEIUS (2) whose daughter was the wife of Pompeius' son Sextus POMPEIUS (5). He commanded a section of Pompeius' fleet in the Adriatic in 49 but by 46 was reconciled with CAESAR (1). In 40 Sextus asked him to negotiate an alliance with ANTONIUS (7) against Octavian (AUGUSTUS), but instead he married his sister SCRIBONIA to the youthful Octavian. Still working for Sextus Pompeius, he went to Asia with him in 36, but joined Antonius the following year. He was consul in 34.

Sejanus, Lucius Aelius (died AD 31) A prefect of the Praetorian Guard in the time of TIBERIUS, he was the son of the Roman knight L. Seius Strabo from Volsinii. After serving in the east under Gaius CAESAR (3), Sejanus was appointed by Tiberius in AD 14 to be his father's colleague as prefect. In 17 his father became prefect of Egypt, leaving Sejanus in sole command. He gradually built up his power, being trusted absolutely by the emperor, and in 23 concentrated the guard in a single camp outside the Viminal Gate of Rome. His power was enhanced by the death of Tiberius' son DRUSUS (4) in 23, whom Sejanus was later believed to have murdered, and the departure of the emperor for retirement at Capri in 26. Sejanus' wish to marry Drusus' widow, GERMANICUS' sister Livilla (LIVIA 3), was, however, rejected by Tiberius. Nevertheless, Sejanus continued to gather power, engineering the banishment of his enemy AGRIPPINA (2) and targeting her children, the heirs to the throne. He held a joint consulship with the absent Tiberius in 31 and was granted the power of a proconsul. But that October the emperor's sister-in-law, ANTONIA (2), worried by Sejanus' rising ambition, warned Tiberius, who arranged Sejanus' downfall by writing to the Senate and sending MACRO, prefect of the city watch, to arrest him and take over his post as prefect of the guard. After a trial before the Senate, Sejanus was executed and his supporters, including Livilla, and his family, were liquidated. Sejanus' fate illustrates Tiberius' mixture of gullibility at the hands of a clever manipulator and inability to trust his own kin. It is debatable whether Sejanus was plotting a coup. See E.T. Salmon (1968) *A History of the Roman World from 30 BC to AD 138*, London: Methuen.

Seleucus 1. IV Philopator ('Father-loving') (*c.*218–175 BC) was a Seleucid king, the second son of ANTIOCHUS (1) III. Having served in military command under his father, he was made joint king after the battle of Magnesia in 189 and succeeded in 187. He was severely constrained in policy at home and abroad by the harsh treaty of Apamea which Rome had imposed on his father, including an indemnity of 15,000 talents; his freedom to move westwards by land or sea was also curtailed by the treaty. He maintained good relations with the independent powers of the east, Macedonia and Egypt. He continued his father's favourable treatment of Judaea, guaranteeing that religious revenues would if necessary be subsidised by his treasury. He was assassinated by his minister Heliodorus, who tried to withdraw the subsidy.

2. V A Seleucid king, the eldest son of DEMETRIUS (7) II, he became king in 126 BC but was killed by his mother, Cleopatra, the next year.

3. VI Epiphanes ('the Glorious') (reigned 96–95 BC) was a Seleucid king of Syria, the eldest son of ANTIOCHUS (6) VIII Grypus. The year after his accession he defeated and killed his uncle, ANTIOCHUS (7) IX, but later in the year was defeated by the latter's son ANTIOCHUS (8) X and expelled from the kingdom.

Sempronius 1, Tuditanus, Gaius (late C2 BC), as consul in 129 was appointed by the Senate to enforce the decisions of the agrarian commission set up by Tiberius GRACCHUS (4). This ploy was designed by SCIPIO (11) Aemilianus, its proposer, to wreck the work of the commission, and after declining to act, Sempronius departed for Illyria where he earned a triumph by his military successes. He wrote historical works of which little survives, including a work on the magistrates.

2, Publius (late C3 BC), after fighting at Cannae in 216, commanded Roman armies in northern Italy from 213, when he was praetor, to 211. He was sent *c.*205 to Macedonia, where he concluded the Peace of Phoenice, which ended the First Macedonian War. He was defeated by Hannibal in Bruttium during his consulship in 204, but subsequently turned the tables on him. In 200 he joined an abortive embassy to PHILIP (1) V.

Seneca 1, Lucius Annaeus (*c.*50 BC–*c.* AD 40), known as the Elder to distinguish him from his more famous son, was a rhetorician of wealthy family from Corduba (Córdoba) in Spain, who early in his life went to Rome to be educated and spent much of his time there, writing and practising rhetoric. We know little of his life. He married a rich woman from Spain named Helvia, by whom he had three sons, Novatus, later named GALLIO, SENECA (2), and Mela, the father of LUCAN.

Of his writings, his historical works have disappeared. His other known work, on rhetoric, was written in his old age for his sons, and consists of an anthology of quotations from speakers of various kinds, with comments and explanations and even exercises. In compiling it he relied on his memory. The title of this work was *The Propositions, Analyses, and Lines of Approach of Practitioners of Oratory*: it was subdivided into twelve books, ten of *Disputations* (*Controversiae*) or debates, and at least two of *Advisory Speeches* (*Suasoriae*), monologues urging a course of action. Of these, five books on the former subject and one on the latter have survived in a mutilated state, together with the prefaces of seven books of *Disputations*. There are abridgments of the other books of *Disputations*. From Seneca's work we can gain an insight into the training of the public speaker and the practice of declamation, which in those days was central to the education of public men as well as a form of entertainment. Though at Rome the use of rhetoric for politics was now obsolete, forensic oratory had replaced it. Fortunately Seneca did not confine himself closely to his subject and his digressions are full of interesting information on the writers and speakers of his age. See J. Fairweather (1981) *Seneca the Elder*, Cambridge: Cambridge University Press; L.A. Sussman (1978) *The Elder Seneca*, Leiden: E.J. Brill.

2, Lucius Annaeus (*c.*3 BC–AD 65), the Younger, the second son of SENECA (1), was an important figure in the history of the Neronian age as well as a considerable writer of plays and philosophical letters. He was born in Corduba (Córdoba) in Spain and brought to Rome for his education by AD 5. He lived there with his aunt, the wife of C. Galerius. Besides rhetoric he made a study of philosophy and came under the influence of the school of SEXTIUS and of DEMETRIUS (4) the Cynic. He went to Egypt where his aunt, whose husband had become prefect in AD 16, took charge of him during a period of illness, and returned with her in 31 when their ship was wrecked and the prefect drowned. With her help he embarked on a public career and engaged in oratory with such success that in 39 he earned the jealousy of the emperor CALIGULA, and was in danger of execution. At an unknown date he married Pompeia Paulina, by whom he had a son, who died in 41. In 41 CLAUDIUS (1) banished him to Corsica for alleged adultery with JULIA (8) Livilla, the sister of Caligula. However, in 49 AGRIPPINA (3), the mother of the future emperor NERO (1), had him recalled to become praetor and her son's tutor. After Nero's accession in 54, Seneca and the prefect of the Praetorian Guard, BURRUS, took the role of Nero's advisers. His influence upon the impressionable youth was such that the first five years of the reign were afterwards considered, e.g. by the emperor TRAJAN, as a 'golden age'. It seems likely that Seneca's exercise of power was private and advisory rather than the holding of any direct political office. But as Nero matured and assumed responsibility for decisions of state, Seneca and Burrus had to humour him and give way to his whims. After Nero's murder of his mother in 59 he surrounded himself with flatterers and Seneca was sidelined. When Burrus died in 62, Seneca asked to be allowed to retire from court, but was refused permission, though he was able to absent himself much of the time and live outside the city. In 64, after the great fire, he surrendered most of his fortune to Nero and lived at court in confinement, seeing a small group of friends. He was accused of involvement in the conspiracy led by PISO (2) and forced to commit suicide, which he did in a manner appropriate to a Stoic philosopher. He was subsequently criticised as a hypocrite for his preaching a life of poverty in contrast to his own life of wealth which he was unwilling to surrender.

He wrote extensively and much of his work has survived; lost works are known to have covered geography, natural history and ethics. The ten extant *Dialogues*, a series of essays written at various dates, are exercises in rhetoric and Stoic moral philosophy. Of these the longest is *Anger*, in three books, dedicated to his brother Novatus. The others are *Providence*, dedicated to his friend LUCILIUS (2), *The Philosopher's Constancy*, to Annaeus Serenus, an officer in the city police (*vigiles*), *Consolation (addressed to Marcia)*, to the daughter of Cremutius CORDUS, who was in mourning for her son. *The Happy Life* was dedicated some time after 58 to his brother Novatus, now known as GALLIO. *Leisure* (mostly lost) and *Peace of Mind* were addressed to Serenus, *The Shortness of Life* to Paulinus, his father-in-law, a prefect of the grain-supply, *Consolation (addressed to Polybius)*, to Claudius' freedman Polybius; it is marred by flattery of the emperor who had banished him. *Consolation (to Helvia)* was addressed to his mother to comfort her during his exile in Corsica. Other writings on moral questions outside this collection are the incomplete *Clemency*, addressed to Nero after his suspected murder of BRITANNICUS in late 55, and *Favours* in seven books, a complex and dry work which tells much about the social rules in contemporary Rome. The *Moral Epistles to Lucilius*, 124 letters in twenty books addressed to his friend Lucilius, are not real spontaneous letters like those of CICERO (1), but self-consciously didactic essays with an ethical purpose, perhaps in the tradition of philosophical 'letters' such as those of Epicurus. Nevertheless, they reveal much humanity in the man and bring him to life and, far from being dogmatic in tone, present arguments for the case they maintain.

He also addressed the eight books of his *Natural Questions*, on the subject of natural phenomena, to his friend Lucilius. Both sets of letters seem to date from the end of his life, the time of his retirement from the activities of the court. The text of the latter work is damaged and corrupt, and its parts are disordered, but despite the intrusion of ethical material there is much of scientific interest in his investigations of nature. The subjects discussed are divided according to their relationship to the four elements of fire, air, water and earth, and the work was influential in the Middle Ages. In startling contrast to these letters is *The Pumpkinification of Claudius* (*Apocolocyntosis*), a satirical work with a serious element in the tradition of the Greek writer Menippus, on the death and deification of that emperor. Ten tragedies were also ascribed to Seneca, nine on themes from Greek myth and the tenth, now proved to be by a different, later hand, on the contemporary theme of OCTAVIA (3), the first wife of Nero. The nine genuine plays were probably not written to be staged, but rather to be recited or read aloud. They are not in the tradition of Classical Greek theatre but probably owe much to imperial Roman precedents such as the *Medea* of OVID and the *Thyestes* of VARIUS Rufus. They have a powerful rhetorical quality, and the influence of VIRGIL's *Aeneid* and OVID's *Metamorphoses* and *Heroines* is also strong. They are written in five acts and include a prologue, choral odes, and much stichomythia; the metre of the dialogues is the iambic trimeter of Greek tragedy. The titles of the plays are *Hercules* or *The Madness of Hercules*, *The Trojan Women*, the unfinished *Phoenician Women*, *Medea*, *Phaedra*, *Oedipus*, *Agamemnon*, *Thyestes* and *Hercules at Oeta*. The relationship of ancient Greek tragedy to these plays is more one of inspiration than adaptation. They are impossible to date accurately. Some seventy-seven epigrams are also attributed to Seneca but, except for three, most of them cannot be considered authentic. See M.T. Griffin (1976) *Seneca: A Philosopher in Politics*, Oxford: Clarendon Press; G.O. Hutchinson (1993) *Latin Literature from Seneca to Juvenal: a Critical Study*, Oxford: Clarendon Press; N. Pratt (1983) *Seneca's Drama*, Chapel Hill: University Press of North Carolina.

Senecio, Quintus Sosius (died *c.*AD 110), was a Roman literary figure and general who served under the emperor TRAJAN. He married a daughter of FRONTINUS, and held a full consulship in 99 at the outset of Trajan's reign and another in 107 with SURA, a mark of the esteem in which the emperor held him. There is some evidence that he was in command of forces during Trajan's conquest of Dacia in 105 and 106. He was a friend of several men of letters including PLINY (2) the Younger and PLUTARCH, who dedicated to him his *Parallel Lives*. He was also a close friend of the emperor HADRIAN, and married his daughter Sosia Polla to the successful general FALCO.

Septimius *see* SEVERUS (1), VABALLATHUS.

Sertorius, Quintus (*c.*126–73 BC), was a Roman knight of Sabine origin from Nursia. Sertorius fought with distinction in the wars against the Cimbri under CAEPIO (3) and MARIUS (1) and in Spain under Titus DIDIUS. After a quaestorship in 91, he stood for the tribuneship in the early 80s but was opposed by SULLA (2), and consequently joined CINNA (2), under whom he helped in the capture of Rome in 87. He put a stop to the indiscriminate slaughter carried out in the city by Marius' followers. As praetor *c.*85 he showed overt disapproval of his side in its conduct of the civil war, and went to Spain as its governor in late 83. He was proscribed by Sulla in 81 and left Spain briefly for Mauretania, where he gained military experience as a guerilla fighter. In 80 he was recalled to Iberia by the Lusitani and the Roman residents who opposed Sulla, and set up a quasi-independent state, gaining support from the local peoples by his fairness and courage. He was joined by many Romans who had been persecuted by Sulla, including many followers of LEPIDUS (3) whom PERPERNA (3) led to Spain. He conducted a brilliant war of irregular tactics against several Roman commanders, and by 77 had control of most of the peninsula, claiming to act as a proconsul of the Roman republic. He set up a senate consisting of Roman and Italian officials and settlers in the province, and insisted on the legitimacy of his position. In 76 he negotiated an alliance with MITHRIDATES (3) VI of Pontus, though refusing to agree to Mithridates' claim to the province of Asia. Despite a victory over POMPEIUS (2) at the battle of the Lauro, from 75 METELLUS (7) Pius in Western Spain and Pompeius in the east wore down Sertorius' forces and his tactics increasingly failed him. He lost much support and under pressure became crueller to his subordinates: Perperna murdered him in 73 and tried to replace him without much success. PLUTARCH wrote his life. See L.A. Curchin (1991) *Roman Spain*, London: Routledge; E. Gabba (1976) *Republican Rome*, Oxford: Blackwell; P.O. Spann (1987) *Quintus Sertorius and the Legacy of Sulla*, Fayetteville: University of Arkansas Press.

Servianus, Lucius Julius Ursus (*c.*AD 47–136) The brother-in-law of the emperor HADRIAN, being married to his sister Aelia Domitia Paullina, he was some thirty years the emperor's senior, but became fatally entangled in a dispute with him over the succession. He had a distinguished career. There is evidence that he was suffect consul in 90, and he replaced TRAJAN as governor of Upper Germany in 98. He was in action with Trajan in the First Dacian War and held a full consulship with SURA in 102. He persuaded Trajan to grant PLINY (2) the Younger the tax immunity of men with three children. Consul for the third time in 134, he was accused in 136 of conspiring with his eighteen-year-old grandson Pedianus Fuscus, Hadrian's closest male kinsman, to make him Hadrian's successor in place of Lucius AELIUS (3), and was put to death.

Servilia (born *c.*100 BC) was ambitious for her family, the patrician Servilii. The daughter of CAEPIO (4) and LIVIA (1), sister of CATO (5), she married M. Junius Brutus to whom she bore M. Junius BRUTUS (4). Her second husband was Decimus Junius Silanus, by whom she had three daughters who married respectively P. Servilius ISAURICUS (2), M. Aemilius LEPIDUS (4) and Gaius CASSIUS (2), CAESAR (1)'s assassin. She was Caesar's mistress for many years, and some suspected that her son Brutus was his. She hated POMPEIUS (2) and made money from the sale of his property in 48. After Caesar's murder she took a role in the plans of the conspirators and presided at a family discussion at Antium involving Brutus, Cassius and CICERO (1). She disappears from view after the battle of Philippi.

Servilius *see* AHALA, CAEPIO, CASCA, GLAUCIA, ISAURICUS, RULLUS.

Sestius, Publius (C1 BC), was a senator and supporter of CICERO (1) in 63 against CATILINE (he served as the quaestor of ANTONIUS (1) Hybrida in the campaign) and, when he was a tribune in 57, in working for his restoration from exile. He organised a band of street fighters against CLODIUS, and in 56 was prosecuted for assault, being successfully defended by Cicero (whose speech, strongly conservative, survives), CRASSUS (3), CALVUS, and HORTENSIUS (2). He was prosecuted once more for electoral bribery when he stood for a praetorship *c*.54 and again acquitted thanks to Cicero. After the battle of Pharsalus he became a supporter of CAESAR (1), but maintained friendly relations with Cicero, who refers to him in correspondence. CATULLUS mocked his boring speeches (poem 44). His son Lucius, one of the assassins of Caesar, was active in the conquest of Further Spain, and the addressee of a fine *Ode* (1.4) by HORACE.

Severus 1, Lucius Septimius (AD 145–211), was an emperor of Punic (Carthaginian) origin from Lepcis Magna in North Africa, though his mother's family had sprung from Italy. His grandfather, Septimius Severus, a Roman knight, had been an important figure in the city of Lepcis during TRAJAN's reign, and was a friend of the poet STATIUS. Severus' second wife was JULIA (10) Domna, by whom he had two sons, CARACALLA and GETA (3). He was made a senator by MARCUS AURELIUS and reached the consulship in 190: his colleague was PESCENNIUS Niger. The following year he governed Pannonia with the help of a fellow African, Q. Aemilus Laetus, the prefect of the Praetorian Guard. In spring 193 the emperor, PERTINAX, was murdered, and on 9 April Severus' troops proclaimed him emperor at Carnuntum (near Hamburg) with a mission to avenge the death of Pertinax. He then marched on Rome with the support of the armies of the northern frontiers and of Clodius ALBINUS (1), the governor of Britain, whom he honoured with the title *Caesar* as a sign that he would be Severus' successor. In June 193 his rival DIDIUS JULIANUS was executed and Severus entered Rome with the support of the Senate. He reformed the Praetorian Guard by dismissing the current force, which had auctioned the empire to Didius, and replacing it with a body twice as strong drawn from the armies he had commanded in Pannonia. He also stationed a new legion in the Alban Hills near Rome and strengthened the city police (*vigiles*). Rome had never been so powerfully garrisoned. He won added support among the military by raising army pay and allowing the soldiers to marry.

During the next twelve months Severus and his generals were busy securing his rule from the attempt to seize it by the claimant Pescennius Niger, now governor of Syria. Though his supporters held Byzantium for several years, he himself was defeated at Issus and fled towards Parthia, but was caught near Antioch and killed. As a result, Severus divided the province of Syria in two, Phoenicia on the coast and Coele Syria inland. He continued to advance eastwards, punishing Antioch for its support of Niger. He took Osroene and in 195, to lend legitimacy to his position and out of respect for tradition, he proclaimed himself the son of Marcus Aurelius, whom he deified, and the brother of COMMODUS, whom he also deified. He took the titles *Parthicus* and *Adiabenicus*. He made his son Caracalla *Caesar*, renaming him Marcus Aurelius Antoninus, and gave his wife the titles *Augusta* and 'Mother of the Army'. Albinus, now disappointed of the succession, turned on Severus and invaded Gaul. The two armies met near Lugdunum (Lyons) in February 197, when Severus defeated Albinus and held a pogrom of his supporters and friends in the Senate and elsewhere. He returned to the east in 197 and extended his conquests, and in January 198 took Ctesiphon, capital of Babylonia. He made his son Caracalla his co-ruler with the title *Augustus*, and made his second son Geta *Caesar*, taking for himself the title *Parthicus Maximus*. He created a new province of Mesopotamia garrisoned by two newly recruited legions. He spent the following year (200) in Egypt (where he established a measure of local government) and after creating senates and councils at Alexandria and in the capitals of the nomes, and after a further year (201) in Syria, returned to Rome in spring 202. He held his third consulship with Caracalla in 202. The senate voted him a triumphal arch and he celebrated the ten-yearly games in honour of his conquests. He also married his son Caracalla to Fulvia Plautilla, the daughter of the prefect of the Praetorian Guard, Gaius Fulvius PLAUTIANUS. Later in the year he went to Africa, revisiting his native city, which he beautified, and campaigning against the peoples of the desert. He spent the following years in Rome and Italy. In 205 Caracalla had his father-in-law Plautianus executed, whom Severus replaced with PAPINIANUS and, as assessors, the great jurists PAULUS and ULPIANUS. He reformed the role of the prefect, making it more administrative and judicial than military, and extended the use of equestrians to high military and administrative functions. In 208 he went with his sons to Britain where he fought two campaigns in Scotland, intending to extend Roman rule to the whole island. In 210 he proclaimed himself and Caracalla victors with the title *Britannicus*, and he gave Geta the rank of *Augustus*. He died on 4 February 211 at York, in the vain hope that he had left his sons effective co-rulers of the Empire. See M. Grant (1985) *The Roman Emperors*, London: Weidenfeld & Nicolson; A.R. Birley (1988) *Septimius Severus: The African Emperor*, London: Eyre & Spottiswoode.

2. Alexander (AD 208–235) was a Roman emperor who reigned from 222 to 235. Originally named Marcus Julius Gessius Alexianus Bassianus, he was the son of the Syrian procurator Gessius Marcianus and JULIA (13) Avita Mamaea. He was adopted in summer 221 by the emperor ELAGABALUS, his cousin, with the name Marcus Aurelius Alexander Caesar. When Elagabalus was murdered the following March, the fourteen-year-old boy became emperor, adding Severus to his name. He was not a free agent, being under his mother's control, but he made a good impression for his modesty and politeness to elder statesmen, who now became influential in the government. CASSIUS (1) Dio, an elderly senator, and others like him, were enrolled into a council of state to advise the emperor and his mother. Dio held a consulship in 229 with Alexander, but had to serve outside Rome because of the threat posed by the guardsmen, who in 223 had killed ULPIANUS, appointed by Alexander and his mother as prefect of the Praetorian Guard. He had dealt with the ringleader of the assassins, Epagathus, by a subterfuge, sending him first to be prefect of Egypt but then luring him to his death in Crete. Alexander was married in 225 to a daughter of Cn. Seius Herennius, but had to send her away in 227 when Seius tried to overthrow him. The reign appeared to posterity as something of a golden age, a time of peace and relative prosperity between two periods of anarchy. During the reign, however, official supervision of trade and industry grew steadily and the coinage was debased. State subsidies of

education and tax rebates granted to guilds and property owners caused a financial crisis that was tackled with difficulty. From 231 to 233 Alexander campaigned against the revived Persian empire under the Sasanids, and managed to hold on to Mesopotamia. In 234 he had to face a serious incursion by the Alemanni. He failed to offer battle and tried to negotiate with the invaders and even buy them off, and his troops in their disillusionment killed him and his mother near Mogontiacum (Maintz). Their leader was a Thracian staff officer named Julius Verus MAXIMINUS (1) whom they elected the next emperor. See M. Grant (1985) *The Roman Emperors*, London: Weidenfeld & Nicolson; R. Syme (1971) *Emperors and Biography*, Oxford: Clarendon Press; A.R. Birley (1999) *Septimius Severus: The African Emperor*, London: Routledge.

3, Flavius Valerius (died AD 307) An Illyrian of humble birth, he became a commander in the army and a friend of the emperor GALERIUS, who demanded that he be created *Caesar* on the retirement of MAXIMIAN. This was done at Milan in May 305, and he was put in charge of Italy and Africa. In July 306 he was made *Augustus* of the west on the death of CONSTANTIUS (1) I, with CONSTANTINE (1) as his subordinate *Caesar.* He tried to interfere in Rome, where MAXENTIUS was proclaimed emperor. In spring 307 he advanced from Milan to the neighbourhood of Rome but was forced to flee when his troops deserted him for Maximian. He took refuge in Ravenna where Maximian compelled him to abdicate and Maxentius later executed him. See M. Grant (1985) *The Roman Emperors*, London: Weidenfeld & Nicolson.

Sextius, Quintus (C1 BC/AD), was a Roman eclectic philosopher who declined to enter public life but founded a school of philosophy that became influential. He was influenced by Stoic and Pythagorean ideas and promoted vegetarianism. He asserted the existence of a soul independent of the body, the transmigration of souls, and recommended an ascetic way of life akin to that of the Cynics. His ideas appealed to SENECA (2) the Younger, Cornelius CELSUS (1), Papirius FABIANUS, and Sotion of Alexandria.

Sextus (C2 AD) was the compiler of an extant collection of sayings and maxims in Greek, known to ORIGEN (1), which was expanded by the addition of Christian material. Rufinus of Aquilea translated it into Latin in the fourth century as *The Ring* (*Anulus*). A Syriac version shows a mistaken ascription to Xystus, a bishop of Rome in the third century. A Coptic version was found in 1945.

Silanus, Marcus Junius (consul 25 BC), was the son of Decimus, the consul of 62. He supported his sister's husband the future triumvir LEPIDUS (4) in 44 but fought for ANTONIUS (7) at Mutina in 43. He broke with the triumvirs and joined Sextus POMPEIUS (5). In 39 he returned to Rome and later threw in his lot with Antonius, but deserted him before the battle of Actium in 31. He served his consulship as AUGUSTUS' colleague and was raised to patrician status.

Silenus (C3–2 BC) was a Greek historian from Caleacte in Sicily who wrote a lost history of his native land. He was one of two Greek historians who were invited to join HANNIBAL's expedition to Italy, and his work, of which very little is left, was used by POLYBIUS and Caelius ANTIPATER (5). It appears to have been in the tradition of romantic historiography, as witness the description of Hannibal's dream as he crossed the Ebro.

Silius, Gaius (died AD 48), while consul designate in 48, went through a form of marriage with MESSALLINA, wife of the emperor CLAUDIUS (1), in the palace while the emperor was at Ostia. TACITUS (1) describes him as most handsome. There was an associated plot to remove Claudius from power or to force him to give up his freedmen ministers. However, the freedman NARCISSUS had the pair liquidated before Claudius could recover from the shock of the revelation.

Silius Italicus (*c.*AD 26–102) was an epic poet who took the Second Punic War as his subject. Tiberius Catius Asconius Silius Italicus, who composed his *Punic War* (*Punica*) in Latin in seventeen books running to 12,000 lines of hexameters, was a public figure, a lawyer who enriched himself in prosecuting the enemies of NERO (1), and was consul in 68, Nero's last year. The following year, when there were four emperors, he was caught up in the turmoil and negotiated on behalf of VITELLIUS (1) with VESPASIAN's brother SABINUS (2). He governed Asia as proconsul under Vespasian in 77. He spent the rest of his life in retirement in Campania, where he had many houses, and undertook his vast poetical work, using LIVY as his main historical source and VIRGIL's *Aeneid* as his poetic model. He knew men like MARTIAL, who praised his epic, and PLINY (2) the Younger, whose letter 3, 7 is our chief source of information about his life. He admired CICERO (1) and bought one of his country villas. He restored Virgil's tomb near Naples, which lay in one of his properties. At the age of 76 he realised that he was incurably ill and starved himself to death.

His poem, which has the faults of bombast and turgidity, was much influenced by the *Civil War* of LUCAN, though it also represents a reaction to Lucan's approach to epic. He brings back the divine apparatus so powerful in the *Aeneid* and introduces stock epic features like the description of Hannibal's shield. The central pivot of the work is the battle of Cannae, which takes up the three middle books; there are seven books on either side. Silius presents HANNIBAL as an almost divine instrument of Junonian wrath against Rome, recalling Dido's curse in *Aeneid*, 4. The Roman resistance to Hannibal's onslaught is led by heroic characters such as FABIUS (8) Maximus and SCIPIO (7) Africanus. See M. von Albrecht (1964) *Silius Italicus* (in German) Amsterdam: Schippers.

Sisenna, Lucius Cornelius (died 67 BC), a Roman historian, was praetor in 78 and was serving under POMPEIUS (2) as a legate in Crete in the year of his death. In 70 he defended VERRES in his trial for misconduct in Sicily. Some fragments of his *Histories* survive. CICERO (1) considered him the best Roman historian to date, and VARRO (3) commemorated him in the title of a dialogue on the writing of history. He modelled himself on Cleitarchus, and his style, including speeches and digressions, which SALLUST (who may have continued his *Histories*) admired, was artificial and mannered: he had a penchant for strange words. His work, in at least twelve books, appears to have consisted mainly of a full account of the Italian Social War and the wars of SULLA (2), and to have been a continuation of the *Histories* of ASELLIO.

Sittius, Publius (died 44 BC), was an adventurer and mercenary soldier from Nuceria in Campania, originally a rich trader of equestrian rank with interests in Spain and Mauretania. He fell under suspicion of being implicated in the conspiracy of CATILINE and, despite the support of CICERO (1), he decided to sell his possessions and emigrate to Mauretania, where he took service under king BOCCHUS (2) with a band of hired troops. He was prominent in an attack on king JUBA (1), the ally of POMPEIUS (2), and fought for CAESAR (1) at the battle of Thapsus (46). He was active in mopping up Pompeian remnants after the battle, and was responsible for the deaths of AFRANIUS (2), Faustus SULLA (1), and METELLUS (11) Pius Scipio. Caesar granted him territory around Cirta (Constantine), which Sittius made into a Roman colony where he settled his men. He was murdered by a Mauretanian chief.

Sophonisba (Sophoniba) (late C3 BC) was the wife of king SYPHAX of the Masaesylii of Numidia, whom she married *c.*206, and a daughter of HASDRUBAL (3). She persuaded her husband to support Carthage in the Second Punic War. She poisoned herself in 203 when her husband's kingdom fell to MASINISSA and the Romans. LIVY tells a romantic story according to which Masinissa fell in love with her and assisted her suicide to save her from imprisonment at Rome.

Soranus of Ephesus (early C2 AD) was a Greek doctor and writer on medicine who studied at Alexandria before going to Rome to practise. His works included the biographies of medical men and discussions of linguistic questions. Two of his works in Greek have survived, *Gynaecology* in four books, and treatises on fractures and bandaging. His *Acute and Chronic Diseases* exists in a Latin translation by Caelius Aurelianus. His *Gynaecology* offers a useful insight into contemporary midwifery and gives a noble specification for the ideal midwife. See O. Temkin (1956) *Soranus' Gynaecology*, Baltimore: Johns Hopkins University Press.

Sosius *see* SENECIO.

Sosylus (C3–2 BC) was a historian from Sparta who accompanied the expedition of Hannibal across the Alps into Italy and wrote a history of the campaign (*Hannibal's Achievements*) in seven books which were heavily drawn upon by POLYBIUS, despite his particular criticism of Sosylus in book 3. 20, 5. A papyrus fragment of Sosylus' fourth book has been found which gives the lie to Polybius' harsh opinion.

Spartacus (died 71BC) was a Thracian gladiator and former auxiliary soldier who served in a gladiatorial school at Capua where in 73 he led an uprising of the mainly Gallic and Thracian gladiators. As the movement grew stronger it was supported by runaway slaves and land-workers, and reached a strength exceeding 70,000 men. Spartacus won several victories, defeated both consuls of the year 72 in battle, and roamed over southern Italy with his huge force. Later in 72 he moved northwards into Cisalpine Gaul, hoping that many of his troops would disperse from there to their native lands. They were, however, unwilling and he had to return to the south where, after winning a victory in Lucania, he wished to transport his army to Sicily. But the pirates on whom he relied for shipping failed him, and he had to face CRASSUS (3) in Lucania, whose absolute victory wiped out the rebellious army. Spartacus was believed to have perished in the battle, though his body was never found. Many survivors were caught, and those whose owners could not be found suffered crucifixion at the hands of Crassus: 6,000 men hanging on crosses lined the Appian Way. POMPEIUS (2) mopped up some of the remnant, for which he claimed an inordinate share of the glory.

Statilia Messallina (C1 AD), the third and last wife of the emperor NERO (1), was a woman of great culture who replaced POPPAEA SABINA in 66. She was the great-great-granddaughter of STATILIUS TAURUS, and became available for the imperial bed when Nero killed her fourth husband, Vestinus Atticus. She accompanied the emperor on his artistic tour of Greece, and after his death remained a focus of literary and artistic life.

Statilius Taurus, Titus (died *c.*15 BC) A military man and loyal follower of Octavian (AUGUSTUS), he was suffect consul in 37 and commanded the fleet in the Sicilian War of 36. He then seized the province of Africa and brought it under his control, and returned to Rome for a triumph in 34. An amphitheatre was built in the Campus Martius to commemorate his triumph. He fought in Illyricum during the next two years and in 31 led Octavian's army in the Actium campaign. In 29 he governed Spain. He had thrice been hailed as *Imperator* by his victorious troops, and held the consulship as Augustus' colleague in 26. He was City Prefect in 16 when Augustus was absent in Gaul, but died before his return.

Statius, Publius Papinius (*c.*AD 45–*c.*96), was a poet whose family came from Naples, where his father, before moving to Rome while his son was an adolescent, had been a schoolmaster. Statius' father had won prizes at Greek festivals for his poetry, but he himself wrote in Latin though he drew on Greek myth for the subjects of his two epics. Statius gained a reputation as a poet when still a young man; he married Claudia, the widow of another poet by whom she had borne a daughter. He took part in official competitions for poetry at Roman games, and won a prize at DOMITIAN's Alban Games, probably in 90, but failed to do so at the Capitoline Games in the same year. Late in life he and his family moved back to Naples where he died just before the death of Domitian.

We have the whole of the epic hexameter poem he wrote on the Theban cycle of Greek myths, the *Thebaid*, his masterpiece. He probably began work on it before 80, and published it *c.*92. The work, in twelve books, is chiefly concerned wth the quarrel of the two brothers Eteocles and Polynices and explores the themes of violence and insanity. Though Statius owed debts to VIRGIL's *Aeneid* (which he acknowledged at the end of the poem), OVID's *Metamorphoses*, LUCAN's *Civil War*, and the tragedies of the Younger SENECA (2), his work displays great originality in terms of the presentation of the conflict and the manner in which the divine apparatus is handled. He introduces an allegorical element in the latter which was influential in the Middle Ages, when his work was popular and he was wrongly believed to have been a Christian. He rivalled Ovid in his technical mastery and style of versification. His *Silvae* (the word has a technical sense: occasional extempore poems) in five books, published between 92 and after his death, consist of thirty-two poems, all except six in hexameters, and cover various subjects, mostly intimately connected with the poet's relatively unexciting life. A poem on sleep (5, 4) is outstanding. He addressed six poems to Domitian, which hindsight may cause modern taste to depreciate. The manuscript of the *Silvae* was discovered by Poggio in 1418. We also have a fragment, one book and 160 lines of the next (probably all he wrote) of the *Achilleid*, an epic poem telling the life of the Greek hero Achilles. The writing is lighter and more charming than the earlier epic. His lost works include an epic poem on Domitian's German campaign, the poems he wrote for festival competitions, and the libretto of the mime *Agave*, which he is said to have written for Paris, a mime actor of Domitian's court. See A. Hardie (1983) *Statius and the Silvae*, Liverpool: Francis Cairns; P.O. Hardie (1993) *The Epic Successors of Virgil*, Cambridge: Cambridge University Press; D. Vessey (1973) *Statius and the Thebaid*, Cambridge: Cambridge University Press.

Stolo, Gaius Licinius (C4 BC), as tribune of the *plebs*, with his colleague Lucius Sextius Lateranus, was reputedly instrumental in the passing of legislation, the Licinian-Sextian Acts (*Leges Liciniae Sextiae*) in 367. These decreed that one consul each year should be plebeian, that individual citizens should be restricted as to their holdings of public land to 500 *jugera* (135 hectares), and a law regulating the repayment of the interest and capital of debts. He lived at a time of political instability, and in the years preceding the passing of the laws he and his colleagues prevented elections being held to the senior magistracies of Rome. Stolo's colleague Lateranus was elected the first plebeian consul, and he himself subsequently became consul. The history of these events is difficult because LIVY is our chief authority and his account is chronologically confused.

Strabo (*c.*64 BC–*c.*AD 24) was a geographer from Amisea in Pontus on the Black Sea. He was educated in Rome, where he studied under teachers of the Peripatetic school including TYRANNIO (1), though his philosophical views were Stoic. He may have derived his approach to the study of geography, which he closely associated with the study of history, from POSIDONIUS, whom he knew while a child and whose work he used. He wrote in Greek: his first work, which is lost, was *Notes on History* (*Hypomnemata*) in forty-seven books, continuing the work of POLYBIUS. He travelled widely: to Egypt, where he stayed for several months while his patron Aelius GALLUS (1) served there as prefect; to Ethiopia and the Yemen; and he made many visits to Rome. He wrote an extant treatise, *Geography*, in seventeen books, of which one, book 7 on Germany, exists only in epitome. He used much material from authors whose work is otherwise lost, and produced what is for us an irreplaceable source of information not only about ancient geography but also about history and the life of his times. However, he seldom claims to have seen at first hand the places he describes, and used much material from the library at Alexandria.

His approach to geographical writing was generally practical rather than theoretical, in comparison with that of his predecessor Eratosthenes, of whose work and ideas he was quite critical, though his own technical and mathematical powers are not above criticism. But he did include a wealth of information on a variety of topics which are strictly extraneous to geography, yet which enrich his work greatly. He made a point of trying to enlighten Greeks and Romans about each other: he almost certainly held Roman citizenship. He understood the need of the rulers and military commanders of the Roman Empire to have accurate geographical information at their disposal. He returned to his native Amisea in 7 BC and remained there until his death.

Suetonius 1. Paulinus, Gaius (C1 AD), as commander with praetorian rank of Roman forces in Mauretania, largely achieved the conquest of the country in 41 and 42, and wrote a description of the Atlas Mountains, which he crossed. As an ex-consul in 58 he was appointed governor of Britain, where he pacified most of Wales. In 60, while campaigning against the Druids of Anglesey, he was recalled to the province by news of the rebellion of BOUDICCA, queen of the Iceni who inhabited Norfolk. Lacking the main body of his army, he could not prevent her with her followers from destroying the towns of Colchester, St Albans and London, the three most important towns of southern Britain. He later concentrated his forces and defeated her army. He treated the British who had taken part in the revolt with extreme cruelty, in which he was opposed by the procurator, Classicianus, who prevailed on NERO (1) to replace Suetonius. He was active in 69 in support of OTHO and, after his fall, VITELLIUS (1).

2. Tranquillus, Gaius (*c.*AD 70–*c.*130), was a writer of biographies in Latin. He was the son of Suetonius Laetus, a Roman knight who had served as a tribune in the Thirteenth Legion at the battle of Cremona in 69. He came from Hippo Regius in Numidia or possibly from Pisaurum in Umbria. He trained as a lawyer and practised the profession at Rome, where he became a friend of PLINY (2) the Younger. Pliny obtained for him *c.*102 a military tribuneship in

Britain, which Suetonius, however, failed to take up. He appears to have accompanied Pliny on his mission to Bithynia in 110. Pliny was also instrumental in obtaining for him the prized tax immunity held by men who had three children. Suetonius held three official secretaryships under TRAJAN and HADRIAN, being placed in charge of the emperor's libraries and archives, and finally as Hadrian's principal private secretary (*ab epistulis*). After his sudden dismissal *c.*122, apparently for being too familiar with the empress SABINA, he devoted himself to writing.

Of his copious output of biographies, the principal surviving work is the *Lives of the Caesars*, of which only the first few pages are missing, consisting of the lives of Julius CAESAR (1) and all the emperors down to DOMITIAN. He dedicated this work to the prefect of the Praetorian Guard, Gaius Septicius Clarus, who lost his post at the time Suetonius was dismissed. During his employment he had the advantage of access to the imperial archives and must have made good use of this invaluable source while he could. Part of his *Lives of Famous Men* (*De Viris Illustribus*), probably an earlier composition treating of the lives of Roman writers including grammarians and teachers of rhetoric, has also survived. The whole work was divided up into groups of biographies by categories of authorship. We have fragmentary lives of the poets TERENCE, HORACE and LUCAN, offering anecdotes and descriptions of physical appearance, and further biographies which are no longer considered to be his, of JUVENAL, PERSIUS, and the Elder PLINY (1). Donatus' life of VIRGIL is thought by some to be derived from Suetonius' lives of the poets. The Christian writer and scholar Jerome drew on this work for information about many poets and orators for use in his *Chronicle*. Much that Suetonius wrote is lost, though many titles are known from the *Suda* and other chance references; some were written in Greek. They include a miscellany entitled *Meadows* (*Prata*), works on Roman customs, physical defects, public shows, public offices, the Roman festivals and the Roman year, and some lexicographic material on Roman dress, geographical names, names of the winds, critical marks used in writing, and grammatical problems. He also wrote on the Greek athletic contests, the famous courtesans, the lives of royalty, and a commentary on the *Republic* of CICERO (1).

His approach to biography was thematic rather than chronological, and his main purpose was to entertain the reader. He produced sensational work packed with gossip and anecdote, and dwelt on the personal habits and physical features of his subjects; the emperors came to life under his pen. He was careful with his facts and sometimes quoted conflicting evidence, but he lacked real historical insight. The usual pattern of his biographies was to give an account of his subject's ancestry, his career before becoming emperor, his career in the purple, and his death, with an account of his physical appearance. Suetonius showed his greatest interest, as evidenced by the length and thoroughness of treatment, in Caesar and AUGUSTUS. He gave a detailed account of TIBERIUS' supposed scandalous life in retirement on Rhodes. The Flavian emperors are dealt with more briefly than the Julio-Claudians. The first substantial writer of biography in Latin, Suetonius was a model for subsequent biographers such as the late fourth-century author of the *Historia Augusta* and even mediaeval writers. The *Lives* were translated in 1606 by Philemon Holland. See A. Wallace-Hadrill (1983) *Suetonius: The Scholar and his Caesars*, London: Duckworth.

Sulla 1, Faustus Cornelius (*c.*88–46 BC), the son of SULLA (2) and METELLA, was given his unusual forename ('lucky') to commemorate his father's success in war. He served as a military tribune in the army of POMPEIUS (2) in the east, and led the unit that captured the Temple in Jerusalem. In 60 BC he held lavish games in honour of his father's memory, and was elected augur. As quaestor in 54 he lent support at their trials to his half-brother M. Aemilius SCAURUS (3), and two years later to his brother-in-law MILO. In the same year he was given the task of rebuilding the Senate House, which the followers of Publius CLODIUS had destroyed. He remained faithful to Pompeius in the Civil War, fought at Pharsalus, and was killed by SITTIUS after the battle of Thapsus.

2. Felix, Lucius Cornelius (138–78 BC), the offspring of an old patrician family and of moderate means, received a good education and developed a love of literature and the arts. He spent his early years in a life of pleasure but, after inheriting considerable wealth from his stepmother, he began a political career. He fought in the army of MARIUS (1) as quaestor in the war against JUGURTHA in 107, and earned his commander's jealousy when, following Sulla's skilful diplomacy, BOCCHUS (1) surrendered Jugurtha to him. He remained in Marius' service, however, in the war with the Cimbri and Teutones until 102, when he left Marius for service under Quintus CATULUS (2), as whose legate he fought at the victory of Campi Raudii in 101 and later drove off the Tigurini in the eastern Alps. He failed to be elected praetor for 98, but thanks to lavish bribery was elected city praetor for the following year. He spent the next five years as proconsul of Cilicia, under orders from the Senate to instal ARIOBARZANES (1) on the throne of Cappadocia, which he did by raising troops locally. There he was visited by a delegation from the king of Parthia who requested friendship with Rome. He returned to Rome *c.*91 and was unsuccessfully prosecuted for his conduct in Cilicia. He also quarrelled again with Marius, over a proposal to allow Bocchus to set up a statue on the Capitol commemorating the surrender of Jugurtha.

The Social War, however, interrupted this growing animosity, and Sulla gained some brilliant victories, defeating the Samnites and taking their capital Bovianum. He was elected consul for 88 with the help of the powerful Metelli, and brought the war to a successful conclusion by taking Nola. His colleague was Q. Pompeius Rufus, whose son married Sulla's daughter. Sulla himself took as his second wife Caecilia METELLA, widow of SCAURUS (2). The Senate then allotted to Sulla the command in the war against MITHRIDATES (3) VI, but a tribune, SULPICIUS (1) Rufus, wishing to curry favour with Marius, had the command transferred to him by the Assembly of the People. After a fracas that threatened his life, Sulla briefly acquiesced in Marius' plan, but being well aware that he had strong support among the six legions destined to fight Mithridates, which he had commanded in the Social War, he fled to Campania to join them. He then marched on Rome, which he captured without difficulty in the first Roman civil war. He purged the opposition, killing Sulpicius, and causing Marius to flee to Africa. By dint of armed force, he then had measures passed that transferred legislative powers from the Tribal Assembly to the Comitia Centuriata subject to a senatorial veto. He reduced the maximum interest payable by debtors to 10 per cent. He made Lucius CINNA (2), the consul-elect, swear to maintain these changes, and departed for the east with his army. He was, however, declared an outlaw and his measures were repealed, but no Roman had the strength to molest him.

He began in 86 by starving into submission Athens, whose port, the Piraeus, he sacked. He won two decisive victories over Mithridates' general ARCHELAUS (1), and expelled Mithridates' followers from Greece. In 85 Sulla advanced slowly to the Hellespont while his legate LUCULLUS

(2) searched the eastern Mediterranean for a fleet and money. He then crossed into Asia and joined in a negotiation between Mithridates and FIMBRIA at Dardanus, in which Mithridates agreed to terms of peace highly favourable to Sulla, who could now turn his attention elsewhere. In 84, he pursued Fimbria to Thyatira where he took the latter's troops from him. He occupied the province of Asia with these forces and imposed a huge fine on the province, including five years' tribute and the costs of the war. In 83, Cinna being dead, he embarked for Italy leaving his legate Murena to rule Asia in his name. Bringing a huge booty, including APELLICON's library and Mithridates' fine of 2,000 talents, he landed at Brundisium in spring and had no trouble with the huge force that CARBO (5) had assembled against him. He was joined by a number of disillusioned aristocrats, including METELLUS (7) Pius, Marcus CRASSUS (3), and the youthful POMPEIUS (2). He tried to compromise with the Italians, and allowed them to keep their hard-won rights, but was harsh to those who continued to resist. On his march through Italy he defeated each consul, Lucius Scipio, and NORBANUS in Campania. Early in 82 Sulla made a dash northwards despite the much better preparations of his enemies, and after defeating MARIUS (2) near Praeneste he entered Rome and then moved quickly to Etruria, where Carbo's army awaited him. Here he won a resounding victory over it, but was dogged by a large force consisting mainly of Italians under the Samnite leader Pontius Telesinus, which had broken away and tried to relieve Praeneste. It then marched on Rome, where Sulla met it beneath the city walls by the Colline Gate. After a bitterly fought battle in which the Samnite contingent, including those who surrendered, was butchered to a man, resistance to Sulla was virtually at an end. With the assistance of the *interrex* Valerius FLACCUS (7), whom he made his deputy, he secured a vote of the Comitia to become dictator for the purpose of reforming the constitution, and was voted immunity for all illegal acts he might commit, past or future. This covered the proscription he inaugurated of those who had opposed him, and which excelled the worst atrocities of Marius and his allies. He confiscated the lands and property of the proscribed and of towns and provinces which had shown favour to the Marians to pay the expenses of his army, to reward his friends, and to meet the need to settle his discharged soldiers. These latter he mainly located in Etruria and Campania, where they were well placed to defend his new order. He took the title *Felix*, 'Lucky', and at the beginning of 81 held a magnificent triumph for his victories over Mithridates. He devoted the remainder of the year to his reforms (see METELLA).

He enrolled some 400 new senators from the equestrians who supported his cause, and enacted legislation to remove power from the Assembly of the People to the Senate, to which he gave the power to veto legislation. He also restricted the powers of the tribunes, depriving them of some of their powers of veto and of the right to proceed to higher magistracies. He removed the control and composition of the standing criminal courts (*quaestiones*) from the Assembly to the Senate. He increased the numbers of senatorial magistrates, the quaestors to twenty and the praetors to eight. The quaestors were now automatically to become members of the Senate on completing their year of office. He thus provided enough qualified men to serve on the senatorial juries and to limit provincial governorships to one year's tenure. He reformed the senatorial political career, making tenure of both the quaestorship and praetorship necessary qualifications for the consulship, the minimum age for which was to be forty-two; a second consulship might only be held after a ten-year interval. He abolished the post of Leader of the Senate, which had been dominant in republican politics, and increased the number of state priests. He established Cisalpine Gaul as a province. He struck coinage bearing his image on his own authority, and abolished the right of the poor to buy cheap grain. He then gave up the dictatorship and was elected consul, with Metellus Pius, for 80, during which he tried to deny his ally Pompeius a triumph for his African campaign. After this he returned to private life. He was influenced in this by a prophecy he had received long before in Cilicia that he would die at the height of his powers. He lived a quiet if extravagant life of study and pleasure in Campania, writing his memoirs in twenty-two books, which were edited by Lucullus, but have not survived. He remarried and died in 78. His splendid funeral was a reminder of the strength of his veterans. His constitutional legislation, which was practical rather than constructive, was mostly unravelled in the following years, and finally demolished by Pompeius and Crassus in 70. It did not succeed in strengthening the senatorial aristocracy or in saving Rome from future civil wars. His administrative changes, however, were long lasting. See Plutarch's *Life of Sulla* and Appian's *History of Rome* on the Civil Wars and the Wars with Mithridates. See also E. Badian (1970) *Lucius Sulla: The Deadly Reformer*, Sydney: Sydney University Press; A. Keaveney (1982) *Sulla: The Last Republican*, London: Croom Helm.

3, Publius Cornelius (died *c.*45 BC), was a kinsman of the dictator SULLA (2). He became rich on the property confiscated from the victims of the proscriptions. He was prominent in the founding of the colony of Pompeii on the Bay of Naples for Sulla's veterans. On being elected consul for 65 with P. Autronius Paetus, he was expelled from the Senate on being found guilty of bribery of the electorate. In 62 he was prosecuted for having supported CATILINE in his conspiracy, and was acquitted by the eloquence of HORTENSIUS (2) and CICERO (1) in the speech *For Sulla*, the latter of whom he rewarded with a huge loan. In 54 he unsuccessfully prosecuted Aulus GABINIUS (2) for the same crime. He fought for CAESAR (1) in the Civil War, where he commanded the right wing at the battle of Pharsalus, and was restored by him to the Senate.

Sulpicia 1. (C1 BC) was the daughter of Servius SULPICIUS (2). Brought up in the house of her uncle MESSALLA (4), she was the only Roman woman of classical times whose poetry has survived. Six poems of high quality in elegiac metre were preserved in the corpus of TIBULLUS' poetry. They are addressed to her lover, a man of the same social class, whom she refers to by the Greek pseudonym Cerinthus. The unconventionality of such compositions by a girl will account for their rarity in the literature that has survived.

2. (late C1 AD) One fragment survives of the work of this poetess who lived during the reign of Domitian. She was commemorated with admiration by MARTIAL (10. 35 and 38), who attributed to her a felicitous combination of erotic passion and matrimonial fidelity. She wrote love poems to her husband, Calenus, and left a reputation that led to the later composition of imaginative imitations falsely attributed to her pen.

Sulpicius 1. Rufus, Publius (early C1 BC), studied law in company with a group of distinguished young men under Lucius CRASSUS (2), and unsuccessfully prosecuted NORBANUS in 95 for treason. He was quaestor in 93 and served as legate to POMPEIUS (4) Strabo in 89 during the Social War. As tribune in 88 he wished to pursue the programme of enfranchisement of Italians advocated but not implemented by Livius DRUSUS (1). He met with opposition from the nobles, and turned to MARIUS (1) and the popular party for support. This alliance led ultimately to his death: violent popular support won him his bill, but in return he had to pass a bill to transfer the command against MITHRIDATES (3) VI to Marius. He had to flee from Rome when SULLA (2) took the city by force: but he was caught at Laurentum and executed. Sulla repealed his law.

2. Rufus, Servius (mid-C1 BC). CICERO (1) greatly admired this fine orator, and correspondence between the two men is extant (Cicero, *Letters to his Friends*, 4. 5 and 12), including Sulpicius' famous consolation on the death of Cicero's daughter, Tullia. He was an expert jurist and was opposed in his prosecution of Lucius MURENA by Cicero, who ridiculed his learning. He was taught by Q. Mucius SCAEVOLA (4), the greatest lawyer of his age, whom Sulpicius came to rival in expertise. He failed to be elected consul for 62, when Murena won the post, and had to wait until 51 for his turn. In the Civil War he was timidly neutral and CAESAR (1) appointed him governor of Achaea in 46. He died in 43 at Mutina while on an embassy from the Senate to ANTONIUS (7). Cicero testified to his greatness in his *Ninth Philippic*. He left many writings on legal subjects, none of which is wholly extant, though his opinions are well represented in Justinian's *Digests*. He taught several pupils including ALFENUS Varus.
See also GALBA, GALLUS (7), QUIRINIUS.

Sura, Lucius Licinius (died *c.*AD 112), an important general of the time of TRAJAN, came from the north-east of Spain. He held three consulships, in 97, 102 and 107, the last as the colleague of his friend Sosius SENECIO. Already highly influential in the reign of NERVA (4), he is said to have persuaded Nerva to adopt Trajan as his heir in October 97; he may have been governing Lower Germany at the time. In the First Dacian War Sura carried out unsuccessful negotiations with DECEBALUS. He was greatly esteemed by Trajan, who granted him a statue and a public funeral. He was a fine orator, moved in literary circles, and was a patron of MARTIAL and a friend and correspondent of PLINY (2) the Younger.

Suren or **Surenas** was the name of a powerful Parthian family, rulers of Seistan and hereditary crowners of the Parthian kings. One of them became kingmaker in the middle of the last century BC, and in 55 overthrew Mithridates III to replace him with ORODES II. In 53 he used his powerful mounted archers against CRASSUS (3), whose invading force he annihilated at Carrhae. He was then at the pinnacle of success, but fear and jealousy combined to bring about his death at the hands of his king.

Syphax (died 201 BC), a king of the Masaesylii in western Numidia, supported Carthage in the Second Punic War until 214, when he made an alliance with the Roman generals in Spain, Gnaeus SCIPIO (1) and Publius SCIPIO (6). He made war on his weaker eastern neighbour, MASINISSA the king of Massyli, who supported Carthage, and drove him out of his kingdom. In 205 he changed sides under the influence of his wife SOPHONISBA, and resisted the Roman invasion of North Africa. He was defeated in 203 by SCIPIO (7) Africanus at the battle of the Great Plains in the valley of the Bagradas and fled back to Numidia, where he was captured by Masinissa and the Romans. The former was awarded most of his kingdom; the latter took him in chains to Italy, where he died at Tibur. His son Vermina later made peace with the Senate and was given a small kingdon in Numidia.

T

Tacfarinas (died AD 24) was a Numidian freebooter and rebel against Roman rule during the reign of TIBERIUS. His origin was obscure and he had been an auxiliary soldier in the Roman army. He was defeated several times by the proconsuls of the province (including BLAESUS, who was proclaimed *Imperator* by his victorious troops) but could not be pinned down until Publius DOLABELLA (5) killed him at Auzia.

Tacitus 1, Publius Cornelius (*c.*AD 54–*c.*120), was the most famous and original Roman historian. He was probably born in Narbonese Gaul and moved to Rome when he was about twenty to embark on a senatorial career. His father was of equestrian status, and his education may well have been completed by QUINTILIAN. The consul AGRICOLA recognised his potential and chose him in 77 to be his son-in-law. He reached the praetorship by 88, and was abroad from 89 to 93, doubtless to hold a command in an imperial province. Thus he was absent from Rome when his father-in-law died. He was by this time a member of a prestigious priestly college, and was gaining a fine reputation at the bar. He had begun to collect material suitable for projected writing. During the period 93–96, DOMITIAN's reign of terror, he kept a low profile and uttered no public criticism; however, the events and feelings of that time marked him for the rest of his life and affected his outlook as a historian and commentator. In 97 he held a suffect consulship and as such pronounced the funeral eulogy of the consul Verginius RUFUS (5). In 100 he joined his friend, PLINY (2) the Younger, in the prosecution of Marius Priscus for his deeds as proconsul of Asia. Seniority brought him the governorship of the province of Asia as proconsul in 112–13. He seems to have had no children, though the emperor TACITUS (2) claimed him as an ancestor.

Tacitus wrote five works of historical and literary importance that have come down to us in part or whole. The first was published in spring 98, *The Life of Julius Agricola*, an appreciation of his deceased father-in-law. It is an invaluable source for the history of early Roman Britain as well as a powerful condemnation of the tyranny of Domitian. The deep affection he shows for the great general lends unity and force to the work. His next work, *Germany*, more accurately *The Origin and Location of the Germans*, published later in the same year, is an ethnographical monograph concerning the peoples of Greater Germany in Tacitus' time. It provides its author with many opportunities to draw comparisons between Roman and German society, often critical of Roman customs. Tacitus had plenty of source material to research this book, in particular the *German Wars* of PLINY (1), the *Notes on the Gallic War* of CAESAR (1) and LIVY's book 104. He probably did not know STRABO's work. His *Dialogue on Orators* is hard to date, 102 now being the usually accepted date. It purports to be a report of a discussion Tacitus heard while a young man newly arrived in Rome. Three speakers offer their own accounts of the decline in the quality of oratory from the time of CICERO (1). Marcus Aper defends contemporary oratory, Vipstanus Messalla pleads for the revival of past morality and education, and Curiatius Maternus provides a rational analysis of the changes in political and social life since republican times, which have rendered oratory superfluous or dangerous. The discussion is graceful, intelligent, and inconclusive.

The two major historical works for which Tacitus is best known, covering the period of imperial government from the outset of TIBERIUS' reign until the fall of DOMITIAN, are the *Histories* and the *Annals*. He began the former, whose original title we do not know, *c.*105 and published it *c.*110. It consisted of some fourteen books, of which the first four and a quarter survive, covering the years 68–70. He then turned to the earlier period of the principate and composed his masterpiece, which he entitled *From the Death of Augustus* (*Ab Excessu Divi Augusti*), and which we know as the *Annals*. It probably consisted of some eighteen books, of which several are not extant. We possess books 1–4 and part of 5, 6, and the second half of 11 and 12 to the middle of 16. It was probably written in the years before his death and may never have been finished. Tacitus was at home in writing of the degenerate age which preceded the laudable era of TRAJAN and HADRIAN in which he lived his later years. He claimed to aim at impartiality and equanimity in his approach to his subject, but was unable to conceal his strong feelings about the cruelty and corruption of the reigns of the Julio-Claudian emperors, in many of whom, and especially Tiberius, he saw the image of the hated Domitian.

Tacitus' handling of the warfare of 69 between the various aspirants to the purple was criticised by Mommsen for its lack of precision. However, in terms of the quality of the narrative and its ability to excite the reader, it excels; Tacitus' agenda was different from that of modern historians. Unfortunately we lack those parts of the *Histories* which refer to the times through which Tacitus himself lived. At the beginning of the work he expressed his intention to go on to write the history of the reigns of NERVA (4) and TRAJAN, but in fact he turned to the earlier period treated in the *Annals*. He regarded the emperors in general and Tiberius in particular as men of corrupt character who sometimes began their reigns with a show of virtue but inevitably dropped the mask to reveal the tyrannical reality. For example, Tiberius began his reign with many a show of republican sentiment, but after his retirement to Capri and the unleashing of SEJANUS, he ended it with a series of treason trials. Tiberius especially evoked Domitian for him. Of the emperors whom Tacitus describes, only VESPASIAN is allowed to have improved during the progress of his reign.

We know very little about Tacitus' sources in composing his historical works. He will doubtless have drawn on the Elder PLINY (1), Aufidius BASSUS (2), CLUVIUS Rufus and FABIUS (11) Rusticus, and the memoirs of men like CORBULO. Mommsen and many later critics have suggested that for much of his narrative Tacitus was content with a single unnamed source, possibly one of the above. The record of proceedings of the Senate was also at his disposal.

Tacitus' style sprang from his intense training in oratory and developed during his career as a writer. His earlier works reveal what was to come, and we already note in the *Agricola* the telling epigram on Roman imperialism put in the mouth of the Caledonian chieftain Calgacus, 'They make a desert and call it peace'. The *Dialogue* stands apart and displays features of a neo-Ciceronian style. His mature style emerges in his two great historical works, particularly the *Annals*. He was influenced by the highly colourful style of SALLUST, who had eschewed longwindedness and sought brevity of expression, though Tacitus took the use of ellipse and compression of language much further than his model. Above all, Tacitus avoided anything that might seem monotonous or hackneyed, and constantly strove for variety. He therefore shunned rhetorical balance or antithesis, and used unusual expressions and strange or poetic forms of familiar words. He also made far greater use of metaphor than his predecessors. His sense of the oral effect of his work, which like most historical writing was designed to be read aloud, encouraged him to practise rounding off each passage with an epigram, even though the epigram occasionally fell flat. In contrast with earlier Latin writers, he tended to express the main idea or action near the beginning of a sentence and then to add subordinate ideas in various ways, often using participles. Thus he was enabled to append comments of his own on the actions of his subjects, or to suggest the motives of the agents or the reactions of those about them. He was deeply interested in the psychology of his subjects, and tellingly explored the characters and motivation of the participants in his narrative. Coupled with a penetrating insight into men's character and the issues of the period, there is a profound pessimism and disillusionment underlying his historical works. His work was largely neglected by posterity, and the church condemned him as an enemy of Christianity (his few comments on it were not favourable): hence the precarious nature of the survival of his works. He came into his own in the Renaissance and has been admired ever since. Gibbon captured something of his spirit in his *Decline and Fall of the Roman Empire*. See F.R.D. Goodyear (1970) *Tacitus*, Oxford: Clarendon Press; R. Syme (1958) *Tacitus*, Oxford: Clarendon Press; T.A. Dorey (ed.) (1968) *Tacitus*, London: Routledge and Kegan Paul; T.J. Luce and A.J. Woodman (eds) (1993) *Tacitus and the Tacitean Tradition*, Princeton: Princeton University Press.

2, Marcus Claudius (reigned AD 275–276), was an elderly senator who was chosen by the Senate in September 275 to take the place of the assassinated AURELIAN. Though reluctant at the age of about seventy-five to assume the responsibility of ruling the empire, he allowed himself to be persuaded and set out with his Praetorian Prefect FLORIANUS (perhaps his half-brother) to deal with a crisis in Asia Minor. Together they proved their mettle by defeating and driving out the Goths who had invaded Pontus. However, in mid-year Tacitus died at Tyana in Cappadocia, almost certainly killed by his troops. Florianus briefly succeeded him.

Tasciovanus (reigned *c.*20 BC–*c.*AD 10) ruled the British nation of the Catuvellauni, which occupied territory to the north of modern London, with its capital at Verulamium (St Albans). He struck coinage based on classical models. He may have been a grandson of CASSIVELLAUNUS, the opponent of CAESAR (1)'s invasion in 54 BC. His son was CUNOBELINUS.

Telesinus, Pontius *see* SULLA (2).

Terence (*c.*195–159 BC) Publius Terentius Afer was a Latin writer of comedies based on Greek plays (*fabulae palliatae*). His last name implies a North African origin: his biography by SUETONIUS (2) claims that he was born in Carthage. He came to Italy as the slave of a senator, Terentius Lucanus, by whom he was given an education and his freedom. He moved among literary circles, being accepted by the members of the family of L. Aemilius PAULLUS (2). It is said that the aediles commanded him to read his first play to the playwright CAECILIUS (5) Statius, who was dining as Terence read, and was so impressed by the work that he invited Terence to join him at the meal. All six plays that he wrote survive: we know their dates from first-century BC production notices preserved with the plays. They were produced by AMBIVIUS Turpio, with music by Flaccus, a slave of one Claudius. In 159 he set out to travel to Greece to collect more material for his work, but disappeared, perhaps in a shipwreck.

His first play, *The Girl from Andros* (*Andria*), was presented at the Megalensian Games in 166. It was an adaptation of two plays by Menander, *The Girl from Andros* and *The Girl from Perinthos*, with an original material at the opening of the prologue. The story, set in Athens, has the usual ingredients of New Comedy, mistaken identity, a seduction, a clever and manipulative slave, and a happy ending. *The Mother-in-Law* (*Hecyra*), first produced at the Megalensian Games of 165, was adapted from a play by Apollodorus of Carystus, though its plot resembles that of Menander's *Arbitration* (*Epitrepontes*). The first production of *The Mother-in-Law* was ruined by competition from a tightrope dancer's act, which distracted the audience. The play was revived twice in 160: the first revival, at the funeral games of Aemilius PAULLUS (2), was again a failure. The plot is concerned with the suspicion of a married man for his wife, who bears a child as a result of a rape, and he leaves her. It turns out, thanks to the help of an honest courtesan, that the child is in fact his, and he had violated her in the dark before he married her. He had also taken a ring from her and given it to his mistress, a courtesan. The play is named after the two mothers-in-law who figure prominently in the action. *The Self-Torturer* (*Heauton Timoroumenos*) was adapted from Menander's play of the same name, and produced at the Megalensian Games in 163. The self-torturer is a man who has driven away his son for forming an unsatisfactory liaison. His neighbour reproves him for his harshness, but is eventually found guilty of equal harshness towards his own son. All ends happily when a lost relationship is revealed. *The Eunuch* (*Eunuchus*) was also adapted from Menander's play of the same name, and was produced with great success at the Megalensian Games of 161, bringing Terence considerable wealth. In the story, a courtesan rescues a young Athenian girl from slavery and dishonour, and an admirer presents the courtesan with a eunuch as a slave. The admirer's brother falls in love with the young slave girl, disguises himself as the eunuch, and has his way with the slave girl. The courtesan reveals the truth about her and brings about the marriage of the seducer with the girl, now proved to be of citizen birth. Terence added a couple of characters, a boastful soldier and a parasite, from Menander's play *The Toady* (*Kolax*). *Phormio* was based on a comedy by Apollodorus of Carystus, *The Claimant*, and was first produced at the Roman Games of 161. The character Phormio is a parasite who becomes involved in a love affair between an orphan and a young Athenian whose father is abroad, and persuades the court to order the marriage of the two under the law that orphaned girls must marry their next-of-kin. This action leads to much intrigue and the revelation to his wife that the girl's father is alive and begot her in an extra-marital affair. Like *The Mother-in-Law*, *The Brothers* (*Adelphoe*), adapted from Menander's *Brothers* and with a scene taken from Diphilus' *Those who Die Together*, was put on at the funeral games of Aemilius Paullus: it had been commissioned by a pair of brothers, Paullus' sons, SCIPIO (11) Aemilianus and FABIUS (5) Maximus. Like the two Romans, who were adopted into separate families, the two sons of Demea are brought up separately, and in very different styles, one by their father and the other by his brother. The tale involves seduction, suspicion, and a change of character on the part of the crusty Demea at the expense of his tolerant brother.

The style of Terence's work is markedly different from that of his predecessor PLAUTUS, and more faithful to the spirit of the original Greek comedies of Menander and his contemporaries, two centuries earlier. His dialogues are closer to natural everyday speech, though his prologues, which are not introductions to the plots, are highly rhetorical. There is less intrusion of Italian material, and the passages with musical accompaniment are reduced in length. He uses simpler metres than Plautus. However, his ability to retain the interest of his audience, and his understanding of the human predicament, are impressive. Several well known sayings derive from his work, such as 'there are as many opinions as there are individuals' (*quot homines, tot sententiae*), and 'I am human: I consider nothing human foreign to me'. He shows a particular sympathy for women for the way men treat them. The appeal of his plays was more to the educated upper classes than the broad populace who found Plautus' works more amusing. The fourth-century commentator DONATUS (1) wrote a commentary on his plays, part of which survives. See S.M. Goldberg (1986) *Understanding Terence*, Princeton: Princeton University Press; G.E. Duckworth (1952) *The Nature of Roman Comedy*, Princeton: Princeton University Press; W. Beare (1964) *The Roman Stage*, London: Methuen; E. Segal (1987) *Roman Laughter*, 2nd edn, Oxford: Oxford University Press; R.L. Hunter (1985) *The New Comedy of Greece and Rome*, Cambridge: Cambridge University Press.

Terentia (*c.*80 BC–*c.*AD 23) was a woman of wealthy and aristocratic background, the first wife of CICERO (1) and mother of his two children. She was a powerful influence on him, strengthening his resolve at moments of crisis such as the conspiracy of CATILINE and his exile. But he came to suspect her of dishonesty in financial matters and divorced her late in 47, though he found it difficult to repay her dowry, which she assigned to BALBUS (1) to repay a debt she owed him. PLUTAR-CH states that she remarried twice, first with SALLUST and then MESSALLA (4), and lived to be 103. See TYRANNIO (2).

Terentius *see* CULLEO, VARRO.

Tertullian (*c.*AD 160–*c.*240) Quintus Septimius Florens Tertullianus was born at Carthage, the son of a Roman centurion. He almost certainly trained and perhaps practised as an advocate, and his writings teem with rhetorical power, argument and irony. It is disputed whether the author of *Legal Problems* in eight books and *Soldiers' Cash Savings* is the same man, but the likelihood is strong. Tertullian wrote in Latin, and after his conversion to Christianity *c.*195 used his formidable talents to defend an ascetic and puritanical tradition in the North African church, asserting that only martyrdom could ensure salvation, and refuting the common charges that the Christians were atheists, magicians and enemies of the state. He grossly exaggerated the extent of the persecution of Christians by the Roman authorities. By 197 he had published *To the Martyrs*, *To the Nations*, and *A Defence* (*Apologeticus*). The last of these is perhaps his most interesting work. It takes the form of a court speech addressed to the civil authorities, the governors of the provinces, in which he sets the record straight about the nature of Christianity, contrasting it with the teachings of the philosophical schools. He asks for protection for Christians from mob violence and eloquently pleads for fair treatment and justice in the tribunals of the Empire, where there was frequent abuse of process against Christians accused of atheism and treason. He then turned to writing about Christian ethics. In several books, including *The Witness of the Soul*, he warned Christians against relying on the arguments of philosophy (though he was happy to accept the support of Stoicism where it agreed with his teachings). He based his own doctrine rigorously on the Bible, asserting that humankind has an innate knowledge of God. He attacked the heretical Gnostic writer Marcion in five books for emending the Christian scriptures and disregarding the Hebrew scriptures, and he condemned the attempts of some Christians to substitute philosophy for faith as the guiding principle of their lives. At some time *c.*206 he became a Montanist (see MONTANUS 2), perhaps because he disapproved of the slackness of the Catholics, but he never broke formally with the church. He wrote further treatises, addressing one (*To Scapula*) to a Roman governor to urge the value of religious freedom, and others to his fellow Christians in support of monogamy and rigorous fasting, and condemning obedience to the civil powers. In *The Flesh of Christ*, *The Resurrection of the Flesh*, *The Soul*, and *Against Praxeas* he developed a doctrine of monism that denied the distinction between body and soul. He also wrote *Chastity* against the reform of Callistus, bishop of Rome, which had relaxed the rules of penitence. Tertullian kept to the teaching that there could be no pardon for those who had committed mortal sins. He eventually abandoned Montanism and founded an even more extreme sect of his own.

He was the first Christian theologian to write in Latin, roughly contemporary with MINUCIUS (2) Felix, who drew on his work. His style is difficult and his vocabulary rich and varied, and he invented many new words. He contributed greatly to the development of the Latin language for theological use. Thirty-one of his works are extant. Many of his principles and prejudices were shared by HIPPOLYTUS. See H. Chadwick (1986) *The Early Church*, 2nd edn, Harmondsworth: Penguin; T.D. Barnes (1985) *Tertullian: A Historical and Literary Study*, Oxford: Clarendon Press.

Tetricus, Gaius Pius Esuvius (reigned AD 270–274), while governor of the Gallic province of Aquitania replaced Victorinus as ruler (styling himself emperor) of the empire in the west, consisting of Gaul, Spain and Britain, which POSTUMUS had seized. He appointed his son as *Caesar* and his successor. He was worn down by warfare with the Germans, and in 274 had to face an invasion by AURELIAN whom he met at Châlons-sur-Marne. He lost his nerve, deserted his army, and surrendered his person to Aurelian, who paraded him in his triumph together with Queen ZENOBIA. Aurelian treated him gently, restored his senatorial status, and made him governor of Lucania. See M. Grant (1985) *The Roman Emperors*, London: Weidenfeld & Nicolson.

Teuta *see* CORUNCANIUS (1), SCERDILAIDAS.

Thrasea Paetus, Publius Clodius (died AD 66), was a Stoic senator, probably from Patavium (Padua). He tried to preserve the dignity of the Senate during the reign of NERO (1), but fell foul of the emperor by his independence of thought and outspoken criticism. Nero prevailed upon the subservient Senate to sentence him to death, and he committed suicide in the presence of his son-in-law, HELVIDIUS (1) Priscus and the philosopher DEMETRIUS (4) the Cynic, but prevented his wife, ARRIA (2), from following her mother's example and joining him in death. He wrote a life of CATO (5) of Utica, the Stoic hero of the previous century, upon whom he modelled his life. The book, which has not survived, influenced PLUTARCH's *Life of Cato*.

Tiberius (42 BC–AD 37) (Tiberius Claudius Nero) was the second Roman emperor. He was born on 16 November 42, the elder son of Tiberius Claudius NERO (3) and his wife LIVIA (2). When Tiberius was three years old and his brother DRUSUS (3) was still in the womb, Nero divorced Livia so that she might marry Octavian (the future emperor AUGUSTUS). Tiberius was brought up, at least after his father's death in 33, in Octavian's house, which as he grew older became more and more like a royal court. He performed his first military duties in Spain in Augustus' presence, and was appointed quaestor in 23, when he was five years younger than the minimum age laid down for the post. In 20 he was sent with an army to Armenia where he crowned the Roman nominee to the throne of that country, TIGRANES (2) III, and received the Roman standards taken from CRASSUS (3) by the Parthians in 53. He had an extremely distinguished military career, beginning in 16 BC with a key command on the northern frontier, in company with his brother Drusus, when he finished the conquest of the Alpine region. In 13 he held the consulship. He then served in Pannonia until 9 BC, when Drusus died, and subjugated the Pannonians and Dalmatians, establishing in 11 the imperial province of Illyricum. Tiberius then took command in Germany until his second consulship in 7, for which he was rewarded with a triumph. After that he received the powers of a tribune (tribunician power) for five years, the basis of Augustus' own authority in Rome, and a special command for diplomatic purposes in the east. He was instructed to restore Roman authority over Armenia, which had been weakened by the death of Tigranes III.

His mission, however, turned into a voluntary retirement in Rhodes. The cause of this development was Tiberius' domestic misery, brought about by his enforced divorce in 11 from Vipsania AGRIPPINA (1), the daughter of AGRIPPA (1) and his first wife Caecilia, by whom he had a son, DRUSUS (4). For dynastic reasons Augustus had compelled him to marry his own daughter JULIA (5), Agrippa's widow, whom Tiberius came to detest. She bore him a son who did not survive. His retirement did not endear him to Augustus, who rejected Tiberius' requests to be allowed to return home. However, Augustus was persuaded by Livia and other members of his family to permit Tiberius to return in AD 2, three years after Julia's banishment for adultery. He only regained Augustus' favour in 4 after the deaths of the latter's grandsons Gaius CAESAR (3) and Lucius CAESAR (8), whom he had made his heirs. Augustus now adopted Tiberius and AGRIPPA (2) Postumus, though the latter quickly fell from favour. Tiberius at the same time adopted GERMANICUS, the popular son of his late brother, and was granted tribunician power for ten years. He was sent again to Germany, where he remained in command from 4 until 6. In the latter year he was summoned to Illyricum to suppress a rebellion there. This occupied him until 9 when he was faced with the task of rectifying the disastrous situation on the German frontier caused by the crushing defeat of Quinctilius VARUS. By 12 he had restored the situation and returned to Rome to a triumph. In 13 he was invested with tribunician and proconsular powers equal to those of the emperor.

In 14, on Augustus' death, the transition of power was smooth, thanks to the powers Tiberius already possessed. Agrippa Postumus was put to death, a murder Tiberius denied ordering. A debate held in the Senate on 17 September is reported by TACITUS (1), and shows Tiberius as being reluctant to adopt all the trappings of monarchy. He certainly dispensed with Augustus' privy council, and restored decision-making to the Senate. He probably hoped for greater collaboration from a servile Senate than it was capable of. On his accession there were serious mutinies on the German and

Danubian frontiers, which were put down with difficulty. He remained in Rome until 23, when he was 64, and during this time he governed with moderation and justice. His policy on the frontiers was to continue that of Augustus as laid down in the latter's political testament, the *Achievements of Augustus*, which Tiberius had probably helped to revise in 13. Thereby he came into conflict with his nephew Germanicus, who fought arduous and ambitious campaigns in Germany before being restained by Tiberius' cautious hand. He appointed Germanicus in 17 to a command in the east, by which Commagene and Cappadocia were annexed as provinces. He had to face the difficulties caused by Germanicus' death in 19 and the accusation of poisoning against PISO (4) brought by AGRIPPINA (2). He made up for the shortage of suitable candidates for governorships by extending the office of those already serving, such as Pontius PILATE; and even allowed some governors to be absent from their provinces. His relations with his mother Livia were poor and it was suggested that he left Rome in 26 to escape from her. He never returned.

There were many problems, often financial, during the reign, and rebellions, which took place in Gaul (in 21) and at Rome, attest the dissatisfaction of many. The provincials felt a heavy burden of tax, and there was temptation on the part of some politicians to enrich themselves by accusing others of treason, and trials before the Senate increased in number and viciousness as the reign progressed. At first Tiberius was lenient to those accused, but after his retirement there was something approaching a reign of terror. On the death of his son Drusus, of whose poisoning by SEJANUS and LIVIA (3) he knew nothing, he went first to Campania, ostensibly to dedicate some temples, and the following year to the delightful island of Capreae. Sejanus, the Praetorian Prefect, had long been the power behind the throne, and encouraged Tiberius' retirement. He now had a free hand. Germanicus' widow Agrippina and sons NERO (4) and DRUSUS (5) were disgraced and exiled (29–30). He asked the emperor's permission to marry Drusus' widow, his mistress Livia, but was refused. Not until 31, when much damage to Tiberius' reputation had already been done, did ANTONIA (2) engineer Sejanus' downfall and death. Sejanus, who had been plotting to seize power for himself, was replaced by MACRO, who exercised a similar power, and held a purge of all those who were suspected of assisting Sejanus. Tiberius died in suspicious circumstances on 16 March 37, while passing a night on the mainland at Misenum, and was succeeded by CALIGULA. The vices attributed to Tiberius in his retirement by SUETONIUS (2) and others are almost certainly false. In fact he was an intelligent and sensitive person who wrote neoteric poetry, held Sceptical philosophical views, was a powerful public speaker, and enjoyed fine art. He was also inclined to irony and often expressed himself ambiguously. Tacitus (*Annals*) regarded him as having ruled well until he allowed Sejanus his head, but as revealing his true colours in the ensuing oppression. See F.B. Marsh (1931) *The Reign of Tiberius*, London: Oxford University Press; B. Levick (1976) *Tiberius the Politician*, London: Thames & Hudson; R. Seager (1972) *Tiberius*, London: Eyre Methuen.

Tibullus, Albius (*c*.54–19 BC), was an elegiac poet of considerable originality. Of equestrian rank, he came from Pedum, between Tibur and Praeneste, where his family owned an estate that suffered in the confiscations of land carried out in 42 by Octavian (AUGUSTUS). He was a protégé of the great literary patron MESSALLA (4) along with OVID (who wrote an elegy on his death) and LYGDAMUS, and was a friend of HORACE, who addressed to him an *Ode* (1, 33) and an *Epistle* (1, 4) which display both sympathetic affection and ironic criticism. In 30 he embarked for Syria with Messalla's retinue but terminated his journey at Corcyra (Corfu), when he fell ill and returned home. In 28 he may have accompanied Messalla in a military role when he was governor of Aquitania. After this he gave up all pretensions to a public career and seems to have buried himself in the country. In his poetry he makes much of this rustic way of life. Three books of elegies were attributed to him, but the last contains poems by other members of Messalla's circle: Lygdamus and SULPICIA (1). It is doubtful whether any poem in this book is by Tibullus, though he may have written a group of elegies on Sulpicia's love for Cerinthus and the penultimate elegy.

In his first book (published *c.*26) Tibullus writes of his love for Delia (a pseudonym: her real name was Plania), whom he longs to share a rustic idyll with him, and for a boy, Marathus. The second, perhaps a posthumous publication, contains a fine description of a country festival, poems for Messalla, and for a mistress he calls Nemesis. He was considered by some contemporaries to be the best of the Roman elegists, and his work is characterised by its plain language, smoothness, and simple elegance. Unlike his contemporary PROPERTIUS, he scarcely uses myth in his poems, but he does regard love as a kind of military service, and the lover as his mistress' slave. His admirers probably saw his work as the Roman answer to the challenge of Greek poetry, and he shows the influence of Hellenistic and earlier Greek models. Modern taste, however, prefers the intellectual challenge of Propertius and the sheer brilliance and wit of Ovid. His appeal to Romans of his time lay in his answer to a problem they felt deeply, their struggle between the call of public duty and their ancestral tie to the land. His work seemed to offer a hope that, civil war being ended, Romans could return to their rural roots. See F. Cairns (1979) *Tibullus: A Hellenistic Poet at Rome*, Cambridge: Cambridge University Press; R.O.A.M. Lyne (1980) *The Latin Love Poets*, Oxford: Clarendon Press.

Tigellinus, Gaius Ofonius (*c.*AD 15–69), was a handsome Sicilian of obscure origin, the son of an Agrigentine exiled to Scylaceum. He was brought up within the households of the husbands of CALIGULA's sisters AGRIPPINA (3) and JULIA (8) Livilla, and was accused of adultery with them both, for which he was exiled by Caligula. CLAUDIUS (1) allowed him to return. He inherited a fortune but lived obscurely until NERO (1), impressed by his horsebreeding successes in Apulia, promoted him to the post of Chief of the City Police (*Praefectus Vigilum*). In 62 he appointed him to replace BURRUS as Praetorian Prefect jointly with Faenius Rufus, and in this post Tigellinus played a crucial role in detecting the conspiracy of Gaius PISO (2), for which he was rewarded with triumphal decorations. He accompanied Nero on his tour of Greece. Notorious for the executions he had caused, he was dismissed by GALBA (1), but saved from death by his powerful friend VINIUS. However, OTHO by popular demand forced him to commit suicide. See K. Wellesley (1975) *The Long Year, AD 69*, London: Elek.

Tigranes 1. II 'The Great' (reigned *c.*100–*c.*56 BC), the son of Tigranes I, king of Armenia, or of Artavasdes I, was held as a prisoner of the Parthians before they gave him the throne of Armenia in return for a slice of its territory. He married Cleopatra, a daughter of MITHRIDATES (3) VI of Pontus, and formed an alliance with him against Cappadocia, bringing the intervention of SULLA (2). In 83 he attacked Parthia, which had to face enemies in the east, and occupied the remnant of the Seleucid empire, Syria, Cilicia and Phoenicia. He founded Tigranocerta in south-western Armenia as a new capital, and peopled it with the inhabitants of cities which had resisted him, Soli and Mazaca. But his alliance with Mithridates proved his undoing, as it led to war with Rome: in 69 LUCULLUS (2) attacked his kingdom and seized Tigranocerta, and in 66 POMPEIUS (2) split him from Mithridates and defeated him, depriving him of all his territory except Armenia. He gave Rome no more trouble, regaining Sophene and fighting the Parthians over border disputes. He was succeeded by his son ARTAVASDES (1) I.

2. **III** (reigned 20–6 BC), a son of ARTAVASDES (1) I, king of Armenia, was captured by ANTONIUS (7) in 34 and taken to Egypt. Octavian (AUGUSTUS) took him to Rome, where he lived until the murder of his brother ARTAXIAS (1) *c.*22 created a vacancy on the Armenian throne. At the request of the Armenians, Augustus sent TIBERIUS in 20 at the head of an army to install him as king. He maintained neutrality though ostensibly an ally of Rome.

3. **IV** (reigned 6 BC–AD 1) inherited the Armenian throne from his father, TIGRANES (2) III, with the support of Parthia, and was joint ruler with his sister Erato. He was deposed in 1 BC when Gaius CAESAR (4) replaced him with Ariobarzanes. However, soon after, his rival was murdered and he returned to power. He died in the defence of the eastern frontier of his kingdom.

4. V (reigned AD 60–61), a member of the Cappadocian royal family and a descendant of HEROD (1), was placed on the throne of Armenia by CORBULO to further the eastern policy of NERO (1). The next year Tigranes rashly attacked Adiabene in Mesopotamia, from which he was driven out by VOLOGESES I, the Parthian king, and penned in Tigranocerta. Corbulo negotiated his release and he left his kingdom.

Timesitheus, Gaius Furius Sabinius Aquila (died AD 243), was an able, even brilliant cavalry officer and administrator of humble origins, who had proved himself under the emperors SEVERUS (2) Alexander and MAXIMINUS (1) in provincial administration, holding a number of procuratorships. In 241 he was appointed prefect of the Praetorian Guard to GORDIAN III, then a youth, who married Timesitheus' daughter. Until his death from illness he was the virtual head of state, restoring the fortunes of the principate and leading a successful campaign against the Persians under ARTAXERXES.

Tincommius (reigned *c.*25 BC–*c.*AD 1) The son and heir of COMMIUS as king of the Belgic Atrebates in Britain, he appears to have had Roman support as a buffer against the Catuvellauni. His brother Eppilius displaced him and drove him into exile.

Tiridates 1. *See* PHRAATES (1).

2. *See* ARTABANUS (1).

3. (mid-C1 AD) was made king of Armenia in 54 by his brother, King VOLOGESES I of Parthia. Temporarily displaced in 60 by the Roman nominee to the throne, TIGRANES (4) V, with the help of the Roman general CORBULO, he was soon restored by Vologeses. He made an agreement with Corbulo to go to Rome and receive the crown from NERO (1), which took place in 66. He lost his kingdom to the Alans in 72.

Tiro, Marcus Tullius (*c.*103–4 BC), was the secretary of CICERO (1), his slave and, from 53 BC, freedman and friend. He was the inventor of a form of Latin shorthand. He caught malaria in 51, a disease which plagued him and worried his master. Before Cicero's murder in 43, Tiro had bought a farm near Puteoli. He published Cicero's *Letters to His Friends* and some of his speeches, and wrote a life of Cicero, which has not survived.

Titius, Marcus (C1 BC), was proscribed in 43 BC and assembled a private fleet. He was captured in 40 by MENODORUS, the ally of Sextus POMPEIUS (4), and spared

by the latter, who had already given refuge to Titius' father Lucius. In 39 he joined Marcus ANTONIUS (7) in the east and served under him in his war with Parthia. In 35 he captured Sextus Pompeius at Miletus and killed him. Antonius appointed him proconsul of Asia but in 32 he deserted Antonius for Octavian (AUGUSTUS) in the company of his uncle, Munatius PLANCUS (1). They reported the existence of Antonius' infamous will, deposited with the Vestal Virgins. Titius was rewarded with a suffect consulship in 31, served at the battle of Actium, and governed Syria as legate at some later date.
See also ARISTO.

Titus (AD 39–81), the second Flavian emperor, was born on 30 December 39 and named Titus Flavius Vespasianus. He was the elder son of VESPASIAN and his wife Flavia Domitilla. His father being then in high favour and a friend of the freedman NARCISSUS, he was brought up with BRITANNICUS at the court of CLAUDIUS (1), and given a good education by Sosibius: he was proficient at singing and playing music, and wrote tragedies and poems. After this auspicious start he married Tertulla Arrecina *c.*62, the daughter of a former prefect of the Praetorian Guard. She died soon after, having borne him a daughter, FLAVIA JULIA. He next married Marcia Furnilla, but divorced her when her family fell from imperial favour. He began the senatorial career but did not advance far, having only reached the quaestorship when his father became emperor. He spent much of his adult life on military service, first as a military tribune in Germany and Britain. It is likely that he became friendly with the Elder PLINY (1) while serving in Lower Germany. In 67 he served under his father in the war to defeat the rebellion of the Jews, and commanded a legion. He acted to heal relations between Vespasian and MUCIANUS, governor of Syria, and was sent with his father's message of support to GALBA (1) in 68, but returned when he received news of Galba's death at Corinth. He continued the siege of Jerusalem, and when his father, aided by Mucianus, made a bid for power in July 69, he remained to command the army in Judaea. Vespasian made him consul for 70 and granted him the powers of a proconsul. In 70 he took Jerusalem and was hailed by his army as *Imperator*. The pro-Roman Jewish historian JOSEPHUS, whom the Flavians befriended, was present and wrote an account of the war.

Titus returned to Rome in summer 71 to share a triumph with Vespasian, who on 1 July, the second anniversary of his accession, confirmed his intention to found a dynasty by conferring on Titus the power of a tribune. There followed six further consulships and the revived censorship, in all of which offices he was his father's colleague. There was no question, however, of joint rule. Titus was appointed prefect of the Praetorian Guard and earned unpopularity in 79 by his ruthlessness in putting down the conspiracy of EPRIUS Marcellus and CAECINA (3) Alienus, if such it was. He was also criticised for openly living at Rome with the Jewish princess BERENICE (2), which he did from 75 until 79, though he ignored her when she visited Rome after his accession.

Titus had an easy transition to power on his father's unexpected death on 23 June 79. His brief reign was marked by good government, respect for the Senate and the rejection of informers with accusations of treason. He deified his father, opened the Colosseum, erected a large bathing establishment nearby and produced lavish games. He worked hard to alleviate the suffering caused by the eruption of Vesuvius in August 79 and the plague and fire at Rome in 80. His early death on 13 September 81 was almost certainly natural, though his brother DOMITIAN, with whom he had shared an uneasy relationship, was suspected by some of poisoning him. He was sincerely mourned and regarded in retrospect as the 'darling of the human race'. See B.W. Jones (1984) *The Emperor Titus*, London: Croom Helm.

Torquatus 1. Imperiosus, Titus Manlius (C4 BC), was an almost legendary Roman hero. The few facts about him are that he was thrice consul, in 347, 344 and 340, and dictator at various times, notably 353 when he forced a hundred-year truce on Caere. In 340, with his colleague Decius MUS (1), he defeated the combined Latins and Campanians at Veseris in Campania and after a further victory at Suessa held a triumph. Stories of fortitude and valour accrued to his name, such as the single combat with a Gallic warrior from which he gained his *cognomen*, derived from the torque worn by Gauls round their necks. He is also said to have executed his son before the battle of Veseris for duelling, giving rise to his reputation for severity.

2, Titus Manlius (*c.*270–202 BC), consul in 235, triumphed after a campaign in Sardinia and closed the gates of the temple of Janus, showing that Rome was fighting no wars anywhere. He held a second consulship with Quintus FLACCUS (2) in 224, when together they subdued the Boii in Cispadane Gaul after the battle of Telamon. In 215 he held a command in Sardinia where he defeated a united Sardinian and Carthaginian army. He was appointed dictator in 208 to organise elections and games.

Traianus, Marcus Ulpius (C1 AD), was the father of the emperor TRAJAN. He was a native of the municipality of Italica near the modern city of Seville, and *c.*67 governed his native province of Baetica as proconsul. He commanded a legion under VESPASIAN in the Jewish War until 69, when Vespasian gave him patrician status and designated him consul for 70. He governed Syria in the mid-seventies and built a road from Palmyra to the Euphrates. He was granted triumphal decorations for his handling of the Parthians. He was proconsul of Asia in 79–80 and was later deified by his son.

Trajan (AD 53–117) reigned as emperor from January 98 to August 117. He was born at Italica near modern Seville in Spain, the son of a distinguished ex-consul, Marcus Ulpius TRAIANUS, whose name he inherited. He entered the military career and had long service (perhaps ten years, as PLINY 2 states) as a military tribune, including service under his father when the latter governed Syria. In 89 he led a force of troops from Spain to Upper Germany to help put down the rebellion of the governor, SATURNINUS (1), against DOMITIAN. He was rewarded with a consulship in 91 and survived the reign of terror that Domitian inaugurated. In 97 NERVA (4) appointed him legate of Upper Germany and shortly afterwards adopted him as his heir and co-ruler. Three months later, while serving his second consulship in 98, he succeeded Nerva. He toured the Balkan provinces, visiting the armies in Moesia and Pannonia, and on his arrival in Rome punished the Praetorian guardsmen who had mutinied against Nerva. By his affability and courtesy, Trajan became very popular, especially with the senatorial class who had hated Domitian, and received from the Senate the title *Optimus Princeps* ('Best of Emperors'). Trajan continued the practice of Nerva, which he solemnised by an oath, not to execute any senator unless the Senate had itself condemned him. In 100 the Younger Pliny, on assuming the consulship, delivered a speech (the *Panegyricus*) in praise of Trajan to the Senate, in which he compared Trajan's conduct favourably with that of Domitian, and thanked him for restoring freedom to the state. Trajan consulted the Senate over policy decisions and treated the house with respect. He replaced the freedmen administrators of CLAUDIUS (1) and NERO (1) with men of equestrian rank, and established new administrative careers in the imperial service.

Trajan's greatest achievements lay in his military operations in Dacia (Transylvania) and on the eastern frontier. He invaded Dacia in 101, and in two years of bitter campaigning reduced DECEBALUS' kingdom to client status. Trajan returned to Rome for a triumph, was invested with the title *Dacicus*, and issued commemorative coins. The arrangement broke down two years later, however, when Decebalus attacked the Roman garrison and in 105 invaded the province of Moesia. Trajan again attacked Dacia, with an enormous army of twelve legions, driving Decebalus out of Moesia and penetrating his kingdom. In 106, after a battle fought near the capital, Sarmizegethuza, the Dacians surrendered and Decebalus, whose treasure was captured, fled and killed himself. Trajan celebrated his victory by erecting in the Roman Forum the famous column bearing his name and illustrated by scenes from the war, dedicated in 113. In 107 Trajan turned the Dacian kingdom into a Roman province under a governor of consular rank, drove out many of the Dacians, and repopulated the area with settlers from the Balkan provinces and Asia Minor, founding colonies and other towns. The wealth of Dacia, including the produce of its gold mines, was used to finance a building programme which included Trajan's Forum in Rome, other public works, poor relief, and bonuses for the troops. Trajan further celebrated the conquest by inaugurating a series of games lasting 123 days.

In the east Trajan seized the kingdom of the Nabataeans in 106 and turned it into a province, Arabia Petraea, adding Damascus to Syria. A dispute arose over Armenia with king Osroes of Parthia, and in 114 Trajan arrived at Antioch to settle the matter. There was civil disturbance in Parthia over the succession, and Trajan used the opportunity afforded by Parthian weakness to incorporate Armenia in the Empire as a province and to attack Parthia through Mesopotamia. At first he had an easy conquest, taking the Parthian capital, Ctesiphon, and placing his own nominee, Parthamaspates, on the throne of Parthia. He turned Mesopotamia into a province and added another province, Assyria, and was voted the title *Parthicus*. He crossed the Tigris, entered Adiabene, and marched down the Euphrates to reach the Persian Gulf, but rebellions broke out in his rear and his line of retreat was only kept open by the efforts of LUSIUS Quietus. In 117 a new rebellion flared up in Judaea, and Trajan appointed Lusius governor of Judaea to quell it. Trajan's eastern policy, however, quickly fell apart. He had stripped the other frontiers of troops for his war, and he had advanced the eastern frontier to a line lacking a natural barrier. His thrust to the east had failed, and his successor abandoned all the new provinces but Arabia. He patched up the problem by restoring his new provinces to the status of kingdoms. In 117 Trajan fell ill and decided to return to Rome, but he died on the way at Selinus in Cilicia on 9 August. He had no children: his wife, Pompeia PLOTINA, who favoured HADRIAN, persuaded Trajan to adopt him on his deathbed.

He had been a very popular emperor, and was highly successful in winning and keeping the affection of Romans and provincials alike. His correspondence with the Younger Pliny (mostly the work of his civil servants) attests his attention to detail and administrative ability, as well as showing the humane, liberal attitude he encouraged his officials to adopt. He enhanced the empire with roads, libraries, baths, many public buildings and monuments, and his magnificent forum. His ashes were buried beneath his column. See L. Rossi (1971) *Trajan's Column and the Dacian Wars*, London: Thames & Hudson; F. Lepper (1948) *Trajan's Parthian War*, London: Oxford University Press; M. Grant (1985) *The*

Roman Emperors, London: Weidenfeld & Nicolson.

Trebonius, Gaius (died 43 BC), was one of the assassins of CAESAR (1). In 55 he was a tribune of the *plebs*, when he proposed a law to appoint POMPEIUS (2) governor of Spain for five years and CRASSUS (3) likewise of Syria. It also confirmed Caesar's command in Gaul and Illyricum for five more years. He served under Caesar as a legate in Gaul from 54 to 50, and besieged Massilia (Marseilles) for Caesar in 49. After holding a praetorship in 48, Caesar sent him to resist the followers of Pompeius in Spain as governor of the southern province, but he achieved nothing. Nevertheless Caesar appointed him, though a 'new man', to a suffect consulship in the last three months of 45. He was aleady plotting against Caesar, and at the assassination he prevented Marcus ANTONIUS (7) from entering the Theatre of Pompeius. He was murdered at Smyrna in his bed by DOLABELLA (4) in 43 while proconsul of Asia. A close friend of CICERO (1), he published a collection of his *bons mots*, which has not survived.

Trogus, Pompeius (late C1 BC), was a scholar from Narbonese Gaul who wrote lost works on biological subjects. He is best known as a historian, his *Philippic Histories* in forty-four books being epitomised quite accurately by Justinus, who added little other than moralising remarks. We have this epitome and the table of contents. The work, in Latin, contains such large digressions from its original subject, the Macedonian monarchy, that it has the nature of a universal history from the early Near East through the Greek states and Hellenistic kingdoms, Parthian origins, the Roman kings, to Spanish and Gallic history including the campaign of Augustus in Spain. He is also quoted by PLINY (1) the Elder.

Tubero, Quintus Aelius (C1 BC), was the son of CICERO (1)'s friend and relative by marriage Lucius Aelius Tubero. When his father was excluded from the province of Africa, which the Senate had appointed him to govern in 48, Tubero accompanied him to the Pharsalus campaign on the side of POMPEIUS (2). They were subsequently pardoned by CAESAR (1). He prosecuted LIGARIUS for helping king JUBA (1) I while he was a legate in Africa, but failed to overcome Cicero's defence. He turned to writing history, and composed a *History of Rome* down to his own day. He also wrote legal works including both public and private law, setting down the duties of a judge and the workings of senatorial procedure. His works are lost, though the jurist POMPONIUS (2) criticised his archaic language. He married a daughter of SULPICIUS (2) Rufus.

Turbo, Quintus Marcius (early C2 AD), was a friend and general of HADRIAN. He was born at Epidaurum in Dalmatia, joined the army and rose to the rank of first centurion (*primuspilus*), from whence he progressed to the unpopular prefecture of transport services and the command of a unit in the city police (*vigiles*). After further responsible positions, TRAJAN appointed him commander of the fleet at Misenum, in which capacity he served in the east during Trajan's Parthian campaign, when he was ordered to suppress Jewish uprisings in Egypt and Libya (116). Having by now become friendly with Hadrian, he was sent in 117 to suppress a rebellion in Mauretania. Next he received an extraordinary command in Pannonia and Dacia with the rank of prefect, supervising the consolidation of the new province of Dacia. In 119 he became prefect of the Praetorian Guard, in which he served until Hadrian grew tired of him. He is an example of a man rising from the ranks to high office.

Turnus (C1 AD) was a satirical writer of the Flavian period. A freedman, he was popular at the court of DOMITIAN and met with MARTIAL's admiration. His brother, Scaevus Memor, wrote tragedies. Our only fragment of his work is in the style of VIRGIL's *Eclogues*.

Tyrannio 1. (early C1 BC) was the nickname of a scholar and teacher, Theophrastus, son of Epicratides, from Amisus on the Black Sea. A pupil of the Greek grammarian Dionysius the Thracian, he was brought as a prisoner to Rome in 72 BC by LUCULLUS (2) and bought as a slave by L. Licinius, who later manumitted him. POMPEIUS (2) encouraged his work, and he received the friendship of CAESAR (1), CICERO (1) and ATTICUS. He held classes in Cicero's house in 56, and arranged the library of APELLICON, which SULLA (2) had brought from Asia Minor to Rome. His writings, which were concerned with poetic metre, Homeric studies, and grammar, have not survived. The grammar, based on the work of the Alexandrian grammarian Aristarchus of Samothrace, was very influential at Rome. He taught the geographer STRABO.

2. (C1 BC) was a Phoenician named Diocles, the son of Artemidorus, who was brought to Rome as a slave and owned by TERENTIA, the widow of CICERO (1). After she freed him, he became a pupil of TYRANNIO (1), from whom he took his nickname, and whose interest in grammar he pursued. His works, on grammar and accentuation, which appear to have been confused with those of his master, have not survived.

U

Ulpianus, Domitius (AD 170–223) (Ulpian), was a jurist from Tyre in Phoenicia who studied under PAPINIANUS. In the reign of Septimius SEVERUS (1) he worked as an equestrian civil servant in the office for petitions (*libelli*), where he wrote answers (*rescripta*) to petitions, becoming the emperor's secretary for petitions (*a libellis*) in 202. After CARACALLA's *Constitutio Antoniniana* of 212, an edict by which Roman citizenship was conferred on all free men in the empire, Ulpianus applied himself to a programme of writing over 200 volumes on Roman law, which emphasised the universal and rational nature of the system, and posited its foundation in natural law. He was later (*c.*221) appointed prefect of the *annona*, managing the supply of cheap grain to Rome, and in 223 SEVERUS (2) Alexander appointed him sole prefect of the Praetorian Guard, at that time both a military and judicial post, virtually the emperor's second-in-command. The troops, who had no respect for him as a soldier and held him responsible for the executions of his predecessors Flavianus and Chrestus, murdered him, probably in late 223, in the presence of Severus and the emperor's mother JULIA (13) Mamaea, who had favoured him. The ringleader, Epagathus, was sent to Egypt as its prefect and then put to death in Crete.

Ulpianus was the most influential of Roman lawyers, with a lofty view of its function and purpose, and his textbooks and commentaries carried great weight. Among other works he wrote eighty-one books of commentaries on the Praetor's edict, which by then had a fixed form and governed criminal as well as civil offences, and fifty-one on the civil law. He also wrote manuals on the duties of governors and other officials. He was one of a handful of earlier jurists whose work was authorised as a valid source by the Law of Citations of AD 426. Two fifths of Justinian's *Digests* consist of extracts from Ulpianus' writings, which are otherwise lost to us. As a lawyer, he appears to have been cautious and rather conservative, avoiding controversial or innovative approaches to his work. His influence was enormous and his work, on account of its clarity and comprehensiveness, was an important factor in enabling Roman law to be passed on so as to become the basis of the mediaeval and modern European systems. See T. Honoré (1982) *Ulpian*, Oxford: Clarendon Press.

Ulpius *see* MARCELLUS (8).

Urbicus, Quintus Lollius (C2 AD), was the governor of Britain who built the Antonine Wall. A Numidian from North Africa, he commanded a legion in Pannonia before serving in the Jewish War of 132, when he was awarded decorations. After holding a consulship *c.*135 he governed

Lower Germany, and in 138 was appointed to govern Britain. He led his troops north and took the lands south of the Clyde and Forth, to protect which he built the turf wall of which vestiges remain. He was later appointed city prefect of Rome.

Urgulania (C1 AD) was a close friend of LIVIA (2) and traded on the connexion. In 16, Lucuis PISO (8) sued her for a debt, but instead of appearing in court she took refuge in the Palace. The emperor TIBERIUS offered to represent her in court, but Livia solved the problem by repaying her debt for her. She once also refused to give evidence before the Senate, which sent a praetor to take her deposition. She married Plautius Silvanus, and her son PLAUTIUS (4) was the father of Plautia Urgulanilla, the first wife of the emperor CLAUDIUS (1).

V

Vaballathus, Septimius *see* ZENOBIA.

Valerian, Publius Licinius (*c.*AD 190–260), was emperor from 253 till his capture in 260. An eminent senator, while acting as the emperor DECIUS' representative in Rome, he was called to assist Trebonianus GALLUS (8), who had succeeded Decius, against a rebellion by the governor of Moesia, AEMILIANUS. He went to Raetia to collect an army, and on the death of Gallus was proclaimed emperor. He led his troops into Italy, where he heard of the murder of Aemilianus by his men. In autumn 253 Valerian and his son GALLIENUS were jointly proclaimed *Augusti*. They had many problems to face, both internal and external. Valerian set out in 254 for the east to tackle the threat from Persia and the Goths. In 257 and 258 he initiated a persecution of Christians, perhaps under the strain caused by the general weakness of the Empire. He made good use of the support offered by Septimius ODAENATHUS of Palmyra, and repelled a Persian invasion of Syria in 257, but in summer 260 was captured by the Persian king SAPOR (1) I while involved in personal negotiations with him, and died in Persia. See M. Grant (1985) *The Roman Emperors*, London: Weidenfeld & Nicolson.

Valerius Aedituus (C2–1 BC) was a poet, the author of two love poems quoted by Aulus GELLIUS (1) (19. 9), one a translation into Latin of a poem by Sappho (later adapted by CATULLUS 1). The style of his work shows features of early Latin.

Valerius Antias (early C1 BC) was a Roman historian whose work is lost apart from quotations in later writers such as LIVY who, though he used his work as a source, carped at his inaccuracy and tendency to exaggerate numbers. It is difficult for us to judge his work, which consisted of some seventy-five books and ran from the foundation of Rome to the time of SULLA (2). He appears to have treated earlier history in a cursive manner and to have written in much detail only about his own times.

Valerius Cato, Publius (*c.*90–*c.*20 BC), a poet and teacher of grammar, was born in Cisalpine Gaul. His writings are all lost, and we rely on SUETONIUS (*Gram.*, 11) for information about him. He wrote a *Protest* about the loss of his inheritance during the dictatorship of SULLA (2), a love-poem, *Lydia*, and a narrative poem, *Diana*, on the myth of Britomaris. He was a close friend (but not the teacher) of several contemporary poets, CATULLUS (1) (see poem 56), CINNA (4), BIBACULUS, Ticida and possibly Cornelius GALLUS (4).

Valerius Corvus (C4 BC) was a partly legendary hero of the wars with the

Gauls, and in 349 is reported by LIVY to have defeated a Gallic champion in single combat with the help of a crow (*corvus*). Besides being an outstanding soldier, he held six consulships between 348 and 299, and won four triumphs. He was also credited with a law (300) granting the right of appeal to the people against the judgment of magistrates.

Valerius Flaccus Setinus Balbus, Gaius (C1 AD), was an epic poet. We know nothing of his life save for a remark of QUINTILIAN (10. 1, 90), written *c.*96, that he had recently died. It has been suggested on flimsy grounds that he was a member of the priesthood (*viri sacris faciundis*) which guarded the Sibylline Books. He wrote the *Tale of the Argonauts* (*Argonautica*) during the Flavian period (70–96), in which he refers to the eruption of Vesuvius in 79. The epic owes a debt to the work of the same name by the Hellenistic Greek poet Apollonius of Rhodes, to VARRO (4) of Atax, and much to VIRGIL. Seven books and a large part of an eighth survive, which may be the sum of his composition, though there is another view that he finished book 8. He set himself a hard task in attempting to tread such a well worn path, and the critics have not spared him. He brought originality to his composition, however, toning down the rhetoric and introducing an occasional note of wry humour. He was a keen observer and an accomplished master of the hexameter. His poem covers the events in the life of Jason, the quest for the Golden Fleece, and the love-affair of Jason and Medea, the latter of whom is portrayed with great sympathy. Valerius was interested in exploring the psychology behind Medea's dilemma when faced with a choice between her father and Jason. Jason, however, is sometimes shown in an unsympathetic light, weak and irresolute, as he contemplates abandoning her. Valerius departed from the traditional story in places, and even invented incidents of his own. In his poem the Argo, the first ship, takes on a novel symbolism, representing a new and expansive phase in human civilisation. There is also a political side to the poem with its account of the origin of war and the development of imperial institutions. There is a note of doom associated with man's overstepping the boundaries of nature with activities such as sailing, and the present age of iron is contrasted unfavourably with the earlier golden age. The work, which was lost until the Renaissance, merits attention.

Valerius Maximus (C1 AD) wrote a handbook of useful quotations in the reign of TIBERIUS, who comes in for much uncritical adulation, and to whom it is dedicated. It appears to have been published after the fall of SEJANUS in 31, as an unnamed conspirator whom Valerius denounces is probably he. The work, entitled *Nine Books of Memorable Deeds and Sayings*, is extant: it is divided up according to subject-matter (mostly moral or philosophical terms such as 'Gratitude' and 'Chastity') and consists of undigested examples from Roman and foreign (mainly Greek) sources, the Roman being pre-eminent. He drew upon writers such as CICERO (1), LIVY, VARRO (3), and Greek authors. Despite its turgid and bombastic style, the work had some success and was known to PLINY (1) the Elder and PLUTARCH. It records many curious events not found elsewhere, but its statements must be treated with caution.

See also FLACCUS, LAEVINUS, MESSALLA, POPLICOLA, PROBUS (2).

Valgius Rufus, Gaius (late C1 BC), was a poet and senator, suffect consul in 12 BC. HORACE respected his judgment in poetry (*Sat.*, 1. 10) and wrote him an Ode (2. 9) to comfort him on the loss of a beloved slaveboy. Valgius wrote elegiac and other poetry and in prose wrote on rhetoric, grammar and medicinal plants. Like AUGUSTUS, he studied under APOLLODORUS

(1), whose work *The Art of Rhetoric* he translated into Latin. Only a few shreds of his elegies survive.

Varius Rufus, Lucius (C1 BC), was a poet and tragedian of the circle of MAECENAS, a friend of VIRGIL, with whom he introduced HORACE to Maecenas. He was a friend of PHILODEMUS and an Epicurean, and *c.*43 wrote a poem, *On Death*, which influenced Virgil's writing. The poem, probably meant to free its readers from fear of death, referred in a disparaging way to Marcus ANTONIUS (7). Horace says in *Ode* 1. 6 that he might write an encomium on AGRIPPA (1), and mentions him (*Sat.*, 1. 10) as an epic poet. His work has not survived, but QUINTILIAN praised his *Thyestes*, which was commissioned by AUGUSTUS and written for the games of 29 BC to celebrate the victory of Actium.

Varro 1, Gaius Terentius (late C3 BC), was praetor in 218 and consul in 216, when he was a general at the disastrous battle of Cannae at which HANNIBAL destroyed the Roman army sent to meet him. Though LIVY disparages him, he clearly had the support of the Senate in facing Hannibal in open combat, and received a vote of thanks from the Assembly of the People. He continued to serve in important commands in Italy, and after the war was sent on diplomatic missions to Greece and Africa.

2. Lucullus, Marcus Terentius (116–*c.*55 BC), was the younger brother of Lucius LUCULLUS (2), adopted by a certain Varro. Like his brother, he was a supporter of SULLA (2), and served as a legate in Sulla's eastern campaign and his invasion of Italy. He and his brother held the aedileship in 79. He was praetor in charge of the court for foreigners in 76, and established a process to try cases of gang warfare. He was consul in 73 with C. Cassius Longinus, and proposed a law to provide the city's poor with cheap foodstuffs. He then held the governorship of Macedonia and extended Roman influence in Thrace and Moesia to the Danube, and returned to triumph in 71. His life was thenceforth blighted by his brother's unpopularity. He supported CICERO (1) against CLODIUS and worked for his recall from exile, using his position as a priest (*pontifex*) to help restore his property.

3, Marcus Terentius (116–27 BC), was a prolific writer and scholar. Born at Reate in the Sabine country, where he was brought up frugally and gained close acquaintance with agriculture, he went to Rome for education at the hands of Lucius AELIUS (1), and then studied under ANTIOCHUS (15) IV of Ascalon, whether at Athens or possibly during the latter's stay in Rome. He fought from 76 to 72 under POMPEIUS (2) in Spain against SERTORIUS, an experience which drew him to Pompeius' side in the forthcoming crisis. He was tribune of the *plebs* in 70, the year of Pompeius' consulship, and served again under Pompeius in his campaign against the pirates in 67, for which he was decorated with a naval crown. In 59, on the founding of the 'triumvirate', Varro was made a member of a board of twenty to supervise the distribution of farmland in Campania to the veterans of Pompeius' wars.

He held a praetorship, and when the civil war broke out in 49, he was Pompeius' legate in Spain in command of two legions. He surrendered to CAESAR (1) at Corduba and, after being pardoned and released, he made his way to Greece to join the Pompeian forces. Like his friend CICERO (1), he took no part in the battle, but saved the lives of many sick men at Corcyra after the battle. ANTONIUS (7) wished to proscribe him, but Caesar prevented his death and allowed him to return to Italy, and in 47 commissioned him to draw up plans for a new public library at Rome. But he had made little progress with the project when Caesar was murdered in 44. In 43, having ransacked

Varro's villa at Casinum, Antonius proscribed him because he owned great estates. But he escaped death by hiding at the house of CALENUS, and thus avoided Cicero's fate. From then on his life on his estates of Tusculum and Casinum was tranquil, spent in study and writing. He is said to have died on 16 January 27.

He was a prolific writer, and composed 630 volumes on a variety of subjects, including 150 volumes of *Menippean Satire*, written between *c.*81 and 67; seventy-six books of *Logistorici* written *c.*44, imaginary dialogues between near-contemporary Romans on a variety of philosophical subjects with examples from history; *Hebdomades*, also known as *Portraits* (*De Imaginibus*), fifteen books dating from 39 containing 700 portraits of famous Greeks and Romans, including an epigram on each one: what the significance of the number seven was in the work we do not know; nine books entitled *Disciplines*, written in his last years; an encyclopaedia of the seven liberal arts 'that every free cultured man should be familiar with'; *Human and Divine Antiquities*, lost twice, the second time by Petrarch, published in 47, in forty-one books: the second half was dedicated to Julius Caesar; smaller works, *The Life of the Roman People*, dedicated to ATTICUS, about the way of life of the Romans, and *The Origin of the Roman People*, in which he tried to explore the history of the race back into the dark ages, and books about the theatre, especially PLAUTUS, whose plays he catalogued: all the above works are lost.

Two of his works still exist in whole or part: a major work, *The Latin Language*, in twenty-five books of which only six (5–10) are partly extant. He tries to account for the origins of words and expressions, often quite fancifully, but adds a great deal of interesting material by the way, concerning early texts, laws and rituals, which make the work invaluable. *Farming* (*De Re Rustica*) is a minor treatise in three books preserved in full, written in 37 when he was eighty: he deals, in dialogue form, with the various topics of the farmer's world. It is debatable whether VIRGIL was influenced by it in writing the *Georgics*; the work displays Varro's interest in detail and in the logical analysis of his subject. He describes his aviary at Casinum in detail. See J.E. Skydsgaard (1968) *Varro the Scholar*, Copenhagen: Munksgaard; E. Rawson (1985) *Intellectual Life of the Late Roman Republic*, London: Duckworth; D.J. Taylor (1974) *Declinatio: A Study of the Linguistic Theory of Marcus Terentius Varro*, Amsterdam: John Benjamins.

4, Publius Terentius (born 82 BC), born at Atax (Aude) in Narbonese Gaul, was a poet of whose life we know only that he learnt Greek at the age of thirty-five. He wrote an epic poem on part of CAESAR (1)'s campaign in Gaul (*The Sequanic War* concerning 58 BC), translated the *Argonautica* of Apollonius of Rhodes, and composed a variety of material including love poems to a woman he calls Leucadia, and a didactic poem on the weather (probably named *Ephemeris*) based partly on Aratus' *Phaenomena*, used by VIRGIL in the *Georgics*, 1. His works are lost.

Varus, Publius Quinctilius (died AD 9), was of an obscure patrician family. In his youth he was associated with VIRGIL (with whom he was a fellow-student in Naples) and HORACE, and enjoyed the patronage of AUGUSTUS. He was TIBERIUS' colleague in the consulship in 13 BC, and married a daughter of AGRIPPA (1). He was proconsul of Africa *c.*6 BC, and was sent the following year to govern Syria, when he put down disturbances in Judaea after the death of HEROD (1) in 4 BC. In AD 9 he was commanding an army of three legions in Germany when he was ambushed and his army was wiped out in the Teutoburger Forest and Rome lost all her territory east of the Rhine. He himself committed suicide. His character is disparaged by VELLEIUS Paterculus. The disaster greatly distressed Augustus, his whole German policy having thus been destroyed.

Vatinius, Publius (mid-C1 BC), was a tribune of the *plebs* in 59 when he served the interests of the 'triumvirs', proposing the laws which granted CAESAR (1) his province of Cisalpine Gaul and Illyricum, and confirming the settlement of the east made by POMPEIUS (2). Pursuing this policy he worked against BIBULUS (1), Caesar's hostile colleague in the consulship, and helped to bring down Vettius. He was attacked in court by CICERO (1) in 56, who in defending SESTIUS impugned Vatinius' reliability as a witness. After his praetorship in 55 he was accused of bribery in the election and was successfully defended by Cicero. He then served under Caesar in Gaul and attained the consulship for 46, a boast for which CATULLUS (1) had lampooned him. He governed Illyricum in 45, surrendered to BRUTUS (4) in 43, and in 42 nevertheless held a triumph for his victories in Illyricum. His friendship for Cicero is attested by their correspondence (*Ad Fam.*, 5. 10).

Veiento, Aulus Didius Gallus Fabricius (late C1 AD), was a courtier of influence in Flavian times. He was exiled in AD 62 for abusing his influence with NERO (1) to sell public offices. He returned and flourished under the Flavians, enjoying three consulships and sitting on DOMITIAN's privy council. He was acceptable to NERVA (4), but was subsequently shouted down in the Senate.

Velleius Paterculus, Gaius (*c.*20 BC–*c.*AD 35), was a historian of military background: his grandfather had been Commander of Engineers to POMPEIUS (2) and BRUTUS (4), and his father a cavalry commander. Velleius followed his father's career, served under Gaius CAESAR (3) in the east (AD 2) and from 4 to 12 served under TIBERIUS in his various campaigns. He returned briefly to Rome in 6 to embark on a senatorial career and was elected quaestor. He participated in Tiberius' triumph in 12, and was appointed praetor for 15. He appears to have published his history in 30 from its dedication to Marcus Vinicius, the consul of that year. His history in two books begins with a sketch of Greek and Roman history to 146 BC (the fall of Carthage, which he saw as pivotal in the history of Rome), but nearly all the text between Romulus and Pydna (168 BC) has been lost. The second book is complete and six times as long as what is extant of the first book: it offers an account of Roman history from 146 BC to AD 30, and is marred by an extravagant bias in favour of Tiberius. His style is sometimes tortuous, but there are useful character sketches of men such as CAESAR (1) and POMPEIUS (2). There are two excursuses, one on Roman colonisation, the other on literature. He is an important historian, having had first-hand knowledge, as a senator and a magistrate, of many of the events he describes. he travelled extensively and is sometimes our only authority for important matters. He fills a significant gap in historiography between LIVY and TACITUS (1). See T.A. Dorey (ed.) (1975) *Empire and Aftermath*, London: Routledge and Kegan Paul.

Ventidius, Publius (*c.*94–*c.*37 BC), was a successful general of humble birth from Picenum. Having started as a transport contractor to the army, he became a client of CAESAR (1), under whom he served in Gaul and by whom he was promoted to the Senate in 47. He reached the praetorship in 43, when after the battle of Mutina he led troops by a forced march to join ANTONIUS (7), and was promoted to a suffect consulship at the end of the same year. The next year he governed part of Gaul and led his army into Italy in 41 without becoming involved in fighting. The triumvirs in 40 in their meeting at Brundisium sent him to rescue the eastern provinces in Asia Minor and Syria which the Parthians had invaded: he drove them out with a series of brilliant victories, the Cilician Gates and Mount Amanus in 39, and Gindarus in 38 (see MALCHUS). He then besieged Samosata where ANTIOCHUS (12) I of Commagene held out. He returned to Rome the same year and celebrated a triumph in November. He was given a public funeral.

Vercingetorix (died 46 BC) was an Arvernian nobleman, the son of Celtillus; he led a rebellion against CAESAR (1) in 52 when the conquest of Gaul was practically complete. He was elected king of the Arverni and commander of a force of allied states. He lost a battle at Noviodunum on the Loire, and adopted a policy of tempting Caesar to battle while depriving him of supplies. He won a modest victory in winter against the besiegers of Avaricum (Bourges), and had success at Gergovia, where Caesar attacked him and was repulsed. The Gauls then rose *en masse* against Caesar, who barely managed to regroup, but won a significant victory near Dijon using German cavalry. Vercingetorix retired into the fortress of Alesia (Alise), which Caesar circumvallated so as to prevent supplies or reinforcements reaching the garrison. Vercingetorix was starved into submission, surrendered, and was paraded in Caesar's triumph in 46 before being executed.

Verres, Gaius (died 43 BC), was a notoriously rapacious governor of Sicily. In 84 he was CARBO (5)'s quaestor, but deserted him for SULLA (2). In 80 he was DOLABELLA (2)'s quaestor in Cilicia, and helped him to plunder the wealth of that province and of neighbouring Asia. However in 79, after they returned, he gave evidence against Dolabella which brought about his conviction for extortion. He was city praetor in 74 when he corruptly sold justice, and from 73 to 70 governed Sicily as proconsul, impoverishing his province by his unrestrained extortions. He spared Messana, but extended his depredations even to Roman citizens. He disregarded a motion of censure of the Senate in 72: his holding the office for three years was abnormal and a disaster for the provincials. He expected to evade condemnation by the use of his great wealth and powerful friends. CICERO (1), who had been quaestor in Sicily in 75, prosecuted him on behalf of the islanders in 70. Verres' advocate, HORTENSIUS (2), designated consul for 69, supported by the powerful Metelli, tried to prolong the case to his year of office, and to have Cicero replaced by a more favourable advocate, Q. Caecilius Niger, but Cicero forestalled him with a powerful speech. Given 110 days to prepare his case, he was ready in fifty days, despite the fact that Verres' successor was a Metellus. POMPEIUS (2) threw his weight behind Cicero, who introduced his case with a brief speech and then produced his crushing evidence, upon which Hortensius abandoned the case and advised Verres to flee. He went to live in Massilia (Marseille) taking most of his loot with him. Cicero agreed to a low assessment of the damages in order to placate Verres' noble friends, but published a second, much more elaborate prosecution speech, to publicise the extent of Verres' crimes. Marcus ANTONIUS (7) is said to have proscribed and killed Verres in 43.

Verrius Flaccus, Marcus (*c.*55 BC–*c.*15 AD), was a scholar and antiquarian. He was a freedman and tutored AUGUSTUS' grandsons Gaius CAESAR (3) and Lucius CAESAR (8). His chief interest was language, about which he wrote a number of lost works, especially *The Meaning of Words*, the greatest ancient dictionary of Latin, known to us from a surviving epitome of the second half made by FESTUS (1), and an abridgment of the latter made by Paul the Deacon (C8). Its arrangement was alphabetical; it included citations from authors, and rare and obsolete words. A man of great erudition, he was interested in antiquities as well as in words, and wrote on *The Etruscans*, on *Memorabilia*, on *Cato's Obscurities*, and on *Orthography* (all lost). He also composed a calendar for Praeneste of which fragments survive.

Verus, Lucius Aelius (130–169 AD), was a Roman 'emperor' as the colleague from 161 to 169 of MARCUS AURELIUS. The son of Lucius AELIUS (3), he was adopted by ANTONINUS Pius in January 138 on his father's death, and named L. Aurelius Commodus. He held the consulship in 154 and, with Marcus, in 161; and on the death of Pius was promoted to be Marcus' colleague as emperor (*Augustus*), taking his name Verus. He was titular commander of the war against Parthia in 162–6, though his subordinate generals were responsible for the Roman success. In 164 he married Marcus' daughter Lucilla at Ephesus, and they had several children. He held a triumph in 166, and unwillingly joined Marcus on the Danube frontier in 168, from which he soon returned in fear of plague. He died from a stroke on the journey and thus relieved the Empire of a man unsuitable to rule it through his indolence and love of luxury.

Vespasian (AD 9–79) (Titus Flavius Vespasianus) was the first emperor of the Flavian house. He was born at Reate in the Sabine country, the son of Flavius Sabinus, an equestrian tax-collector in Asia and Gaul, and his wife, Vespasia Polla, whose brother was a senator. He was brought up by his father's mother. His brother, SABINUS (3) also followed a senatorial career. Vespasian served as a military tribune in 27 in Thrace, was quaestor *c.*35 in Crete, aedile in 38 and praetor in 40. He married Flavia DOMITILLA, by whom he had three children, TITUS, DOMITIAN and DOMITILLA, but his wife and daughter died before he became emperor. He received the support of NARCISSUS, the freedman secretary of state of CLAUDIUS (1), who arranged for him to command a legion in the invasion of Britain in 43. He remained on the island until 47 and conquered the territory of the south-west, probably installing COGIDUBNUS as king of the Atrebates. He was honoured for this success with triumphal decorations, was a suffect consul in 51, and frequented the imperial court where Titus was educated with BRITANNICUS. He was appointed proconsul of Africa *c.*62, but fell out of favour while AGRIPPINA (3), who had hated Narcissus, held sway at court. In 66 he was in attendance on NERO (1) as he toured Greece, but offended the emperor by his behaviour and had to leave court. Later in the year, however, he was sent to Judaea to suppress the rebellion of the Jews. Highly successful in containing the insurrection, he began to besiege Jerusalem and, after difficulties with MUCIANUS, the governor of Syria, achieved reconciliation and the two joined forces, recognising in turn the three emperors GALBA (1), OTHO and VITELLIUS (1).

In spring 69, however, the two men changed their policy and decided to use the forces at their disposal to make a bid for the purple on behalf of Vespasian, who had the advantage of being a successful general, popular with the troops, and in the public perception was uncontaminated with the excesses of the reign of Nero. Vespasian's ally, Ti. Julius ALEXANDER (3), the Prefect of Egypt, arranged for his troops to proclaim Vespasian emperor on 1 July 69, from which he dated his reign. Alexander also detained grain ships bound for Rome, causing the threat of a famine. The rest of the army in the east quickly followed suit, and were joined by the army on the Danube. With the latter, Marcus Antonius PRIMUS invaded Italy and in October defeated Vitellius at Bedriacum near Cremona, which his troops sacked. Primus reached Rome on 21 December, defeated the troops loyal to Vitellius, who had lynched Vespasian's brother Sabinus, and took the reins of power temporarily until

Mucianus arrived to act as Vespasian's regent. The Senate immediately voted Vespasian all the powers by now associated with the imperial function, yet he insisted on counting his years of office from July. The enactment was very broad and sanctioned all the new emperor's acts from the date of his proclamation. Vespasian suffered from a lack of prestige as compared with all his predecessors, and sometimes made a virtue of his plebeian origin; but his position was well fortified by this legislation, of which a fragment is extant.

Vespasian visited Egypt, where he raised much money by selling off the imperial estates, and remained in the east until mid-70, when he entered Rome. Mucianus then faded away, and the following year Titus returned from victory over the Jews to a triumph and his appointment as prefect of the Praetorian Guard. Vespasian ruled for ten years, and embarked on a sensible policy of consolidation. He reformed the army, ending the dangerous practice of stationing auxiliary units in the lands of their origin. Nor did he allow them to be commanded any longer by men of their own nationality, influenced by the experience of the rebellion of CIVILIS and CLASSICUS which was put down by CERIALIS in 70. He strengthened the frontiers by advancing to better lines in Britain and Germany, and he brought Lesser Armenia and Commagene into the Empire. He increased taxes and revoked immunities on a wide scale, and with the money thus gained he restored the deficiencies caused by Nero's extravagance and the devastation of the Civil Wars, and rebuilt the Capitol, founded the Colosseum (the *Amphitheatrum Flavium*), built a new forum, and a new temple of Peace. He thus acquired an unfair reputation for avarice, but resisted an attempt by the Senate to trim his expenditure. He was consul, six times with Titus as his colleague, every year of his reign except 73 and 78. As censor with Titus in 73–4 he brought new blood from Italy and the provinces into the Senate, and gave Latin rights and other privileges to communities in the provinces. He reorganised the army, relocating the legions of Vitellius in places where they could not be a threat, and splitting the army of Syria into three. He promoted the arts and education, founding chairs of philosophy and rhetoric in important cities and granting teachers tax privileges. Though he was a poor speaker, he could quote Homer and had his sons well educated. The reign was peaceful and a relief after Nero and the civil wars, though Vespasian had to put the Senate in its place, and in 79 Titus summarily executed CAECINA (3) Alienus and forced EPRIUS Marcellus to commit suicide. Vespasian died on 23 June 79 and was later deified by Titus, who succeeded him, the first natural son to succeed his father to the purple. See J. Nicols (1978) *Vespasian and the Partes Flavianae*, Wiesbaden: Steiner; M. Grant (1985) *The Roman Emperors*, London: Weidenfeld & Nicolson.

Vibius Crispus, Lucius Junius Quintus (C1 AD), was an influential senator in the reign of VESPASIAN, who admired him for his wit and held him in great affection. He held three suffect consulships, in 61, 74 and 83. He was proconsul of Africa (71) and legate of north-eastern Spain in 73. He was the patron of both the Plinys and of Verginius RUFUS (5).

Vindex, Gaius Julius (died AD 68), was of Gallic extraction from Aquitania and of royal blood. His father was a senator. He was NERO (1)'s governor of Central Gaul (Lugdunensis) when in 68 he rebelled and appealed for support. His appeal was heeded by GALBA (1) and some Gauls, especially the inhabitants of Vienne, but by no other office-holders nor by the people of Lugdunum (Lyons). He was routed at Besançon by Verginius RUFUS (5), governor of Upper Germany, and killed himself.

Vinicius, Marcus (late C1 BC), a 'new man' from Campania, was suffect consul in 19. As governor of Illyricum in 13 he assisted AGRIPPA (1) to launch the Pannonian campaign which TIBERIUS completed. In AD 1 or 2 he was appointed commander of the army on the Rhine. At some time before this he had commanded operations on the Danube. His son, Publius, who admired the work of OVID, flourished under Tiberius, and his grandson, Marcus, supported VELLEIUS Paterculus, who dedicated his history to him.

Vinius, Titus (C1 AD), was jailed in AD 39 in Germany as a military tribune for adultery with the wife of his commanding officer. CLAUDIUS (1) freed him and appointed him legate of a legion, but he was accused of stealing a gold cup at the emperor's feast. However, he successfully governed Narbonese Gaul. He joined GALBA (1)'s rising against NERO (1), and later recommended him to adopt OTHO. Ironically, he was killed in 69 along with Galba by Otho's troops.

Virgil (Publius Vergilius Maro) (70–19 BC), a Latin poet, was born at Andes, a village near Mantua in Cisalpine Gaul, on 15 October 70. His father, sometimes said to have been a potter, was of equestrian rank and married a woman named Magia; she remarried after his death. His father was rich enough to send Publius for his education to Cremona, from where he graduated to a school of rhetoric in Milan. After a year or so there, aged eighteen, he went on to Rome and thence to Naples, where he joined an Epicurean community under Siro. He also came under the influence of the Greek poet PARTHENIUS, who introduced him to the Callimachean ideal of poetry and the works of other Hellenistic poets. After the civil war of 42, much land was confiscated around Mantua and Cremona for the veterans of the victorious leaders of the Caesarian party, ANTONIUS (7) and Octavian (see AUGUSTUS), and it seems that his father's estate suffered in this way: it was confiscated by ALFENUS Varus, and it is probable that Virgil was subsequently given monetary compensation by the intervention of Octavian. Henceforth Virgil lived in Rome and Naples. During this time, with the support and encouragement of his friend Asinius POLLIO (1), to whom he addressed three of the poems, Virgil was composing his first serious poetry, the *Bucolics* (*Herdsmen's Poems*) or *Eclogues* (*Excerpts*, from his way of releasing extracts or single poems before he published the whole work), superficially pastoral poems in the style of the *Idylls* of the Greek poet Theocritus. In two of them, however, the land confiscations are a serious issue. Three contemporary Romans who are referred to in the *Eclogues*, VARUS, Pollio and Cornelius GALLUS (4), are known to have been involved in confiscating land. His real patron at the time was probably already Octavian, who is referred to indirectly as a 'god'.

The *Eclogues* were published *c*.38, (though individual poems or pairs had been circulated before then) and Virgil read them aloud in a theatre to an enthusiastic but critical audience. They attracted the attention of MAECENAS, already an active patron of poets (under Octavian's aegis), whose circle Virgil joined and thus became intimate with other literary figures. At about this time Virgil and VARIUS introduced HORACE to Maecenas, and in 37 all three poets accompanied Maecenas on a journey to Brundisium, described in a satire by Horace, for a negotiation with Antonius at Tarentum. Virgil had already embarked on his second major work, the *Georgics*, four long poems about husbandry and the Italian countryside, which he published in 29 and read to Octavian, recently returned from his campaign against CLEOPATRA (4) VII. Octavian rewarded him generously and encouraged him to further endeavour by giving him an immense sum of money, 10,000,000 sesterces. He was by now famous and had many influential friends. In the following years Virgil embarked on the *Aeneid*, or at any rate on an epic which turned into that poem. Augustus, who may be said to have commissioned the poem, is said *c*.25 to have requested to see samples of the work, but Virgil had nothing he considered worth showing his patron. At this time PROPERTIUS, another poet of Maecenas' circle, wrote in book 2 of his *Elegies* that a greater poem than Homer's *Iliad* was being born. As his work progressed, Virgil in 23 read some parts of the early books to Augustus and his family: OCTAVIA (2) fainted at the mention, in book 6, of her son MARCELLUS (7) who had recently died. In the spring of 19 he set out for Greece, having completed a draft of the epic, planning to spend three years in that country improving his draft. But at Athens that summer he met Augustus, who was about to return to Rome from a tour of the east, and changed his plans, resolving to return to Italy with the emperor. He caught a fever during an excursion to the Megarid, but proceeded with his journey. By the time he reached Brundisium he was seriously ill, and died there on 20 September. Virgil was buried near Naples (Parthenope). His epitaph, probably composed by a friend, ran: 'Mantua gave me life, Calabria carried me off, Parthenope now holds me. I sang of pastures, farmlands, and rulers'. In his otherwise generous will he ordered the *Aeneid* to be destroyed. Much of our information about him comes from a dubious source, the *Life of Virgil* by DONATUS (1). There was an ancient tradition that Virgil was tall, slender and strong. We have portraits showing a thin-faced, swarthy man, but we do not know how reliable such evidence is. He never married and had few friends; Horace left memorials of his affection for Virgil in *Ode* 1. 3 and *Satire* 1. 5, 40ff.

His *oeuvre* consists of the three major works mentioned above; apart from four epigrams in the *Catalepton* dedicated to his friends, it is doubtful whether he wrote any of the other poems in the *Virgilian Appendix*, a collection of later poems in various metres on widely differing subjects which were wrongly attributed to him.

The first *Eclogue* sets the tone of the collection of the ten pastoral poems: two herdsmen meet and talk of the unseen power, far away in Rome, which controls their lives, disastrously for one of them, who is being driven from his land. The poem is about the helplessness of ordinary folk in the face of power, and the unfairness of life to the weak. Thus Virgil changes the rustic vein of Theocritus and, in the guise of the pastoral, illustrates a contemporary tragedy. *Eclogue* 9 returns to the theme of dispossession: unlike Theocritus, Virgil arranged his country poems with meticulous care so as to present the reader with a clear train of experience, and significantly these dark poems, 1 and 9, frame the collection. There is further careful arrangement: 2 and 8 are connected by their subject-matter, the lamentations of tragic lovers; while 3 and 7 have a shared structure in the patterns of the herdsmen's songs, one song responding to another. *Eclogues* 4 and 6 display more elevated themes and style, the former, with an echo of CATULLUS (1)'s *Theseus and Ariadne* (64), about the forthcoming birth of a baby and the return of a golden age, considered by many to refer to the expected offspring of Antonius and Octavia (see ANTONIA 1); the new 'golden age', a theme encouraged by the Caesarian triumvirate, was symbolised on their coinage. *Eclogue* 6 follows Callimachean principles, and in Silenus' song (based on Apollonius' *Song of Orpheus*) Virgil presents his audience with poetry which is learned, strange, outrageous, and ultimately about poetry itself: it contains a strong reminiscence of the opening of Callimachus' *Aetia* (*Causes*). Indeed, the poems belie their appearance and subtly undermine the townsman's dream of a rural idyll: unlike their Theocritean models they are sophisticated works written for an urban audience. *Eclogue* 5 is central to the scheme, a poem in honour of the traditional country god Daphnis, in the form of two closely parallel songs in his praise sung in fellowship by two rustic poets. The poem hints delicately at Virgil's admiration for Julius CAESAR (1). *Eclogue* 10, the plaint of Gallus, stands outside the general structure of the collection and relates mainly to 5, replacing the joy of that poem with sadness and introspection.

Virgil composed the *Georgics* between 37 and 29, when it was published. The rate of composition averaged a line a day. The models for the work were both Latin and Greek (but not fifth-century Athenian) poetry and prose: the *Georgica* of Nicander, of which only fragments remain, the *Phaenomena* of Aratus about astronomy and meteorology, the four books of *Causes* (*Aetia*) of Callimachus (the profoundest influence), the *Works and Days* of Hesiod, Homer's poems the *Iliad* and *Odyssey*, and *The Nature of Things* by LUCRETIUS, which had shown the possibility of a didactic poem being emotionally moving and conveying a message of almost religious intensity; but the influence of that poem on the *Georgics* is shallow and mainly stylistic. The treatise *Farming* by VARRO (3), published just before Virgil began to write the *Georgics*, was the main prose influence, but the contrast between them is striking: no farmer could have used the *Georgics* as a real textbook. He also drew on material from the works of Theophrastus. There are also echoes of a multitude of Greek and Roman authors. The poem is far from being a real didactic work (its audience was urban and sophisticated), and its true theme is the glory of the Italian countryside and the worth of its inhabitants: in book 2 Virgil gave expression to encomia of the beauties and richness of the land. It also starkly conveyed the uncertainty of the political situation, especially in the violent closing lines of book 1 and the prayer at line 500. The end of the work, however (4. 559ff.), written after the victory at Actium, looked forward to brighter prospects. Book 1, where Hesiod's influence is at its strongest, deals with the subject of growing crops and the calendar of annual tasks; much use is made of Aratus in the second half of the book in dealing with weather lore. There is also reference to Eratosthenes' *Hermes* and its treatment of the five climatic zones. The tone of book 1 is pessimistic and gloomy, making a point of the unseasonable storm which destroys the crops, the fruit of so much effort, and the civil war which, despite men's careful study of signs and portents, destroys the state. Book 2 shows a similar pessimism, describing the sexual urge which brings disaster to farm animals, the pestilence which attacks them, and finally the plague which kills men. Book 3 is different in tone, but deceptive: the book is concerned with the work of the grower of vines and fruit trees, but the process of grafting is suggested as being a perversion of the natural order: man dominates nature by an almost military force. And it is an artificial, man-made landscape that is admired in the section praising the Italian countryside. Both this and the praises of rustic life at the end of the book take the reader out of the real world and into a world of fantasy and illusion. In book 4 Virgil treats of beekeeping, but his main interest is still humankind. The first part deals in detail with the nature of honey bees and their husbandry. The mythical Aristaeus is introduced because of the story that his bees were suffering disease and death until he discovered the nature of his fault and the action needed to overcome it. He had unwittingly caused the death of Eurydice, wife of Orpheus, whose vain search for his wife in the Underworld is described by sea-god Proteus with great drama and beauty. Aristaeus uses a technique (of Virgil's invention) involving a dead ox to recreate his swarm of bees. The episode of Orpheus and Eurydice owes much to Catullus 64, and probably to the work of Gallus. Again, the theme is that of contrasted failure and success. The *Georgics* is arguably the most original poem ever written in Latin.

In writing the *Aeneid*, Virgil departed from the Callimachean principles of his earlier work and composed an epic in twelve books of hexameters, ostensibly modelled upon Homer's *Odyssey*, seeking to provide Rome with a monumental national poem to rival the Homeric epics in Greek. The subject, however, did not come from Roman history: instead, Virgil went back to the heroic age of the Homeric poems and made his work a sequel to the *Iliad*, just as the *Odyssey* was. The difference was that his story was told from the Trojan point of view, and the connection between Troy and the earliest ancestors of the Roman people (a purely fictitious kinship, borrowed from the *Annals* of ENNIUS) was assumed as axiomatic for the story. Like the *Odyssey*, the *Aeneid* is neatly divided into two halves, the first being a wandering journey from Troy and the second a homecoming. The technique of starting the narrative in the middle of events and recounting in a flashback what had preceded also resembles the *Odyssey*: in the *Aeneid* Virgil puts an account of the fall of Troy and of his subsequent wanderings into the mouth of Aeneas as he talks to Queen Dido of Carthage at a banquet. The hostility of the goddess Juno to Aeneas is established in the first book, where Aeneas is washed up on the coast of north Africa near Carthage: the support of his mother, Venus, who helps him in the form of a huntress, is also made clear (cf. the hostility of Poseidon to Odysseus, and the support of Athena, in the *Odyssey*). The book ends with the welcome Aeneas receives from Dido, queen of Carthage, who gives him and his people hospitality for the winter, falls in love with him, and seeks to unite the Trojans with her own Punic (Phoenician) refugees from persecution in the founding of Carthage. In books 2 and 3 Aeneas tells Dido and her courtiers the story of the sack of Troy seven years earlier, the escape of a remnant of the Trojans under his leadership, and of the voyage they eventually undertook to find somewhere new to settle, since Troy itself was now forbidden them. Aeneas' father Anchises dies in Sicily. Book 4, somewhat reminiscent of the love story of Jason and Medea in Apollonius of Rhodes' *Argonautica*, tells of the love of Dido and Aeneas, and its premature end when Jupiter sends Mercury to warn Aeneas that he must leave Carthage and proceed to Italy, his destined home. Dido commits suicide with his sword on their bed, atop a pyre of wood. The treatment of this love-story has attracted much criticism in modern times, but Romans would have regarded a marriage between Dido and Aeneas as a betrayal of his sacred mission. The episode serves to hint at the future enmity between Rome and Carthage. Book 5 describes the voyage to Italy by way of Sicily, where they celebrate funeral games for Anchises. The account of these games is based on the funeral games of Patroclus in the *Iliad*. In book 6 the Sibyl of Cumae, a prophetess, takes Aeneas to the Underworld to see the spirits of the dead and the yet unborn: his resolve is strengthened by the revelation of the Roman state his descendants are destined to found and of its achievements. In this book Virgil makes use of ideas and theories, including the recycling of souls, taken from Pythagorean and other sources.

The second half of the epic, superficially resembling the second half of the *Odyssey* as a kind of homecoming, also recalls the *Iliad* in the scenes of warfare and battle that it contains and in the confrontation of the two heroes. Unlike the *Iliad*, it ends with the death of the loser, Turnus. In book 7 Aeneas and his followers land at the mouth of the Tiber, are briefly welcomed by Latinus, king of the Latin nation, whose daughter Lavinia

Aeneas proposes to marry, but soon confront the hostility of local Italian peoples: Rutulians led by prince Turnus, Lavinia's betrothed, Volscians led by Camilla, and Etruscans led by Mezentius. In book 8 Aeneas, assisted by the god of the Tiber, departs to make an alliance with Arcadian Greek settlers led by Evander. Vulcan makes a new shield for Aeneas, which is described in detail (it depicts scenes from Roman history including Actium) like that of Achilles in the *Iliad*. Book 9 describes the siege of the Trojan camp by the Rutulians, relieved in book 10 by the return of Aeneas and new allies, including the Etruscan Tarchon. Turnus kills Pallas, son of Evander, and Aeneas kills Mezentius and his young son Lausus. In book 11, a single combat is arranged between Aeneas and Turnus to settle the war, which takes place in book 12, with an interruption caused by the interference of Juturna, the sister of Turnus. Aeneas is wounded but cured by Venus, the city of Latinus is burnt by the Trojans, and the two heroes finally meet in combat. Aeneas wounds Turnus, who begs for mercy. But Aeneas notices the baldric of Pallas, which Turnus wears, and slays him in anger for his friend.

The poem, subtle and moving, was a worthy successor to Homer's epics, and immediately found a place at the heart of the Roman literary canon. Virgil conveyed in the poem a strong feeling of the tragedy of human suffering as well as the greatness of the foundation of the Roman race. His Aeneas is anything but romantic: he resembles a struggling pilgrim uncertain of his goal but determined not to be diverted from his quest. Virgil delineated future events and historical characters by subtle means, such as the parade of the souls in the Underworld and the pictures on Aeneas' shield. The poem displays a strong sense of fate, which is connected in an unspecified way with Jupiter's will. Thus Virgil creates a powerful impression of a unified thread of Roman history down to Augustus' new order, and a patriotism that embraced Italy as a whole. Virgil does not always succeed in the portrayal of distinct characters, and his use of divine machinery is banal. He died dissatisfied with the work, which he regarded as incomplete, and is said to have given instructions in his will that the *Aeneid* should be destroyed. Augustus charged Varius and Plotius Tucca to prepare it for publication, adding nothing, but removing anything they thought below the quality of Virgil's best work.

Virgil was the greatest of Rome's poets, a man of immense talent who composed poetry of great diversity and wonderful richness and subtlety of language. He had a fine ear for the music of words and a deep understanding of his Greek models, which he equalled and even transcended, especially in the pathos and depth of feeling conveyed in his sublime poetry. See J. Griffin (1986) *Virgil*, Oxford: Oxford University Press; W.F. Jackson Knight (1966) *Roman Virgil*, 2nd edn, Harmondsworth: Penguin; W. Berg (1974) *Early Virgil*, London: Athlone Press; D.R. Slavitt (1991) *Virgil*, New Haven: Yale University Press; B. Otis (1963) *Virgil: A Study in Civilised Poetry*, Oxford: Clarendon Press; R. Jenkyns (1999) *Virgil's Experience*, Oxford: Clarendon Press; P. Levi (1998) *Virgil: His Life and Times*, London: Duckworth; W. Clausen (1987) *Virgil's Aeneid and the Tradition of Hellenistic Poetry*, Berkeley: University of California Press; K.W. Gransden (1990) *Virgil: the Aeneid*, Cambridge: Cambridge University Press; P.R. Hardie (1986) *Virgil's Aeneid: Cosmos and Imperium*, Oxford: Clarendon Press; F. Cairns (1989) *Virgil's Augustan Epic*, Cambridge: Cambridge University Press.

Viriathus (*c.*180–139 BC) was a shepherd who became the war leader of the Lusitanians against Roman oppression. He escaped from the massacre conducted in 150 by Servius GALBA (4), and by 147 had rallied his countrymen and trained a small mobile force in guerrilla tactics so well that he won a series of victories over Roman commanders, ranging all over the peninsula, thus encouraging the Celtiberians in 143 to take up arms again against the Roman invader. In 141 he defeated the consul Q. Fabius Maximus Servilianus and had his force of 20,000 men at his mercy. Against his own principles he negotiated a treaty with the Romans, which the Senate and Popular Assembly went on to ratify, gaining the recognition of Lusitanian freedom and alliance with Rome. In 140 Fabius was succeeded by Servilius CAEPIO (2), who persuaded the Senate to ignore the treaty and renew hostilities. Though outmanoeuvred by Viriathus, Caepio bribed his troops to desert him, and then bribed his servants to murder him in his sleep. The Lusitanians were thus brought under Roman rule. Viriathus is still honoured as a hero in Portugal.

Vitellius 1, Aulus (AD 15–69), was emperor for part of the year 69. The son of VITELLIUS (2), he was a prominent courtier under the emperors CALIGULA, CLAUDIUS (1) and NERO (1), and held the consulship in 48. He then governed Africa as proconsul, serving his brother, who succeeded to the post the following year, as his legate. In November 68 GALBA (1) appointed him legate of Lower Germany, and with uncharacteristic vigour he set about winning the favour of the garrison by generous promises. At the beginning of the next year his army proclaimed him emperor, and he gathered further support from Upper Germany, Gaul, Spain and Africa. He placed Fabius Valens and CAECINA (3) Alienus in command of his forces: they defeated those of OTHO at Bedriacum near Cremona in April 69. They then marched in disorderly fashion to Rome, which they reached in July. Otho had killed himself in April and the Senate recognised Vitellius' principate, but VESPASIAN was declared emperor by troops in the east in July. Vitellius' reign went rapidly downhill: he had no money to pay the largesse he had promised his men; he dismissed the Praetorian Guard and replaced it with an enlarged body consisting of sixteen cohorts of soldiers from Germany. He killed some centurions of the legions on the Danube for supporting Otho and thus gained that army's enmity. The forces of Vespasian began to close in, but Vitellius failed to guard the Alpine passes, which Antonius PRIMUS easily crossed. A second battle took place in October near Bedriacum, in which Vitellius' army, under Valens and Caecina, was routed. In December, as Vespasian's army approached Rome and most of his followers except his praetorians had deserted Vitellius, Flavius SABINUS (2), City Prefect and Vespasian's brother, persuaded him to abdicate. However, the Roman mob attacked Sabinus and his men and forced them to take refuge in the Capitol, which was burnt. The city fell to Primus' troops, whom Vitellius' men could not resist. He himself was maltreated, insulted, and killed. See M. Grant (1985) *The Roman Emperors*, London: Weidenfeld & Nicolson.

2, Lucius (died *c.*AD 51), of equestrian background from Luceria in Apulia, was a powerful courtier under the emperors TIBERIUS, CALIGULA and CLAUDIUS (1). He held the consulship three times, in 34, 43 and 47. He worked hard while legate of Syria from 35 to 37, when he negotiated with the king of Parthia, ARTABANUS (1) II, to concede control of Armenia to Rome, and he removed Pontius PILATE from his post as procurator of Judaea, where he had done so much to offend the Jews, and sent him to Rome for trial. TACITUS (1) the historian gives a mixed verdict on him, accusing him of sycophancy and yet praising his integrity. In 43 he acted as Claudius' deputy in Rome while the emperor was absent in Britain, and he was Claudius' colleague as censor in 47. He spoke publicly on behalf of the

Senate in support of Claudius' marriage with AGRIPPINA (3). He was honoured with a public funeral.

Vitruvius (C1 BC) was a Roman writer on architecture and civil engineering whose cognomen may have been Pollio. He served under CAESAR (1) as a military engineer, and built a basilica (law court) at Fano on the Adriatic coast which has not survived. His extant work, a treatise in ten books on *Architecture* (*De Architectura*), includes much incidental information including urban planning, surveying, decoration, astronomy, physics, mechanics and military engineering. He drew heavily on the Hellenistic Greek writer HERMOGENES (1) and others, and seems to have wished to impress Octavian (AUGUSTUS) to whom he dedicated the work. He is aware of the Roman technique of building with concrete, though he has reservations about it. But his work is not a manual for professionals, though it has much to offer interested laypeople. It provides invaluable information about ancient building methods and materials, the architectural orders, and the rules of proportion.

Vitruvius' breadth of interest in topics as wide-ranging as medicine, the weather, philosophy, and many branches of science, all of which he saw as relevant to his subject, makes his book a source of great diversity and interest. His approach to his subject was encyclopaedic and his work is systematic and thorough. He took trouble to explain connections which sometimes seem far-fetched to a modern mind, such as his insistence on the relevance of early Greek scientific theories about matter to the use of bricks, Plato's abstract geometry to surveying, astronomy to the use of sundials, and even astrology to lifestyle. It is noteworthy that he recommends for practical use theories which Greek philosophers had formed for no practical purpose at all. His book had great influence, especially in the Renaissance. See H. Plommer (1973) *Vitruvius and Later Roman Building Materials*, Cambridge: Cambridge University Press.

Volero, Publilius (C5 BC), a tribune of the *plebs* in 472–1, was believed in later times with Publilius PHILO (1) to have established the right of plebeians to appeal from the decisions of magistrates to the tribunes, to have inaugurated 'plebiscites' (votes of the assembly to give legal force to a resolution already passed by the patrician senators), and to have increased the number of tribunes to five. He was also believed to have founded the tribal assembly known as the *Comitia*.

Vologeses I (reigned AD 51–80) was a Parthian king who disputed control of Armenia with Rome. In 54 he made his brother TIRIDATES (3) king of Armenia: his action was challenged by NERO (1), who in 58 sent his general CORBULO to intervene. As a result Tiridates fled, and in 60 Corbulo installed the pro-Roman TIGRANES (4) V. Meanwhile Vologeses was occupied with a war against his son Vardanes, but returned to confront Caesennius PAETUS (1), governor of Cappadocia, whom Nero sent in 62 to maintain Roman influence and who capitulated shamefully to Vologeses. A vestige of honour was, however, retrieved by Corbulo, now governor of Syria, when Tiridates agreed to go to Rome to be crowned by Nero, an event which took place in 66. VESPASIAN sent Vologeses aid against an invasion by the Alans. Vologeses was a nationalist who reduced the Greek influence in his kingdom: he first issued coins bearing inscriptions in the Pahlavi language.

Volusius *see* MAECIANUS.

Vonones *see* ARTABANUS (1).

Vulso 1, Gnaeus Manlius (early C2 BC), was a general in the war with ANTIOCHUS (1) III. During his consulship in

189, he succeeded SCIPIO (4) Asiagenes in Asia Minor after the defeat of Antiochus, and marched his army from Ephesus to Ancyra (Ankara), plundering along his way, and won two important victories over the Galatians. In 188 he met Antiochus at Apamea, where with the assistance of ten commissioners from the Senate he made a treaty with the king. He returned to Rome in 187, having suffered the loss of many men and substantial booty. He claimed a triumph on his return which, despite the opposition of the commissioners led by Aemilius PAULLUS (2), was granted. LIVY attributes to the return of this army the coming of oriental luxury to Rome.

2. *See* REGULUS (1).

X

Xanthippus (C3 BC) was a Spartan mercenary commander who was hired by Carthage to fight in the First Punic War. After reforming the Carthaginian army he led it to a brilliant victory in 255 against REGULUS (1), taking advantage of the elephants and cavalry that were at his disposal. He may have gone from Carthage to Alexandria, for Ptolemy III used a man of the same name in controlling the lands beyond the Euphrates.

Z

Zenobia (C3 AD) was a queen of Palmyra, the second wife of ODAENATHUS. After her husband's death in suspicious circumstances in 267, she proclaimed her younger son, Septimius Vaballathus, king with his father's titles, while effectively ruling herself. This situation was tolerated as long as she protected the eastern frontier, but in 270 Zenobia seized the chance offered by the death of CLAUDIUS (2) II and occupied Egypt and a large part of Asia Minor. AURELIAN could not accept this usurpation, attacked her in 272, and besieged her in Palmyra. She now took the titles *Augustus* and *Augusta* for her son and herself. She was captured, but her life was spared as the city fell. She was paraded in Aurelian's triumph in 274.

Glossary

Academy, academic The school established by Plato (*c*.429–347 BC) in Athens, and its later adherents.

Aedile A junior magistrate at Rome. Originally there were two aediles elected to support the tribunes, attend to the plebeian temples and cults, and to execute decisions of the tribunes. In 367 BC two patrician aediles were added, the curule aediles, but they too were eventually shared with the plebeians. The aedileship, originally the lowest rung on the ladder of the senatorial career, became superior in rank to the tribunate.

Assembly The *Comitia Centuriata* was an assembly of citizens which voted in 193 'centuries', allocated among them according to wealth and age, so that the richest and oldest had the greatest voting force and the poorest, being all enrolled in one century, were effectively powerless. It met outside the city boundary, usually in the Campus Martius, and passed laws, elected magistrates such as the consuls, praetors and censors, acted as a court of ultimate appeal for capital offences, and declared war and peace. Two other *comitia* existed, the *Comitia Curiata*, whose functions were mainly religious, and the *Comitia Tributa*, where voting took place by tribes, and which acted with greater despatch than the *Centuriata*. It elected the lower magistrates, was a court for non-capital offences, and, when composed only of plebeians, enacted plebiscites; it made laws when composed of the whole people. The political powers of these assemblies effectively ended at the start of the principate, when AUGUSTUS and his successors effectively deprived them of their now much diminished powers.

Augurs The officially appointed diviners who regulated some religious practices and ceremonies and inaugurated new temples and public buildings. They normally acted as a college, consisting of fifteen men in the time of SULLA (2) and sixteen under CAESAR (1). They could also act individually, and sometimes declared the proposed actions of magistrates inauspicious.

Augusta An honorific title given to many consorts of emperors, equivalent to 'empress'.

Augustus A title, meaning 'divinely ordained', which was conferred by the Senate on the first emperor, Gaius Julius Caesar Octavianus (AUGUSTUS), in 27 BC, and thereafter assumed by all succeeding emperors. The title virtually means 'emperor'. See **Caesar**.

Caesar The family name of Julius CAESAR (1) which was inherited by the Julio-Claudian emperors by virtue of adoption by their predecessors until CLAUDIUS (1) I, who took the name as a title. This precedent was followed by his successors, so that the name came to be seen as a title equivalent to 'emperor'. In the later Empire (see DIOCLETIAN), *Caesar* was a title given to the heirs and deputies of the *Augusti*, the senior rulers in East and West.

Campus Martius ('Field of Mars') An open area along the river Tiber where Roman citizens exercised for military training and where meetings of the *Comitia Centuriata* were held. In later times it became the site of the camp of the Praetorian Guard. The area was gradually filled with monumental buildings commemorating imperial successes before and during the principate. See **Capitol.**

Capitol The smallest and most central of the seven hills of Rome, adjacent to the Roman forum. On it stood a very ancient temple of Jupiter Best and Greatest, Juno and Minerva. It was the centre of the national cult and here consuls and governors took vows and made sacrifices. It was the goal of triumphal processions, which began in the Campus Martius.

Careers (*Cursus Honorum*) There was a distinct senatorial career open to members of certain families which evolved and became standard in the late republic. After military service as a tribune, and possibly minor civil administrative posts, the quaestorship was held between twenty-seven and thirty years of age; the aedileship and tribunate of the *plebs* would follow (the latter only in the case of plebeians); the praetorship, and finally the consulship was held at around forty-two. These offices were normally held for a year. Ex-consuls might, if required, be elected censors. Provincial governorships, with the titles of propraetor and proconsul, would, in many cases, be interspersed with the senior posts. The quaestorship qualified its holder for a seat in the Senate. All these posts were unpaid, though the unscrupulous, of whom there were many, could make a fortune in provincial administration. An equestrian career, including governorships of minor provinces, was developed during the early principate.

Censor A non-executive office to which a pair of senior ex-consuls could, every four or five years, be elected for an eighteen-month term by the Assembly of the People. The task of the censors was to regulate the membership of the citizen body (the census) and especially the Senate, and purge it of corrupt or undesirable members. Censors also had the task of collecting dues and making contracts for the leasing of land and tax-collecting contracts on behalf of the state. The last censors were elected in 22 BC, after which the emperors exercised their powers.

Client In the system of patronage, a powerful element in Roman society especially of imperial times, the client was a citizen of lower status who was attached to a patron, a more influential or richer citizen, by ties which often depended on family connection, heredity, or financial dependence. The client was expected to perform certain services for his patron such as lending political support if asked, and in cities would call upon his patron to offer his services each day in return for a dole of cash or food. The formality of the tie can be exaggerated, and should not be confused with political friendship (*amicitia*), a feature of republican political life. A 'client king' was nominally the ruler of his kingdom but effectively under Roman control as far as military and foreign affairs were concerned.

Consul After the fall of the monarchy the Romans established a joint annual magistracy shared by two elected senators to act as the head of the executive and to lead the armies in war. They were originally called *praetors* ('leaders') but the term *consul*, whose origin is obscure, replaced the older word. Their power was that of the king, limited by their annual term and duality. Until 153 BC they came into power each year on 13 March; thereafter they took power on 1 January. They were elected by a special session of the Centuriate Assembly called by a consul, dictator, interrex, or military tribune holding consular power. After the beginning of the principate their powers and influence declined markedly.

Cynic The name given to the philosophy established by Diogenes of Sinope (*c*.400–*c*.323 BC), so called because of his allegedly shameless behaviour. We have virtually no writings of the Cynics, and the nature of their beliefs is controversial and difficult to retrieve. More a way of life than a school of philosophy, Cynicism seems to have consisted of living according to nature in a primitive way.

Decree, ultimate decree A resolution of the Senate which, though lacking the force of law, was made to advise the magistrates who, as members of that order, felt constrained to obey the decree. When it had been implemented it gained the force of law unless it was vetoed by a competent magistrate such as a tribune. In HADRIAN's reign and thereafter some decrees gained immediate legal force. The 'ultimate' decree instructed the consuls to see that the republic suffer no harm, and after its institution by Lucius OPIMIUS to deal with Gaius GRACCHUS (1) was considered to confer emergency powers on the consuls, including those of life and death.

Deification The procedure for declaring an emperor divine and assigning him a cult. It began with the deification of Julius CAESAR (1) by AUGUSTUS (then Octavian) in 44 BC. Many of the more successful and popular emperors were deified, usually to strengthen the position of their relatively weak successors. Such were Augustus, CLAUDIUS (1), VESPASIAN, TITUS, TRAJAN and HADRIAN. Some of their wives or mothers were also deified, such as LIVIA (2).

Denarius A Roman monetary unit represented by a silver coin, the standard of the Roman monetary system. During the imperial period the value of these coins was progressively devalued.

Dictator An irregular magistrate of the Roman republic whom the elected magistrates could appoint with senatorial authorisation in an emergency of the state to replace the consuls for a limited period, six months at most. Himself the infantry commander, he was assisted by his deputy, the Master of the Horse. A special dictator could be appointed to conduct elections when necessary.

Eclectic An approach to philosophy wherein aspects of different systems are combined at the discretion of the thinker.

Elegiac A poetic metre involving the use of alternate hexameter and pentameter lines. Originally a sung lament, it came to be used for epitaphs and other inscriptions and also for poems on a variety of subjects, including the erotic.

Emperor Though the later career of Julius CAESAR (1) prefigured the nature of the emperor's power, it was AUGUSTUS who founded the principate with his constitutional reforms in 27 and 23 BC. Taking the 'republican' title *Princeps*, he kept the power of a tribune, allowing him to initiate and veto legislation, and of overriding military power, allowing him control of all the garrisoned provinces. He was therefore the permanent commander of the entire Roman army. Stability was created, a court like that of a king was quickly established round the emperor, and by the end of Augustus' reign nobody could remember any other system of government.

Epicurean Used of the philosophy of the Greek thinker Epicurus (341–270 BC), an atomist who added a moral and social dimension to the system devised by Leucippus and Democritus, whom he was, however, unwilling to acknowledge as his masters. It is mainly known to us through the poem of LUCRETIUS, *The Nature of Things*.

Epigram A short poem on a single theme. The literary epigram developed in Greece from the writing of inscriptions, including epitaphs, usually in the elegiac metre. It was greatly extended in Hellenistic and Roman times when a variety of metres was used.

Epithalamium A poem or song celebrating a wedding, traditionally sung outside the bridal chamber.

Epyllion A modern term for a miniature epic poem which, however, instead of relating a story as a complete narrative, concentrates on a single episode or scene from a myth and often dwells on the scene and the emotions of the characters concerned.

Equestrian The equestrian order, the knights, second to the senatorial order, originally consisted of men of the census or income bracket sufficient to enable them to keep and equip a horse to enable them to serve in the cavalry. The order in late republican and imperial times included some very rich men who ran the commercial life of Rome. The qualification for membership in the late republic was 400,000 sesterces. There was also an equestrian career of public service, mainly in the military and the provinces. Equestrians, who were appointed by the censors and distinguished by the wearing of a ring, were socially the equals of senators and often intermarried with them: indeed, the sons of senators, before entering the Senate, had the status of knights.

Ethnarch The ruler of a nation. In the east, especially Palestine, a title given to the equivalent of a minor client king, such as ARCHELAUS (6), son of HEROD (1) the Great.

Gnosticism A set of religious teachings involving a belief in the fundamentally evil nature of the world and the redemption of humankind by a redeemer. It originated in the east and was based partly on the Hebrew Scriptures, especially the Book of *Genesis*. Gnostics drew on Platonic theories of duality and an evil principle governing the world, on the teachings of Zoroaster and Mithraism, Judaism, Christianity and the Hermetic corpus of texts. The power of the teachings is suggested by the strength of opposition expressed by philosophers such as PLOTINUS, and in the Pauline letters.

Hendecasyllables A verse metre of Greek origin, used for light-hearted subjects, used by CATULLUS (1), MARTIAL and others. The line contained eleven syllables arranged in a distinctive metrical pattern.

Hexameter The verse metre used in writing epic, didactic and satirical poetry. The hexameter line had a falling rhythm and consisted of four feet which could be either dactyls (¯ ˇ ˇ) or spondees (¯ ¯), a dactylic fifth foot, and finally a spondee or trochee (¯ ˇ) in the sixth foot.

Iambic A verse metre common in plays, consisting usually of six feet with a rising rhythm (ˇ ¯). A *scazon* or 'limping iambic' reverses the rhythm in the last foot, which is a trochee.

Interrex A Roman republican solution to the problem of the death of both consuls in office. The patrician senators elected from their own number men to hold this office (*interreges*), who then held consular power for five days each. Their principal responsibility was to hold elections to make good the deficiency of consuls.

Jurist An expert in the law, though not necessarily an advocate. After the early republic, when knowledge of legal procedures was the monopoly of a few patrician priests, there arose a class of respected lawyers (*iurisconsulti*) who were capable of advising litigants and judges, and often acted as teachers of law and writers on the subject.

Law A bill passed by the popular assembly, either the *Comitia Centuriata* or the *Comitia Tributa Populi* had the force of law (*lex*) and was so named. It was generally known by the name(s) of its proposer(s).

Legate The deputy of an army commander or of a provincial governor; the word literally means 'entrusted'. The governors appointed by emperors to administer the imperial provinces on behalf of the emperors were legates, as were the commanders of legions under the principate.

Master of the Horse *See* **Dictator.**

Metre In Latin and Greek literature, the fixed pattern of light and heavy syllables, arranged in 'feet' or metrical units, making up rhythmical 'lines' or verses, which produce the effect of poetry. See **hexameter, iambic, hendecasyllables.**

New Man A senator who was the first member of his family to be elected to that body.

Patrician In the early days of the republic, the patricians were members of a restricted number of privileged families with special rights to property and voting power. Before 445 BC, patricians and plebeians were not allowed to intermarry. Patricians monopolised the priesthoods and consequently exercised much political power. The plebeians seceded from Rome at least three times in protest against their lack of rights, and each time gained ground. The last secession was in 287 BC. The distinction became less and less important as the patrician families died out. It was obsolete from *c.*AD 100 onwards.

Patron *See* **Client.**

Peripatetic The name given to the school of philosophy founded by Aristotle (384–322 BC) at the Lyceum in Athens, so-called from the covered walks (*peripatoi*) there in which the members of the school could stroll as they talked.

Plebiscite A resolution of the plebeian assembly (*Comitia Tributa Plebis*) which, if ratified by a resolution of the patricians in the Senate, became binding with the full force of a law. From 287 BC they were equivalent to laws (*leges*).

Plebs Those Roman citizens who were not patricians (q.v.) were members of the *plebs*.

Pontifex, Pontifex Maximus The college of *pontifices* consisted of three patrician priests, three *flamines* or priests specific to particular gods, the Vestal Virgins, minor priests, and an officer called the *rex sacrorum* who performed the priestly functions of the former king. Their role was advisory and concerned broadly religious and family matters. The college was reformed in 300 BC and became open to plebeians: membership was prized and distinguished men sought it. In the later republic membership of the college, and its leading position, the *Pontifex Maximus*, came to be elected by a popular vote of half of the voting tribes of the Assembly. The prestige of the *Pontifex Maximus* grew until AUGUSTUS took it for himself and made it virtually a chief priesthood. Thereafter all the emperors down to Gratian (AD 359–383) held the post.

Praetor Though the title originally denoted the office that became the consulship, from 367 BC a new, lower annual office was created which took over the title 'praetor'. The function of the praetor thus became differentiated from that of the consuls, and was mainly exercised at Rome. A major duty was administration of the law, though when both consuls were away at war the praetor was the chief magistrate of the city. After the First Punic War (*c.*244) an extra praetor was added to supervise foreigners at Rome, and thereafter the number increased in stages to ten or twelve, briefly sixteen under CAESAR (1). They were used for governing provinces and leading armies, and the post became a prerequisite for the consulship. The praetorship was the first post to offer a man administrative power, legal and military, and ex-praetors could govern provinces (q.v. proconsul) and lead armies.

Praetorian Guard The headquarters of a Roman general, usually a praetor or consul, was known as his *praetorium*, and the praetorian cohort was the small guard which in republican times accompanied the general. After the civil wars, when generals had often kept large bodyguards, AUGUSTUS created the Praetorian Guard of nine cohorts (each of 1,000 men) which he stationed in a camp outside the city in the Campus Martius.

Prefect A term of wide application, simply meaning 'in charge'. It was often used in a military context: in republican times, the Italian auxiliary units of the Roman army were commanded by prefects, as were cavalry units. The commander of the Praetorian Guard was a prefect of equestrian rank, and the joint prefecture of two men, like the consulship, was instituted by TIBERIUS. The term was extended to governorships, e.g. of Egypt after AUGUSTUS' conquest in 31 BC, and the City Prefect, an old regal institution revived by Augustus, was the emperor's deputy at Rome, responsible for public order. In imperial times these great prefectures were often held by senators.

Principate The system of government established by AUGUSTUS with the emperor (*Princeps*) at its head. Other terms used to denote the imperial position were *Imperator*, *Augustus* and *Caesar*.

Proconsul, propraetor Promagistrates were created in the second century BC as the number of external provinces increased and the number of praetors available to govern them was kept static. A man who had held the praetorship and so exercised *imperium* (administrative power) was considered capable of governing a province as a propraetor (the term used in lesser provinces) or as a proconsul (in the major provinces, such as Asia and Africa). In later times the proconsulship was confined to ex-consuls. It should be noted that the governorships of provinces were essentially military appointments, commanding troops, and having authority over the non-citizens in the province. This situation changed under the principate.

Procurator An agent or representative; under the principate the procurators, usually men of equestrian rank, were the emperor's civil servants. In some small imperial provinces they acted as governors; in larger ones they acted as financial officers supervising tax collection and the maintenance of the army. This function was also extended to the senatorial provinces. Procurators were sometimes put in charge of public works.

Proscribe, proscription The process of declaring a citizen outlawed. As a result, he could be killed with impunity and his property was confiscated to the state and auctioned. The most famous proscriptions were those of SULLA (2) in 82 and the Triumvirs in 43 BC.

Quaestor The lowest rank of the senatorial career, an annual office held after a military tribunate or some other junior administrative post: by the reforms of SULLA (2) it gave entry to the Senate. The post originally had a financial function, which was extended to military and judicial duties. The number of quaestors was eventually increased by Sulla to twenty. The post was usually held for one or two years, either at home or in the service of a provincial governor. A quaestor deputised for his superior officer if he was unable to act. The term was also used for municipal treasurers.

Rhetorician A specialist in the art and theory of rhetoric or public speaking, and in particular a teacher of rhetorical skills, which were considered supremely important in ancient cities, especially democratic ones.

Scazon *See* **Iambic**.

Secretaries of State The imperial secretaries *a libellis*, *a rationibus*, *ab epistulis* and *a studiis*, mainstays of the civil service, were of equestrian rank except for the imperial freedmen employed by CLAUDIUS (1) and NERO (1). For further information, see CLAUDIUS (1).

Senate, senator The Senate was originally the advisory body of the kings, and later of the consuls. It grew from being a relatively small body of rich men chosen by the consuls in the early republic to a much larger assembly of ex-magistrates who were wealthy, aristocratic, and politically experienced. The Senate did not legislate, but produced *senatus consulta* (which the tribunes could veto), influential advice for the magistrates. Membership, which was normally for life, was regulated by the censors, whose duty it was to expel miscreants. Members had to be qualified by wealth to be equestrians, but unlike equestrians were not allowed to trade. CAESAR (1) increased the Senate to 900 members. Senators wore a broad purple stripe on their togas, and special shoes. They were not allowed to leave Italy without permission. Meetings of the Senate, which were held in sacred buildings, were private and consisted of a consultation of the members who spoke in turn, each from his seat. A record was kept of their proceedings. Before the principate, in some areas of government, such as foreign policy, the work of the magistrates, and military matters, the Senate had final authority. AUGUSTUS modified the composition and size of the Senate, and his successors constantly introduced new blood. He increased the effective legislative role of the Senate by the virtual elimination of the Popular Assembly, though he and his successors assumed most of the important powers which the republican Senate had held.

Sesterces The main unit of coinage under the principate: originally a quarter of a silver denarius, it was devalued under NERO (1) so that the relationship was 5:32. There were several other coins in use, from the gold *aureus* to the copper *as*.

Stoa, Stoic The followers of the philosopher Zeno of Citium took their name, Stoics, from the *Stoa Poikile* ('painted colonnade') on the edge of the market-place (*agora*) of Athens, where they met in the early third century. The philosophical system became very influential and popular with educated Romans.

Suffect A substitute for the holder of a magistracy, who took the place of the latter upon his resignation or incapacity. Under the principate it became common for the consuls of the year to retire after two or three months to be replaced by a fresh couple of consuls, who themselves retired and so on. This greatly increased the available number of men of consular rank, which qualified them for governorships and posts in the imperial service.

Tetrarch In Syria and Judaea a tetrarch was appointed to rule a quarter of the kingdom: the word means 'ruler of a quarter'. The title was sometimes applied loosely to any subordinate ruler in the Roman imperial system in the east.

Tribe A division of the Roman citizens, originally territorial and based on residence, of which there were thirty-five by 241 BC. Their main function was for the purpose of voting in the Assembly, in elections, in recruitment to the army, and for taxation. Membership of a tribe was a prerequisite for citizenship.

Tribune 1. of the *plebs* This office, usually held for a year, probably began with the first secession of the plebeians in 494 BC, and by 449 there were ten tribunes with equal powers. What their relationship was to the tribes is unclear. The function of the tribunes was to protect and represent the plebeians, and by an oath sworn by the *plebs* their persons were sacrosanct. They gathered important powers within the city of Rome: the right (held individually by each tribune) to veto legislation, senatorial decrees, or the acts of any magistrate; the right to summon meetings of the Assembly and of the Senate; and the right to enforce decisions of the Assembly. In the later republic tribunes gained the right to sit in the Senate and influence its business. During the late second century their activities were often turbulent, especially concerning the reforms of the GRACCHUS family and the career of SATURNINUS (2), and SULLA (2) reduced their powers drastically. They were restored by 70 BC, but lost their importance under the principate, though the emperors used the powers of the tribunate as a main source of their own power.

2, Military Originally the commanders of the tribal contingents in the Roman army, in later times there were six tribunes appointed to act as the officers of each legion. They had to be men of equestrian rank with at least five years' military experience, and two tribunes commanded the legion in rotation. Under CAESAR (1) and in the principate the tribunes' importance declined and the legions were commanded by legates. At this time one of the six legionary tribunes was usually the son of a senator embarking on the senatorial career.

Triumph A procession led by a victorious commander from the Campus Martius to celebrate and offer thanks for his victory to Jupiter in his temple on the Capitol. The victory had to be substantial, involving the deaths of 5,000 of the enemy. The triumphator rode in a four-horse chariot, dressed in a purple robe, with a slave who held a laurel wreath over his head and reminded him that he was mortal. His troops followed and sang songs which humorously insulted the triumphator. To be eligible for a triumph, the general had to gain permission from the people to keep his military power within the city boundary, to have won his victory acting as a magistrate of the Roman People, and to have concluded the war. There was also a lesser victory ceremony, an ovation. AUGUSTUS and his successors did not recognise the right of anybody outside the imperial family to a triumph, though 'triumphal decorations' could be awarded to their legates.

Triumvir, triumvirate The triumvirate ('board of three men') best known to history is the one created in 43 BC consisting of Octavian (AUGUSTUS), ANTONIUS (7) and LEPIDUS (4). They were granted consular powers as long as their office ran (it was renewed in 37 and expired in 32) with the purpose of restoring republican institutions. The earlier 'triumvirate' of CAESAR, POMPEIUS and CRASSUS had no official or legal standing. The institution of boards of three for various administrative purposes was well known in Roman political life.

Vestal Virgins Six priestesses of senatorial family who spent at least thirty years of their lives in the service of the goddess Vesta (and the Roman state) tending the everlasting flame on her hearth, making the salted grain for use in public sacrifices, and performing other religious duties. They could be punished for impurity by being buried alive in the Field of Wickedness outside the Colline Gate of Rome.

Appendix I

Chronological table of Roman history

BC

509	Traditional date of the founding of the Republic.
494	First secession of the *plebs* and creation of the tribunes.
471	Law of Publilius and VOLERO.
451/0	The rule of the *Decemvirs*, a board of ten men with consular powers. Publication of the Twelve Tables of Law.
449	Second secession of the *plebs*.
445	The military tribunate: military tribunes with consular powers. Rome defeats Aequi and Volsci on the Algidus.
390	Battle of the Allia: the Gauls sack Rome (387 according to POLYBIUS).
386	Rome defeats the Latins, the Volsci and the Hernici.
367	Restoration of the consulship: one consul to be a plebeian. Curule aedileship created.
366	Creation of Praetorship.
358	Treaty renewed between the Romans and the Latins.
354	Alliance of Rome and the Samnites.
351	Falerii and Tarquinii make a forty-year peace with Rome.
348	Rome and Carthage renew treaty.
343–1	First Samnite War.
340–38	Rebellion of Latins.
339	Laws of Publilius PHILO (1).
338	Dissolution of the Latin League.
326–304	Second Samnite War.
321	Samnites defeat Rome at Caudine Forks.
315	Samnite victory at Lautulae.
314	Roman victory at Tarracina. Capua taken.
312	Appius CLAUDIUS (4) the Censor begins construction of Appian Way.
310	Roman incursion into Etruria: she makes treaties with Perusia, Cortona, and Arretium. Roman navy: duoviri navales appointed.

BC	
306	Third treaty with Carthage.
304	FLAVIUS publishes the legal procedures and the dates propitious for legal action. Rome defeats the Aequi and ends the Samnite War. Alliance with Marsi, Paeligni, Marrucini and Frentani.
300	VALERIUS CORVUS' law on appeals, OGULNIUS' law on priesthoods.
298–90	Third Samnite War.
295	Roman victory at Sentinum over the Gauls, Samnites and Umbrians.
290	Rome annexes the Sabines as citizens without voting rights.
287	Last secession of the *plebs*. Law of dictator HORTENSIUS (1) to support plebeian rights.
283	Rome defeats Etruscans and Gallic Boii at Lake Vadimo.
282	Rome assists Thurii against the Lucanians.
280	PYRRHUS invades Italy and defeats Rome at Heraclea.
279	Pyrrhus defeats Rome at Asculum. Rome makes a new treaty with Carthage. Pyrrhus crosses into Sicily.
273	Egyptian envoys in Rome.
272	Death of Pyrrhus. Papirius CURSOR (2) takes Tarentum.
268	Rome gives the Sabines full citizenship. Colonies founded at Beneventum and Rimini.
264	Rome in alliance with Mamertines of Messina. Appius CLAUDIUS (5) sent to Sicily. The First Punic War between Rome and Carthage begins.
263	HIERON of Syracuse becomes an ally of Rome.
262	The Romans capture Acragas (Agrigento).
260	Roman naval victory at Mylae.
257	REGULUS (1) wins naval victory off Tyndaris.
256	Naval victory of Ecnomus. Regulus lands in Africa and defeats the Carthaginians. He winters at Tunis.
255	Regulus defeated and captured. Rome wins naval victory off Cape Hermaeum. Fleet wrecked at Pachynus.
254	Rome takes Panormus (Palermo).
250	Roman victory at Panormus: siege of Lilybaeum (Marsala).
249	CLAUDIUS (10) defeated on sea at Drepana.
248	Hieron renews his alliance with Rome.
247	HAMILCAR Barca starts Carthaginian offensive in Sicily.
244	Rome builds a new fleet and founds colony at Brundisium.
241	CATULUS (1) defeats Hanno off Drepana. End of First Punic War: Rome occupies Sicily.
238	Rome occupies Sardinia and Corsica.
237	Hamilcar goes to Spain.
235	Carthaginian conquests in Spain.

BC	
232	FLAMINIUS passes a law to distribute territory taken from the Gauls to citizens in small lots.
230	Death of Hamilcar; Hasdrubal becomes the Carthaginian commander in Spain.
229	First Illyrian War.
228	Demetrius is made ruler of Pharos. Teuta, queen of the Illyrians, surrenders: the Illyrian coast becomes a Roman protectorate. Rome sends an embassy to Athens and Corinth.
227	Institution of four praetors: two of them are appointed to govern Sicily and the newly created province of Sardinia.
226	Treaty between Rome and Hasdrubal: the Ebro to be the frontier between them in Spain.
225	Rout of Gauls invading Italy.
223	FLAMINIUS defeats the Insubres.
222	Battle of Clastidium: Insubres surrender.
221	Death of Hasdrubal: HANNIBAL replaces him in Spain.
220	Flaminius is censor and begins the Via Flaminia.
219	Hannibal besieges Saguntum, taking it in November. Second Illyrian War.
218	Second Punic War breaks out. Hannibal marches from Spain to Italy and wins battles of Ticinus and Trebia (December).
217	Hannibal crosses the Apennines, wins battle of Lake Trasimene. FABIUS (8) Maximus is appointed dictator. Roman naval victory off the Ebro.
216	Carthaginian victory at Cannae. Capua and other central Italian cities rebel against Rome.
215	Hannibal in southern Italy. Together, SCIPIO (1) and SCIPIO (6) defeat HASDRUBAL (2) near Dertosa in Spain. Syracuse allies with Carthage. Law of OPPIUS (1) to restrict luxury.
214	Laevinus in Illyria. SYPHAX allies with Rome.
213	Marcellus besieges Syracuse. Hannibal seizes Tarentum. Philip captures Lissus in Illyria.
212	Romans besiege Capua. Carthage makes peace with Syphax. LAEVINUS makes treaty with Aetolians.
211	Syracuse falls to the Romans: Archimedes killed. The two Scipios defeated and killed in Spain. Hannibal marches on Rome: Capua falls. GALBA (3) replaces Laevinus in Greece.
210	NERO (2) holds the Ebro frontier until SCIPIO (7) Africanus lands at Emporium. Romans take Agrigentum and Aegina.
209	Scipio captures New Carthage. Rome retakes Tarentum.
208	Scipio wins a victory at Baecula: Hasdrubal marches north and winters in Gaul. PHILIP (1) V wins victories over the Romans by land. Laevinus wins a naval victory off the coast of Africa.

BC	
207	Hasdrubal is defeated and killed on the Metaurus. Philip raids Aetolia.
206	Scipio wins victory at Ilipa in Spain, takes Gades, founds Italica, returns to Rome. Aetolians make peace with Philip.
205	Rome makes peace of Phoenice with Philip. Scipio as consul recaptures Locri and in Sicily. MAGO in Liguria.
204	Scipio lands in Africa. Cato brings Ennius to Rome. Death of Livius ANDRONICUS.
203	Scipio defeats Syphax, wins victory at the Great Plains. Carthage breaks truce. Mago defeated in Gaul. Recall of Hannibal.
202	Scipio wins battle of Zama. Armistice and peace treaty with Carthage.
201	MASINISSA becomes king of enlarged Numidia. ATTALUS (1) and the Rhodians seek Roman help against Philip.
200	After an ultimatum, the Romans declare war on Philip, the Second Macedonian War. Philip takes Abydos. GALBA (3) in Illyria. Roman embassy to ANTIOCHUS (1) III, who wins victory at Panion. Revolt of the Insubres.
199	The Aetolians ally with Rome. Galba campaigns in Macedonia.
198	The Achaeans ally with Rome. CATO (4) in Sardinia. Number of praetors raised to six. FLAMININUS wins a victory on the Aous.
197	Romans defeat Philip at battle of Cynoscephalae. Peace made between Rome and Macedonia. Accession of EUMENES II of Pergamon. CETHEGUS (2) defeats the Insubres.
196	Flamininus proclaims 'freedom of the Greeks' at the Isthmian Games. Romans settle Greek affairs. Antiochus advances into Thrace and meets Roman embassy at Lysimachia. Hannibal begins political reforms at Carthage. MARCELLUS (4) defeats the Insubres.
195	NABIS of Sparta defeated, submits to Rome. Antiochus makes peace with Egypt. Hannibal is exiled and joins Antiochus at Ephesus. Masinissa begins to raid Carthaginian territory. Cato quells revolts in Spain.
194	Roman troops evacuated from Greece. Antiochus in Thrace and reopens negotiations with Rome. Rome at war with the Lusitani.
193	Aetolians offer support to Antiochus. Nabis violates his treaty with Rome and attacks the Achaeans. Breach between Antiochus and Rome.

BC	
192	Nabis is defeated and dies. Antiochus at instigation of the Aetolians crosses to Greece (October). Antiochus declares war on Rome (November).
191	Romans defeat Antiochus at Thermopylae. Eumenes and the Rhodians join Rome. Antiochus' fleet is defeated at Coryrus. Rome refuses Carthaginian offer to pay off the whole indemnity. SCIPIO (12) NASICA defeats the Boii. Reform of Calendar.
190	Antiochus' fleets defeated at Side and Myonesus. Scipios land in Asia and defeat Antiochus at Magnesia.
189	Campanians enrolled as Roman citizens. Ambracia falls, the Aetolians submit to Rome. Manlius VULSO (1) defeats the Galatians.
188	Rome makes treaty of Apamea with Antiochus: affairs of Asia settled.
187	Via Aemilia built. Rome expels the Latins from the city.
186	The Ligurians defeat Marcius PHILIPPUS (4). Roman embassy sent to Philip V. The rites of Bacchus made illegal.
184	Cato is censor. Philip's son Demetrius is sent to Rome as a hostage. Death of PLAUTUS.
183	Death of Scipio Africanus.
182	Death of Hannibal in Bithynia.
181	War against the Celtiberi. BAEBIUS' law against electoral corruption. Philip campaigns in the Balkans.
179	PERSEUS' accession as king of Macedonia. GRACCHUS (3) ends Celtiberian War by treaties.
177	GRACCHUS (3) subdues rebellion in Sardinia.
173	The Latins are struck off the rolls of citizens.
172	Roman mission to Greece, instigated by Eumenes' complaints against Perseus.
171	Third Macedonian War breaks out between Rome and Perseus. Perseus wins victory in Thessaly.
169	Romans under Philippus attack Macedonia, Genthius of Illyria supports Perseus. War between Syria and Egypt. Death of Ennius.
168	Battle of Pydna: Aemilius PAULLUS (2) defeats Perseus and ends Macedonian independence. Rome weakens Pergamon and Rhodes.
167	Romans plunder and enslave Epirus. They divide Macedonia into four and Illyria into three protectorates. Hostages of the Achaean league including POLYBIUS deported to Italy. Perseus' library brought to Rome.
166	Maccabee risings in Palestine. TERENCE's *Andria*.

BC	
163	Roman mission to weaken Syria. Seleucid regent Lysias defeats the Hasmoneans in Palestine.
161	Expulsion of Greek philosophers and teachers from Rome. Rome makes treaty with Judaea.
160	Defeat and death of Judas Maccabaeus. Accession of ATTALUS (2) II of Pergamon.
159	PRUSIAS (2) II of Bithynia compelled to make peace with Pergamon. Death of Terence.
157	Judaea becomes an independent state headed by the high priest. Roman campaign in Dalmatia.
155	Embassy of the philosophers (Carneades, Critolaus and Diogenes) to Rome. Dalmatia subdued.
154	War breaks out with the Lusitani. Massilia seeks Roman help against the western Ligurians.
153	Consuls enter office on 1 January. War with the Celtiberi.
151	Return of Achaean hostages from Italy to Greece. Carthage declares war on Masinissa.
150	Masinissa defeats Carthage. Alexander BALAS becomes king of Syria under the protection of Egypt.
149	Third Punic War. Rising in Macedonia under Andriscus. (Fourth Macedonian War). Sparta secedes from the Achaean League: Diaeus urges war.
147	VIRIATHUS begins resistance against the Romans in Lusitania. SCIPIO (11) Aemilianus besieges Carthage.
146	Sack of Carthage and creation of province of Africa. War between Rome and the Achaean League: defeat of Diaeus by Mummius. Sack of Corinth. Macedonia is turned into a Roman province.
143	Celtiberian revolt. Numantine War.
142	First stone bridge over the Tiber.
139	Ballot for elections introduced by the law of Gabinius. Accession of ATTALUS (3) III of Pergamon.
138	Death of Viriathus, leader of the Lusitani.
133	Land bill of Tiberius GRACCHUS (4) passed instituting land commission. Gracchus murdered on the eve of elections. Attalus III wills his kingdom to Rome.
132	The consuls POPILLIUS and RUPILIUS preside over a court of inquiry to punish the supporters of Gracchus. Revolt of ARISTONICUS in Pergamon after the death of Attalus.
131	CARBO (1) passes a law to extend voting to legislation.
130	PERPERNA during his consulship defeats Aristinicus of Pergamon.

BC

129	Death of Scipio Aemilianus. Defeat of Sempronius Tuditanus in Illyria. Perperna and Manius Aquilius reorganise province of Asia. Senate refuses to confirm gift of Phrygia to Mithridates V of Pontus. PTOLEMY (4) VIII restored to his throne, but civil war in Egypt continues. Death of Carneades.
126	Aliens forbidden access to Rome.
123	First tribunate and legislation of Gaius GRACCHUS (1).
122	Gracchus is tribune for second year but fails to get his legislation passed and is not reelected. The Balearic islands conquered. First use of the ultimate decree. Gracchus murdered in riot. OPIMIUS executes Gracchan supporters. Defeat of Arverni and Allobroges. Assassination of Mithridates V of Pontus at Sinope.
119	MARIUS (1) in his tribunate legislates to improve voting procedures and check bribery of voters. The Gracchan land commission abolished.
118	Death of MICIPSA, king of Numidia. Joint rule of ADHERBAL, HIEMPSAL (1) and JUGURTHA.
116	After the death of Hiempsal, Jugurtha consolidates his power: a senatorial commission in Numidia.
115	MITHRIDATES (3) VI seizes power in Pontus and inaugurates his policy of expansion.
114	The Sordisci of Macedonia defeat CATO (1). Marius in Spain.
113	Cimbri defeat CARBO (4) in Noricum. Jugurtha sacks Numidian capital Cirta.
112	Rome declares war on Jugurtha.
111	Temporary truce with Jugurtha; land law passed at Rome.
110	Jugurtha sacks the camp of Aulus Albinus.
109	METELLUS (5) wins successes against Jugurtha. Death of PANAETIUS.
107	Marius' first consulship: he enlists a new army of volunteers from lower classes, succeeds Metellus, and takes Capsa.
106	Marius and SULLA (2) in western Numidia: BOCCHUS (1) surrenders Jugurtha to Sulla.
105	Cimbri and Teutones destroy a Roman army at Arausio (Orange).
104	Second slave war in Sicily. Marius reorganises the Roman army. Election for priestly colleges established by law.
103	SATURNINUS (2) passes a law regulating grain distribution. A court established to deal with treason.
102	Marius defeats the Teutones near Aquae Sextiae (Aix-en-Provence). ANTONIUS (5) fights the pirates in Cilicia.

BC	
101	Marius and CATULUS (2) defeat the Cimbri near Vercellae. Mithridates and NICOMEDES II of Bithynia partition Paphlagonia and occupy Galatia.
100	Legislation and fall of Saturninus. AQUILLIUS (2) ends Second Sicilian Slave War.
98	Marius departs for Asia.
96	Sulla installs ARIOBARZANES (1) on the throne of Cappadocia.
95	Rome orders Mithridates to leave Paphlagonia and Cappadocia.
94	Death of NICOMEDES III.
91	DRUSUS (2)'s tribunate, he attempts reforms but is assassinated. Social War breaks out: massacre of Romans at Asculum.
90	Law of Julius CAESAR (5) offers citizenship to all communities not in revolt. Roman reverses.
89	Asculum captured; victory of POMPEIUS (5) Strabo and Sulla.
88	War ends with suppression of the Samnites. The tribune SULPICIUS (1) Rufus proposes laws to enrol new citizens in every tribe and replace Sulla with Marius in Asia. Sulla marches on Rome and repeals Rufus' laws. Sulla strengthens Senate: Marius flees. Mithridates overruns Asia Minor and massacres Roman and Italian residents. He besieges Rhodes.
87	CINNA (2) seizes power, Marius returns; Sulla's supporters in Rome massacred. Sulla lands in Greece and besieges Athens which supports Mithridates.
86	Death of Marius, consulships of Cinna until 84. Sulla takes Athens, wins further battles in Greece, brings Mithridates to terms: treaty of Dardanus. Restoration of NICOMEDES IV and Ariobarzanes. Rhodes rewarded.
84	Cinna killed, CARBO (5) sole consul: new citizens distributed through all tribes.
83	Sulla returns to Italy and gains support of POMPEIUS (2). Murena starts Second Mithridatic War.
82	Battle of Colline Gate, Sulla destroys his enemies and inaugurates proscription. Pompeius settles Sicily for Sulla. Murena driven from Cappadocia. SERTORIUS leaves for Spain.
81	Sulla dictator to reform constitution: reforms criminal law. Pompeius defeats the Marians in Africa. SERTORIUS driven from Spain by Annius Luscus.
80	Sertorius returns to Spain to raise an army and lead revolt of the Lusitani. PTOLEMY (7) XI, Sulla's nominee to the throne of Egypt, is murdered by the Alexandrians and PTOLEMY (8) XII the Piper seizes the throne. CICERO (1) delivers the court speech *In Defence of Roscius of Ameria*.

BC	
79	Sulla returns to private life. Sertorius defeats METELLUS (7) Pius.
78	Death of Sulla. Aemilius LEPIDUS (3) aims to overthrow Sullan constitution. Lepidus, defeated by Pompeius and CATULUS (3), dies in Sardinia. Pompeius appointed to govern Spain and crushes a rebellion in Gaul on the way there.
76	Sertorius wins successes against Pius and Pompeius. Sertorius makes an alliance with Mithridates.
75	The law proposed and passed by Aurelius COTTA (1) removes disabilities of tribunes.
74	Nicomedes IV of Bithynia dies and bequeaths his kingdom to Rome: Mithridates declares war on Rome and invades Bithynia: LUCULLUS (2) appointed to oppose him. The praetor ANTONIUS (6) is given a roving commission to deal with the pirates.
73	SPARTACUS leads a rebellion of slaves in southern Italy at Capua. Lucullus' successes.
72	Spartacus defeats Cassius Longinus at Mutina. Perperna murders Sertorius but is himself defeated by Pompeius, who pacifies Spain. Lucullus drives into Pontus; his brother Marcus ravages Thrace. Antonius defeated by Cretan pirates.
71	CRASSUS (3) overwhelms Spartacus in Lucania. Lucullus settles the debt problem of Asia. His forces reduce Amisus and other Pontic towns. Mithridates flees to Armenia.
70	Consulship of Pompeius and Crassus. Full powers restored to the tribunes. Law of Aurelius Cotta reconstitutes criminal courts. Trial of VERRES for extortion in Sicily.
69	Lucullus invades Armenia and captures Tigranocerta.
68	Lucullus captures Nisibis: his army suffers discontent. Mithridates returns to Pontus.
67	Legal reforms governing praetors' edicts. Law of GABINIUS (2) gives Pompeius authority to rid the Mediterranean of the pirates.
66	Law of MANILIUS (1) empowers Pompeius to crush Mithridates: he replaces Lucullus, and makes an alliance with Phraates III, king of Parthia. Mithridates is finally defeated and abandons his kingdom. CATILINE's first conspiracy.
65	Pompeius campaigns against Iberi and Albani.
64	Pompeius overthrows Seleucid power in Syria. Law of Papius expels non-citizens from Rome.

BC	
63	Cicero's consulship. He defends RABIRIUS (1) and MURENA. Caesar elected *Pontifex Maximus*. Pompeius in Damascus and besieges Jerusalem. End of Hasmonean power. Conspiracy of Catiline: execution of conspirators left in Rome. Death of Mithridates.
62	Pompeius organises his conquests: he makes Syria, Cilicia, and Bithynia provinces, and appoints several client kings. In December he returns to Italy and disbands his army. Catiline defeated and killed at Pistoria. CLODIUS profanes the *Bona Dea* festival.
61	Trial and acquittal of Clodius. Caesar governs Further Spain. Pompeius, whose decisions are opposed by the Senate, holds triumph in September. Aedui appeal to Rome to save them from the Sequani and ARIOVISTUS.
60	Secret agreement between Caesar, Pompeius and Crassus ('first triumvirate'). Helvetii decide to migrate to western Gaul.
59	Caesar's consulship and legislation; Pompeius marries JULIA (4). Senate recognises PTOLEMY (8) XII as king of Egypt. Caesar obtains Gaul and Illyricum as his province for five years.
58	Clodius as tribune destroys opposition to the 'triumvirate'. Cicero goes into exile. CATO (5) annexes Cyprus. Ptolemy driven from Alexandria. Caesar defeats Helvetii and Ariovistus.
57	Cicero's return to Rome. Ptolemy flees to Rome. Caesar defeats the Nervii and Belgae.
56	Conference of Luca extends the 'triumvirate' for five years. Caesar's campaigns against the Veneti and Morini.
55	Consulship of Pompeius and Crassus who renew triumvirate dispositions. Pompeius consecrates his theatre. Caesar massacres the Usipetes and Tencteri, bridges the Rhine and raids Britain.
54	Pompeius proconsul of Spain but stays near Rome and governs through legates. Julia dies (September). Caesar invades Britain but is forced to retreat by revolt of north-eastern Gaul. Crassus in Syria prepares his attack on Parthia. Gabinius, proconsul of Syria, restores Ptolemy. Riots prevent consular elections.
53	Consuls not elected till July. Rioting between gangs of Clodius and MILO. Crassus defeated and killed at Carrhae (May): CASSIUS (2) reorganises remnant of army. Unrest in Gaul: Caesar pacifies Senones, Carnutes and Nervii. He bridges the Rhine again and writes *On Regularity*.

BC	
52	Pompeius sole consul till August. Milo's men kill Clodius (January): Milo prosecuted and retires to Massilia. Pompeius legislates against electoral irregularity. VERCINGETORIX's unsuccessful rebellion in central Gaul.
51	Optimate moves in Senate against Caesar: he suppresses revolt of the Bellovaci. Parthians invade Syria. PTOLEMY XIII and CLEOPATRA VII become joint rulers of Egypt.
50	CURIO (2) proposes that both Caesar and Pompeius lay down their commands, but veto is applied. The consul MARCELLUS (1) bids Pompeius save the republic (November). Caesar organises Gaul and crosses Rubicon.
49	Pompeius leaves for Greece (January). Caesar's eleven-day dictatorship: he passes emergency legislation. He wins battle of Ilerda and siege of Massilia. Curio killed in Africa.
48	Caesar consul: insurrection of Caelius and Milo. Caesar lands in Greece, Dyrrachium, victory at Pharsalus (June). Pompeius murdered in Egypt (September). Caesar lands in Egypt, Alexandrian War. Death of Ptolemy XIII; Caesar replaces him with Ptolemy XIV. PHARNACES wins battle of Nicopolis.
47	Caesar is dictator in absentia. He defeats PHARNACES at Zela, settles Asia Minor and Syria. He quells mutiny in Campania. He sails for Africa (October).
46	Caesar wins battle of Thapsus (February) and creates province of New Africa. Cato's suicide. Caesar celebrates four triumphs. Calendar reform. Caesar leaves for Spain (November).
45	Caesar, dictator for third and fourth times, wins battle of Munda (March).
44	Caesar, dictator for life, rejects royal crown (February). His assassination (15 March). The Popular Assembly appoints ANTONIUS (7) to a five-year command in Gaul. Octavian's return to Italy. Cicero's *Philippics*.
43	Battle of Mutina: Antonius' siege is raised. Octavian consul (August); triumvirate of Antonius, Octavian and LEPIDUS (4) (October): proscriptions and death of Cicero (December). BRUTUS (4) in Macedonia, Cassius in Syria.
42	Battle of Philippi: suicides of Brutus and Cassius (October). Sex. POMPEIUS (4) controls Sicily.
41	War of Perusia in Italy. Antonius, in Asia Minor, meets Cleopatra at Tarsus and visits Egypt.
40	Octavian receives surrender of Perusia. Pact of Brundisium (October). Antonius marries OCTAVIA (2). Parthian invasion of Syria and Asia Minor. Senate appoints HEROD (1) king of Judaea.

BC	
39	Pact of Misenum with Sex. Pompeius (4) (April). AGRIPPA (1) campaigns in Gaul. VENTIDIUS defeats Parthians at Mt Amanus.
38	Octavian marries LIVIA (2). Sex. Pompeius defeats Octavian's fleet off Messina. Ventidius' further success and death of Pacorus at Gindarus.
37	Pact of Tarentum between triumvirs. Herod and Sosius capture Jerusalem (July). 'Marriage' of Antonius and Cleopatra.
36	Octavian receives sacrosanctity of a tribune. Campaigns against Sex. Pompeius. Lepidus defeats him but is deprived of triumviral power. Antonius suffers reverses in Armenia.
35	Sex. Pompeius killed in Asia.
34	Octavian operates in Dalmatia. Antonius invades Armenia and captures ARTAVASDES (1). Antonius' triumph in Alexandria and Donations. SALLUST dies.
33	Rome gains Mauretania on death of BOCCHUS II. Antonius campaigns in Armenia.
32	Antonius divorces Octavia: his will is published at Rome.
31	Agrippa storms Methone in Peloponnese; Octavian lands in Epirus. Battle of Actium (September).
30	Octavian receives tribunician power for life. PHRAATES (1) captures Media and restores ARTAXIAS (1) to throne of Armenia. Octavian takes Alexandria: suicides of Antonius and Cleopatra.
29	GALLUS (4) crushes a revolt in Egypt. Revolt of Morini and Treveri in Gaul. CRASSUS (4) operates in Balkans. Dedication of temple of Divus Julius.
28	MESSALLA (4) in Aquitania. Octavian and Agrippa hold census. Senate reconstituted.
27	Constitutional settlement: division of provinces between AUGUSTUS and the Senate. He has proconsular power for ten years. Augustus' tour of Gaul and Spain begins.
26	Disgrace and suicide of Gallus.
25	Marriage of JULIA (5) and MARCELLUS (7). Augustus makes JUBA (2) II king of Mauretania. Galatia annexed on death of Amyntas. Augustus returns from tour. GALLUS (1)'s expedition to Arabia Felix.
23	Illness of Augustus. Conspiracy of CAEPIO (1) and Murena. New constitutional settlement: Augustus gives up consulship and takes overriding proconsular power and full tribunician power. Death of Marcellus. Agrippa sent east as vice-regent.
22	Augustus takes responsibility for grain supply at Rome. He begins his tour of Greece and Asia.

BC

21	Marriage of Julia and Agrippa.
20	Agrippa quells disturbances in Gaul and Germany. TIBERIUS enters Armenia and crowns TIGRANES (2). Building of temple of Mars Ultor on the Capitol.
19	Return of Augustus, death of VIRGIL (September). Agrippa pacifies Spain. BALBUS (2)'s expedition against the Garamantes.
18	Augustus' power extended for five years. Agrippa is co-regent. Augustus' legislation.
17	Augustus adopts his grandsons Gaius and Lucius. Augustus holds *Ludi Saeculares.*
16	Noricum incorporated in the empire. Agrippa sent back to the east. Augustus begins tour of Gaul.
15	Tiberius and DRUSUS (3) defeat Raeti and advance to the Danube. Agrippa in Jerusalem.
14	Agrippa installs POLEMO (1) as king of Bosporan kingdom.
13	Return of Augustus: his power extended for five years. Return of Agrippa. PISO (7) quells rising in Thrace. Theatre of Marcellus dedicated.
12	Augustus becomes *Pontifex Maximus*. Death of Agrippa. Tiberius' command in Pannonia. Drusus dedicates altar to Rome and Augustus near Lyons, and campaigns in Germany till 9.
11	Tiberius divorces Vipsania AGRIPPINA (1) to marry Julia.
9	Death of Drusus in Germany. Dedication of *Ara Pacis Augusti.*
8	Augustus' power extended for ten years. Tiberius operates against the Sugambri in Germany. Deaths of MAECENAS and HORACE.
7	Tiberius' triumph. Rome divided into fourteen regions for administrative purposes.
6	Tiberius receives tribunician power for five years. He retires to Rhodes.
4	Death of Herod.
2	Augustus, consul for thirteenth time, receives title *Pater Patriae* ('Father of the Fatherland'). Exile of Julia.

AD

1	Gaius Caesar in Syria.
2	Return of Tiberius from Rhodes. Death of Lucius Caesar at Massilia. Gaius Caesar negotiates with Phraataces, king of Parthia, and awards the throne of Armenia to Ariobarzanes, king of Media.
3	Augustus' power extended for ten years.

AD

4	Death of Gaius Caesar in Lycia. Tiberius adopted by Augustus and granted tribunician power for ten years. GERMANICUS, adopted by Tiberius, invades Germany as far as the Weser.
5	Tiberius reaches the Elbe.
6	Revolts in Pannonia and Illyricum. Maroboduus recognised as king of the Marcomanni. Judaea organised as a province by QUIRINIUS, legate of Syria.
8	Pannonians capitulate. OVID banished to Tomis.
9	Revolt in Dalmatia crushed. ARMINIUS defeats VARUS in Germany and destroys three legions.
12	Tiberius triumphs for his Illyrian campaign.
13	Augustus' power extended for ten years. Tiberius, his partner in power, receives tribunician power for ten years and proconsular power equal to that of Augustus.
14	Death of Augustus (August). Tiberius, now emperor, appoints SEJANUS to head the Praetorian Guard. Mutinies in Pannonia and Germany. DRUSUS (4) sent to deal with crisis in Pannonia, Germanicus invades Germany.
15	Germanicus invades territories of Chatti and Lower Germany. Achaea and Macedonia become imperial provinces.
16	Germanicus again invades Germany, but is recalled.
17	Germanicus' triumph: he is sent to the east. Gnaeus PISO (4) appointed legate of Syria. Deaths of LIVY and Ovid.
18	Germanicus enthrones ARTAXIAS (2) in Armenia. He makes an unauthorised tour of Egypt.
19	Jews banished from Rome. Arminius killed by his kinsmen. Piso leaves Syria. Germanicus dies at Antioch (October).
20	Trial and suicide of Piso.
21	Tiberius retires to Campania. Rising of SACROVIR and allies in Gaul.
22	Praetorian camp built in Campus Martius. Drusus receives power of a tribune.
23	Death of Drusus (September).
24	DOLABELLA (5) defeats and kills TACFARINAS in Mauretania.
26	Tiberius retires to Capri.
28	Death of Livia. Banishment of AGRIPPINA (2) and her son NERO (4) Julius Caesar.
31	Fall of Sejanus, to be replaced by MACRO.
36	Crucifixion of JESUS. Removal of PILATE from Judaea by VITELLIUS (2), governor of Syria.
37	Death of Tiberius (March); accession of CALIGULA (Gaius), who makes CLAUDIUS (1) his fellow-consul.
38	Death and deification of Gaius' sister JULIA (7) Drusilla. Trouble between Jews and Greeks in Alexandria.

AD	
39	Gaius leaves for Gaul and invasion of Britain (September). Raids into Germany. Conspiracy of LENTULUS (6) Gaetulicus and LEPIDUS (7) to kill Gaius in Germany: execution of them and exile of Gaius' sisters.
40	Gaius returns to Rome (August) after failure of plan to invade Britain. Execution at Rome of PTOLEMY (12) king of Mauretania. Risings in Judaea against Gaius; embassy of Alexandrian Jews. AGRIPPA (3) I receives kingdom of HEROD (2) Antipas.
41	Murder of Gaius (January); Claudius I made emperor. He settles disputes between Jews and Greeks in Alexandria and adds Judaea and Samaria to Agrippa's kingdom. Chauci defeated.
42	Failed revolt of SCRIBONIANUS in Dalmatia. Mauretania reorganised as two provinces.
43	Successful invasion of Britain under Aulus PLAUTIUS (1). Claudius at Colchester.
44	Achaea and Macedonia transferred to the Senate. Agrippa dies; Judaea annexed.
46	Thrace an imperial province.
47	Ovation of A. Plautius. Claudius holds *Ludi Saeculares*. CORBULO subdues Frisii.
48	Fall and death of MESSALLINA. Claudius marries AGRIPPINA (3).
49	SENECA (2) recalled from exile, made praetor, and tutor to Domitius (NERO 1), son of Agrippina.
50	Claudius adopts Nero and makes him the guardian of BRITANNICUS.
51	BURRUS appointed Praetorian Prefect. VESPASIAN consul. Defeat of CARATACUS in Wales.
53	Marriage of Nero and OCTAVIA (3). Parthians occupy Armenia and TIRIDATES (3) recovers his throne.
54	Claudius dies, poisoned by Agrippina. Nero has Claudius deified.
55	PALLAS removed from office. Britannicus poisoned. Corbulo appointed to command against Parthians.
57	Nero orders senators and knights to participate in the games.
58	Nero refuses perpetual consulship; proposes abolition of all indirect taxes. Corbulo takes Artaxata. Arrest of PAUL at Jerusalem.
59	Nero has Agrippina murdered; introduces Greek games to Rome. Corbulo takes Tigranocerta.
60	The *Neronia* instituted. Corbulo completes subjugation of Armenia; is appointed to govern Syria.

AD	
61	Revolt of Iceni under BOUDICCA and Trinovantes. VOLOGESES, king of Parthia, supports the invasion of Adiabene by Tiridates and threatens Syria. Corbulo obtains a treaty recognising the status quo.
62	Death of Burrus and fall of Seneca. Octavia divorced, banished and murdered. Tigellinus Prefect of Praetorians. Paetus in Cappadocia. Nero marries POPPAEA. Paul reaches Rome.
64	Fire at Rome (July). Persecution of Christians.
65	Conspiracy of PISO (2) (April). Suicides of Seneca and LUCAN. Death of Poppaea.
66	Nero crowns Tiridates king of Armenia at Rome. Nero's tour of Greece: he proclaims Greece free. Suicide of PETRONIUS (1). Rebellion throughout Palestine.
67	Corbulo's forced suicide. Vespasian appointed to command in Judaea (February). JOSEPHUS surrenders to him.
68	Nero returns to Italy, dies in June. GALBA (1) accepted by Senate and Praetorians as emperor: enters Rome in Autumn. Rebellion of Vindex in Gaul put down by Verginius Rufus.
69	Fall and death of Galba (January): Praetorians install OTHO. VITELLIUS (1) proclaimed in Germany, his forces defeat Otho's at Cremona (April). Civilis' rising on the Rhine. Vespasian proclaimed in Alexandria and east (July). His forces, mainly from Danube, beat those of Vitellius at Cremona (October). Vitellius dies (December).
70	MUCIANUS reaches Rome (January). Vespasian reaches Rome (summer). Rebellions of Julius CLASSICUS and CIVILIS in Gaul. TITUS besieges Jerusalem (spring) and takes it (September). Capitoline Temple restored.
71	Titus returns to triumph and receives tribunician and proconsular powers. Expulsion of astrologers and philosophers from Rome.
75	AGRIPPA (4) II and BERENICE (2) visit Rome. Alani invade Armenia and Media.
78	Conspiracy of EPRIUS Marcellus and CAECINA (3) Alienus. Agricola appointed governor of Britain.
79	Death of Vespasian (June); Titus' accession. Eruption of Vesuvius (Aug.); destruction of Pompeii and Herculaneum. Death of PLINY (1).
80	Fire at Rome: destruction of the Capitoline Temple. Inauguration of the Colosseum.
81	Death of Titus (September): Domitian's accession.
83	Domitian's triumph over the Chatti.

AD	
85	Domitian takes censorship for life. DECEBALUS defeats legate of Moesia.
88	*Ludi Saeculares* held. Dacians defeated at Tapae.
89	Domitian returns and holds a triumph. Edict against astrologers and philosophers. Failed rebellion of SATURNINUS (1).
92	Palatine palace completed. Domitian campaigns against the Suevi and the Sarmatae.
93	Death of Agricola. Trial and condemnation of Baebius MASSA for extortion in Spain.
95	Expulsion of philosophers from Italy.
96	Murder of Domitian (September): accession of NERVA (4).
97	Land laws. Rising of Praetorians against Nerva. Adoption of TRAJAN.
98	Death of Nerva and accession of Trajan (January). TACITUS (1)'s *Germania.*
99	Return of Trajan to Rome from Germany.
100	The *Panegyric* of PLINY (2).
101	Trajan begins his Dacian campaign.
102	Decebalus capitulates to Trajan.
105	New war against Decebalus.
106	Capture of Sarmizegethusa and suicide of Decebalus. Dacia organised as a province. Arabia annexed.
109	Trajan dedicates monument at Adamklisi to Mars Ultor.
111	Pliny sent to govern Bithynia.
112	Trajan's Forum dedicated.
113	Armenia and Mesopotamia annexed.
116	Rebellion in the east against Rome. Jewish revolt spreads from Cyrene to Egypt and Cyprus.
117	Trajan dies in Cilicia (August): accession of HADRIAN.
118	Hadrian reaches Rome (July).
121	Hadrian visits the western provinces. Rough date of death of Tacitus.
122	Hadrian visits Britain, commences the Wall. Second revolt of Mauretania.
124	Hadrian in Asia Minor.
129	Hadrian at Athens.
130	Hadrian founds Antinoöpolis. Aelia Capitolina founded on the site of Jerusalem.
131	Jewish revolt under Bar Cosiba.
134	The Alani invade Parthia.
135	Hadrian finally defeats the Jews, expels them from Judaea, and organises Syria Palaestina as a province.
136	Hadrian adopts Lucius AELIUS (3) as Caesar.

AD	
138	Death of L. Aelius (January): ANTONINUS Pius adopted as co-regent (February). Death of Hadrian (July). Accession of Antoninus Pius.
139	Lollius Urbicus subdues southern Scotland, builds Antonine Wall. Hadrian's Mausoleum dedicated.
140	First consulship of MARCUS AURELIUS.
145	Marcus marries ANTONINUS' daughter FAUSTINA.
152	Peace re-established in Mauretania.
159	Dacia divided into three provinces.
161	Death of Antoninus (March): accession of Marcus Aurelius. Lucius VERUS receives the title *Augustus*.
162	Parthia declares war on Rome and invades Armenia. Lucius Verus sent to meet the invasion.
163	Armenia regained.
164	Defeat of the Parthians: destruction of Seleucia and Ctesiphon.
165	Spread of plague from Seleucia to Asia Minor and beyond.
166	Roman successes in Media. L. Verus returns and celebrates triumph with Marcus (October).
167	Plague in Rome. German invasion of northern Italy.
168	Marcus and L. Verus successful in driving out the Germans.
169	Death of Verus (January). War continued against Germans and Sarmatians until 175.
173	Revolt in Egypt.
175	Revolt of AVIDIUS CASSIUS, governor of the Eastern Provinces (April), who was killed in July. Marcus and COMMODUS go to the East.
176	Marcus and Commodus hold triumph (December).
177	Commodus made *Augustus*. Roman victory over the Mauretanians.
178	Unrest of Marcomanni and other Danube nations. Marcus and Commodus go to the frontier (August).
180	Death of Marcus (March): accession of Commodus. Pacification of Danube frontier. PERENNIS appointed to head Praetorian Guard.
182	Conspiracy and execution of LUCILLA, Commodus' sister.
185	Execution of Perennis: Cleander replaces him as Prefect.
186	PERTINAX suppresses army mutiny in Britain.
188	Roman victory against revolt in Germany.
190	Execution of Cleander. Pertinax crushes disorders in Africa.
192	Murder of Commodus (December).

AD	
193	Pertinax emperor (January); murdered by Praetorians (March). Didius Julianus emperor April–June. Accession of Septimus SEVERUS (1): he marches against PESCENNIUS Niger, proclaimed emperor in Syria. Siege of Byzantium begins.
194	Severus defeats Pescennius at Issus and crosses the Euphrates.
196	CARACALLA proclaimed *Caesar.* Byzantium falls.
197	Caracalla made joint emperor (*Augustus*). Defeat of Albinus near Lyons (February). Britain made into two provinces. Severus returns to the East.
202	After two years in Egypt, Severus returns to Rome.
203	Dedication of the Arch of Severus in Roman Forum. ORIGEN (1) head of catechical school in Alexandria.
204	Severus in Africa.
205	Consulship of Caracalla and GETA (3). Murder of PLAUTIANUS by agency of Caracalla.
208	Severus leaves Rome for Britain.
211	Death of Severus at York. His sons leave for Rome.
212	Caracalla murders Geta and becomes sole emperor (February). The Antoninian Constitution makes all free men citizens.
213	Caracalla defeats the Alemanni.
214	Edessa becomes a Roman colony.
215	Caracalla winters in Antioch and then advances to the eastern frontier of Adiabene in Mesopotamia.
217	Caracalla assassinated near Carrhae (April) MACRINUS proclaimed his successor, but is defeated near Nisibis (summer).
218	Macrinus defeated and killed at Raphaneae (May) and ELAGABALUS is proclaimed emperor.
219	Elagabalus travels from Nicomedia to Rome.
222	After adopting his cousin Alexander, Elagabalus is murdered with his mother JULIA (12) Soaemias. Alexander becomes emperor as SEVERUS (2).
223	ULPIANUS, jurist and prefect of the Praetorian Guard, is murdered by his men.
226	ARTAXERXES I (Ardashir) is crowned king of kings in Persia.
229	Consulship of Severus Alexander and CASSIUS (1) Dio.
230	The Persians invade Mesopotamia and besiege Nisibis.
231	Severus Alexander leaves Rome for the east (spring).
232	Failure of Roman campaign against Persians. Origen is banished from Alexandria.
233	Alexander returns to Rome.
234	Campaign against the Alemanni. The Thracian MAXIMINUS (1) proclaimed emperor by the Pannonian legions in their disgust at Alexander's weakness.

AD	
235	Alexander and his mother JULIA (13) Mamaea murdered by the troops near Maintz (March). Maximinus confirmed as emperor by the Senate. He wins victory over the Alemanni. He enforces laws against the Christians.
236	Campaigns against the Sarmatians and Dacians.
238	Senate, opposed to Maximinus, appoints GORDIAN I and his son to rule. They are assassinated by Capellianus, legate of Numidia. Next the Senate appoints PUPIENUS and BALBINUS (April). Maximinus is murdered while besieging Aquilea (May). The Praetorians kill Pupienus and Balbinus and raise GORDIAN III to the purple (July). Threats by Goths and Carpi.
240	MANI begins to preach in Persia. SAPOR (1) I becomes king of Persia.
242	TIMESITHEUS, the prefect of the Praetorian Guard, leads campaign against Persia.
243	Successes of Timesitheus and his death.
244	Murder of Gordian III in Mesopotamia. Accession of PHILIPPUS (1) (Philip the Arab), who makes peace and goes to Rome.
245	Wars on the Danubian frontier until 247.
247	The emperor's son made *Augustus*. The city's millennium celebrated.
248	DECIUS re-establishes order in Moesia and Pannonia. Origen publishes *Against Celsus*.
249	Decius forced to assume the purple (June) and defeats and kills Philip near Verona (September). Gothic incursions. Decius persecutes the Christians.
251	Decius is defeated and killed on the Danube. Trebonianus GALLUS (8) proclaimed: his son, Volusianus, is made *Augustus*.
252	Large-scale barbarian invasion from the north. The Persians drive out Tiridates and take Armenia, and attack Mesopotamia.
253	AEMILIANUS is proclaimed emperor: he kills Gallus, but three months later is murdered by his troops. VALERIAN proclaimed emperor in Moesia. The Senate appoints his son GALLIENUS a second *Augustus*. Goths attack Asia Minor. Origen dies.
254	Invasion of the Marcomanni as far as Ravenna. Goths devastate Thrace. Sapor takes Nisibis.
256	Gothic attack on Asia Minor by sea.
257	Valerian persecutes the Christians. Renewed Persian invasion.
258	Gallienus defeats the Alemanni.
260	Sapor captures Valerian. Gallienus ends persecution of Christians. Rival emperors proclaimed: MACRIANUS and QUIETUS (2) in the east, POSTUMUS in Gaul. Revolts in Pannonia.

AD	
261	Macrianus killed in battle against AUREOLUS. Quietus executed at Emessa.
262	Successes of ODAENATHUS of Palmyra against the Persians. The Arch of Gallienus dedicated.
267	Gothic invasion of Asia Minor. Assassination of Odaenathus; Zenobia replaces him in name of her infant son Vallabathus.
268	Gothic armies active in the Balkans and Greece. After defeating them at Niš, Gallienus is murdered at the siege of Milan (August). CLAUDIUS (2) II emperor: he puts Aureolus to death.
269	Postumus killed. Romans win successes against the Goths.
270	Claudius dies at Sirmium (January). AURELIAN defeats the attempt of Quintillus to replace his brother. Aurelian defeats the Juthungi. Zenobia's troops enter Alexandria. Death of PLOTINUS.
271	Aurelian's new walls round Rome. Aurelian proceeds against Zenobia.
272	Death of Sapor I of Persia; accession of Hormizd I.
273	Aurelian destroys Palmyra. Hormizd dies, replaced by Vahram I.
274	TETRICUS reconciled to Aurelian, who recovers Gaul. Aurelian's triumph and reform of the coinage. He builds a temple to the Sun.
275	Aurelian is murdered in Thrace. TACITUS (2) is made emperor (September).
276	Tacitus dies at Tyana: His half-brother FLORIANUS seizes power, but is killed at Tarsus. Accession of PROBUS (1). Vahram II of Persia.
277	Probus clears Gaul of Germans and Goths.
278	Probus pacifies Asia Minor.
282	Probus is murdered and succeeded by CARUS (October).
283	Carus is murdered near Ctesiphon, succeeded by his sons CARINUS (west) and NUMERIAN (east). Vahram II makes peace with Rome.
284	Numerian killed in Bithynia and succeeded by Diocles (November).
285	Diocles defeats Carinus on the Margus. Diocles takes name DIOCLETIAN.
286	MAXIMIAN defeats the Gallic Bacaudae (brigands) and receives the rank of *Augustus*.
288	Revolt of CARAUSIUS. Diocletian places Tiridates III on throne of Armenia. He suppresses a revolt in Egypt.
289	Diocletian's campaign against the Sarmatians. Carausius defeats Maximian.

AD	
292	Further campaign against the Sarmatians.
293	CONSTANTIUS (1) and GALERIUS appointed Caesars of the West and East respectively. ALLECTUS kills Carausius. Vahram II and III of Persia are succeeded by Narses I.
296	Constantius recovers Britain from Allectus.
297	Galerius makes war on Narses. Diocletian's edict against the Manichaeans (March). Rebellion of Achilleus in Egypt, suppressed by Diocletian the following year.
302	Death of Narses.
303	Persecution of Christians at Nicomedia.
305	Diocletian and Maximian abdicate (May). Constantius and Galerius succeed them as *Augusti*, SEVERUS (3) and MAXIMINUS (2) Daia as *Caesars*.
306	Constantius dies at York. His soldiers proclaim CONSTANTINE (1) I emperor of the west. MAXENTIUS proclaimed *Princeps* at Rome, supported by his father Maximian. Severus invades Italy.
307	Constantine marries Maximian's daughter FAUSTA (2), and recognises Maxentius as *Augustus*. Defeat and death of Severus. Galerius enters Italy but withdraws to Pannonia.
308	The conference of Carnuntum: LICINIUS declared *Augustus*.
310	Maximian, captured at Massilia, commits suicide.
311	Galerius issues edict of toleration of Christianity. Galerius dies. Persecution resumed. Suppression of rebellion in Africa.
312	Constantine defeats Maxentius at the Milvian Bridge (October). Death of Maxentius.
313	Meeting of Constantine and Licinius at Milan. They partition the Roman Empire. Licinius defeats Maximinus at Adrianople (April): Maximinus commits suicide at Tarsus.
314	Christian Council of Arles. Constantine makes successful war on Licinius.
315	Arch of Constantine erected at Rome.
317	The sons of Constantine and Licinius are declared *Caesars*.
320	Licinius harasses the Christians.
324	War between Constantine and Licinius. Constantine wins victory of Chrysopolis. Banishment and execution of Licinius. Creation of new capital of Constantinople begins.
325	Christian Council of Nicaea.
330	Constantine moves his capital and residence to Constantinople.
337	Death of Constantine: the Empire divided between his three sons, CONSTANTINE (2) II in the west, CONSTANS and CONSTANTIUS (2) II in the east.

AD	
340	Constans defeats Constantinus II at Aquilea and becomes ruler of the west.
350	Revolt of MAGNENTIUS, who kills Constans.
351	Battle of Nursa in Pannonia: Constantius defeats Magnentius and rules the whole Empire till 360.
355	Constantius makes JULIAN *Caesar.*
357	Julian defeats the Alemanni near Strasburg.
359	War with Persia.
360	Julian proclaimed *Augustus* by his troops, revives traditional religion.
361	Death of Constantius before the two emperors can clash.
363	Julian's expedition against Persia, his death. End of dynasty established by Constantine. Peace with Persia. JOVIAN becomes emperor, reverses Julian's religious policy in favour of Christians.
364	Death of Jovian.

Appendix II

List of the Roman emperors

AD

Augustus	27 (BC)–AD14
Tiberius	14–37
Gaius (Caligula)	37–41
Claudius	41–54
Nero	54–68
Galba	68–69
Otho	69
Vitellius	69
Vespasian	69–79
Titus	79–81
Domitian	81–96
Nerva	96–98
Trajan	98–117
Hadrian	117–138
Antoninus Pius	138–161
Marcus Aurelius	161–180
Lucius Verus	161–169
Commodus	177–192
Pertinax	193
Didius Julianus	193
Clodius Albinus	193–197
Pescennius Niger	193–194
Septimius Severus	193–211
Caracalla	198–217
Macrinus	217–218
Elagabalus	218–222
Severus Alexander	222–235
Maximinus	235–238
Gordian I and II	238
Balbinus/Pupienus	238
Gordian III	238–244
Philip	244–249
Decius	249–251
Gallus	251–253

Volusianus	251–253
Valerian	253–260
Aemilianus	253
Gallienus	254–268
Claudius II	268–270
Quintillus	270
Aurelian	270–275
Tacitus	275–276
Florianus	276
Probus	276–282
Carus	282–283
Carinus	283–285
Numerian	283–284
Diocletian	284–305
Maximian	286–305
Constantius I	293–306
Galerius	293–311
Maximinus Daia	311–313
Constantine I	311–337
Constans	337–350
Magnentius	350–353
Constantine II	337–340
Constantius II	337–361
Julian	361–363
Jovian	363–364

Appendix III

Maps

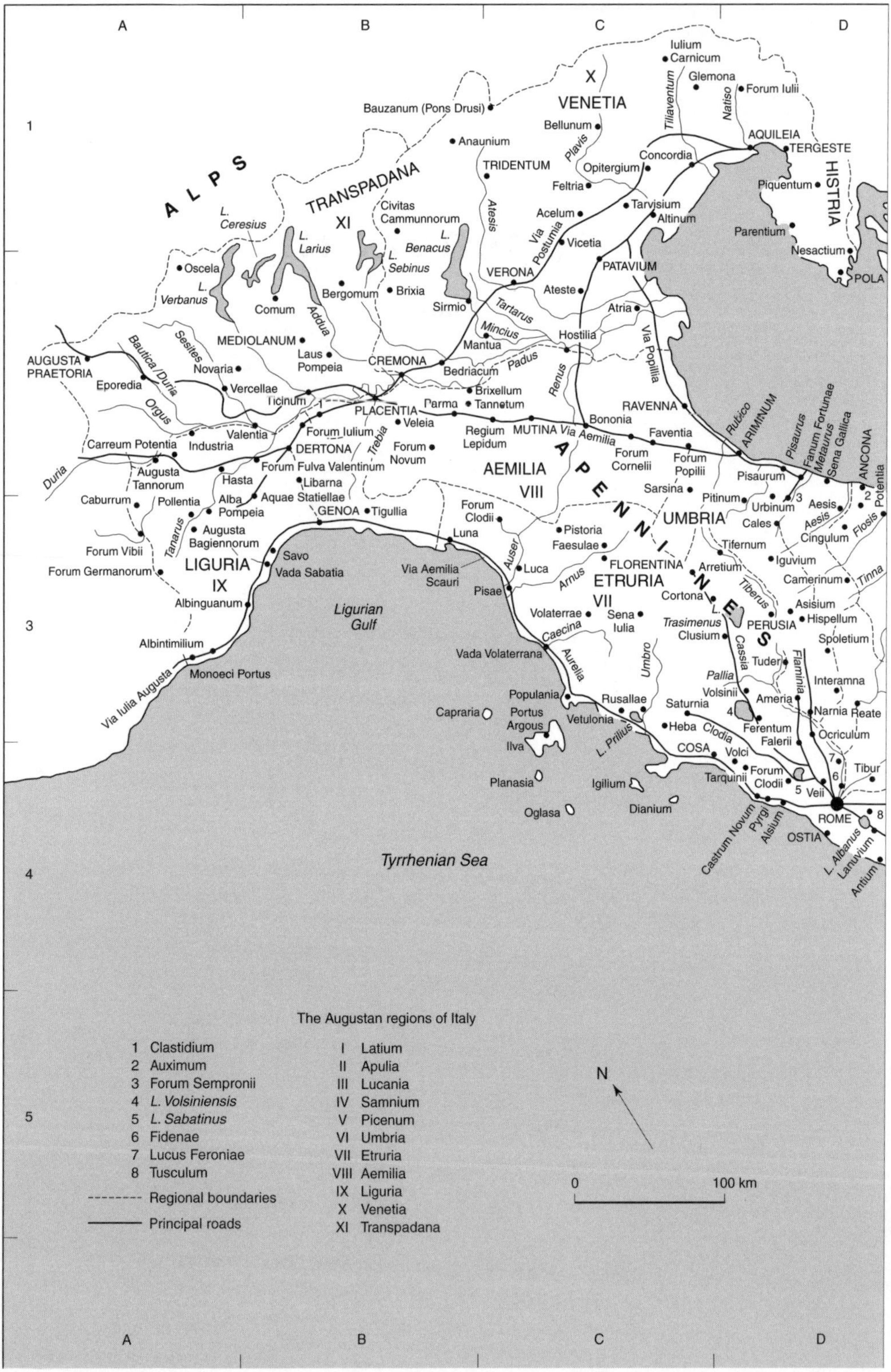

Map 1 Italy in the age of Augustus
Source: R.J.A. Talbert (ed.) (1985) *Atlas of Classical History*, London: Croom Helm

E
F
G
1
2
3
4
5
6
Adriatic Sea
Diomedaea Is.
Firmum Picenum
Falerio
Truenius
Castrum Truentinum
PICENUM
ASCULUM
Hadria
V
Interamnia
Aternum
Amiternum
Aternus
SAMNIUM
Histonium
CORFINIUM
Alba Fucens
Sulmo
L. Fucinus
Sagrus
IV
Teanum
Larinum
Sipontum
Aufidus
Arpi
Salapia
Cannae
Barium
APULIA
Canusium
Caelia
LUCERIA
Herdonia
II
CALABRIA
BRUNDISIUM
Lupiae
Rudiae
Uria
Carsioli
Liris
Aufidena
Aesernia
Bovianum
Saepinum
Praeneste
Sora
Arpinum
Atina
Aquinum
Casinum
Venatrum
Allifae
I
Fregellae
LATIUM
Trerus
Cales
Teanum
CAPUA
VENUSIA
Via Appia
Bantia
Aeclanum
BENEVENTUM
Bradanus
TARENTUM
Appia
Forum Appii
Suessula
Abellinum
Casuentus
Metapontum
Potentia
Uzentum
Tarracina
Fundi
Formiae
Minturnae
Volturnus
Volturnum
Casilinum
Nola
Via Annia
Heracleia
Circeii
Nuceria
Neapolis
Atina
Aciris
Tarentine Gulf
Cumae
MISENUM
Pompeii
Silarus
Grumentum
LUCANIA
Siris
Surrentum
Aenaria
Paestum
Crathis
Pandateria
PUTEOLI
CAMPANIA
III
Velia
Buxentum
Pontia
Capreae
Blanda Iulia
Cosentia
Croton
BRUTTIUM
Via Annia
Clampetia
Tempsa
Terina
Scylacium
Vibo Valentia
LOCRI EPIZEPHYRII
RHEGIUM

Map 2 The Roman Empire in AD 211
Source: R.J.A. Talbert (ed.) (1985) *Atlas of Classical History*, London: Croom Helm

E
F
G
Approximate provincial boundaries
Provincial capital or main centre
Legionary base
Legionary base and provincial capital
BELGICA
Province
Armenia
'Client kingdom'
QUADI
Other territories/ peoples
0
500 km
1
2
4
5
6
IAZYGES
Potaissa
Apulum
ROXOLANI
DACIA
Sarmizegetusa
DOBRUDJA
BOSPORAN KINGDOM
Viminacium
Singidunum
Danube
Durostorum
Novae
MOESIA SUPERIOR
MOESIA INFERIOR
BITHYNIA AND PONTUS
Amastris
THRACE
Satala
MACEDONIA
Perinthus
Nicomedia
CAPPADOCIA
Armenia
Thessalonica
GALATIA
EPIRUS
Ancyra
Melitene
Nicopolis
Pergamum
Caesarea (Mazaca)
Samosata
ACHAEA
ASIA
Resaina
Corinthus
Ephesus
Tarsus
MESOPOTAMIA
Singara
CILICIA
Antioch
Myra
CYPRUS
SYRIA COELE
2 legions
Raphaneae
CRETE
LYCIA AND PAMPHYLIA
Gortyn
Paphus
Tyre
SYRIA PHOENICE
Caparcotna
Caesarea
CYRENE
Bostra
Euphrates
SYRIA PALAESTINA
Aelia Capitolina
Cyrene
ARABIA
Alexandria/ Nicopolis
EGYPT
Nile

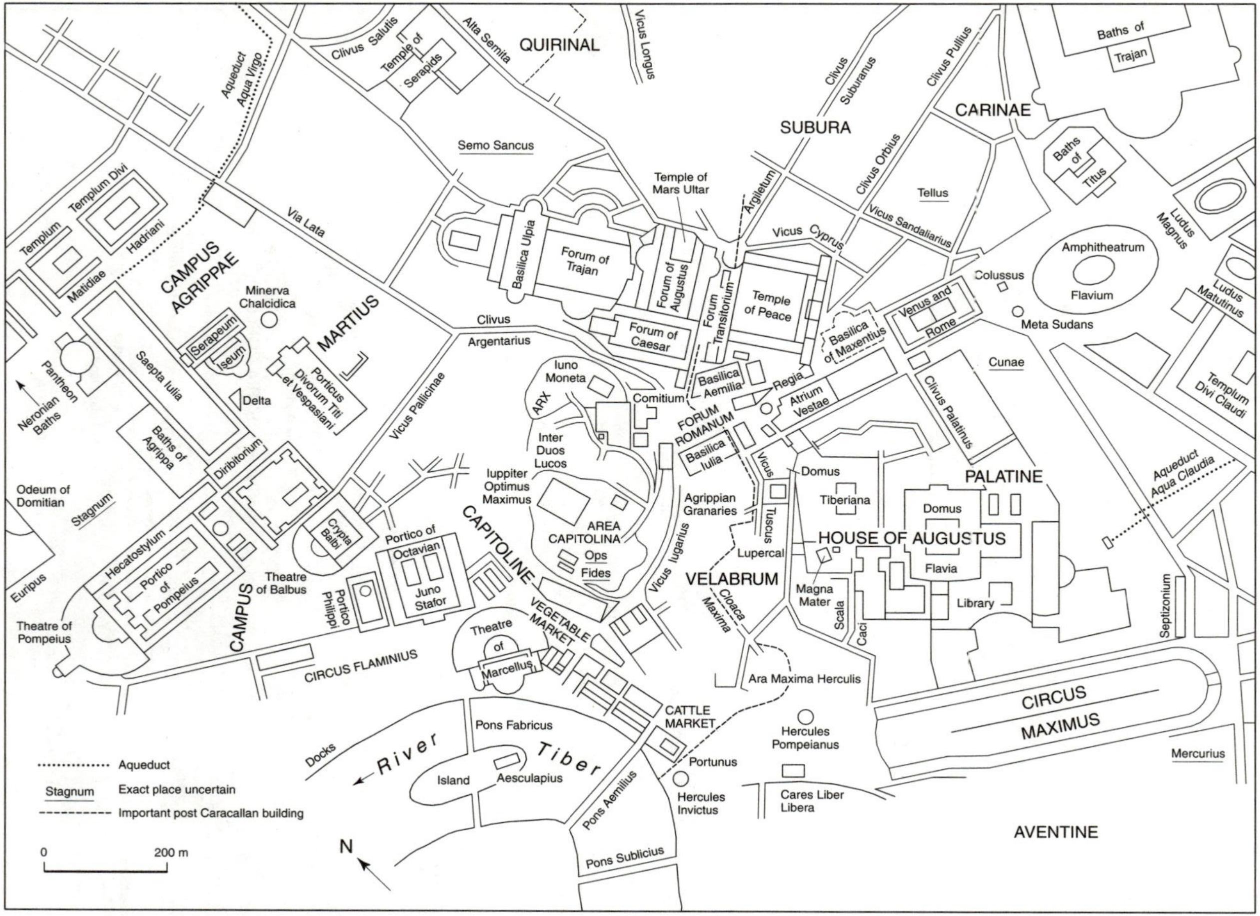

Map 3 The centre of Rome in the age of Caracalla
Source: R.J.A. Talbert (ed.) (1985) *Atlas of Classical History*, London: Croom Helm